Business and Society

Dimensions of Conflict and Cooperation

Edited by

S. Prakash Sethi
Baruch College, CUNY

Cecilia M. Falbe
State University of New York at Albany

Lexington Books
D.C. Heath and Company/Lexington, Massachusetts/Toronto

Library of Congress Cataloging-in-Publication Data

Business and society.

   Includes index.
   1. Industry—Social aspects—United States. 2. Business and politics—United States.
I. Sethi, S. Prakash. II. Falbe, Cecilia M.
HD60.5.U5B853   1987   658.4'08'0973   86-45548
ISBN 0-669-13207-1 (alk. paper)

Published simultaneously in Canada
Printed in the United States of America
Paperbound International Standard Book Number: 0-669-13207-1
Library of Congress Catalog Card Number: 86-45548

The paper used in this publication meets the minimum requirements of American National Standard for Information Sciences—Permanence of Paper for Printed Library Materials, ANSI Z39.48-1984.

87 88 89 90 8 7 6 5 4 3 2 1

Contents

Introduction

What is socially responsible behavior? How can it be measured? What are the factors—internal and external—that determine and differentiate corporate responses in a given situation? Questions such as these fuel the debate on how economic institutions should act in society.

What is seen as acceptable corporate social performance is influenced by a variety of corporate stakeholders who differ in their expectations of a share in a corporation's output and their role in determining the sharing process itself. Social performance is defined in a narrow economic and legal sense by traditional stakeholders, for example, stockholders and others who view the corporate role as almost exclusively in the economic arena. Other stakeholders, for example, employees, consumers, community residents, and various interest groups, define social performance in broader terms. In their view, social returns are as important, and for some, more important than economic returns. Each of these stakeholder groups measures acceptable social performance as acceptable in terms of meeting its own needs.

Increasingly, corporations have come to recognize that in both the marketplace and in the sociopolitical arena, economic and noneconomic factors interact in a manner that influences corporate survival and growth. Instances abound where business fortunes have been radically altered by changes in the legislative and regulatory environment, which in turn has been influenced by changing public perceptions of societal needs on the one hand and corporate behavior on the other. Thus, decisions relating to corporate strategies, and even tactics, must consider not only economic factors, but equally important, sociopolitical factors. Studies show that an increasing part of chief executives' time is now devoted to managing the public-affairs function, that is, corporate responses to changing legal and sociopolitical environments.

A corporation, as a social organism, must meet societal expectations in order to maintain its franchise. In a dynamic social system these expectations constantly change and consequently so has the role of corporations in society. It is generally accepted that the corporation's narrow economic role, (that is, maximization of profits) at all costs and to the exclusion of all other goals—if ever such a goal was seriously considered even by corporations outside the narrow confines of rhetoric for self-justification—must be tempered not only by existing legal constraints, but also by changing societal expectations that have not yet been codified into new laws. There is ample historical evidence to show that whenever corporate performance has fallen behind societal expectations, corporations have been encumbered with greater regulation, for example, workplace safety, auto-emission standards, and regulation of the nuclear industry.

Since the mid-1960s, there has been tremendous progress in our understanding of the role of business and society in the traditional sense of economic activities, and in the more subtle and complicated sense of what impact these economic activities have on all other social arrangements. What started out originally as an attempt to ask corporations to do more to ameliorate the second-order effects of their activities (for example, environmental pollution), coincided with the early 1960s social activism surrounding the Vietnam War. Over the years activism has evolved into not simply a voluntary activity on the part of the corporations but a systematic undertaking. The question of what roles corporations play in economic and sociopolitical domains has become an integral part of social debate in determining national priorities at the governmental level, and has been made part of the government's monitoring and regulatory function. Many societal concerns have become institutionalized (for example, the Occupational Safety and Health Administration, the Product Safety Commission, the Environmental Protection Agency). In the legislative area there also has been a tremendous concern for protecting the rights of individuals.

In the public arena we have seen the emergence of a whole new set of institutions, that is, public-interest groups and private voluntary organizations (PVOs) that are nonrepresentative in the sense that their members represent a set of ideas rather than traditional stakeholder concerns. These institutions use both the legislative processes and public pressure to bring about or institutionalize regulatory mechanisms for dealing with corporations. The spectrum of these organizations ranges from traditional environmental groups, such as the Wildlife Federation and Natural Resources Defense League, to religious groups that take their concerns for the poor and the oppressed and bring them to bear on a number of other social issues. The latter can be seen in terms of the church involvement in disarmament and the debate over apartheid in South Africa.

In response, companies have started developing systems to deal with the impact of external groups, both on their activities in the market and public-policy arena, and within the organization as they pertain to strategy, structure, and decision-making processes. A whole field of public-affairs management or social-issues management has evolved.

As we approach 1990, we seem to be reaching another turning point. As the traditional social issues have become institutionalized in the form of regulatory agencies and interest groups, we now look at the impact corporations have on the formulation of public policy, and how public policy in turn impacts corporate behavior. We are now beginning to see the integration of public-policy issues as part of the management and strategic planning process itself.

Disenchanted with the apparent failure of many large government programs, the public responded favorably to the promise in the early 1980s of reduced government intervention in business and social affairs. Support grew for deregulation and privatization in the interest of greater productivity. The inability of government to solve social problems was recognized. Now there is debate over the extent to which business can undertake social-responsibility programs in light of global competition. The present turbulent business environment requires corporations to be more efficient in order to survive. This is viewed by some as a rationale for discontinuing or modifying programs that were developed as a response to activism in the 1970s. However, many corporations are continuing social programs and undertaking new efforts without government pressure. This is but one sign of the progress that many corporations have made in response to social demands.

These divergent views have, of necessity, generated creative dialogue and a high level of intellectual activity. However, they have also served to move our focus away from the core issue. What can be reasonably expected of corporations as important social institutions, and how might that role be evaluated and rewarded? Thus, we see the possibility of corporations being praised by one group for their socially responsible behavior in an area, while other groups criticize their behavior as socially irresponsible in another area. The problem is not easily resolved. Some corporations defend or explain their questionable market and social behavior as reflecting the standards, or shortcomings, of the larger society from which they draw their physical and human resources. Others argue that corporations must exemplify a higher level of social accountability and thereby display characteristics of leadership that are commensurate with their role as powerful economic institutions.

Current approaches to analyzing corporate social performance can be classified into two broad categories. The first assumes that it is the external environment that is dominant in affecting changes in corporate behavior. This is a "window-in" approach and does not deal adequately with the internal corporate structure and how this structure responds rationally and thereby adapts to the external environment. This approach treats internal organizational processes as a "black-box" model whereby external constraints are treated as given, and corporate performance is observed and classified. The links among corporate characteristics, the environment, and corporate responses are rarely examined or even postulated. Differences in corporate responses and their possible causes, a corporation's propensity to take risks, and the means by which the corporation perceives changes in external sociopolitical environment remain to be examined.

The "window-out" approach is internally focused and emphasizes the effects of structural design, leadership style, and organizational culture on corporate performance in response to externally defined constraints on corporate behavior. The window-out approach has been confined largely to measures of corporate economic performance with less attention being paid to measuring its effectiveness in dealing with sociopolitical dimensions of the external environment.

The window-in approach to corporate social performance has been influenced by a variety of intellectual orientations, notably macroeconomics, political science, law, sociology, moral philosophy, and theology. Underlying this approach are two broad axioms:

1. The corporation is a rational institution primarily motivated by self-interest. Therefore, it would adjust its behavior and respond to whatever constraints its external environment imposed on it.

2. Being a self-serving institution, it follows that a corporation would be unlikely to initiate changes in its behavior that are not called for by the external environment and, therefore, are viewed by the corporation as contrary to its self-interest.

The window-out approach focuses on the ways in which the underlying processes of internal elements of a corporation adapt to a changing external environment. The primary intellectual influences emanate from such fields as social psychology, sociology, and law, and reflect themselves in organizational theory and behavior. The emphasis here is to view the external environment as a constraint whose adverse impact must be limited so that the organization can obtain necessary resources, pursue its own goals, and manage its affairs relatively free from outside intervention.

To the best of our knowledge, this book is the first attempt to consider these divergent views, providing the student of business and public policy with a comprehensive look at the multifaceted nature of the issues. The arrangement of this book shows how we, the editors, view the future order. We believe that in order to fully appreciate the complexity of the effect of the environment on organization social performance, the reader must have some conceptual and theoretical foundation. The first chapter of this book deals with the ideological underpinnings of business and society. The articles address the concept of the legitimacy of the corporation in society, the range of corporate behavior that underlies societal acceptance, and the interplay between societal and business values.

Important analytical schemes have been developed for describing the environment and types of corporate responses. Chapter 2 brings together several of these analytical frameworks. Within these, the student can look at the relationships between different aspects of business and society concerns, and view types of social issues and their evolution.

Clearly ideological underpinnings and models would have to relate to a sense of both individual and institutional ethics. Since there are no completely acceptable measures of accountability, there is an emphasis on societal expectations and their fulfillment, and ethics becomes a key issue. Ethicists, moral philosophers, and theologians are concerned with issues of ethical norms—individual and communal—and how they are enhanced or subverted by corporate behavior both within and outside its boundaries. Chapter 3 addresses the debate regarding corporate social responsibility that covers such issues as how the discussion of CSR has evolved, and what are some of the economic and noneconomic arguments for corporations to behave in a socially responsible or responsive manner. The articles examine what business ethics is and how it can be employed by organizations.

One of the ways to look at why corporations should behave differently is the notion of market failure and regulation. In chapter 4, business and government relations are examined, in terms of market control versus control by authority, that is, public policy and regulation. In a democratic society market control is preferred, and only in areas where market failure occurs is there support for government regulation of business. The reverse side of market failure is also addressed in chapter 4—under what conditions does government regulation create its own failures that the market has to address. Within this framework, we examine some of the new initiatives regarding regulation being presented in Congress and by the federal administration. In addition, the notion of how waste and fraud in government can be minimized is considered from the view of business representatives and private citizens. We also question some of the areas where the conventional wisdom of government doing the job may not be so logical—thus, the debate over privatization.

Issues involved in the relations between corporations and their stakeholders are presented in chapter 5. Stakeholders are defined as those directly involved in the corporation such as stockholders and employees, and also those from the broader societal context. The evolving role of boards of directors is discussed along with the notion of shareholder democracy. Employee relations are discussed in terms of the whistleblower and his protection, and the relations between work-related ethical attitudes and profitability. These selections emphasize the obligation of corporations to protect stakeholder interests. Moving into the external arena within which companies operate, the parts played by the church and public-interest groups, that is, the rationality, credibility, legitimacy, and effect of their role in the public-policy process, are considered (chapter 6).

An analysis of corporate response patterns to external pressures is found in chapter 7. The window-out approach emphasizes that internal factors influence the way the organization perceives the environment. Internal processes also influence the set of responses that organizations perceive as available to them, including the perception of the need for change and the attention an issue will receive from top management. The issues in chapter 7 include a discussion of the circumstances that give rise to business-society conflicts and ways corporations can resolve conflicts. We examine how companies can go about scanning their environment so they maintain an advance warning system. We also look at crisis management when companies tend to ignore the simmering, long-term issues. The chapter concludes with a discussion of how one can go about integrating social issues management and strategic management.

As a society, we have to decide what kind of deterrents or mechanisms we will use to curb deviant or socially undesirable corporate behavior. Chapter 8 presents material on the scope of corporate violations of the law and the controversy surrounding the relatively new approach to combating that crime, for example, the Racketeer Influenced and Corrupt Organizations Act (RICO).

Another way corporations have responded to external pressures is by becoming politically active. Thus, we consider the activities of large corporations in the political arena, that is, the use of economic power to achieve political influence in the determination of a nation's public-policy agenda and social priorities. This line of inquiry considers such issues as the politicalization of corporations, for example, political action committees and lobbying, including grassroots lobbying. There has been tremendous debate on the role of Political Action Committees (PACs). Chapter 9 deals with the nature and extent of corporate participation in the political process and some of the issues that arise as a consequence of this involvement. We examine the rationale for corporate activism, public attitudes toward PACs and how PACs might become more ethical and socially responsible.

Clearly, one of the major problems in dealing with the gap between societal expectations and corporate performance has to do with effective communication of corporate activities to various constituent groups. Similarly, in-house corporate communications are equally important to ensure that the employees and managers have a common vision of what is expected of them and the institution, and to ensure that creatively conceived plans do not fall down at the implementation stage because of poor communication. Chapter 10 examines two major issues dealing with corporate external communications—advocacy advertising and how business deals with the news media.

In chapter 11, we look at the international dimensions of business-society nteraction. Increasingly, business scholars have come to recognize the need for linking economic and sociopolitical variables in the external environment with the concepts of strategy implementation and organization control. Corporate economic performance cannot be isolated from its sociopolitical underpinnings. This has become particularly important in the context of the changing nature of international competition. With this important issue in mind, changing rules of international corporate behavior and the problems of conducting business in countries torn by internal political strife are discussed.

The material presented in the book, authored by academics and executives, gives the reader exposure to a broad range of issues and provides the basis for class discussion on the changes taking place in the increasingly complex relationship between business and society. The United States is no longer, if it ever was, an insulated nation. What used to be international competition is very much domestic competition. We are competing in U.S. markets with the Japanese, the Europeans, and other third country-based multinationals. These companies bring with them different manufacturing technologies as well as a whole new way of managing business and corporate culture, thereby radically altering the rules of the game.

We are also entering a new industrial age driven by computer-integrated manufacturing technology and information systems. Issues of business and society for U.S. corporations extend beyond the United States. All these changes require a reexamination of the sources of conflicting pressures exerted on corporations and of managerial responses to stakeholder demands.

We wish to thank the authors who contributed their work to the anthology. In particular, we wish to thank James Carman, Gerald Cavanagh, Robert Chatov, Neils Christiansen, William Frederick, Robert Harris, Sharon Meluso, Rafael Pagan, Jr., Paul Steidlmeier, Kenneth Walters, and Oliver Williams for preparing original papers for the book. Our appreciation is also extended to a number of authors who adapted portions of newly published works especially for this collection and to those who prepared extensive revisions of previously published papers. We wish to acknowledge the capable research assistance of Joseph Mancheno and Francis Honegan. Frances Krull, Michelle Edwards, and Rosa Estrada typed papers and graciously handled a number of administrative details that facilitated the completion of this project.

1
Ideological Underpinnings of Capitalism

Toward a Theology of the Corporation
Michael Novak

Our task is to set forth some steps toward a theology of the corporation. We need such a theology so that the ministers who serve businessmen and workers might be able to preach more illuminating and practical sermons and so that critics might have at their disposal a theologically sound standard of behavior for corporations.

For many years one of my favorite texts in scripture has been Isaiah 53:2–3: "He hath no form nor comeliness; and when we shall see him, there is no beauty that we should desire him. He is despised and rejected of men; a man of sorrows, and acquainted with grief; he was despised, and we esteemed him not." I would like to apply these words to the modern business corporation, a much despised incarnation of God's presence in this world.

When we speak of the body of Christ, we ordinarily mean the church, both invisible and visible, both sinless and marred by sin. God calls His followers to bring His presence to their work, to their daily milieu, to history. This is the doctrine of Christian vocation. A liturgy does not end without a word of mission: "Go out into the world of daily work to carry the peace and love of Jesus Christ." I do not mean by this to suggest that the Christian form is the only form of speech for this fundamental attitude. A sense of vocation infuses Jews, Muslims, and others of religious faith. Many who are not religious also regard their work as useful and ennobling. They feel called to the task of making life better for their fellow human beings. But I am a Catholic Christian, and it is better to speak in the idiom with most meaning for me than to pretend to an idiom that, by virtue of being no more than a common denominator, would appear superficial to all of us.

To work in a modern business corporation, no one need pass a test of faith or even reveal his or her religious convictions to others. But it would be a mistake to permit the business corporation's commendable acceptance of religious pluralism to mask the religious vocation that many see in it.

The Multinational Corporation

In speaking of the corporation, I will concentrate on those large business corporations that are found among the 300 or so multinational corporations, two-thirds of which are American.[1]

The reason one must first consider these big corporations is that all but very strict socialists seem to be in favor of markets, ownership, cooperatives, and small business. Religious socialists like John C. Cort favor the private ownership of small businesses, ownership through cooperatives, and some free-market mechanisms.[2]

What are multinational corporations? They are not those which merely sell their goods in other lands, buy goods from other lands, or trade with other lands. Multinationals are corporations that build manufacturing or other facilities in other lands in order to operate there. The building of a base of operations in other lands is an important condition for qualification as a multinational corporation in the strict sense. One should not think only of factories; banks and insurance firms—important for local investment—may also establish such operations.

The training of an indigenous labor and managerial force is not a strictly necessary condition for a corporation to be considered multinational, but it is a common characteristic, particularly of American companies. Thus multinationals make four chief contributions to the host country. Of these the first two, (1) capital facilities and (2) technological transfers inherent in the training of personnel, remain forever in the host country, whatever the ultimate fate of the original company. In addition, products manufactured within the nation no longer have to be imported; thus (3) the host nation's problems with balance of payments are eased. Finally, (4) wages paid to employees remain in the country, and local citizens begin to invest in the corporation, so that most of its future capital can be generated locally.[3] These are important factors in any accounting of the relative wealth transferred to and from the host country and the country of the corporation's origin. Critics sometimes concentrate only on the flow of return on investment. They commonly neglect to add up the capital investment, training, balance-of-payments relief, salaries, and stimulation of local investment.

Almost all of the 200 American multinationals are to be found among *Fortune's* 500 industrial companies, though a few are among the largest banks and insurance firms. What less-developed countries want most today is manufactured goods, at prices made possible by local production, and the financial services of banks and insurance companies.

Generally speaking, only a company of the size represented by the *Fortune* 500 has the capital and skills to accept the risks of operating in an unfamiliar culture. As it is, 40 percent of all foreign sales of U.S. multinationals are in Western Europe, and another 25 percent are in Japan, Canada, Taiwan, Hong Kong, South Korea,

Australia, and other industrial nations. Most concerns about the multinationals, how-ever, focus on their role in the developing nations. Only about 12 percent of the busi-ness of U.S. multinationals is to be found in Latin America, and only a tiny fraction in Africa. Vast expanses of the whole world never see an American multinational.[4]

The vast majority of U.S. corporations are not multinationals. Many that could be do not wish to be, believing the headaches more costly than the rewards. Some that are multinationals refuse to build operations under unstable conditions, such as those characterizing most of the developing nations. That is why such a small proportion of overseas activity by U.S. multinationals is to be found in Latin America and Africa.

Other contextual matters should be noted. In most nations of the world—notably the socialist nations—private corporations are not permitted to come into existence. Only a few nations produce privately held corporations. Furthermore, some nations which do so (the United States) were formerly colonies, and some others (Hong Kong) still are colonies. Since economic development depends to a large extent on home-based privately held corporations, differences in moral-cultural climate are significant. Some cultures seem to develop far higher proportions of skilled inventors, builders, and managers of industry than others do. In some cultures, the work force is more productive than in others.

Over time, education and training may provide new moral models and fairly swift cultural development. Simultaneously, of course, such developments may pro-voke intense conflicts with guardians of the earlier cultural order. It cannot be stressed too often that corporations are not merely economic agencies. They are also moral-cultural agencies. They may come into existence, survive, and prosper only under certain moral-cultural conditions.

It goes without saying that private corporations depend on a nonsocialist, non-statist political order. Insofar as socialist governments in Yugoslavia and elsewhere are now experimenting with autonomous economic enterprises, taking their signals from a free market, and rewarding their managers and workers according to profit and loss, they are moving toward a democratic capitalist-political order. As their middle class grows, so will the demand for further political rights, due process, democratic methods, free press, and freedom of worship. Economic liberties re-quire political liberties, and vice versa. Historically, not only has private business enterprise grown up with liberal democracy, it has also been the main engine in destroying class distinctions between aristrocrats and serfs, by making possible per-sonal and social mobility on a massive scale.

The private business corporation is particularly active among Americans. As Oscar Handlin has pointed out, the United States in 1800, with a population of just over 4 million, already had more corporations than all the nations of Europe combined.[5] Some of these corporations began to grow into large-scale organizations—roughly, following the railroads—at the end of the nineteenth century.

Nearly all American corporations, and particularly those in the *Fortune* 500, originated around a novel invention. They grew in sales, size, and capital either through products never before known or through novel processes for producing them.

Entire industries, like those for airplanes, automobiles, oil, gas, electricity, television, cinema, computers, copiers, office machinery, electronics, and plastics, are based on corporations initially formed by the American inventors of their products.

Theological Beginnings

In thinking about the corporation in history and its theological significance, I begin with a general theological principle. George Bernanos once said that grace is everywhere. Wherever we look in the world, there are signs of God's presence: in the mountains, in a grain of sand, in a human person, in the poor and the hungry. The earth is charged with the grandeur of God. So is human history. If we look for signs of grace in the corporation, we may discern seven of them as follows.

Creativity

The Creator locked great riches in nature, riches to be discovered only gradually through human effort. John Locke observed that the yield of the most favored field in Britain could be increased a hundredfold if human ingenuity and human agricultural science were applied to its productivity.[6] Nature alone is not as fecund as nature under intelligent cultivation. The world, then, is immeasurably rich as it comes from the Creator, but only potentially so. This potential was hidden for thousands of years until human discovery began to release portions of it for human benefit. Yet even today we have not yet begun to imagine all the possibilities of wealth in the world the Creator designed. The limits of our present intelligence restrict the human race to the relative poverty in which it still lives.

In 1979 Atlantic Richfield ran an advertisement based on a theme first enunciated, as far as I can tell, by Father Hesburgh of Notre Dame, namely, that 40 percent of the world's energy is used by the 6 percent of the world's population residing in the United States.[7] This way of putting the facts is an example of the cultivation of guilt that Professor Bauer has described.[8] A moment's thought shows that it is a preposterous formulation.

What the entire human race meant by energy until the discovery of the United States and the inventions promoted by its political economy were the natural forces of sun, wind, moving water, animals, and human muscle. Thomas Aquinas traveled on foot or by burro from Rome to Paris and back seven times in his life. The first pope to be able to make that voyage by train did so six centuries later, in the mid-nineteenth century. Until then, people traveled exactly as they had done since the time of Christ and before—by horse and carriage, by donkey, or by foot. History for a very long time seemed relatively static. The social order did not promote inventions and new technologies, at least not to the degree lately reached. The method of scientific discovery had not been invented.

In 1809 an American outside Philadelphia figured out how to ignite anthracite coal. The ability to use anthracite, which burned hotter and more steadily than bituminous coal, made practical the seagoing steamship and the locomotive. In 1859 the first oil well was dug outside of Titusville, Pennsylvania. Oil was known in biblical times but used only for products like perfume and ink. Arabia would have been as rich then as now, if anybody had known what to do with the black stuff. The invention of the piston engine and the discovery of how to drill for oil were also achieved in the United States. The first electric light bulb was illuminated in 1879 in Edison, New Jersey.

After World War II the U.S. government dragooned the utilities into experimenting with nuclear energy. They knew nothing about it. They did not need it. They did not want it. Oil and coal were cheap. The government, however, promoted the peaceful uses of the atom. Thus 100 percent of what the modern world means by energy was invented by 6 percent of the worlds' population. More than 60 percent of that energy has been distributed to the rest of the world. Though the United States can, of course, do better than that, we need not feel guilty for inventing forms of energy as useful to the human race as the fire brought to earth by Prometheus.

The agency through which inventions and discoveries are made productive for the human race is the corporation. Its creativity makes available to mass markets the riches long hidden in Creation. Its creativity mirrors God's. That is the standard by which its deeds and misdeeds are properly judged.

Liberty

The corporation mirrors God's presence also in its liberty, by which I mean independence from the state. That independence was the greatest achievement of the much-despised but creative 6 percent of the world's population. Advancing the work of their forebears, they invented the concept and framed the laws that for the first time in history set boundaries on the state, ruling certain activities off-limits to its interference. Rights of person and home, free speech in public, free press, and other liberties came to be protected both by constitutional law and by powerful interests actively empowered to defend themselves under that law. Legal autonomy was such that even the king could not forcibly enter the home of a peasant; a peasant's home was as protected as a duke's castle—rights that the colonists in America demanded for themselves. Private business corporations were permitted to become agents of experimentation, of trial and error, and for good reason: to unleash economic activism. The state retained rights and obligations of regulation, and undertook the indirect promotion of industry and commerce. The state alone was prohibited from becoming the sole economic agent. A sphere of economic liberty was created. The purpose of this liberty was to unlock greater riches than the world had ever known. Liberty was to be an experiment, which Adam Smith and others advocated, that might (or might not) prove to be in accordance with nature and with the laws of human society. Pleading for room to experiment, their practical, empirical arguments flew in the face of entrenched ideological opposition. The case for liberty prevailed.

The foundational concept of democratic capitalism, then, is not, as Marx thought, private property. It is limited government. Private property, of course, is one limitation on government.[9] What is interesting about private property is not that *I* own something, that *I* possess; its heart is not "possessive individualism," in C.B. MacPherson's phrase.[10] It is quite the opposite. The key is that the state is limited by being forbidden to control all rights and all goods. It cannot infringe on the privacy of one's home or on one's right to the fruit of one's labors and risks. Herbert Stein has a useful definition of capitalism: "The idea of a capitalist system has nothing to do with capital and has everything to do with freedom. I think of capitalist as a system in which ability to obtain and use income independently of other persons or organizations, including government, is widely distributed among the individuals of the population."[11]

Stein's idea is the distinctively American way of thinking about private property. In this framework, property is important less for its material reality than for the legal rights its ownership and use represent and for the limits it imposes on the power of the state. Such liberty was indispensable if private business corporations were to come into existence. Such corporations give liberty economic substance over and against the state.

Birth and Mortality

In coming into being with a technological breakthrough, and then perishing when some new technology causes it to be replaced, a typical corporation mirrors the cycle of birth and mortality. New corporations arise every day; dead ones litter history. Examining the *Fortune* 500 at ten-year intervals shows that even large corporations are subject to the cycle: new ones keep appearing, and many that were once prominent disappear. Of the original *Fortune* 500, first listed in 1954, only 285 remained in 1974. Of the missing 215, 159 had merged, 50 had become too small or gone out of business, and six were reclassified or had unavailable data.[12] Recently, Chrysler has been number 10. Will it by 1990 be gone from the list? Will Ford be gone from the list? It is entirely possible. As products of human liberty, corporations rise and fall, live and die. One does not have in them a lasting home—or even an immortal enemy.

Social Motive

Corporations, as the very word suggests, are not individualistic in their conception, in their operations, or in their purposes. Adam Smith entitled his book *An Inquiry into the Nature and Causes of the Wealth of Nations*. Its social scope went beyond individuals and beyond Great Britain to include all nations. The fundamental intention of the system from the beginning has been the wealth of all humanity.

The invention of democratic capitalism, the invention of the corporation, and the liberation of the corporations from total control by state bureaucracies (although some control always, and properly, remains) were intended to be multinational. Smith foresaw an interdependent world, for the first time able to overcome immemorial famine, poverty, and misery. He imagined people of every race, every culture, and every religion adopting the new knowledge about the causes of wealth. One does not need to be Christian or Jewish, or to share the Judeo-Christian world view, to understand the religious and economic potency of the free economy. Smith did not exactly foresee Toyota and Sony. But he certainly would have been delighted to add a chapter to his immense study showing how the Japanese demonstrated the truth of his hypothesis.[13]

Social Character

The corporation is inherently and in its essence corporate. The very word suggests communal, nonindividual, many acting together. Those who describe capitalism by stressing the individual entrepreneur miss the central point. Buying and selling by individual entrepreneurs occurred in biblical times. What is interesting and novel—at least what struck Max Weber as interesting and novel—is the communal focus of the new ethos: the rise of communal risk taking, the pooling of resources, the sense of communal religious vocation in economic activism. To be sure, certain developments in law and in techniques of accounting had to occur before corporations could be institutionalized in their modern form. In this sense, too, they are social creations.

Corporations depend on the emergence of an infrastructure in intellectual life that makes possible new forms of communal collaboration. They depend on ideas that are powerful and clear enough to organize thousands of persons around common tasks. Moreover, these ideas must be strong enough to endure for years, so that individuals who commit themselves to them can expect to spend thirty to forty years working out their vocation. For many millions of religious persons the daily milieu in which they work out their salvation is the communal, corporate world of the workplace. For many, the workplace is a kind of second family. Even those who hate their work often like their co-workers. This is often true in factories; it is also true in offices. Comradeship is natural to humans. Labor unions properly build on it.

Insight

The primary capital of any corporation is insight, invention, finding a better way. Insight is of many kinds and plays many roles: it is central to invention; it lies at the heart of organization; it is the vital force in strategies for innovation, production, and marketing. Corporate management works hard at communal insight. Constantly, teams of persons meet to brainstorm and work out common strategies.

Insight is the chief resource of any corporation, and there cannot be too much of it. Its scarcity is called stupidity.

Karl Marx erred in thinking that capital has to do primarily with machinery, money, and other tangible instruments of production. He overlooked the extent to which the primary form of capital is an idea.[14] The right to patent industrial ideas is an extremely important constitutional liberty. It is indispensable to the life of corporations, as indispensable as the copyright is to writers. Money without ideas is not yet capital. Machinery is only as good as the idea it embodies. The very word *capital*, from the Latin caput, meaning "head," points to the human spirit as the primary form of wealth. The miser sitting on his gold is not a capitalist. The investor with an idea is a capitalist. Insight makes the difference.

A momentary digression. Money was more material before capitalism, when it was gold and silver coin, than it came to be afterward. Under capitalism, perhaps a majority of transactions are intellectualized "book" transactions. Moreover, paper money is necessary, as are stocks, bonds, constitutions, and legal contracts. Materialism is more and more left behind as money depends for its value less on material substance than on public confidence, the health of the social order, the stability of institutions. Let these be threatened and investments flee because deteriorating social health reduces the value of the amounts registered on paper. Materially, money is often "not worth the paper it's printed on." Its real value depends on sociality, trust, a sense of health and permanence. In this respect, a theological treatise on the symbolic nature of money is badly needed. Such a treatise would have to deal not only with the fact that most money exists only in the intellectual realm but also with the impersonality of money, which transcends discrimination based on race, religion, sex, or nationality, and with money's remarkable indeterminacy, according to which its moral value springs from how persons, in their liberty, use it. Money opens a vast range of freedom of choice. Accordingly, it is more closely related to insight and liberty than to matter. It no longer functions as it did in biblical times.

The Rise of Liberty and Election

A corporation risks liberty and election; it is part of its romance to do so. Tremendous mistakes in strategy can cripple even the largest companies. Easy Washing Machines of Syracuse once made an excellent washing machine, but Maytag's discovery of a new technology took away part of Easy's market. Easy had all its assets sunk in a plant it could not redesign quickly enough to incorporate the new technology, and the company collapsed. Thus a sudden technological breakthrough, even a relatively minor one, can cripple a company or an industry. A simple strategic mistake by a team of corporate executives about where to apply the company's energies over a year or two can end up dimming the company's outlook for many years. A failure to modernize can bring about bankruptcy. The corporation operates in a world of no scientific certainty, in which corporate leaders must constantly make judgments about reality when not all the evidence about reality is in. Such leaders argue among themselves about strategic alternatives, each perhaps saying to himself, "We will see who is right about this," or "The next year or two will tell." But a judgment must be made and the investment committed before the telling is completed. Thus decision makers often experience the risks inherent in their decisions. At the very least they always face the risk of doing considerably less well than they think they are going to do.

In these seven ways, corporations offer metaphors for grace, a kind of insight into God's ways in history. Yet corporations are of this world. They sin. They are semper reformanda—always in need of reform.

Problems of Bigness and Other Accusations

Big corporations are despised and rejected even when the market system, small businesses, and private ownership are not. Some religious socialists do not absolutely reject certain elements in the democratic-capitalist idea. But they often bridle at the big corporations. Their accusations against such corporations—many of them as true as charges made against the universities or against any large institution— are many.

One accusation is that the corporations are autocratic, that internally they are not democratic. In trying to decide how true this charge is, one could undertake a survey of the management techniques of the *Fortune* 500 corporations. How are they actually managed? How does their management differ in practice from the internal management of universities, churches, government agencies, or other institutions? Let us suppose that some autocrats still function in various spheres of authority today, including business. What sanctions are available to autocrats within a corporation? Leadership in all spheres today seems to depend on large areas of consensus; leaders seem to "manage" more than they "command." I have roughly the same impression of the chief executive officers I have met as of the American Catholic bishops I have met; namely, that out of the office, as Schumpeter says, "they would find it hard to say boo to a duck." Few, as I see them, are autocrats. Would that the world still saw the likes of Cardinals Spellman, Connell, Cushing, and Gibbons; or of industrial autocrats like Carnegie, Mellon, and others. Such types seem to have perished from the earth. In their place are men who, if you saw them in sport shirts at a Ramada Inn, would make you think you had dropped in on a convention of real-estate agents from Iowa. Very pleasant, nice men, they are nowhere near as assertive as journalists. They do not often have the occupational arrogance of academics. But empirical tests are in order to see how many autocrats are in corporations, in comparison with any other sphere of life.

A second frequent accusation against big corporations is the alienation their employees experience in the workplace. To what extent is such alienation caused by the conditions of modern work under any existing system or under any imaginable system? Do laborers in auto factories in Bratislava or Poznán work under conditions any different from those faced by laborers in the United States? One ought to compare hours of work, conditions of the workplace, salaries, working procedures, and levels of pollution. These is no evidence that any real or imagined socialism can take the modernity out of modern work. Nor is boring work unique to the modern factory; it surely dominated the ancient work of European peasants and continues to dominate the fourteen-hour day of the modern potato farmer. Farming is not, in my experience, inherently less alienating than working seven hours, with time off for lunch, on an assembly line. Alienation is not a problem peculiar to capitalism or to corporations. Is work less alienating within a government bureaucracy? Instead of condemning political activists or politicians to jail for various crimes, suppose one simply condemned them to filing the correspondence of congressmen from states like Ohio and Arkansas for periods of up to three months.

A third accusation against corporations is that they represent too great a concentration of power. What is the alternative? There is indeed a circle within which small is beautiful, a relatively small and beautiful circle. But "small is beautiful" does not apply across the whole large world. When Jane Fonda and Tom Hayden made their pilgrimage to seventy-two cities carrying the word on economic democracy, they did not fly in airplanes made in small stores. Their travel arrangements were not made by small organizations working off a telephone in a back room, but by agencies with computers and Telex connections to operating stations in all airlines and in all airports, giving them the instantaneous information required to synchronize such a trip in a very short time.

Socialist economist Robert Lekachman has argued that the big corporations should be reduced in size to more manageable proportions.[15] Maybe so. To my mind the question is a practical, experimental one. Consider the largest of all corporations, General Motors. It is already broken up into more than 200 units in more than 177 congressional districts in the United States. Its largest single facility, in Michigan, employs no more than 14,000 people. Many universities—the University of Michigan and Michigan State, to name two—comprise human communities two or three times that size. Corporations already follow the principle of subsidiarity far more thoroughly than Lekachman seems to take into account. One might argue that they should be still smaller. Yet one must note that the smaller U.S. auto companies—American Motors, Chrysler, and Ford—are apparently in danger of perishing because of inadequate capital to meet the enormous expenses of retooling for new auto technologies. The foreign auto companies competing with General Motors (even in the United States) are also very large. If small is beautiful, beauty seems precarious indeed; big may be necessary.

In practice, I cannot imagine how human capacities and human choices of the sort needed by mass markets could still be made available except through large organizations. Small organizations may suit a small country, but it seems to me absurd to imagine that a continental nation with a population of 220 million can be well served in all respects only through small organizations in small industries. If somebody can invent a system of smallness, fine; I am not, in principle, against it. I just cannot imagine that it can work in practice.

Corporations are further accused of being inherently evil because they work for a profit. Without profit no new capital is made available for research, development, and new investment. Further, there is a difference between maximization of profit and optimization of profit. To aim at maximizing profit—that is, to obtain the greatest profit possible out of every opportunity—is to be greedy in the present at the expense of the future. The profit maximizer demands too much for products that can be produced more cheaply by somebody else and in the process narrows his market and destroys his reputation. Inevitably, he damages himself and, in time, destroys himself. Adam Smith made this point a long time ago, and history is replete with examples of it. By contrast, to optimize profit is to take many other factors besides profit into account, including long-term new investment, consumer loyalty, and the sense of a fair service for a fair price.

The profit motive must necessarily operate in a socialist economy, too. Every economy that intends to progress must have as its motive the ability to get more out of the economic process than it puts in. Unless there is a return on investment, the economy simply spins its wheels in stagnation, neither accumulating nor growing. Capital accumulation is what profits are called in socialist enterprises. If the Soviets invest money in dams or in building locomotives, they must get back at least what they invest or they lose money. If they do lose money—and they often do—then they must draw on other resources. And if they do that throughout the system, economic stagnation and decline are inevitable. The same law binds both socialist and capitalist economies. Economic progress, growth, and forward motion cannot occur unless the return on investment is larger than the investment itself.

It is true that under socialism profits belong to the state and are allocated to individuals by the state for the state's own purposes. Such a procedure can be institutionalized, but the costs of enforcing it are great. It tremendously affects the possibilities of liberty, of choice. It deeply affects incentives and creativity.

Objections to corporations are many. Some are clearly justified. Some are spurious. A full-dress theology of the corporation would properly evaluate each one fairly, from many points of view. A convenient summary of some of them is to be found in *The Crisis of the Corporation*, by Richard J. Barnet.[16] Barnet makes three major accusations: (1) that the multinational corporations have inordinate power; (2) that they weaken the powers of the nation-state; and (3) that their actual practice destroys several myths about corporations.

The power of the multinational corporations, Barnet believes, springs from their ability to internationalize planning, production, finance, and marketing. In planning, each part can specialize, so that the whole pursues profit maximization. In production, resources from various lands are integrated. In finance, computerization allows multinational corporations to take advantage of fluctuations in capital markets. In marketing, goods and consumption are standardized.[17]

From another point of view, these accusations seem to list advantages. Any economic organization that can work as Barnet describes would seem to be well placed to produce the maximum number of goods at the lowest cost. This efficiency should have the effect of making the most practical use of scarce capital, while increasing that capital through profitable investment. (We have already noted an important difference between profit maximization and profit optimization.) The purpose of an interdependent world economic order is to match off the strengths of one region with those of another: a region with capital reserves and high labor costs is needed by a region without capital reserves but cheap labor. The cost of ignoring each other would be high for both regions. Cooperation should produce benefits for both.

Barnet argues that the powers of nation-states are weakened because multinational corporations make intracorporate transfers of funds without the knowledge of national governmental bodies. In addition, he asserts, they shift production to low-wage areas with fewer union troubles; move productive facilities to regions where tax advantages are greatest; have no loyalty to any one country; and use dominance in one national market to achieve dominance in others because they can out-advertise smaller local companies.[18]

If all of these assertions are true, at least sometimes and in some places, not all of their effects are evil. Consider, for example, the competition between Japanese, European, and U.S. automobile manufacturers. The new reality is that market competition has been internationalized. Every such new development has advantages and costs. It appears that U.S. citizens benefit by quality and cost from this competition. Obviously, foreign auto workers would seem to benefit. Unless U.S. manufacturers can do better, U.S. auto workers will continue to suffer.

Would the world be a better place if each nation-state tried solely to protect its own industries? At various times, protectionism has triumphed. Nations do have the power to expel, close out, restrict, and nationalize foreign industries; often they do. This course, too, has costs as well as advantages. Barnet does not show that its costs are lower than those of the competition he opposes. No matter how Chrysler advertised during 1979, it did not seem to move the cars it tried to sell. Advertising is far less exact than he imagines.

Barnet argues, finally, that monopolization undercuts competitive free enterprise. He concedes that monopoly scarcely exists, but hastens to substitute for it oligopoly (four major firms, for example, controlling a majority of sales in several industries), whose "effects are much the same."[19] He argues that efficiency is undercut by intracorporate transactions (as when tax laws encourage the shipment of products over long distances, when similar products could be acquired locally);[20] that income distribution between the top 20 percent and the bottom 20 percent of income earners in the United States has "remained the same for forty-five years";[21] and that democracy is not enhanced by a free economy.[22]

Since Barnet himself is in favor of state monopolies in the socialist pattern, his objections to oligopolies do not have an authentic ring. Surely, four large companies in an industry are better than one state monopoly. Moreover, in the international field, the three major U.S. automobile companies, for example, compete not only with each other but also with Volvo, Fiat, Peugeot, Volkswagen, Toyota, and many others. In other industries, international competition is also a reality.[23]

It is true that prices in a complex, highly technological industry are not a simple matter, but it goes too far to suggest that they are no longer a useful indicator of cost and value. Consumers today make economic choices not only between cars to buy but between buying a car and investing the money, or building an addition on the house, or doing something else. In seeking the consumers' dollars, producers compete not only with others in their own industries but also with other industries altogether. Pricing, however sophisticated the process through which prices are calculated, still affects the decisions of purchasers, as alternative marketing strategies amply demonstrate.

With respect to income distribution, most socialists today recognize that incomes are not and cannot be perfectly equal. They certainly are not in socialist countries. If persons at the top end of the income ladder receive eight times as much as those at the bottom, it follows that the total share of income of those at the top will be significantly higher than that of a similar cohort at the bottom. This relationship is strictly arithmetical. Imagine that Barnet himself earns $50,000 a year from his salary and royalties. This income would rank in the top 3 percent of all U.S. households, seven times as high as the official poverty level for a nonfarm family of four.[24] Arithmetically, his class—say, that of the top 5 percent— must accumulate a disproportionate share of all U.S. incomes.

There is a further point. One must not compare only percentiles—snapshots of groups at one point in time. As a graduate student at Harvard Law School, Barnet's income was certainly lower than it is now; it may even have been below the poverty level (though this did not, except technically, make him poor). At each decade thereafter one would expect his income to place him in a different percentile. While percentiles may remain relatively constant, individuals (at least in a free, mobile society) rise and fall between them. Moreover, a family's relative wealth in the long run—over, say, three generations—largely depends on the sort of investment it makes with available funds. Investments in consumption at each moment preclude growth; investment in education, property, and the like make future material improvement probable. Thus, in many families, one generation works not solely for itself but for its future progeny. As it happens, families once wealthy sometimes experience economic decline, and families once poor sometimes become better off than in earlier generations. One must track not simply the statistical percentiles but the rise and fall over time of individuals and families within these percentiles. One would expect some individuals and families to be more intelligent, wiser, and luckier over time than others. Inequality of income is no more a scandal than are inequalities of looks, personality, talent, will, and luck. Inequality of income appears to be an inevitable fact in all large societies.

There is a peculiar historical link—which even Marxists recognize—between the emergence of liberal democracy in Great Britain, the United States, the Netherlands, and a few cognate lands and the emergence of a free economy. One might be satisfied to stress the historical character of the link. But it also seems to have a necessary conceptual character. If individuals lack fundamental economic liberties (to earn, spend, save, and invest as they see fit), they necessarily have few effective political liberties. If they are dependent on the state for economic decisions, they must be wards of the state in other matters. Moreover, to believe that state bureaucrats are competent to make economic decisions for the common good is to make a great leap of faith, when one considers the actual economic well-being of workers in the U.S.S.R., Poland, Cuba, and Yugoslavia. Even the democratic socialists of Sweden and West Germany insist on vital economic liberties for individuals and corporations.

Socialist societies do not permit private corporations to exist. They operate on the assumption that state officials know best what is for the common good. In reflecting on their actual practice, one may come to believe that democratic capitalism is more likely to meet the goals of socialism—plus other goals of its own—than socialism is. The social instrument invented by democratic capitalism to achieve social goals is the private corporation. Anyone can start one; those who succeed in making them work add to the common benefit. Yet corporations do not live (or die) in a vacuum. They must meet the demands of the moral-cultural system and of the political system. While corporations spring from some of our most cherished ideals about liberty, initiative, investment in the future, cooperation, and the like, they must also be judged in the light of our ideals. They are moral-cultural institutions, as well as economic institutions. Their primary task is economic. One cannot ask them to assume crushing and self-destructive burdens. Yet they are more than economic organisms alone and must be held to political and moral judgment.

Three Systems—Three Fields of Responsibility

The most original social invention of democratic capitalism, in sum, is the private corporation founded for economic purposes. The motivation for this invention was also social: to increase the wealth of nations, to generate (for the first time in human history) sustained economic development. This effect was, in fact, achieved. However, the corporation—as a type of voluntary association—is not merely an economic institution. It is also a moral institution and a political institution. It depends on and generates certain moral-cultural virtues; it depends on and generates new political forms. In two short centuries, it has brought about an immense social revolution. It has moved the center of economic activity from the land to industry and commerce. No revolution is without social costs and sufferings, which must be entered on the ledger against benefits won. Universally, however, the idea of economic development has now captured the imagination of the human race. This new possibility of development has awakened the world from its economic slumbers.

Beyond its economic effects, the corporation changes the ethos and the cultural forms of society. To some extent, it has undercut ancient ways in which humans relate to each other, with some good effects and some bad. After the emergence of corporations, religion had to work on new psychological realities. The religion of peasants has given way to the religion of new forms of life: first that of an urban proletariat, then that of a predominantly service and white-collar society. The productivity of the new economics has freed much human time for questions other than those of mere subsistence and survival. The workday has shrunk, and weekends have been invented. After work, millions now take part in voluntary activities that fill, in effect, another forty-hour week (associations, sports, travel, politics, religion, and the like). Personal and social mobility has increased. Schooling has become not only common but mandatory. Teenagerhood has been invented. The stages of human life have drawn attention with the emergence of the private self.

But the corporation is not only an economic institution and a moral-cultural institution: it also provides a new base for politics. Only a free political system permits the voluntary formation of private corporations. Thus, those who value private economic corporations have a strong interest in resisting both statism and socialism. It would be naive and wrong to believe that persons involved in corporations are (or should be) utterly neutral about political systems. An economic system within which private corporations play a role, in turn, alters the political horizon. It lifts the poor, creates a broad middle class, and undermines aristocracies of birth. Sources of power are created independent of the power of the state, in competition with the powers of the state, and sometimes in consort with the powers of the state. A corporation with plants and factories in, say, 120 congressional districts represents a great many employees and stockholders. On some matters, at least, the districts are likely to be well-organized to express their special political concerns. Political jurisdictions often compete to attract corporations, but their arrival also creates political problems.

Corporations err morally, then, in many ways. They may through their advertising appeal to hedonism and escape, in ways that undercut the restraint and self-discipline required by a responsible democracy and that discourage the deferral of present satisfaction on which savings and investment for the future depend. They may incorporate methods of governance that injure dignity, cooperation, inventiveness, and personal development. They may seek their own immediate interests at the expense of the common good. They may become improperly involved in the exercise of political power. They may injure the conscience of their managers or workers. They are capable of the sins of individuals and of grave institutional sins as well. Thus, it is a perfectly proper task of all involved within corporations and in society at large to hold them to the highest moral standards, to accuse them when they fail, and to be vigilant about every form of abuse. Corporations are human institutions designed to stimulate economic activism and thus to provide the economic base for a democratic polity committed to high moral-cultural ideals. When they fall short of these purposes, their failure injures all.

Private corporations are social organisms. Neither the ideology of laissez faire nor the ideology of rugged individualism suits their actual practice or their inherent ideals. Corporations socialize risk, invention, investment, production, distribution, and services. They were conceived and designed to break the immemorial grip of mercantilist and clerical systems on economic activity. However, they cannot come into existence, and certainly cannot function, except within political systems designed to establish and to promote the conditions of their flourishing. Among these are a sound currency, a system of laws, the regulation of competitive practices, the construction of infrastructures like roads, harbors, airports, certain welfare functions, and the like. The state, then, plays an indispensable role in democratic capitalism. The ideals of democratic capitalism are not those of laissez faire. The relations between a democratic state and a social market economy built around private corporations are profound, interdependent, and complex.

The ideals of democratic capitalism are not purely individualist, either, for the corporation draws on and requires highly developed social skills like mutual trust, teamwork, compromise, cooperation, creativity, originality and inventiveness, and agreeable management and personnel relations. The rugged individualist of an earlier mythology may be an endangered species.

Great moral responsibility, then, is inherent in the existence of corporations. They may fail economically. They may fail morally and culturally. They may fail politically. Frequently enough, they err in one or all these areas. They are properly subjected to constant criticism and reform. But types of criticism may be distinguished. Some critics accept the ideals inherent in the system of private business corporations, and simply demand that corporations be faithful to these ideals. Some critics are opposed to the system qua system. Among these, some wish to restrain, regulate, and guide the business system through the power of the state and/or through moral and cultural forces like public opinion, shame, ridicule, boycotts, and moral suasion ("do not invest in South Africa," for example). In the theory of mixed systems, the ideal of democratic capitalism shades off into the ideal of democratic socialism—one leaning more to the private sector, the other leaning more to the public sector. Still other critics wish to make the business system directly subject to the state. These last may be, according to their own ideals, corporate statists or socialists. They may be state socialists or local participatory politics socialists. Criticism from any of these quarters may be useful to the development and progress of democratic capitalism, even from those who would wish to destroy it.

There is plenty of room and plenty of evidence for citing specific deficiencies of corporations: economic, political, and moral-cultural. To be sure, there is a difference between accusations and demonstrated error. Like individuals, corporations are innocent until proved guilty. A passionate hostility toward bigness (or even toward economic liberty), like a passionate commitment to statism, may be socially useful by providing a searching critique from the viewpoint of hostile critics. But unless it gets down to cases and sticks to a reasoned presentation of evidence, it must be recognized for what it is: an argument less against specifics than against the radical ideal of democratic capitalism and the private corporation. It is useful to distinguish these two types of criticism, and it is helpful when critics are self-conscious and honest about which ideals actually move them. To criticize corporations in the light of their own ideals, the ideals of democratic capitalism, is quite different from criticizing them in the name of statist or socialist ideals incompatible with their existence. Clarity about ideals is as necessary as clarity about cases.

Theologians, in particular, are likely to inherit either a precapitalist or a frankly socialist set of ideals about political economy. They are especially likely to criticize corporations from a set of ideals foreign to those of democratic capitalism. To those who do accept democratic-capitalist ideals, then, their criticisms are likely to have a scent of unreality and inappropriateness. Wisdom would suggest joining argument at the appropriate level of discourse—whether the argument concerns general economic concepts, whether it concerns the rival ideals of democratic capitalism and socialism, or whether it concerns concrete cases and specific matters of fact. Each of these levels has its place. Wisdom's principal task is *distinguer.*

Managing a free society aimed at preserving the integrity of the trinitarian system—the economic system, the political system, and the moral-cultural system—is no easy task. An important standard set by Edmund Burke is cited as the epigraph of a masterly work by Wilhelm T. Röpke:

> To make a government requires no great prudence. Settle the seat of power; teach obedience: and the work is done. To give freedom is still more easy. It is not necessary to guide; it only requires to let go the rein. But to form a *free government;* that is, to temper together these opposite elements of liberty and restraint in one consistent work, requires much thought, deep reflection, a sagacious, powerful and combining mind.[25]

To govern a free economy is yet more difficult than to form a free government. It is hard enough to govern a government. The difficulty is multiplied to govern a free economy—to establish the conditions for prosperity, to keep a sound currency, to promote competition, to establish general rules and standards, to keep markets free, to provide education to all citizens in order to give them opportunity, to care for public needs, and to provide succor to the unfortunate. To have the virtue to do all these things wisely, persistently, judiciously, and aptly is surely of some rather remarkable theological significance. It may even represent—given the inherent difficulties—a certain amazing grace. To fall short is to be liable to judgment.

Christians have not, historically, lived under only one economic system; nor are they bound in conscience to support only one. Any real or, indeed, any imaginable economic system is necessarily part of history, part of this world. None is the Kingdom of Heaven—not democratic socialism, not democratic capitalism. A theology of the corporation should not make the corporation seem to be an ultimate; it is only a means, an instrument, a worldly agency. Such a theology should attempt to show how corporations may be instruments of redemption, of humane purposes and values, of God's grace; it should also attempt to show corporations' faults. Corporations may be seen as both obstacles to salvation and bearers of God's grace. The waters of the sea are blessed, as are airplanes and plowshares and even troops making ready for just combat. A city in Texas may be named Corpus Christi, and a city in California, Sacramento. Christianity, like Judaism, attempts to sanctify the real world as it is, in all its ambiguity, so as to reject the evil in it and bring the good in it to its highest possible fruition.

Most Christians do not now work for major industrial corporations. Instead, they work for the state (even in state universities), for smaller corporations, restaurants, barbershops, and other businesses. Still, a Christian social theology that lacks a theology of the large corporation will have no effective means of inspiring those Christians who do work within large corporations to meet the highest practicable Christian standards. It will also have no means of criticizing with realism and practicality those features of corporate life that deserve to be changed. Whether to treat big corporations as potential vessels of Christian vocation or to criticize them for their inevitable sins, Christian theology must advance much further than it has in understanding exactly and fairly every aspect of corporate life. The chief executive officer of General Electric needs such a theology. So do those critics of the corporation at the Interfaith Center for Corporate Responsibility. If we are to do better than clash like ignorant armies in the night, we must imitate Yahweh at Creation when he said, "Let there be light." We have not yet done all we should in casting such light.

Notes

Reprinted with permission from Michael Novak, "Toward a Theology of the Corporation," in *Toward a Theology of the Corporation* (Washington, D.C.: American Enterprise Institute, 1981), pp. 33–55. Copyright © 1981 by American Enterprise Institute.

1. Sperry Lea and Simon Webley, *Multinational Corporations in Developed Countries: A Review of Recent Research and Policy Thinking* (Washington, D.C.: British-North American Committee, 1973), p. 1.

2. See John C. Cort, "Can Socialism Be Distinguished from Marxism?" *Cross Currents* **29** (Winter 1979–1980): 423–434.

3. Ronald E. Muller estimates that 80 percent of the capital raised by multinational corporations in Latin America is local: "We find initially that, for the period from 1957 to 1965, of the total U.S. investment in Latin America only 17 per cent of the actual financial capital investments ever came from the United States. When we look at the manufacturing sector for the same period, we find that 78 per cent of all U.S. corporate investments were financed not from U.S. savings but from Latin American savings." "The Multinational Corporation: Asset or Impediment to World Justice?" in *Poverty, Environment and Power,* ed. Paul Hallock (New York: International Documentation on the Contemporary Church—North America, 1973), p. 42.

4. U.S. Bureau of the Census, *Statistical Abstract of the United States,* 1979, (Washington, D.C.: U.S. Department of Commerce, 1979), table 944.

5. Oscar Handlin, "The Development of the Corporation," in *The Corporation: A Theological Inquiry*, ed. Michael Novak and John W. Cooper (Washington, D.C.: American Enterprise Institute, 1981).

6. John Locke, *Second Treatise of Civil Government* (New York: Macmillan, 1947), p. 20.

7. Theodore Hesburgh, *The Humane Imperative: A Challenge for the Year 2000* (New Haven, Conn.: Yale University Press, 1974), p. 101.

8. P.T. Bauer, "Western Guilt and Third World Poverty," in *The Corporation*, ed. Novak and Cooper.

9. See Paul Johnson, "Is There a Moral Basis for Capitalism?" in *Democracy and Mediating Structures: A Theological Inquiry*, ed. Michael Novak (Washington, D.C.: American Enterprise Institute, 1980), pp. 49–58.

10. C.B. MacPherson, *The Political Theory of Possessive Individualism: Hobbes to Locke* (New York: Oxford University Press, 1962), p. 263.

11. Herbert Stein, *Capitalism—If You Can Keep It* (Washington, D.C.: American Enterprise Institute, 1980), p. 6.

12. "The 500: A Report on Two Decades," *Fortune*, May 1975, p. 238.

13. Per capita savings deposits in Japan at the end of 1977 were $9,531, compared with $4,354 in the United States. See *Facts and Figures of Japan* (Tokyo: Tokyo Foreign Press Center, 1980).

14. "Economy is essentially the transformation of natural forces and natural goods into forces and goods that serve humanity. It is an order created by thinking people, and one that has developed as a result of people's intellectual and spiritual growth. Further, it should be clear that when we regard economy as the creation of thinking human beings, economic wealth becomes nothing more than the transformation of natural wealth. There is no material wealth except that of nature and that created by humans from nature." Stephen B. Roman and Eugen Loebl, *The Responsible Society* (New York: Regina Ryan Books/Two Continents, 1977), pp. 22–23.

15. "A second characteristic I would seek from socialism is a reduction in the scale of the corporation in our country. Now, this is not 'small is beautiful.' I do not think you are going to build large aircraft with E.F. Schumacher's intermediate technology—nor, for that matter, large computers in local workshops. Nevertheless, by every account, the scale of the large corporation is much less related to technological economies of scale than to various advertising, marketing, financial, and legal benefits—including the opportunity to control markets.

"Now, free enterprise economists, of course, would be alarmed by the idea of limiting the size of corporations. I would argue that competition only works where it exists; and the scale of the large organization frequently limits the amount of effective competition that can occur. Diminishing the average size of the productive units would increase their number, and thereby the potential for competition." Robert Lekachman, "The Promise of Democratic Socialism," in *Democracy and Mediating Structures*, ed. Novak, p. 40.

16. Richard J. Barnet, *The Crisis of the Corporation* (Washington, D.C.: Institute for Policy Studies, 1975).

17. Ibid., pp. 7–8.

18. Ibid., pp. 8–11.

19. Ibid., p. 14.

20. Ibid., pp. 16–17.

21. Ibid., p. 20.
22. Ibid., pp. 21–22.
23. Lester Thurow, "Let's Abolish the Antitrust Laws," the *New York Times*, October 19, 1980.
24. "The poverty threshold for a non-farm family of four was $7,412 in 1979." U.S. Bureau of the Census, *Money Income and Poverty Status of Families and Persons in the United States: 1979 (Advanced Report)* (Washington, D.C., 1970), p. 1.
25. See Wilhelm T. Röpke, *A Humane Economy: The Social Framework of the Free Market* (Chicago: Henry Regnery, 1960), facing p. 1; the quotation is from Edmund Burke, *Reflections on the Revolution in France* (1790).

Bibliography

Barber, Richard J. *The American Corporation: Its Power, Its Money, Its Politics*. New York: E.P. Dutton, 1970.

Berle, Adolf A., Jr. *The Twentieth Century Capitalist Revolution*. New York: Harcourt, 1954.

Brozen, Yale; Mott, William C.; Tyrmand, Leopold; St. John, Jeffrey; Shenfield, Barbara; and Howard, John A. *Corporate Responsibility: The Viability of Capitalism in an Era of Militant Demands*. Rockford, Ill.: Rockford College Institute, 1978.

Davis, John P. *Corporations: A Study of the Origin and Development of Great Business Combinations and Their Relation to the Authority of the State*, 2 vols. New York: Putnam, 1961, reprint of 1905 edition.

Davis, Joseph S. *Essays in the Earlier History of American Corporations*, 2 vols. Cambridge, Mass.: Harvard University Press, 1917.

Drucker, Peter F. *Concept of the Corporation*. New York: John Day Co., 1946.

Finn, David. *The Corporate Oligarch*. New York: Simon & Schuster, 1969.

Frank, Isaiah. *Foreign Enterprise in Developing Countries*. Baltimore: Johns Hopkins University Press, 1980.

Galbraith, John Kenneth. *The New Industrial State*. Boston: Houghton Mifflin, 1967.

Hessen, Robert. *In Defense of the Corporation*. Stanford, Calif.: Hoover Institution Press, 1979.

Hewlitt, Sylvia Ann. *The Cruel Dilemmas of Development: Twentieth-Century Brazil*. New York: Basic Books, 1980.

Hunt, Bishop C. *The Development of the Business Corporation in England; 1800–1967*. Cambridge, Mass.: Harvard University Press, 1936.

Hurst, James Willard. *The Legitimacy of the Business Corporation in the Law of the United States, 1780–1970*. Charlottesville, Va.: University Press of Virginia, 1970.

Kristol, Irving. *Two Cheers for Capitalism*. New York: Basic Books, 1978.

Manne, Henry G., and Wallich, Henry C. *The Modern Corporation and Social Responsibility*. Washington, D.C.: American Enterprise Institute, 1972.

Moore, Wilbert E. *The Conduct of the Corporation*. New York: Random House, 1962.

Moran, T.H. *Multinational Corporations and the Politics of Dependence: Copper in Chile*. Princeton, N.J.: Princeton University Press, 1974.

Novak, Michael, and Cooper, John W., eds. *The Corporation: A Theological Inquiry*. Washington, D.C.: American Enterprise Institute, 1981.

Powers, Charles W. *Social Responsibility and Investment*. Nashville, Tenn.: Abingdon, 1971.

———, and Vogel, David. *Ethics in the Education of Business Managers.* Hastings-on-Hudson, N.Y.: The Hastings Center, 1980.

Sigmund, Paul E. *Multinationals in Latin America: The Politics of Nationalization.* Madison, Wisc.: University of Wisconsin Press, 1980.

Vernon, Raymond. *Sovereignty at Bay: The Multinational Spread of U.S. Enterprises.* New York: Basic Books, 1971.

Walton, Clarence. *The Ethics of Corporate Conduct.* Englewood Cliffs, N.J.: Prentice-Hall, 1977.

Williams, Oliver F., and Houck, John W. *Full Value: Cases in Christian Business Ethics.* New York: Harper & Row, 1978.

Values and Morality in Corporate America

Gerald F. Cavanagh, S.J.

The values and morality of individuals are affected by external events: history, family, opinion leaders, and a wide variety of other influences. One strong influence is little acknowledged: the organization in which people work. Our values, and our morality in turn, heavily influence the many choices that we make each day of our lives. Often these values are opaque to us; we are not aware of the values that drive our own lives.

This article attempts to shed some light on how current American business values have developed. It will examine the effect on our values of:

1. history, social movements, and U.S. geography;
2. the groups and organizations to which we belong;
3. advertising and the values it presents.

We will then proceed to examine the influence that our values have on:

1. attitudes toward work (both blue-collar and managerial);
2. the distinction that we make between law and morality;
3. moral decision making within the firm.

In brief, this article tries to uncover the elements that have gone into influencing our business values,[1] and will then seek to assess the influence that those values and this morality have on our work and environment.

A value system or ideology is the foundation upon which decisions, business or otherwise, are made. Values become so much a part of us that we are often unaware of their precise content and impact. Like the way we type or operate an automobile, we only become explicitly aware when we are asked to explain how we do it. Without knowing that procedure, it would be impossible to drive. Without a value system or ideology, it is impossible to make consistent and reasonable decisions on important alternatives.

An ideology is a coherent, systematic, and moving statement of basic values and purposes. It is an organized set of values held by a group, and the members of the group support one another in that ideology. An ideology asks and provides answers to such questions as: What are the most important values and activities to me? How do I explain those values and activities to those of other cultures or generations? How do I defend my life and values when they are criticized either from within the group or from outside?

Morality and *ethics* will be used interchangeably in this article. Ethics is the more common term, so let us define it. Ethics are the principles of conduct that govern a person or a group. Ethics enable an individual or group to decide whether a certain act or policy is morally right or wrong (that is, ethical or unethical). In most cases this judgment is easy to make (for example: "It is wrong to lie about a fellow worker"). There are ethical judgments, on the other hand, far more difficult to make. Judgments on values and priorities differ. Full data are not always available, and pressures on the individual can limit freedom. This uncertainty often leads Americans to cynicism with regard to the application of ethics. Since it is often difficult to agree on ethical norms, these individuals often put ethics aside. However, events such as General Dynamics' overcharges, E.F. Hutton's check kiting, overseas bribes (Exxon, Northrup, or Westinghouse), marketing faulty products (Firestone 500 tires), and exaggerated and even false claims in advertising (Warner-Lambert's Listerine) have all caused us to ask firms and executives to act in a more ethical and statesmanlike manner.

Our sense of ethics grows out of our past. We learn what is right and wrong in our early years, and these notions mature as we gather new evidence and experience. At each stage we are heavily influenced by our environment. As with cultural values, so too with ethical values, it is easier for us to see the ethical blindspots of other peoples. For example, we find it hard to understand how authorities in the Soviet Union can so blatantly violate human rights. Our stereotypes, and sometimes our experiences, tell us that bribery is common in Latin America and in the Arab states. It is more difficult for us to recognize our own ethical blindspots. It is far easier for citizens of other cultures to point them out to us.

It is in an attempt to better understand, not only the blindspots, but the entire complex of our American ideology, values, and ethics, that this article is written. Hence, we will examine, in a brief form, some of the events, people, and issues that have given us our current business ideology.

History as Prelude

Western attitudes have been influenced by the ancient Greeks. For them, the life of the craftsman, farmer, and worker had little dignity.[2] It was menial, dirty, and demeaning; the fact that this work was done by slaves, and that citizens were not required to do such work, influenced the disdain they showed for work.

For the ancient Hebrews, work was more accepted as an integral part of their lives. Although work was necessary, it was also a hardship (Gen. 2:15). Early Christians built on the Hebraic tradition of work, trade, and commerce. These early Christians were themselves workingmen: fishermen, herdsmen, tentmakers, and so on. It is not surprising that their attitudes were sympathetic to work and the life of the worker (Mark 6:3; Acts 18:2; Luke 12:41–49).

The unique contribution of Christians toward work attitudes was that work was done in order to not only provide the necessities for self and family, but also so that the goods produced could be shared in love with one's fellows. The work ethic of Christianity as an ideal has the same love ethic as does the larger life of the Christian.

The Benedictine monasteries were gatherings of monks who dedicated their lives to working and praying together. They are credited with being the first (that is, in the Ninth Century) to order the workday and to systematically use labor-saving devices.[3] The monks brought a more positive attitude toward work. With this as a background, let us look at that familiar description of the American work ideology: the Protestant ethic.

New World Values

Saving, working hard, and a strong personal value system were all encouraged by the traditional Protestant ethic. The Protestant ethic developed largely in North America. This new physical setting provided seemingly limitless land and resources and few natural barriers. This presented a challenge to the hearty, to those who were willing to risk. The effect of the frontier on the American mentality has been well-developed by Frederick Jackson Turner.[4] The new lands to farm, mine, and settle seemed to be without limits.

The immigrants brought with them to the new world many of the ideals that were to become the Protestant ethic, and that so heavily influenced American life. Puritan divine Cotton Mather (1663–1728) was among the first to spell out the root values of the Protestant ethic. The Christian had two callings: a worldly calling to work and another to worship God. They were equally important.

Before the American Revolution, Benjamin Franklin helped to publicize the values of the Protestant ethic. In doing so he shifted these values from a religious to a secular foundation. Some of Franklin's musings have become a part of our popular mind, such as "Diligence is the mother of good luck," or "Little strokes fell great oaks."[5]

Even before this period, Martin Luther (1483–1546) and especially John Calvin (1509–1564) set the stage in Europe for these values. Luther acknowledged that trade was acceptable, and preached vehemently against idleness and covetousness. Although Luther did not allow lending at interest and looked to the simple farmer as the ideal, his new "Protestant" position set the merchant and the cities free from religious authority.

Calvin was born in a city and blessed the work of not only the craftsmen and farmers, but also the merchants and bankers. John Calvin is thus the central figure in the development of the Protestant ethic.[6] Calvin's central theological position is predestination. God, in his infinite wisdom, knows all things. He therefore knows whether an individual will be saved or damned. So there is nothing individuals can do to effect their destiny. However, we may obtain some indication of whether we are numbered among the saved or the damned: the extent to which God showers his blessings on us. That is, if we are successful in our life and work, this is a sign that we are probably among the elect. Given this way of God's indicating who is saved, it is not surprising that Calvinists, and their direct descendants, the Puritans, exerted every effort to be a worldly success, so that this might be a sign to all that they were among those who were to be saved.

John Locke (1632–1704) also had a considerable influence on American values. English-born and Oxford-educated, Locke focused on a person's rights to private property. Locke saw property as basic to other rights, for example, to life, to housing, and to food. If a person had property, he could provide a home, a garden, and a living for self and family.

The grandfather of modern economics, Adam Smith (1723–1790) was the first to clearly articulate free enterprise values.[7] As a moral philosopher himself, he pointed out the value of specialization of labor. Through his now famous "invisible hand," materials, labor, ingenuity, and other resources would be guided to provide for the needs of men and women; and, in so doing, they would be most efficiently utilized.

Only the Fit Survive

Following on Smith, Herbert Spencer (1820–1903), also an Englishman, proposed a harsh "survival of the fittest" philosophy. Taking his inspiration from Charles Darwin's then current notions of evolution, Spencer saw human beings as evolving, too. This bettering of the human race became known as "social Darwinism." The weaker, handicapped, less alert persons should not be supported. Indeed, if the race was to improve, only the stronger, more intelligent and cleverer were to be encouraged; their rewards would come naturally. It was up to society, for the sake of its long-term health, not to support the weak or handicapped or less able. Thus, through social Darwinism the race and society as a whole would improve.

The basic content of the Protestant ethic[8] could be summarized as underscoring the importance of:

1. hard work,
2. self-discipline and self-reliance,
3. saving and planning ahead,

4. competition,
5. honesty and observing the "rules of the game."

In turn the Protestant ethic was supported by these convictions:

1. A person's hard work is generally met with success.
2. Working at one's own self-interest automatically benefits the greatest number (the "invisible hand" of Adam Smith).
3. Each individual has a chance to be successful.
4. Only the most able and the most motivated will survive. The system will weed out the weak, and the strong will remain (the "survival of the fittest" of Herbert Spencer).

Building on this foundation, the values of "American individualism" emerged, articulated by Ralph Waldo Emerson and Henry David Thoreau.[9] Their view was based on the conviction of the natural goodness of the individual. The main elements of their views could be summarized as:

1. The primacy of the individual, the person.
2. The denial of social restraint: society and the group has an inhibiting effect on the individual; it is a necessary burden that must be borne.
3. Each individual had best pursue her/his own well-being.

According to both the Protestant ethic and American individualism, the government's role ought to be minimal. Among its more important functions is that of protecting the individual's private property.

A Rich Person's Right to Wealth

A poor immigrant from Scotland, Andrew Carnegie, was able to put together U.S. Steel and amass a fortune.[10] As one of the famous "robber barons" at the turn of the century, Carnegie was quite satisfied that his thousands of workers got subsistence wages, while he himself had millions at his disposal. He was convinced that the poor worker did not know how to wisely use the extra dollars anyway; it would be used merely for excessive eating and drinking.

On the other hand, the wealthy person recognized an obligation that comes with such wealth. It is only the wealthy who can endow libraries and universities. The money is better distributed when an individual can accumulate large amounts, according to Carnegie, so that he can accomplish great things. Carnegie thus defended his fortune, his right to have it and dispose of it as he saw fit.

Carnegie here demonstrates another aspect of an ideology: it is constructed to rationalize and defend a socioeconomic system. For Carnegie and other capitalists, it gave them a justification for their immense wealth, even in the face of thousands of their workers who were very poorly paid.

Decay of the Protestant Ethic

Even from its earliest days, many feared that the Protestant ethic was not stable and would eventually collapse. Both John Calvin and John Wesley noticed that religious ideals urged men and women to be hard-working, self-disciplined, and frugal. Yet as they became successful, so, too, came more material goods to enjoy and thus less of a need to be self-disciplined and frugal. The very success that the Protestant ethic brings to the individual tends to undermine the ethic values themselves.[11]

Capitalism and free enterprise require a high degree of flexibility and innovation to make the system successful. Creative men and women must be willing to invest their time, energy, and talents into producing goods and services for society. Hungry people tend to have more energy if they see that it will provide them a return. Men and women who are relatively well taken care of may lose the motivation to invest themselves wholeheartedly in work. A generation ago, the well-known economist, Joseph Schumpeter,[12] expressed these fears. He also pointed out that many intellectuals (such as educators, the middle-class, professionals) have little sympathy for capitalism. Since it is a system geared to production, and has little in the way of an ideology to support and protect itself, it is highly vulnerable. He contrasts it with Marxism, where individuals are asked to sacrifice today in order to make a better life for others or for tomorrow. They are urged to work to help the most disadvantaged and oppressed peoples; this sparks idealism and a willingness to work hard for something outside oneself. Capitalism has little of that idealism; it has nothing that might call out the very best in men and women.

Current Free Enterprise Ideology

What now remains of the Protestant ethic values? What remains of the values of American individualism? Many would say that precious little is left of the Protestant ethic—especially among those not directly affected by the Great Depression. Probably more remains of individualism: the primacy of the individual person, the suspicion of society and the government, and the encouragement of "enlightened self-interest."

Hard work is rarely considered to be its own reward in our society. Except for the occasional craftsman, professional, or entrepreneur, work is losing its quality of fulfilling a human need and expressing a person. Work becomes a trade-off for what it will buy. We work so that we will have more to spend.

Spending and consumption have become our goals. Rather than saving and planning ahead for the rainy day, we are encouraged to buy on time. We purchase something and pay for it over its lifetime. Self-reliance and self-discipline are giving way to a growing sense of entitlement. Increasingly we Americans feel that we are owed a job, housing, education, and medical care. These are seen less as goals that we must work hard to achieve, and more as rights that are due to us. Whereas thrift and restraint were once predominant, now we witness individuals seeking self-fulfillment. One hundred and fifty years ago Alexis de Tocqueville pointed out that American enlightened self-interest would inevitably lead to selfishness.[13] The pursuit of self-fulfillment is not far from selfishness.

Influence of the Group: Socialization

Organizations generally provide an "orientation" for new employees and managers. An orientation is essential if the new person is to learn what is expected in the way of performance and attitudes. Each organization has its own job descriptions, work times, communication systems, and reward structures.

The individual quickly learns that success at one's job requires that one master the expectations, both explicit and implicit, of one's superiors. Although no organization can operate without some consensus and cooperation from its members, this consensus often extracts its price from the individual.

The price can express itself in several ways:

1. excessive attention to procedures and rules, and the resulting loss of creativity and incisiveness;

2. an anxiety as to whether performance is measuring up to expectations (sometimes shown in ulcers or heart trouble);

3. a diminution of one's own values and purposes which in turn can result in sacrifice of family, friends,[14] and one's own ethics.

Among managers 60 to 70 percent "feel pressured to compromise personal ethics to achieve corporate goals."[15] More than half of this group also feel that most managers would not refuse orders to market off-standard and possibly dangerous items.

How could managers, who generally pride themselves on their independent judgment, be willing to compromise their own principles in such a fashion? An organization has its own pressures. The judgments of peers and superiors have a powerful effect within the organization.

Laboratory research on how judgments and values are formed may shed some light on this process. Solomon E. Asch set out to examine the influence the group has on the judgment of the individual.[16] He obtained volunteers among engineering students at MIT; each group of seven to nine men was enlisted to do "psychological experiments in visual judgment." The groups were arranged in semicircles, and they were shown two cards. The first card bore a line several inches long. The second card bore lines of three distinctly different lengths on it, and each individual was asked to pick which of the three lines was the same length as the line on the first card. However in each group all of the individuals but one were "confederates" and had been instructed to pick the same wrong line. The one exception was seated near the end of the semicircle. The length of lines was easily distinguishable. Acting individually, a person would pick the right line 99 percent of the time. The question here was: How often would the pressure of the others' consistently wrong answers sway subjects to alter their own judgments?

In a society that prides itself on being individualistic (and this would be especially true among MIT engineering students), only 25 percent braved the opinion of the group, stuck to their own judgments, and picked the right line. Seventy-five percent erred in the direction of the majority.

The opinions of the group can have powerful influence on judgments. When the individual is so greatly influenced by the judgment of the group we lose the benefit of the individual's independent assessment of reality. It is thus not difficult to understand how an individual can be co-opted into actions that she or he might individually consider to be quite unethical: the judgment of others and the pressure of the group are powerful forces.

Representing Business to the Community

For most Americans their most immediate contact with business and much of their impression of the businessperson is obtained from advertising. Surely we all know individual managers and merchants, but our image, especially of larger companies, is formed to a great extent by advertising. If advertising and advertisers should appear to be more hard-sell than informative, more manipulative than honest, more trivial than substantive, then Americans may begin to think of businesspersons as largely hirelings: bright and articulate, but not balanced and trustworthy. This image would do serious harm to the business community.

Unfortunately, the level of confidence that Americans have in business leaders and advertisers seems to support this fear. While the leaders of business firms had the confidence of more than half of the American people in 1966, this has dropped to 18 percent having confidence sixteen years later. Leaders of other institutions also have lost the trust of the American people, but no group so much as advertisers. Only 11 percent of Americans had a great deal of confidence in them.[17] Advertisers are among the least trusted groups in the United States.

This severely negative attitude surely affects public confidence toward business in general. Advertisers, who are hired to provide the link to consumers, to communicate the benefits of the product and the firm, are not doing this well. Rather than provide information on products, advertisers often set out to avoid product specifications and to concentrate on how the product will make one happier, sexier, and more enviable. Leo Burnett, past president and chairman of the advertising agency that bears his name, spells this out: "Don't tell people how good you make goods; tell them how good your goods make them."[18]

By any measure, we find that Americans are distrustful of advertising. In national polls, more than half feel that advertising does not present a true picture of the product advertised. More than two-thirds thought that "advertising causes people to buy things they don't need" and that government intervention is necessary in order to get essential information.[19]

Given the fact that advertising touches the citizen and the consumer so intimately, and that citizens often judge business as a whole on the basis of the advertising they experience, one would think that advertisers would take special care to be truthful, substantive, and ethical. Moreover, one would expect that advertising firms on their own would try to be leaders in ethics. This does not seem to be the case. In fact, even though advertising is constantly in the public eye and is closely monitored by the Federal Trade Commission for unfair and deceptive advertising, the industry does not seem to be a model of honest, trustworthy behavior among American business firms.[20]

If indeed Americans come to think of business as focused largely on short-term profits, half-truths, and exaggeration, trust in the system may decline even further. Trust and confidence is absolutely essential if the business system is to maintain legitimacy and operate effectively. The legitimacy of any system, whether political or economic, is quickly eroded if the public loses confidence in the operation of that system. Indeed the greatest cost to all citizens may be this loss of trust in the economic system.

Effect of Advertising on Values

The effect that advertising has on our values is a vital question for all citizens and consumers. However, it is also an issue for which it is difficult to establish a causal connection.

We do know, however, that advertising very often intentionally appeals to social status or fear of ridicule.[21] Advertisers can give us the impression that if we are unhappy or sick or feel ugly, they have just the right product for us. Something we can purchase (provided it is the right brand) can solve our problems.

Advertisers have commonly been accused of being creators of dissatisfaction. The image they often present of slick, beautiful, immaculately groomed and dressed men and women is an unreal picture of the world—either as it is or as it should be. This image can create unattainable expectations and frustration, especially for the young and the less affluent.

Advertising also encourages consumption, and this in a time of diminishing resources. Automobiles, plastics, and other petroleum users are still being touted, long after the oil firms themselves have ceased directly pushing their own products. Advertising and the lifestyle it encourages and promotes also present an image of Americans as being materialistic, shallow, and self-centered people.[22] On the other hand, advertisers will tell us that they do not create these values; they merely reflect and build on the values that they find already present. I would suggest that advertising solidifies and reinforces those embryonic materialistic and self-centered values that we find in all people, especially the less mature. Advertising values image over information, sports cars over people, attractive appearance over theater and art, toothpaste and deodorants over reading. It supports the image of a self-centered, acquisitive, and selfish person.

Advertising firms are now hired to provide an image for and to "sell" political candidates.[23] In the last two decades we have been subjected to thirty-second television ads in place of in-depth discussion of complex issues. We are presented with a few words and an attractive face, and thus are expected to elect that person to an important office. A thirty-second ad hardly provides the time or atmosphere to discuss complex issues. Even worse, if the ad is successful, it often communicates that the issues are really quite simple and solutions are easy.

Advertisers sometimes act as if, like engineers and accountants, they are "value-free." They are professionals and they offer their skills and knowledge without regard to the merits of a particular firm or product.[24] Few professionals today hold this position. They are well aware that any significant management decision has ethical implications that must be considered in weighing that decision. It is unclear whether advertisers also recognize this.

Let us now examine the effect of values and ideology on work and work performance.

Values and Work Performance

Studies of blue-collar workers over the last two decades show that a significant majority do not enjoy their work.[25] Even though they did not get satisfaction out of their work, studies twenty years ago showed that people would continue to work even if they inherited a large amount of money. Current experience witnesses large numbers retiring well before 65 years of age. This phenomenon presents three problems:

1. It shows that these workers are not getting much satisfaction from their work.
2. It is expensive; it adds to the cost of operation.
3. It thus contributes to the decline in productivity.

Focusing on rather immediate self-fulfillment in the workplace is quite different from the hard work, self-discipline and self-reliance called for in the Protestant ethic. It is true that entry-level jobs today in large firms rarely provide the satisfaction that more responsible positions provide. Trust, discretion, and responsibility generally come after some years of good job performance.

Satisfaction from work generally comes when that work is seen in a larger context. Work can give dignity, a sense of accomplishment, a sense that one's life is fruitful and that one is providing for others' needs. Thus strong personal goals and values are important to providing a foundation for a satisfying work life. However, this sort of satisfaction requires a broader view and a longer time frame than merely a year or two.

Immediate Gratification and Top Management

Management decries the need for immediate self-fulfillment, the short time perspective, and the growing sense of entitlement of workers—whether they be blue-collar or white-collar. However, managers themselves are subject to many of the same pressures and thus also create pressures for those they manage. The desire to have immediate results, looking to year-end return, and being judged on this quarter's accomplishments can easily lead management into the same sort of press for immediate results and short time perspective.

William C. Norris, founder of Control Data, says that we have become a "risk avoiding, selfish society."[26] In his words, "Too few of us are ready to take the risks necessary to solve our problems. We lack the will." He points out that one of the major shortcomings of our society is that "everyone is out for himself." In industry, to obtain needed new products or services, a firm acquires a small company in place of investing and risking its own resources in research and innovation.

This indictment is even more troublesome in the case of management, since it is precisely its charge to look to the long-term health and growth of the firm. Nevertheless, the desire to show increasing year-end returns on investment often leads management to underfund research and development, from which possible rewards are far in the future—in the job tenure of someone who would follow and reap the rewards. Such a disposition can cause management to invest in projects that will show a quicker return and to avoid investments whose return may be a decade away. If an able, energetic, and competitive manager is on a fast track, he or she probably has evidence that his/her performance is going to be judged by the year-end financial returns in his/her division.

International Telephone and Telegraph (I.T.T.) is a classic example of a firm that emphasizes annual growth in earnings, and which has ignored long-term public support for the firm. It has tried to influence elections and to punish "uncooperative" governments in Chile and Ecuador. It tried to bribe the Nixon regime and succeeded in getting it to call off the Hartford Fire Insurance anti-trust case. After severe public criticism, the I.T.T. board replaced Harold Geneen as president.

The Securities and Exchange Commission (SEC) filed suit against I.T.T. for, among other things, lying about its improper overseas payments. In an unusual move, the SEC asked the court to appoint a special investigator in order to obtain information on I.T.T.'s influence peddling and its illegal and unethical deals. It also asked that special outside directors be appointed to I.T.T.'s Board.[27]

I.T.T.'s manipulations have been highly publicized. Many Americans read about these unethical and illegal acts and generalize to all corporations. Surely all corporations should not be condemned because of the actions of a minority. Yet confidence in our business system is critically influenced by what people read in the newspapers and see on television. A lack of honesty merely adds to the lack of credibility and trust. Management knows it must balance short-term goals with the long-term future of the firm. Moreover, it is in looking to these longer-term issues, and anticipating solutions before legislation is necessary, that management will be able to keep more of its prerogatives.

Long-Term Planning and Ethics

The Protestant ethic is no longer a common ideology for Americans. In fact the shift from saving and self-denial to consumption and "buy now, pay later" is due in a large part to our own business system. Advertising and inflation tell us that we are foolish if we do not spend our money on goods and services rather than putting it in a bank or in securities. Spending and consumption, and the immediate gratification that goes with them, also stem from the desire for self-fulfillment. This new ethic has grown amongst the rubble of fallen institutions: government, churches, and business. Without a sense that someone or something is looking out for long-term good ("the common good"), the only option that seems safe is one of self-interest and self-fulfillment.

Hence, values today are not commonly held; they are largely personal. In fact, the very word *values* connotes something not objective and common, but rather subjective and unique to each person. We pride ourselves on our pluralism, yet with such rampant pluralism, how can effective policy—either in business or government—be formulated? Some common set of values is essential for managing any organization.

Long-range planning based upon intelligent, cooperative ethical values can help in increasing productivity and solving social problems. Various worker participation programs demonstrate the value of cooperation in the private sector. Quality of worklife programs have changed the organizational climate at some General Motors (GM) facilities. At GM's Detroit Gear and Axle, the plant manager split the seven thousand workers into seven smaller business units. Each of these "small businesses" has its own marketing, financial, and other information that it needs to plan. The assembly line itself was broken into about sixty-five teams, each of which put an entire brake system together and checked it for quality. The workers thus became more concerned about the quality of their product.[28] At another GM assembly plant, Pontiac Fiero, some fifty workers volunteer to call purchasers of the auto to find out if there have been any difficulties with the auto. Thus, any complaints reach the plant floor in a fraction of the time, and have an urgency since they are relayed by other assembly workers.[29]

Legislation and Regulation

Management generally prefers addressing social issues by developing its own policies and initiatives rather than having government intrude with regulations. However, in some areas such as pollution control and equal employment opportunity, there is a need for governmental regulation. In a highly competitive industry or where social mores are very strong, such as equal employment opportunity, it seems reasonable that the same objective requirements be placed on all firms. In a competitive industry, if only one firm internalizes its social costs, its production costs would be forced above those of its competitors. Competitors, by placing a portion of their costs of production on society as a whole—for example, dirty water or toxic waste—are thus able to sell their product at a lower price. Hence, the argument for government regulation: it places costs where they should be.

On the other hand, all agree that it is best to keep these governmental interventions to a minimum. Government regulations are costly and troublesome. In addition, big government is often bureaucratic, inflexible, not efficient, and not even always sensitive to public needs. It would be better if we could accomplish the same objectives without government intervention.

The only effective alternative to government regulation is management initiatives. In areas where the public is about to make new demands, or indeed, in anticipation of such demands, corporate management can and does take the initiative. Some firms do a social audit, have independent directors on their board audit, nominating, or ethics committees, and encourage genuine two-way communication with their shareholders, employees, customers, and other stakeholders. These firms are going beyond what the law presently requires and are responding on their own initiative to their various publics.

Management can elect to take these initiatives for a number of reasons:

1. Management hears the growing demands of its public and takes the initiative as a public relations posture to quell social pressures.

2. Management anticipates regulation and hopes to forestall it.

3. Management judges that it is the right thing to do; that is, shareholders deserve the information, consumers have a right to know . . . etc.

This last position involves an ethical judgment. It is not always acknowledged as an ethical judgment. As a business decision, it can often be defended more readily if it is supported by a long-term financial argument.

Law or Ethics

When an environmental or social issue arises, often the first question that management asks is: What does the law say? While this question is important in outlining the limits of what the corporation may or may not do, it does not answer the question of what it *should* do. Too often we seem to believe that if an act is legal, it is therefore ethical. The law is a floor; it tells us what must be done. It says nothing with regard to what is the more desirable behavior.

To act only when the law requires action merely encourages more legislation and regulation. So, while we agree that there is often too much regulation, nevertheless, our own attitudes and policies encourage more regulation.[30]

How can we best bring ethical values to bear on corporate policy decisions? Most firms have developed codes of ethics for employees; these have been updated over the years.[31] However, formulating ethical codes does not make corporate decisions more ethical.

Managing by adherence to ethical principles is more complex and difficult, but obviously necessary. Indeed, in many firms, top management has taken strong stands on certain issues, such as equal employment opportunity, kickbacks, or product quality. Some firms, such as Levi Strauss, factor ethical and socially responsible behavior into their reward system. Promotions and pay increases are based not merely on the annual profitability of the unit, but also on the ethics and social responsiveness of the individual manager. Some tests of the ethics of a firm are:

1. What milieu or organizational climate has been created in the firm? Is the climate supportive of the ethical manager, or is it a climate exclusively of bottom line, short-term financial returns?

2. Does the middle manager feel that he is often forced to compromise his own values because of the pressure of the firm for short-term results and profitability?

3. As inputs to complex decisions, do managers look only to the law, or do they look to ethical principles above and beyond the law?

4. Would top management be satisfied and even proud to have their decisions known by a wider group? For example, would they be embarrassed if a local TV station did a feature on a current issue and their decision?

In a firm, there must be a balance between short-term profitability and looking to the long-term life of the firm. This latter view includes acting on ethical principles, and thus requires the gearing of the organization to act according to these ethical principles. What elements are present in the individual and the organization that contribute to ethical or unethical behavior? In a laboratory situation business researchers have found several factors in the environment that influence ethical decisions. Threat of punishment and informal organizational policy have a strong direct effect. These researchers also found that individual values do indeed have a significant impact on personal ethical behavior within the firm.[32]

In these same laboratory experiments the business researchers found that as competitiveness increased, the level of ethical behavior dropped. Moreover, if unethical behavior takes place and is rewarded (that is, rewards are given for profits in spite of unethical behavior), the unethical behavior is reinforced. Unethical behavior can be conditioned or encouraged by the organizational climate and expectations.

Ethical Decision Making

Beyond ethical codes and a basic human decency, there are some ethical principles that can be of help to businesspeople in decision making. It is beyond the scope of this article to do much more than point directions.

The classical ethical traditions are:

1. Utilitarianism
2. Theories of rights
3. Theories of justice

All problems are not equally well handled by any one approach. Indeed, some problems require an emphasis on one theory, other problems another. So, it benefits the decision maker to have a basic understanding of each approach.[33]

Utilitarianism is a direct descendant, along with classical economics, of Adam Smith's principles of moral philosophy. Utilitarianism calls for "the greatest good of the greatest number." In any decision, those with the responsibility for the decision are to consider the well-being of all those who would be affected by that decision, and to try to estimate the relative benefits and costs of the decision to all those affected. It then would be the obligation of that decision maker to decide in favor of the option that provides the most net benefits. Utilitarianism essentially asks that a cost/benefit analysis or assessment be done, and it thus involves the difficulties that face the social audit, especially problems of measurement.[34]

Theories of rights are generally easier to apply. Rights look to the protection of an individual's personal rights (for example, life, safety, privacy, good name) or property rights. The United States Bill of Rights and the United Nations Declaration of Human Rights are developed from a set of rights that are considered to be fundamental for all human beings.

Theories of justice provide standards of equity, fairness, and impartiality. Justice seeks to provide for an equitable distribution of society's benefits and burdens. Justice theories are becoming more prominent and have recently received renewed attention from both scholars and practitioners.[35]

The above outline is only that. If interested in pursuing the question, the reader is urged to seek out some of the growing literature on business ethics.[36]

Conclusion

The Protestant ethic gave Americans a self-discipline, a willingness to sacrifice current gain for the sake of greater opportunity later. This provided the flexibility, the innovation, and the willingness to risk that had been the hallmark of the United States, and has produced our industrial base.

Values of spending, consumption, immediate gratification, and self-fulfillment, and the professional manager's goals of short-term return, have had a more recent influence on the business system and on individuals. These new values bring with them a press for immediate satisfaction, and a quick return on work efforts. There is now less saving, and thus less available for investment. This has slowed our growth rate and lowered our productivity.

However, there is no consensus on these current values. Generally, values are naively seen as subjective and vague, and therefore of little use for decision making and policy formation. This posture puts us adrift without ethical guidelines.

The dramatic difference in organizational climate and reputation between firms headed by the minority of short-sighted, self-seeking managers demonstrates the influence of a developed sense of ethics and humane values. While good ethics do not always bring a financial return, they are at least a long-term investment.

The ethics of most American managers are actually quite good. However, the manager generally is not at ease with the concepts, language, and models of ethical analysis. Hence, financial, marketing, and production information and criteria tend to crowd out the ethical issues. A familiarity with the principles and the language to express one's self would put the manager in a better position to present an intelligent and intelligible ethical analysis.

Notes

1. This historical and cultural material is covered in detail with references to original sources in Gerald F. Cavanagh, *American Business Values* (Englewood Cliffs, N.J.: Prentice-Hall, 1984).

2. Plato, *The Laws of Plato,* tr. A.E. Taylor (London: Dent, 1934); Aristotle, "Politics," in *Basic Works of Aristotle,* ed. Richard McKeon (New York: Random House, 1941).

3. Lewis Mumford, *Techniques and Civilizations* (New York: Harcourt Brace, 1934), p. 14.

4. *The Frontier in American History* (New York: Holt, 1920).

5. *The Autobiography and Other Writings* (New York: New American Library, 1961).

6. See Max Weber, *The Protestant Ethic and the Spirit of Capitalism,* tr. Talcott Parsons (New York: Scribner, 1958), pp. 35–41.

7. Adam Smith, *Wealth of Nations,* ed. J.C. Bullock (New York: Collier, 1909).

8. See Cavanagh, *American Business Values,* pp. 38–40, 47–48, 102–104.

9. Ralph W. Emerson, *The Conduct of Life and Other Essays* (London: Dent, 1908), pp. 190–213.

10. Andrew Carnegie, "Wealth," in *Democracy and the Gospel of Wealth,* ed. Gail Kennedy (Lexington, Mass.: D.C. Heath, 1949).

11. Max Weber, *Protestant Ethic,* pp. 35–41.

12. *Capitalism, Socialism and Democracy* (London: Allen & Unwin, 1943).

13. *Democracy in America,* tr. Henry Reeve (New York: Knopf, 1946), p. 98.

14. See William E. Henry, "Executive Personality and Large-scale Organizations," in the *Emergent American Society,* Vol. 1, by W. Lloyd Warner et al. (New Haven: Yale Press, 1967), p. 275. See also Cavanagh, *American Business Values,* pp. 70–74.

15. "The Pressure to Compromise Personal Ethics," *Business Week,* Jan. 31, 1977, p. 107.

16. Solomon E. Asch, "Opinions and Social Pressure," in *Science Conflicts and Society* (San Francisco: Freeman, 1969), pp. 52–57.

17. Louis Harris Survey, 1978 and 1982.

18. Leo Burnett, *Communications of an Advertising Man* (Chicago: Leo Burnett & Company, 1961), p. 243.

19. William J. Wilson, "Consumer Reality and Corporate Image," in *The Unstable Ground: Corporation Social Policy in a Dynanic Society,* ed. S. Prakash Sethi (Los Angeles: Melville, 1974), pp. 490–491; also Stephen Fox, *The Mirror Makers: A History of American Advertising and Its Creators* (New York: William Morrow, 1984), p. 328.

20. Federal Trade Commission Act, Section 5.

21. James U. McNeal, "You Can Defend Advertising—But Not Every Advertisement," *Business Horizons,* September–October, 1981, pp. 33–37.

22. Cavanagh, *American Business Values,* pp. 177–182; also G. Moschis and R. Moore, "A Longitudinal Study of Television Advertising Effects," *Journal of Consumer Research,* December, 1982, pp. 279–284.

23. William Sachs, *Advertising Management* (Tulsa: Pennwell, 1983), pp. 441–442; see also Joe McInnis, *The Selling of the President 1968* (New York: Trident, 1969).

24. Michael Schudson, *Advertising—The Uneasy Persuasion: Its Dubious Impact on American Society* (New York: Basic Books, 1984).

25. *Work in America,* ed. James O'Toole et al. (Cambridge, Mass.: MIT Press, 1973), pp. 9–10; also "Satisfaction on the Job: Autonomy Ranks First," *New York Times,* May 28, 1985, p. 21.

26. William C. Norris, "A Risk-Avoiding, Selfish Society," *Business Week,* January 28, 1980, p. 20.

27. "I.T.T., Exxon on the Spot," *Business Week,* Nov. 13, 1978, p. 101. "High Politics at I.T.T.," *Fortune,* August 13, 1979, pp. 31–32. "Harold Geneen's Tribulations," *Business Week,* August 11, 1973, pp. 102–110, 148. Anthony Sampson, *The Sovereign State of I.T.T.* (New York: Stein & Day, 1973).

28. John Simmons and William Mares, *Working Together* (New York: Alfred A. Knopf, 1983), pp. 49–71; see also the new classic by Thomas J. Peters and Robert H. Waterman, Jr., *In Search of Excellence* (New York: Harper & Row, 1982), pp. 167–168.

29. "A GM Plant with a Hot Line Between Workers and Buyers," *Business Week,* June 11, 1984, p. 165.

30. Christopher Stone, *Where the Law Ends: The Social Control of Corporate Behavior* (New York: Harper & Row, 1975); see also Gerald F. Cavanagh, "The Common Good as an Effective Moral Norm for the U.S. Businessperson," in *Catholic Social Teaching and the Common Good,* ed. John Houck and Oliver Williams. In Press.

31. Seventy-three percent of corporations surveyed have a written code of ethics (Princeton, N.J.: Opinion Research Corporation, 1980). See, for example, Caterpillar Tractor Company's *A Code of Worldwide Business Conduct,* revised May 1, 1982.

32. W. Harvey Hegarty and Henry P. Sims, "Unethical Decision Behavior: An Overview of Three Experiments." Paper presented at the Social Issues Division, Academy of Management, Atlanta, August 11, 1979.

33. For an additional explanation of this approach, see Gerald F. Cavanagh, Dennis Moberg, and Manuel Velasquez, "The Ethics of Organizational Politics," *The Academy of Management Review,* July, 1981; Gerald Cavanagh, *American Business Values,* Chapter 5, "Ethics in Business" (Englewood Cliffs: Prentice-Hall, 1984); and Manuel Velasquez, *Business Ethics: Concepts and Cases* (Englewood Cliffs, N.J.: Prentice-Hall, 1982).

34. American Institute of Certified Public Accountants, *The Measurement of Corporate Social Performance* (New York: AICPA, 1978); also David H. Blake, William C. Frederick,

and Mildred S. Myers, *Social Auditing: Evaluating the Impact of Corporate Progress* (New York: Praeger, 1976).

35. John Rawls, *A Theory of Justice* (Cambridge, Mass.: Belknap Press, 1971).

36. In addition to *American Business Values* and *Business Ethics: Concepts and Cases* cited above, see also Richard T. DeGeorge, *Business Ethics* (New York: Macmillan, 1986); Thomas Donaldson and Patricia H. Werhane, *Ethical Issues in Business* (Englewood Cliffs, N.J.: Prentice-Hall, 1983); and W. Michael Hoffman and Jennifer M. Moore, *Business Ethics: Readings and Cases in Corporate Morality* (New York: McGraw-Hill, 1984).

2
Models of Business and Society Interaction

A Conceptual Framework for Environmental
Analysis of Social Issues and Evaluation of
Business Response Patterns
S. Prakash Sethi

Business institutions in the United States and other industrially advanced countries have suffered a marked loss in social credibility. While business institutions justifiably take credit for tremendous strides made in living standards, they are accused of causing a host of environment-related and sociopolitical problems and of being insensitive to societal needs. Considerable pressure is put on business institutions to improve their management of social issues, and many institutions, especially large corporations, have taken steps to deal with a variety of social issues. The types of issues that business should tackle and the adequacy of their responses have spawned a whole new field of study, grouped under the rubric of business and society. However, a relative lack of development of a conceptual and analytical framework has hampered a systematic study of comparison and evaluation of corporate social responses and the environmental conditions that lead to the success or failure of specific responses to societal problems.[1, 2] This article attempts to develop an analytical framework to facilitate comparisons of business institutions and of the nature of business responses to social pressures under varying situational contexts and environmental conditions.

The Framework

The analytical framework proposed here is classificatory. The classes are broadly defined because both the types of issues covered and the environmental context within which they must be analyzed are so complex. Sociocultural and political phenomena, involving interactions among human beings and social institutions, are difficult to analyze in precise quantitative terms. Arbitrary precisions in the definition of variables are just as likely to conceal valuable information as to elucidate. A showing of causal relationships among variables so defined may be erroneous, since the underlying variables are interdependent. One should be wary of words that *simplify* when the reality they are presumed to describe is *complex*. Precision, under these circumstances, tends to force one into fixed positions that are intellectually difficult to defend and emotionally difficult to withdraw from. Thus, a framework that attempts to develop a broad classificatory scheme is the only approach both feasible and of some practical value.

The Social Context of Corporate Performance

An evaluation of corporate performance or the performance of any other social institution must be to a large extent culturally and temporally determined. A specific action is more or less socially responsible *only* within the framework of time, environment, and the nature of the parties involved. The same activity may be considered socially responsible at one time, under one set of circumstances, and in one culture, and socially irresponsible at another time. No system for evaluating corporate social performance can therefore ignore the cultural and sociopolitical environment, and the criteria used must necessarily be general and flexible.[3]

Nevertheless, a classificatory scheme must at least have stable classifications and stable meanings if we are to make valid cross-cultural comparisons. The categories for classifying corporate activities should be stable so that while the nature of those activities and public expectations may change, the scheme should be able to accommodate them to make historical comparisons. The definitions of various classes should be such that they can be applied across firms, industries, and social systems.

The framework developed herein meets these criteria and suggests a rationale by which corporate activities can be analyzed in terms of social relevance so that comparisons over time and across industries and nations are possible. The framework consists of two sets of components. The first deals with categorization of the types of corporate responses. These are defined not in terms of specific activities, but in terms of types of underlying rationale applied in responding to social pressures. The second component deals with the definition of the external environment or the context within which the corporate response is being made and evaluated. The emphasis is not on the specifics of a particular social situation or problem, but on the generalized external conditions created by a multitude of acts by various social factors that are essentially similar within a given temporal and contextual frame.

This approach enables us to determine a logical and therefore acceptable external criterion against which a corporation's performance can be measured in a societal context. Thus it becomes an important complement to research and writing dealing with the issue of the measurement of corporate social performance generally treated under the somewhat misleading title of *corporate social audit.*[4, 5, 6, 7, 8, 9, 10, 11]

Dimensions of Corporate Social Performance

Business responds to two kinds of social forces: market and nonmarket. In the case of market forces, a firm adapts by varying its product, service, promotion, and price mix to meet changing consumer needs and expectations. Adequacy of response can be measured in terms of profitability and growth of the firm. All market actions have some nonmarket or indirect consequences for the society. These second-order effects are generally termed *externalities* (for example, pollution) and have traditionally been borne by society as a whole.

There have been increasing societal pressures in every industrialized nation for business to minimize the second-order effects of its activities and also to take a more active part and assume greater responsibility for correcting the social ills that inevitably do occur. It is the business response to the nonmarket forces, commonly termed *social responsibility* and *social responsiveness of business,* that is the focus of our inquiry.

Corporations, like all other social institutions, are an integral part of a society and must depend on it for their existence, continuity, and growth. They therefore constantly strive to pattern their activities so that they are in congruence with the goals of the overall social system.

It would improve our understanding of the situation if we were to analyze the logic of business actions in terms of the role of business in society. Business is a social institution and therefore must depend on society's acceptance of its role and activities if it is to survive and grow. At any given time there is likely to be a *gap* between business performance and societal expectations caused by certain business actions or changing expectations. A continuously widening gap will cause business to lose its legitimacy and will threaten its survival. Business must therefore strive to narrow this legitimacy gap in order to claim its share of society's physical and human resources, and to maintain maximum discretionary control over its internal decision making and external dealings.[12] The quest for legitimacy by the corporation and doubts by its critics about the legitimacy of some of its actions are at the core of the entire controversy pertaining to the concept of corporate social performance.

One way to evaluate corporate social performance is shown in table 1. Given that both corporations and their critics seek to narrow the gap between corporate performance and societal expectations, the social relevance and validity of any corporate action depends on one's concept of legitimacy. Viewed in this respect, corporate behavior can be described as a three-stage phenomenon based on the changing notion of legitimacy from very narrow to very broad. Legitimization involves the types of corporate activities as well as the process of internal decision making;

Table 1
Business Strategies for Narrowing the Legitimacy Gap

Business Performance	Legitimacy Gap	Societal Expectations

1. Does not change performance, but changes public perception of business performance through education and information.
2. If changes in public perception are not possible, change the symbols used to describe business performance, thereby making it congruent with public perception. Note that no change in actual performance is called for.
3. Attempt to change societal expectations of business performance through education and information.
4. If the three case strategies are unsuccessful in completely bridging the legitimacy gap, bring about changes in business performance, thereby closely matching it with society's expectations.

the perception of the external environment; the manipulation of that environment—physical, social, and political—to make it more receptive to corporate activities; and the nature of accountability to other institutions in the system. The corporate behavior thus determined can be defined as social obligation, social responsibility, or social responsiveness.[13]

Corporate Behavior as Social Obligation

Corporate behavior in response to market forces or legal constraints is defined as *social obligation.* The criteria for legitimacy in this arena are economic and legal only. Milton Friedman[14] and Henry Manne[15] believe that a corporation is a special-purpose institution and that it leaves this arena at its own risk. The legitimacy criteria are met by the corporation through its ability to compete for resources in the marketplace and through conducting its operations within the legal constraints imposed by the social system.

This simplistic argument hides much more than it explains. Competition for resources is not an adequate criterion. Corporations constantly strive to free themselves from the discipline of the market through increase in size, diversification, and generation of consumer loyalty by advertising and other means of persuasion. But even in an ideal situation, the ethics of the marketplace provide only one kind of legitimacy, which nations have been known to reject in times of national crisis or for activities deemed vital to the nation's well-being.

The legality of an act cannot be used as a criterion. Norms in a social system are developed from a voluntary consensus among various groups. Under these conditions, laws tend to codify socially accepted behavior and seldom lead social change. The traditional economic and legal criteria are necessary but not sufficient conditions of corporate legitimacy. The corporation that flouts them will not survive; even the mere satisfaction of these criteria does not ensure the corporation's continued existence.

Corporate Behavior as Social Responsibility

Second, most of the conflicts between large corporations and various social institutions during the last two decades or so in the United States and other industrialized nations of the free world fall into the category of *social responsibility*. Although relatively few corporations have been accused of violating the laws of their nations, they have been increasingly criticized for failing to meet societal expectations and failing to adapt their behavior to changing social norms. Thus, social responsibility implies bringing corporate behavior up to a level where it is in congruence with currently prevailing social norms, values, and performance expectations.

Social responsibility does not require a radical departure from normal patterns of corporate activities or behavior. It is simply a step ahead—before the new societal expectations are codified into legal requirements. While the concept of social obligation is proscriptive in nature, the concept of social responsibility is prescriptive.

Corporate Behavior as Social Responsiveness

The third stage of the adaptation of corporate behavior to social needs is in terms of *social responsiveness*. The process of adaptation is only partially served if corporations confine changes in behavior to those concerns that emanate from their actions in the marketplace—those related to their business activities. Examples of such behavior are installing devices to remove pollutants from factory smokestacks or paying immediate and fair compensation to victims of pollution or product-related injuries.

The issue in terms of social responsiveness is not how corporations should respond to social pressures, but what their long-run role in a dynamic social system should be. The corporation here is expected to anticipate the changes that may be a result of the corporation's current activities, or they may be due to the emergence of social problems in which corporations must play an important role. Again, while social responsibility-related activities are prescriptive in nature, activities related to social responsiveness are proactive, that is, anticipatory and preventive in nature.

Table 2 summarizes dimensions and attributes of corporate behavior under the three stages just discussed. These dimensions are not intended to be inclusive, but are indicative of the type of analysis that this framework makes possible. Additional categories can be developed relating to specific activities in which a business is engaged. Such an approach may indeed be desirable when this framework is to be applied to evaluate the behavior of specific companies and industries.

The External Environment

We must also develop a schema to distinguish among the various external environments—physical, economic, and sociopolitical—within which a given corporate

Table 2
A Three-Stage Schema for Classifying Corporate Behavior

Dimensions of Behavior	Stage One: Social Obligation Proscriptive	Stage Two: Social Responsibility Prescriptive	Stage Three: Social Responsiveness Anticipatory and Preventive
Search for legitimacy	Confines legitimacy to legal and economic criteria only; does not violate laws; equates profitable operations with fulfilling social expectations.	Accepts the reality of limited relevance of legal and market criteria of legitimacy in actual practice. Willing to consider and accept broader—extra legal and extra market—criteria for measuring corporate performance and social role.	Accepts its role as defined by the social system and therefore subject to change; recognizes importance of profitable operations but includes other criteria.
Ethical norms	Considers business value —managers expected to behave according to their own ethical standards.	Defines norms in community related terms, that is, good corporate citizen. Avoids taking moral stand on issues which may harm its economic interests or go against prevailing social norms (majority views).	Takes definite stand on issues of public concern; advocates institutional ethical norms even though they may seem detrimental to its immediate economic interest or prevailing social norms.
Social accountability for corporate actions	Construes narrowly as limited to stockholders; jealously guards its prerogatives against outsiders.	Individual managers responsible not only for their own ethical standards but also for the collectivity of corporation. Construes narrowly for legal purposes, but broadened to include groups affected by its actions; management more outward looking.	Willing to account for its actions to other groups, even those not directly affected by its actions
Operating strategy	Exploitative and defensive adaptation. Maximum externalization of costs.	Reactive adaptation. Where identifiable, internalize previously external costs. Maintain current standards of physical and social environment. Compensate victims of pollution and other corporate-related activities even in the absence of clearly established legal grounds. Develop industry-wide standards.	Proactive adaptation. Takes lead in developing and adapting new technology for environmental protectors. Evaluates side effects of corporate actions and eliminates them prior to the action being taken. Anticipates future social changes and develops internal structures to cope with them.

response to a set of social problems must be evaluated. This has been accomplished by dividing the elapsed time between the emergence of a problem and its solution and ultimate elimination into four categories or stages: (a) preproblem, (b) identification, (c) remedy and relief, and (d) prevention. There is some overlap because social problems do not fall neatly into discrete groups, nor can they always be solved in distinct successive steps. However, the arrangement facilitates our analysis of environmental conditions and the adequacy of various corporate responses.

The Preproblem Stage

In the process of manufacturing and marketing, business firms are constantly engaged in a series of transactions with individuals and social groups. These transactions have certain direct and indirect adverse effects on the parties involved. The first type pertains to the normal leakages and shortfalls found in any manufacturing activity and is unavoidable. The second type of negative side-effect pertains to actions by individual firms to cut corners in product quality, service, or manufacturing processes either under competitive pressures or to increase short-run profits. Taken individually, each incident is not significant in terms of its impact either on the corporation or the affected party. However, when similar acts are performed by a large number of companies and continued over a long period, their cumulative effect is substantial. When that happens, a problem is born.

The elapsed time at the preproblem stage is probably the longest of all the four steps, although there is a tendency for the time span to become narrower with increasing industrialization. Most individuals and institutions respond to the problem passively. Their efforts are aimed at adaptation, and the problem is treated as given. Elevation to the problem identification stage varies with different cultures and is based on the relative sociopolitical strength of the affecting and affected groups, the availability of necessary expertise to various groups, the relative size of the affected area relative to total area and population, the existence of mass communication systems in the society, and the access to media by various groups.

The Identification Stage

Once the impact of a problem has become significant enough there is a drive among the affected groups to define it, identify its causes, and relate it to the source. This is one of the most difficult stages in the whole process. First, the business entity could not have known of the problem because technology for its detection did not exist. Therefore, the most responsible businesses following the best safety procedures will be found years later to have polluted the environment, exposed their workers to rare forms of cancer, or sold potentially dangerous products. In most cases, direct linkages between cause and effect are all but impossible to find. The best that can be accomplished is to show through inference and statistical weight of evidence that a given source was the major contributor to the problem.

Second, a given adverse effect can be caused by a variety of sources or factors, and direct linkages are therefore impossible to establish. An example is cigarette smoking and lung cancer. Despite overwhelming statistical evidence, tobacco companies in the United States maintain that no direct cause-and-effect relationship has been established between smoking and cancer.[16] A third difficulty arises when no adequate definitive proof is possible because the symptoms appear years later, for example, cancer caused in workers in manufacturing processes using asbetos fiber[17] or polyvinyl chloride.[18] A fourth difficulty deals with situations in which irreparable damage has been done by the time proof is available, and no corrective or preventive measures are possible, for example, the use of fluorocarbons in aerosol sprays and their impact on the ozone layer of the stratosphere.[19]

The definition of the problem may also involve the vested interest or value-orientation of a particular group. Thus conservationists may bemoan the logging of virgin redwoods and call it a national calamity, whereas local communities and loggers may want to preserve their jobs and may therefore resist the establishment of a redwood national park. What is a problem to one group may appear to be an obstruction to another.[20]

The Remedy and Relief Stage

Once a causal linkage has been established, the question of compensatory and/or punitive damages to the affected parties must be considered. This stage is marked by intense activity by the various parties to the conflict, with many questions involved. One is the determination of the injured parties and the extent of their damage. A second question has to do with the assumption of responsibility for payment of claims—the company and the insurance carrier. An equally important third issue is the role played by courts, legislatures, and executive and administrative agencies of the government.

Certain interrelated issues must be considered. For example, is it socially desirable to make companies pay all the costs of a particular type of pollution not intentionally created? If a particular business or industry is forced to pay the total cost, how will this affect workers, stockholders, and lenders whose livelihood and life savings may be dependent on the profitability of that business or industry? The effect of the health of a particular industry on the total economy is also important in considering who should pay for the damages. Thus, government sometimes may be called upon to subsidize payments regardless of which party is at fault. An example is the U.S. government subsidies to support pension payments to coal miners who had contracted black lung disease during a particular time period.

The Prevention Stage

At this point the problem has achieved a level of maturity. The causal sources are either well established or easily identifiable. The attempt now is to develop long-range programs to prevent the recurrence of the problem. These include development of substitute materials, product redesign, restructuring organizations and decision-making processes, public education, and emergence of new special-interest groups to bring about necessary political and legislative changes. It should be noted that the prevention stage is not sequential, but generally overlaps with the problem identification and remedy and relief stages. The prevention stage, in order to be successful, calls for two changes: a qualitative change in the value sets of business and government, and a modification of the social arrangements among various groups in the social system.

The prevention stage is marked by uncertainty and difficulty in making an accurate appraisal of potential costs and benefits. The strategies to be pursued by society would, of necessity, involve unproved technologies and unfamiliar sociopolitical arrangements. Thus, it is not uncommon to find a high degree of self-righteousness in the pronouncements of various groups, which may be long on rhetoric but short on substance. Groups tend to advocate solutions that favor their particular viewpoint while understating the potential costs to those groups having opposing viewpoints. The ideological antibusiness bias of certain groups at this stage could be as harmful to the development of socially equitable and technologically feasible long-term solutions as the tendency among some business people to resist every demand for change as not technically feasible, expensive, or unnecessary.

Applying the Framework

The analytical model described above can be used both to understand better how social conflicts develop and how firms respond to predict the effectiveness of particular corporate response patterns to different stages of conflict resolution. In this section, the application of the framework is demonstrated in analyzing a major social conflict involving the operations of large corporations in less developed countries. The conflict had to do with the sale of infant formula foods, and the analysis was carried out by Sethi and Post.[21] Two other studies have applied this framework in comparing the responses of the United States and Japanese business corporations to societal pressures in their respective countries[22] and in analyzing the performance of regulatory agencies in the United States.[23]

The Situational Context: Evolution of the Infant Formula Controversy

The first criticism of the industry and its promotional activities can be traced to the late 1960s when Dr. Jelliffe, Director of the Caribbean Food and Nutrition Institute in Jamaica, conducted research studies. His findings and criticism culminated in an international conference of experts in Bogota, Colombia in 1970, under the auspices of the U.N. Protein Calories Advisory Group (PAG), and a follow-up session in Singapore in 1972. The PAG issued an official statement (PAG Statement #23) in 1973 recommending that breastfeeding be supported and promoted in less-developed countries (LDCs) and that commercial promotion be restrained, industry and/or LDC governments.

The first public identification of the issue occurred in 1973 with the appearance of several articles about the problem in *The New Internationalist*.[24] This, in turn, spurred Mike Muller to undertake a series of interviews and observations that were eventually published in 1974 as a pamphlet titled *The Baby Killer*[25] with a German translation published in Switzerland under the title, *Nestle' Totet Kinder* (Nestle Kills Babies). Nestle's lawsuit against the public action group that published the pamphlet produced a period of intense advocacy surrounding the trial in the Swiss courts. Thus, between 1974 and mid-1976 when the case was decided, the issue received considerable international media coverage.

Institutionalized pressures began in earnest in 1975 when shareholder resolutions were filed for consideration at the annual meetings of the American infant formula companies. This pressure has continued, and several institutional investors (universities, the Rockefeller and Ford Foundations) have taken positions questioning the responsiveness of the firms to the controversy. Church groups, through the Interfaith Council on Corporate Responsibility of the National Council of Churches, have led the fight to coordinate the shareholders' campaigns. Most recently, some public interest groups have launched a campaign to boycott Nestle products in the United States. At the LDC level, the government of Papua New Guinea recently passed a law declaring baby bottles, nipples, and pacifiers health hazards and their sale restricted through prescription only. The objective was to discourage indiscriminate promotion, sale, and consumption of infant food formulas.[26]

The preproblem stage of the infant formula case existed prior to the 1970s. During this time, the adverse impacts on LDCs were not yet articulated. By the early 1970s, the identification stage had been reached, as professional criticism grew and articles and stories began to appear in the mass media.

The remedy and relief stage seems to have begun in 1975, primarily through the Nestle trial in Switzerland and the shareholder resolutions filed in the United States. The life cycle of the controversy has not yet reached the preventive stage.

The Nature of Corporate Response

The multinational corporation's (MNC) response during the preproblem stage was of the social obligation type, responding only to prevailing law and market condition. The principal industry effort during the problem identification stage was participation in the conference sponsored by PAG. Abbott (Ross), American Home Products (Wyeth), and Nestle each sent representatives to these meetings as did a number of British, European, and Japanese companies. For most companies, this seemed to mark a decision point between the social obligation phase and the social responsibility phase. Only a few firms, notably Abbott (Ross), moved to an approach that included steps to mitigate their negative impact in the LDCs. For American Home Products (AHP, Wyeth), Borden, Nestle, and others, this did not occur until 1974 when first plans were occurring for the formation of an international trade organization.

In November 1975, representatives of nine MNC manufacturers met in Zurich, Switzerland, and decided to form an international council to be known as the International Council Infant Food Industries (ICIFI). Nestle, AHP (Wyeth), and Abbott (Ross) participated in these discussions along with several European and four Japanese companies. Others, such as Borden and Bristol Myers, sent representatives to the sessions, but chose not to participate actively or join the council. ICIFI urged its members to adopt a code of marketing ethics, requiring the members to recognize the primacy of breastfeeding in all of their product information and to eliminate in-hospital promotion and solicitation by personnel who were paid on a sales commission basis. For those companies that joined, it appears to have marked a passage into the social responsibility phase where efforts were undertaken to mitigate negative social impacts.

There was criticism of the ICIFI code from the beginning and Abbott (Ross) withdrew from the organization, arguing that the code was too weak. The company then adopted its own more restrictive code, which included a provision prohibiting consumer-oriented mass advertising. Additional criticisms have led to some incremental changes that have strengthened the professional character of sales activity, but have not yet proscribed all consumer-oriented mass advertising; indeed, the critics continue to charge that the response at the user level has been insufficient. As a public issue matures, companies may adopt actions that operate to prevent further growth in the legitimacy gap by minimizing or eliminating the underlying sources of criticism (prevention stage). In 1977, Abbott (Ross) announced its intention to commit nearly $100,000 to a breastfeeding campaign in developing nations, budgeted $175,000 for independent research on breastfeeding, infant formula, and LDCs, and announced a plan for a continuing cooperative effort to review the situation with its critics. ICIFI has also begun working informally with international health agencies to prepare educational materials for use in LDCs and is supporting scientific research about breastfeeding, infant formula products, and LDC environments.

Borden has also moved from the social obligation to social responsibility stage. The company did not have shareholder resolutions filed with it until 1977. The filing seems to have facilitated a management review of promotional strategies in LDCs. Abbott (Ross) Laboratories' attempt to act in ways that will create positive impacts in LDCs thereby signals a shift to a social responsiveness stage. Granting that there is some danger of sending double signals to its sales force, the company seems to have adopted a posture that will permit it to sell its products in appropriate circumstances, while assisting the LDCs to encourage breastfeeding where that is most appropriate. Table 3 describes the patterns of responses from social obligation

Table 3
Socio-political Dimensions of Infant Formula Foods Controversy:
Patterns of Industry Responses (5 MNCs)

Patterns of Industry Response	Stages of Conflict Evolution			
	Preproblem Stage (Pre-1970)	*Identification Stage (1970)*	*Remedy and Relief Stage (1976)*	*Prevention Stage (1977–)*
Social obligation (do what is required by law)	Bristol-Myers (Mead Johnson Div.) Borden Nestle– American Home Products (Wyeth Lab.) Abbott (Ross Lab.)	Bristol-Myers (Mead Johnson Div.) Borden Nestle– American Home Products (Wyeth Lab.)	Bristol-Myers (Mead Johnson Div.) Borden	Bristol-Myers (Mead Johnson Div.)
Social responsibility (mitigate negative impacts)		Abbott (Ross Lab.)	Nestle– American Home Products (Wyeth Lab.)	Borden Nestle– American Home Products (Wyeth Lab.)
Social responsiveness (promote positive change)			Abbott (Ross Lab.)	Abbott (Ross Lab.)

to social responsiveness as the evolution of the controversy moves from the preproblem to prevention stage.

Conclusion

The framework developed in this article has been shown to have wide applicability in analyzing social systems within and between nations. My current research is designed to further elaborate the framework to study the interaction between external environment on corporate structure and internal decision making. Studies are also under way that apply this framework to a comparative analysis of children's television programming and advertising in different countries[27] and social performance evaluation of specific regulatory agencies in the United States.[28]

Notes

This article was first published in volume 4 of *Academy of Management Review* (1979).

1. Lee E. Preston and James E. Post, *Private Management and Public Policy: The Principle of Public Responsibility* (Englewood Cliffs, N.J.: Prentice-Hall, 1975).

2. S. Prakash Sethi, "An Analytical Framework for Making Cross-Cultural Comparisons of Business Responses to Social Pressures: The Case of the United States and Japan," in Lee E. Preston (ed.), *Research in Corporate Social Performance and Policy* (Greenwich, Conn.: Jai Press, 1978), pp. 27–54.

3. Dow Votaw and S. Prakash Sethi (eds.), *The Corporate Dilemma: Traditional Values Versus Contemporary Social Problems* (Englewood Cliffs, N.J.: Prentice-Hall, 1973), pp. 9–45, 167–191.

4. Clark Abt, *Social Audit* (New York: American Management Association, 1977).

5. Raymond A. Bauer and Dan H. Fenn, Jr., *The Corporate Social Audit* (New York: Russell Sage Foundation, 1972).

6. Meinolf Dierkes and Raymond A. Bauer, *Corporate Social Accounting* (New York: Praeger, 1973).

7. Ralph W. Estes, *Corporate Social Accounting* (Los Angeles: Melville Publishing Co., 1976).

8. David F. Linowes, *Strategies for Survival* (New York: American Management Association, 1973).

9. Lee J. Seidler and Lynn L. Seidler, *Social Accounting: Theory, Issues, and Cases* (Los Angeles: Melville Publishing Co., 1975).

10. S. Prakash Sethi, "Corporate Social Audit: An Emerging Trend in Measuring Corporate Social Performance," in Dow Votaw and S. Prakash Sethi (eds.), *The Corporate Dilemma: Traditional Values Versus Contemporary Problems* (Englewood Cliffs, N.J.: Prentice-Hall, 1973), pp. 214–231.

11. Allan D. Shocker and S. Prakash Sethi, "An Approach to Incorporating Social Preferences to Developing Corporate Action Strategies," in S. Prakash Sethi (ed.), *The Unstable Ground: Corporate Social Policy in a Dynamic Society* (Los Angeles, Calif.: Melville Publishing Co., 1974), pp. 67–80.

12. S. Prakash Sethi, "Dimensions of Corporate Social Performance: An Analytical Framework for Measurement and Evaluation," *California Management Review*, Spring, 1975, pp. 58–64.

13. Ibid.

14. Milton Friedman, *Capitalism and Freedom* (Chicago: The University of Chicago Press, 1962).

15. Henry G. Manne and Henry C. Wallich, *The Modern Corporation and Social Responsibility* (Washington, D.C.: American Enterprise Institute for Public Policy Research, 1972).

16. S. Prakash Sethi, *Promises of the Good Life: Social Consequences of Private Marketing Decisions* (Homewood, Ill.: Richard D. Irwin, Inc., 1979).

17. Paul Brodeur, *Expendable Americans* (New York: The Viking Press, 1974).

18. Paul H. Weaver, "On the Horns of the Vinyl Chloride Dilemma," *Fortune*, October, 1974, p. 150.

19. "Why Aerosols Are Under Attack," *Business Week*, February 17, 1975, pp. 50–51.

20. S. Prakash Sethi, *Up Against the Corporate Wall: Modern Corporations and Social Issues*, 3rd ed. (Englewood Cliffs, N.J.: Prentice-Hall, 1977).

21. S. Prakash Sethi and James E. Post, "Infant Formula Marketing in Less Developed Countries: An Analysis of Secondary Effects," In Subhash C. Jain (ed.), *Research Frontiers in Marketing: Dialogues and Directions*, 1978 Educators' Proceedings, Series #43 (Chicago, Ill.: American Marketing Association, 1978), pp. 271–275.

22. S. Prakash Sethi, "Dimensions of Corporate Social Performance."

23. Carl L. Swanson, "An Analytical Framework to Appraise the Performance of Regulatory Agencies in the Context of the Public Interest," in Jeffrey S. Susbauer (ed.), *Academy of Management Proceedings*, 1978, pp. 260–264.

24. "The Baby Food Controversy," *The New Internationalist*, August, 1973, p. 10.

25. Mike Muller, *The Baby Killer*, 2nd ed. (London, England: War on Want, 1975).

26. "Baby Bottles Banned in New Guinea," *The Dallas Morning News*, November 3, 1977, p. 8-C.

27. Diane Bagot, "Children's Television: Advertising and Programming, A Cross-Cultural Study," Working Paper, School of Management, The University of Texas at Dallas, 1978.

28. Carl L. Swanson, "Regulatory Agencies in the Context of the Public Interest."

Social (and Other) Issue Management

W. Howard Chase
Thomas Howard Chase

Gertrude Stein's memorable definition of a rose lends itself to paraphase: "An issue is an issue is an issue." Thus, with respect for this anthology's concentration on social issues and their management, I am constrained to say that the disciplines involved in issue/policy management are identical, whether the issue involved is social, political, economic, or technological.

This chapter is devoted primarily to a meticulous tracing of management techniques from the earliest identification of an issue to the CEO-approved action program to do something about it. Therefore, a word about issue management models is in order. I define a model as essentially a photograph of past experience and judgment. Unless a model is so derived, it can hardly serve as roadmap for issue analysis and issue action. The model that deserts past experience and judgment runs the risk of being inapplicable to the real world.

The model presented here has five major components:

1. issue identification;

2. issue analysis;

3. issue change strategy options, or more simply, selecting highest priority issues for appropriate action;

4. CEO-approved issue-action programming;

5. continuing evaluation of all previously accepted issue positions, in light of changing social, economic, political, and technological change.

Careful analysis will show that the derivative models of issue management that have appeared since 1977 are based on the five disciplines just listed. Some of them have the virtue of looking simpler. The issue-management process model discussed in this article is a fundamental reaffirmation of the right of every citizen and every organized group to participate in public-policy formation—not merely to react to policy made by others.

The structural flaw in simplified models is their failure to designate the issue manager as the executor of issue-action programming. This flaw delegates the issue analyst to a permanent or advisory role, and assumes that some higher executive will manage the issue-action program. The difference between *issue advisor* and *issue manager* is important—the first *theorizes* and the second *acts*. The essential difference between issue management and traditional public relations and public affairs is that the two named professions largely reflect and project policy positions determined by others. The issue manager is a participant in the policy formation.

Ever since Alfred G. Sloan, former chairman and CEO of General Motors, helped invent the modern corporation, the evolution of business organizations has been in the direction of increased systematization. That is, the management of each of the traditional "four Ms"—money, men, machines, and marketing—depends more and more on the application of a systematic approach to decision making. It is inconceivable that the financial vice-president or the plant manager would proceed in their functions without a system to guide them, or that the director of marketing would introduce a new product without the testing and validation that any marketing system demands.

The modern corporation is never static. Advanced leadership now recognizes and acts on the increasing impact the public-policy process has on every facet of the organization. When Sloan was building cars and developing the means to sell them, he did not have to contend with the Environmental Protection Agency (EPA), the Occupational Safety and Health Administration (OSHA), the National Highway Safety Administration, the Consumer Product Safety Commission, and other agencies, commissions, and administrations of modern government. In hindsight, it is remarkable that process-minded business leadership in the 1970s did not develop a systems approach to public policy-issue identification, analysis, priority setting, and action programming, in order to reach its basic goal—survival and a return on investment adequate to maintain and expand productivity to meet the needs of society.

The United States did not move in the direction of policy-issue identification largely because no such system for the management of public policy existed. I believe the *Chase/Jones issue-management process model*, developed in 1976, provides that system. (See figure 1.) Although only a few years old, it has already been tested by many large and small corporations. The model developed out of a combination of real-world experience, intellectual curiosity, and scholarship. It draws on the academic research of social scientists; on the practical experience and intuition of line management; on the acknowledged skills of public relations, public affairs, and communications; and on the specialized knowledge of other staff professionals. The model provides the system for management of the corporate response to public-policy issues. It consists of four sets of concentric rings connected by large arrows.

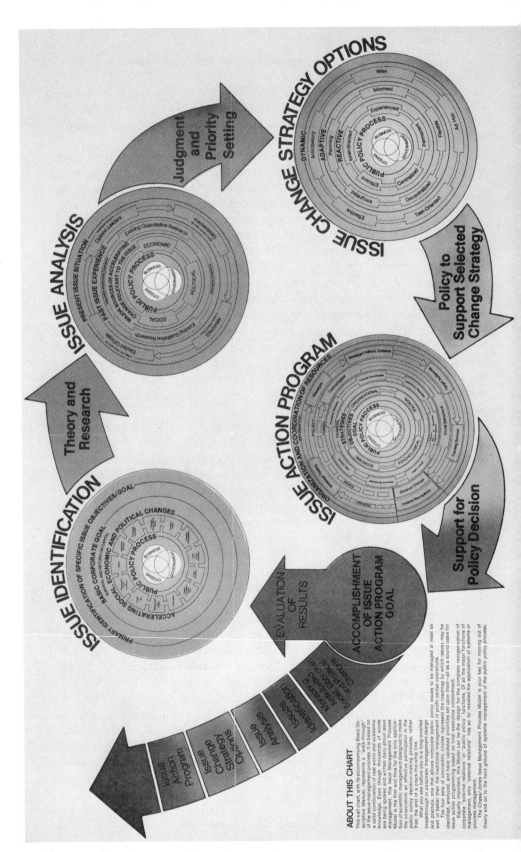

ISSUE ANALYSIS

ISSUE CHANGE STRATEGY OPTIONS

Judgment and Priority Setting

Theory and Research

ISSUE IDENTIFICATION

ISSUE ACTION PROGRAM

Policy to Support Selected Change Strategy

Support for Policy Decision

EVALUATION OF RESULTS

ACCOMPLISHMENT OF ISSUE ACTION PROGRAM GOAL

ABOUT THIS CHART

This wall chart, with its accompanying Basic Descriptive Manual, represents a "walk-through" of the issue management process. It is based on a solid combination of real world and academic knowledge. Even though thousands of words are being spoken and written about issue management, this Issue Management Process Model is the first and thus far the only application of scientific management designed to make the corporation an effective participant in the public policy decision-making process, rather than the end of a crack-the-whip line.

What you see before you is a long-awaited breakthrough in corporate management and practice, one that any competent public policy issues set upon them—at all as a sound basis for issue settlement and appropriate corrective comment.

The four sets of concentric circles represent the roadmap by which issues may be identified, analyzed, and have validated priorities set upon them—at all as a sound basis for issue settlement and appropriate corrective comment.

Equally important, this Model can be the design for the complete reorganization of corporate "external relations"—or "public policy" functions. Of all the major functions of management, only "external relations" has so far resisted the application of systems or process management.

The Chase/Jones Issue Management Process Model is your key for moving out of theory and on to the hard ground of systems management of the public policy process.

CATEGORIES IN THE CHASE/JONES MODEL

(The lettered and numbered entries are main categories. The un-lettered or numbered entries are subcategories and should be visualized as flowing one into another in a circular fashion.)

A. Issue Identification
  1. Primary Identification of Specific Issue Objectives/Goal
  2. Basic Corporate Goal—Survival and Return on Capital
  3. Accelerating Social, Economic and Political Changes
     Inflation—Distributive Economy—Knowledge Explosion—Changing Social/Ethical Values—Pluralistic Politics—Changing Demographics—Limits to Growth Movement—Energy Concerns—Impacts of Increased Leisure Time—Conservation—Redistribution of Wealth—Quality of Life—Institutionalized Activism by Government
  4. Public Policy Process
     Citizens—Business—Government

B. Issue Analysis
  1. Present Issue Situation
     Elected Officials (Legislative Trend Analysis)—Opinion Leaders (Leadership Surveys)—Gatekeepers (Media Content Analysis)—Electorate (Public Opinion Surveys)
  2. Past Issue Experience
     Existing Qualitative Research—(association membership experience)—Existing Quantitative Research—(association experience)
  3. Major Sources of Accelerating Change Relevant to the Issue
     Social—Economic—Political
  4. Public Policy Process
     Citizens—Business—Government

C. Issue Change Strategy Options
  1. Dynamic
     Anticipatory—Wise—Ad Hoc—Task-Oriented—Effective
  2. Adaptive
     Planning—Informed—Flexible—Decentralized—Integrated
  3. Reactive
     Inner-directed—Experienced—Permanent—Centralized—Efficient
  4. Public Policy Process
     Citizens—Business—Government

D. Issue Action Program
  1. Organization and Coordination of Resources
     Information: Messages—Message Delivery Systems—Target Audiences—Tracking Surveys—Desired Perceptions—(redesign)—Message Testing
     Project: Technological—Social Behavioral—Desired Change—(redesign)
     Human: Purchasing > Suppliers—Financial > Stockholders—Consumers > Marketing—Government > Executive and Legislative Branches—Judicial > Legal—Personnel > Employees—Labor > Unions
     Financial
  2. Strategies
     Organizational—Political—Psychological—Economic
  3. Objectives
  4. Goal
  5. Public Policy Process
     Citizens—Business—Government

Source: Copyright © 1977 by W. Howard Chase and Barrie L. Jones.

Figure 1. Chase/Jones Issue Management Process Model

The sets of rings are labeled issue identification, issue analysis, issue change-strategy options, and issue-action program. All are read and followed in the same way, from the innermost circle outward. The large arrows indicate the direction of the flow from one step, or set of rings, in the issue-management process, to the next. A closer examination of each step follows.

Issue Identification

The *issue-identification module,* the first step in the issue-management process, is vital in that it forces its user to find out what issues are confronting him or her in what number. This module, like the other three in the Chase/Jones model, starts at its center with the continuous interaction of the three constituent parts of the public-policy process: citizens, business, and government. This process is at the heart of all four steps in the model and is represented graphically as three interlocking circles. Central to the model is the fact that any attempt to deal with any one of these interrelated forces to the exclusion of any of the others, as well as intervening institutions (for example, church, media, unions, and so forth), is counterproductive, expensive, and doomed to failure if true public policy management is to be achieved.

The next ring outward is *accelerating social, economic, and political changes.* Within this ring are the names of thirteen trends that have significant impact on the operation of any business or institution. Others may be added, for example, federal centralization. Some will directly affect a business and some will not. At seminars conducted by Howard Chase, groups of executives have named 56-120 separate, identifiable trends relevant to them and their companies.

The rise of the public-interest or issue-advocacy group is a by-product of corporate unwillingness or inability to recognize the effects of trends on its future profitability and even its existence. Recognition of these trends and their impact on business is a vital step towards achieving *basic corporate goal*—survival and return on capital.

Obviously, with so many issues competing for attention, some basic decisions will have to be made. No organization, not even the largest, has the resources to effectively manage all the issues confronting it. The next ring outward, *primary identification of specific issues,* provides the preliminary opportunity to determine which issues the organization must respond to, may choose to respond to, and those of only peripheral impact and importance.

This process of sorting out what is really important to the organization in the public-policy arena is invariably an eye-opener. It forces the manager to put priorities on not only those issues that can be reduced to dollars and cents, but also on much broader issues having impact on the society at large. This priority exercise will naturally result in the grouping of issues related to each other, and the simmering down of those the corporation can intelligently deal with at one time. At this stage, those issues of most importance to the corporation are ready to cross the large arrow labeled *theory and research* into the issue-analysis module. From here, the model deals with single issues. Each issue emerging from the issue-identification phase will undergo, separately, the last three operations of the model, where the corporate response to each issue will be managed by a system, just as any other concern of the corporation.

Issue Analysis

The arrow leading to the issue-analysis module, theory and research, is precisely what the issue is subjected to in the issue-analysis step. Starting again at the center, you will find the triad of the public-policy process. Again, keep in mind that the interrelated and interdependent triad—citizens, business, and government—represents forces whose actions or inactions make public policy.

The first task of the issue-analysis phase is to determine where the issue arises and draws its importance. The first ring, *major sources of accelerating change relevant to the issue,* is where this determination begins. Within this ring are listed the three generic sources of ferment affecting the public-policy process on every issue—the social, economic, and political trends and forces that govern our lives.

Once the primary sources of change have been determined, we can move to the next ring, *past-issue experience.* Within this ring are two large boxes. The first, *existing quantitative research,* is connected by narrow bands containing *internal experience* and *external experience.* It is within the past-issue experience ring that existing knowledge of the issue is compiled into useful form. This information may come from within the organization (internal experience) or from other sources beyond the corporation's own resources (external experience). Existing quantitative research is easier to describe than *existing qualitative research* (the second box). This research can include public opinion or other types of surveys by Harris, Yankelovich, Opinion Research, and so on, from external sources, and estimates of costs, employment impact, and effects on sales and marketing plans from internal sources. Depending on the size of the corporation, internal sources might also include analytical data from states where the public-policy decision has already been made and laws or regulations passed.

Existing qualitative research includes the knowledge that pertains to an issue that has not been subjected to scientific rigor, yet is important to an understanding of the issue's evolution and future development. Qualitative research from external sources might include a review of recent periodical literature to see what is being said about an issue in influential magazines or journals. Internally, it certainly includes drawing on the special or generalized knowledge of employees concerning the issue in question. Past successes and failures in dealing with particular issues can be carefully analyzed, adding to the arsenal of existing research.

With this compilation of past-issue experience, the issue manager can move to the next ring outward, *present-issue situation*. By this point in the analysis of an issue, the issue manager should have a fairly clear idea of the origins and evolution of the issue. By studying past-issue experience, he or she should be able to further refine the issue and its impact on the organization. This refinement is necessary to avoid expensive waste in analysis of the present-issue situation.

The last ring in this issue-analysis module, *legislative-trend analysis*, provides the means to determine the salience of the issue through scientific research. The four boxes within the ring contain those groups to be surveyed and the methodologies to be used when necessary. The four groups to be monitored in this ring are *opinion leaders, gatekeepers, electorate,* and *elected officials*.

Opinion leaders are those individuals within a community, state, or nation who exercise an unusually high degree of influence over the opinions, and hence the votes, of others. Leadership surveys help determine the views of these leaders, who might include members of the media and representatives from public-interest groups, politics, business, labor, the law, and the church.

Gatekeepers are the newspaper editors and other media personnel who determine what does and does not get public attention; these gatekeepers exercise great influence in setting the public-policy agenda. A study done by Barrie L. Jones for the U.S. Beverage/Container Industries indicates a correlation as high as 94 percent between published opinion, as measured by media-content analysis, and all obtainable clippings concerning an issue. The results of these analyses will help predict shifts in public opinion.

Public-opinion polls range from the familiar Gallup and Roper polls to highly specific and frequently unpublished surveys commissioned privately by businesses or other groups. Usually, the more specific the survey is, the more it costs. Surveys should be used when necessary, but not without a clear idea of the information sought.

Legislative-trend analysis serves to determine the position of elected officials on the issue under study. Many large companies have this function built into their government relations programs. They can also use anti-industry ranking of legislators, published by many public-interest groups, and a computer-based methodology, voting behavior-path analysis.

The result of the issue-analysis module will be comprehensive examination of all aspects of the issue and its impact on the organization. This module is especially important because, as different issues emerge from it in organized form, it becomes possible for the corporation to proceed with *judgment and priority setting*, as the large arrow indicates. It is the issue analysis that allows the manager to place priorities on the issues and to allocate resources in the most cost- and time-effective manner.

Issue-Change Strategy Options

The large arrow leads to the next module, *issue-change strategy options*. It is here that basic decisions are made on the corporation's response to the challenges posed by any particular issue. In effect, in this module the organization decides whether to fight at all, and if it does, where and when. Issue-change strategy options are those reasonable courses of action open to the corporation after evaluation of the issue-analysis findings

The three rings in this module represent the three modes of response available to the corporation as it faces an issue. From the center outward, they are the *reactive*, the *adaptive*, and the *dynamic* modes.

The reactive response to an issue is demonstrated when management says, "Let's stonewall this one." The word *reactive* has acquired a bad connotation in management literature, but there are times in the issue-management process when the reactive mode will be the proper one. If the issue-analysis process shows an issue to be tangential to the aims of the organization and its constituents, or if rigorous analysis of the issue indicates that it will indeed "blow over," then the issue manager may properly decide to remain in the reactive mode, particularly if corporate action or response might have the effect of reinforcing the issue's importance in the public-policy arena.

The adaptive response implies an openness to change through constructive dialogue and accommodation, within or outside of government intervention. The National Coal Project is a good example. It began in 1976 with a meeting between a top executive of Dow Chemical and a former president of the Sierra Club. The objective was to come up with an accommodation between coal companies and conservation groups so that the nation might move ahead in the development of its coal resources in ways acceptable to both parties. More than a year of meeting and debate, sponsored by Georgetown University, resulted in an outstanding two hundred points of agreement between the sides—two hundred steps the nation can take to use its coal reserves to the optimum advantage of both public and private interests. Participants in the National Coal Project found that concurrent concern for the environment, combined with dismay about the nation's energy situation, made a flexible, nonideological review possible. The combined knowledge of the coal industry and the conservations could yield better solution than either could alone, and at far less cost than through adversary procedures.

To be dynamic in issue-management terms means having the ability to choose the time, place, and method for solution of the problem. Examples of a purely dynamic approach are rare. Most often, the issue manager will find himself using elements of each mode—the reactive, the adaptive, and the dynamic—as he approaches an issue. Selection among issue change-strategy options does not necessarily represent absolute or mutually exclusive decisions.

The purpose of the issue-change strategy options module is to clarify to the organization itself what its options are and to enable it to decide what policy it should pursue regarding any particular issue. The result of this part of the process should be a clear and concise policy and a statement of the desired effect of management decisions. This is symbolized by the large arrow, *policy to support selected change strategy,* leading to the issue-action program.

Issue-Action Program

The issue-action program begins with the statement of a clear and specific goal that the organization is capable of achieving within a reasonable length of time. Objectives usually cover a shorter time period and represent those steps which, subject to quantitative review, help fulfill the corporate goal. Of course, not all aims or ends of action can be subjected to quantitative review; thus, a clear statement of the subjective actions required to reach the objectives might be included in the action-program plan.

In the *strategies* ring are listed those four strategies that support the objective: *organizational, political, psychological,* and *economic.* Selecting from among these strategies, either singly or in combination, requires an interdisciplinary outlook including elements of political science; organizational development; real-world, bottom-line economics; and a sensitivity to the findings of social scientists. Once the strategies are selected, *organization and coordination of resources* begins. This appears just inside the outermost ring of the issue-action program module. Within this circle are four subrings labeled *financial, human, project,* and *information.* These are categories of tactics for effecting the results of the issue-action program.

The innermost of the four subrings, financial, is the simplest to define in traditional terms. How much money is the organization willing to commit to a specific issue? The realistic issue manager, like a plant manager facing a production decision, must operate within budgetary constraints in planning the issue-action program.

In the human subring are listed some of the familiar corporate functions and the constituencies with which they deal. Labor/unions, purchasing/suppliers, financial/stockholders, marketing/consumers, and personnel/employees are typical examples, but this ring also includes relationships such as legal/judicial and government/executive and legislative branches. Human resources could also include many more relationships, for example, press relations/financial editors, sales/wholesalers, and so forth. The model shows that the corporation has available to it more constituencies than some public relations or public affairs departments are now reaching, and there are built-in bridges to these constituencies already in place. The issue manager should realize that the person or department in daily contact with these constituencies is usually the best conduit for the information and point of view the organization wants to convey, and also will be the best source of feedback for the organization. A task-force approach to issue-action programming is necessary, with members drawn from wherever relevant skills and experience may be found in the organization. Old division of line and staff have no place in public-policy management. The issue manager must have access to all talent and knowledge available in the corporation, and should be given the responsibility and authority to use all of these resources to reach the public-policy goal.

The next ring involves project resources. Projects are deeds—real actions of the organization that bear on the issue at hand. The model divides projects into two types: technological and social/behavioral. An example of the technological project is Reynolds Metal's successful establishment of recycling centers for aluminum cans. These centers began as an exercise in public relations to provide the company with a visible answer to its litter-minded critics; now they have become self-sustaining profit centers.

The National Bank of Detroit's (NBD's) Criminal Justice Forum program is an example of a social/behavioral project. NBD, whose main office is in center-city Detroit, felt that the soaring crime rate and the resulting social unrest in Detroit and throughout Michigan were a threat to its own business as well as to society. NBD organized and funded a series of public forums at which nearly 20,000 citizens heard the facts, discussed them, and then acted with votes and letters to change those parts of the criminal justice system that were failing in practice. The citizen input generated by the forums has resulted in several new laws in Michigan, with several more pending passage.

The arrow in the ring connecting the technological and the social/behavioral projects leads to a box labeled *desired change* in public policy. If the desired change is not affected by the projects in place, then the next step is *redesign*, as indicated by the broken arrow. If the project fails, the manager should find out where it was weak and change it for the better. This process is continuous; any project can be improved.

The information ring is based on Harold D. Lasswell's classic communication theory: who says what, through what channels, to whom, and to what effect. Starting with *messages testing,* the arrow leads to the decisions of what *messages* are to be communicated by corporate and third-party speakers, by what *message-delivery systems,* to what *target audiences,* and to what effect. *Tracking surveys* are the means by which the issue manager can judge the effectiveness of each of the elements. If the *desired perceptions* are not attained, *redesign* of the information system is in order. Again, this is a continuous process.

The large arrow coming out of the issue-action program module, reading *support for policy decision,* leads to *accomplishment for issue-action program goal,* the immediate aim of the issue-management process. But another arrow leads back to issue identification, the very first step in the process. The model is unique in that it not only acts as a roadmap for issue mangement, but it also serves as an issue performance-evaluation system. If the program has fallen short of its goal, its weaknesses can be pinpointed by going back through the process and checking each step against the model's guidelines. False steps will be apparent, and the process can go on again, strengthened and corrected. The broken arrow leading away from the accomplishment circle begins the process again, with other issues to contend with on other grounds.

The tour in this article of the Chase/Jones issue-management process model has been linear, moving from one ring to the next in order. The reason the model has been produced in the form of concentric circles is because the process is not always linear. The system process is fluid, involving people, money, management, and changing conditions in the public-policy process itself. The Chase/Jones issue-management process model represents a continuous and ongoing management process.

Models of Management and Society

Lee E. Preston
James E. Post

> The ideas of economists and political philosophers, both when they are right and when they are wrong, are more powerful than is commonly understood. Indeed the world is ruled by little else. Practical men, who believe themselves to be quite exempt from intellectual influences, are usually the slaves of some defunct economist.
>
> —J.M. Keynes, 1936, in *The General Theory of Employment, Interest and Money*

Our basic concepts and understandings about the nature of the world affect our thinking and behavior in powerful, but often unrealized ways. If one believes that illness is caused by evil spirits, then it is rational to call in the witchdoctor at the first sign of a fever; if one understands illness in terms of germs and infections, then an antibiotic may be preferred. We often refer to summary descriptions of our basic concepts as *models* because they are simplified and brief sketches of complex, and perhaps even obscure, relationships. Models are not intended to be complete descriptions of reality; they are, however, useful devices for highlighting fundamental and critical relationships, and for contrasting one basic conceptual scheme with another.

In this essay we draw on terms from systems theory to describe and contrast some important models of the relationship between individual managerial units (firms) and their host environments (society). Each of the models presented has had considerable historic influence, and each captures significant dimensions of observable experience. However, each of them is incomplete in important respects, and they have to be combined and supplemented with additional elements in order to provide a basis for serious analysis.

We begin with a presentation of the *legal model* of the private business organization in our society. This conception is of intrinsic importance; moreover, it emphasizes the fact that the fundamental existence of managerial units as we know them rests on their acceptance by society and, in the case of corporations, their specific authorization in public policy. The remainder of the article presents several fundamental and sharply contrasting conceptual models in which the legal, economic, and social characteristics of microunits are combined and emphasized in various ways. The *market contract model*, familiar from traditional economic and political theory, is contrasted with its classic opposite, the Marxian model of *exploitation*. These two historic conceptions—which, upon examination, turn out to have some important features in common—are shown to be quite distinct in both assumptions and implications from the now-popular idea of a *managed society*, as suggested by the *technostructure model* based on the analyses of Burnham and Galbraith. Finally, elements from these several prior models are combined into our own synthetic model, which is based on the concept of *interpenetrating systems*.

Models of Social Systems

A *system* consists of two or more components or subsystems that interact with each other and that are separated from their larger environment by a boundary. Systems that are completely self-contained, involving no interactions with the environment, are described as *closed*. Although a purely closed system is only a theoretical possibility, the degree to which a system is closed or open provides an important basis for analysis. Any *open* system—which includes any system that can be actually observed—is involved in some sort of transformation of inputs received from the larger environment into outputs discharged into that environment. The boundary of the system filters the type or kinds of inputs that the system can receive from the environment and the outputs that can be discharged. The boundary also determines the time rate of flow of input and output between the system and its environment. This general system conception is, of course, now widely used throughout the physical, biological, and social sciences.[1]

Social systems are invariably open and involve the exchange of inputs and outputs with the larger environment. Some individual social systems may be extremely and continuously open—with many different types of inputs and outputs crossing their boundaries at all times—while others are relatively closed or only periodically engaged in interactions with the environment. A household of family members intimately involved in the life of its local community is an example of an extremely open microsystem, a small subsystem functioning within the larger social framework. The same family living in a remote location and with infrequent and highly specialized contacts with the outside world might constitute a system almost closed.

Large elements of the social environment—communities, industries, regions, and so on—and even society itself are described as macrosystems or *suprasystems*, involving numerous large and complex subsystems as internal components. Some macrosystems exist only through the independent interactions of their subsystem components and without any overall locus of direction or control. *Dominant suprasystems*, however, are those which, once developed, take on an independent existence and exert a degree of control over their internal components. The national economy of the United States is a suprasystem in which central control or dominance is almost entirely lacking; even the economy-wide impact of federal government activity is only one among many influences at work within the aggregate. By contrast, a centrally planned economy is a dominant suprasystem; the overall plan is used to guide the activities of the subsystem components. Our own federal government could also be described as a dominant suprasystem originally formed through the interaction of the component (subsystem) states.

Systems are said to be *interpenetrating* when more than one distinct system, neither totally contained by nor containing the other, is involved in a single event or process. As Parsons states: "Where it is necessary to speak of two or more analytically distinguishable relational systems as *both* constituting partial determinants of process in a concrete empirical system, we speak of the systems as *interpenetrating*."[2]

Our own analysis of the management-society relationship is cast in terms of this interpenetrating systems concept. Therefore, we wish to distinguish as sharply as possibly between an *interpenetrating systems model*, in which two separate systems determine a single process, and two more familiar conceptions: *collateral systems models*, in which two or more systems are engaged in transformation and exchange relationships with each other; and *suprasystems models*, in which the activities of subsystems and components are dominated by system-wide authority or influence. These three general classes of models are illustrated in figure 1.

The Legal Model

The legal framework of our society is a suprasystem in which the authority of the state is used to preserve a stable and harmonious social order. In some instances— as, for example, with respect to criminal activity—state authority is exercised directly. In others, however, the state merely maintains a system of guidelines and institutions (laws and courts) through which individual parties can engage in collateral interactions to preserve and pursue their own interests and resist the impositions of others.[3]

The status of a business enterprise within the legal framework is a fundamental aspect of its existence. In general, the establishment and growth of private firms has been encouraged by our legal system, although private operations have been prohibited in some areas (not only criminal activity, but also postal service and national defense). At the heart of the relationship between the business firm and the legal system is the concept of *legal entity*. An entity is anything that possesses the quality of oneness and may therefore be regarded as a single unit. A legal entity is any unit recognized in law as having the capacity to possess legal rights and to be subject to legal obligations.[4] A legal entity is thus able to acquire, own, and dispose of property; it can enter contracts, commit wrongs, sue and be sued.

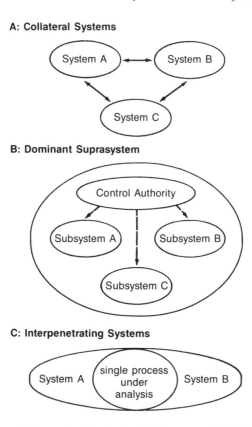

Figure 1. Basic Social Systems Models

Human beings are legal entities of natural origin, possessing legal capacity and legal status. A proprietorship is such a natural person participating in market transactions as a business on a regular and continuing basis. A proprietorship is thus responsible for meeting all the obligations of a business firm, as well as those of an individual, as prescribed by law. Partnerships are associations of individuals participating in market transactions as a business on a regular and continuing basis. They are generally viewed as not having an independent legal existence apart from their members. Since a partnership is not a legal entity in itself, its obligations and responsibilities are those of the individual partners, each of whom—like the proprietor—is fully responsible both as an individual and as a business firm.

Although proprietorships and partnerships are much more numerous than corporations, the latter are clearly the dominant form of business unit in terms of economic influence. Corporations account for an overwhelming share of the revenues and assets of all business enterprises, and their pervasive importance in our society is even greater than simple numerical measures would indicate. However, each organizational form has certain particular advantages and disadvantages in specific situations; and once a legal form has been adopted by a firm, the form itself may have an important effect on the organization's capacity for and direction of future development. The essential feature of the *corporate form* is that it separates the existence and responsibilities of the organization from those of its individual human participants. Whereas the law simply recognizes and sanctions the existence and economic activity of individuals in the proprietorship and the partnership, the corporation exists as a creation of law.

The development of new forms of business organization and relationships has been described as an aspect of the enlargement of options available to individuals in the pursuit of their individually conceived purposes. Thus, the earlier common-law tradition of agreements and legal associations among individuals enforced by the judiciary gradually gave way to the development of collective organizations on the one hand and to an expanding role for the legislative arm of the state on the other. As Hurst comments: "It was inevitable that the legislature play a larger part in regard to corporation law. It did not lie in judicial power to grant charters, and men saw issues in this field too broad and turbulent to fit within the confines of lawsuits."[5] Thus, the state became the creator of new forms of organization, and widespread adoption of general incorporation statutes has greatly broadened the privilege of corporate form and served to popularize it.

The source of corporate existence is the *charter.* Unlike proprietorships and partnerships, which can arise without the formality of public approval, corporations cannot legally exist without governmental authorization. The chartering process serves to confirm publicly the view that the economic system and the organizations participating in it are performing a social function that is endorsed by society's political arm, the state. Corporate charters are either *restricted* or *general* in their terms. Restricted grants limit the types of activities that the corporation may perform. Thus, hospitals and schools, nonprofit charities, and municipalities are each chartered to perform specific types of activities. Should the grants become outdated or merit modification, resort must be had to the public-policy process in order to secure change. General grants, however, rely on the larger system within which the chartered unit will be participating to stimulate the unit to act in a manner that will prove socially beneficial. General grants are, in effect, licenses for the corporation to act as its management sees fit, the assumption being that management's choice of activities will constitute a rational response to the stimuli generated by society as a whole and hence serve a social purpose.

The Market-Contract Model

The expectation that legal business entities will interact with each other, so as to reveal and respond to social needs, rests on an important historical idea that we shall term the *market-contract model.* This model underlies the traditional doctrines of liberal economic and political theory. It is made explicit here so that the similarities and differences of other models to be presented can be clearly indicated.

The essential idea of the market-contract model is that each participant in the economy—down to the individual firm, household, and productive worker—obtains its share of the benefits available in society by providing goods and performing services that are desired by other social entities and individuals. The firm or individual makes, in effect, a market contract with other members of society, provides them with something they desire on terms more favorable than they can obtain elsewhere, and obtains its own share of the social product from them in return. As Adam Smith described the situation: "Every man . . . lives by exchanging, or becomes in some measure a merchant, and the society itself grows to be what is properly called a commercial society."[6]

According to the market-contract model, a business firm comes into being because it can perform desired functions for other members of society on favorable terms. If the market will sustain the enterprise, it continues and perhaps thrives. If tastes change, costs rise, or more favorable competitive alternatives appear, it declines and then must find some other functions to perform, or it will simply pass out of existence. Any problems that cannot be resolved by the market test must be referred elsewhere—to the political decision-making system, for example—or left to private social action and charity. Issues of social involvement are fully resolved by the basic test that some specific task must be performed on terms that at least some customers are willing to pay.

The pure market-contract model is amoral and pragmatic, since, as Adam Smith pointed out:

> It is not from the benevolence of the butcher, the brewer, or the baker, that we expect our dinner, but from their regard to their own interest. We address ourselves not to their humanity but to their self-love, and never talk to them of our own necessities but of their advantages. Nobody but a beggar chooses to depend chiefly upon the benevolence of his fellow citizens.[7]

The social philosophy associated with the market-contract model is not, however, pessimistic or critical. On the contrary, the interplay of forces of self-interest is thought to lead as if by an "invisible hand" to a harmonious outcome for society as a whole. In the most idealistic version of the analysis, competition assures a close relationship between prices and costs; the accumulation of capital permits mechanization and the division of labor; and increasing productivity results in "the progress of opulence" over time.

Whether or not these conclusions can be fully anticipated, one key feature of the market contract model for present purposes is its assumption of a complete and sharp distinction between each market contracting unit, from the individual worker to the largest enterprise, and all other units and individuals within the system. It is a *collateral-systems model* in which each component entity is isolated from every other one, and interactions take place *only* by means of transactions. This assumed separation and isolation extends even to government itself, which, in the pure market contract analysis, is essentially a subsystem among other subsystems. It performs the key functions of maintaining law and order and providing public services, but its relationship with the other units of society comes down essentially to market exchange. Although Adam Smith himself, and most other writers in the liberal tradition, expressed strong personal views as to the proper (and improper) role of the political state, the model itself implies that the state should provide such services as the members of society desire, and on terms that they are willing to pay. Social decision making through the political process exists entirely apart from the market-contracting system, and the latter is seen as the principal and most desirable form of social coordination and decision making. Any impact of government or other forms of collective social direction on the market-contract process and its results can be unambiguously termed *interference*.

The Exploitation Model

Diametrically opposed to the market-contract model is a conception of the management-society relationship as a system of exploitation. Although this conception has its roots in the Marxian analysis of capitalist exploitation, it is equally applicable to the self-interested social dominance of dictators, commissars, and bureaucrats. (An old socialist joke has it that "Capitalism is the exploitation of man by man; socialism is the reverse.")

In the elementary Marxian exposition, capitalistic production inevitably involves the exploitation of labor by the capitalist (that is, the owner-manager) class. Marx viewed the value of all goods and services as due ultimately to the labor required to produce them. The capitalist hires labor and purchases materials in order to resell the resulting products at prices higher than costs, thus obtaining a a profit. His object is not the production process itself (the production of commodities), but only the profit obtained (the production of capital). Each addition to capital increases the ability of the capitalist to employ labor and to expropriate additional surplus value (that is, profit) arising as a result of production; and each round of production and sales increases the stock of capital and hence the capacity for exploitation by the capitalists. "Accumulate accumulate! That is Moses and the prophets!"[8]

The basic exploitation model was subsequently extended by Marx, and even more vigorously by Rosa Luxemburg, to include an emphasis on interracial and international relationships, particularly imperialism. "Capital, impelled to appropriate productive forces for purposes of exploitation, ransacks the whole world. . . ."[9] A half-century later an African representative to a conference on multinational corporations declared that a small nation is "virtually at the mercy" of such corporations in their "eminently rational" search for efficiency and profits. "No matter how one looks at it, foreign investment involves exploitation (in the Marxist sense) of the resources of the host country."[10]

In its modern version the *exploitation model* describes any situation in which a dominant social or economic class controls society for the pursuit of its own particular interests, extracting all available socioeconomic benefits for use toward those ends. In this sense the exploitation model underlies the common conception of both the nineteenth-century "robber barons" in the United States and the political and administrative leaders in Nazi Germany and Stalinist Russia. It also accounts for the attitude, reflected previously, of many less-developed host countries toward large international firms operating within their borders. The essential idea is that there are two types of collateral subsystems—exploiting units and exploited units—and that the exploiting units use their dominant power position to extract maximum benefits and thus maintain and enlarge their spheres of special interest.

The elementary Marxian notion of exploitation grew out of—and, indeed, in opposition to—the market contract notions of the classical economists, whose work Marx described as "learned disputation [about] how the booty pumped out of the labourer may be divided, with most advantage to accumulation, between the industrial capitalist and the rich idler."[11] However, the Marxian analysis shares with the earlier model a basic amorality. Marx viewed "the evolution of the economic formation of society . . . as a process of natural history," in which the individual cannot be held "responsible for relations whose creature he socially remains."[12] The notion of social responsibility (or irresponsibility) as an aspect of private business management would have been as foreign to Marx as to Adam Smith.

In all other respects, however, the Marxian model presents the sharpest possible contrast to the liberal conception of a harmonious society based on market-contract relationships. Where Smith—and liberal economists down to the present—viewed business profits as essentially rewards for successful accomplishment of socially desired tasks and indicators of direction for needed economic expansion, for Marx the rate of profit was synonymous with "the intensity of exploitation." This reversal of relationships replaced the inherent harmony of the classical conception with a system of inherent conflicts and contradictions leading to ultimate collapse. According to the idealized market-contract model, an entire economy in which each individual and organization operates on the same (that is, market contract) economic principle is viable and stable. By contrast, the Marxian model identifies two distinct groups—the exploiters and the exploited—and holds that "capitalism . . . depends in all respects on non-capitalist strata and social organizations existing side by side with it."[13] The capitalist system eventually collapses either because all possible exploitation possibilities are used up or because political and social revolution is brought about by the exploited groups themselves.

The Technostructure Model

The market contract and exploitation models of the management-society relationship share a second characteristic in addition to the absence of moral and ethical content. They assume a clear and sharp separation between the ownership-control element of each individual managerial unit and the rest of society within which that unit operates. For Adam Smith, each economic unit, including the household, exists in isolation and relates to the rest of society through the mechanism of market exchange. Similarly, for Marx, each capitalist unit—and the capitalist class as a whole—is sharply distinguished from the rest of society and relates to it through the process of exploitation.

Both of these collateral-systems models contrast sharply with suprasystems models in which society as a whole is shown to be functionally integrated and managed by some dominant control authority or group. Centralized control by the state would, of course, constitute one form of suprasystem dominance. However, since there seems to be no widespread opinion that such a model would describe our current society, it does not require development here. However, the now-popular conception of an integrated society consisting primarily of large managerial organizations and dominated by their collective staffs of high-level professionals is a suprasystem model of some significance. Borrowing Galbraith's term, we refer to this conception as the *technostructure model.*

The technostructure model was first developed in Burnham's *The Managerial Revolution* (1941), and was more recently presented in Galbraith's *The New Industrial State* (1967). Both of these authors started with the familiar idea of the separation of ownership and control in the large business enterprise and the associated development of a professional managerial class. They then argued that the elite of the managerial class, whom Galbraith termed the *technostructure,* not only take over individual organizations within society, but these large organizations simultaneously expand and develop interconnections so that the technostructure gradually comes to dominate society as a whole. This domination, however, is not essentially exploitative; neither can it be described in market-contract terms. On the contrary, in the process of taking over society, the technostructure comes to be taken over *by* society, embracing social goals and objectives even as it shapes tastes and values through its own behavior. Eventually, the individual manager, the technostructure as a group, the large organization, and society as a whole tend to merge into a single decision-action system in which particularistic goals, efforts, and rewards cannot be readily identified.

As Galbraith describes the process,

> The individual member of the Technostructure identifies himself with the goals of the mature corporation as, and because, the corporation identifies itself with goals which have, or appear to him to have, social purpose. . . .
>
> It is the genius of the industrial system that it makes the goals that reflect its needs—efficient production of goods, a steady expansion in their output (and) . . . consumption, . . . technological change, autonomy for the technostructure, an adequate supply of trained and educated manpower—coordinate with social virtue and human enlightenment. . . .
>
> Given the deep dependence of the industrial system on the state and . . . its identification with public goals and the adaptation of these to its needs, the

industrial system will not long be regarded as something apart from government. . . . Increasingly it will be recognized that the mature corporation, as it develops, becomes part of the larger administrative complex associated with the state. In time the line between the two will disappear. Men will look back in amusement at the pretense that once caused people to refer to General Dynamics and North American Aviation and AT&T as *private* business.[14]

The Galbraithian vision may yet be rather far from reality in the United States, and its details correspondingly indistinct. By contrast, a similar technocrat-manager development has frequently been noted to be a characteristic feature of present-day Japan. *Japan Incorporated* has gained unquestioned use as a

description of one of the world's largest economies as though it were a single, coordinated, centrally managed business unit. . . . This relationship is not comparable to that of a socialist economy, with the state in control . . . nor yet analogous to the United States in the late nineteenth century, with government essentially an instrumentality of big business.[15]

On the contrary, the similarity of personal goals, training, and experience among Japanese political, economic, and social leaders apparently accounts for the overall harmony and broad social comprehensiveness of their viewpoints.

An Interpenetrating Systems Model

The two classic models of market contract and exploitation contain several important truths. One is that the managerial unit is, to some extent, a distinct element within society, not simply an operating mechanism within some larger rationalized and controlled system. Another is that there are elements of quid pro quo (exchange), as well as elements of power and advantage (exploitation), in most important social relationships. At the same time, the extreme separation of the mangerial unit from the rest of society, whether for purposes of pure exchange or unfettered exploitation, required in these models contrasts too sharply with common experience reflecting cohesiveness and a broad commonality of interest—and hence bases for cooperation rather than conflict—along social entities. In contrast, the full-blown technostructure model appears to overstate both the integration and the rationality of social relationships and to underestimate the importance of pluralism, adaptability, initiative, and innovation. Hence, we present here a synthetic model, less precise than any of those previously discussed, although admitting all of them—as well as many other variations and combinations—as special cases.

Our model is based on the concept of *interpenetrating systems*. We assume that the larger society exists as a macrosystem, but that individual (and particularly *large*) mirco-organizations also constitute separable systems within themselves, neither completely controlling nor controlled by the social environment. As Cohen and Cyert describe the situation,

The organization and the environment are parts of a complex interactive system. The actions taken by the organization can have important effects on the environment, and, conversely, the outcomes of the actions of the organization are partially determined by events in the environment. These outcomes and the events that contribute to them have a major impact on the organization. Even if the organization does not respond to these events, significant changes in the organizational participants' goals and roles can occur.[16]

To illustrate the interpenetrating system concept, assume that some firm—an independent entrepreneur or one already organized—decides to pursue a particular path of technological research and development. The firm will draw information and resources—as well as ideas about commercially useful development paths—from the larger society. But the larger society will not in any concrete or conscious way control the development paths pursued—neither their direction nor their success. The development project may yield only trivial results, or none at all. In contrast, it may yield an innovation comparable to the automobile, the computer, or the electric lamp. In the latter case, the firm does not simply exchange the resulting product in a collateral relationship with the rest of society—neither does it do so on a harmonious market-contract basis nor in order to expropriate the surplus value. On the contrary, the introduction of the innovation by the microunit generates both new flows of activity and substantial structural changes within the macrosystem itself. It is this ability of one system to change the *structure* of the other, and not simply to alter the volume or character of inputs and outputs, that distinguishes the interpenetrating systems model from simpler collateral or suprasystems conceptions.

The interpenetrating systems model also facilitates the analysis of the changing role of society, as expressed through formal public policy, *vis-à-vis* the managerial organization. In the market contract model, the state itself is merely one among many separate system units, collecting taxes and tolls in return for services rendered. However, the development of social concern for working conditions, culminating in public policy actions to limit the hours of work or provide protection for health and safety, cannot be described in market-contract (still less in exploitation) terms. On the contrary, we require a model that permits society to influence and constrain—but not necessarily dominate or control—an area of activity formerly reserved to the firm exclusively. Similarly, attempts by individual organizations to affect the course of public policy—whether by bribery or persuasion—may be described as an expansion of managerial activity into the decision system of society at large. In neither example does one system necessarily come to control the other completely, even with respect to the specific matter involved and certainly not in *all* matters. Nor can the relationship between the systems be described in the simple terms of input-output or exchange. On the contrary, the concept of interpenetration seems to be, if less precise, the more accurate general form of the relationship between micro-organizational management and its social environment.

An interpenetrating systems model opens up the possibility—which has, in fact, become a necessity—of considering the potential differences, conflicts, and compatabilities among the goals of micro-organizations and those of society at large. In both the market contract and exploitation models it is assumed that organizations are responsive to their own individual goals and that these goals are balanced (favorably or unfavorably) with those of other system components through the exchange process. In the fully developed technostructure model there can be no goal disharmony; the goals of the managerial class and those of industrial society as a whole have, through the process of adoption and adaptation, become the same. By contrast, the interpenetrating systems model can accommodate both the separateness and possible conflict of managerial and societal goals on one hand and the process of managerial/societal goal adjustment on the other. Society may take into account and seek to influence the goals of the managerial units; and they, in turn, may take into account and seek to influence those of society at large. Neither are the two systems completely separate and independent nor does either control the other; their relationship is better described in terms of interpenetration. As Virgil B. Day, vice-president of General Electric, has remarked:

> The social and economic responsibilities of the corporation have been so broadened and interwoven in the public's expectations . . . that it no longer makes sense, if, indeed, it ever did, to talk as if they could be separated.[17]

> Every corporation has not only a legal charter, but also a form of social charter, that is, the charter of public expectations of corporate performance. These expectations derive from the current set of social values and national goals; and, as these values and goals change so too will the social charter of the corporation.[18]

Notes

This article is a slightly modified version of Lee E. Preston and James E. Post, "Models of Management and Society," in *Private Management and Public Policy: The Principle of Public Responsibility,* © 1975, pp. 14–28. Adapted by permission of Prentice-Hall, Inc., Englewood Cliffs, N.J.

1. Classic references to general systems theory include: K.E. Boulding, "Toward A General Theory of Growth," *The General Systems Yearbook I* (Ann Arbor, Mich.: Society for General Systems Research, 1956), pp. 66–75; E. Nagel, *The Structure of Science* (New York: Harcourt, Brace, 1961); L. Von Bertalanffy, "An Outline of General System Theory," *British Journal of Philosophical Science* (1950), **1** 134–165; L. Von Bertalanffy and A. Rappaport, eds., *The General Systems Yearbook* (Ann Arbor, Mich.: Society for General Systems Research, 1956), annual editions. Our own orientation and terminology is derived from F. Kenneth Berrien, *General and Social Systems* (New Brunswick, N.J.: Rutgers University Press, 1968).
2. Talcott Parsons, "An Approach to Psychological Theory in Terms of the Theory of Action," in *Psychology: A Study of Science,* ed. Sigmund Koch (New York: McGraw-Hill, 1959), pp. 612–711. Quote from p. 649; italics in original. See also Talcott Parsons, "A Paradigm for the Analysis of Social Systems and Change," in *System, Change, and Conflict,* ed. N.J. Demerath and Richard A. Peterson (New York: The Free Press, 1967), pp. 189–212.

For an interesting application of this concept, see Raymond G. Hunt and Ira S. Rubin, "Approaches to Managerial Control in Interpenetrating Systems: The Case of Government-Industry Relations," *Academy of Management Journal,* **16**(2) (1973), 296–311.

3. See Harold J. Berman and Wiliam R. Greiner, *The Nature and Functions of Law,* 3rd ed. (Mineola, N.Y.: The Foundation Press, Inc., 1972), especially Chap. 1.

4. Len Young Smith and G. Gale Roberson, *Business Law,* 3rd ed. (St. Paul, Minn.: West Publishing Company, 1971), p. 720.

5. James Willard Hurst, *Law and the Conditions of Freedom in the Nineteenth-Century United States* (Madison: University of Wisconsin Press, 1956), p. 15.

6. Adam Smith, *The Wealth of Nations,* ed. Edwin Cannan (New York: Random House, 1937), p. 22.

7. Ibid., p. 14.

8. Karl Marx, *Capital,* ed. Frederick Engels, trans. Samuel Moore and Edward Aveling (New York: Random House, 1906), p. 652. (This edition contains one volume only.)

9. Rosa Luxemburg, *The Accumulation of Capital,* trans. Agnes Schwarzchild (New York: Monthly Review Press, 1964), p. 358.

10. *Wall Street Journal,* January 29, 1973, p. 1.

11. Marx, *Capital,* p. 653.

12. Ibid., p. 15.

13. Luxemburg, *The Accumulation of Capital,* p. 365.

14. John Kenneth Galbraith, *The New Industrial State* (Boston: Houghton Mifflin, 1967), pp. 166, 343, and 393. See also James Burnham, *The Managerial Revolution* (New York: John Day Company, 1941). The trend toward a managerial (rather than purely capitalist) society had been earlier detected by Marx, who should perhaps be viewed as the precursor of Berle and Means (*The Modern Corporation and Private Property,* 1932) as well as Burnham and Galbraith. Citing a now-forgotten "Mr. Ure," Marx states that "the industrial managers, and not the industrial capitalists, are 'the soul of our industrial system' . . . The labour of superintendence, entirely separated from the ownership of capital, walks the streets. . . . It is private production without the control of private property." Karl Marx and Friedrich Engels, *Capital,* vol. 3 (Chicago: Charles H. Kerr & Company, 1906), pp. 454–455.

15. James C. Abegglen, "Japan, Incorporated: Government and Business as Partners," in *Changing Market Systems . . . Consumer, Corporate and Government Interfaces,* 1967 Winter Conference Proceedings Series, No. 26 (Washington, D.C.: American Marketing Association, December 27–29, 1967), pp. 228–232. Quote from p. 228. See also Eugene J. Kaplan, *Japan: The Government-Business Relationship* (Washington, D.C.: U.S. Department of Commerce, February 1972). A sharp contrast is provided by the recent *America, Inc.,* which takes an essentially exploitation-model view of business, political, and media leadership in our own society. See Morton Mintz and Jerry S. Cohen, *America, Inc.* (New York: Dial Press, 1971), paperback ed.

16. Kalman J. Cohen and Richard M. Cyert, "Strategy: Formulation, Implementation, and Monitoring," *The Journal of Business* **46**(3) (1973), 352. See also, Paul R. Lawrence and Jay W. Lorsch, *Organization and Environment: Managing Differentiation and Integration* (Boston: Division of Research, Graduate School of Business Administration, Harvard University, 1967); Neil W. Chamberlain, *Enterprise and Environment* (New York: McGraw-Hill, 1968); J. David Singer, *A General Taxonomy for Political Science* (New York: General Learning Press, 1971).

17. Virgil B. Day, "Management and Society: An Insider's View," *Management and Public Policy* (Proceedings of a Conference, School of Management, State University of New York at Buffalo, September 1971), pp. 155–175.

18. Virgil B. Day, "Business Priorities in a Changing Environment," *Journal of General Management,* **1**(1) (1973), 48.

Strategic Uses of Public Policy
Donna J. Wood

We are used to hearing business leaders complain about the burdens of government regulation—high costs, strategic delays, endless disputes over definitions and details, voluminous paperwork and reporting requirements. Yet we also hear the same spokespeople arguing for an industrial policy—suggesting that consumers are best served by heavily regulating certain industries (for example, telecommunications)—or pleading for a federal rule on some health or safety issue that can protect them from charges of negligence and can also serve as a minimum standard of performance for an industry.

As examples of the business community's frequent desire to benefit from regulation and public policy, consider the following recent news items:

1. Businesses support the Occupational Safety and Health Administration's (OSHA) intent to "issue new rules that will require manufacturers to tell their workers about the health hazards of dangerous substances they handle on the job. The initial toll for industry will be $600 million." Business leaders are hoping to avoid stricter and nonuniform state regulation (*Business Week*, November 7, 1983).

2. Wisconsin's Department of Agriculture, Trade and Consumer Protection raided a Milwaukee grocery store and "confiscated alleged contraband shipped across the border from Chicago. The agents' haul: a 175-pound cache of imitation cheese. Wisconsin, where dairying is a $3-billion-a-year business and the state's largest industry, regards imitation cheese in much the same way as the federal government looks upon counterfeit money" (Buss 1981).

3. The Reagan administration proposes to drastically reduce enforcement of the Federal Alcohol Administration Act, which regulates the alcoholic beverage industry. The industry, however, is resisting; the "Washington counsel of the Wine and Spirit Wholesalers of America, said he would 'absolutely' oppose any move to reduce the regulation" (Taylor 1982).

The evidence concerning the costs of regulation is fairly substantial. Few people would argue that government regulations are not costly and burdensome (see

De Fina 1977; Weidenbaum 1981; Bevirt 1978; Leone 1977). The argument, however, that government regulation on balance is more costly than beneficial has yet to be justified. Most such arguments address so-called social regulations—regulations designed to offer diffuse benefits to a large segment of the population or to protect the public welfare (Wilson 1974). But when most of the public discussion seems to focus on regulatory costs and burdens, it is easy to overlook the facts that businesses often find it in their interests to request regulation, and that the government (including Congress and the regulatory agencies) often finds it in the public interest to grant these requests.

Businesses' involvement in U.S. public-policy processes is not a new development, although it may seem so, because businesses have not exhibited consistent, visible political participation. The roots of businesses' political activities are embedded deep in the U.S. social structure. After a period of apparent quiescence (or perhaps invisible activity) in political affairs, U.S. business leaders have recently displayed great interest in entering the political arena openly and in defending the legitimacy of their involvement. Convincing evidence of this trend can be seen in the tremendous growth in political-action committees, public-policy committees of corporate boards, Washington, D.C., offices and corporate lobbyists, and public-affairs management.

Much scholarly attention has been paid to the political activities of businesses in recent years. The academic literature has focused mainly on the areas of business-government relations, the political economy of regulation, agenda-building and the development of public-policy issues, corporate-social responsibility and responsiveness in political affairs, and the ability of businesses to use regulation and public policy as tools for achieving their strategic objectives. There are many reasons, of course, for the burgeoning interest in businesses' political roles, including the abuse—deserved and undeserved—heaped upon big businesses in the 1960s and early 1970s; the economic uncertainties of the late 1970s and 1980s; the growth of federal-budget deficits; the ascendance of the Republican party and the "new right"; and the increasing turbulence of international business.

Continuing concerns about the legitimacy of the political participation of business suggest that some basic questions remain unanswered. How far can business leaders afford to go in using their influence with legislators, regulators, and others in government? How can they afford not to be involved in public-policy matters that will affect their operating and strategic policies, their market positions and product offerings, and their profits? What options do they have for political involvement that will help them to move in advantageous strategic directions and at the same time help to balance the competing demands of their stakeholders? Is it desirable (or inevitable) for businesses to use the powers of government to advance their private interests?

Readers who are familiar with these issues will not be surprised that businesses have responded to an increasingly uncertain and threatening environment in part by seeking to use political processes for their own ends. It is not widely known, however, that the strategic uses of regulation and public policy by businesses have a long and distinguished history in the United States. Business leaders have been aware for over a century that public policy affects the allocation of society's resources and thus affects businesses' ability to fulfill their goals and objectives. They have always guarded and exercised their political roles; in some eras they have simply done so more quietly.

This article examines several theories of regulatory origins and processes. Each theory appears to have serious flaws, but modern and historical evidence suggests that the strategic uses perspective—the idea that businesses can attempt to seize competitive advantage through legislation and regulations—serves as a powerful explanation of much seemingly contradictory business behavior in the public-policy arena.

The Public-Outrage Hypothesis: Crisis and Scandal as Incentives to Legislate

Conventional wisdom often asserts that Congress typically passes public-interest legislation only when it is forced to do so by the weight of public opinion, which peaks during or after some major crisis or scandal. This assertion then becomes the assumption on which critics of regulation can argue that public-interest (or social) laws are typically the outcomes of ill-considered Congressional response to public outrage, and thus are poorly thought-out, impractical, and unnecessarily costly. The public-outrage assumption and the antiregulatory arguments based on this assumption have been very strongly defended by critics of pharmaceutical regulation (see Peltzman 1974; Temin 1980; Grabowski 1976; Grabowski and Vernon 1983), as well as advocates of deregulation in areas such as pollution control and occupational safety and health.

Marvur Bernstein's (1955) analysis of the independent regulatory commissions stands as the leading work promoting the idea that regulation is spawned by public outrage over a crisis or scandal. Bernstein's analysis was attuned to the argument that regulation is imposed to correct some defect of the market or to protect in some other fashion the public interest. He maintains that "frequently twenty years or more may be required to produce a regulatory statute" (p. 75). The first stage of "slowly mounting distress over a problem," according to Bernstein, is followed by "recognition of acute distress," prompted by a scandal or an economic grievance. Organized groups then swing more heavily into action, demanding a legislative solution to the problem and ultimately achieving this objective:

> The forces resisting regulation are powerful and ingenious, and are overcome only by the effective efforts of advocates of reform, sustained by a favorable public response to their demands and led by a strong president. These proponents lay their emphasis on securing the enactment of a law and obtaining public recognition of the claims of certain groups for protection against abusive business practices. (p. 76)

Bernstein's organic metaphor of the regulatory cycle continues through adolescent, adult, and senile elderly phases. It is, of course, less a theory of agency origin and development than it is a set of observations on the ebb and flow of regulatory effectiveness. Note that Bernstein asserts that the problems resulting in a public outcry for regulation are nothing more or less than "abusive business practices." By suggesting thus that business and the public are opposing forces in the development of regulatory laws, he greatly oversimplified the policy-making process and laid the groundwork for capture theories of regulation, which we will examine in a later section.

History seems to offer some support for Bernstein's ideas, and yet the evidence is distressingly equivocal. Consider, for example, the three major federal laws regulating interstate commerce in food and drugs—passed in 1906, 1938, and 1962. Each was passed within a year of shocking public disclosures, but each also evolved over long periods of time, was the subject of intense public and private scrutiny and debate, and served interests far beyond those of the public.

In the case of the 1906 Food and Drug Act, concerns about the safety and quality of foods and medicines were certainly evident, but they were not the sole, or even the most important, impetus to the law's passage. Business leaders' desires to preserve honest competition and to protect export markets, and the desires of individual food and drug businesses to achieve competitive advantage by having competing products treated punitively or banned, played a significant role in the passage of this early piece of social-regulatory legislation (Wood 1985, 1986). Far from being a kneejerk reaction to an immediate crisis, the Pure Food Law was the outcome of a twenty-five-year struggle among numerous interested constituencies (Wiley 1929; Anderson 1958; Bailey 1930).

The 1938 Food, Drugs, and Cosmetics Act (which replaced the 1906 Act) was passed shortly after disclosure of over one-hundred deaths from a poisonous proprietary elixir. This Act required that drugs be tested for safety before being marketed, corrected some enforcement deficiencies of the 1906 Act, and added requirements for accurate labeling, factory inspections, and quality standards for food and drug components. It was strongly supported by the Food and Drug Administration, consumer advocates, and many food and drug manufacturers (Cavers 1939).

The 1962 amendments to the Food, Drugs, and Cosmetics Act originated in 1957 in Senator Estes Kefauver's Subcommittee on Antitrust and Monopoly, although the issues the amendments sought to address emerged much earlier—in 1951—with Federal Trade Commission investigations into drug pricing. The amendments were initially intended to prevent alleged anticompetitive tendencies in the pharmaceutical industry, including price-fixing, reciprocal licensing, and excessive profits. Consumer-protection elements were insignificant in early versions of the bill. In 1961, the world learned with horror about the thalidomide tragedy originating in Europe. Because their mothers took the drug in early pregnancy, an estimated ten thousand babies worldwide were born with the severe physical deformities of phocomelia, or were stillborn (Harris 1964; Insight Team 1979).

Amid public pressure arising from this tragedy, industry representatives and members of Congress agreed to retain some consumer-protection aspects (such as the requirement for premarket testing of drug efficacy) in exchange for dropping all antitrust provisions (Harris 1964), and so the bill was passed.

The public-outrage perspective has some valuable functions when writers who are intent on other analytical or political purposes make an obligatory nod to history. It can serve as the foundation for a tidy (though perhaps mythical) stream of historical continuity, from which it can be argued that when Congress acts to satisfy public outrage, it acts incautiously and without due regard for the long-range consequences of law and public policy. The assumption can then serve as the basis for decrying social legislation and regulation, and for constructing a negative cost-benefit ratio showing convincingly that consumers as well as businesses are hurt by such ill-conceived acts of Congress and the regulatory agencies. In the case of many social laws and regulations, however, the assumption and its resulting arguments are far more convenient than they are accurate.

It is now well-established for some regulatory laws (for example, the Interstate Commerce Act of 1887) that businesses actively promote federal legislation and regulation when it is apparently in their interests to do so (Harbeson 1967; Hilton 1966; Kolko 1965; Purcell 1967). The recent demands of chemical manufacturers for federal rules on warning labels for toxic chemicals in the workplace and the cooperation of over-the-counter drug manufacturers in developing standards for tamper-proof packages (in the wake of the 1983 Tylenol deaths) are more current examples. But in other cases, including food and drug legislation, few analysts seem aware that businesses have any vested interests in securing passage of a federal law. A crisis or scandal, as it turns out, can serve to push Congress into action on legislation that has been stalled as competing interest groups battle to secure their desired positions. Such events, however, rarely generate public policy, and thus cannot serve as an adequate explanation of regulatory origin.

A major problem with the public outrage of public policy is that it typically assumes—at least implicitly—that the public has sole claim to outrage in public-policy disputes. This is clearly untrue, as we will see later. Further, such theories tend to treat business, government, and the public as unrealistically discrete entities when in fact they are no more than abstract and overlapping collections of innumerable interests.

"Adversarial" and "Partnership" Hypotheses: A Sector Approach to Business-Government Relations

Business, government, and the public are often spoken of as if they were clearly distinct social units—with some functional overlaps and interdependencies, but with different and sometimes incompatible interests and memberships. When business leaders are appointed to high government positions, and when former politicians become corporate executives, lobbyists, and consultants, there are murmurs (and sometimes shouts) of conflict of interest. When environmental or consumer-protection groups win a legislative or regulatory victory, complaints are heard about the antibusiness intentions of these public-interest groups. This way of thinking about social institutions can be called a sector approach to social structure.

Viewed in terms of distinct sectors, the social system is divided like a pie, with each slice representing a sector that has a distinguishing characteristic or set of features. In the overlapping sector perspective, a Venn diagram can be used to show that sectors have distinctive functions but may have overlapping memberships. Each institutional sector is seen as being distinct from all others because it is responsible for performing certain tasks so that the society's work can be accomplished through a specialized division of labor (even though individual people hold overlapping sector memberships because of their activities and interests).

This primitive way of categorizing social institutions and their primary tasks is at work whenever one hears statements to the effect that business and government rely on each other (are partners) or have incompatible mandates (are adversaries). Such statements, and the sectoral view of the social system that undergirds them, represent two common hypotheses about the nature of business-government relations—the adversarial hypothesis and the partnership or community-of-interest hypothesis.

Federal and state governments play two direct, formal, reciprocal roles for businesses. First, they guarantee the rights and privileges that are essential for the proper functioning of capitalistic enterprise. Second, they enforce the fulfillment of those obligations to the society or portions of the society that restrict business activities. When government is viewed as an agent of social control, it is clear that these two functions represent government's double-sided efforts to make sure the institutional bargain or social contract is fulfilled by all societal actors.

Guaranteed rights and privileges include the right to own, alter, and dispose of property as one sees fit and the right to enter into contracts and expect them to be fulfilled. Restrictive obligations include the duty to use one's own property in a manner that does not harm the interests of others, as well as the responsibility to avoid interfering with the property of others without their permission. One's right to own property means that one is obliged to forfeit any claim to the property of others, except as the claim can be upheld in the courts. Contracts, equally, are subject to the requirement of reciprocity. The right to enter into contracts is meaningless if the contractors cannot be held to the terms of the contract (Anderson 1981).

The reciprocity of rights and obligations is sometimes overlooked by analysts who pose models of the business-government relationship based only on one of the governmental roles just defined. For those who see the government as a police officer, checking to make sure that businesses fulfill their obligations—demanding, for example, that labels be accurate and that companies refrain from engaging in anticompetitive behaviors—the adversarial model of business-government relations seems most appropriate. For those who tend to focus on government's role as the guarantor of rights and privileges—guarding, for example, the individual's right to privacy or the organization's right to have contracts enforced in court—the partnership or community-of-interest model seems to be more adequate.

The adversarial model puts business and government against each other as virtual enemies, and suggests that the mandates and principal interests of these two societal sectors are not only different, but are often diametrically opposed. Business's search for profits may necessarily conflict with government's mandate to protect the public welfare; or the antagonism may lie instead in the argument that market forces require businesses to use resources in efficient and effective ways, but that government organizations have no such incentives. Government in the adversarial view can be seen as a hostile or punishing parent, or an implacable bureaucratic antagonist, or, at best, a deeply resented irritant to businesses.

The partnership or community-of-interest model views business and government as intertwining and complementary units of the social system, striving for the same ultimate goals, each benefitting substantially from the activities of the other. The jointly held goals can be as specific as increasing productivity and gross national product or as global as protecting "the American way of life." Government in the partnership model is seen as a working marriage partner, a supportive friend, a reliable party to an informal contract of reciprocal benefit with businesses, or—in the more negative view—a corrupt and compliant bedfellow of big business.

Both positions can lay claim to considerable evidence. The adversarial model's supporters can point to a national psychology of individual liberty and the notion that the best government is the least government, along with the ideology of free enterprise and laissez faire economics. They can claim, with substantial justification, that the federal government's regulatory efforts in the past two decades have been extremely costly and sometimes punitive. They can point to numerous issues on which business and government representatives disagree sharply (for example, tax policy, budget deficits, allocation of governmental resources, and regulatory requirements).

Supporters of the partnership model can draw on the functionalist analysis of systemic division of labor (that is, complex systems require specialized but interdependent institutions) for theoretical and ideological support, and they observe that the tasks of business and government are inextricably intertwined—one could not survive without the other. With respect to regulation, partnership advocates point to the many examples of industry-sought regulatory activities, along with the benefits that businesses may reap from regulation (Anderson 1981; Davis and Frederick 1984).

In recent years, federal protection of markets (a feature of the partnership model) has become a major issue of international trade. Negotiated voluntary-import quotas have afforded U.S. auto manufacturers some temporary relief from foreign competition. Provisions allowing for sanctions against foreign firms shown to be "dumping"—selling their products below cost in the United States—have assisted numerous industries, including steel and textiles (Mervosh and Jones 1985). With increasingly alert and aggressive foreign competitors, however, protectionism can backfire. Asian textile firms, for example, have been shifting some of their operations to Europe to get around U.S. import restrictions on Asian-produced fabrics and clothing (Elliott and Melcher 1985). In such cases, the demands for even more protectionist policies typically increase.

Because both models seem to fit reality and have such clear evidence to support them, it is apparent that neither model adequately describes the relationship between businesses and government, either as institutions or as organizations. Both the partnership and the adversarial models assume that all business organizations and all government organizations, respectively, are enough like each other, expressing similar or identical interests, to be grouped together into categories called *business* and *government* without further distinctions being made among them.

This simple typology of the social system is inadequate if one truly wishes to understand how business organizations influence and are affected by public policy, and how government organizations influence and are affected by corporate policy and activities. Businesses are of many different types: small, large, or medium; employing many people or only a few; labor-intensive or capital-intensive; privately or publicly owned; single-business enterprises or conglomerates. They design, manufacture, advertise, transport, sell, finance, install, maintain, alter, or destroy things; they rely on domestic or on foreign markets or on some mix of both; they are profitable or not; they are located in major cities or in farmlands; and so on. Given the great diversity among business organizations, it is difficult to argue that all businesses, or perhaps even a majority of businesses, could be in agreement on most public-policy issues. And the history of federal and state regulation shows clearly that businesses have rarely spoken with a unified voice on matters of public policy (see, for example, Magaziner and Reich 1982).

Consulting, engineering, and manufacturing firms have been the financial beneficiaries of pollution-control regulations that have proven to be so costly for other businesses. Small businesses, appreciative of special tax credits and low-interest loans given to them by the government, may resent and resist any proposal that similar benefits should be provided to their larger competitors. Profitable firms may lobby against federal bailouts of failing companies like Chrysler or Continental Illinois, arguing that the incentive to succeed is diminished if failure is to be so well-cushioned. Given the great diversity of interests, competitive conditions, resource needs, and clout within the American business community, is it reasonable to talk about *business* as though these substantial differences did not exist among the organizations making up the economic sector of society?

The same argument can be applied to the monolithic use of the concept of *government.* State and local governments do not have precisely the same interests, abilities, or structures as the federal government. The legislature, the courts, and the executive agencies cannot be expected to agree on all public-policy questions. Even two agencies under one administration may act against each other's interests, as is so vividly illustrated by the long-standing controversy over the surgeon general's report on the health effects of cigarette smoking, on the one hand, and the continuation of federal subsidies for the tobacco industry, on the other (Miles 1982).

The sectoral approach to a social system has some appeal when the task is to make rough distinctions among social institutions at the most abstract level. Applying such an approach to real-world questions, however, is clearly inappropriate. Of what use is it to say, "Business wants X, Government wants Y, Consumers want Z," if those institutions are each composed of organizations and persons with widely varying interests and goals?

Interest Groups and the Public Interest

Both of the sector-based hypotheses about the nature of the business-government relationship depend on a conceptual distinction between public interests (the official domain of the government) and private interests (the purview of businesses and other nongovernment entities). In the sectoral view, the reason the two sectors are distinct (whether the relation is defined as adversarial or partnerlike) is that their interests are fundamentally different—the governmental sector serving the interests of the abstract whole, and the business sector serving individual interests.

Depending on one's view of the relationship between self-interest and public interest, these two interests may or may not be seen as compatible. If the utilitarian/ laissez faire position is taken that the cumulative effect of independent, self-interested acts is to provide the maximum social benefit, then the partnership model of business-government relations is likely to be favored because the interests of business and government are seen as being compatible, although different. If one contends, however, that self-interest and public interest are contradictory at times—that a prisoner's dilemma exists in the relations between two sectors—then the adversarial model of business and government interaction will seem more appropriate.

The public interest, however, is a peculiar concept. The interests so described can refer to diverse elements of the population—for example, voiceless or powerless citizens, powerful business conglomerates, groups who seem to uphold "the American way of life" (for example, family farmers), groups who speak against American values, imperfectly informed consumers—and even to nonexistent elements, such as future unborn generations. The term can refer to values, ideals, concepts, hopes, material objects, money, or the health or lives of persons themselves. The public interest can be articulated diffusely or specifically, abstractly or concretely. Indeed, in political terms, the public interest is a very useful concept for defending and justifying almost any action or decision; it expresses a deeply held if poorly defined value in American culture. It can be an almost irrefutable justification; no one could be against the public interest.

However, no one has been able to precisely define *public interest.* The term takes on an incredible array of meanings in use. Therefore, it must be used with great caution by analysts and scholars. In particular, the distinction between public interests and private interests has been troublesome. It could be argued, on the one hand, that public and private interests had become blurred but are now re-emerging as distinct, identifiable sets of objectives. To support this view, evidence could be produced to show that the onslaught of legislation and regulations designed to implement socially desired goals (such as environmental protection and equal employment opportunity) is creating a context in which public and private interests are clearly at war and some hard choices have to be made. It could also be argued that public and private interests are blurring and overlapping more than ever before. For evidence, one could point to the "revolving door" of high-level personnel between businesses and government agencies, the national defense positions of certain key industries, and the arguments of scholars such as Schultze (1977) and Lindblom (1978) that government must serve the interests of businesses in order to secure the public interest.

I must agree with R. Edward Freeman (personal communication 1984) that the public interest is little more than a bad faith concept, both analytically and in practice. Although the concept can be taken to mean that public-policy processes should (or do) normally have beneficial outcomes, the truth of this definition is open to question on many fronts. Democratic procedures (majority rule, electoral college, representative legislatures) deny the possibility of rule by a dictatorship, that is, it is not possible that one person's preferences are always (or even usually) implemented. However, the same processes of democracy also deny any general public-interest outcomes, that is, democratic procedures make it highly unlikely that public-policy outcomes can be seen as beneficial to all or perhaps even most segments of the public. That which the majority agrees on may benefit or serve the interests of only a very small portion of the society, and, of course, it may harm the interests of some societal segments.

The public interest, then, is not useful as an analytical or theoretical concept. But as a condensation symbol (see Edelman 1964, 1971)—a linguistic tool that connotes a rich muddle of political and emotional meaning—it has been extremely useful to various interest groups and policy-making bodies precisely because of its broad appeal and its intransigence to specific definition. Instead of using the public interest as an analytical tool, it is more useful to examine how various interest groups actually make use of the concept in their own political pursuits.

The public interest is often linked to so-called social legislation and regulations, but it need not express interests contrary to those of businesses. Social regulation is defined as regulation that seeks to implement noneconomic goals and values. Commonly cited examples are the "Big Four" regulatory agencies of the 1970s: the Consumer Products Safety Commission, the Equal Employment Opportunity Commission, the Environmental Protection Agency, and the Occupational Safety and Health Administration. Other agencies, such as the Food and Drug Administration, are sometimes included in the roster of social-regulatory agencies.

Special-interest groups are often held responsible for the origin, growth, and costliness of these agencies. These groups, allegedly representing the public interest, are often accused by critics of the agencies of acting against the public interest by creating an environment in which U.S. businesses cannot operate efficiently or effectively, and thus cannot compete well in domestic or international markets. Social regulations have been blamed for the downturns and poor showings of the steel and auto industries, among others; for high unemployment rates; for excessive costs to consumers; for declines in product innovation; and for a host of other economic and social ills.

Consumer-protection groups, environmentalists, and other interest groups have long sought to use the power of government to accomplish their aims. The interests of these groups have often been articulated in terms of the public interest, and have been accepted by some lawmakers in that light. Parents of children with rare diseases have lobbied the government for more federal funding for research and medical care costs; it is in the public interest that the physical well-being of persons be valued highly. Highway safety advocates have pushed for mandatory seat belt use and for built-in safety equipment in automobiles; it is in the public interest that lives not be lost needlessly in auto accidents. Diabetics lobbied intensively for the Food and Drug Administration to abandon its proposed ban on saccharin; it was in the public interest that the rights of this minority be protected in a democratic system.

The idea that business is also an interest group surfaces whenever we hear about the business community's views on some proposed or enacted public policy. And business's position on public-policy issues can also be phrased in terms of the public interest. However, this monolithic view of business as a sector, as we have seen, is not very useful in understanding either business-government relations or the development of public policy. Individual businesses can constitute independent interest groups, and they can combine with other businesses or with nonbusiness groups to form coalitions with the purpose of influencing legislation or regulation. And of course, their interests may or may not reflect the public interest.

All interest groups, including businesses, represent human and organizational actors who can have significant input into the development and resolution of public-policy issues. One of the fascinating features of interest groups is not that they try to influence the government to act one way or another, but that they may have very intricate interactions and arrangements among themselves that can affect the actions they take and that can change independently of the government's actions. Interest groups may mobilize advocates who can provide material, interpersonal, or moral resources; they may enter a public-policy controversy at any point and in many different fashions; they may form coalitions with other groups, including some whose fundamental interests are radically different from their own; they may agree to disagree among themselves on issues that are tangential to the issue that brought them together, or they may simply pretend to ignore peripheral issues; they may also make separate deals with various coalition members and shift allegiance from one coalition to another. They can align with, backstab, support, cheat, work for, and fight against each other; they can change political positions and coalition memberships with lightning rapidity. There is nothing monolithic about interest-group politics, in theory or in practice.

In the last section, we saw that both the partnership and the adversarial models of business-government relations require a monolithic and therefore inaccurate typology of social institutions. It seems much more useful and desirable to accept the idea that businesses can be independent interest groups, that they all do not have the same interests, and that they seek to have a voice in the affairs of government in much the same way that other interest groups do. That is, businesses will seek government assistance and intervention in the marketplace when it seems to be in their interests to do so and when they perceive that they have the capability to intervene. When businesses perceive government policies and practices as harmful to their interests, they will oppose such policies and practices. Clearly, this hypothesis does not suggest, as the sector hypotheses do, that all or even most businesses will act politically as a unit.

This self-interest model of business-government relations allows for adversarial and partnerlike interactions to occur. It admits a certain symbiosis in the relationship, but it does not demand that partners never fight viciously or exhibit radically different interests and behaviors. Most importantly, it does not assume—indeed, it denies the likelihood—that all businesses or all government units will act together as a coherent faction, will have the same interests, or will be ranged against representatives of the opposite institution on public-policy matters. It permits pluralistic politics to operate among the business community (and among government units as well). It is this model of self-interested groups and organizations involved in a pluralistic system of identifying and deciding on public-policy issues that lies at the heart of the idea that businesses can and do use the powers of regulation and public policy strategically to further their own competitive goals and objectives.

"Benefits to Industry" Hypotheses: Capture and Economic Theories of Regulation

The idea that industries request regulation by the federal or state governments is traditionally associated with the theory of economic regulation, which emerged in part as a response to earlier capture theories of regulatory origin. A brief review of these two theoretical perspectives will be useful in setting the stage for more recent developments in the strategic uses of regulation (see Posner 1974 for a thorough discussion).

Essentially the capture argument suggests that Congress's apparent intent (to protect the public interest) in passing a regulatory law is easily and routinely thwarted during the law's implementation, when its language must be decomposed into specific regulations and when enforcement procedures must be developed and applied. Inadequate technical expertise among agency personnel and the rotation of executives between the industry and the regulating agency, among other factors, are thought to enhance the ability of industry representatives to gain concessions and delays, to write their own regulations, and to dictate rules and procedures to the agencies that supposedly oversee their activities (Mitnick 1980). The Food and Drug Administration, for example, has recently initiated a pilot project with Abbott Laboratories and Research Data Corp. (RDC) to see if the use of computers can substantially speed the new drug-approval process, as RDC claims in its pitch to sell the FDA on its information services (Port 1985). Such cooperative efforts could be construed as signs that the agency has been captured by the firms it is supposed to regulate.

Barry M. Mitnick (1980, p. 95) says that the capture perspective maintains that "the regulatory mechanism is basically workable and desirable but is somehow 'captured' by the regulated parties so that it serves their interests rather than the public interest. According to Mitnick (1980, p. 95), capture can be accomplished in several ways:

1. The industry can control the regulatory agency directly.

2. Agency and industry activities can be coordinated to serve private interests.

3. The agency can be neutralized via ineffective personnel or via the lack of any true authority to impose sanctions on regulated businesses.

4. Regulators can be co-opted so that they view regulation from the industry's perspective.

5. A reward system can be established that leads inevitably to a partnership between business and government representatives.

The capture argument can provide a possible explanation for why industry representatives might be less than vigilant in opposing laws that are designed to restrict their activities. If business leaders perceive strong public opinion in favor of a law, if they see that their own opposition to such a law could damage their public image, and if they are willing to try to control the law's effect on them during the implementation phase, then there is little incentive for business leaders to oppose publicly any law that is commonly seen as being in the public interest, particularly if there is strong public sentiment, media attention, or broad-based coalitions supporting the law. Instead, business leaders can express general, ambiguous support for social laws, or they can keep silent altogether, and enter the public-policy process during the implementation phase, when they can be much more effective in securing their private interests with little public opposition (or even awareness).

The capture argument cannot be used consistently to explain business behavior (particularly a lack of interest) in relevant public-policy matters. In some cases, it is hard to determine the degree to which businesses are supportive of a law, and even if most affected businesses are quiescent, it is certainly impossible to discern the motives for such behavior. Further, in cases where affected businesses have relatively little experience in dealing with regulatory agencies, the capture motive, however appealing, is unlikely as an explanation of business behavior during the legislative and rule-making phases. Nevertheless, there are numerous allegations of captured agencies, especially those that regulate specific industries like banking, transportation, and space exploration. Are these agencies acting contrary to the public interest when they act in the interests of the industries they regulate?

The economic theory of regulation holds that the capture argument is misguided at best. This perspective maintains that industries actively seek to use the coercive powers of the government to guarantee protection and advantage for themselves. In this view, "regulation . . . tends to be *sought* by industry for its own protection and subsequently serves this purpose" (Mitnick 1980, p. 111, emphasis added). There is no need for an industry to wait until the implementation phase to have an impact on regulatory practices—no need to capture the agency while no one is looking—because much regulation was desired and requested by the regulated industry itself.

What could an industry possibly gain by being heavily regulated? George J. Stigler (1971, p. 3), the originator of the economic perspective on regulation, identifies four types of benefits that businesses can achieve through regulatory protection:

1. direct subsidy
2. control over entry
3. powers affecting substitutes and complements
4. price-fixing

To these benefits others can be added. Posner (1974) has suggested that benefits accrue to regulated industries indirectly as well as directly, because regulations establish the groundwork for "shared rules of behavior" among all (or the most powerful) members of an industry (Mitnick 1980, p. 117). Shared rules may or may not allow an industry to function as an informal cartel; but in all cases, such rules define the boundaries of permissible competitive practices and impose legal limits on free competition. When honest businesspeople, for example, find themselves unable to compete with their less scrupulous counterparts, they may look to the government to define and enforce new rules of competitive behavior that will force all their competitors to do business as they wish it done. Following the 1983 Tylenol deaths, virtually the entire over-the-counter drug industry worked hand-in-hand with government to develop tamper-proof packaging regulations that would offer better consumer protection as well as help shelter businesses from liability suits. (However, during the second wave of Tylenol deaths in 1985–1986 when Johnson & Johnson ended production of capsule products, many firms in the industry declined to follow suit, even though there was some prospect of regulations confirming Johnson & Johnson's decision. The economic theory of regulation has difficulty explaining this sort of event.)

Federal affirmative-action guidelines, particularly the use of timetables and quotas, serve as another example of how industries can benefit from the uncertainty-reduction features of shared legal rules. The Justice Department under the Reagan administration has been working diligently to overturn two decades of public policy favoring affirmative action (Dwyer 1985). Many businesses, and powerful lobby groups such as the National Association of Manufacturers, are firmly opposed to this plan: as *Business Week* reported,

> Business and civil rights groups are making separate last-ditch efforts to kill a new executive order that would repeal the current federal regulations requiring contractors to maintain affirmative-action goals and timetables. Explicit affirmative-action rules now shield businesses from reverse-discrimination suits. Corporate lawyers fear a flood of litigation if the rules are rescinded. ("Employment," 1985, p. 53)

The U.S. Chamber of Commerce stands virtually alone among business groups in favoring the proposed executive order, and many of its members are not pleased with the Chamber's stance (Wildstrom and Dwyer 1985). As *Business Week* reporter Paula Dwyer notes (1985), "corporations are comfortable with the current rules and like the certainty of statistics that show progress."

It is important to remember that industries may battle each other over rules that will have differential effects on their member firms. In 1983, for example, the U.S. Supreme Court ordered the federal Department of Transportation to come up with standards for automatic crash-protection devices in cars, overriding President Reagan's intent to avoid such regulations and resurrecting the controversy over air bags and passive restraints. Detroit auto makers, long opposed to mandatory passive restraints, were challenged this time not primarily by consumer groups but by insurance firms. Led by State Farm Mutual Automobile Insurance Co., the insurers fought for regulations they believed would lower their own operating costs by reducing auto-related deaths and injuries (*Business Week*, July 11, 1983).

The empirical evidence that has been marshaled in support of the economic theory of regulation includes Stigler's (1971) analyses of motor carrier regulation and occupational licensing, several studies of railroad companies' actions to secure passage of the Interstate Commerce Act (Benson 1955; Harbeson 1967; Hilton 1966; Kolko 1965), and Nordhauser's (1973) study of federal oil regulation. Among these and similar works, there are two quite different normative assessments of the findings that regulatory agencies serve the interests of regulated businesses. One view, which is common among older historical works, is that economic regulation and "captured" agencies are perversions, that the purpose of government is to serve the needs and interests of the people and not those of special interests, such as businesses (see, for example, Kolko 1963). On the other hand, Stigler (1971, p. 17) calls this perspective "the idealistic view of public regulation," and says that "so many economists, for example, have denounced the ICC for its pro-railroad policies that this has become a cliche of the literature. This criticism seems to be exactly as appropriate as a criticism of the Great Atlantic and Pacific Tea Company for selling groceries." Why should businesses not seek to use the power of government to serve their own interests? And why should business interests be defined automatically as contrary to the public interest?

The economic theory of regulation has some distinct advantages as an explanatory theory. It does not depend on a narrow definition of "the public interest" as the interests of consumers or some other nonbusiness group. Industries or business coalitions may represent the public interest just as consumer or labor groups may. And, unlike capture or public-interest approaches to regulation, it treats government power as a resource that can be the object of negotiations and varied outcomes. As Goldberg (1976) has noted, many economists, assuming that regulation is intended to correct marketplace abuses or misallocations of resources, may see outcomes such as barriers to entry or price-fixing as "failures of regulation." But is it unrealistic to propose that the businesses and industries receiving the benefits of reduced competition and greater environmental certainty would consider such outcomes to be a resounding success? Perhaps the theory's principal advantage is that it seems to be so well-supported by historical as well as more recent research (although Posner 1974 suggests that the economic theory has the critical disadvantage of seeming to accommodate almost any set of data).

The economic perspective on regulation has traditionally been applied to agencies such as the Interstate Commerce Commission and the Civil Aeronautics Board (now defunct)—regulatory bodies that control a single industry tightly and have relatively weak consumer-benefit justifications to offer. Can this perspective serve as an adequate explanation for the initial development of social legislation and regulation with strong consumer-benefit aspects? Two problems exist.

First, most social legislation is not targeted to a single industry but applies across the board to many industries (Weidenbaum 1981, p. 19). How could firms in all these industries have acted together to seek regulations that would be mutually beneficial? Second, analysts have some difficulty in seeing social legislation as anything but that. Some laws, such as the Occupational Safety and Health Act and the Consumer Product Safety Act, seem to stand as hallmarks of the pure intent of Congress to protect consumers, workers, and the public against fraudulent or dangerous business practices. How can such laws be claimed also as economic legislation to benefit industry? Considerable evidence that social laws can be so viewed is found in studies of early social regulation in the United States. Modern researchers have discredited the idea that most social legislation during the Progressive Era resulted from efforts of reformers to protect consumers and workers from the ravaging horrors perpetrated by big business, and that such laws represented victories of "the people" over "the interests" (Hays 1957; Wiebe 1962; Weinstein 1968). McCraw (1975), reviewing many historical descriptions of U.S. regulation of business, says that "taken as a whole, historical writing offers few clear patterns of regulatory behavior, except that it demonstrates the inadequacy of either 'capture,' the 'public interest,' or the two in tandem as satisfactory models."

Benson (1955) found that the Interstate Commerce Act was "hardly a victory by the 'people' over the 'corporations,' but instead a fight over who would receive what proportion of the new wealth generated by the economic explosion of the period." Vogel (1981, p. 164) has suggested that a true polarity of interest between business and other interest groups was not visible in U.S. politics until the late 1960s. Comparing social regulation from an interest group perspective in the Progressive Era, the New Deal, and the 1970s, Vogal asserts:

> During all three periods the pattern of government intervention significantly influenced the distribution of political power among various interest groups. In the Progressive Era, these shifts largely occurred within the business sector; the conflicts over antitrust policy, federal regulation of the railroad and banking industries, and tariff rates pitted particular segments of the business community against other profit-sector enterprises, both large and small.

The polarity, or class conflict, of which Vogel writes in his analysis of business-government relations in the 1970s—a clear dichotomy of interest between businesses and the public—was not a factor, contrary to common belief, in earlier social regulatory laws. The interests of businesses, consumers, and other interested parties can be—and often have been—compatible and occasionally identical.

When businesses and industries involve themselves in public-policy controversies, are they seeking legislation that would allow the development of cartels operating under shared rules, that is, are they seeking the security and certainty of being a regulated industry? In part this is true. Or instead, is each organization seeking legislation that would benefit it more than its competitors? This perspective can also find support. In many public-policy issues, the businesses involved do not fight in harmony against a government perceived as oppressive; they fight among themselves to seize comparative advantage through the power of regulatory legislation.

The "Strategic Uses" Hypothesis: Public Policy and Competitive Advantage

If it is too monolithic to view all businesses as a single sector with similar interests, this view can be equally inappropriate for all businesses within a single industry. A quick look at retailing provides an example. In this industry there are upscale department stores (Niemann Marcus, Bloomingdale's), mid-scale chains (Sears, JCPenney), discount chains (K-Mart, Zayre), and a host of small chains and individually owned stores, catering to specific clienteles and selling a wide variety of goods. Could all these kinds of stores be expected to have the same interests in regulation and public policy?

Organizations operating in the same industry are not all alike. Each will have distinct competencies to exploit; each will attempt to maximize the value to be obtained from geographic location, personnel, experience, interpersonal connections, product or service characteristics, the demographics of their markets, and a multitude of other factors. Even their approaches to environmental conditions may be different.

Further, in this age of mergers and acquisitions, what used to be a straightforward sorting of firms into industries is no longer as simple. Sears, for example, is not merely a consumer-goods retailer; it has expanded into insurance, financial services (including stockbroking and a general-purpose credit card), optical care, and space leasing. Is Sears still to be classified as a retail enterprise? How do such conglomerate parents identify and defend the public-policy interests of their various business units?

Intra-industry differences in firms can be substantial. Firms that are attuned to significant environmental developments will attempt, according to the strategic-uses hypothesis, to use regulation to achieve comparative advantage—an edge over their competitors—by avoiding or minimizing the costs and obtaining the benefits of regulation. As Mitnick (1981) points out, "expenditures that are perceived by some firms as costs are received by others as benefits" (p. 71). In an important sense, the strategic-uses perspective views regulation as little more than one environmental condition among many. The state of customer demand, interest-rate levels, or any other environmental condition, a single regulation, or a set of regulations can have very different strategic implications for individual firms within an industry.

There is a distinct contrast between the economic perspective on regulation and the strategic-uses perspective. The idea that companies can benefit from regulation is not new; it has long been accepted by those who promote the economic theory of regulation. But this theoretical approach concentrates on regulatory benefits to an *industry* (or, at least, to an industry's dominant firms). The strategic-uses perspective, in contrast, proposes that regulation can be used by individual firms as a competitive tool, just like any other management tool. The firms attempting to use regulation and public policy to their own advantage need not be the industry leaders; they could have virtually any position in the industry, including the least profitable, the smallest, or the most likely to fail. And they need not be working together to achieve common benefits.

What might be some of the strategic advantages that firms could seek through attempting to influence law and regulation? Competitive advantage can take many forms. Mitnick (1981, p. 76) proposes that the strategic benefits of regulation will tend to be reaped by "larger firms, firms with particular technologies or locations, and firms with certain specialized expertise." Mitnick points out, for example, that regulation may force innovation, "providing unforeseen opportunities for profit" (p. 72). Cost reductions and profitable ventures from projects such as energy conservation and materials recycling are positive outcomes of environmental-protection regulations. It is also plausible that regulation may benefit one or a few firms in an industry by requiring the use of a technology that these firms—but not others in the industry—have already mastered. In this case, the firms having the mandated technological expertise hold a substantial advantage over their competitors, who must purchase, install, and learn to use a new technology.

Leone (1979) observes that regulation changes the cost structure of industries and thus can provide unexpected benefits to firms that are well-positioned to take advantage of their competitors' financial difficulties or their own particular strengths. As an example, he cites the pulp and paper industry's mandate to comply with water-pollution regulations, and points out that "almost 80% of the industry's capacity will incur essentially uniform cost increases, while some 20% of capacity will be very costly to clean up" (p. 65). Needless to say, the 20 percent of the industry that incurs excessive clean-up costs will be in some competitive difficulty, because price increases are likely to be more than the extra clean-up costs for the 80 percent, but less than the extra costs for the 20 percent (Leone 1977, p. 66).

Regulation may create new markets for enterprising companies that can provide products and services to help other companies conform to regulatory demands (Mitnick 1981). In 1983, for example, *Business Week* (Sept. 19, 1983) reported that "disposing of toxic wastes is a dirty, smelly, and potentially deadly undertaking. But with public opinion, growing government regulation, and an expanding economy all pointing to increasing demand for hazardous waste disposal services, the outlook has never been rosier for the handful of public companies in this business" (p. 102).

Regulation may allow firms to gain good will among stakeholders by demonstrating their willing compliance with law and regulation (Freeman 1984; Emshoff and Freeman 1979; Sturdivant 1979). During the early stages of the Third World infant formula controversy, Abbott Laboratories secured considerable good will among many stakeholders by agreeing to abide by an international code of marketing ethics when no other company in the industry was willing to do so (Molander 1980). Strictly speaking, the code was voluntary rather than government-imposed regulation, but the comparative advantage to Abbott was the same.

Regulation may favor certain businesses because of their geographic location. Manufacturing plants located in relatively unpolluted areas with free-flowing winds may have an easier time meeting air pollution control standards than their competitors located where temperature inversions are common or other sources of pollution are significant. Certainly any firm already possessing in-house expertise that is required to comply with regulation is in an advantageous position relative to other firms, who must contract with outside agents or search for and employ experts—both relatively costly processes—to gain the necessary expertise.

Laws and regulations may be advocated by businesses if they promise to reallocate costs that seem too burdensome for them to bear alone. Record and music publishing companies, for example, have pushed for a federally levied royalty on the sale of blank tapes and tape recorders. The royalty, opposed by tape and recorder manufacturers, is justified as compensation for royalties lost when people make their own recordings of published music (Dunn 1985). In a better-known case, chemical and oil firms have tried to diffuse the costs of toxic waste cleanup by promoting a bill that would create a value-added tax on all manufacturing to pay for the federal government's Superfund program. A strong coalition of businesses with little or no history of pollution is opposing these efforts (Recio 1985).

Public policy is often invoked against companies by their competitors who believe they have been harmed by the target firm's activities or who see a chance to gain legally sanctioned competitive advantage. The Reagan administration's loosening of Federal Trade Commission controls over deceptive advertising, for example, unleashed a flood of company-against-company legal challenges. American Home Products sued Johnson & Johnson for implying in its Tylenol ads that ibuprofen, used in AHP products, irritates the stomach. J&J countersued. U-Haul International Inc. won $40 million in compensatory and punitive awards from Jartran Inc., based on the latter's advertising claim that its rental trucks were newer and easier to drive than U-Haul's. Jartran appealed the federal court decision (Dugas and Dwyer 1985). Food manufacturers and retailers wrangled with each other recently over aspartame, G.D. Searle & Co.'s new chemical sweetener. Retailers, represented by the Food Marketing Institute's Community Nutrition Institute, sued in U.S. district court "to force the FDA to hold hearings on the safety of aspartame," a move deemed unnecessary by Searle and the FDA (*Business Week*, Jan. 30, 1984, p. 24). In another instance, a *Business Week* editorial argued against weakening the antitrust laws and spoke favorably of Congress's apparent inclination "to resist . . . a plea by some business groups to limit damages in the treble-damage private antitrust suits that make up the bulk of antitrust legislation." As the editorial pointed out, "business sophisticates are well aware that [private suits] are a potent—and legitimate—competitive weapon. In fact, most such suits are brought not by consumers but by competitors. And that's really a free market" (*Business Week*, Dec. 9, 1985, p. 142).

Failing companies, when they can argue successfully that their demise would be detrimental to the national welfare, can obtain government protection in the form of loan guarantees, direct subsidies, deferment of tax obligations, and favorable trade restrictions. Chrysler Corp. and Continental Illinois are among the most notable recent beneficiaries of such government assistance. The protection afforded to bankrupt firms under the reorganization provisions of Chapter 11 can actually save failed companies from the death that would be their natural fate in a truly free market, as the recent cases of Johns-Manville (asbestos) and A.H. Robins Co. (the Dalkon shield) demonstrate (see *Business Week*, Sept. 2, 1985, p. 38). Their competitors, understandably, may not appreciate the government's willingness to resurrect the dead.

Several features distinguish the strategic-uses perspective from that of the economic theory of regulation. There is no presumption that the firms in an industry act together to seek or to benefit from regulation; within an industry, some firms will seek regulations (although they may not seek the same ones), some will oppose any regulation, and some will be quiescent from ignorance or intent. It is not necessary to show that regulation has been sought by businesses in order for them to benefit from it; firms may choose to be inactive during the policy-making phase, or they may be unaware that changes are occurring, but they can still seek to obtain benefits from regulation after the law has passed. Further, there is little or no free-rider problem as there is with both the capture and the economic hypotheses; the actions of one firm will not necessarily benefit all firms in the industry—indeed, the whole point of using regulation strategically is to outwit the competition.

There already exists some historical evidence that businesses have recognized that regulation could serve strategic functions since before the turn of the twentieth century. Vietor (1977, pp. 47–66) examined the events and conditions preceding passage of the Hepburn Act of 1906, which gave the Interstate Commerce Commission (ICC) the power to set rates. Vietor concludes:

> The findings show that support for federal rate regulation came from shippers suffering competitive dislocations due to rate structures unsuited to changing market conditions. Opposition to greater federal control came from shippers and railroads that benefited from the existing ICC-enforced rate market configurations. This evidence explains Progressive Era politics as a response to the rapidly changing conditions of the market economy, rather than with the value-laden rhetoric of liberal reform or conservative triumph.

Vietor's study is often cited as support for the economic perspective on regulation; but actually, what he shows is that rate regulation by the ICC was an outcome desired only by some members of the rail transport industry—it was, in fact, an attempt on the part of some companies to gain a competitive edge within the industry by obtaining strategic benefits from regulation.

The idea of strategic uses of regulation is a way of expanding the economic theory of regulation from strictly economic to social regulation as well. Posner (1974, p. 353) notes that "the 'consumerist' measures of the last few years—truth in lending and in packaging, automobile safety and emission controls, other pollution and safety regulations . . . —are not an obvious product of interest group pressures, and the proponents of the economic theory of regulation have thus far largely ignored such measures." Posner has proposed that regulation can serve as a substitute for the uncertainty-reduction features of an industry cartel, and that "the demand for regulation (derived from its value in enhancing the profits of the regulated firms) is greater among industries for which private cartelization is an unfeasible or very costly alternative" (p. 345). In the absence of conditions favoring the emergence of a cartel, firms will enter the political process to obtain favorable regulation, which can take many forms (for example, subsidies, gifts, import-export controls, price-fixing, standard-setting, and so on). Any regulatory form, including those favorable to cartel-like operations, is likely to have differential effects on industry members "when there is significant asymmetry among the positions of industry members." Thus, each firm has an incentive to participate in a coalition because each wants to have its own best-suited regulatory form adopted. "This suggests that it may be cheaper for large-number industries to obtain public regulation than to cartelize privately" (Posner 1974, p. 346).

Leone (1977) points out the desirability of recognizing that regulation is inevitable:

> One need not enthusiastically embrace government controls to recognize that regulations are a growing and permanent reality. Managers who respond to these controls as if their only impacts were measured in administrative red tape and higher production costs will continue to think of these regulations as a nuisance to be "managed around" rather than as a reflection of fundamental changes in the economic environment. (p. 66)

Thus the regulatory boom—like any other change in the economic environment—creates costs for some, opportunities for others, and challenges for all.

From a managerial perspective, the strategic use of regulation and public policy offers a practical, sensible, positive approach to business-government relations and to the government's regulatory functions. The strategic use of regulation to promote the competitive interests of individual businesses is by no means a new idea. To be sure, the current business environment is different from that existing at the turn of the century. But the tradition of businesses employing the powers of government to achieve comparative advantage is well-developed, if not very well-known.

Interests and Outcomes in Public-Policy Controversy

Despite recent federal moves toward deregulation and regulatory reform, it is safe to assume that the business environment will continue to be heavily regulated. Explaining the behavior of firms in such an environment, however, has not proven to be a simple task. Some perspectives on public policy, as we have seen, find their roots in a confrontational approach to political efficacy, in the idea that government is essentially unresponsive to the desires of constituencies and must be forced into action (Cobb and Elder 1972). The public-outrage hypothesis of the origin of social regulation is so founded, and it therefore cannot be relied on to explain the development of controversial issues that proceed in a different manner. The economic perspective on regulation, however, is based on the idea that government and business tend to be mutually supportive, and that government will be responsive to an industry's requests for protection and stability. The economic perspective has much to offer as an explanatory tool, but it cannot easily accommodate the different competitive interests of businesses within a regulated industry.

Where there are two clearly antagonistic camps of politically active groups and individuals and a single issue, the development of public policy can be modeled rather neatly. In many instances, however, numerous issues arise, separately and in tandem with others; many parties enter the controversy with a host of motives and interests that do not necessarily remain the same throughout the period before passage of the law; many parties change their positions, sometimes more than once; and the many issues that are involved became solidified as a single issue—if at all—only in the very last stages of public and legislative debate.

It is unproductive, theoretically and practically, to draw the battle lines so tightly into pro and con on a policy issue. Indeed, it might be reasonable to speak of an issue set rather than a single issue in many cases. Extrapolating directly from the concept of a role set, the idea of an issue set allows us to see that numerous conflicting or imperfectly compatible opinions can be expected on any given policy issue and that there is no a priori reason to deny legitimacy to any of these opinions. For public-policy analysts, solidification of issues into pro and con positions obscures the processes of negotiation, compromise, and reiteration that reflect political realities.

Given that so many issues can be at stake in the development of public policy, it should not be surprising that outcomes are rarely entirely satisfactory to any interest group. However, many groups involved in a controversy may achieve some of their objectives and thus be able to take some satisfaction from the outcome of their efforts. It would be remarkable if so many actors, with so many different interests and interactions among themselves, could achieve an outcome that would please all or even most of them (Maitland, 1983).

The strategic uses of regulation perspective does not depend on assumptions of combative or cooperative relations between businesses and government units. It does rely on the idea that the pursuit of self-interest can lead to many different types of relations between businesses and government organizations. It allows each organization to be perceived as an entity independent of all others; it recognizes that firms need to adapt to environmental conditions and to take advantage of opportunities that arise. And it respects the fact that organizations have objectives that often put them at odds with other organizations, particularly their competitors. The strategic use of regulation and public policy, as we have seen in the past and will continue to see, is essentially a story of competition and efforts to gain competitive advantage within the boundaries of law and public policy. It takes public policy out of the realm of the abstract and places it directly in the setting of environmental management.

Note

This article is adapted from Donna J. Wood, *Strategic Uses of Public Policy: Business and Government in the Progressive Era*. Boston: Pitman, 1986.

References

Anderson, Oscar E., Jr. *The Health of a Nation: Harvey W. Wiley and the Fight for Pure Food*. Chicago: University of Chicago Press, 1958.

Anderson, Ronald A. *Government and Business,* 4th ed. Cincinnati: South-Western, 1981.

Bailey, Thomas A. "Congressional Opposition to Pure Food Legislation." *American Journal of Sociology* **36** (July, 1930):52–64.

Benson, Lee. *Merchants, Farmers, and Railroads: Railroad Regulation and New York Politics, 1950-1977.* Cambridge, Mass.: Harvard University Press, 1955.

Bernstein, M.H. *Regulating Business by Independent Commission.* Westport, Conn.: Greenwood Press, 1955.

Bevirt, Joseph L. "The Cost Impact of Federal Government Regulation on the Dow Chemical Company." *Proceedings of the American Statistical Association* (1978):354–358.

Business Week (July 11, 1983), "No End in Sight for the Air Bag Blowup," p. 30.

Business Week (Sept. 19, 1983), "An Improving Environment for Waste Disposal Stocks," p. 102.

Business Week (Nov. 7, 1983), "An OSHA Rule Industry Wants Despite the Cost," p. 47.

Business Week (Jan. 30, 1984), "A Bitter Dispute over Nutrasweet's Safety," pp. 24–25.

Business Week (Sept. 2, 1985), "A.H. Robins Files for chapter 11," p. 38.

Business Week (Oct. 14, 1985), "Employment," p. 53.

Business Week (Dec. 9, 1985), "Save What's Left of Antitrust," p. 142.

Buss, Dale D. "To Dairymen's Dismay, Imitation Cheeses Win Growing Market Share." *The Wall Street Journal* (July 20, 1981).

Cavers, David F. "The Food, Drug and Cosmetic Act of 1938: Its Legislative History and Its Substantive Provisions." *Law and Contemporary Problems* (Winter, 1939):2–42.

Cobb, Roger W., and Charles D. Elder. *Participation in American Politics: The Dynamics of Agenda-Building.* Baltimore: Johns Hopkins University Press, 1972.

Davis, Keith, and William C. Frederick. *Business and Society: Management, Public Policy, Ethics,* 5th ed. New York: McGraw-Hill, 1984.

De Fina, Robert. "Public and Private Expenditures for Federal Regulation of Business." Working Paper No. 22. Center for the Study of American Business, Washington University, St. Louis, November, 1977.

Dugas, Christine, with Paula Dwyer. "Deceptive Ads: The FTC's Laissez-Faire Approach is Backfiring." *Business Week* (Dec. 2, 1985), pp. 136, 140.

Dunn, D.A. "A Music-Industry Bill that's Striking the Wrong Chord." *Business Week* (Nov. 18, 1985), p. 45.

Dwyer, P. "Ed Meese is Taking a Jackhammer to Affirmative Action." *Business Week* (Sept. 2, 1985), p. 41.

Edelman, Murray. *The Symbolic Uses of Politics.* Urbana: University of Illinois Press, 1964.

Edelman, Murray. *Politics as Symbolic Action: Mass Arousal and Quiescence.* New York: Academic Press, 1971.

Elliott, Dorinda, with Richard A. Melcher. "Hong Kong's End Run around U.S. Protectionism." *Business Week* (Aug. 16, 1985), p. 45.

Emshoff, James R., and R. Edward Freeman. "Who's Butting into Your Business?" *The Wharton Magazine* (Fall, 1979):44–59.

Freeman, R. Edward. *Strategic Management: A Stakeholder Approach.* Boston: Pitman, 1984.

Goldberg, Victor J. "Regulation and Administered Contracts." *Bell Journal of Economics and Management Science* **7** (Autumn, 1976):426–448.

Grabowski, Henry G. *Drug Regulation and Innovation.* Washington, D.C.: American Enterprise Institute, 1976.

Grabowski, Henry G., and John M. Vernon. *The Regulation of Pharmaceuticals: Balancing the Benefits and Risks.* Washington, D.C.: American Enterprise Institute, 1983.

Harbeson, Robert W. "Railroads and Regulation, 1877–1916: Conspiracy or Public Interest?" *Journal of Economic History* **27** (June, 1967):230–242.

Harris, Richard. *The Real Voice.* New York: Macmillan, 1964.

Hays, Samuel P. *The Response to Industrialism, 1885–1914.* Chicago: University of Chicago Press, 1957.

Hilton, George W. "The Consistency of the Interstate Commerce Act." *Journal of Law and Economics* **9** (October, 1966):87–113.

Insight Team, Sunday Times of London. *Suffer the Children: The Story of Thalidomide.* New York: Viking Press, 1979.

Kolko, Gabriel. *The Triumph of Conservatism.* Glencoe, Ill.: Free Press, 1963.

Kolko, Gabriel. *Railroads and Regulation, 1877–1916.* Princeton, N.J.: Princeton University Press, 1965.

Leone, Robert A. "The Real Costs of Regulation." *Harvard Business Review* (Nov./Dec., 1977):57–66.

Lindblom, Charles E. "Why Government Must Cater to Business." *Business and Society Review* **27** (Fall, 1978):4–6.

McCraw, Thomas K. "Regulation in America: A Review Article." *Business History Review* **59** (Summer, 1975):159–183.

Magaziner, Ira C., and Robert B. Reich. *Minding America's Business: The Decline and Rise of the American Economy.* New York: Harcourt Brace Jovanovich, 1982.

Maitland, Ian. "House Divided: Business Lobbying and the 1981 Budget." In Lee E. Preston (ed.), *Research in Corporate Social Performance and Policy,* vol. 5. Greenwich, Conn.: JAI Press, 1983, pp. 1–26.

Mervosh, Edward, with Norman Jones. "The New Trade Strategy: Reagan Tries to Contain Protectionist Fires, But It May Be Too Late." *Business Week* (Oct. 7, 1985):90–96.

Miles, Robert H. *Coffin Nails and Corporate Strategies.* Englewood Cliffs, N.J.: Prentice-Hall, 1982.

Mitnick, Barry M. *The Political Economy of Regulation: Creating, Designing, and Removing Regulatory Forms.* New York: Columbia University Press, 1980.

Mitnick, Barry M. "The Strategic Uses of Regulation—and Deregulation." *Business Horizons* (March, 1981):71–83.

Molander, Earl C. *Responsive Capitalism: Case Studies in Corporate Social Conduct.* New York: McGraw-Hill, 1980.

Nordhauser, Norman. "Origins of Federal Oil Regulation in the 1920s." *Business History Review* **47** (Spring, 1973):53–71.

Peltzman, Sam. *Regulation of Pharmaceutical Innovation.* Washington, D.C.: American Enterprise Institute, 1974.

Port, Otis. "Curing Drug-Approval Delays with Computers." *Business Week* (Sept. 2, 1985):77.

Posner, Richard A. "Theories of Economic Regulation." *Bell Journal of Economics and Management Science* **5** (Autumn, 1974):335–358.

Purcell, Edward A., Jr. "Ideas and Interests: Businessmen and the Interstate Commerce Act." *Journal of American History* **54** (Dec. 1967):561–578.

Recio, Maria E. "No One Wants to Pay for a Bigger Superfund." *Business Week* (Sept. 23, 1985):40.

Schultze, Charles L. *The Public Use of Private Interest.* Washington, D.C.: The Brookings Institution, 1977.

Stigler, George J. "The Theory of Economic Regulation." *The Bell Journal of Economics and Management Science* **2** (Spring, 1971):3–21.

Sturdivant, Frederick D. "Executives and Activists: A Test of Stakeholder Management." *California Management Review* **22** (Fall, 1979):53–59.

Taylor, Robert E. "U.S. Plans to Deregulate Alcohol Industry, But Suppliers and Retailers Oppose Move." *The Wall Street Journal* (Feb. 12, 1982):18.

Temin, Peter. *Taking Your Medicine: Drug Regulation in the United States*. Cambridge, Mass.: Harvard University Press, 1980.

Vietor, Richard H.K. "Businessmen and the Political Economy: The Railroad Rate Controversy of 1905." *Journal of American History* (June, 1977):47–66.

Vogel, David. "The 'New' Social Regulation in Historical and Comparative Perspective." In Thomas K. McCraw (ed.) *Regulation in Perspective: Historical Essays*. Cambridge, Mass.: Harvard University Press, 1981, pp. 155–186.

Weidenbaum, Murray L. *Business, Government, and the Public*, 2nd ed. Englewood Cliffs, N.J.: Prentice-Hall, 1981.

Weinstein, James. *The Corporate Ideal in the Liberal State: 1900–1918*. Boston: Beacon Press, 1968.

Wiebe, Robert H. *Businessmen and Reform: A Study of the Progressive Movement*. Cambridge, Mass.: Harvard University Press, 1962.

Wildstrom, Stephen H., and Paula Dwyer, with Michael A. Pollock. "Why the Chamber of Commerce is Losing Its Audience." *Business Week* (Dec. 23, 1985):30.

Wiley, Harvey Washington. *The History of a Crime Against the Food Law*. Washington, D.C.: author, 1929.

Wilson, James Q. "The Politics of Regulation." In James W. McKie (ed.), *Social Responsibility and the Business Predicament*. Washington, D.C.: Brookings Institution, 1974, pp. 135–168.

Wood, Donna J. "The Strategic Use of Public Policy: Business Support for the 1906 Food and Drug Act." *Business History Review* **59** (Autumn, 1985):403–432.

Wood, Donna J. *Strategic Uses of Public Policy: Business and Government in the Progressive Era*. Boston: Pitman, 1986.

3

Corporate Social Responsibility and Business Ethics

Business Ethics: Reconciling Economic Values
with Human Values

Paul Steidlmeier

Some 2,300 years ago the Greek philosopher Socrates was forced to commit suicide by drinking the hemlock. (His story is told in *The Apology* by Plato.) His crime was passionate devotion to the search for truth and a morally good life. Socrates maintained that the unexamined life is not worth living. His examination took the form of dialogue aimed at ferreting out the difference between peoples' opinions (*doxa*) and correct understanding (*episteme*). Obviously his approach annoyed the authorities of the day. Three things about Socrates' legacy are worth noting. First, ethics for him was essentially a positive search for the good life (where one's actions are in accord with the truth). Second, he was neither a dogmatist nor content with what he already knew. Rather, he was a relentless questioner and searcher for wisdom. Third, he was committed to dialogue.

This spirit of inquiry provides my starting point for discussing business ethics. Ethics in my view is essentially positive and creative, searching out the truth for human fulfillment and choosing it as good and beautiful. The purpose of ethics is practical. Following Aristotle (*Nichomachean Ethics*, Book VI), it seeks the full flowering of the human person, excellence in the actualization of human capacity. In this context the discussion of moral virtues (life giving patterns of behavior) and vices (destructive patterns) takes place. Unfortunately most discussions of business ethics have concentrated on the latter. Business ethics is often negative and guilt-ridden. In concentrating on what should not be, no clear positive and creative vision has emerged of what should be. Furthermore, a good deal of business ethics discussions are needlessly defensive and dogmatic.

Why has business ethics taken such a negative turn? How might the state of the question (as the scholastic philosophers put it) be fruitfully transformed? How might the social activity of business ethics be positively structured? These questions provide the focus of this essay. I approach them by considering (1) the historical background to the question; (2) the search for ethical norms; (3) an analysis of business activities in terms of economic values; (4) a probing of these same activities in terms of human development; and (5) processes of business ethics defined as precisely a *social* activity.

Historical Background to the Question

At the very time business ethics is becoming more established in academic circles and in management training seminars, a crisis is emerging regarding its foundations. There are several reasons for this.

First, business is dynamic and rapidly changing. However, a good deal of business ethics discourse is cast in static terms. In Western civilization there is a long tradition of questioning business activities. Ethical treatises on private property, just price, just wages, usury, and so forth are well-known. However, in distinction from the tradition, contemporary business ethics is not primarily focused on small businesses and shopkeepers. Rather the focus is on the large corporation (big business). For its part, the corporation, especially since 1945, is a new type of social agent, quite distinct from anything that preceded it. The term *business* does not mean the same thing in 1986 as it did in the times of Smith (1800s), Calvin (1600s), Aquinas (1200s), Augustine (400s), new testament times (100s), or the period of Socrates (500 B.C.). The structural institutionalization of *property, prices, interest,* and *markets* have all changed dramatically. The nonhistorical approaches to these issues, which characterize many orthodox capitalists as well as socialists, are necessarily wide of the mark.

Second, modern business, as a new type of large, complex organization (LCO), has been seeking approval. It has never overcome the public's lurking suspicion of selfish profiteering and dirty tricks. Other large, complex organizations (for example, churches) have by no means been free of social injustices. Churches have mounted many a holy war and imposed inquisatorial discipline. Nation states have committed every imaginable excess in the name of patriotism, manifest destiny, and so forth. Strange to say, these LCOs have found legitimation an easier task than businesses have, for they ennoble their causes in terms of self-transcendence and a manifestly greater good. They have saints and heroes; business has not been so fortunate.

The issue here is the ultimate philosophical basis of legitimate authority and economic power in society. Robert Nisbet (1977) put the matter clearly from the business point of view:

> One of the persistent mysteries of Western intellectual history has been the question of why capitalism, with its unique record in the production of goods and services and its utterly vital role in making possible the liberal democracies of the

West, has been almost from its beginning the object of continuing attack. Why from the outset was it faced with the radical question of whether it could continue to justify itself by spreading the employment of goods it was able to produce to the great mass of mankind? . . . There are exceptions—Adam Smith preeminent—but . . . down to the present the prevailing attitude of intellectuals toward business-men and what they do has been negative. It has ranged from contempt and caricature to outright hostility and attack. With today's big and growing government effec-tively in the hands of the intellectuals who dominate congressional, judicial, and presidential staffs, we may expect this attitude to become more rather than less evident. (p. 28)

Nisbet's statement points out the notable success of the capitalist system. However, he says nothing about the social relations that accompanied its develop-ment (colonialism, the slave trade, the exploitation of workers). There are also prob-lems today: power abuse, persistent losers in the system, discrimination, and pollu-tion. If the contributions of the system are to be taken seriously, so are its defects. Some businessmen would maintain that market values and ethical values are mutually exclusive realms. Others recognize only the positive aspect of business and ignore the negative. Such approaches are necessarily incomplete. The result is that the modern corporation lacks legitimization.

This raises a third historical point. With the evolution of the modern corpora-tion in the 1800s, business ethics has been intertwined with the law. The avalanche of legislation from the end of the Civil War to the present clearly attests to this fact. There are two problems with this connection: (1) the law is taken as a proxy for ethics—whatever is legal is thought to be all right, and (2) the legal approach reinforces an approach to ethics as essentially negative: ethics about what is forbidden.

Fourth, business ethics today is rooted in an implicit analytical apparatus which is inadequate. Much of business ethics discourse is rooted in parable and symbol rather than critical and rational thought. The dreams and stories of the hard-working, thrifty workers; entrepreneurs; frontier people; and other heroes of the marketplace are well-known. Lurking behind them is a rational model of the economic person: a self-interested, isolated individual, who first computes prospective economic benefits and costs, and then chooses freely and rationally between alternative courses of action. Hirschman (1985) and Hosmer (1984) have rightly criticized this model of human behavior as too reductive.

Fifth, together with the rational model and the myths of the economic per-son, one finds the analogy of business activities to individual behavior. Drucker (1981) maintains that there is no ethics but individual ethics. Coye (1986) takes a similar approach but gives more attention to the corporation as an environment that is conducive or not conducive to individual morality. Others have recourse to legal tradition. Goodpastor and Matthews (1982) explore the analogy of the corpora-tion and the moral person and succeed in clarifying its logical meaning. However helpful these thinkers are in clarifying the terms, their approaches remain too in-dividualistic in my opinion. In the 19th century, there was perhaps more logic to the analogy of the moral person as well as individual responsibility, but less so today. In the end, the reduction of business ethics to a framework modeled on individual choice leads to hopeless confusion and loses any significant sense of social ethics. Social ethics is not mere individual concern about social issues (individual actions that affect others), but socially structured reflection, dialogue, and action. As will be discussed later, many moral agents are involved in an interactive social process (see figure 1). Unless the social rather than individual nature of business ethics is addressed, the true meaning of economic freedom and competition in a social sense will be missed.

Sixth, there is a tendency to view business as off by itself. In such an analytical apparatus a narrow vision of the social contract is operative. The world of owners, managers, suppliers and customers is hypothetically imagined as if it could exist in a state hermetically sealed off from the rest of society.

Finally, among discussions on business ethics there is no consensus on what the term means. In interviewing many business poeple and academics as well as surveying over 150 textbooks, Lewis (1985) has demonstrated that there is little agreement on either precise norms or delineation of responsibilities.

The Scandal of Philosophy: Are There Any Norms?

Most business ethics texts present a buffet of ethical theories that are not harmonious with each other. The analytical tasks are to see, judge, and act (see figure 1B). The "scandal of philosophy," as modern thinkers put it, is that philosophers, over a span of thousands of years, have been unable to reach any uncontestable conclusions regarding norms of ethical behavior. That is, there is no sure guide to seeing, judging, and acting. Such a state of affairs has only hastened the appeal of businesspeople to legal norms, on the one hand, and introduced a sort of intuitive relativism in moral judgment, on the other (Donaldson and Werhane 1983, pp. 19–21).

Academic philosophy is in a sort of crisis of its own. It has become more and more a discipline in its own right, focusing on textual and historical studies, logic, and methodology. There is merit to such endeavors, of course, but in the meantime philosophy as a social activity of reflectively searching out the meaning of human experience—specifically in areas such as business, medicine, law, and so forth—has suffered.

The scandal of philosophy is based on false premises: that philosophy is primarily an academic discipline and that it should provide fixed principles or a blueprint for human behavior. Those scandalized by the lack of a blueprint suffer from false expectations. They treat life (and being) more as a problem to be solved by techniques rather than as a mystery whose meaning is to be searched out, and creatively, as well as continually, reshaped in freedom. My approach to philosophy is dynamic, as the phrase "love of wisdom" suggests. It is a human search for meaning and,

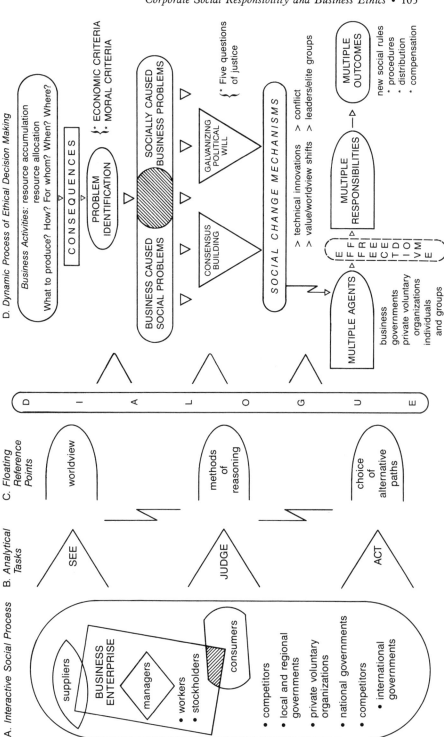

Figure 1. Dynamic Aspects of Business Ethics Decision Making

therefore, will always inherently be unfinished. This means that business ethics is not cut and dry. It represents a dynamic human activity that is moored to floating reference points. What are these reference points (see figure 1C).

First, is the world-view of the participants and associated moral goals guiding their inquiry—world-view points to the philosophical quest for so-called "first principles" to which philosophers from Aristotle, to Augustine, Aquinas, Descartes, Kant, and Hegel, and contemporary thinkers have devoted themselves. Ethical inquiry is itself rooted in a grounding vision of human flourishing. The traditions of Western civilization (rooted as they are in Greco-Roman and Judaeo-Christian thought) present a grounding vision of personal excellence within community (emphasizing friendship, fellowship, justice, and the common good). The ethical quest for first principles is part of what is called *ontology* or *metaphysics*, the study of ultimate reality and meaning. It is more than a curiosity that these terms are popularly associated with magic and the occult. The neglect of grounding world-view in much of business ethics today means that it is characterized by what Heidegger called "the forgetfulness of being." Ethical discourse is reduced to opinion polls and behavioral surveys. It is unmoored from any sense of ultimate reality and fulfillment. These issues are not easy. They raise the problem of justification of one's ethical position (Goodpastor, 1985).

At this point I wish to emphasize that world-view is a reference point of pivotal importance in business ethics. In business ethics all ethical statements have an implicit world-view. Different world-views lead to different moral imperatives for human behavior. For moral behavior is precisely seen as achieving some sort of excellence and actualization of ultimate reality. For example, caste discrimination is only intolerable if one believes in the fundamental dignity of all persons, either because all are children of God (a theological reason) or members of the same species (a philosophical reason). If one believes in reincarnation together with a caste structure of human interaction, then there is no moral imperative for a Brahmin to treat an untouchable as a Brahmin. In one case, there is an imperative of equal social consideration. In the other, there is not. The issue will only be resolved by scrutinizing first principles.

The second floating-reference point of business ethics is found in accepted methods of reasoning. How does one figure out what sort of activities are good and bad (with reference to world-view)? Many religious groups as well as utopian movements and political parties have solved the issue for the masses through the imposition of authority and discipline, although ethicians want to know the logic of decision making. They want to know the reasons why. Concretely, in stating the facts and proposing moral solutions, they want to know what attention is paid to (1) empirical analysis of behavior; (2) historical analysis and symbolic modes of expression; and (3) rational critical analysis. For example, in the South African example of apartheid, the behaviorist-empirical approach will yield a model of behavior between the races and ethnic groups as well as a statistical profile of those observed. But there is much more to the "fact" of apartheid. Narrative historical method changes the picture. Afrikaans tell their history of settling the land before others. Their stories and heroes, their symbolizations of themselves (as bearers of a certain civilization) and others, are an intrinsic part of the facts. While Zulus may agree with them on an empirical study, on narrative-historical levels they will present a widely different set of facts. The contrast is precisely over the genesis and meaning of the "facts."

Meaning is also gone over from a critical-rational point of view. This approach mediates the concrete reality with ultimate reality and world-view. Hence, for Christian Afrikaans apartheid is grounded in a particular theology of creation that justifies the separation of the races. Those who object to apartheid cite precisely *contradictions in principle* between Christian ideals of equality and fellowship, on the one hand, and systematic discrimination, on the other. The position of foes of apartheid can be put in syllogistic form:

All persons possess equal dignity in community as children of God.

Apartheid treats people as things and denies their dignity.

Therefore, apartheid should be abolished.

Presuppose that people agree that apartheid is wrong. How to do it? That is not clear. Selecting the appropriate moral action is the third floating-reference point of business ethics. Those against apartheid are precisely divided between those who want the business community to withdraw investment and trade from South Africa and those who see it as one of the more progressive forces in that society and want it to remain to exercise leverage (Hennessey 1985; Williams 1985). Ethics is a creative and practical art. Great care must be exercised so that proposed solutions are not worse than the evil they are trying to eliminate—the aftermath of many modern revolutions clearly attests to this. To conclude, moral actions should be consonant with world-view and be grounded in solid methods of reasoning. In addition, they should be technologically feasible and systems-manageable. Those are difficult qualities to assure. On the practical level, ethical action only can be approached in terms of probabilities and in an experimental fashion.

Ethics in general, and business ethics in particular are dynamic and practical in the sense just discussed. What follows about the nature of business ethics? First, it deals with probabilities. Dealing with probabilities does not mean that people are not knowledgeable. Rather, their knowledge is not exhaustive and is subject to a certain range of variability as unknown factors become known. Second, business ethics is primarily a social process of communal reflection on the adequacy of world-views, methods of reasoning, and proposed courses of action. It continually focuses on all three reference points in processes of public dialogue. Third, the task of ethics is not merely eliminating evil (liberation) but creatively imagining alternatives and bringing them to be. Ethicians cannot remain content with denunciation of evil— they must become artisans of a new order. Fourth, as communal action, the primary object of business ethics is to change the rules of the game by which society is ordered. In doing so, business ethics is really a process of social change, which entails a wide variety of agents and related responsibilities, actions, and multiple outcomes. With apartheid, the change affects not only business, but all of politics and culture. The agents are international, national, and grass roots. They range from politicians and business leaders to church leaders, the press, and ethnic leaders, each with their own responsibilities. The actions engaged include legal reforms, boycotts, protest, and intellectual studies. There are multiple outcomes, ranging from a new geopolitical situation to changing economic structures.

Business Activities and Economic Values

Business and economics have firm (but often unacknowledged) roots in philosophy. These roots become clear in the discussion of values. Both capitalist and socialist economic theories clearly relate economic values to human values and well-being. In this section I clarify the corporation's social role with respect to economic values.

As Samuelson (1978) points out in his introduction to economics, any economic system addresses itself to three fundamental questions: what to produce, how to produce it, and for whom. The basic functions of a corporation in society directly affect the way these questions are answered in an economic system. A corporation, after all, does not operate in a vacuum but in the social context of government, interest groups, and consumer demands. Responsibility is accordingly shared for how the fundamental questions are answered. The individual enterprise is to be held accountable according to the measure of its actual participation in society and share in power and authority.

In determining its market line and deciding what to produce, a corporation performs the economic function of allocating scarce resources for a particular purpose in view of perceived demand. Thus, an enterprise may allocate resources for luxury cars rather than buses. Clearly, demand is not the same as needs, but represents the goods and services consumers seek, are willing to pay for, and do pay for.

Two principal issues are involved in the production of required goods and services in an economic system. First is the macroeconomic issue of how the economic system itself is organized—whether it is socialist or predominantly private enterprise. The other principal issue is the microeconomic aspect of the problem: what commodity shall the firm produce, and with what technology? For example, if an agribusiness concern decides to allocate land for tomato production, its next step must be to decide to engage in such production in a more labor-intensive or capital-intensive way. As a stream of goods and services is generated in an economic system, it is appropriate to ask for whose benefit they are generated and to examine the general distribution of economic benefits and costs in the corresponding society.

The important issue, therefore, is to determine appropriate criteria for analyzing a corporation's social responsibility as the corporation addresses the three questions of what to produce, how to produce it, and for whom.

What is it fair to ask of a corporation? Business has traditionally responded by pointing to its economic efficiency, a concept that encompasses both technical and allocative efficiency (Friedman 1962, p. 133). Technical efficiency demands that the production process of any business get the most out of a fixed set of resources. Thus it measures output per unit of input: tons of wheat produced per hectare, per labor hour, per dollar of capital investment. But it also refers to the way the product itself generates goods and services. For example, one corporation may produce a car that goes 40 miles per gallon of gas, while another produces a similar car that goes 15 miles per gallon of gas. Obviously, the first car is more efficient in the way it uses fuel. It is fair and reasonable to ask corporations in both the private and the public sector to allocate scarce resources in the most efficient manner—a manner that optimizes the input-output relation both in the production process itself and in the performance of the product.

Allocative efficiency calls for making the most profit out of a given fixed output or spending the least possible amount of money on it. Profit maximization and cost minimization are related but not identical goals. At any rate, in allocative efficiency the amount of output remains fixed, and one then compares cost or profit per unit with other possible ways of producing the product. An example of this sort of efficiency is found in the international steel industry. Whereas some U.S. interests claim that the Japanese are "dumping" steel, the Japanese claim that it is not simply a matter of marketing strategy, but rather they are more price-efficient; that is, they can produce a ton of steel at less cost because their plants are technologically superior to U.S. plants. The notion of allocative eficiency does not simply focus on increasing gross output. Neglecting such efficiency would mean higher costs for consumers, reduced investment for jobs, and less tax revenue.

Can the case rest? No. The reason is that it is valid to pose another series of questions regarding these very same economic activities and performance. These questions focus on the *quality* of relations between people participating (either directly or indirectly) in these activities and affected by their outcomes. That is, the basic corporate economic activities are subject to economic scrutiny in terms of efficiency and ethical scrutiny in terms of what happens to people in the process.

Business Activities and Values of Human Development

Given a view of social relations in which market values and ethical values coexist, one can discern a wide variety of problems that surface in the marketplace (Blostrom 1975; Donaldson and Werhane 1983; Luthans and Hodgetts 1976; Sethi 1982; Sturdivant 1985). The problems are categorized as follows. First, is consumerism, which deals with such matters as deceptive advertising, pricing policy, product quality, safety, service, and issues of fraud. Second, is the issue of resource use and the environment, where the focus is on pollution and waste of scarce resources through inefficient or frivolous use. Third, are issues affecting labor, such as job safety, wages, worker welfare and pensions, job security, meaningfulness of work, and the export of jobs abroad. Fourth, is the issue of responsibility to shareholders; here, the concerns are profits and growth, disclosure, and shareholder democracy regarding such issues as investment in South Africa. Fifth, there are problems related to poverty and social inequality: in the cities the issues are the obsolescence of urban capital, urban poverty, the corporations' relations to local governments; in the regional scene the issues are plant location and abandonment, profiteering, transfer pricing, technology transfer, and job creation. Sixth, is the perversion of the public purpose through bribery, fraud, tax evasion, misallocation of resources, and exploitative development. Seventh, there is the issue of industrial democracy or codetermination of economic structures by workers and management. Finally, there are problems of equal opportunity and compensation as related to social discrimination based on race, sex, or creed.

In the problems in the marketplace (just discussed), two general groupings emerge: (1) business actions that cause social-ethical problems (for example, pollution); and (2) problems caused by society (for example, poverty and discrimination) in which business is a significant social agent. It is one thing to identify problem areas and another to come up with solutions. The former task of denunciation is relatively easy. The latter task of creating answers is quite formidable.

Ethicians must be precise about what social ends and goals are being sought, and what are fair expectations of business in achieving them. I make an approach to these issues by first reviewing the business literature and then setting forth my own position. Traditional market economics is not devoid of an ethical position. The content of liberal ethics is frequently cast in terms of a business creed (Cavanagh 1976, chapter 2). Several values lie at the heart of the traditional approach. The ethical rules that developed from them tended to focus on seven issues:

1. protecting the interests of property owners by promoting efficiency, reducing costs, and thereby increasing profits;

2. encouraging respect for the rights of private property;

3. refraining from anticompetitive practices;

4. guarding the freedom of labor, owners, and consumers, and discouraging government interference;

5. honoring contracts and refraining from fraud or coercion;

6. developing personal honesty, responsibility, and industriousness;

7. encouraging private contributions to charity.

This ethic was and is enormously appealing to the dominant North American cultural view of reality for a simple reason: the historical forces that created the ethic were the same forces that molded American traditions (Bellah et al. 1985, chapter 2). The stress on the importance of profit and competition, for example, goes back to the social Darwinists and to the eighteenth-century economist Adam Smith. The values of individual freedom and minimal government interference can be traced to Mill and Bentham in the eighteenth century and to Locke and Hobbes in the seventeenth. The virtues of the work ethic have their sources in the early New England Puritan settlers, a group that in turn sprang out of the Protestant Reformation. The importance of charitable contributions derives from Judaeo-Christian scriptures, which urge a concern for the poor, the orphaned, the widowed, and the oppressed. The foundation set on honoring contracts is deeply rooted in the common law and Roman law traditions out of which North American legal institutions grew.

The private enterprise system has profound roots in narrative traditions that serve to legitimate the system. The great hero in North America is the self-made man who by hard work and thrift pulls himself up by his bootstraps. The market system manifests itself in the story of the frontier and the land of opportunity, in consumer sovereignty and dollar votes, in the myth of progress and the American way of life, in the legend of God's blessing of America. There are stories that never entered the mainstream: the Indians' story of their homeland was drowned out by the white story of the frontier and development, the story of the slaves by the claims of manifest destiny, the story of the sufferings of the coal miners by the myth of progress.

The traditional business creed, then, has profound historical, religious, and philosophical roots. Because this view is so deeply ingrained in American thought, it has an almost irresistible appeal. Why, then, is it being questioned even within business circles? Quite simply, a new generation of businessmen are admitting openly that their private decisions have some public effects, and they realize that it is not in their long-term political and economic interests to ignore them (O'Toole 1979; Bower 1983).

The main problem with the liberal creed is found in assumptions made about social power. We do not find in economic theory any significant account of power in social relations. In classical economic thought the very theory of the marketplace assumed that power was not a problem; it assumed that competition was perfect and that power (over prices, market access, information, and so forth) was, therefore, fairly equally distributed. Should problems have arisen due to dysfunctions, then it was assumed that power abuses would have been held in check by the countervailing system of civil authority or by the particular Christian social conscience that characterized nineteenth-century social values.

In neoclassical economic thought, power in the marketplace is circumscribed by very much the same assumptions. Yet the social conscience permeating the fabric of society has changed and become, behaviorly at least, more pragmatic, individualistic, and utilitarian. The traditional values of nineteenth-century Western

Christianity have become more eroded in a pluralistic and increasingly secular society. That is, world-view has changed. Traditional sociocultural constraints on economic power abuse have become ineffective. Other restraints have increasingly come into existence. If one examines the history of business in the United States in the last one hundred years, it is clear that the checks on power and the redressing of social injustices have resided in legal institutions rather than in voluntary restraints.

Contemporary business circles are correctly preoccupied with their legal environment. Business circles understand power better than economic theorists, who assume power is no problem. Indeed, Mintzberg (1983) makes the case for corporate social responsibility in terms of self-interest, sound investment policy, and, more important, the likelihood of future government interference.

The issue is the quality of markets. As George Lodge has pointed out, among business people there is an increasing recognition that a new business ideology must evolve (Lodge 1975; Goodpastor 1985; Chamberlain 1977). The market is not hermetically sealed off from society; business is seen as having an ever wider social contract with the public regarding overall social priorities. Accordingly, business tries to be a good citizen on the basis of what it sees as mutual self-interest it shares with larger segments of society. This new business ideology, called *corporatism*, (O'Toole 1979), profoundly believes in private enterprise and in the institutions of market and corporation. Furthermore, it sees the corporation as both the most efficient manager possible of economic resources and as a good citizen in helping to resolve broader social problems. The corporation's primary responsibility, however, remains economic efficiency. Its broad social responsibilities are understood as analogous to taxation within a framework of social benefits and costs that accrue to all members of society and are to be distributed fairly.

However, in contemporary society there is a chorus of dissent even to this model of corporate social responsibility. It is difficult to generalize about protests, because they range from socialism to religious communitarian ethics, but two major configurations have emerged: ecohumanism and egalitarianism.

Those of a socialist persuasion, exemplified in North America by people such as Michael Harrington, have never accepted the logic of business in either the traditional or corporate form. For them the issue turns to equality—equality of opportunity and equality in distribution. What they suggest is a refashioned notion of social justice based on new patterns of social participation and resource distribution. This call has been taken up by various groups, although not all have the same agendas. Under the label of humanism one sees the "green movement" of ecology and environment that puts emphasis on the physical quality of life and the benefits of appropriate technology and small-scale participation by all in society, as opposed to vast bureaucratic forms of management. Under this label there are also forms of humanist-communitarian ethics based on more explicit notions of social justice and the overall development of the person. Whereas all of these various groups express quite different viewpoints, they all pose the fundamental problem of social justice.

Social justice (in distinction from mere economic efficiency) deals with much more than a firm and its technical economic performance. Social justice takes a broad view of the entire exchange system and judges the interrelations among the goals, structures, and functions of a firm and the goals, structures, and functions of other groups and persons in society as a whole. Herein lies a difficulty. The general definitions of technical and allocative efficiency have gained wide acceptance in our society. However, in the world today with its many views of ultimate reality, personal meaning, and cultural values, the concept of justice remains decidedly pluralistic. In the business literature one does not find a general explanation of social responsibility on which all agree.

Communitarian approaches to social justice in modern times have generally regarded strict economic efficiency as a necessary but not sufficient condition of general economic justice. The task is to creatively think through problems in terms of the ethical values one seeks. The question of social justice is very complex. The language of moral analysis is by no means standard. Values underpinning the criteria of justice in contemporary society are quite pluralistic. My world-view is rooted in Judaeo-Christian traditions as well as Aristotelian traditions and contractarian thought. It embodies a communitarian ethic (in contrast to individualism, emotivism, or utilitarianism). The guiding world-view expresses general norms such as do not harm others (the Ten Commandments), and do good to others (the Beatitudes and the Good Samaritan). The reasons for not doing harm as well as doing good when able to are grounded in the ideal of community. Malfeasance destroys community. The building up of a community characterized by love, justice, and peace calls for beneficient actions. Related to this general world-view are three other considerations. These are the universal destination of all the goods of creation, the inalienable dignity of the person, and the common good. Each of these notions has sparked the development of a considerable body of literature too extensive to explore adequately here.

In speaking of social justice, what are the main questions to be faced? In justice discourse there is an underlying question of general social equality and the legitimacy of social differences: do all persons and peoples deserve the same social consideration and treatment? The question is whether all persons and peoples are truly subjects of their political and economic structures and institutions or merely subject to them. My position is that all persons and peoples do deserve the same social consideration and treatment. The reasons are based on the world-view just discussed.

Equal social treatment raises themes that one finds recurrent in contemporary literature: liberty versus dependency; participation versus emargination; meeting needs versus deprivation; the duty to contribute to the common good versus apathy or unconcern; and due legal process versus arbitrary processes of sanctions and rewards. Each point poses a different question of general social equality. The positive content of the notion of justice can be made more specific in terms of these themes.

Liberty versus Dependence: Are all persons and peoples to enjoy the same degree of liberty and self-determination? My approach to community affirms the rights of peoples, and of individuals and groups within peoples, to self-determination. The argument is based on the fundamental dignity of the person. In this way the freedom of the oppressed and dependent takes priority over the licentious liberty of the powerful.

Participation versus Emargination: Are all persons and peoples to enjoy the same opportunities to participate in social structures? Emargination denies individuals and groups equal opportunity and the right to participate fully in political, economic, and social life. Pushed to the edges of these social structures and institutions, the emarginated must endure all the duties and strictures of society without receiving any of the benefits. My approach affirms the right of poor and emarginated individuals and groups to participate in social structures in the face of their exclusion from these benefits by the powerful. Again, the argument is based on the dignity of the person. Also, emargination destroys community.

Deprivation versus Equality of Distribution: Should all persons and peoples receive the same amount of resources, goods and services, and power attached to social offices? Deprivation underscores the case of those who live in indigence and cannot meet their needs on either an individual or national level, while others enjoy enormous wealth. Regarding distribution of resources, and goods and services, my position affirms the priority of the needs of the poor over the mere wants of the rich. But a fair formula of distribution takes account of other factors as well. There are four criteria. The priority is given to needs and then to effort within a context of equal opportunity. Those who make a greater effort deserve more. Claims based on meritocracy (the best and the brightest) and even historical privilege (nobility) are recognized but are conditioned by the common good and the moral obligation to do good. The priorities in this approach are needs, effort, merit, and privilege, in that order. This does not preclude differences, but conditions them. The reasoning for this is based on the dignity of the person, the universal destiny of the goods of creation, and the prerequisites for a flourishing community. I realize this aspect of my position is very controversial. I have set forth my position in greater detail elsewhere (Steidlmeier 1984, pp. 88*ff*.). It is an articulation of a communitarian ethic.

Apathy and Egoism versus Contribution and Duty: Should all persons and peoples be required to make the same effort to contribute to society's well-being? The plight of the poor is often met with apathy and unconcern on the part of those who are wealthy. A communitarian approach stresses the duty of all to make a contribution to society according to abilities and finds the refusal to do so, whether deriving from egoism or apathy, an unacceptable position. There is a social duty to be responsive to the overall common good and to contribute according to one's ability. More is asked of those who have more. Such a golden-rule ethic derives from the prerequisites of community.

Dissent and Due Process versus Coercion: Should all persons and peoples enjoy the same degree of due process regarding sanctions, retribution, incentives, and compensation in social structures? Economic and political sanctions against those who break the social rules of the game can only be considered unjust if the rules of the game are themselves just. Coercive sanctions and unfair schemes of incentives that treat individuals, groups, and people as things, or as instruments for either individual, group, or national self-interest, are unacceptable. In the face of unjust rules of the game, dissent is a duty. Again the reasoning is based on human dignity in community.

How one answers these five questions directly depends on world-view. Based on a communitarian world-view they yield concrete (as well as controversial) criteria for evaluating ethical problems in business. It is difficult to establish such principles as valid goals. It is even more difficult to figure out how to achieve them.

The ethical realities of justice only come clear in a concrete situation. Abstract principles are like a skeleton in comparison with the realities of life. What purpose do they serve? They provide some good questions to be raised in case analysis. Ethics is a practical and painstaking analysis of concrete experience, that is, an art that can only be carried out through case analysis. There is a long history of case analysis in Western philosophical, Christian, and rabbinical traditions. The object is to figure out what sort of behavior would be moral or the best in a concrete situation, given the types of questions that ethical principles based on one's world-view suggest. The case tradition has not been all positive. Indeed the word *casuistry* (derived from the Latin *casus* meaning case) has come to denote the fudging of ethical principles through self-interested rationalizations and deceit. Case analysis is obviously subject to such twists and turns. Socrates himself focused on the bias of the Sophists. Bias is a real problem especially when one is intimately involved with a case. Nonetheless, case studies remain the only adequate grounds for the concrete task of ethical decision making. The object of case analysis is to sort out values, ends and means, responsibilities in terms of correlative rights and duties, and fair distribution of benefits and costs. Such tasks may be guided by principles, but they are very concrete and practical.

Processes of Business Ethics

Business ethics is about special problems of human development and fulfillment that arise in the ordinary course of economic activities. Business ethics can obviously focus on moral qualities of a particular type of economic system. Such considerations lie outside of the scope of this article. I presuppose and favor a democratic society whose economy is based on private enterprise and market institutions. A case is made for public policy in terms of market imperfections, externalities, and public goods.

I reject individualist approaches to business ethics, which either claim that all ethics is individual or that business is morally analogous to an individual moral person. My position is that business ethics is social; hence, it represents a social process. In clarifying this process I refer to two cases: apartheid, a social problem in which business is involved; and environmental pollution, a social problem that business causes.

What is the primary focus of business ethics? It is to change the rules of the game by which business institutions, in particular, and society, in general, are governed. What are the rules of the game?

The five questions listed in the previous section focus on the rules of the game. For example, take apartheid in South Africa (a social problem): (1) What liberty or self-determination do black people have? (2) What opportunities do blacks have as compared to whites? (3) What resources do blacks have to meet their needs? Or what do they receive in proportion to their efforts? (4) Who is able to help in solving the problems of the blacks and are they helping? (5) Is there due legal process? If one holds a communitarian ethic, the judgment on apartheid cannot be negative on every level.

Next, take pollution (a business-caused problem): (1) Are people free to choose the quality of the environment? (2) Are people who are affected by pollution able to participate in processes to do something about it? (3) How are the benefits and costs of pollution distributed? (4) Are those who are able to resolve the problem doing what they can? (5) Is the legal system fair in terms of sanctions and compensation?

People will respond to these questions in different ways depending on their world-views. As mentioned earlier, the world-view problems must be thrashed out, for they are critical to establishing the legitimacy or illegitimacy of the rules. Rules of the game are legitimated (or delegitimated) by world-view and related cultural values. The general social culture is vast and complex and contains many subcultures. The rules of the game cover procedures (liberty, opportunity, due legal process) as well as the distribution of outcomes and resources. They exist on corporate and broader social levels. Conflicts can arise between institutional rules and corresponding cultures. For example, conflict between social rules on pollution and corporate practice can create conflicts in managers and even lead to whistleblowing. In South Africa, conflict between religious rules of fellowship and social apartheid can create conflict in those who try to follow both.

The first task of business ethics is to scrutinize the rules of the game. This is accomplished by providing the grounds for either legitimation or delegitimation of the operative rules in terms of the five questions of justice. Legitimation is carried out both in rational/critical modes of thought as well as in historical, narrative, and symbolic presentations of models of reality. I mentioned earlier how the discussion of apartheid goes on at all levels at once. The same happens with pollution where discussion ranges from progress and the meaning of development to economic growth and the quality of life.

The result of scrutinizing the consequences of business activities in terms of underlying rules of the game will be a clear identification of the ethical problem.

This is a complex process of social dialogue. In the end, the problem will be identified as primarily a socially caused problem (such as apartheid) or a business-caused social problem (such as pollution) (see figure 1D). Once the problem is identified, people must figure out what to do about it. This is a period of dialogue focused on building consensus and galvanizing political will.

The second task of business ethics is to clarify the roles of all the individuals involved in a business ethics problem. I do not maintain that social problems are reducible to individual responsibilities (for the rules of the game and cultural legitimation are precisely *shared* behavioral routines and *shared* patterns of meaning). But individual roles and responsibilities are highly important. They are also difficult to spell out in detail. Prime Minister Botha, Bishop Tutu, and literally thousands of others have significant roles to play in apartheid. None has total control. In fact, so far the focus of their activities has principally been the rules of the game, legitimation, and due process (or the lack thereof) mentioned previously. The pollution case likewise draws in corporate engineers and consultants, managers, community leaders, ecologists, politicians, and government civil service and other interest groups.

These tasks of business ethics suggest something about the process of business ethics. The process includes problem solving and much more. It is fundamentally about social change (Buchholz 1982, chapter 5). Social change is brought about by a number of mechanisms. First, there is technical innovation. In the case of apartheid, modern communications media play a vital role. In pollution, the technology to dispose of toxic wastes is pivotal. Second, values are a catalyst for social change. They are directly linked to world-view and ethical principles. The value of human dignity is the basis of anti-apartheid. Values of ecology, stewardship of the earth, and environmental protection are basic to antipollution movements. Third, social conflict (not necessarily violent) stimulates social change. This is increasingly coming to the fore in South Africa. Also, the environmental movement has made use of both demonstrations and legal conflicts to accentuate their stand.

Finally, great leaders and elite groups (whether in educational, religious, or other circles) can spark change. Black consciousness in South Africa owes its development to courageous leaders, who were almost alone in going against the tide decades ago. The rise of the environmental movement was likewise stimulated by small groups who became ecologically conscious and slowly disseminated their position.

As a complex process of social change, business ethics in the cases of pollution and apartheid involve a wide variety of multiple agents on both individual and group levels, as well as local, domestic, and international levels. In addition, each of these protagonists is involved in an innumerable variety of actions, spanning private voluntary initiatives, public policy and legislation, and measures to change not only corporate but industry-wide practices. All the actions explained here lead to a wide spectrum of outcomes on economic, political, and sociocultural levels. Efforts to end pollution create new economic enterprises, new public policy to protect the environment, and new relations between society and nature. Ending apartheid will radically change political institutions, economic opportunities, and the cultural vision of South African society.

Business ethics is not merely a quick fix for a problem. It is a long historical process of social change. Unlike individual ethics (where responsibility is primarily vested in one person and where the time-frame is relatively short), a problem in business ethics manifests many responsibilities and a life-span of ten years to generations. Apartheid problems have existed for more than forty years; the resolution process could easily last another fifteen to twenty-five years. Environmental pollution problems seem to have a minimal span of ten years. Certain toxic wastes still elude solutions although they have been a problem for many years.

Business ethics is also concerned with individual change within social change. The process is itself social. It involves many years of dialogue to establish the nobility of ultimate ends and values, the adequacy of proximate ends, the suitability of means, the development of social consciousness, the worthiness of the intentions of those who act or fail to act, the fairness of consequences, and the degree of effective freedom of various agents. As business ethics moves from initial question to consensus and political will, it aims to see (to grasp the facts of the problem as best as possible), to judge (to morally evaluate the problem) and to act (to galvanize the political will to create a better alternative). It is necessary to stimulate awareness of the issue, to develop a consensus to change it, and to figure out appropriate strategies and a fair sharing of social benefits and costs in changing the issue. None of these points is easy; the last one is especially difficult.

Suggestions for Corporations

The main questions for corporations is how to prepare themselves for and insert themselves into the social-ethical process. First, corporate leaders must clarify their world-views and related ethical principles. As Miesing and Preble (1985) have demonstrated, business philosophies right now are in a confusing state. Both formal seminars (Jones 1982) as well as general business education should be revamped. Second, ethical considerations should not be added on as an afterthought (Pastin 1984, 1985; McCoy 1985). Ethics is not an add-on to economic functions. It is inherent to them. It cannot be handled by the public relations part of the firm, but only by managers and others concerned about asking the right questions. How to do this is not clear. Carroll and Hoy (1984) have, however, made some interesting suggestions on integrating such policy into strategic management. They combine policy formulation on the macro level with implementation devolving on the corporation's micro level. They make the same point that Pastin and McCoy make: ethics must be part of the strategy from the beginning.

The institutionalizing of new forms of management are still being tested. This should not be surprising, given the new sociological nature of the corporation. Filios (1984) has assessed the potential of social audits; Maitland (1985) brings out the difficulties of business self-regulation; Cressey and Moore (1983) discuss the relevance of codes of conduct. Two points run through these articles. Ethical action that incurs costs and weakens profits weakens the position of management. Solutions that are not industry-wide also weaken management in terms of competitiveness in the marketplace.

These observations reinforce my position that business ethics is primarily concerned with changing the rules of the game. Specifically, the conduct of the industry, not just the corporation or the individual, must be changed. The willingness of shareholders, workers, and the public to equitably share the costs in terms of lower dividends and wages and increased costs at the consumer level is part of any sensible solution. The generation of society-wide benefits calls for an equitable society-wide sharing of costs.

Business would be well-served if it would not be defensive about questions of ethics, but rather undertake ethics in the positive spirit of Socrates: the unexamined life of our structures and institutions is not worth living. In this light McCoy (1985) calls for a proactive rather than a reactive stance. Business leaders are members of many other institutions besides their own enterprises. They would be well-poised, in all of their roles, to be parts of the creative processes of business and social ethics. Some will find McCoy's proactive stance distasteful just as people found the original quest of Socrates a bothersome attack on their institutions. But others will be invigorated by the challenge to be artisans of justice and peace in a dynamic and developing society.

References

Andrews, Kenneth R. 1984. "Difficulties in Overseeing Ethical Policy," *California Management Review*, **27** (4), 134–146.

Beauchamp, Tom L., and Norman E. Bowie. 1983. *Ethical Theory and Business*, 3rd ed. Englewood Cliffs, N.J.: Prentice-Hall.

Bellah, Robert N. Richard Madsen, William M. Sullivan, Ann Swidler, and Steven M. Tipton. 1985. *Habits of the Heart: Individualism and Commitment in American Life.* Berkeley, Calif.: University of California Press.

Blostrom, Robert L. 1975. *Business and Society: Environment and Responsibility*, 3rd ed. New York: McGraw-Hill.

Bower, Joseph C. 1983. "Managing for Efficiency, Managing for Equity," *Harvard Business Review*, **61**, 83–90.

Buchholz, Rogene A. 1982. *Business Environment and Public Policy.* Englewood Cliffs, N.J.: Prentice-Hall.

Carroll, Archie B., and Frank Hoy. 1984. "Integrating Corporate Social Policy Into Strategic Management," *The Journal of Business Strategy*, **4** (3), 48–57.

Cavanagh, Gerald. 1976. *American Business Values in Transition.* Englewood Cliffs, N.J.: Prentice-Hall.

Chamberlain, Neil W. 1977. *Remaking American Values.* New York: Basic Books.

Coye, Ray. 1986. "Individual Values and Business Ethics," *Journal of Business Ethics,* **5** (1), 45–49.

Cressey, Donald R., and Charles A. Moore. 1983. "Managerial Values and Corporate Codes of Conduct," *California Management Review,* **25** (4), 53–77.

Donaldson, Thomas, and Patricia H. Werhane. 1983. *Ethical Issues in Business—A Philosophical Approach.* Englewood Cliffs, N.J.: Prentice-Hall.

Drucker, Peter. 1981. "What is Business Ethics?" *The Public Interest,* **3,** 18–56.

Filios, Vasilio P. 1984. "Corporate Social Responsibility and Public Accountability," *Journal of Business Ethics,* **3** (4), 305–314.

Friedman, Milton. 1962. *Capitalism and Freedom.* Chicago: University of Chicago Press.

Goodpastor, Kenneth E. 1985. "Business Ethics, Ideology and the Naturalistic Fallacy," *Journal of Business Ethics,* **4** (4), 227–232.

Goodpastor, Kenneth E., and John B. Matthews, 1983. "Can a Corporation Have Conscience?" in T.L. Beauchamp and Norman E. Bowie, eds., *Ethical Theory and Business,* pp. 68–80.

Hennessey, John W., Jr. 1985. "Ethical Aspects of the South African Investment Debate on American University Campuses," mimeograph, Dartmouth College, Hanover, N.H.

Hirschman, Albert O. 1985. "Against Parsimony: Three Easy Ways of Complicating Economic Decisions," *Economics and Philosophy,* **1** (1), 7–21.

Hook, Sydney. 1967. *Human Values and Economic Policy.* New York: New York University Press.

Hosmer, Larue T. 1984. "Managerial Ethics and Microeconomic Efficiency," *Journal of Business Ethics,* **3** (4), 315–328.

Jones, Donald G. 1982. *Doing Ethics in Business.* Cambridge, Mass.: Oelgeschlager, Gunn and Hain.

Kossell, Clifford. 1981. "Global Community and Subsidiarity," *Communio* **8** (2), 37–50.

Lewis, Phillip V. 1985. "Defining Business Ethics—Like Nailing Jello to a Wall," *Journal of Business Ethics,* **4** (5), 387–394.

Lodge, George. 1975. *The New American Ideology.* New York: Alfred Knopf.

Luthans, Fred, and Richard M. Hodgetts. 1976. *Social Issues in Business.* New York: MacMillan.

McCoy, Charles S. 1985. *Management of Values—The Ethical Difference In Corporate Policy.* Marshfield, Mass.: Pitman.

McMahon, Thomas F. 1985. "The Construction of Religious Tradition to Business Ethics," *Journal of Business Ethics,* **4** (4), 341–344.

Maitland, Ian. 1985. "The Limits of Business Self-Regulation," *California Management Review,* **27** (3), 132–146.

Miesing, Paul, and John F. Preble. 1985. "A Comparison of Five Business Philosophies," *Journal of Business Ethics,* **4** (6), 465–477.

Mintzberg, Henry. 1983. "The Case for Corporate Social Responsibility," *The Journal of Business Strategy,* **4** (2), 3–15.

Moser, Martin. 1986. "A Framework For Analyzing Corporate Social Responsibility," *Journal of Business Ethics,* **5** (1), 69–72.

Nader, Ralph. 1984. "Refining Corporate Governance," *California Management Review,* **24** (4), 126–133.

Nisbet, Robert. 1977. "Capitalism and the Intellectuals," *Wall Street Journal,* September 16.

O'Toole, James. 1979. "What's Ahead for the Business-Government Relationship?" *Harvard Business Review*, **57**, 94–105.

Pastin, Mark. 1984. "Ethics as an Integrating Force in Management," *Journal of Business Ethics*, **3** (4), 295–305.

——. 1985. "Management Think," *Journal of Business Ethics*, **4** (4), 341–344.

Pemberton, Prentiss L., and Daniel Rush Finn. 1985. *Toward a Christian Economic Ethics— Stewardship and Social Power*. Minneapolis, Minn.: Winston Press.

Rawls, John. 1975. *A Theory of Justice*. Cambridge, Mass.: Harvard University Press.

Samuelson, Paul. 1977. *Economics*. New York: McGraw-Hill.

Sethi, S. Prakash. 1982. *Up Against The Corporate Wall*, 2nd ed. Englewood Cliffs, N.J.: Prentice-Hall.

Sethi, S. Prakash, and Nobuaki Namiki. 1983. "Managing Public Affairs: The Public Backlash Against PAC's," *California Management Review*, **25** (3), 133–144.

Steidlmeier, Paul. 1984. *Social Justice Ministry: Foundations And Concerns*. New York: Le-Jacq Publishing Co.

Stevens, Edward. 1979. *Business Ethics*. New York: Paulist Press.

Sturdivant, Frederick D. 1984. *Business and Society, A Managerial Approach*, 3rd ed. Homewood, Ill.: Richard D. Irwin.

Williams, Oliver F. 1985. "Investments in South Africa—A Christian Moral Argument," mimeograph, Notre Dame University.

Confronting New Threats to Business: Ethics as a Tool for Predicting and Managing Social Issues

Mark Pastin

Ethics is a powerful tool for predicting social issues that will affect corporations in coming years. Because ethics focuses on the most basic principles of individuals and organizations, changes in ethics have broad impacts on corporations. Social changes often can be first detected by observing what ethical issues are at hand. One social function of ethics is to provide a forum for arguing basic changes. Ethical discussion does not move quickly, so such discussion may predate an actual shift in ethics, or fundamental principles, by years. Thus, observing on-going discussions of ethics allows us to see what fundamental social changes are coming.

Many of the changes that affected corporations in the 1970s were preceded by intense ethical discussion that was largely unnoticed by business. Intense discussion of obligations to preserve the quality of the environment preceded an effective environmental movement, and regulation, by almost ten years. Active discussion of women's rights preceded the women's movement by at least five years. When society decides that things should change, there is a cost of lubricating the change

None of us wants to pay for the lubrication. Since business has said little about the changes, taking a reactive posture at best, we often ask it to lubricate the change. There is no question that the cost of environmental protection has been shifted to business. Business is bearing a lot of cost for correcting past discrimination. (Of course, part of these costs may be passed along to consumers.) This may or may not be good. Managers should have seen these shifts coming.

Our aim is to use ethics to look ahead at emerging social issues and at ongoing ethical discussions that are the leading edge of these issues. By using ethics to uncover emerging social issues, managers can foresee these issues better and can manage them better. In order to use ethics to look ahead, we need a working definition of ethics. Whereas ethicists make ethics appear hopelessly complex, we adopt a simple definition for our purposes. Ethics focuses on the most fundamental principles of individuals and organizations. This implies that both individuals and organizations have ethics.

The *ethics of a person* is the set of basic ground rules by which that person acts. When we talk about the ethics of a person, we are talking about the principles that the person's actions reveal to be fundamental for that person. We call these principles the person's *ground rules*. Ground rules delimit those actions that are possible for a person and those that are not. Just as the rules of a game determine what moves are possible and what each move means, so a person's ground rules determine what actions the person may take and what these actions mean.

The *ethics of an organization* is the set of basic ground rules by which the organization acts. There are fundamental principles, or ground rules, by which organizations act. 3M has an ethics of innovation, Motorola an ethics of participation, and Amtrak an ethics of survival. Like the ground rules of individuals, organizational ground rules determine what actions are possible for the organization and what these actions mean.

This simple model of ethics as ground rules provides a basis for using ethics to foresee social issues and to take steps to better manage them. When we use ethics to make predictions by looking around, we look for perturbations in the business environment that signal shifts in ground rules. Two obvious perturbations in the business environment are corporate tragedies and rapidly changing technologies. These phenomena are closely connected, and both signal emerging types of social issues. The factors that make tragedies hard to foresee and manage are the factors that make new technologies threatening. These factors include entrenched corporate cultures, a management style that precludes asking hard questions, and ethical illiteracy.

Possibilities of Corporate Tragedies

Dealing with tragedies is one of the greatest challenges for contemporary managers. Despite the fact that businesses have faced a large number of tragedies in recent years

(Tylenol I and II, Bhopal, E.F. Huttons's check-kiting problems, Three-Mile Island), managers resist thinking about tragedies. It is as if managers have an unspoken compact with life stating that the world is an orderly and predictable place in which the worst will not happen to them.[1] This unspoken compact keeps managers from taking the possibility of tragedy seriously. Their resistance to thinking about tragedies is reinforced by the fact that tragedies typically involve an element of evil.[2]

The unspoken compact is a basic principle or ground rule. You can see this by rephrasing. "These unthinkable things *shouldn't* happen to us" or even "Unthinkable things can't happen to us." It is appropriate to think of tragedies in terms of the ethical concept of evil. Evil is that which falls outside the ground rules. Evil tears our ground rules apart by demonstrating that these rules cannot always be counted on.

The association between new technologies and tragedies is through evil. If the thought of bureaucracies tracking your every move from birth to death by using increasingly powerful information systems does not strike you as clearly evil, then the prospect of designing children (using rapidly developing genetic-engineering techniques) to make them "better" surely will. New technologies stun our low-tech ethics, violate our ground rules, and invite application of the term *evil*.

Evil is hard to think about. Almost every corporate tragedy from thalidomide to Bhopal was forewarned. It may seem that this is merely hindsight. But often the warnings were so obvious and/or uncannily accurate that we can only conclude that managers *refused* to consider them. Richardson-Merrell may not have been forewarned of the dangers of thalidomide, the drug that caused the birth of countless stillborn and deformed children in the late 1950s. However, no sooner were the results of this tragedy in when Richardson-Merrell marketed a cholesterol-repressing drug called MER/29 that blinded many people who took it. In the face of one tragedy, the company obviously did nothing to prevent the same thing from happening again. To view this as the unchained profit motive requires that we assume incredible stupidity on the part of Richardson-Merrell executives. A more likely explanation is that they simply could not consider the possibility that their products were evil. They did not ask: Will this happen again?

The Richardson-Merrell tragedies are not an atypical case. In a seminar for executives on thinking about the unthinkable, we review a minor tragedy at Warner-Lambert. An explosion at a Freshen-Up manufacturing facility severely burned fifty-four employees and killed six.[3] In reviewing this case, the executives are outraged that Warner-Lambert did not heed countless warnings that such an explosion might occur. An exercise asks participants to pretend that some such problem could arise in their firms. At least 90 percent of the participants are shocked to find that they are ignoring warnings in their own firms, at least as strong as those in the Warner-Lambert case. Why? After some futile attempts at buck passing, the groups generally conclude that they just cannot bring themselves to think about these things.

If we are to use ethics to think constructively about present and future tragedies, we need a typology distinguishing the types of tragedies that corporations confront. The most important distinctions concern the degree of salience of tragedies at a given time and the extent to which the tragedy is specific to a given firm at a given time. A tragedy is salient at a given time if the tragedy has already surfaced and requires immediate management attention. Ethical thinking can help determine whether a tragedy that is salient at a given time is an anomalous event or reflects a shift in ground rules indicating that the company can expect more events of the same kind. Thus, at the time of the accident at Three-Mile Island, this tragedy had salience but it also signalled a shift in the ground rules of public discussion of nuclear power. An interesting and important question is whether the Bhopal tragedy, which retains salience, signals a shift in the ground rules governing offshore operations of U.S. firms.

Some tragedies have little or no salience at a given time, but they have high potential salience. Thus, some tragedies may have no more present salience than the thought that there is a potential for a tragedy concerning an actual or prospective product, operation, or research program. Tragedies having high present salience and high potential salience require the immediate attention of management as well as intense thinking about how to address possible future tragedies. Tragedies having low present salience but high potential salience present traps for managers. Because these tragedies do not require present management attention, there is a tendency to ignore them no matter how strong indications are that such tragedies will have salience at a later time. There is ample evidence that the tragedy Bhopal fell into this category for at least a year before it occurred. And the recent National Aeronautics and Space Administration (NASA) hearings strongly suggest that the Challenger tragedy was in this category for some time before the launch. Low present salience, high-potential salience tragedies are often first reflected as challenges or conflicts at the level of ground rules.

The second basic distinction among tragedies concerns their specificity. Some tragedies may have a very powerful effect on a particular firm but relatively little effect on an industry at large. The Warner-Lambert tragedy is an example of a tragedy that had a powerful effect on one company but limited effect on the industry. However, tragedies that initially affect one company—and not always critically—may have powerful industry-wide and cross-industry impacts. The accident at Three-Mile Island, which probably does not qualify as a tragedy considered in isolation, had disastrous impacts on the nuclear power industry as a whole. Tragedies multiply their effect across an industry or industries when the tragedy calls ground rules into question (for example, the ground rule that we must accept risks with little question in order to avoid the negative consequences of an energy short fall). Managerial attention usually focuses on tragedies resulting directly from the activities of their own firms. But since tragedies resulting entirely from the activities of other firms may have even greater impacts on a given firm, managers must be alert to tragedies that reflect basic changes in ground rules (figure 1).

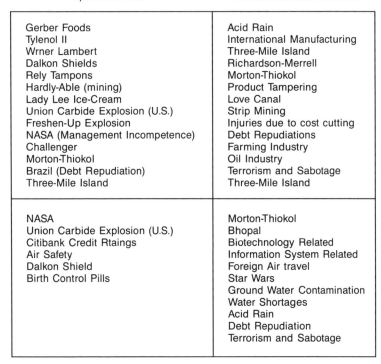

Specific to Firm	General to/across Industries
Gerber Foods Tylenol II Wrner Lambert Dalkon Shields Rely Tampons Hardly-Able (mining) Lady Lee Ice-Cream Union Carbide Explosion (U.S.) Freshen-Up Explosion NASA (Management Incompetence) Challenger Morton-Thiokol Brazil (Debt Repudiation) Three-Mile Island	Acid Rain International Manufacturing Three-Mile Island Richardson-Merrell Morton-Thiokol Product Tampering Love Canal Strip Mining Injuries due to cost cutting Debt Repudiations Farming Industry Oil Industry Terrorism and Sabotage Three-Mile Island
NASA Union Carbide Explosion (U.S.) Citibank Credit Rtaings Air Safety Dalkon Shield Birth Control Pills	Morton-Thiokol Bhopal Biotechnology Related Information System Related Foreign Air travel Star Wars Ground Water Contamination Water Shortages Acid Rain Debt Repudiation Terrorism and Sabotage

*High
Present
Salience* (applies to the first row)

Note: These categories are not exclusive. A tragedy may have both high present salience and high potential salience (Brazil, debt repudiation). A tragedy may be specific to a particular firm and also general to an industry or industries (Three-Mile Island).

Figure 1. Typology of Tragedies

This typology enables us to see that there are many tragedies implicit in new technologies. It is predictable that the biotechnology industry will produce an environmentally harmful organism, just on the statistical basis of the number of experiments occurring together with the fact that every industry faces its worst accident at least once. This is a tragedy with low present salience but high potential salience. It is also likely to be a tragedy not specific to a particular firm or firms but to the entire biotechnology industry. It is predictable that a factory robot will go crazy and injur a number of people, on much the same basis. Again, this tragedy has only modest present salience but high potential salience. It is a tragedy of great generality affecting more than a firm or firms, in fact, affecting several industries. Ethics is a good tool of forecasting and management with respect to tragedies having high generality and low present, high potential salience.

Ethics as a Tool for Meeting Tragedies

How can ethics help business deal with the evil of tragedies? Tragedies are unpredictable in specific terms, but they can be foreseen by type. Businesses are more vulnerable to tragedies as they rely more and more on new technologies in both products and manufacturing. This fact can be recognized. We can anticipate, to some extent, the directions from which tragedies will come. Not every accident or disaster is a tragedy. An accident/disaster differs from a tragedy in that a tragedy violates ground rules. So ethics tells us to anticipate tragedies by focusing on events that will upset our ground rules and the ground rules of society at large.

Can ethics help us do more than anticipate? Use ethics to assess the tragedy in Bhopal. Many died in Bhopal, but many benefitted from Union Carbide's presence in India by having jobs and the fundamentals that jobs provide. It is possible that Union Carbide saved more lives in India than were lost in the accident. Union Carbide might not have had a location in India if U.S. safety standards had to be observed there. And if Union Carbide did not exist in India, many people might be unemployed. This is tough reasoning; ethics requires as much. It does not necessarily excuse Union Carbide. Even if Union Carbide saved more lives than were lost in the accident, it still may have unnecessarily lost lives.

I do not recommend that Union Carbide press the issue of trade-offs publicly. But it can press industry organizations to make the point. The tragedy in Bhopal has high generality affecting all chemical manufacturers (through insurance rates), all companies with overseas operations, and all companies in high-risk businesses. Companies in high-risk businesses need to initiate public discussion of the risk-benefit trade-offs of their activities. And such companies, not individually but through organizations, need to establish agreements with affected constituencies. Who picks up the pieces in case of an accident? Do you want us here badly enough to insure us? Fair agreements are possible in this domain. Some utilities have made agreements with residents near nuclear facilities to pre-indemnify them for risk in return for guarantees not to litigate. Agreements must be made prior to tragedies.

Business should also seek agreements with consumers. Products have risks and consumers know it. Our regulatory system does not grant consumers the right to take risks. They are instead protected against risks. When protection inevitably fails, someone gets blamed. Since the consumer could not assume risk, and regulators were trying to protect the consumer, guess who is found guilty? Business must reopen discussion of whether consumers are to be allowed to take risks. If Rely Tampons had been labeled "New Product Subject to Further Testing," they would still have found a market. If people buy sports cars, they will take other risks for style, convenience, or simply to experiment. Allowing consumers to take risks will prove essential as products resulting from new technologies proliferate.

Most important, the reciprocity of rights and responsibilities needs to be re-argued and reestablished. The Tylenol case was a shock because a part of our ground rules, a part honored even by murderers and rapists, was violated. Who is responsible for this? Can packaging really protect us against psychopaths? If we want products offered in convenient, inexpensive ways, we must accept reciprocal responsibility for the safety of the marketplace.

In short, the strategy is to think ethically, using ethics to open discussion with stakeholder groups. What does ethics say about this accident or risk? Is there an agreement worth establishing? These questions will not eliminate corporate tragedies, but they make it possible to think about them, ask questions that need asking, and assume a nonreactive posture. This approach must also be used in dealing with tragedies resulting from application of new technologies, such as bioengineering. These new technologies will be at issue in an increasing number of tragedies.

New Technologies: Information Tragedies

Information systems, computers, and biotechnology will make or break many businesses, including businesses not directly involved in these technologies. The outcome depends on the ability to get ahead of these technologies by thinking ethics.

We focus on the new technologies of information and bioengineering. We look at information technologies because they are changing the ground rules by which we live and work. We look at biotechnologies because they show us what we must do if we are to have a say over the ground rules by which we will live and work. Both technologies can produce tragedies. Information technologies can produce incremental tragedies—tragedies that occur and are virtually unnoticed. These tragedies have low salience now but their aggregate affect gives them high potential salience and generality. Biotechnologies can produce tragedies that make Bhopal seem unimportant. Although these tragedies have minimal present salience, their potential salience and generality cannot be estimated.

At a major computer firm, applicants for the position of manager for product development, mini-computers, are being considered. The division manager favors Linda Berman. She is a bright, articulate, and energetic interviewee. However, the recruiting officer is bothered by what is revealed by a routine check with Person Search, a computerized screening system. Ms. Berman was once genetically profiled for an insurance check. Tests indicate she has nearly a 100 percent chance of developing Huntington's Chorea by age forty. She is thirty-seven.

When the results of this check are reported to the division manager, he is disappointed. The manager for product development must hold the position three to five years if the company is to benefit from hiring this person. The division manager knows such checks are often inaccurate. Even if he reviews the information with Ms. Berman and finds it inaccurate, she will likely be resentful. He hires someone else. The truth? Since Ms. Berman's father died of Huntington's Chorea, an insurance company once screened her blood. The results were misread as "positive." This mistake is unfortunate, but we recognize that the overall benefits of information technologies exceed the mistakes. We are less aware of the benefits of biotechnologies, but we accept on faith that benefits are forthcoming.

Personnel departments do use screening services, and the services do make grievous undiscovered errors. They assemble databases by "cleaning" data from tapes supplied by personnel departments, credit companies, insurance companies, and other sources. Checking data case by case is impossible. Ms. Berman's case shows the potential for abuse of biotechnologies coupled with information systems. Genetic screening to determine the chances of inheriting Huntington's Chorea will soon be common. Genetic tests for a predisposition to diabetes, depression, alcoholism, Alzheimer's disease, various forms of cancer, and hyperactivity may soon surface. The issue of using such tests for insurance and personnel checks is being debated. A recent *Wall Street Journal* asks whether an employee who knows his genes predispose him to Alzheimer's disease has the right to withhold this information from his employer.[4] The article questions the employee's right to withhold the information, implying a presumptive right for the employer to know. Where did this right come from?

Managers who want to manage new technologies, rather than be managed by them, must use ethics to ask some key questions. We suggest three general questions about information systems:

Can information networks become communities?

Where does responsibility reside in an information system?

Can we manage without individuals?

We can not answer these questions, but we can use ethics to start thinking about them.

Can Information Networks Become Communities?

We create information networks but not information communities.[5] Networks link people who share common information interests and standards. There are networks for lawyers (Lexis), doctors (Medicus), stockbrokers (Dow Jones), philosophers (Philosophers' Index), econometricians (DRI), owners of Osborne computers (users' group), hackers (bulletin boards), and almost every group of information users. Although information carried by a network should have economic value, to justify the cost of the network, it cannot be intensely proprietary. This is critical to the comparative competitive positions of network members. Stockbrokers do not share names of their best clients.

Communities differ ethically from networks. The ethics of a community is nonutilitarian. Diverse people are accepted as part of a community. Communities encompass old and young, rich and poor, smart and stupid. In the best case, a community accepts each member as a whole person and not on the basis of their utility to the group.[6] Information networks are not communities because network users have only narrow utilitarian relationships to each other. The fact that information networks are not communities explains why people guiltlessly steal (copy) software, add inaccurate data to databases (census takers, insurance investigators), and break into systems (hackers and embezzlers). The user has no nonutilitarian ethical relationship to other users—nothing to feel guilty about and no one to be responsible to.

Should we try to transform information networks into communities? We might not want to trade the efficiency of a network for the inefficient integrity of a community. There is a middle ground—something more responsible than a network and more efficient than a community—this is, an agreement, a social contract among users of a network. An agreement establishes rights and responsibilities without the inefficiencies of a community.

Where Does Responsibility Reside in an Information System?

Recall Linda Berman. Who is responsible for her situation? Those who entered false data? These data collectors may have done their best to gather needed data, often at Ms. Berman's request. Is it those who sell data without verifying it? Data clearinghouses cannot check the accuracy of all data without making their services inordinately expensive. Is it those who use the data to make important decisions? People are not always truthful about themselves, and decision makers need to know who is lying and who is not. Perhaps Ms. Berman is responsible for not checking the information herself. Even if this were possible, it would be a full-time job for Ms. Berman or for anyone. We must put the responsibility where it belongs—everywhere. An agreement or ground rules are necessary to emphasize responsibility for each of our information acts.

Can We Manage without Individuals?

This is the important question. What does it mean? Privacy is one issue. Why does each culture have a domain of personal privacy, even if there is wide divergence on what is kept private. One explanation is that private information is the capital from which we create close relationships. The closer someone is to you, the more you share personal information with that person. All cultures value close relationships; all allow individuals a domain of information to use selectively in forming relationships.[7]

We are rapidly narrowing the domain of private information. Without privacy, there is little individuality. Trust is replaced with regulation. Organizational processes, such as performance appraisal, take on an adversarial, formal character. Entrepreneurship, which is business's way of giving expression to individuality, is threatened by this loss of privacy.

Information systems have eliminated part of the ethics of capitalism, the "ethics of the second chance." Most entrepreneurs fail before succeeding. Failing teaches them how to succeed in bold ventures. Information systems lessen the opportunity to learn by failing. Entrepreneurs need capital. Those who supply capital want to know the record, and they can now examine it in detail. The same is true inside organizations; those who get to try new ideas have records of success. If you want to be an entrepreneur, you must take risks.

The leveling effects of information systems are not restricted to entrepreneurship. When it becomes an obvious social fact that records cannot be buried and that deviant actions will stay with a person indefinitely, there will be even greater pressures for conformity with a concomitant loss of diversity and social vitality.[8] The tragedy of information systems is a quiet tragedy—the extinguishing of the very individuality that makes our business and government institutions work. This is a tragedy having little salience until the aggregate, very general effects become undeniable.

Information systems shorten the range of management thinking. Managers can now monitor many quantifiable factors hourly. Managers respond to what they can measure. When to intervene? If a unit's performance is off for a quarter? A month? A day? It is hard to resist intervening, even if time could be spent on something less measurable such as a new product idea or a vague but promising marketing plan. Investors like information. If the quarterly figures are down, they move their money. Those who invest on behalf of pensioners, policy holders, and charities have a fiduciary responsibility to move funds based on the most current information. They cannot afford to consider the long-term interests of companies in which they invest. For this reason managers think in quarterly terms. If investors had the same information on a monthly, weekly, daily, or hourly basis, they would respond, and so would managers. Managers' ability to think in strategic and qualitative terms decreases in direct proportion to the advance of information systems.

Let us summarize our conclusions concerning critical questions about information systems: Can information networks become communities? We opted for ground rules for information users rather than full-scale communities. Where does responsibility reside in an information system? Individuals are responsible for each of their information acts. Can we manage without individuals? We cannot. The ground rules that are agreed on must affirm that information, about or created by a person, is that person's most valued private property, his or her human capital.

Biotechnology Tragedies

There are two key ethical indicators of the future of biotechnologies: the incredible anticipatory wave of biotechnology regulation, and the increasing number of corporate tragedies. How do corporate tragedies relate to biotechnologies? What topics could be less connected than the low-technological tragedy in Bhopal and biotechnology? Consider the following wire service report:

WIDER GOVERNMENTAL REIN URGED OVER BIOTECHNOLOGY

Representative Gerry Sikorski said he was impressed by the potential of bio-technologies, but "the Union Carbide disaster in India is all too fresh in our minds to view any technological innovation without due respect for the uncertainties associated with its use" (UPI, 12/12/84).

The inference from Bhopal to biotechnology is a flat non sequitur. But it is understandable in ethical terms. Tragedies violate our ground rules and thus are perceived as evil. Biotechnology exceeds our ground rules and so invites application of evil. The association is through perceived common evil and the need to rationalize the evil. When we confront evil, we seek external factors to explain the evil and revalidate our ground rules. Business is often the handiest villain to accuse.

Public debate over biotechnologies has consisted mainly of irrational attacks. Will gene splicing produce Frankenstein monsters? Business discussion of biotechnologies is confined to glowing reports of potential benefits and arguments over whether new life forms are patentable. These issues miss the major questions posed by biotechnologies. What questions might we ask about biotechnologies? While biotechnologies promise to revolutionize agriculture (synthetic animal super-growth hormones), energy production (synthesized fuel alcohol), and medical diagnostics, we focus on human-genetic engineering. The following questions fundamentally challenge our ground rules.

Is genetic self-improvement worth it?

Will industry's next basic technology be controlled by the public sector?

Is biotechnology an action item for business?

Genetic Self-Improvement

Biotechnologies will have their greatest impact on humans rather than on the environment. For example, a genetic trigger seems to tip the anabolism (growth, development) versus catabolism (decline, death) balance in favor of catabolism. If we learn to jam this trigger, life may be prolonged indefinitely. We may be faced with such problems as having to fit people who are two-hundred years old into pension plans. Once it is practical to predetermine the gender of children, we may face great imbalances in the workforce.

The likely scenario is that incremental progress in biotechnology will lead to full-scale human engineering and leveling. Biogenetic techniques will first be applied to agriculture, provoking events of low present salience such as the open-environment release of unapproved antifrost bacteria in Oakland, California. Biotechnologies will also be used to treat some of the diseases known to be genetically determined. This step will provoke events of only moderate salience, such as recent discussion of the availability of human growth hormone. Through a number of steps, each provoking events of only moderate salience, we will eventualy alter the human genome to the point that we have significantly altered the nature of human life, quite possibly for the worse.[9] Incremental steps will produce a radical shift, which may go undetected until it is irreversible.

There are deeper reasons to avoid thinking about biotechnologies. The critical questions stupify our standard positions. What is a market approach to designing people? Markets produce things efficiently *for people*. Should markets produce people? For whom? What is a socialist stance on biotechnology? Allocate "good genes" to those who *need* them; withhold them from those favored by nature? Do we design people for the common good? These questions mock our ground rules.

Technology Control by the Public Sector

The alternative to letting biotechnology run us is to control it by regulation. This approach is favored by governments and legal and scientific authorities. Business has been silent on this topic, with a few exceptions. The exceptions concern patenting new life forms, attempts by certain states to ban bioengineered products, and a recent attempt to block mixing of the genetic matter of humans with that of animals (using human growth hormone genes to enlarge hogs). Business accepts massive government regulation of biotechnology as a given. Several executives, noting the rapid proliferation of regulations and agencies enforcing regulations on biotechnology, have called for the appointment of a special counselor to the president on biotechnology, to sort out the already-congested regulatory environment.[10]

No nonregulatory approach to biotechnology has been proposed. The broader issues remain untouched, except by those fanning public fears of catastrophes. This silence will prove costly. The government is already immersed in briefing documents and proposed biotechnology regulations. In addition to current regulatory claims on biotechnology by the National Institutes of Health (Recombinant DNA Advisory Committee), the Environmental Protection Agency (administration of the Toxic Substances Act), the Department of Agriculture, and the Occupational Safety and Health Administration, Senators Florio, Gore, and Durenberger, have proposed new legislation aimed at biotechnologies.[11]

Biotechnology as an Action Item

Few executives regard biotechnology as an action item. Despite the dense regulatory atmosphere being created, specific issues have low present salience. Only biotechnology companies such as Cetus, Genetech, and Vega place bioethics regulation anywhere on their agendas. Ignoring bioethics is a mistake. Biotechnology is critical to business—not just to biotechnological companies. It is critical to those who will give credit, insure, package, market, and produce in the new business environment. The first biotechnological tragedy will have temendous impact in the industry as well as in related industries (agriculture, drugs, energy).

One strategy is to profit from the ethical confusion about biotechnologies. One firm has anticipated the inevitable outrage about unethical information practices by designing an ethical information system. The system documents the source and estimated accuracy of inputs and locates responsibility for data inputs, exits, and changes. As outrage over information abuse grows, this system will create demand among "high-image" information users (insurance companies, brokerages). No firm now seeks an ethics-based competitive advantage in biotechnology.

Another strategy is self-regulation. This strategy might be combined with the first strategy, since there is profit in organizing and managing industrial organizations. While self-regulation is usually preferable to government regulation, it is still control. It often blocks the market. A meeting of high-level biogenetics researchers at the Asilomar Conference established research safety standards. It seemed that self-regulation might work in biotechnology. As the industry has developed, interest in self-regulation has waned. It can wait until the industry has its Three Mile Island.

Business must use ethics to think about biotechnology. This technology may not be allowed to develop. Why did the Chinese, who once had the world's greatest navy, become a fourth-rate naval power, and, consequently, a technologically backward country? The Chinese navy was regulated out of existence (during the Ming Dynasty) because of fear of the unknown and the desire to fund social programs rather than technology. The U.S. nuclear power industry has been largely regulated out of existence. When nuclear power is discussed, the issue of what we have foregone by terminating this industry is not considered.

Biotechnology may halt when it has its first tragedy. No one in the industry acknowledges that sooner or later there will be a disaster. Why? Probabilities. No industry has developed without a disaster. The chances of particular disasters are small, but, in aggregate, a tragedy is certain. Everyone in biotechnology needs to think about what will happen when tragedy comes, even if it does not come to their firm. When there is a tragedy it will be general—to the biotechnology industry at the very least—and very salient.

Biotechnology illustrates that many important ethical issues confronting business are inherently general; they are not internal to individual firms. Critics of business can easily divide and conquer on these issues. Witness, for example, international payments, excess profits, and executive severance pay. Business values must figure in discussions of issues central to our social and economic vitality. The job of business is to solve problems profitably. Business does not think well collectively, nor should it. Business speaks most eloquently through products. However, some issues are settled before there are products to speak, leaving only the marketplace of ideas. Business has lost the edge in this market through reactiveness. It has allowed its critics to argue fundamental changes in the ground rules of our society, while remaining silent or reacting at best. Business must reacquaint itself with the language of ethics and re-enter the discussion of society's ground rules.

An Ethical Framework for Tragedies and New Technologies

We have emphasized that ethics can be a powerful tool for foreseeing and managing crises and for participating in debates concerning the development of new technologies. We now provide a framework for using ethics to play these roles. The concept of ethics is refined as ground rules, and ethical models for thinking systematically about ethical issues are outlined. We look more closely at ground rules—what they are and how to find them. We sharpen our ability to observe ground rules with a process for reverse-engineering the actions of persons and organizations to find the underlying ground rules.

Actions have their roots in decisions. Of course, we do not make a conscious decision every time we act. But we do consciously decide before important actions, and less significant actions reflect past conscious and implicit choices. Thus, the best place to find our ground rules is in our decisions. A decision has several components. A decision occurs when we face alternatives or think we face alternatives. One component of a decision is to try to determine what the alternatives are. We sometimes do not correctly assess the alternatives. We may think an alternative is open to us when it is not. More often, we incorrectly assess alternatives by overlooking critical ones. Assessing alternatives is a key area in which ethics can improve business performance.

Once we have surveyed the alternatives, we must see what each alternative offers. At this point ground rules enter the picture. In assessing alternatives, there are two key questions: How much value do I see in each alternative? and What do I have to do to pursue each alternative? Answers to the first question reveal one kind of ground rule—ground rules of *value*. To reach a decision, and act, we rate some alternatives as more desirable than others. For example, someone who chooses a career as a stockbroker takes risks to pursue a mixture of wealth and independence. (Ground Rule = It is worth it to take risks to prosper and to be free of control.) Someone else facing the same career alternatives might decide to be a finance professor. That person places more value on security and on satisfying curiosity. (Ground Rule = Once basic needs are met, it is important to discover the principles by which things work.) Factual issues concerning career opportunities and abilities are important. Once we consider the facts, what we count as desirable/valuable and undesirable/not-valuable orders the alternatives.

Answers to the second question reveal a second type of ground rule—ground rules of *evaluation*. We may see one alternative to be the most desirable and yet choose another. To pursue the most desirable alternative we must do things we ordinarily would not do. It is not that the option involves too much work, a kind of work we do not like, or risks we do not want to take. That is part of assessing how desirable an alternative is. Rather, there are things that we will not do to obtain even the most desirable outcomes because we evaluate these actions as unacceptable in principle. At one point, the chief executive officer of a major hotel chain realized that the way to produce the outcome he judged as most desirable for the firm was to move into the casino business. He had no objection to people being in the casino business. But he did not believe in gambling or promoting gambling himself, so he presented the casino option to his board as the best option, and resigned. The casino option violated his ground rule: I will not profit from others doing what I will not do.

At the heart of every decision, and every action resulting from a decision, are ground rules expressing what we value and what we will do to get what we value. To find your ground rules, squeeze the factual assumptions out of your decisions; the ground rules are the residue that drives the decision. Organizations have the same kinds of ground rules. But just as it is hard to find responsibility in organizations, it is also hard to find the ground rules. Organizational decisions are made by people and groups of people. The trick is to find out who makes the decisions, and to pick through diversions to see how decisions are made and evaluated. Familiarity with basic ethical models will assist you in this reverse-engineering process of looking at actions and decisions, squeezing out factual assumptions, and finding the underlying ground rules. We outline three basic ethical models known as end-point ethics, rule ethics, and social-contract ethics to uncover ground rules.

End-Point Ethics

End-point ethics sharpens our ability to uncover ground rules of value. End-point ethics states that a person, organization, or society should do what promotes the greatest balance of good over harm. But whose good and whose harm counts? This is a fundamental question in ethics and in all complex management decisions. We approach this question through a three-step decision process.

The process starts by asking who we should consider in decision making. End-point ethics says "everyone." But it is impossible to consider everyone in formulating an employment policy or a market strategy. "Everyone" is thus usually read as "everyone seriously affected." This is better than a general "everyone," but still not very helpful. Is everyone who is seriously affected by a decision affected in the same way? And who is the judge of what effects are serious? In short, everyone seriously affected is a large, heterogenous group. The best way to determine who to consider is in terms of *stakeholder groups*. Ask, "Who has an identifiable stake (or interest) in this decision?" and "What is that stake (interest)?" In this way, you can list the critical stakeholder groups, and assess the consequences for each group.

End-point ethics says choose the action that promotes the greatest balance of good over harm for everyone. Greatest compared to what? If there is but one possible course of action (*not acting* is a course of action), then that course of action is best by default. But every actual decision involves many alternatives. The action that produces the greatest balance of good over harm is that action among the alternatives that produces the best balance. The second step of our decision process is to identify the alternate courses of action. The direction, "Identify the alternatives open to you and the firm," is too broad to be practical (there are countless alternatives) and too vague (plausible, innovative alternatives are hard to come by). How do you rule out frivolous or implausible alternatives? And how do you identify the critical but obscure alternatives, which may be optimal?

Our decision process adds substance to the directive to consider the alternatives. The second step is elaborated as follows. Identify the alternatives you consider most plausible. Then determine what alternatives each stakeholder group considers plausible. If practical, key stakeholder groups should be directly queried. There are two advantages to querying key stakeholders. You may find that the alternatives you regard as optimal meet strong resistance in stakeholder groups needed to implement them. And, those with a different stake in the decision may see important alternatives that you have overlooked.

Identifying stakeholders and alternatives does not constitute a decision. The end-point model directs, "Choose the alternative that leads to the greatest balance of good over harm for everyone." Who is to say what is a good or harmful outcome? There are two approaches to this question: democracy and authority. Democracy says, "Ask what each stakeholder group considers a good outcome and a harmful one. Choose the outcome that maximizes the balance of good over harm, all stakeholder groups considered." Authority says, "It is the manager's responsibility to decide what outcomes to seek (good) and what outcomes to avoid (harm). So decide." The best approach is to first ask what the stakeholder groups see as good and harmful outcomes, prioritize the stakeholder groups (stakeholder groups are not created equal for managers), and then use authority.

This end-point process is useful to managers in foreseeing and managing tragedies and new technologies in two ways. First, it focuses attention on just those stakeholders usually hidden from managers' attention. Low present salience, high potential salience tragedies show first in stakeholder groups outside of the current management picture. Potential biotechnological tragedies may show first in such stakeholder groups as parents groups or antitechnology gadflies. Second, by forcing managers to consider a broad range of alternatives, managers get a glimpse of potential tragedies and technological developments as well as potential ways to meet tragedies and use technologies.

Rule Ethics

Rule ethics states that a person or organization should do what is required by valid ethical principles. Furthermore, a person or organization should refrain from doing anything contrary to valid ethical principles. If end-point ethics attunes us to the ground rules of value stakeholders, rule ethics attunes us to the stakeholders' ground rules of *evaluation*. Rule ethics focuses attention on what approaches the stakeholder groups consider acceptable or unacceptable in pursuit of their values. We build on our end-point decision process to uncover the ground rules of evaluation—the particular rule ethics—of stakeholder groups.

The rule ethics process works as follows. Consider a decision facing your organization. First identify the groups that have a significant stake in the decision (as in the end-point process). Then try to write the ground rules unique to each stakeholder group. Remember to focus on the actual ground rules, not the professed ground rules. Now take on an advocacy stance on behalf of each group. Use that group's ethics to argue that the decision most likely to be made is unethical. Keep trying until you make a case that you could present on behalf of that group in a public forum. If you do a good job with this process, you have also done a good job of forecasting. You are very likely to see the arguments you raised on behalf of various groups again if you proceed with the decision. You now know where they come from and what ground to meet them on.

One feature of ethical rules—particularly ground rules of evaluation—contributes so much to the ethical indictment of business that we single it out for special attention. Ethical rules may be of two kinds: *categorical* or *prima facie*. Categorical rules allow absolutely no exceptions. Most ethical rules are not categorical. For example, the rule that one should keep promises has clear exceptions. In fact, sound ethics requires that this rule sometimes be broken. Suppose I promise to sell a patent to a friend. After making the promise, I learn that he is selling technology to the Soviet Union for military uses. He probably befriended me just to learn what I know about guided missiles. I am obligated to break my promise to him, and, if possible, sell him a very misleading fake patent.

The rules that one should keep promises and tell the truth are not categorical—they are prima facie rules. These rules can, and sometimes must, be violated in favor of more pressing obligations. Prima facie rules support the belief that other things being equal, one should keep promises, tell the truth, obey the law, and so on. A common and effective strategy for ethically attacking business is to indict a firm or executive for violating a commonly accepted ethical rule. The trick is that although the rule is commonly accepted (do not lie, bribe, violate the law), it is a prima facie rule, which sometimes must be violated to uphold ethics. And the complex circumstances in which tragedies arise and new technologies provoke criticism do not conform to simple maxims. Businesses and executives typically respond to such attacks in economic, legal, or other defensive terms, suggesting that they acted unethically. Once it is realized that violating an ethical rule may be ethical, or even ethically required, you may be able to take a positive stand without conceding ethics to the critic.

Rule ethics helps managers foresee and manage tragedies and the development of new technologies by bringing the ethical codes of stakeholder groups to the surface. This helps managers see conflicts among ethical rules that precede fundamental shifts in ground rules. Further, by enabling managers to recognize the distinction between prima facie and categorical rules, managers can seek a fairer hearing in crises and argue for more flexibility in allowing the development of new technologies.

Social-Contract Ethics

We conclude our survey of ethical models with social-contract ethics. Social-contract ethics sees the ethical rules we live by as products of implicit contracts. It emphasizes that social contracts are not explicitly negotiated, although they may be subject to intentional change. Social contracts are carried by the cultures of the groups, organizations, and society to which we belong. Every organization is a web of implicit contracts. When we enter an organization, we also enter a set of contracts. The social contract is an implicit agreement about the basic principles, or ethics, of the group.

If we take the ground rules of value and evaluation uncovered by end-point and rule ethics to express implicit contracts governing various stakeholder groups, then social-contract ethics provides a standard for judging whether these contracts are sound. Social-contract ethics states that a contract is sound if parties to the contract enter the contract freely and fairly. Since social contracts are not explicitly negotiated, social-contract ethics asks what parties would agree to in a hypothetical negotiation. Obviously, there is room for debate over what someone would agree to. The only reliable test is negotiation. Even if contracts will not actually be negotiated, social-contract ethics helps us judge whether to support standing contracts or to seek their change or demise.

A contract has no standing unless the involved parties entered it freely. *Freely* is open to interpretation. If I hold a gun to your head, you may "freely" agree to pay me a thousand dollars for a copy of today's paper. Your agreement is free in that it is not an involuntary reflex. You could have refused and faced the consequences, but no one would ethically criticize you for submitting to this agreement.

Social-contract ethics says that contracts must be both free and fair. A contract need not be fair in the sense that everyone fares equally well under it. A contract allows people to pursue interests cooperatively or competitively, without expectation that each party will reap the same rewards. A contract is fair if the parties freely agree to the contract even if their roles might be switched upon its enactment. In a labor negotiation, this means that a contract is fair if the negotiators would agree to it not knowing if they would be assigned to labor or management upon ratification. To find out if existing contracts are fair, assume the position of the different affected parties and ask how you would view the contract from each position.

When end-point and rule-ethics models are combined with social-contract ethics, we have a powerful tool for understanding tragedies and new technologies. When social-contract ethics is applied to the ground rules of value and evaluation of the stakeholders in a business or industry, we can see the conflicts and changes underway in these rules. Where the rules are perceived as unsound within or among stakeholder groups, there is a likelihood of fundamental change. Such change will surface in the form of social debate and uncertainty. When a firm or industry is susceptible to a kind of event that will challenge ground rules that are foundational for stakeholder groups, the preconditions for viewing the events as tragedies are met.

When new technological developments render standing contracts unfair, unfree, or otherwise unsound, the developments will meet strong resistance. End-point ethics and rule ethics bring ground rules to the surface. Social-contract ethics helps us see where those rules are unstable, open to social debate, in conflict, or fragile in the face of change. These are the areas that are ripe for tragedies and strident resistance to new developments.

Social-contract ethics suggest strategies for managing tragedies and new technologies. The suggested strategy for managing tragedies is to address perceived unfairness in relations with stakeholder groups on a continuing basis. For example, companies that are in businesses which inevitably impose risks to consumers (such as drug companies) must broach the issue of shared risk with affected stakeholder groups before the risks are realized. As some companies have discovered, there are powerful support groups—those who have considerable need for risky or experimental drugs—who can help establish a fair balance of assumed risk. The suggested strategy for managing new technologies is to expose the ethical issues implicit in these technologies before the public feels that regulation is the only way to gain a measure of control. The unlikely strategy of many companies is to try to sneak changes by so they are unnoticed, and then face up to the strident response later. But stakeholder groups demand their say and have learned to use the legal and political systems to gain it. Our ground rules cannot adapt to the challenges posed to them by new technologies if consideration of these challenges is postponed until we must choose between our ethics and the technologies. Again, some stakeholder groups will naturally favor change. These groups cannot enter the pro side of the debate if there is no debate.[12]

The Next Ethics

The best use of ethics in management is to provide a framework for asking questions. The less clear the issues facing us, the more important it is to ask good questions. The social issues that will critically affect organizations in the future are certainly not clear. Thus, our focus has been on using ethics to ask questions about these issues.

The three ethical models considered are intended to capture the elements of ethics as it has evolved to the present. These models can serve as important tools in foreseeing and managing the critical issues that business will face. But ethics too will evolve, the ground rules we have today do not address many of the issues we will face, since new technologies give us powers we have not yet thought about exercising. Our ground rules have evolved for two purposes: defining and protecting rights of individuals and groups against each other, and allocating scarce resources. We inherit conflict-resolution and scarcity-management ethics. The problems of new technologies are problems of design. They are problems of designing agreements to block the encroachment of information systems, and problems of designing the environment we will live in. We have no ethics of design.

We call the next ethics an ethics of design. It is an ethics of design because the hard choices we confront are design choices. Since the forms of organization we have do not work, as evidenced by intense interest in almost any new organization form, we must design new organization forms. Since information systems that rest on our existing agreements provoke a plague of abuse and crime, we must design new ground rules—a new ethics—of information. Since our ground rules for new technologies breed tragedies, regulations, and no control, we must design an ethics to guide use of these technologies. Since biotechnologies allow us to design ourselves and our environment, we either devise an ethics of design or accept an ethics of willful prejudice.

Revolutions respect the past, if only by reacting against it. The next ethics will respect our present ethics, even though it will arise as a criticism of this ethics. We conclude by speculating on that criticism and its likely outcome.

End-point ethics is to be criticized for telling us to maximize the common good, without telling us why more is better, or what to seek more of. It tells us to drive in a straight line as fast as possible, but it offers no direction. Rule ethics is to be criticized for telling us to act on principle, while providing a variety of conflicting principles. When faced with this criticism, it becomes inflexible and demands faith. As much as we long for the old principles to work, they do not tell us to whom information belongs, what agreements should govern new organizations, and what we should and should not genetically design. Today, if we are to act on principle, we must first choose the principle. On what principle do we choose principles?

Social-contract ethics is to be criticized for telling us to uphold agreements we would freely and fairly choose, without telling us what to agree about. Agreements produce orderly arrangements among individuals already bound together by something. They do not create that something. To view fair agreements as an end in themselves is to commit the classic fallacy of confusing means and ends.

We speculate that an ethics of design will be an ethics of stakeholder agreement—of cross-stakeholder contracts of a comparatively explicit kind. This is a development of social-contract ethics to allow fundamental value differences to coexist by being "negotiated out." Agreements must be based on an alignment of differing stakeholder group values. Agreements will be judged on their ability to support mutually purposeful action. This development of end-point ethics gives up the ghost of the common good in favor of aligned pursuit of stakeholder values. This ethics will put a premium on action based on principles. Since the principles by which we should act are not settled, principles will be close to the surface of social life. We will tolerate different principles, but can only hold those who use tolerance to excuse ethical opportunism in contempt. This is a development of rule ethics with respect for principled action supplanting the hopeless search for the one and only set of right principles.[13]

We speculate that this ethics of design may emerge to meet the criticisms and weaknesses of current ethical models and address the ethical problems of the present and future. We do not argue that this is the only plausible ethics of design. And we do not argue that the chances are great of this ethics emerging. That would carry us from speculation to fantasy. There is no question that ethics as we know it is as likely to persist as the steel mills of Pittsburgh. We do not know what factors produce and direct ethical change. So we have made the only assumption available to someone who accepts responsibility, and hence choice, in the matter of ground rules we live by. We can, by our intentions and actions, influence the outcome of ethical debate.[14]

Notes

This article is based on Mark Pastin, *The Hard Problems of Management.* Jossey-Bass Publishing, 433 California Street, San Francisco, Calif., 1986.

1. Mitroff, I.I., and R. Kilmann. 1984. "Corporate Tragedies: Teaching Companies to Cope with Evil," *New Management,* **1**(4), 48–53.
2. Mitroff, I.I., and R. Kilmann. 1984. *Corporate Tragedies.* New York: Praeger, pp. 63–77.
3. Sethi, S.P. 1982. *Up Against the Corporate Wall.* Englewood Cliffs, N.J.: Prentice-Hall, pp. 99–117.
4. Bishop, J.E. 1984. "Should Employers Be Told?" *Wall Street Journal,* Sept. 12, p. 1.
5. Mason, R.O. 1983. "Designing Information Communities: Ethical Issues in the Information Age." Working Paper, Management Information Systems. Tuscon: University of Arizona, pp. 1–5.
6. Ibid., p. 2.
7. Fried, C. 1970. *An Anatomy of Values.* Cambridge, Mass.: Harvard University Press, pp. 137–154.
8. Kent Greenwalt's view as discussed in Burnham, D. 1980. *The Rise of the Computer State.* New York: Random House, p. 47.
9. Wade, N. 1979. *The Ultimate Experiment.* New York: Walker, pp. 151–152.
10. Jefferson, E. 1984. "Biotechnology Advance Will Require End to Regulatory Limbo," *Financier,* Oct. 1, pp. 21–24.
11. Ibid., p. 22.
12. These models are elaborated in Pastin, M. 1986. *The Hard Problems of Management: Gaining the Ethics Edge.* San Francisco: Jossey-Bass.
13. Ibid., pp. 172–197.
14. Stephen J. Snyder of Arizona State University provided research assistance relating to corporate tragedies.

Theories of Corporate Social Performance
William C. Frederick

Theories of corporate social performance try to explain, rationalize, and, in some cases, advocate societal values that are essential to the human condition, but are sometimes ignored or overridden by business. Three such theories about the social performance of U.S.-based corporations have been developed since the beginning of the twentieth century. The theory of *corporate social responsibility (CSR1)* emerged first, attaining its greatest popularity among corporate executives and academic scholars during the 1950s and 1960s. The theory of *corporate social responsiveness (CSR2)* appeared during the early 1970s, overlapping but not entirely replacing the notion of social responsibility. The theory of *corporate social rectitude (CSR3)* began to take shape during the mid-1970s, fueled by swelling concern about the ethical quality of corporate performance.

All three theories presently exist side by side, duplicating one another to some extent, while each still retains a distinctiveness reflecting unique philosophical orientations and institutional purposes. Each of these theories of corporate social performance reveals much about the relations between business firms and the societies in which they conduct business. To the perceptive observer, they also demonstrate both the opportunities and the limitations of making deep inquiry into the nature of business enterprise as practiced in the United States.

Business and Society Thought

The origin of business and society thought in the United States is both intriguing and surprising. The idea that corporations have social responsibilities that go beyond the pursuit of profits is heard in the early years of the twentieth century from business executives themselves—from the very persons who might normally be expected to think only of their responsibilities to stockholders. These top-level business representatives, usually men who had profited handsomely from their jobs and positions, spoke of the need to temper profits and corporate power with a concern for the broader public welfare.

This puzzling beginning of social responsibility thinking is explained by remembering the context in which business firms were operating at the time. The late nineteenth and early twentieth centuries were a time of intense concern and even fear about the economic and social consequences of the giant industrial combines being formed by financial magnates and industrial leaders. When the U.S. Steel Corporation was formed in 1901, many observers saw in it a threat, not just to competitive enterprise, but to a democratic way of life. Looming corporate power, growing by leaps and bounds, particularly when linked with the known financial abuses of the robber barons, might well overwhelm Jeffersonian ideals, put many communities under the corporate heel, complete the subjugation of working people, and even capture the seats of governmental power.

One result of these fears was liberal and radical criticism directed against business. A further result was the extension of antitrust laws, banking regulations, food and drug regulations, and public utility guidelines to a wider range of business firms. In this climate of increasing public alarm about business power and of expanding government control, we find business executives beginning to speak of their social responsibilities. Their ideas laid the foundations of what we now recognize as the classic or conventional theory of corporate social responsibility.

Corporate Social Responsibility

Two major principles supported the theory of corporate social responsibility: the charity principle and the stewardship principle. Both were paternalistic expressions of established corporate power. For convenience and clarity, this particular interpretation of corporate social responsibility is called CSR1.

The *charity principle* obligated the well-to-do to extend comfort to those less fortunate. For wealthy individuals, this meant sharing a self-determined portion of their riches with the poor or with community institutions and organizations less well-off. Those temporarily out of work, physically handicapped, chronically ill, or too old to hold a job qualified for such charitable aid. So too did community institutions who ministered to such groups, such as the church, the mission, the settlement house, and, by the 1920s, the new Community Chest movement.

Soon these community needs outgrew the wealth of even the most generous wealthy individuals. Sometime during the 1920s, the business firm itself became a potential source of charitable support. From this time on, charitable obligations to the unfortunate were seen as an important additional responsibility incurred by the business community. This was one of the two major meanings that corporate social responsibility assumed in the classic or conventional theory.

The *stewardship principle* was equally important. Derived from an ancient, even biblical precept, it allowed corporate executives to view themselves as stewards or fiduciary guardians of society's resources. As such, they held those resources in trust, to be used for whatever legitimate purposes might be implicit in private ownership of productive resources. Foremost among those purposes was profit making, which was a consequence of the prudent use of the resources one owned or controlled. As the biblical parable of the talents demonstrated, slothful or careless use of one's God-given talents led to waste, whereas honest and wise applications multiplied the bounty at one's command. Above all, therefore, a business firm's main responsibility to society was to invest its resources wisely and prudently. In that way, society's wealth (as well as the business firm's) would multiply.

But business trusteeship or stewardship implied the existence of responsibilities and obligations that went beyond the firm itself. These powerful corporations that had struck such fear in the hearts of the public were, due to their size, clearly in a position to influence the quality of life of many participants in society. Employees, suppliers, competitors, customers, and local communities were often at the mercy of decisions made in corporate board rooms. Would it not be true that a faithful steward of society's resources should consider the interests and needs of all these other groups that depended so heavily and directly on business decisions and policies? The answer was yes, just so long as meeting these broader obligations did not interfere with the primary aim of the firm to turn a profit on its operations.

Thus were established the two primary components of the classical theory of corporate social responsibility. The charity principle urged business firms to take a generous attitude toward society's unfortunate ones. The stewardship principle urged them to consider the interests of others in society as part of their trusteeship duties.

Core Components of CSR1

This social responsibility theory caught on and was accepted by increasing numbers of corporate leaders during the 1950s and 1960s. As a fully developed doctrine, corporate social responsibility rested on six fundamental precepts.

Power begets responsibility. Since business firms, especially the largest corporations, control such large amounts of wealth and since their decisions and policies affect the economic livelihood of so many persons in society, business executives automatically incur a degree of responsibility that matches their power. They are then obligated to wield their power and influence in responsible ways, trying at all times to keep power and responsibility in balance.

A voluntary assumption of responsibility is preferable to government intervention and regulation. CSR1 theory from its early twentieth-century beginnings has reflected the natural fear felt by business leaders when confronted with social criticism and competing power centers. The preservation of business's power of decision has been paramount. For that reason, CSR1's advocates have always been able to sway some business leaders to their side by arguing that government intervention may occur in the absence of voluntary social actions.

Voluntary social responsibility requires business leaders to acknowledge and accept the legitimate claims, rights, and needs of other groups in society. These groups include employees, trade unions, customers, suppliers, competitors, local communities hosting business operations, and the general public. The ultimate curb placed on the ability of business to respond to these claims was the firm's economic base, particularly its profit position. But within those limits,

CSR1 theory urged business decision makers to broaden their view beyond market-defined responsibilities. Here, in modern garb, were the two core principles of charity and stewardship.

Corporate social responsibility requires a respect for law and for the rules of the game that govern marketplace relations. Fraud, dishonesty, not honoring legal contracts, price-fixing, or any other anticompetitive or antimarket practices are forbidden. The reasons are simple and straightforward: adherence to both the legal and the market rules of the game is essential if business is to enjoy the necessary degree of political and economic stability that permits the pursuit of profits.

An attitude of "enlightened self-interest" leads socially responsible business firms to take a long-run view of profits. This posture may require a company to incur short-run costs in order to act responsibly (for example, to contribute to a local charity or to recall a defective product that threatens customers' health or safety), thus reducing profits in the short run (which usually means for as long as one to four accounting quarters). However, in the long run these added costs will be recovered and the company will continue to make profits due to its improved public image and the increased public confidence that flows from such socially responsible acts.

Greater economic, social, and political stability—and therefore a lower level of social criticism directed toward the private enterprise system—will result if all businesses adopt a socially responsible posture. This precept—actually a warning—flowed naturally out of the collective business memory of times past when sharp questions had been raised about the ability or willingness of private enterprise to meet the needs of society. The Progressive Era of the early twentieth century, the depression years of the 1930s, and the tumultuous 1960s had produced torrents of radical criticism of the capitalist system. In such a context of social criticism, CSR1 offered a welcome alternative to government intervention in private affairs, as well as shelter from the charge that a heartless, profit-minded business system cared so little for the general public that it deserved to be abolished or severely curbed. All that was needed to counter such criticism, according to CSR1 doctrine, was for business to accept its social responsibilities.

The Attack on CSR1

To understand the many criticisms directed against the classical doctrine of corporate social responsibility, one must remember that its chief supporters were business executives who wanted to preserve the private enterprise system and their favored position within it. Therefore, anyone who was the least bit dubious about how well free enterprise or corporate executives could meet both economic and social needs was likely to oppose the idea.

An odd coalition of critics pummeled the doctrine with great enthusiasm. Included among the opponents were leftist critics ("It's a capitalist smokescreen hiding profits and greed"); free-market advocates ("It reduces market efficiency"); liberal critics ("Its impact is marginal"); and a large but unknown number of hard-nosed business executives ("It's impractical, too costly, and unworkable"). Among all the points raised against the theory, three major shortcomings proved to be the most troublesome to its supporters.

The Definition Problem. Foremost was the problem of defining just what corporate social responsibility means. Operationally, what is the content and substance of socially responsible actions? Charitable or philanthropic contributions would seem to qualify, as would any law-abiding behavior or general adherence to the rules of the marketplace. But, some asked, if these actions also added to the company's profits, would they still be counted as socially responsible or could they be considered smart business tactics? This led some scholars to argue that only those actions that required some financial sacrifice by the firm could be classified as socially responsible. If, for example, a contribution to a local art museum helped create a pleasant community, thereby aiding the company in attracting and holding employees, then it would be simply a sophisticated extension of the company's personnel policies having little to do with social responsibility.

In addition to the substance of CSR1, questions arose about its scope and magnitude. Just how far out into the social world must a company reach in order to be thought socially responsible? Where were the boundaries of proper action? For example, how clean should the air be made, how many minorities should be hired, or how many industrial accidents and injuries should be avoided for a company to be classified as socially responsible? Does social responsibility require business to tackle all of society's problems or just a few of them? Which ones? The answers were not obvious.

Others wondered whether social responsibility referred only to voluntary acts, rather than those things required by law. If a person or a company is forced by law to do something, how can we know whether it was done in the spirit of social concern or whether it was just a matter of legal compliance? Still other skeptics believed that only individual persons, not companies, could be held responsible for their acts. The corporation, after all, was known to be an artificial person, nothing but a legal fiction or a structural shell, which assumed its true meaning and purpose only when populated by real live persons. Its actions and policies were directed by individual managers, and it was these actual human beings who were responsible for what the company did or did not do. Moreover, corporations might allow the actual human decision makers to hide behind the artificial corporate facade and thus escape the accountability they owed to society for the decisions they made. Until these questions of definition could be clarified—the content, the scope, the motive force, and the actors involved—the notion of social responsibility would remain vague and highly subjective.

The Trade-off Problem. Another worrisome dilemma was deciding how to balance economic needs against social demands. Making the workplace safer costs money. How can a firm decide whether the investment is worthwhile? This question raises another: how is the value of human life or human wellness to be measured? Do they have infinite value, taking precedence over all other considerations? If their value can be calculated, should it be stated in economic (that is, dollar) amounts? If human life is assigned a financial value, then it would be easier to decide whether an investment to save lives or preserve health is worthwhile. A business analyst might then compare the monetary costs of safety investments against the financial returns to be expected. If the financial ratio is positive, then the firm would know whether it should proceed to invest its funds for this social purpose.

Most business executives know that a storm of public criticism would envelop their firms if they appeared to be so callous of human life and safety as to apply this type of cost-benefit reasoning to decide how to allocate economic resources for social needs. But even if they dared to do so, they would still face some perplexing questions. Where pollution clean-up expenditures that are imposed on an economically marginal but still profitable plant would result in its closure, is the clean air worth the loss of the plant's jobs? Until the science of economic and social measurement can provide socially acceptable answers to such questions, both business and society will have much difficulty in dealing with the trade-off between desirable social goals and perhaps equally desirable economic goals. In the meantime, socially concerned business executives cannot know with certainty whether they should get involved socially or how much money they can legitimately and prudently spend for such purposes.

The Moral Justification Problem. The most serious problem encountered by academics, even among those who favored corporate social responsibility, was the doctrine's failure to enunciate a clear moral principle that could guide business decison makers to act in socially responsible ways. "Doing good" is generally admirable but one must have some moral basis for doing so. The most that could be said was that charity and stewardship are extensions of biblical precepts and, as such, they act as the ultimate moral justification of social responsibility. Some said this reasoning did not have a broad enough moral base. They cited two reasons: (1) charitable acts carried out by corporate stewards-trustees are limited by the company's need to make profits, as well as by the fiduciary responsibility that managers have to stockholders, and (2) the amount and direction of corporate charity extended depends on the subjective social views and personal value preferences of top corporate executives.

The first point amounted to saying that the moral actions of social responsibility are always limited by available economic resources, which means that morality is a function of economic factors. This materialistic view would be unacceptable to many who believe that morality must precede all other considerations. The second point squeezed the moral basis of social responsibility into another narrow channel. Since the personal values of most corporate executives are private matters, unknown and inaccessible to the general public, and perhaps not even well understood by the executives themselves, the moral basis for corporate decisions is almost totally subjective. The moral justification given for corporate acts could be as varied as the lives and values of the executives making the decisions. Unless we psychoanalyze all such executives, there would be no way to grasp the moral principles they are using to make socially responsible decisions. Additionally, any given company would then be dependent on the moral whims of its top managers who may or may not be interested in social concerns.

Thus, on both practical and intellectual grounds, doubt was cast on this first attempt to advocate an expanded social role for the corporation. These doubts subtly undermined the theory's intellectual foundations without noticeably diminishing the ranks of its supporters, and the theory lives on today as a favorite among many academicians and corporate executives. It was less a matter of intellectual weakness, and more a matter of the swelling social tumult that occurred during the 1960s, that produced yet another theory of corporate social performance.

Corporate Social Responsiveness

Beginning around 1970, a new strain of thought crept into the deliberations about business's role in society. More frequently, one began to hear the phrase *corporate social responsiveness* in place of *corporate social responsibility*. This subtle change of phrasing heralded the arrival of a new theory of corporation-society relations.

Corporate social responsiveness (CSR2) turned out to be much more pragmatic, much more action-oriented and results-oriented—in general, more managerial in tone and intention—than the older notion of corporate social responsibility. The managers of socially responsive companies exhibit an analytic approach to social problems and favor forecasting techniques that might help the organization anticipate emerging social demands. They are less reactive and more proactive as they face a turbulent social environment. And, perhaps fatefully, CSR2 managers are not inclined to concern themselves with the underlying moral justification for their socially responsive efforts. In their pragmatic way, they are satisfied to respond where response seems to be needed, without worrying much about the grounds for doing so.

CSR2 managers attempt to develop organizational mechanisms and behavioral patterns that will enable their company to respond to social demands. They look upon social problems as they do marketing, production, or financial problems, believing that there is a managerial solution to be found. What is required is agreed-on goals, the assignment of priorities, the creation of organizational authority and responsibility, the allocation of budgetary resources, the assurance of rewards for effective performance, and the monitoring and evaluation of results. When the organization is restructured along these lines, its ability to be socially responsive increases.

From CSR1 to CSR2: The Underlying Cause

A full understanding of the corporation-society relationship as it is approached in American society is not possible without seeing why this new theory of corporate social responsiveness appeared in the early 1970s. During the 1960s business was subjected to social pressures and demands on a scale and with an intensity rarely experienced before. The charges were brought by civil rights advocates, environmentalists, consumer activists, women's rights advocates, union members demanding greater workplace safety, young people feeling excluded, and antiwar protesters. The demands for action and for reform were central and mainstream, not marginal or discretionary. Social critics wanted to change business's production technology, the design of products, the pricing of goods and services, its personnel practices, the markets served, the allocation of capital, and the make-up of the corporation's official governing body, the board of directors. This was not the mild menu of charitable helpfulness that CSR1's supporters had in mind when they had urged business to be socially responsible. These demands were penetrating and threatening, challenging the inner precincts of corporate power, authority, and privilege. A failure to respond skillfully and effectively could unhinge the system.

A struggle and social upheaval on this scale—one that shakes the foundations of a culture as did the 1960s disturbances—can only be a welling-up of values that are frustrated and long restrained, values that refuse to be denied any longer, values that are thought to be so central to the lives of many persons that they will brook little or no opposition to their fuller expression and realization. Here we see the full significance of the social protest movements of the 1960s. They were the carriers of newly invigorated social values, the vehicles through which bold and forthright value proclamations and claims were made.

Few of these values were new but they now found a new expression and took new forms. Minorities and women proclaimed equality, opportunity, and freedom for themselves to be central values. Consumers pushed for effectiveness, reliability, safety, and legal-ethical recourse as guiding values in the marketplace. Employees demanded dignity, humanity, safety, wellness, involvement, and participation as guiding values at work. Environmentalists wanted more attention given to ecological care, esthetics of nature, preservation of the biosphere's living space, and wellness and health. Young people sought earlier involvement in society's major institutions; older persons struggled for continued participation beyond society's stereotyped termination points; peace activists insisted that foreign policy be pursued diplomatically rather than by resorting to armed force. Beyond these characteristic values that inspired and energized the major social movements were many others shared among these and other groups: a mistrust of concentrated power; a demand to know what goes on behind the bureaucratic walls of both business and government; a retreat from traditional values and privileges; an emphasis on the quality of human relations rather than the quantities of material goods in defining the good life; and a generalized preference (perhaps even a nostalgia) for the humane values typical of small-scale life rather than the impersonal procedures often found in mammoth business and government institutions.

These were the value themes that required a corporate response. For these kinds of pressures, the older CSR1 doctrine was almost totally inadequate as a guide to corporate action. Here were enormously threatening forces pounding at the corporation's front doors. The protesters demanded action, not charity. They questioned the authority and motives of corporate trustee-stewards, doubting that they acted in the public interest. The critics acted with the fury, if not the biblical authority, of Christ driving the money changers from the temple. They were not to be placated by the generalities typical of CSR1 thinking. Clearly, something better was needed. CSR2—that is, a theory that could provide both the reasons and the means as well as the limits of corporate social response—was the result. Coming as it did in the early 1970s, this new formulation brought some sense of relief, if not hope, to the beleaguered boardrooms of corporate America.

CSR2's Micro and Macro Dimensions

CSR2 theorists, while agreeing on the central need for an effective corporate response, followed somewhat different paths for achieving it. One group emphasized changes to be made in the structure and everyday procedures of business corporations. Another group of theorists believed that the best social response could be found in the realm of public policy. The former looked inward to a reform of the corporation itself; the latter looked outward for guidance on social matters. The first group focused on the micro (that is, the single company) dimension of corporate social action; the second group emphasized the macro dimension where collective actions might be taken.

The Micro Organizational Dimension. Here the focus is on the single company and its ability to achieve significant levels of social responsiveness. Robert Ackerman and Raymond Bauer (1976) were among the first to recommend that corporations strive for responsiveness rather than responsibility. Ackerman's research revealed a three-stage sequence through which companies tended to move—from the first stage where a social policy was formulated through an organizational learning stage to a third stage representing the company's institutionalized commitment to meeting social demands. His advice to corporate managers was act early in the life cycle of any social issue in order to enjoy the largest amount of managerial discretion over the outcome.

Ackerman and Bauer (1976) identified three obstacles to be overcome: (1) the dispersed and decentralized managerial authority of a divisional corporate structure well suited for attaining economic goals but poorly organized for social responses, (2) an accounting system adapted for measuring and controlling financial data but unable to compute social factors with precision, and (3) an organizational incentive system that rewards economic performance but does not do very well in recognizing or rewarding social performance. A company has a better chance of moving to stage three of social responsiveness if it redesigns its corporate structure by assigning explicit organizational authority to someone for grappling with social issues, if it adopts social auditing as a supplement to its standard accounting systems, and if it gives explicit rewards for social achievement or doles out punishments for failure to attain social goals.

Other business school scholars, most notably James Post, enriched CSR2 theory by demonstrating the different strategic postures assumed by companies when faced with pressing social demands. Some corporations were reactive to social change, refusing to acknowledge and sometimes even failing to see the need to reform normal business practice. Others knew that social changes were occurring but tried to turn those trends to the firm's advantage; often these companies acted proactively but without much concern for the public interest. A third type of social strategy was interactive; it was found where a company, while acting in its own interest, nevertheless made major efforts to harmonize its needs with those of the public. Post's findings suggested that an interactive strategy would bring more lasting benefits to both business and society. Along with others whose research discovered similar patterns of corporate social response, he pointed the direction for companies who needed to take action (Post 1978).

It was natural that these views of needed corporate restructuring to meet social demands would sooner or later be combined with the notion of long-term business planning. From a company point of view, all aspects of the environment in which it operates—social and political as well as economic and technological—deserve close attention if plans and operations are to succeed. Thus emerged greater collaboration between the advocates of strategic planning, such as George Steiner and Edward Freeman (Freeman 1984), and the supporters of social responsibility.

When these views were combined with the organizational reforms recommended by Ackerman and Bauer, the scholarly case for social responsiveness became stronger and began to attract the attention of corporate practitioners. It was they, after all, who needed the help that CSR2 theory could provide. Here was a way for a firm to manage its relations with the social environment, rather than to submit to a pounding from unfriendly forces or simply to respond hastily to the perceived needs of the moment.

The Macro Public-Policy Dimension. In order to understand why public policy was seen as one answer to the social problems confronting business—and why therefore it became an increasingly important part of CSR2 thinking—one must follow the events of the late 1960s and early 1970s. Social activists had been pressuring business to take direct action on a whole range of social problems. Due to the persistence of traditional thinking within the corporation plus organizational inertia and competitive market forces, the corporate response had been sluggish. Even Ackerman and Bauer (1976) had recognized that the best of the socially responsive companies might take as long as six to eight years to reach the highest levels of organizational commitment. As a result, many of the protests moved from the corporate boardrooms to the political arena. If business will not respond directly and expeditiously, said the leaders of the protest movements, they can be made to respond to legal requirements and government mandates. By 1970, this trend toward politicizing the social reform of the corporate system reached its high-water mark, as revealed in landmark studies by Edwin Epstein (1969) and David Vogel. Public policy rather than direct action was now to be the way to bring the business system to heel.

If Ackerman and Bauer (1976) were the progenitors of CSR2's micro dimension, then Lee Preston and James Post (1975) were largely responsible for laying the theoretical foundations of the macro dimension. Their *interpenetrating systems model* held that business and society mutually influence one another, neither one controlling the other but each capable of making significant inroads on the other's actions. Through a business firm's primary market-oriented relations with employees, customers, creditors, suppliers, and others, it created one set of interpenetrating links with society. These linkages might be supplemented by secondary relations if a company's profit-making efforts created negative impacts in society; in these cases, business incurred a social or public responsibility for the social problems its operations had created. Hence, business's relationships with society were of two kinds, one mediated through the marketplace (the primary relations) and another requiring nonmarket mechanisms (the secondary relations). In these two spheres, the interests of business and society interpenetrated one another. The outcome would depend on the relative strength and effectiveness of market institutions and nonmarket institutions in coping with the social problems at hand.

Where questions arose in the business mind about what social actions to take and how far their firms should go in trying to satisfy social demands, this model could be used to provide the answers. Guidance on how far the company should go in its ameliorative efforts is to be found, not in the individual social consciences of its top managers, but in public policy. That is, a company official should ask, What does the law require me to do about discrimination, industrial accidents, environmental pollution, and the host of similar problems plaguing society? What have Congress and the state legislatures set as targets? What regulatory standards have been issued? What have the courts ruled? What does general public opinion support?

Preston and Post preferred to speak of the principle of *public* responsibility because they thought it avoided some of the vagueness and subjectivity implicit in the older CSR1 rubric of *social* responsibility. Additionally, it conveyed the notion that both the content and the scope of business's responsibilities to society are to be found in public policies and political processes. Altogether, this approach was believed to be more specific, more direct, and more accessible to public participation than CSR1's reliance on voluntary private actions to solve social problems. Business and society thought had taken a giant leap forward.

The Pluses and Minuses of CSR2 Thought

The gains from CSR2 thinking are quite significant when compared to the older theory of corporate social responsibility.

Business managers are much more comfortable in dealing with the tangibles of social response than with the imponderables of social responsibility. As a result, they are more inclined to take action.

Business researchers are encouraged to help business firms develop tools and techniques of social response—environmental scanning, social forecasting, issues management, and social auditing.

Academic research also can reveal the many constraints on organizational responsiveness and what might be done to overcome them—the one-sided incentive systems that fail to reward social performance, an organizational design that works well for economic purposes but not for social purposes, and the lack of precision in measuring social factors and setting priorities for them. Here are problems to be solved rather than philosophic principles to be debated.

Another gain is the realization that business operates within a complex sociopolitical system of governmental institutions and public opinion. It is unrealistic to believe that any large corporation can do business without being affected by this network of political and social institutions. Much that the public wants from business is funneled through public-policy institutions, as well as being expressed by purchases in the marketplace.

Perhaps the central significance of CSR2 thought was its attempt to identify institutional structures through which insistent social values could have practical impact in the business arena. Some placed their faith in a more socially responsive corporate structure, believing that business could and would learn to listen and respond to the rising social clamor. Others preferred greater reliance on public policy and representative political processes to bring new social values into the midst of business operations. Business moderates spoke of the need for greater collaborative efforts—a partnership—between business and government. With something to be said for each of these institutional arrangements, CSR2 theorists had moved the debate over business's social interactions from abstract philosophic speculation to operational choices about the best way to link business with society.

CSR2's major theoretical shortcoming was its apparent inability to specify the substantive meaning of social responsiveness. It had offered three basic ways—individual company actions, public-policy guidelines, and government-business cooperation—to bring about greater social response from business.

What it did not make clear, though, was the operational definition of social responsiveness. Did business have to respond to *all* social demands made on it in order to be considered socially responsive? Or should it pay attention only to the most powerful and well-organized of its critics? Or if public-policy guidelines adopted by one presidential administration are subsequently changed by another, or modified by congressional action, or overturned entirely by court decisions, does this mean that social responsiveness is only a relative term that must take its basic meaning from the political mood of the moment? And if business is successful in imposing its own views on public policy, might that not lead business simply to reject the social demands to which a response is needed? Or if social response is to be a function of success in redesigning the organization to make it more open and receptive to social demands, what happens to social responsiveness when a company's management decides it is satisfied with the company as it is? In all these cases, the real meaning of social responsiveness seems to slip out of one's grasp. It varies from time to time, from company to company, from issue to issue. Worse yet, it seems to depend largely on the meaning that business is able and willing to give it. But the public has rarely been satisfied to let business have such undiluted power over social priorities.

The central theoretical shortcoming here is a failure to recognize and advocate a value system or a set of social priorities that would give substantive, operational meaning to social responsiveness. Such a value system cannot come solely from within the corporation's own precincts, for that would only perpetuate the tensions between business and its social critics. Nor can the society's priorities be set only by listening to business's critics, for that would in many cases impose unacceptable economic and social costs on both business and society. What is needed are consensual criteria of social performance that give full scope to the values that help sustain the life and the continuity of human communities. Corporate social responsiveness surely must find its meaning both outside the boundaries of an economically focused corporate culture but also sufficiently inside that culture to allow business to perform economizing functions that contribute vitally to societal life.

The quest for a normative or ethical core of standards rooted in both business and society was neither the goal nor the achievement of CSR2 theorists. Their contribution was positive enough without this further theoretical need. Other scholars were working on the normative questions that would give substantive meaning to the idea of social betterment. The work of this latter group signaled the emergence of a third phase of thinking about the corporation and its relation to society.

Corporate Social Rectitude

Corporate social rectitude (CSR3) had developed a value component and an ethics component by the mid-1980s. Although related to one another, value and ethics components were not quite identical. Although both were ultimately focused on the normative aspects of business operations, the two theoretical components had been produced by different sets of scholars and drew on distinctive bodies of literature and research.

The Value Component of CSR3

The fundamental premise of CSR3 theory is that business is inescapably bound up with social values and cannot be understood without taking them into consideration. Value-free business decisions do not and cannot exist. Therefore, it becomes vitally important for the values on which business policies and actions are based to be made explicit. Only in that way can society know whether business is safeguarding, or possibly endangering, the values that are essential to an organized, humane existence for all members of society. When this point of view is taken, an attempt is made to discover the values that are embedded in business custom and practice—the ones that guide the decisions of business professionals—and how they differ from the competing values held by groups in society who criticize business performance.

One broad group of management theorists, led by Gerald Cavanagh, S. Prakash Sethi, and Robert Heilbroner, has argued that the traditional value system of business—the one based on profit, economic growth, technological efficiency, and financial performance—is inadequate to meet the needs of society. A single-minded focus on economic factors, according to this view, overlooks or may override values that are of central importance to others in society. Minorities and women may prefer equitable treatment to pure economic efficiency. Environmentalists may seek clean air rather than maximum economic growth. Employees may put their health and safety ahead of an employer's efforts to lower production costs by eliminating safeguards on machinery. Consumers may prefer safe and reliable products, even if they cost more, to those that fail to meet minimum standards of performance. If business does not heed these social value preferences, it will lose the public's confidence. Here was a direct indictment of the central values on which business decisions were based.

Meanwhile, others were working to clarify the values at work inside the corporation and particularly inside the minds of corporate managers. George England's pioneer research revealed the pragmatic inclinations of managers and their tendency to emphasize those values that promoted the interests of their companies. Subsequent studies by Barry Posner demonstrated the somewhat uniform clusters of values that impel managers in their decision making, as well as the unique influence that might be exerted by the values embedded in the cultures of "excellent" companies. These researchers were not openly critical of managers' values or behavior, but their findings tended to show that managers' on-the-job values could channel corporate decisions toward company goals without full consideration of the needs and values of other groups in society.

The Ethical Component of CSR3

Ethics is as important as values in making judgments about corporate behavior. Corporations are regularly accused of acting unethically and are occasionally even praised for making ethical decisions. If these kinds of ethical judgments are to be made, then one needs a clear idea of just what is meant by ethics. What does it mean to say that a corporation or its managers have acted unethically? When does an action become ethical? And what factors are most likely to encourage unethical behavior by people in the business world?

The answers to these questions have come largely from a number of professional philosophers, including Richard DeGeorge, Tom Beauchamp, Norman Bowie, Thomas Donaldson, Patricia Werhane, Kenneth Goodpaster, and Manuel Velasquez. From the mid-1960s to the mid-1980s, these philosophers began to apply their theories of ethics to the business scene. They found that most business decision makers relied almost completely on *utilitarian* ethics. This meant that they justified their actions by judging whether the economic benefits outweighed the economic costs. A business firm that is successful in an economic sense is one that has made a whole series of such decisions. The end result is a surplus of benefits over costs—a profit.

While this kind of ethical reasoning is a normal part of a private business system, it did not satisfy the applied philosophers. They pointed out that two other modes of ethical reasoning are possible and desirable. One emphasizes the rights of individuals and groups in society. In order to be considered ethical, a decision must recognize and respect the rights of other persons and groups to life, freedom, participation, development, security, and other conditions essential to human life. These rights must be protected and preserved, even if it becomes very costly to do so—even if the costs outweigh the benefits. The rights of the weakest members of society, even if they are not organized to protect those rights, are as important as those of the strongest in society who know and can defend their rights. It is the ethical responsibility of business decision makers to respect basic human rights, regardless of the costs they may have to incur in doing so.

The applied philosophers also thought that business decision making would be improved ethically if managers would consider social justice when preparing policies or corporate actions. This involves questions of how the benefits and burdens in any given society are distributed throughout the population. Since income and wealth are unevenly distributed in most societies, many people and various groups suffer lower standards of living and have fewer opportunities than others at the top of society's income pyramid. Philosophers wonder whether this kind of unevenness is fair; they insist that the reasons for inequality be fully explained and defended on rational and logical grounds. The demands of racial minorities, women, and others who suffer discrimination are largely demands for social justice, that is, an insistence that they not bear an unfair share of life's burdens while others take most of the benefits.

The ethical duty of corporate managers, therefore, is to draw on all three modes of ethical reasoning—utilitarianism, human rights, and social justice—in establishing a company's policies and in making decisions that affect others in society. To limit oneself to traditional cost-benefit analysis may result in overlooking the rights of some persons or may give insufficient attention to social justice. For example, closing a plant because it is not as profitable as a company would like (utilitarian reasoning) may jeopardize employees' rights to jobs or pensions (rights reasoning) or may put too much of the burden on the local community and not enough on the company (justice reasoning).

Making decisions from this broader ethical perspective would infuse a sense of moral goodness into corporate affairs that is often lacking or underemphasized. It would increase the likelihood that companies would act with rectitude, that they would show greater respect for others in society, that the values they promote would be more nearly consonant with those of their major social stakeholders. This focus on rectitude—on a pervasive sense of rightness, respect, and humanity—distinguishes this approach to the corporation-society relationship from its predecessors, CSR1 and CSR2. Here, values and ethical considerations are put at the center of a company's concerns, its policies, and its major decisions. This value-centered corporate focus is the essential meaning of CSR3 thinking.

In viewing the social performance of corporations, society looks for more than mere responsibility and more than mere responsiveness. Society wants corporations to act with rectitude, to refer their policies and plans to the most fundamental moral principles of humankind. The phrase *corporate social rectitude* captures and preserves this normative perspective on corporate social performance.

CSR3's Unfinished Task

CSR3's two streams of thought—one focusing on values and the other on ethics— one developed by management scholars and the other by philosophers—have developed in parallel fashion. They have not intersected one another to any significant extent. Both have been critical of corporate social performance but for different reasons. Ethicians are openly critical of business for basing so many of its decisions on utilitarian grounds. However, value theorists say that corporate officials often pay too much attention to the needs, goals, and values of their organizations while ignoring social needs and values. The approaches, the literature base, and the attitudes of the two groups are not the same. For the most part, they belong to different professional associations, have different research interests, read different professional journals, and rarely see one another (even if on the same campus).

In spite of these differences, CSR3 scholars are united in one fundamental way: they are trying to find and establish systematic ways to make normative (that is, ethical or value) judgments about business's social performance. In this respect, they resemble some of the earlier but unsuccessful efforts of CSR1 theorists to identify broad moral principles that would justify the demands of society for corporate social responsibility. If the ethics theories of the philosophers and the value theories of the management scholars could be joined together, the long search for a moral basis of corporate social performance might be brought much closer to its goal. Then one might be better able to define corporate social responsibility in specific, substantive terms by referring business behavior to a set of ethical and value criteria that would protect, preserve, and promote humane social needs and practices. That is the major unfinished task for this latest phase of thinking about the relation of corporation and society.

However, to reach that goal—to develop what might be called a *generic theory of corporate social responsibility*—will require going beyond the present perspectives and methods of the ethicians and the students of management values. The latter group are too immersed in the values and practices of corporate culture, and they tend to be too defensive of its core values. The philosopher-ethicians, however, are too far removed from the managerial scene, too biased against the materialistic values at work there, and too burdened with their own intellectual and philosophical traditions. Neither group is likely to generate the needed concepts or analytical insights that could move theory to a desired level. Both groups have done enough; both have advanced the business and society field beyond where it was during an earlier time; both can be proud of their work. It remains now for others to build on their accomplishments and to carry inquiry into yet another phase of thinking about the corporation and society.

The Future of Business and Society Theory and Practice

The future directions of business and society thought should be very carefully charted by everyone who wishes to bring greater clarity to this important sphere of business's operations. The theoretical gains that have been made so far—those embodied in CSR1, CSR2, and CSR3—should be preserved but not enshrined, valued but not worshipped, recognized as analytic tools rather than everlasting truths.

Exploratory Steps for Scholarly Inquiry

Explore links between the scientific-technological process and human values. Past studies of this relationship have emphasized the negative effect science and technology exert on values. A closer look may reveal that positive human values lie at the root of all scientific and technological endeavors. In that case, the continued advance of science and technology could be seen as the source of many of society's new value yearnings, as well as providing some of the means by which those value expressions can be made whole within the human community.

Use the concept of corporate culture to reveal the kinds of values embedded in business practices, decisions, and policies. Values are more than the mere personal preferences of their individual human carriers, because values are phenomena learned from one's social and cultural heritage. The values present in any single company's culture tend to outlast the individuals who express them at any given time. These values have a continued life that becomes an important part of the company's traditions and customs. It is this embedded pattern of lasting values that often provides individual company managers with their decision-making orientation and inclination. The key to the value judgments made by business managers may well be found in a company's culture rather than in the psyches of individual managers.

Become familiar with the literature of moral reasoning and adapt it for use within the corporation. Individuals learn notions of morality in progressive stages as they mature physically and socially. A knowledge of this process and how it can affect the ability of corporate managers to reason their way through a moral dilemma can be a powerful analytic aid in understanding how and why certain value judgments are made within the business system.

Reexamine the concept of utilitarian ethical reasoning, particularly its relation to the instrumental logic that undergirds scientific and technological processes. Business usage of utilitarian reasoning is typically limited to calculations based on monetary measurements, and for this reason it frequently falls woefully short of capturing all of the important qualities that should enter into human value judgments. But utilitarian reasoning holds more promise than this somewhat cramped version permits. The utilitarian's insistence on considering the consequences —good and bad—that flow from a contemplated action or decision is closely akin to the scientist's need to examine all possible factors that may explain a given phenomenon or relationship. Whereas the former may be freighted with normative meaning and the latter may seem to be merely descriptive, the logic of linking means and ends to one another in a consequential way underlies both processes. For this reason, utilitarian reasoning may not deserve the negative press it has been given by the philosopher-critics of business. It may, on the contrary, be an essential mode of reasoning, not just in business, but in human affairs generally.

Demystify the concept of human rights by seeing these rights less as absolutist claims and more as human needs that help define an organized, humanely intelligent community life. Absolutist claims of any sort tend to be at odds with the realities of life in a risky, constantly changing world. Subjecting business decision makers (or any other institutional leaders) to strict, unbending, absolutist rules may be less serviceable for meeting important human needs than a more flexible approach that applies maximum human intelligence and judgment to each situation as it arises. This is not a plea for a situational ethics that recognizes no general or lasting standards of value. Rather, it is an invitation to view human rights as created objects of culture that are subject to the same discipline of intelligent reasoning as other aspects of our lives.

Define social justice as the recognition of instrumentally legitimate claims of social groups to share in the bounty created by society, as well as a need to shoulder some of the unavoidable burdens and risks that arise. The intention here is to avoid linking the idea of social justice to a social class system based on power, privilege, and prestige. Questions of justice can and should be couched as questions of intelligent participation and involvement in life's benefits and burdens, without invoking social class status to bolster one's claims or to reject another groups' claims. Justice has more to do with social involvement than with social status.

Practical Steps for Corporate Managers

It is important that management theory contribute to the work of managers. That is its ultimate justification. To achieve this goal, managers and scholars need to communicate with each other, to try to understand the work each does, and to offer candid judgments about how meaningful the efforts of the one are to the other. If managers are to benefit from what has been learned by management scholars during eight decades of thinking and writing about the business and society relationship, they might consider taking the following actions. Doing so would bring their companies closer to being the kind of organization society wants business to be.

Adopt a strategy of social response and of ethical action whose purpose would be to improve a company's ability to cope with social demands and ethical problems. Central to this strategy is an understanding of the dominant values of the company's culture and how they are related to competing social values.

Study the ethics awareness programs and the social response strategies of other companies. Some of these firms have been remarkably successful, not just in weathering an immediate ethics crisis, but in sensitizing their managers and employees to the ongoing importance of ethical and social factors in day-to-day decision making. Those lessons can be adapted to the special needs and characteristics of any company.

Establish an ethics outreach activity that brings the company into direct contact with some of the toughest ethics challenges of the day. These include plant closings, shifting production to foreign nations, on-the-job drug usage, operating in nations with repressive regimes, and other complex ethics puzzles. Hiding or running away from such issues will only postpone the time when they must be faced.

Listen to philosopher-ethicists who have been wrestling with ethics issues that arise in business. Their theories, concepts, and research are not a bottomless pit of vague abstractions. They are rather a source of analytic tools that can cut to the core of many ethical dilemmas faced by business managers every day.

Listen to management scholars in business schools who are working to convert social and ethical theories into managerially meaningful guides to action and decision. Much has been learned about corporate social responsibility, corporate social responsiveness, and corporate social rectitude—what they mean, their limits, and their possibilities. This knowledge could be added to the data base on which managers depend as they make decisions and establish policies for their companies.

The concerted efforts of academicians and management practitioners will be needed to drive theory and practice in desired and necessary directions. Doing so will carry immense rewards for both groups—and for society as a whole—for it will aid the business corporation in responding to humane needs and essential social values.

Bibliography

Corporate Social Responsibility

Bowen, Howard R. *Social Responsibilities of the Businessman* (New York: Harper, 1953).
Committee for Economic Development. *Social Responsibilities of Business Corporations* (New York: Committee for Economic Development, 1971).
Friedman, Milton. "The Social Responsibility of Business Is to Increase Its Profits," *New York Times Magazine*, September 13, 1970, pp. 33, 122–126.

Corporate Social Responsiveness

Ackerman, Robert W., and Raymond A. Bauer. *Corporate Social Responsiveness: The Modern Dilemma* (Reston, Va.: Reston, 1976).
Buchholz, Rogene A. *Essentials of Public Policy for Management* (Englewood Cliffs, N.J.: Prentice-Hall, 1985).
Epstein, Edwin M. *The Corporation in American Politics* (Englewood Cliffs, N.J.: Prentice-Hall, 1969).
Freeman, R. Edward. *Strategic Management: A Stakeholder Approach* (Boston: Pitman, 1984).
Preston, Lee E., and James E. Post. *Private Management and Public Policy: The Principle of Public Responsibility* (Englewood Cliffs, N.J.: Prentice-Hall, 1975).

Corporate Social Rectitude

Cavanagh, Gerald F. *American Business Values* (Englewood Cliffs, N.J.: Prentice-Hall, 1984).
Donaldson, Thomas. *Corporations and Morality* (Englewood Cliffs, N.J.: Prentice-Hall, 1974).
Elbing, Alvar O., and Carol J. Elbing. *The Value Issue of Business* (New York: McGraw-Hill, 1967).
Post, James E. *Corporate Behavior and Social Change* (Reston, Va.: Reston, 1978).
Sethi, S. Prakash. *Up Against the Corporate Wall*, 4th ed. (Englewood Cliffs, N.J.: Prentice-Hall, 1982).
Velasquez, Manual. *Business Ethics: Concepts and Cases* (Englewood Cliffs, N.J.: Prentice-Hall, 1982.)

The Structure of Business and Corporate Responsibility

Ian Maitland

Self-regulation by business is often invoked as an alternative to more big government, but it has never lived up to its promise. This article argues that the undersupply of business self-regulation is explained by the fact that its benefits typically take the form of public goods. It is notorious that public goods, because they are vulnerable to free-rider problems, are inefficiently supplied by the market. Ironically, then, the principal means that we rely on to regulate business—the market—undercuts business's capacity for self-regulation in cases of market failure. The extreme fragmentation of business in the United States and the barriers we have placed in the way of interfirm collective action have left us heavily dependent on government to regulate market failures. In other societies, collective action by business, typically administered by a peak organization, has limited the role of government.

The Case for Business Self-Regulation

The lasting appeal of the concept of business self-regulation is not hard to understand. In a liberal democracy, there are limits to the extent to which socially responsible behavior can be ordered by law. Beyond a certain point, the costs of expanding the apparatus of state control become prohibitive—in terms of abridged liberties, a swollen bureaucracy, and sheer inefficiency. It follows that we would all be better off if corporate behavior could be regulated by the promptings of a corporate conscience rather than by the heavy hand of government regulation.

To its advocates, the virtues of self-regulation, or corporate social responsibility, are self-evident. These virtues promise simultaneously to allay business fears of further government encroachment and to restore the public's faith in business. What is more, they ask of business only that it behave in its own enlightened self-interest. Although this entails a radical break in the way the manager has conceived of his or her role, it does not make any impossible or self-contradictory demands that an imaginative manager cannot adapt to. In any case, the new awareness of the fragility of the physical environment, the quantum leap in power in the hands of large corporations, a new American ideology, and so forth all demand no less.

The period from the mid-1950s to the mid-1970s saw a stream of proposals for the moral reconstruction of the corporation. The principal obstacle for self-regulation was diagnosed as managers' single-minded preoccupation with profit maximization. This, in turn, was attributed to intellectual shortcomings—managers' insularity, their failure to keep up with changing values, their inability to see their role in a system-wide perspective—and to managers' attachment to an outmoded ideology, which defined the public interest as the unintended outcome of the pursuit of selfish interests. Also implicated were the organizational structure and culture of the modern corporation that supposedly embodied and perpetuated this orientation to profit. Thus, the advocates of self-regulation saw their task as proselytizing and scolding managers into a broader definition of the management role and drawing up blueprints for the socially responsible corporation.

This most recent wave of enthusiasm for self-regulation has largely receded, leaving behind few enduring achievements. The exhortations appear to have fallen on deaf ears, or at best to have had a marginal impact on corporate conduct. The primacy of profit maximization remains unchallenged and we continue to rely—and will do so for the foreseeable future—on legal compulsion administered by the state to regulate the undesirable consequences of economic activity.

This article argues that responsible corporate conduct cannot simply be willed or exhorted into existence by appeals to the public interest or to firms' enlightened self-interest. It depends on the creation of institutional conditions under which business can behave responsibly as a matter of self-interest. In the United States such conditions are conspicuously lacking. The next section employs a prisoner's dilemma model to explore the very real constraints that the operation of a market economy imposes on managers' ability to consider noneconomic values or objectives.

A Prisoner's Dilemma Model of Corporate Irresponsibility

An individual firm's interests as a competitor in the marketplace often diverge from the same firm's interests as a part of the wider society (or, for that matter, as a part of the business community). In the latter role the firm is likely to welcome a cleaner environment, but in its role as a competitor in the marketplace it has an interest in minimizing its own pollution abatement costs. It may philosophically favor a free market, but it will probably lobby in favor of protection for itself.

The firm's interests as part of a broader group typically take the form of collective or public goods. Using a rational choice model of behavior, Mancur Olson has demonstrated that it is not in the interest of a group member (let us say, the firm) to contribute to the costs of providing such goods.[1] Public goods—for example, a clean environment or a free market—are goods that are available to all firms regardless of whether they have contributed to their upkeep or refrained from abusing them. Since the availability of public goods is not contingent on a firm having contributed, each firm has a rational incentive to free-ride, that is, to leave the costs of providing public goods to other firms. But, of course, if each firm succumbs to this temptation, as it must if it acts in its own rational self-interest, then the public goods will not be provided at all. Thus, even when they are in agreement, "rational, self-interested individuals will not act to achieve their common or group interests."[2] In a rational world, Olson concludes, "It is certain that a collective good will *not* be provided unless there is coercion or some outside inducement."[3]

The typical objectives of business self-regulation and responsible corporate behavior are public goods. Olson's theory, therefore, provides a basis for explaining why business self-regulation appears so hard to achieve. As Russell Hardin has pointed out, the logic underlying Olson's theory of collective action is identical to that of an *n*-person prisoner's dilemma (PD).[4] The strategy of not contributing toward the cost of a public good dominates the strategy of paying for it, in the sense that no matter what other firms do, any particular firm will be better off if it does not contribute.

Both Olson's theory and the PD have been criticized on the grounds that their assumptions regarding human motivations (that is, that they are invariably rational and self-interested) are unduly strict. But even under a modified version of the PD, which relaxes these harsh motivational assumptions, an undersupply of business self-regulation is still to be expected: Runge has argued that what appear on the face to be PDs on closer inspection reveal themselves to be "assurance problems" (APs).[5] According to the AP, the group member—that is, the firm—does not withhold its contribution to a public good based on a rational calculation of the costs and benefits involved (as with the PD), but rather does so because it is unable to obtain the necessary assurance that other firms will contribute their fair share. The AP substitutes the more lenient assumption that firms prefer equal or fair shares for the PD's assumption that they invariably try to maximize their individual net gain. Under the AP, we can expect firms to regulate their own behavior in some larger interest so long as they are confident that other firms are doing the same.

But in a market economy, because decision making is highly dispersed, the prediction of other firms' behavior becomes problematic. As a consequence, an individual firm cannot be sure whether it is placing itself at a competitive disadvantage by unwittingly interpreting its own obligations more strictly than its competitors are doing. In these circumstances, all firms are likely to undertake less self-regulation than they would in principle be willing to accept.

In spite of their differences, both the PD and the AP involve problems of collective action. In the case of the PD, it is always in the rational interest of each firm to put its own individual interests ahead of its collective interests. In the case of the AP, coordinating firms' expectations regarding fair shares is a concern. Accordingly, the suboptimal supply of business self-regulation can be explained largely in terms of the barriers to collective action by firms.

Approaches to Self-Regulation

There are three levels of self-regulation: the firm level (corporate social responsibility); the industry level (industry self-regulation); and at the economy level (business self-regulation). Only at the third level is the necessary collective action likely to be of a socially benign variety.

Corporate Social Responsibility

Contemporary advocates of corporate social responsibility acknowledge the difficulties implementing it, but they go on to proclaim the inevitability of corporate responsibility. Advocates say it has to work because nothing else will. At best, the law elicits grudging and literal compliance with certain minimal standards when what is needed is corporations' spontaneous and whole-hearted identification with the goals of the law.[6] As Christopher Stone says, there are clear advantages to "encouraging people to act in socially responsible ways because they believe it the 'right thing' to do, rather than because (and thus, perhaps, only to the extent that) they are ordered to do so."[7]

Advocates of social responsibility have offered a number of prescriptions for the moral reconstruction of the corporation, including overhauling firms' financial reporting systems, requiring greater disclosure, strengthening protections for whistle-blowers, instituting corporate social audits, increasing shareholder democracy, reforming the board of directors, mandating public directors, and so on. One critic has argued that nothing short of the divestiture of divisionalized corporations will suffice to make them responsive to the communities in which they operate.[8] But these proposals exaggerate the extent to which corporate responsibility can be produced by manipulating the corporation while leaving the context in which it operates unchanged.

The irony is that corporate irresponsibility is largely a product of our own making. The principal means we (the people) rely on to regulate corporate conduct in the public interest—namely the competitive market—undercuts the ability of firms to regulate themselves in cases of market failure. In effect, we have sought to make the logic of the prisoner's dilemma work for us (much as the district attorney does in the paradigmatic case of the PD).[9] We have isolated firms from one another so that they cannot coordinate their behavior to our detriment. Although we have been successful in creating truly competitive markets, we have limited firms' capacity to take into consideration anything but profits. And by placing obstacles in the way of cooperation between firms, we have also impeded their ability to coordinate their behavior in the public interest.

The decentralized structure of the United States economy makes the provision of any public goods problematic. The point is not just that firms find it difficult to act in the public interest; they find it just as difficult to act in the interests of their industry or of the business community. James Q. Wilson has described that, lacking any enforcement authority, trade associations have been beset with free-rider problems.[10] Trade association attempts to restrain price competition have been frustrated by the absence of "sanctions with which to ensure that collective benefits would override individual rationality" (p. 149). Wilson concludes that "business associations have on the whole been . . . least successful when they have had to rely on voluntary agreements" (p. 151).

This point is also illustrated by cases where competitive pressures have prevented firms from acting responsibly even when it would be in their economic interest to do so. Robert Leone has described how aerosol spray manufacturers were reluctant to abandon the use of fluorocarbon propellants (which were suspected of depleting the ozone layer in the stratosphere) even though the alternative technology was cheaper. The problem was that "any individual company that voluntarily abandoned the use of such propellants ran the risk of a sizeable loss of market share as long as competitors still offered aerosol versions of their products [which the public valued for convenience]."[11] In situations of this kind it is not unusual for responsible firms, aware of their own helplessness, to solicit regulation in order to prevent themselves from being taken advantage of by competitors who do not share their scruples about spoiling the environment or injuring the industry's reputation. Thus, aerosol manufacturers did not oppose the ban on fluorocarbons in spite of the tenuous scientific evidence of their dangers.

Similarly, following the Tylenol poisonings, the pharmaceutical industry sought and obtained from the Food and Drug Administration (FDA) a uniform national rule on tamper-resistant packaging. Prior to that, firms had not wanted to risk exposure to sabotage, but no individual firm wanted unilaterally to incur the expense of tamper-resistant packaging.[12] In the 1930s, the Pharmaceutical Manufacturers Association endorsed FDA regulation of drug advertising after one firm had dishonestly attacked the reliability of a competitor's products.[13] This list of examples could be extended almost indefinitely.

In a market economy, firms are usually unable to act in their own collective interests because responsible conduct risks placing themselves at a competitive disadvantage unless other firms follow suit. Where there is no well-defined standard that enjoys general acceptance, it will take some sort of tacit or overt coordination by firms to supply one. Even if that coordination survives the scrutiny of the Antitrust Division and the Federal Trade Commission (FTC), compliance will be problematic because of the free-rider problem. Arrow has pointed out that a "code [of behavior] may be of value to . . . all firms if all firms maintain it, and yet it will be to the advantage of any one firm to cheat—in fact the more so, the more other firms are sticking to it."[14] The paradox results that the voluntary compliance of the majority of firms may depend on the coercive imposition of the code of behavior on the minority of free-riders. Thus, although it is fashionable to view voluntarism and coercion as opposites—and to prefer the former for being more humane and, ultimately, effective—they are more properly seen as interdependent.[15]

Industry Self-Regulation

Responsible corporate conduct must ultimately be backed by coercion. This raises the question of who is to administer the coercion. Is self-regulation by a trade association or other industry body a practical alternative to government regulation? The classic solution to the public-goods dilemma is "mutual coercion, mutually agreed upon."[16] The possibility of "permitting businesses to coerce themselves" has been raised by Thomas Schelling who notes "the appeal of such an approach to firms which are prepared to incur costs but only on condition that their competitors do also."[17] Murray Weidenbaum has proposed that trade associations become the moral conscience of the business community.[18]

Industry self-regulation in the United States has, in fact, commonly risen in response to the public-goods problem. David A. Garvin explains the development of self-regulation in the advertising industry in this way.[19] Michael Porter has noted that self-regulation may be of particular importance to an emerging industry that is trying to secure consumer acceptance of its products. At this stage of its life cycle, an industry's reputation could be irretrievably injured by the actions of a single producer.[20] Thus, the intense self-regulation in the microwave industry is understandable in terms of the industry's need to "overcome the inherent suspicion with which many people view 'new' technology like microwave ovens."[21]

Nevertheless, industry self-regulation remains the exception in the United States. This is so because it is a two-edged sword: the powers to prevent trade abuses are the same powers that would be needed to restrain trade. Apart from the obvious cases like restrictions on entry (into an industry or occupation) and cooperative price-setting, even some of the apparently innocuous examples reviewed by Garvin had antisocial consequences. Bans on advertising have resulted in higher prices, and voluntary product standards have limited the range of product types that firms offer, thus making it easier to monitor and detect competitive moves.[22] According to Thomas Grumbly, quality grading of oranges and tomatoes in California has restricted competition.[23]

Because of the potential anticompetitive implications of industry self-regulation, its scope has been strictly limited. Antitrust laws have significantly circumscribed the powers of trade associations. Legal decisions have proscribed industrywide attempts to eliminate inferior products or impose ethical codes of conduct.[24] Major oil firms were frustrated by the antitrust statutes when they tried to establish an information system to rate the quality of oil tankers in an attempt to reduce the incidence of oil spills from substandard vessels.[25] Airlines have had to petition the Civil Aeronautics Board for antitrust immunity so that they could discuss ways of coordinating their schedules in order to reduce peak-hour overcrowding at major airports.[26]

In short, industry or trade associations appear to hold out little promise of being transformed into vehicles for industry self-regulation. The fear is too entrenched that industry self-regulation, however plausible its initial rationale, will eventually degenerate into industry protectionism.

Business Self-Regulation

If self-regulation at the level of the individual firm is of limited usefulness because of the free-rider problem, and if industry self-regulation is ruled out by antitrust considerations, we are left with self-regulation on a business-wide basis, presumably administered by a confederation or peak organization. An encompassing business organization of this sort would be less vulnerable to the antitrust objections that can be leveled at industry associations. This is so because the diversity of its membership would inhibit such an organization from aligning itself with the sectional interests of particular firms or industries. Because it would embrace, for example, both producers and consumers of steel, it would be unable to support policies specifically favoring the steel industry (a cartel, tariffs, and so forth) without antagonizing other parts of its membership that would be injured by such policies. A business-peak organization would thus be constrained to adopt a procompetitive posture.[27]

How might a peak organization contribute to resolving the assurance problem and the prisoner's dilemma? In the case of the AP, we saw that the principal impediment to cooperation is imperfect information. Obviously coordination is impossible if others' behavior cannot be predicted. By defining a code of responsible corporate conduct—and/or making authoritative rulings in particular cases—a peak organization might substantially alleviate this difficulty. Especially if it were equipped to monitor compliance with the code, it could provide cooperating firms with the necessary assurance that they were not shouldering an unfair burden.

The point here is not that a peak organization would necessarily be more competent to make ethical judgments or that its code would be ethically superior; it is that the code would be a common one that would enable firms to coordinate their behavior. As we have seen, where there is a multiplicity of standards, there is effectivley no standard at all, because no firm can be confident that its competitors are playing by the same rules.

So far we have assumed that each firm wants to cooperate (that is, to contribute to the realization of the public good, in this case by acting responsibly) provided other firms do the same. As long as there is some means of coordinating their behavior, then firms can be counted on to cooperate. What happens if we allow for the likelihood that, while most firms may be disposed to comply with the code, some number of opportunistic firms will choose to defect? A code of conduct—even if only morally binding—may exert considerable pressures on would-be defectors. Such a code embodies good practice and so serves as a standard against which behavior can be judged in individual cases. Consequently, firms that violate the code are isolated and the spotlight of public indignation may be turned on them.

All the same, minus coercion, codes of conduct are inherently unstable. The defection of even a handful of firms would undermine the social contract on which the consent of the majority was based. The majority's continued compliance would be likely to be conditional on the code being effectively policed. Therefore, it seems inconceivable that business self-regulation could be based on moral suasion alone. As John Rawls says,

> Each person's willingness to contribute is contingent upon the contribution of the others. Therefore to maintain public confidence in [a common agreement] that is superior from everyone's point of view, or better anyway than the situation that would obtain in its absence, some device for administrating

fines and penalties must be established. . . . In a well-ordered society the required sanctions are no doubt mild and they may never be applied. Still, the existence of such devices is a normal condition of human life even in this case.[28]

Thus, if we modify the AP to reflect the real-world probability that some number of opportunistic firms will disregard the code, the case for investing the peak organization with some powers of compulsion becomes unanswerable. The case is stronger still if we accept the axiom of the PD that firms will invariably defect when it is in their narrow self-interest to do so. Some form of authority to enforce the terms of the social contract then becomes indispensable.

To summarize, under the original AP a peak organization (or some functional equivalent) is essential to self-regulation because it provides the information that enables firms to coordinate their behavior. Under both the modified AP (in which the heroic assumption that firms universally want to cooperate is abandoned) and the PD, a peak organization is also necessary but must be given teeth in order to secure firms' compliance. Before considering the prospects of such an organization evolving or being created in the American context, we must address the objections that (1) such a formidable concentration of power would be as likely to be used in an irresponsible manner as a responsible one, and (2) a powerful peak organization would weaken representative democracy. Since no true peak organizations exist in the United States, these questions are best answered in the light of the experience of other countries.

The Behavior of Peak Organizations

Peak, or encompassing, organizations are not merely larger special-interest organizations; by virtue of the breadth and heterogeneity of their membership, they are transformed into a qualitatively different phenomenon. Indeed, peak organizations are likely to exert pressure on the behavior of their members in the direction of the public interest.

In the interests of its own stability, any organization must resist efforts by parts of its membership to obtain private benefits at the expense of other parts. It follows that the more inclusive or encompassing the organization, the larger the fraction of society it represents, and so the higher the probability that it will oppose self-serving behavior by sections of its membership that inflict external costs on the rest of society. Its own size means that it must internalize many of the resulting external costs. The costs of pollution or workplace injuries, for example, are not just borne by some undifferentiated public or society, but by other managers, stockholders, workers, and so forth. Thus, according to Mancur Olson, encompassing organizations are less likely than narrow-based ones to further the economic interests of their members in ways that reduce overall levels of social income and wealth.[29]

> The incentives facing an encompassing . . . organization are dramatically different from those facing an organization that represents only a narrow segment of society. . . . The members of the highly encompassing organization own so much of the society that they have an important incentive to be actively concerned about how productive it is. . . . The [encompassing] organization has not only an incentive to at least consider the effect of its policies on the efficiency of the society, but also an incentive to bargain with other substantial organized groups in the interests of a more productive society. The really narrow special-interest group usually does not have an incentive to do even that.

According to Olson's logic, the existence of a powerful business peak organization should promote convergence between the interests of business and other social groups and so lessen the need for coercive regulation.

This expectation can be tested in a crude fashion by examining the admittedly fragmentary evidence concerning the behavior of peak organizations abroad. The officers of business peak organizations in Germany, Japan, and Sweden have a quasipublic conception of their role that is far removed from the American interest group model. In Germany, according to Andrew Shonfield, the two business *Spitzenverbande* "have typically seen themselves as performing an important public role, as guardians of the long-term interests of the nation's industries."[30] Gerard Baunthal notes that, "To avoid giving an impression that it is an interest group with base, selfish and narrow aims, the BDI [Confederation of German Industry] constantly identifies its own goals with those of the entire nation."[31] And, David Bresnick has examined the role of the national confederation of employers and trade unions of six countries in the formation and implementation of youth employment policies. In Germany, these policies were largely made and administered by the confederations themselves. Bresnick says,

> The system in Germany has evolved with minimal government regulation and maximum protection of the interests of the young, while promoting the interests of the corporations, trade unions and the society in general. It has reduced the government role to one of occasional intervenor. It has taken the government out of the business of tax collector and achieved a degree of social compliance that is extraordinary.[32]

A similar account is given by Ezra Vogel concerning the role of the Japanese business peak organization, *Keidanren*.[33] Keidanren concentrates on issues of interest to the business community as a whole and "cannot be partial to any single group or any industrial sector" (p. 114). Vogel reports that Japanese business leaders are surprised at "the extent to which American businessmen thought only of their own company and were unprepared to consider business problems from a broader perspective" (p. 115). In Japan, "This higher level of aggregation of interests within the business community tends to ensure that the highest level politicians also think in comparably broad terms" (p. 116).

Perhaps the fullest account of the role played by a peak organization in the regulatory process is to be found in Steven Kelman's comparative case study of occupational safety and health rule making in Sweden and the United States.[34] Remarkably, Kelman found that the content of the regulations in the two countries was rather similar and in both cases tended to favor more protective alternatives over less protective ones. But the resemblances ended there. According to Kelman:

The regulations were fought persistently in the United States but accepted meekly in Sweden.

Occupational Safety and Health Administration was bound by a detailed set of procedural requirements while ASV (its Swedish counterpart) was bound by virtually none.

Occupational Safety and Health Administration adopted a far more punitive approach to compliance than ASV did.

Lawyers and courts were pervasively involved in both rule making and compliance in the United States and virtually uninvolved in Sweden.

In short, American business got a set of regulations just as strict as the Swedish ones, and after a rancorous and costly rule-making process. The American regulations were then administered in a more coercive, inflexible, and adversarial spirit. In his introduction to Kelman's study, James Q. Wilson notes the irony that social democratic Sweden showed

a willingness to accommodate business views, an inclination to make policy behind closed doors, and a readiness to accept business assurances of compliance that, if they occurred in this country, would bring forth immediate charges of collusive behavior and irresistible demands for congressional investigations.[35]

A key factor in the ability of business and government in Sweden to reach agreement on health and safety standards was the dominant role played by SAF—the Swedish employers' federation. SAF enjoyed a virtual monopoly on the representation of business's interests in the rule-making process. On the rare occasions when individual firms or industry associations participated, the likelihood of agreement being reached decreased markedly.[36]

In conclusion, while the data reported here—on Swedish, German, and Japanese peak organizations—are too unsystematic to constitute a strict test of my hypotheses concerning the behavior of peak organizations, they do shed a revealing light on the role that such organizations might play in the United States. In administering a system of self-regulation, a peak organization would be in a position to take into account a broader range of interests than is catered for by our present structures of interest representation. A peak organization might promote more harmonious business-government relations without entailing the cooptation or capture of one by the other.

The Prospects for Business Self-Regulation

What are the prospects for a system of self-regulation, administered by a business peak organization, taking root in U.S. soil? In the United States, peak organizations are notoriously weak. The dilemma faced by a peak organization—indeed by any voluntary association—is the problem of collective action identified earlier. A peak organization exists to represent the common interests of a sector of society, in this case, the business community. But it is precisely these interests that are most vulnerable to the free-rider problem. That is, each firm has an incentive to leave other firms to pay the costs of maintaining an organization that works for their common interests. James Q. Wilson has examined the history of business associations in the United States and has found that while "some trade associations did emerge out of a common recognition of the gains that will accrue to combined efforts . . . [all] suffered from the problem of the 'free-rider.' "[37] Wilson notes that the free-rider problem is especially severe in the case of peak organizations, because "no single businessman has an incentive to contribute to the attainment of what all would receive if the organized political efforts are successful."[38] In these circumstances, he goes on, "the creation and maintenance of an association such as the [U.S.] Chamber, which seeks to represent all business in general and no business in particular, has been a considerable achievement."[39]

If obtaining adequate financial support from the business community is problematic, then imagine how much more difficult it would be for a peak organization to try to impose its standards and rulings on autonomous firms. If it is to overcome the free-rider problem, the peak organization would need to have at its disposal private benefits or selective incentives unavailable outside the organization that are sufficiently attractive to induce firms to comply.[40]

Selective Incentives

What incentives might a hypothetical business peak organization use in order to secure firms' compliance with its code of conduct? Students of business associations have identified an array of incentives—or sanctions—that are commonly used to attract and hold members. These include selective access to information under the association's control (about government actions, technical developments, commercial practices), regulation of jurisdictional disputes between members, and predatory price (cutting, boycotts, withdrawal of credit, public disparagement, fines, social status, and conviviality). Purposive incentives—"intangible rewards that derive from the sense of satisfaction of having contributed to the attainment of a worthwhile cause"—have provided at least a transient basis for organization. But, in the absence of major external threats, associations relying on such incentives have typically recruited only a fraction of their potential members.[41]

For the most part, associations have found these incentives to be of limited usefulness in influencing members' behavior. Wilson says of the cotton industry in the early 1900s that "[t]hough it was in the interest of the industry as a whole to have a uniformly high price level, it was to the advantage of each individual firm to undercut that level, and the association had no sanctions with which to ensure that collective benefits would override individual rationality."[42] The use of some incentives was ruled out by antitrust considerations; other incentives involved services that firms could just as easily obtain through the market; and still other incentives were used sparingly because of the fear that they would create bitterness and distrust within the organization.

The difficulties encountered by trade associations that have tried to influence their members' behavior are compounded in the case of a would-be peak organization. A peak organization has access to fewer selective benefits with which to maintain members' allegiance, and its goals are even further removed from the immediate concerns of most firms. As we have seen, these goals tend to be public goods, and so the resulting benefits cannot be withheld from firms that do not pay their way.

A Corporatist Solution

In the United States, interfirm collective action—associations, cartels, collusions—has proved highly unstable. Firms have been far more successful at achieving common goals when they have enlisted government to administer and police their agreements for them. As Wilson remarks, "Business associations have on the whole been far more effective when they have tried to reach their objectives through obtaining favorable legislation and least successful when they have had to rely on voluntary agreements."[43]

If trade associations have generally been ineffective except when their authority has been underwritten by the government, it follows that a peak organization is *a fortiori* likely to be dependent on government support. And, in fact, in Western Europe, "many of the peak associations . . . reached their hegemonic status with major contributions from the more or less official recognition of key government agencies."[44]

What form would such public support have to take in the United States? Public support might involve waiving antitrust laws in the case of the peak organization, for example, by permitting the organization to punish free-riding behavior by imposing fines or administering boycotts; or, alternatively, government might grant the organization certain prerogatives, for example, privileged access to key policy deliberations or agency rule making. The organization might use these prerogatives to obtain leverage over recalcitrant firms; or the government might require, as in Japan,[45] that every firm be a registered member of the peak organization. All these actions would serve to strengthen the peak organization vis-à-vis its members.

However, the prospects of a corporatist solution along these lines being adopted in the United States are very slight. In the first place, as Salisbury says, "American political culture is so rooted in individualist assumptions that [interest] groups have no integral place."[46] In contrast with Europe, associations have not been officially incorporated into the process of policy formation; bureaucrats in the United States deal directly with constituent units—individual firms, hospitals, universities—not with associations. Given the dubious legitimacy of interest organizations in general, it seems improbable that semi-official status or privileged access would be granted to a peak organization.

A second obstacle is the structure of U.S. government. The fragmentation of power in the U.S. system—federalism, separation of powers, legislators nominated and elected from single-member districts—has created multiple points of access for interests that want to influence the policy process. Wilson has persuasively argued that a country's interest group structure is largely a reflection of its political structure. Thus a centralized, executive-led government is likely to generate strong national interest associations and, conversely, "the greater decentralization and dispersion of political authority in the United States helps explain the greater variety of politically active American voluntary associations."[47] In the American context, then, it is virtually inconceivable that a peak organization could secure a monopolistic or privileged role in public policy making in even a few key areas; but without superior access of this sort a peak organization is deprived of one of the few resources available to influence its members' behavior.

Conclusion

The thesis advanced in this article is that responsible corporate conduct cannot simply be willed or exhorted into existence by appeals to the public interest or firms' so-called enlightened self-interest. Instead, responsible corporate conduct depends on the creation and maintenance of particular institutional conditions under which business can behave responsibly as a matter of self-interest.

In our atomistic market economy, firms are bound to take a partial or parochial view of their behavior and its consequences. For the most part, their own actions, seen in isolation, have imperceptible impacts for better or for worse on the general welfare. Firms may well deplore the consequences that result when all firms engage in irresponsible actions, but so long as they have no control over other firms' behavior they have no incentive to behave responsibly themselves. In such circumstances, social responsibility is not rational but irrational. The firm that practiced it would be doubly penalized, first by foregoing the benefits of irresponsible behavior, and second by having to share in the decline in general welfare.

Is this dilemma inescapable? This article has outlined a solution that might permit firms to coordinate their behavior in their own larger interests and the public interest while minimizing the risk of abuse in this coordination. Such a benign outcome could be obtained by permitting collective action to be administered by a business-wide peak organization. At this level of coordination, a competitive market economy could coexist with effective self-regulation. However, the United States, given its distinctive political institutions, is likely to be inhospitable to such an arrangement.

Notes

This article is a revised version of "The Limits of Business Self-Regulation," *California Management Review*, **27** (3), Spring 1985.

1. Mancur Olson, *The Logic of Collective Action* (Cambridge, Mass.: Harvard University Press, 1965).
2. Ibid., p. 2.
3. Ibid., p. 44.
4. Russell Hardin, "Collective Action as an Agreeable *n*-Prisoner's Dilemma," *Behavioral Science*, **16**:472–479 (1971).
5. C. Ford Runge, "Institutions and the Free Rider: The Assurance Problem in Collective Action," *Journal of Politics*, **46**:154–181 (1984).
6. Henry Mintzberg, "The Case for Corporate Social Responsibility," *Journal of Business Strategy*, **14**:3–15 (1983).
7. Christopher Stone, *Where the Law Ends* (New York: Harper Torchbooks, 1975), p. 112.
8. Mintzberg, "Corporate Social Responsibility," p. 11.
9. In the prisoner's dilemma, two prisoners are interrogated separately about an armed robbery they are charged with committing. Given the strength of the case against them, each can expect to get one year in jail for fire-arms possession, but only so long as neither confesses. The D.A. offers each of them a deal: if either turns state's evidence against the other, all charges against that person will be dropped, but his partner will be convicted and will face a ten-year sentence. However, if both confess, both will be convicted and will receive reduced sentences of six years each. Plainly, what is in the narrow self-interest of each prisoner (each is better off confessing no matter what his partner does) is in conflict with what is in their collective interest (between them they serve a total of only two years if neither squeals). See Hardin, "Collective Action," p. 2.
10. James Q. Wilson, *Political Organizations* (New York: Basic Books, 1973), chapter 8.
11. Robert A. Leone, "Competition and the Regulatory Boom," in Dorothy Tella, ed., *Government Regulation of Business: Its Growth, Impact, and Future* (Washington, D.C.: Chamber of Commerce of the United States, 1979), p. 34.
12. Susan Bartlett Foote, "Corporate Responsibility in a Changing Legal Environment," *California Management Review*, **26**:217–228 (1984).
13. Paul Quirk, "Food and Drug Administration," in James Q. Wilson, ed., *The Politics of Regulation* (New York: Basic Books, 1980), pp. 191–235.
14. Kenneth J. Arrow, "Social Responsibility and Economic Efficiency," *Public Policy*, **21**:315 (1973).
15. See Thomas Schelling, "Command and Control," in James Q. McKie, ed., *Social Responsibility and the Business Predicament* (Washington, D.C.: Brookings, 1974), p. 103.
16. The phrase is from Garrett Hardin's "The Tragedy of the Commons," *Science*, **162**:1247 (1968).
17. Schelling, "Command and Control," p. 103.
18. Murray Weidenbaum, *The Future of Business Regulation* (New York: Amacon, 1979), p. 110.
19. David Garvin, "Can Industry Self-Regulation Work?" *California Management Review*, **25**:42 (1983).
20. Michael Porter, *Competitive Strategy* (New York: Free Press, 1980), p. 230.

21. Thomas P. Grumbly, "Self-Regulation: Private Vice and Public Virtue Revisited," in Eugene Bardach and Robert Kagan, eds., *Social Regulation: Strategies for Reform* (San Francisco: Institute for Contemporary Studies, 1982), p. 97.

22. Garvin, "Can Industry Self-Regulation Work?" pp. 39–40.

23. Grumbly, "Self-Regulation," p. 98.

24. Garvin, "Can Industry Self-Regulation Work?" p. 155.

25. Ibid., p. 156.

26. Christopher Conte, "Transport Agency's Dole Vows to Restrict Traffic at 6 Busy Airports if Carriers Don't," *Wall Street Journal*, August 16, 1984, p. 10.

27. Mancur Olson, *The Rise and Decline of Nations* (New Haven, Conn.: Yale University Press, 1982), pp. 47–48.

28. John Rawls, *A Theory of Justice* (Cambridge, Mass.: Harvard University Press, 1971), pp. 269, 270.

29. Olson, *Rise and Decline*, pp. 47–48.

30. Andrew Shonfield, *Modern Capitalism* (New York and London: Oxford University Press, 1965), p. 245.

31. Gerard Baunthal, *The Federation of German Industries in Politics* (Ithaca, N.Y.: Cornell University Press, 1965), pp. 56–57.

32. David Bresnick, "The Youth Employment Policy Dance: Interest Groups in the Formulation and Implementation of Public Policy." Paper presented at the American Political Science Association meetings in Denver, Colo., September 2–5, 1982, p. 33.

33. Ezra Vogel, *Japan as Number 1* (New York: Harper Colophon, 1979), chapter 5.

34. Steven Kelman, *Regulating America, Regulating Sweden: A Comparative Study of Occupational Safety and Health Policy* (Cambridge, Mass.: MIT Press, 1981).

35. Ibid., p. x.

36. Ibid., pp. 117, 158–161.

37. Wilson, *Political Organizations*, pp. 34, 146–147, 153–156 *passim*.

38. Ibid., p. 153.

39. Ibid., p. 161.

40. This is the argument of Olson's *Logic*. This section draws on James Q. Wilson, *Political Organizations;* and Robert H. Salisbury, "Why No Corporatism in America?" in P. Schmitter and G. Lehmbruch, eds., *Trends Toward Corporatist Intermediation* (Beverly Hills: Sage, 1979).

41. Wilson, *Political Organizations*.

42. Ibid., p. 149.

43. Ibid., p. 151.

44. Salisbury, "No Corporatism," p. 215.

45. Vogel, *Japan as Number 1*, p. 112.

46. Salisbury, "No Corporatism," p. 222.

47. Wilson, *Political Organizations*, p. 83.

4

Business-Government Relations

The Political Economy of Regulation:
An Analysis of Market Failures

Robert G. Harris
James M. Carman

This article is concerned with the social control of business in a predominantly market economy. Charles Lindblom (1977) has identified five major methods of social control: authority, exchange, persuasion, morality, and tradition (custom). Authority, (that is, most of what we call public policy) is difficult to establish and expensive to administer. Furthermore, in societies that value the rights and freedoms of individuals, there are strong preferences for restricting the use of authority. A central postulate of democratic theory, therefore, is that authority ought to be employed only when other methods of social control fail. Therein lies the logic of this article.

Of the five types of social control, we are concerned primarily with the interaction between authority and market exchange. It is our view that the relationship between public policy and markets (that is, between authority and exchange in Lindblom's terms) can be characterized in the following way. In a market economy, the authority of the state is employed to create and protect the property and other rights requisite to market exchange. Individuals, acting alone or in voluntary association, produce, exchange, and consume goods and services. As long as these private actions are consistent with social values and goals, there is a strong argument against public intervention. If failures occur, however, authority is employed to correct them (by modifying existing markets, creating new markets, or substituting authority for markets). But as markets sometimes fail, so too do political remedies. We must choose, then, among highly imperfect institutions; we make these choices in the belief that, in any particular set of circumstances, one method of control may produce better results than another.

Here and in the succeeding article in this book we present a conceptual scheme for identifying and classifying the effects and interactions between exchange and authority as methods of social control. Our approach in this endeavor is institutional (see Arndt 1981) and can be illustrated as follows:

Legal Framework	→	Market Exchange	→	Market Failures	→	Regulatory Responses	→	Regulatory Failures	→	Public Choice

Although the linear representation here is simple, it represents a highly complex, interactive process, providing a general framework for analyzing the ways in which society makes trade-offs between two allocative mechanisms: market exchange and political authority. We do not mean to imply, however, that the scheme presented here actually describes that process.

Although democratic societies may have a strong value preference for relying on private exchange as a method of social control, markets do not exist in a state of nature; they must be created. Unless there is a system for creating and protecting property rights, one has nothing to exchange (or at least one is constantly threatened by involuntary loss of the potential objects of exchange).[1] Furthermore, in a developed economy, where exchange is seldom extemporaneous and often complex, the state must provide a set of contractual rights and a system for enforcing them. Even the most extreme libertarian grants these as legitimate functions of the state. What is important to our argument is that these political acts are inherently regulatory in function, if not in intent; that is, the way in which property and contract rights are (or are not) defined has enormous consequences for the actions of market agents and outcomes of market transactions.

The role of the state in creating markets is critical to our understanding of market failures. In many cases, failures result not because a market is working improperly, but because the market does not exist, is incomplete, or is presently constrained by regulation. Thus, we need to distinguish between the inherent limits of markets and the failures of existing markets. If the failures are inherent in market exchange as a method of control, that suggests using a nonmarket solution. If the failure is one of existing markets, one option is to extend, or modify, existing property, contract, or liability rights.

Types of Markets

Before proceeding to market failures, it may be helpful to present a very brief classification of types of market linkages. David Revzan was fond of defining a market as a "meeting of minds." But in advanced societies these meetings occur in an extraordinary number and complexity of ways. Although highly simplified, this myriad of market types can be categorized as follows:[2]

Auction markets: in the ideal case, the identities of the buyer and seller are unknown to each other; a disinterested auctioneer simply matches up buy and sell orders; terms of trade do not take account of past or future transactions (for example, commodities, securities markets).

Bidding markets: like auction markets in some respects, but with one crucial difference—the auction is conducted by either the buyer or the seller, who is therefore not a disinterested intermediary (for example, oil leasing, government procurement).

Relational markets: there is a personal (though not intimate) relationship between the buyer and seller, who meet by phone or by mail; furthermore, by relational, we mean that the terms and conditions of any single transaction are influenced by prior or potential transactions between the same parties (for example, retail goods and services markets).

Contractual markets: there is a contractual relationship between buyer and seller that transcends a single transaction, but is limited to one or a few objects of exchange (for example, long-term supply contracts).

Franchise markets: there is a contractual relationship between buyer and seller that transcends a single transaction and covers a wide range of goods and/or services, including supplies, advertising, architectural services, financing, management services (for example, retail franchises).

Obligational markets: there is a contractual relationship between buyer and seller spanning a period of time; the conditions of exchange include provisions that shift the locus of control over, but not ownership of, the object exchange to the buyer (for example, employment contracts, which give the employer authority over the employee; equity investment, in which the shareholder gives to managers control over the use of the capital).[3]

There is one other characteristic of markets that is critical to our analysis of the authority-exchange relationship, namely their interconnectedness. Each market has its own institutional characteristics, rich and complex, changing and developing over time. Markets are also connected to many other markets, some in a direct fashion, more in indirect ways. Just as the intended, beneficial consequences of market outcomes are transmitted across markets, so too are market failures. Accordingly, in analyzing and deciding public policies toward markets, we must take explicit account of these interdependencies. These intermarket effects may be classified as horizontal or vertical. For example, undue bargaining power in a labor market clearly affects the prices of the products of the producers, and thereby the sales of complementary and substitute goods and services. Thus, public policies can, and often do, attempt to remedy failures in one market by modifying outcomes in related markets. By the same measure, public policies directed at correcting a failure in one market will have side effects in other markets.

The Ideal Market

As there are strong value preferences for one method of social control over another, so there are value preferences and differences in perceptions about how each of these control methods does or ought to work. There are norms about what constitutes a fair exchange and a recognition that certain conditions must apply, more or less, in order for a control method to work the way it is supposed to. In the case of market exchange, classical political economy defines this ideal type as the perfectly competitive market, and specifies the following conditions for market success:

Perfect competition: subjects to the exchange should have relatively equal bargaining positions (that is, neither should have power over the other).

Perfect information: subjects should be fully informed about the object of exchange and about other exchange possibilities (for example, the prices and product attributes of substitutes).

Absence of externalities: all of the consequences of the exchange process (including pre-exchange production and post-exchange consumption or use) should be internalized in the exchange.

Divisibility: the object of exchange must be divisible into exchangeable units.

Excludability: the subjects of exchange can exclude nonsubjects from the benefits of the exchange.

Zero transactions costs: there are no barriers to exchange, so that the market instantaneously clears at a price that equilibrates current supply and demand conditions.

Zero entry barriers: there are no long-run supply constraints that inhibit additional production when demand exceeds supply in the short-run.

Economic rationality: subjects to the exchange act to maximize their individual self-interest, as measured in materialistic terms (that is, utility maximization by consumers, profit maximization by producers).

Fair distribution of wealth and income: distribution of economic resources available for exchange is consistent with social consensus of fairness; in a market economy, that means that each individual has wealth and income corresponding to his production of economic goods and services.

These are ideal conditions that never literally hold true in any market; there is considerable controversy regarding the extent to which these conditions typically hold true in markets. Indeed, this difference in opinion is a major component of political ideology: the libertarian believes markets to be almost always nearly perfect (at least if given sufficient time to reach equilibrium), whereas the liberal (as the term is presently employed) believes that markets are often fundamentally flawed. Hence, the libertarian favors exchange over authority as a control mechanism, while the liberal often favors authority over markets.

Types of Market Failures

Although ideological differences involved in this debate often color perceptions of what is actually happening, the measurement problem of determining when a market should be considered a failure may be a more serious impediment to public choice between exchange and authority than are ideological differences. While we will expand on this point now, the typology of market failure should be free of value considerations. By market failure (the reader might prefer to substitute market imperfections), we mean to identify those possible instances in which the ideal conditions for a market success do not hold. We do not mean to suggest that in each instance a regulatory response is desirable.

In our typology, we specify the nature of the failures as they relate to the classical ideal conditions for market exchange. This is a descriptive, not normative, statement. Although we have attempted to develop a descriptive typology that is unambiguous, inclusive, and mutually exclusive, we readily acknowledge that any particular attribute or outcome of market exchange could be classified in a number of other ways.[4]

Because of their classical roots, the ideal conditions overemphasize static, structural market attributes and underemphasize dynamic and functional considerations. It is not our intent to champion that perspective; we recognize, for example, that the dynamic benefits of economic profits flowing to research and development and thence to product improvements, or products and services, are real. The question is, How imperfect can markets be before they become socially undesirable? In attempting to answer that question, scholars have attempted to define a concept of workable or effective competition in a market, then to address the measurement suggested by that definition. One definition that is useful for present purposes (but certainly not easy to make operational) is that competitive market exchange is workable when there is no regulatory response that would result in greater social gains than social losses (Markham 1950).

Such a rule could be applied in deciding whether to intervene in a given market, and in choosing among regulatory responses. In response to dangerous drugs, for example, we might prohibit their exchange, require sellers to disclose information regarding the dangers of consuming their products, or leave the market alone. the choice among these options depends on the perceived harms of the market solution, as compared to the costs of exercising authority to modify market outcomes. We address regulatory failures, and the implications of those failures for public policies toward markets, in the succeeding article. The typology of market failures is presented in table 1. The remainder of this section is a discussion of the elements of the type typology, and illustrative examples of each type.

Table 1
Types of Market Failures

Type of Failure	Nature of Failure	Examples of Failure
Imperfect competition		
Natural monopoly	Economies of scale	Electric utilities
Monopoly(sony)	Bargaining power	Standard Oil (pre-1912)
Oligopoly(sony)	Interdependent conduct	Tobacco
Monopol(son)istic competition	Transaction costs; excess capacity	Retail sale of convenience goods
Excessive competition	Fluctuating supply/demand	Trucking
Anticompetitive conduct	Collusion; predation	OPEC cartel; AT&T; MCI
Imperfect information		
Bounded rationality	Uninformed exchange	Professional services
Information costs	Uninformed exchange	Life insurance
Asymmetric information	Unequal bargaining	"Lemons"
Misinformation	Misinformed exchange	Wonder bread
Lack of information	Uninformed exchange	New therapeutic drugs
Side effects		
Internalities	Transmittal of costs to nonsubjects	Health effects of tobacco
Negative externalities	Overconsumption; costs imposed on nonsubjects	Air pollution; communicable diseases
Positive externalities	Underconsumption; benefits accrue to nonsubjects	Innoculations against communicable diseases
Public goods	Indivisibility; nonexcludability; zero MC	Street lighting; parks; national defense
(De)merit goods	Divergence of private wants, social values	Education; (gambling)
Income maldistribution		
Factor market failures	Any of above	Employee discrimination
Economic vs. social value	Earned income not equal to social worth	Children; disabled; "superstars"
Intergenerational transfers	Inconsistency with value that income be "earned"	Inheritances; socially advantaged upbringing

Source: From *Journal of Macromarketing*, vol. 3, no. 1 (Spring 1983), p. 53.

Imperfect Competition

In order for market exchange to function well as a method of social control, subjects of exchange cannot have unequal bargaining positions (since we assume that self-interest would cause them to exploit that bargaining advantage, resulting in unfair terms of exchange). Although we might measure bargaining position or power directly, we can more easily infer it from the structure of the market, that is, the number and size distribution of buyers and sellers in the market, and the conditions of entry into and exit from the market. The classical definitions of industrial organization identifies those market structures in which market failures are most likely.

Natural Monopoly. Natural monopoly is due to economies of scale (or scope in a multiproduct producer) relative to total market demand, which only one (or a few) producer(s) can produce at minimum cost. When these economies are of dominating importance, markets fail because too many firms will produce at costs exceeding the minimum achievable (technical inefficiency), or too few firms will exist in the market (so each seller will market power). Examples are electric utilities, postal services, and highway systems.

Monopoly (sony). Although a monopoly is not achieved by economies of scale, one seller (buyer) has power in the exchange because it is the sole available subject to exchange. Libertarians argue that the only monopolies are created by government. Liberals argue that there are no monopolies only because the antitrust laws have prohibited them. In any event, we cannot think of any clear cases of monopoly that are not based on economies of scale.

Oligopoly (sony). Whether natural (economies of scale) or not, sellers (buyers) have power in the market because there are too few sellers (buyers). Thus, while there may be some gains from economies of scale, there will be a concomitant increase in the market power of the oligopolists. Examples of oligopoly are tobacco, cement, and paper carton markets. Examples of oligopsony are labor markets in which a few employers account for a large share of total employment.

Monopolistic (sonistic) Competition. Even though there are a large number of sellers (buyers), they have some power over buyers (sellers) because transactions costs inhibit competition. Examples are retail markets in which shopping costs are high relative to the total transaction value (for example, convenience goods).

Excessive Competition

If supply or demand fluctuates unpredictably over time, there may be excessive entry by producers during peak demand, resulting in excess capacity during off-peak demand. Furthermore, if capital is specialized, supply adjustments may take longer than the duration of the fluctuation and prices will be driven below long-run average costs. Or, if storage costs are high, producers may sell output below costs to avoid those costs. In addition to the instability in supply and loss of income by producers, excessive competition may induce producers to reduce the quality of their service, perhaps with jeopardy to consumers. Examples are agricultural markets (for example, the hog cycle) and trucking and airline (pre-regulation) companies.

Anticompetitive Conduct

Because of the potential economic gains, sellers (buyers) may commit acts in concert with (collusion) or against (predation) other sellers in order to enhance their position in the market. In the short run these acts may raise (collusion) or lower (predation) prices and correspondingly reduce or increase output relative to the competitive levels. By modifying the market structure, both collusion and predation raise prices and reduce output in the long run. There are numerous examples in both product and service markets. There is one other class of anticompetitive behavior, unfair trade practices (for example, misleading advertising), which we treat as an informational failure rather than as a competitive failure.

Imperfect Information

In order for markets to work well, subjects to exchange must be fully informed about the object of exchange and about conditions and objects in other markets; ideally, information is perfect and costless. In highly localized, premodern economies, buyers and sellers may have had something approaching perfect information. But in developed economies, with geographically dispersed markets, complex goods and services produced by very large, anonymous organizations, and many available substitutes and complements, information is highly imperfect and very costly. There are several distinct types of information failures:

Bounded Rationality. Even if information was costless, it would not be perfect, in that information has value only if the subject has the knowledge needed to use the information. Given the limits of individuals to analyze, store, and retrieve information, we can predict that many exchange transactions will not be fully informed. An example is the prescription of surgical services by the doctor (seller) when the patient (buyer) lacks knowledge (and often the emotional or physical stamina to procure it) required to assess needs for, or benefits of, those services. Closely related to bounded rationality is the problem of cognitive dissonance, which causes individuals to fail to acknowledge (or even receive) information even when it is presented to them. An example is the consumers who will not accept scientific evidence of the health effects of smoking.

Information Costs. Even when information is readily available, it is seldom costless. Because of the money and opportunity costs of obtaining information, subjects to exchange often act without full information. The problem is most serious when: (1) the product or service is purchased infrequently; (2) performance characteristics are difficult to evaluate either before or soon after purchase; (3) the rate of technological change is rapid relative to the interval between purchases; and (4) the terms of exchange change rapidly relative to the purchase interval. Examples are life insurance and automobile tires (Holton 1978, 1981).

Asymmetric Information. Because there are economies of scale in the collection, storage, retrieval, and analysis of information, subjects who engage in many exchanges involving the same object will typically have an information advantage. Thus, because a producer typically sells more of a given object than a consumer buys, there often exists an asymmetry between producers and consumers. Moreover, self-interest causes producers to exploit this information advantage in the exchange process. Note two important exceptions to this rule of asymmetry. In industrial markets, purchasing agents specialize in particular goods or services, so the buyer may have better (or at least as good as) information than the seller. In factor markets, buyers may have considerably better information about working conditions (for example, toxic fumes or hazardous machinery) than the seller of labor services, or better information about the financial condition and prospects of the company than the seller of capital.

Misinformation. Because information is costly but often essential to exchange, subjects have economic incentives to provide information to other potential subjects to exchange. Sellers advertise and promote their products by providing information about the attributes of their products, and the ways in which they satisfy buyers' needs or wants. Sellers also provide information about the offerings of other sellers, either explicitly (as in comparative advertising) or implicitly (as in persuading consumers to buy one class of objects rather than another). Unfortunately, sellers also have economic incentives to misinform potential buyers about their products or the products of others. For the very reason that buyers lack information about the relative merits of available products, they are often unable to distinguish good information from bad information. Examples of misinformation are when sellers use advertising to create the impression of product differentiation (and a corresponding willingness to pay higher prices) for homogeneous products; when professionals advise clients to purchase services not needed by the buyer; when employers mislead workers about the health effects of workplace pollution; when managers mislead shareholders about the terms of an acquisition offer.

Lack of Information. As human knowledge is limited, important information about a product does not exist. The fact that both seller and buyer are equally ignorant is of no relief in such cases. This problem is especially relevant to the negative attributes (or side effects) of objects of exchange. Examples are when long-term effects of therapeutic drugs and effects of asbestos on workers' health are not known.

Information as Object of Exchange. When information is itself the object of exchange, there are severe limits as to what information about the product can be revealed without revealing the product itself. Furthermore, once revealed, the cost of reproducing information is often so low that the producer of the information has difficulty internalizing the value of his product. We will discuss this issue further under the section entitled "Public Goods."

Side Effects

All goods have their bads, in their production, their consumption, or both. Sometimes those side effects accrue to subjects of the exchange (internalities); often they accrue to individuals who are not subjects to the exchange (externalities). In either case, market exchange is often imperfect because the terms of exchange will probably not incorporate all of the consequences of the production and consumption of the object of exchange.

Internalities. If the side effects are borne by a subject of exchange (for example, the consumer of the product or the provider of labor services), and there is no information failure (that is, the subject is aware of the side effect and incorporates that information in the exchange terms), then there is no immediate market failure. But side effects can be transmitted through other markets; if, for example, the side effect raises health care costs but insurance premiums are not sensitive to the higher risk, then the internality is externalized in the form of higher premiums to other individuals.

Another type of internality imposes negative side effects on other users (whether as producers or consumers) when too many users attempt to consume a service at the same time. This congestion effect is not really an externality, since the costs are borne by those involved in the exchange process. Examples of internalities are waiting lines at banks and highway congestion.

Negative Externalities. When negative side effects of production or consumption are borne by nonsubjects, resource allocation will be distorted by overproduction and overconsumption. Examples are pollution by manufacturing plants, automobiles, or smokers; reckless driving; transmitting contagious diseases due to improper sanitation by providers of personal care services.

Positive Externalities. When some of the positive effects of production or consumption are realized by nonsubjects, underproduction and underconsumption result. Examples are innoculation against contagious disease reduce the probability of incidence to the uninnoculated as well as to the innoculated; education (presumably) benefits all members of society, in addition to the person receiving the education.

Public Goods

In order for exchange to function well, the objects of exchange must be private, in the sense that they are divisible into exchangeable units and that nonsubjects can be excluded from the benefits of exchange. By public goods, we mean economically valuable goods or services that are characterized by indivisibility and nonexcludability. When goods cannot be privatized for these reasons, exchange fails because of the free-rider problem. Although individuals would benefit from the provision of the good, none has an adequate incentive to purchase the good; no one individual can afford to purchase the entire (indivisible) good, but if enough others purchase the good, the nonpurchasers can still enjoy the benefits. Examples are street lighting, urban "green space," and national defense.

As already noted, information is a most important class of public goods. Intellectual products (for example, books), inventions, and production know-how (that is, trade secrets) are all instances of public goods that are characterized by indivisibility and nonexcludability. When information is an important attribute of an object of exchange, markets fail because free-riders can obtain the value of the product without buying from the seller. Brand names and corporate good will are instances of public goods from which markets cannot exclude other subjects (for example, competitors) from realizing the benefits.

Two additional features of public goods should be noted. First, there is seldom an absolute barrier to excludability; rather there would be a waste of economic resources in excluding on-purchasers (for example, shading, directing, or placing street lighting to privatize the benefits). Second, by definition of indivisibility, the marginal costs of providing the goods to consumers is (until a congestion point) near zero. So, although we could use pricing to limit entry to parks, it would violate one norm of competitive markets: that price reflect the marginal social cost of production.

(De)Merit Goods

The normative theory of exchange assumes that individuals are economically rational: that individuals are capable of knowing what is good for them (or bad for them) and acting accordingly. On this premise are based the principles of individual freedom and consumer sovereignty. In all societies, however, value conflicts exist between individual and social preferences about economic goods and services, often because the production or consumption of economic goods runs counter to noneconomic (for example, religious or ethical) social values.[5] Markets are not capable of providing optimal allocation of resources if social, rather than personal, values are used as the welfare criterion. So, although black markets may work exceedingly well for some products and services, they fail as a means of social control by providing too many demerit goods and too few merit goods. Examples of demerit goods are gambling, prostitution, alcohol, tobacco, and recreational drugs. An example of merit goods is education (even if there are no externalities, society believes that individuals are better off with an education, whether or not the individual is of the same opinion).

Rents

While exchange is premised on the existence of scarcity (if all goods were limitless, there would be no need for private property and no need to exchange), the normative theory of exchange assumes that, over the long run, there are no inherent limits to the production of any particular object of exchange. Indeed, one chief attribute of markets is that prices send signals to potential producers indicating the need for additional production, inducing entry, capacity, and returning the market to equilibrium. Markets fail when there exists a long-run inelasticity of supply, preventing production from expanding sufficiently, so that existing producers realize prices exceeding the competitive level. Whereas monopoly profits result from an inelastic demand curve (which by definition indicates that the market is not perfectly competitive), rents are attributable to an inelastic supply curve. Examples are petroleum, natural gas extraction, and urban land markets.

We should note here that scarcity-induced rents are very often generated by authority, rather than by market failures. In these instances, there are no natural limits on the factors of production (or at least those limits would be reached at a higher level of output). Rather, there are regulatory constraints that prohibit or inhibit access to, or use of, the factors required to increase production and eliminate rents. Examples are housing rents due to zoning laws that restrict the density of housing units, and petroleum extraction rents due to limiting access to oil reserves.

Maldistribution of Income and Wealth

Exchange is a method of allocating and distributing resources: how much of which goods get produced and by whom are they consumed. Allocation is the domain of intermediate and final goods and services markets, whereas distribution is principally controlled in factor markets. In a market system, society believes that income—personal control of exchangeable goods and services—ought to be a function of the individual's economic contribution to society. But our ethical system also believes that each person has an inherent value, quite apart from his or her economic worth. Thus, markets fail when there is an incongruence between economic and social value, or when income does not reflect true economic value. Aid to Dependent Children, for example, is a social program predicated on the belief that a child's value is not reflected in the low income of his or her parent(s).

Failures in Factor Markets. As already noted, all the market failures just classified exist in factor markets. When they occur, there is a misallocation of resources (too many objects will be produced if the workers are underpaid; or, fixed factors will be underutilized if workers are paid more than their production justifies). Moreover, imperfections in factor markets will affect the distribution of wealth and income among factors.

Discrimination. One particular factor market failure is discrimination, which violates the normative standard that subjects are economically rational (that is, personal attributes of subjects should have no effect on the terms of exchange). When discrimination occurs, individuals may be unable to sell their labor services, or may have to sell them at a less than fair price. Discrimination also occurs in labor-related consumer markets, such as schools and universities. When the sellers of educational services discriminate against potential consumers on noneconomic grounds, there is a misallocation of educational resources and the possibility of losses in income-earning potential by those discriminated against.

Social versus Economic Value. Even if factor markets were perfect, individuals might not possess sufficient economically valuable resources to earn an income that is consistent with social values. There are three main classes of individuals for whom this is likely to be true: children, who have yet attained economic value; disabled, who for reasons of physical or mental impairment have limited economic value; and elderly, whose economic value has declined due to age. There may also be cases where individuals earn more than what society deems the individuals are worth. An example is highly paid celebrities.

Intergenerational Transfers. One other source of distributional market failures is attributable to differences in interpersonal transfers of wealth. Here there is a conflict between the norm of individual freedom (control over the use of resources includes the right to give them to others) and the norm that individuals' income should reflect their own economic contribution to society. Hence, one rationale for inheritance taxes (quite apart from raising revenues) is to prevent individuals from receiving substantial unearned income. Note that these transfers include services (for example, a good upbringing, which enhances income-earning potential) as well as tangible assets (for example, a money inheritance).

Notes

An earlier version of this article was published in the *Journal of Macromarketing* in Spring 1983.

1. For a more thorough discussion of the relationship between property rights and marketing systems, see Carman (1982).
2. This system of classification is consistent with the types of marketing channels identified in Carman (1982), page 206.
3. According to Williamson's view (1975), this amounts to a substitution of hierarchy for market as the means of control (as in the distinction between MacDonald's franchised outlets and their company-owned outlets). Because there is a market for employees to manage and staff company-owned, we view hierarchy and market as complementary means of control.
4. For the classic typology of market failures, see Bator (1958).
5. For an excellent review of sumptuary laws, see Hollander (1982).

Bibliography

Arndt, Johan, "The Political Economy of Marketing Systems: Reviving the Institutional Approach," *Journal of Macromarketing*, Fall 1981.

Bator, Francis E., "Anatomy of Market Failure," *Quarterly Journal of Economics*, August 1958, pp. 351–379.

Breyer, Stephen, *Regulation and its Reform*. Harvard University Press, Cambridge, Mass., 1982.

Carman, James M., "Private Property and the Regulation of Vertical Channel Systems," *Journal of Macromarketing*, Spring 1982.

Caves, Richard E., and Marc J. Roberts, eds., *Regulating the Product: Quality and Variety.* Ballinger, Cambridge, Mass., 1975.

Coase, R.H., "The Problem of Social Cost," *Journal of Law and Economics* **3** (October 1960):1–44.

Commons, John R., *Legal Foundations of Capitalism.* University of Wisconsin Press, Madison, 1959.

Crozier, Michel, *The Bureaucratic Phenomenon.* University of Chicago Press, Chicago, 1964.

Fritschler, A. Lee, and Bernard H. Ross, *Business Regulation and Government Decision Making.* Winthrop Press, Cambridge, Mass., 1980.

Hawley, Ellis, "Three Facets of Hooverian Associationalism," in *Regulation in Perspective,* Thomas K. McCraw, ed. Harvard University Press, Cambridge, Mass., 1981.

Hemenway, David, *Industrywide Voluntary Product Standards.* Ballinger, Cambridge, Mass., 1975.

Hollander, Stanley C., "Sumptuary Legislation—Demarketing by Edict," presented to the Seventh Annual Macromarketing Seminar, Boulder, Colo., 1982.

Holton, Richard H., "Advances in the Backward Art of Spending Money," in *Regulating Business: The Search for an Optimum.* Institute for Contemporary Studies, San Francisco, 1978.

Holton, Richard H., "Public Regulation of Consumer Information: The Life Insurance Case," in *Regulation of Marketing and the Public Interest,* P.E. Balderston, J.M. Carman and F.N. Nicosia, eds. Pergamon Press, New York, 1981.

Lindblom, Charles E. *Politics and Markets.* Basic Books, New York, 1977.

Markham, J.N., "An Alternative Approach to the Concept of Workable Competition," *American Economic Review* **40** (June 1950):349–361.

McCraw, Thomas K. (ed.), *Regulation in Perspective: Historical Essay.* Harvard Business School Press, Boston, 1981.

Mueller, Dennis C., *Public Choice.* Cambridge University Press, Cambridge, 1979.

Olson, Mancur, *The Logic of Collective Action.* Harvard University Press, Cambridge, Mass., 1965.

Samuels, Warren, *The Classical Theory of Economic Policy.* World Publishing Company, New York, 1966.

Schelling, Thomas C., "On the Ecology of Micromotives," *The Public Interest,* Fall 1971, pp. 59–98.

Schmalansee, Richard, *The Control of Natural Monopolies.* Lexington Books, Lexington, Mass., 1979.

Schultze, Charles L., *The Public Use of Private Interest.* Brookings Institution, Washington, D.C., 1977.

Weldenbaum, Muarry L., *Business, Government and the Public.* Prentice-Hall, Englewood Cliffs, N.J., 1981.

Williamson, Oliver E., *Markets and Hierarchies: Analysis and Antitrust Implications.* Free Press, New York, 1975.

Wilson, James Q., ed., *The Politics of Regulation.* Basic Books, New York, 1980.

Wolf, Charles, Jr., "A Theory of Nonmarket Failure: Framework for Implementation Analysis," *The Journal of Law and Economics,* October 1978, pp. 107–139.

The Political Economy of Regulation: An Analysis of Regulatory Responses

James M. Carman
Robert G. Harris

Since markets cannot function without a system of property and contract rights, there are no pure market economies.[1] What we mean by a market economy is that society has a strong value preference for using exchange as the method of resource allocation, distribution, and social control, and markets are in fact the predominant means of social control. Conversely, there is no economy without markets, but nonmarket economies are those in which there is a normative preference for using authority, tradition, or persuasion, rather than exchange, as the primary means of social control.

We have already assumed that the United States is a market society in that there is a preference for market solutions. However, that leaves an enormous range of differences over the extent to which, and the actual cases in which, authority will be used to create, modify, or substitute for markets. As markets are exceedingly varied and complex, so too are the instruments of authority. Furthermore, there are few cases in which a single type of authority is employed; regulations come in bunches. In any particular market there is a nexus of rights and regulations that affect the subjects, objects, and medium or terms of exchange.

As background to our discussion of the types of regulation, there are several important dimensions of authority worth delineating. The first dimension is a continuum from private to public exercise of authority. Perhaps the most private of political institutions is the family, in which certain individuals have authority over other individuals, as a consequence of public policy and private economic power. Next, there are private associations, to which the members contract certain elements of authority, but only under the auspices of a more general social contract (for example, rights of religious association, labor unions, or private property associations). In some cases, however, the state can make membership in these private associations mandatory (that is, as a condition of having an exchange relationship) as in closed shops in labor markets, or membership in professional societies as a condition for selling the corresponding professional services. In some cases, private associations are assigned regulatory functions by the state, giving them a quasipublic character (professional licensing bodies). Finally, even at the public level of authority, one can distinguish regulations by the scope of the political authority (as in city, county, state, regional, and national governments). In some cases, political jurisdiction has inherent rights under the prevailing social contract (the national and state governments). Other units of government do not have sovereignty, but have been delegated their authority by some higher level of government (for example, city charters granted by states).

Along a second dimension of political authority are regulatory instruments that are more or less compatible with exchange. Although continuous, we can distinguish five discrete categories:

1. *Market creating:* public policies designed to create markets by establishing rights, incentives, and opportunities for exchange (for example, creating a market for air pollution rights).

2. *Market facilitating:* policies that promote or improve the operation of markets by reducing transactions costs, enhancing incentives, or internalizing benefits and costs (for example, public investment in transportation to expand the geographic scope of markets by reducing transport costs).

3. *Market modifying:* regulations that attempt to change the conduct of the subjects, objects, medium or terms of exchange, in order to produce outcomes different from those the market would otherwise produce (for example, agricultural marketing orders).

4. *Market substituting:* policies that create substitutes for markets; instruments of political authority are used to allocate or distribute resources or control conduct of individuals or organizations; outcomes are achieved by the exercise of authority rather than by exchange, (for example, the provision of public school education through rationing rather than through market exchange).

5. *Market proscribing:* policies that attempt to prohibit exchanges by particular subjects or of particular objects, with no attempt to use authority as a substitute method for achieving a given outcome; rather, authority is used in an effort to prevent that outcome from occurring (for example, laws prohibiting the sale of dangerous drugs).

A third dimension along which policies differ is their respective degree of coercion or compulsion. At one extreme, there are laws or policies carrying virtually no compulsion, because they are superfluous (that is, people would have acted in the legally prescribed way with or without the law); unenforced (for lack of adequate enforcement capacity, prosecutorial discretion or social consensus that it is a bad law); or though enforced, the sanctions imposed are not sufficiently severe to have much effect on conduct. At the other extreme, policies can be extremely coercive, when enforcement and sanctions are highly effective and the conduct prescribed or proscribed by the law is greatly different from individual preferences. Most laws, of course, lie in that middle ground in which individuals' conduct is modified, but with no great sense of loss of personal freedom due to a high degree of compulsion. When categorizing policies with respect to coerciveness, it should be noted that laws often require us to do what is good for us and others; we are happy to comply with the law, and happy to have the law so that others will comply as well (for example, traffic laws).[2]

These three dimensions of authority—the degree of publicness, the degree of compatibility with exchange, and the degree of compulsion—explain much of the ideological battle over the use of authority in general, or the selection of public policies in particular. Libertarians prefer instruments of authority that are more private and less public, most compatible with markets, and least coercive. Conservatives tend to prefer policies that protect prevailing property interests (whether compatible with markets or not) and that are coercive (for example, heavy penalties for socially unacceptable behavior). Liberals tend to favor public authority instruments that constrain, replace, or limit the scope of exchange. One might characterize the recent wave of neoliberalism as a shift in liberal thought toward public policies more compatible with, rather than hostile toward, market exchange and private incentives.

Types of Regulations

We have attempted to order our typology of regulations along these three dimensions. Thus, we have arranged policy instruments from most to least compatible with markets, from most private to most public, and from least to most cohesive. This is done for the sake of logical organization, not necessarily as a reflection of our own ideological preferences.

One is tempted to argue that a particular type of regulatory response is most appropriate to deal with a particular type of market failure; certainly there are those who offer specific responses as a panacea. If this were so, then we could map the responses onto the failures and provide a guide as to what kind of response to use on any particular problem. But political reality is quite the contrary: there is no one-to-one correspondence between each respective type of market failure and regulatory response. Although certain responses may be recognized as more appropriate, and hence more often used in response to particular market failures, public policy makers have historically applied almost every type of response to each type of market failure. Table 1 summarizes the types and categories of regulatory responses to market failures.

Legal Rights

In a market-oriented economy, legal rights are essential to the creation and functioning of markets. The definitions of these rights sometimes determine whether exchange will even occur; more often, they affect the terms of exchange. They do so by designating property that can be exchanged (property rights) and are protected (criminal law); assigning transactions and compliance costs (contract rights); defining liability for intended or unintended consequences of exchange (liability rights); allowing, facilitating, or denying associational rights (corporate law, collective bargaining rights); delineating the range of applicability of the rights; and establishing the rules of evidence, proof, proceeding, and standing (civil and administrative procedural rights and due process rights).

Table 1
Types of Regulations

Type of Response	Variations	Examples
Legal rights	Property rights	Land ownership
	Contracts rights	Compliance enforcement
	Associational rights	Public utility franchises
	Procedural rights	Rule-making participation
	Due process	Corporation as "person"
Information responses		
Promoting markets—	Protection from liability	Consumer reports
	Allowing cooperative action	Better Business Bureau
Disclosure	Available on request	Worker health records
	Public reporting	SEC Financial reports
	Provision in exchange	Labeling laws
Content	Specific	Sugar content of food
	Comprehensive	Therapeutic drug insert
Protection	Privacy rights	Confidential records
	Accuracy of information	Credit reporting
	Agreement of owner	Patents, trademarks
Public provision	Available on request	Consumer buying guides
	General dissemination	Auto safety records
	Mandatory consumption	Public health education
Standards		
Compliance	Voluntary	Uniform package sizes
	Mandatory	Milk processing
Object of standard	Producers	Occupational licensing
	Production process	Food processing
	Product	Auto safety standards
	Consumption process	Speed limits
	Consumer	Drivers' licensing
Source of standard	Market incentives	CP/M° operating system
	Private provision	Underwriter's laboratory
	Exchange transactions	Procurement standards
	Private collective action	FASB account principles
	Public agencies	Restaurant sanitation
Nature of standard	Performance	Allowable emissions
	Design	Catalytic converters
Taxes/subsidies		
Form of transfer	Money payments	Income tax, Soc. Security
	Stamps, coupons	Food stamps
	Discounts	Senior citizens/transit
	Services in kind	Indigent medical services
Method of transfer	Incentive for private action	Charitable deductions
	Internal cross-subsidies	Regulated prices
	Rationing	Import quotas
	Direct	Income tax, Soc. Security
Object of transfer	Exchanged objects	Sales, excise taxes
	Production process	Effluent charges/subsidies
	Factors of production	Personal income tax
	Ownership	Property taxes
		Corporate income tax

Type of Response	Variations	Examples
Controls on collective action		
Horizontal structure	Prohibiting mergers	Sherman Act
	Public franchise	"Regulated" industries
Vertical structure	Prohibiting mergers	Clayton Act
Horizontal conduct	Limits on investment	Joint venture restrictions
	Limits on collusion	Price fixing
	Exemptions from limits	Agricultural cooperatives
Vertical conduct	Limits on cooperation	Boycotts
	Limits on private restraints	Resale price maintenance
	Limits on differences in terms of trade	Price discrimination; exclusive dealing
Price controls		
Compliance	Voluntary	Wage, price guidelines
	Incentives	"Tax Incentive Plan"
	Mandatory	Published tariffs
Source of controls	Contractual	Uranium contract case
	Private cooperation	Food marketing coops
	Public sanction of associational control	State liquor boards
	Public agencies	Public utility commissions
Nature of controls	Price information	Posting, public provision
	Allowable price range	ICC zone of reasonableness
	Public approval of prices	Public utility commissions
	Price setting	Postal rates
Applicability	Seller-specific	Electricity rates
	Class of sellers	Truck rates; minimum wage
	General	Wage/price freeze
Allocative controls	Price subsidies	Food stamps
	Mandate exchange	Common carrier obligation
	Restricting exchange	Rationing coupons
	Proscribing exchange	Cocaine, child labor
Public provision	Quasipublic enterprise	ComSat
	Public enterprise/prices	TVA
	Public agency/user charges	Highways, universities
	Public agency/rationing	Social service agencies

Source: From *Journal of Macromarketing*, vol. 4, no. 1 (Spring 1984), pp. 50–51.

In the U.S. legal system, these rights are defined and protected through a hierarchy of common, administrative, statutory, and constitutional laws. All of these evolve historically, which is to say that precedence and tradition are powerful determinants of legal policies and their interpretation by legislative, judicial, executive, and administrative agencies. The continual redefinition, expansion, or contraction of legal rights reflects prevailing social consensus, legal and political theory, and the perceived effects of current and potential definitions. Although legal instruments of authority are seldom selected solely on the basis of their effects on exchange relations, it is undeniable that they have important exchange-regulatory intent and consequences.

Information Responses

Authority can be used in a variety of ways to generate and disseminate information. Within this category, there is a hierarchy of responses that merely create or extend markets to those that inhibit markets in information, and to those that substitute public for private provision of information.

Information Markets. By means of property rights (or exemptions from liability), authority can be used to facilitate private markets for information, in which individuals exchange for the information needed to make rational decisions in exchange transactions (consumer reports). Policies can also facilitate the voluntary, private provision and production of information by exempting such activities from general proscriptions against cooperation among competitors (Better Business Bureau).

Disclosure. Authority can require disclosure of information by the possessor of the information. This typically means that subjects to exchange must provide information regarding the object or terms of exchange. Variants of disclosure requirements include: making information available on demand (allowing workers to inspect health and safety records), public reporting (filing 10-K financial statements), and providing specific disclosure (packaging or labeling laws). The required content of disclosure may range from very narrow (salt content of foods) to very broad (all known attributes and side effects of a therapeutic drug). Authority can also be used to prevent private associations from inhibiting the flow of information (for example, recent Federal Trade Commission rulings prevent professional societies from banning price advertising in their professional codes of ethics).

Protection of Information. Because of the public good aspects of information, authority can be used to prevent the collection or dissemination of information. These remedies include protection against unwarranted intrusions into personal affairs (rights of privacy, confidential records); proscriptions about the accuracy of information content (personal or corporate credit reports); or use of the information without the agreement of the owner of the information (patents, trademarks, copyrights, trade secrets).

Public Provision of Information. Political authority can also be used to actually provide information about the subjects, objects, or terms of exchange to the general public or to specific audiences. The public provision of information can take the form of general distribution through public media (automobile safety records and crash test results); distribution of materials on request by individuals (agricultural market-information services); or mandatory consumption of information by individuals in government institutions (public-health information in public schools).

Production of Information. Government can regulate information by requiring private parties to produce (or government can produce) information that might not otherwise exist. Required product testing by private parties or government agencies is the most prominent instance of information production by exercise of authority.

Standards Remedies

Even if information were free, human rationality is limited, so more information is not necessarily better. In complex market economies, the frequency and complexity of exchange generates information overload. In recognition of these limits, authority is employed to reduce the need for information by creating standards applicable to exchange relations. By indicating that the object of the standard meets or exceeds some threshold level on one (or more) attribute(s), subjects of exchange need less or no information about that attribute. Unfortunately, standards are so varied and complex that they cannot be reduced to a linear hierarchy of types. Rather, we identify the several dimensions on which standards differ and discrete categories of standards.

Compliance. Standards can range from purely voluntary (uniform package sizes) to highly mandatory, meaning that products failing to meet the standard are excluded from legal markets (for example, milk standards).

Object of the Standard. Standards can be applied to the producers (professional certification or licensing), the production process (workplace safety standards), the product (auto safety standards),[3] the consumption process (highway speed limits), the consumers (driver's licensing), and the complementary goods and services (highway safety standards, lead content of gasoline). The oldest use of standards regulates the quantities, rather than qualities, of goods exchanged (standard weights and measures). In traditional regulation (the regulated industries in transportation, communications, energy distribution, and financial services), authority is used to comprehensively regulate the production and provision of goods and services, although we sometimes separate responsibility for quality regulation from quantity and price regulation between agencies (Federal Aviation Administration regulates airline safety, whereas the Civil Aeronautics Board regulates entry, exit, quantity, and price of service).

Source of Standards. We can also distinguish standards by the process by which standards are developed, promulgated, and/or enforced. Standards are regularly generated by market processes, of course, when firms have incentives to standardize product attributes even though no authority requires them to do so (as in the adoption of PC-DOS operating systems for sixteen-bit microprocessors). Authority can be used to promote private contractual standards (legally enforceable exchange terms, as in procurement contracts or collective bargaining agreements) and private associational standards (promulgated by industry trade association, privately or publicly enforced, as in SEC-encouraged standards generated by the Financial

Standards Accounting Board).[4] Standards are promulgated and enforced by public agencies (usually with private participation), as in public health and sanitation standards for restaurant and personal care establishments.

Nature of Standards. We can also categorize standards as performance-oriented, design-oriented, or ingredient-oriented. Performance standards establish threshold levels for outcomes, while leaving producers or consumers discretion as to the method of achieving the specified performance (for example, specifying the units of emitants allowed from a factory). Design standards require that the object of the standard be manufactured or operate in a specific way (for example, requiring manufacturers to install catalytic converters to control emissions). Ingredient standards specify actual, minimum, and/or maximum ingredients required in order for the product to be sold, or in order to be designated by a commonly accepted name (for example, mayonnaise).

Taxes and Subsidies

There are three general purposes served by government fiscal policies and operations: allocation, distribution, and stabilization. Government collects revenues to cover the costs of government; to redistribute income among individuals; and to stabilize prices, reach full employment, and reach full economic growth. Our concern here is with the use of taxes or subsidies as the means of correcting market failures, that is, with the regulatory functions of fiscal policies. In thereby limiting the discussion, we do not mean to suggest that there are not other important functions of taxes and subsidies.

Taxes and subsidies are logically similar, although of opposite sign. The one logical difference between them as instruments of authority is that, in any given instance, there is almost always a higher degree of coercion attached to taxes than to subsidies. Someone eligible for Social Security payments can simply not request them, or refuse them if offered, with no legal sanction. One does not have the same option with respect to payment of Social Security taxes, however. Having acknowledged this distinction, it will greatly expedite the discussion to treat taxes and subsidies as roughly equivalent instruments of public policy, except that in one case the transfer of resources is negative, in the other, positive.

Form of Transfer. Taxes or subsidies can take one of several forms. The most commonly used means of transfer is money (or near-money) payments (as in Social Security). The second form of transfers is stamps or coupons, which can be spent like money, but only for the purchase of specified goods or services (food stamps, educational vouchers). The third form of transfer is through the price mechanism, that is, modifying the terms of exchange so that the subjects pay (receive) less (more) than the market-determined price (senior citizen discounts). If these exchanges are made at a zero price, we can classify them as a fourth form of transfers, namely the direct provision of goods and services (indigent medical services, urban playgrounds).

Method of Transfer. Authority can be used directly or indirectly to tax and subsidize. Indirect methods include creating incentives for private, voluntary transfers among individuals and associations (charitable giving promoted by tax deductibility). Transfers can also be achieved by regulating the prices of goods and services (long distance telephone users being taxed to subsidize local telephone users). Another indirect public method of transfer is to ration or restrict markets, so as to affect the income of factors in the market (subsidizing the domestic auto producers, shareholders, and employees by import quotas on Japanese autos). Finally, transfers can be made directly (income taxes, Social Security payments).

Object of Transfer. Transfers vary in the object and range of their applicability. One generic class of transfers is directed toward objects transferred in exchange; goods and services are taxed or subsidized, either in general (sales tax) or specific (excise tax). Taxes or subsidies can be applied to the side effects of production, consumption, or exchange (effluent taxes, emission-control subsidies). Another category of transfers is tied to the ownership (rather than transfer) of goods (property taxes). Another generic class of transfers is related to the earnings of factors of production (personal income, capital gains taxes). Finally, transfers can be directed at producing agencies (corporate income taxes, subsidies to mass transit agencies or universities).

Controls on Collective Action

Given the nature of the consumption, production, and exchange processes, collective organizations are a virtual necessity in modern economies. Collective action has three main purposes: (1) to realize economies of scale in production, (2) to internalize the benefits of productive actions, and (3) to change the balance of power between participants in the exchange process. The state allows and encourages collective action by a variety of regulatory instruments already covered, including associational rights.[5] Surely the most important of these are the rights of incorporation granted to companies and labor unions (including limited liability and equity ownership and transfer rights in the first case, collective bargaining and grievance procedural rights in the second). Authority also promotes collective action by use of taxes and subsidies: by granting subsidies to collective agents (government grants to private social service agencies or research institutes), by exempting contributions to collective from taxation (contributions to charitable agencies are tax deductible, whereas contributions made directly to needy individuals are not), and by exempting collective agencies from taxation (tax exempt status of nonprofit organizations). In addition to these regulatory instruments, authority is used to control markets and market failures by directly shaping the structure of markets and controlling the conduct of organizations in the following ways.

Horizontal Structure. In order to affect bargaining positions in the exchange process, authority shapes the structure of competitors (buyers or sellers). While property rights and the rights of incorporation create a presumption that organizations may grow and expand without further approval, authority can be used to specifically deny such expansion when it threatens the competitive process (antitrust laws on mergers and acquisitions). A more restrictive class of structural controls are entry and exit regulation, which strictly limit the opportunity of producers to enter a market, or to exit from it (public franchises in transportation, communications, and financial services).[6] Although authority primarily has been concerned with power within a given market, there are also controls that span markets, since power in one market might give an unequal bargaining position in another market (restrictions on conglomerate mergers, restrictions on the activities of bank-holding companies).

Vertical Structure. All markets exhibit a high degree of vertical interdependence, with goods moving through many successive transactions from the original source to the final consumer. Accordingly, authority can be employed to regulate the vertical structure of markets, especially those involving economic organizations on both sides of exchange. Structural controls may specify the conditions under which firms will be allowed to vertically integrate across channel levels, or actually prohibit such vertical integration (statutes on vertical mergers).

Horizontal Conduct Controls. In order to shape market structure, authority allows, encourages, and prohibits competitors from cooperating in various ways. To promote the flow of information and the establishment of standards, competitors are usually allowed to cooperate in those areas. Cooperation in research and development, investments in productive capacity, and marketing activities may be allowed or denied (joint-venture regulations). Because of its onerous effects on bargaining, cooperation on the design of the product or on the terms of exchange (especially price) is often prohibited (Sherman and Clayton proscriptions against restraints in trade). In cases where there is a perceived imbalance in bargaining positions, however, cooperation among competitors is allowed, usually by exemption from laws prohibiting such cooperation (antitrust exemptions granted to agricultural marketing cooperatives, the rationale for which is the market failure of excessive competition; buying cooperatives).

Vertical Conduct Controls. In recognition of the complexity of channels of distribution, the state regulates relations among members of the channel, by allowing acts of cooperation (cooperative advertising), denying other acts of cooperation (boycotts), prohibiting certain restrictions in the terms of trade (resale price maintenance), and setting limits on discriminatory treatment in the terms of trade (Robinson-Patman proscriptions on price discrimination, provisions in the proposed AT&T consent decree requiring local operating companies to provide equal access to competing long-distance signal carriers).

Price Controls

Because prices are so central to the allocative functioning of markets, and so critical to the distributional consequences of exchange, authority is used to influence or determine the prices at which exchanges occur. As already noted, prices may be influenced by the imposition of taxes or granting of subsidies, and by controls on the structure of markets and the conduct of subjects in markets. In addition, there are class-of-authority instruments aimed more or less directly at prices themselves, either because other forms of control have failed to produce the desired result or because price controls are preferred to alternative forms of control.

There are a number of dimensions on which price controls vary, and the number of permutations across dimensions is very large. Rather than identifying discrete types of price controls, we will discuss the dimensions that characterize any particular control instrument, and attempt to identify the variants on each dimension.

Compliance. Price controls range from purely voluntary (wage and price guidelines), to quasi-voluntary (use of economic incentives to induce particular pricing behavior, the Tax Incentive Plan for restricting wage increases in labor markets), to mandatory (published tariffs in regulated industries).

Source of Controls. As with standards, prices can be established, and compliance enforced, in a number of ways. The most private method of price control is private exchange, as enforced by contractual rights (long-term supply contracts). Prices also can be established by private agreement among competitors (producer cartels), although this form of price control is often precluded by controls on collective action. Authority can be used to establish or sanction price controls (fee schedules established by professional societies), which means that public authority is employed to enforce compliance with the controls. Price controls can be established by private agencies or association, but submitted to public authority for approval and implementation (state liquor control boards). Finally, price controls can be generated and enforced by public agencies, although usually with procedural rights assuring private participation.

Nature of Controls. Although price controls are always directed at the price terms of exchange, they vary in the manner by which the intended results are achieved. The most marketlike forms of price control are related to price information: requiring disclosure (price posting of wholesale liquor prices to dealers or posting of gasoline prices at the pump); precluding private control on disclosure (banning professional code limits on price advertising); and public provision (comparative price studies published by government agencies). Direct intervention in the pricing process includes establishing a zone within which private parties can set prices (the zone of reasonableness recently adopted by the Interstate Commerce Commission); requiring specific approval of privately set prices (most administrative agencies only approve prices, not actually set them); and establishing the price at which goods or services will be exchanged (postal rates, minimum wages).

Applicability of Controls. Price controls can be applied very narrowly to a specific transaction, or to all transactions between a particular seller (buyer) and its buyers (local telephone rates are seller-specific). More generally, price controls can be applied to all sellers (buyers) in a broad class (motor carrier rates). The most general type of price controls applies to whole sectors of the economy, or even, hypothetically to all prices in the economy (general price freeze). While price controls are most often applied to goods and services in intermediate and final markets, they can also be used in factor markets (minimum wage laws, interest rate ceilings).

Direct Allocative Controls

Prices and rationing are alternative means of allocating or distributing resources. Although rationed goods often carry prices, the defining characteristic of rationing is that exchange is no longer a purely voluntary act by the parties to the exchange: there is some compulsion (in addition to economic incentives) at work on either or both sides of the transaction. Rationing can be implemented directly by public agency or through private exchange transaction channels (public schools versus educational vouchers for private schools). Furthermore, rationing can be positive or negative: it can be used to facilitate the transfer of resources or restrict exchange transactions. We can distinguish the following type of allocative controls.

Price Subsidies. As we indicated previously, subsidies can be granted in the form of stamps or coupons, which can be used along with money in the purchase of specified goods or services. The function of the subsidies in these cases is to increase the ration of those goods to the recipients of the coupons (that is, relative to their ration under market prices). This form of rationing is not intended to limit or restrict the allocation of goods to nonrecipients of the subsidies, although it may have that effect (by increasing the demand for, and therefore market-equilibrating price of, the subsidized goods). It should be noted that this form of rationing may actually be intended to subsidize the producers of the goods, rather than the consumers (hence the support of agricultural lobbies for the food stamp program).

Mandating Exchange. Goods and services also can be positively rationed by requiring sellers to exchange with specified buyers (either at a privately negotiated price or at a regulated price). This form of rationing is commonly employed in public utilities and common carriers, wherein franchised producers are required to provide services on demand to all potential buyers within their franchise area, and at published tariffs. As in price subsidies, the intent of this rationing is to increase, rather than decrease, the volume of exchange; it may also have the effect of restricting exchange (some classes of buyers usually pay implicit taxes in order to subsidize the provision of services to customers whose revenues do not cover the cost of service).

Restricting Exchange. In the event of excess demand for goods, allocative controls can be used to restrict production, exchange, and/or consumption of certain goods and services. Under these controls, money alone is an insufficient means of payment; stamps, coupons, or some other evidence of authority is also required (ration coupons during World War II). Allocative controls also can be applied to factor markets, as in laws regulating hours of employment, or credit allocation.

Proscribing Exchange. The most market-delimiting form of allocative controls is the prohibition of (legal) exchange of goods and services. This form of control is typically directed at those instances in which there is a substantial conflict between market outcomes (in the absence of controls) and prevailing social values (that is, demerit goods). The most emphatic application of this form of control is embodied in the Emancipation Proclamation, which forbade exchange of human beings, and in the labor laws designed to protect children from exploitation in labor markets. As applied to consumer markets, proscriptive controls apply to goods (dangerous drugs) and services (prostitution). We might add that market responses to these prohibitions is a rather striking example of the limits of enforcement and level of compliance with acts of authority.

Government Provision of Goods and Services

As has been noted in the previous sections on regulatory responses, authority can be exercised by allowing, encouraging, or requiring specified conducts or outcomes of private parties, or it can be implemented by the state itself. Depending on the actual configuration of public action, then, authority is more or less consistent with market exchange. When the government is merely providing information that facilitates and improves the operation of markets, there is no conflict between politics and markets. The government can also influence market outcomes by its own actions in the marketplace, as in the use of procurement standards to influence product design (for example, purchasing government auto fleets with air bags to help auto makers on the scale necessary to economically offer them as an option to other customers).

Beyond these market facilitating acts, though, government can be directly involved in markets by substituting for them. Through the use of public enterprise, for example, the government grants to itself the franchise necessary for transacting in that market (postal services). By holding the rights of ownership to itself, government can more or less exclude the enterprise from capital markets and substitute public authority for market control of the firm; along this dimension are quasipublic enterprises (ConRail, ComSat) and government enterprises (U.S. Postal Service).

Having established agencies of government as the provider of goods and services, these agencies differ in whether their output is exchanged through markets with prices (public universities), quasiprices (user charges such as gasoline excise taxes), or rations (social services).

Types of Regulatory Failures

This section presents a typology of regulatory failures—that is, how and why public actions intended to correct market failures (at least purportedly) fail to achieve their goals. This section provides guidelines for deciding when regulatory action may be justified and for choosing among alternative regulatory responses.

To set the stage for this typology, we provide a summary of regulatory responses and market failures. While we would expect fundamental rights and the common law to affect virtually all types of market failures, it would seem logical that other regulatory responses would be used to solve specific types of market failures. Table 2 shows quite a different picture. It is possible to cite instances in which each type of regulation is being used in response to each type of market failure.

Thus, while we will say something about the design of regulatory responses and their likelihood of success, it is not possible to specify a single kind of remedy that should be applied to each particular type of market failure: the uses of regulatory instruments are more pervasive, and their success or failure more complicated. Key questions that should be addressed in evaluating regulatory responses are:

> Are the consequences of a market failure sufficient to justify the cost of the regulation and the performance that it can reasonably be expected to achieve?

> Do the apparent shortcomings of a given regulation stem from its design or implementation, or are they inherent in the nature of the original market failure?

> Are there other regulatory responses that would be more likely to achieve better performance or be more cost effective?

> Will a regulatory response that is successful in the short term prove to be a failure over the longer term?

> Are there secondary or aggregate effects of a regulation on the marketing system or other social systems that outweigh the direct or immediate effects of the regulation?

Public Choice Failures

While most public-policy analyses are typically cast in terms of economic efficiency, fairness, freedom, and equity are criteria that are more basic to a democratic society. Indeed, the most fundamental basis for a market economy is that only a free-market

Table 2
Typology of Market Failures and Regulatory Responses

Regulatory Responses	Types of Market Failures							
	Monopoly Power	Anticompetitive Conduct	Excessive Competition	Imperfect Information	Externalities/Side Effects	Public Goods	(De) Merit Goods	Income Distribution
Legal rights and liabilities	Unenforceable contracts (e.g., cartels)	Criminal antitrust statutes	Bankruptcy laws	Product liability; commercial libel limits	Nonsmoking workplace rights	Antidiscrimination laws	Controlled substance criminal liabilities	Limits on right-to-fire employment-at-will
Information	Line-of-business reporting	Ban of professional advertising restrictions	Licensing boards' information services	Cigarette packaging/advertising warnings	Toxic waste "site right-to-know" ordinances	Public health information	Ratings of movies	State employment agencies
Standards	Electric utility service reliability	Fair trade laws	Aircraft maintenance standards	Funeral industry disclosure requirements	Automobiles catalytic converters	Federal highway design standards	State accreditation of schools	Equal opportunity employment standards
Taxes/subsidies	Excess profits tax (WWII)	Antitrust civil fines	Local air service subsidies	FDA's "failure-to-disclose" fines	Fines for air/water effluent violations	Tax exemption of non-profit schools	National endowments for arts/humanities	A.I.D., Medicare
Controls on/rights of collective action	Antitrust/restraint of trade	Boycott restrictions	Legal cartels (agricultural marketing boards)	Class action product liability	Class action environmental suits	Permit control on parades/demonstrations in public places	Antitrust exemption for newspapers	Labor union organizing, collective bargaining
Price controls	Utility rate regulation	Predatory pricing limits	Minimum rate regulation	State insurance regulation	Peacetime price/wage controls	Deposit bottle bills to combat litter	State liquor price controls	Lifeline utility rates
Allocative controls	Equal carrier access (telephone)	Antidumping provisions	Entry controls (taxi, motor carrier permits)	Prescription drugs	Offshore drilling rights	Allocation of radio and TV broadcast license	Public school attendance requirements	Import preferences to Third World countries
Public provision	Highways; municipal electric utilities	Law concerning political debates on TV	Depository insurance; crop loans	Consumer buying guides	Public schools and higher education	National parks and forests	Public schools and higher education	Social welfare services

system is consistent with political freedom and individual liberty. Moreover, democratic societies regularly use methods of organization and control that are not efficient in the narrow sense of the term. Perhaps the best example of inefficiency in a democratic society is an election. Imagine bearing the costs of having millions of people go to the polls when a small random sample of the population could produce the same result at a fraction of the cost, although with some small margin of sampling error. In democratic societies, we do use representational methods to increase efficiency over ongoing town meetings. In addition to elections, our primary institutions of public choice are legislatures, judiciaries, and executive agencies. As with markets, we can identify the ideal character of these institutions, but we use those ideals as standards against which to measure or compare realities. As markets fail, so do the institutions and instruments of authority. Some failures are inherent in the public-choice process itself.[7]

Transaction Costs. Public choice is a costly proposition, regardless of the method or object of choice. For this reason, public choices have a natural longevity, the duration of which is determined by a subsequent act of public choice that eliminates, modifies, or substitutes for prior choice. While in markets we often make frequent, periodic choices (which store to shop at, which brand of soft drink to buy), we make public choices much less frequently. By and large, prevailing policies are the accumulation of prior public choices. As circumstances change over time, we should expect that, even if the policy were once appropriate, it will become less so over time. But because of the transactions costs of public choice, we do not spontaneously change policies in accord with changing circumstances.

Electoral Failures. Elections play three different roles in public choice: (1) by referenda, voters actually decide public policy; (2) by electing legislators, voters decide who will make policy decisions; and (3) by electing executives, voters decide who will make and/or implement policy decisions. Although there are some similarities between markets and elections (enough so that modern political economists refer to the supply of and demand for political services and the marketing of candidates), there are some fundamental differences.

The most critical difference between markets and politics is that there can be no exchange; candidates for elected office can promise to support certain policies or promote certain values if elected, but they cannot offer anything specific in exchange for someone's vote. Even if such a promise were made, it would be an unenforceable contract between the parties (which is not to deny that such promises have been made, and parties have attempted to enforce such contracts, albeit in violation of the law). In short, elections lack the reciprocity essential to exchange.

Elections differ most from markets in their inherently collective nature. Whereas market exchanges are acts of private, individual choice, elections must necessarily be acts of public, collective choice (Olson 1971). Unless we impose a rule of unanimity (which would make public choice impossible in most electorates), election results will favor some individuals over others. Indeed, a central feature of the social contract in democratic societies is that individuals agree to accept the results of elections, even when they lose.

As a consequence of majority rule, the result of an election is a public good in that an individual voter can neither determine the outcome nor be excluded from incurring the benefits or costs of the outcome. As a public good, the electoral process suffers from the problem of free riders. No matter how or even whether one individual votes, the outcome will be the same. So even though elections may have very important consequences for individuals, they have little incentive to become well informed, or even participate in the process.

Even when citizens do vote, elections suffer from a number of problems not unlike market failures. There are very serious information failures: compared to most economic products and services, public choices are exceedingly more complex. In order for elections to work well, voters must understand the nature and consequences of alternative votes; such information is always costly, time-consuming to process, often unavailable, and sometimes misleading. Issues of public choice are on occasion so complex that not even the experts fully understand the alternatives, much less the electorate.

Another electoral failure relates to the bundling of issues. Although market goods are a bundle of desired attributes, we typically have considerable choice among bundles. Indeed, some tied sales are illegal. In elections, we are usually limited to two (or other small number) of choices: yes or no on referenda, Democratic or Republican representation. Because an elected official will represent his/her constituency on countless issues of public choice, it is a certainty that there will be differences between the votes or the legislator (or the acts of an executive or judge) and the preferences of any given voter. Thus, bundling forces individuals to make difficult trade-offs among issues; they may favor one candidate's stand on transportation policy, another on energy policies.

Alternatively, some voters may use a choice process that places such importance on a particular high saliency issue that the candidates' position on that single issue may determine their vote. The result may be that the winning candidate, while favoring the right position on the single issue, may have positions on other issues that are at odds with the majority of the electorate.

Legislative Failures. Once elected, legislators ideally act in the interests of a majority of their constituency, although that necessarily means action against the interests of some constituents on any given issue. Moreover, we assume that legislators are not fundamentally different from other individuals, so we expect them to behave (if sometimes opportunistically) in their own self-interest. Given the costs of conducting electoral campaigns, and the need for organized support to overcome information failures, one significant failure is the influence of resourceful, vocal, well-organized citizens in the legislative process. Legislators also suffer from information failures, in that the issues they decide are extremely complex individually, and usually bundled together in legislative acts.

Other legislative failures relate to their representational and organizational structure. These structural failures include: (1) the overrepresentation of rural interests in the U.S. Senate or state senates (that is, citizens in jurisdiction with small populations have far more senators per capita than those in populous jurisdictions); (2) the committee and seniority systems concentrate power in the hands of a minority of representatives, whose interests (or even whose constituents' interests) are not necessarily those of a majority of the electorate; and (3) the complexity and number of issues is such that elected representatives increasingly depend on staff whose private interests (for example, future employment with lobbying organizations) may differ from constituents' interests.

Jurisdictional Failures. Whether public choice is made directly through elections or through representation, it can create externalities not dissimilar to those found in market systems. Externalities occur because public policies of a given jurisdiction can have effects on citizens or activities in other jurisdictions. Examples of these externalities include air or water pollution moving across state lines, liberal corporate charter provisions causing companies to incorporate in a state other than the one in which they principally do business, and interstate differences in taxes or subsidies causing personal movement to lower tax or higher welfare states. At the highest level, jurisdictional failures arise among nation states, where the consequences of regulatory or market failures of one country may fall on the populace of other countries. Indeed, nationalistic self-interest might seek such results, especially when reciprocity or retaliation is improbable.

Design Failures

As we have shown in table 2, many different types of regulation are used to prevent, modify, and shift the costs/benefits of each type of market failure. Regardless of the type of the intent or method of regulation, policies fail in part because policy makers often lack the information needed to (1) correctly assess the nature and extent of the market failure, (2) evaluate the direct effects of alternative responses, (3) evaluate the side effects of alternative responses, (4) correctly predict the incidence of costs and benefits of the regulation, or (5) simply design a regulatory response that will solve the market failure. In some cases, the necessary information is simply not available (that is, it lies beyond the limits of human knowledge or is prohibitively expensive to obtain). In other cases, the problem is one of information asymmetry: the parties to be regulated have, or control access to, the information needed for the policy design, but the public policy makers do not. Participants in the policy design process will exploit this asymmetry to gain strategic advantage. These information failures, combined with the legislative failures just described, lead to, ex post, poorly designed regulation.

A special kind of information failure concerns external and side effects. Efforts to regulate one market or product almost inevitably affect other goods or markets. Regulating auto emissions by requiring the installation of catalytic converters dramatically shifts the demand for converters while decreasing the demand for research and development into superior methods of emission control. There is virtually no limit to these side effects, as they are transmitted, like ripples, from one market to another. In the worst cases, negative effects are amplified in magnitude; in such cases, regulation may be successful where it was intended, but still is a failure overall because the indirect effects outweigh the direct benefits.

Even where there are discernible benefits of regulation, there are always costs as well. The self-evident costs are those incurred by the government in implementing a policy, but these are sometimes small relative to the total costs, which include the costs of complying with the regulation by private parties. Because the costs and benefits of a regulation are seldom, if ever, borne by the same parties in the same proportions, there are inevitably distributional consequences of regulation, whatever their primary purpose may be.[8]

Implementation Failures

Once policies are selected, through the democratic public-choice process (either in the present or very distant past), they must be implemented to have an effect on private conduct or market outcomes. The legislature delegates responsibility for implementation to an agency of the government, a quasipublic agency (one with legal powers granted by the state), or a voluntary association of individuals. Although legislative enactments sometimes contain specific provisions regarding delegation, more often acts are implicitly delegated on the basis of general principles (or laws) of delegation. Thus, the implementation of contract compliance provisions falls to the judicial system as a matter of constitutional principle. Sometimes legislative acts create new agencies for implementation of the policies in the act, although even then legislatures are constrained by legal separation of power, jurisdictional rights among units of government, and the organization of those units.

Although there are a large variety of institutional mechanisms for implementing public policies, we will concentrate our attention by grouping into four classes: judicial agencies, bureaucratic agencies, public boards, and private associations. While all of these suffer from more or less the same generic institutional failures (mainly, information failures, transactions costs, free riders and agent-principal problems), the manifestations of these failures differ across institutional types. It is because of these differences that we choose one agency of implementation over another in order to minimize the failures and improve performance and outcomes.

Judicial Failures. The distinguishing characteristic of judicial agencies is that they implement policies by deciding whether parties have, in a given instance, complied with prevailing policies (constitutional, statutory, administrative, or common law). The parties engaged in the process can be individuals, associations, or other public agencies. Typically, these decisions are made in an adversarial process, which has a number of institutional implications.

First, principals in the dispute (plaintiff, prosecutor, or defendant) are represented by agents (lawyers) who receive income for their services. Self-interested behavior of agents often conflicts with the interests of the principals (for example, expending resources to appeal a decision that will surely be upheld).

Second, the adversaries in the dispute represent only two of the interests affected by the decision; there are externalities of judicial acts both positive and negative (for example, establishing a precedent that will be used in future cases). One of the most frequently cited failures of regulatory agencies is of this sort: the tendency of agencies to be captured by well-organized interested parties, to the exclusion of other interests.

Third, the information available to the decision maker (judge, jury, or regulatory commission) will depend in large part on the evidentiary submissions of the parties, with consequent information failures. Information needed for a good decision may not exist, or it may be concealed. The quality of the information presented is dependent on the representational abilities of the agents and the resources of the principals; if there is an imbalance in abilities or resources, the decision process may not be fair.

Finally, there are inherent limits of judicial decisions (as opposed to executive actions); courts have very limited enforcement capabilities. Though actions can be prevented (injunctions), courts are generally limited to punishing or compensating for acts that have already occurred. When those acts have irreversible, irreparable, or otherwise noncompensable consequences, courts cannot remedy them.

Bureaucratic Failures. Responsibility for interpretation and implementation of public policies are commonly assigned to agencies of government. The standard organizational form of these agencies is bureaucratic, hence the classification of the failures associated with implementation by public agencies. Because individuals in bureaucracies are self-interested, a most significant class of bureaucratic failure is the pursuit of organizational objectives contrary to the objectives of the public policies (Crozer 1963). One prominent instance of such behavior is budget-maximization, but there are many others as well: promoting policies that will further the career objectives of agency employees, acting favorably toward parties for financial gain or future employment prospects, or interpreting policies in a manner consistent with personal values, but inconsistent with the social values on which the policies are premised (Fritschler and Ross 1980; Wilson 1980).

Bureaucracies also fail due to information failures. As they often are dependent on regulated industries for data and analysis, they are subject to opportunistic behavior by those parties. In any case, the issues they must decide and the actions they must take to successfully implement policies are complex, sometimes beyond the limits of bounded rationality.[9]

The most widely noted failure of bureaucracies is their cost, which is indeed staggering (add up the combined expenditures of all levels of government). But as recent studies have shown (Weidenbaum 1981), the costs of bureaucracy are quite small compared to the costs of compliance with the regulations they impose. Even so, these costs must be measured in relative terms, since alternative institutional forms are not costless.

Finally, there are bureaucratic failures of a jurisdictional kind, due to overlapping jurisdictions across agencies or levels of government (for example, attempts by the CAB, FAA, and OSHA to regulate airline working conditions; or the myriad of environmental reports and approvals required for new factory construction). Although many of these are instances of turf protection by agencies, they also result from the inherent structure of governmental authority in a society that values separation of powers and checks and balances. Even in societies of this persuasion, however, there are organizational alternatives. In the United States, the checks are principally through a congressional committee; in the United Kingdom, the checks are principally through the Exchequer; in India, the checks are principally through purposely given overlapping authority to agencies in other ministries.

Quasipublic Agency Failures. One common technique to get around the suboptimization, information failures, and high cost of bureaucracies is the public board. In this structure, private citizens are appointed to sit on a regulatory board. In some cases they serve for only expenses; in other cases they may receive a fee. However, they are not career civil servants. These appointments should reduce costs. The citizens are appointed because, when viewed as a whole, they represent the broad interests of the society, and therefore, are unlikely to seek objectives other than those of society. They are also selected because they have some expert knowledge in the field they are appointed to regulate. Thus, they should overcome some informational failures, and if provided with some agency staff support, they should at least be able to ask the right questions.

Unfortunately, such boards can exhibit failures on all counts. First, since they are expert, active citizens, they are busy. They may not always have the motivation to prepare their positions and decisions as carefully as the society would like. Thus, the staff involvement and costs are as great or greater than if the board were not there. Second, how does an executive branch select a board that represents society, is motivated to serve, and is expert in the special field (as well as active in the right political faction)? The answer is often to pick persons from the field being regulated. Even if true public members are on such boards, they often defer to the expertness of the industry members. Thus, such boards often use their additional information to serve the special interests of the regulated rather than the interests of the society.

Private Association and Self-Regulation Failures. The problems just cited may not be serious if the regulation is concerned with efficacy, internal equity, health, and safety with regard to the practice of a particular profession. In such cases, responsibility for implementing public policies is often granted to private associations in such professions. Normally, these delegations of authority involve individuals or organizations with economic interests affected by the policy, for example, professional licensing boards and agricultural marketing boards. Here, one of the failures of public boards becomes far more serious in such attempts at self-regulation. Clearly, the association's authority can be used in the self-interest of the members of the association without regard to unrepresented interests. This problem is exacerbated by the problems of bounded rationality and asymmetric information. The costs or benefits of authority are usually distributed very unevenly, for example, the benefits of milk price-supports accrue mainly to a few thousand producers, while the costs are borne by tens of millions of consumers. In these circumstances, it is quite rational for the producer group of individuals to devote their time, energy, and resources to the formation and implementation of authority, while the rest of society ignores the situation.

Another class of failures of self-regulation relates to the appointed citizens' limited authority. When we delegate authority to private associations, we specifically limit that grant, either in the terms of the act authorizing the delegation or by more general legal principles. Thus, private remedies sometimes fail because the private association lacks the authority to obtain a sufficient degree of compliance for its policies. This is especially true when there are public goods at issue, as when the benefits or costs of labor organizing for collective bargaining accrue to all employees, whether or not they participate in the organizing and bargaining process.

Finally, policy implementation by a private association often fails due to agent-principal problems. Authority is seldom exercised directly by the members of an association. Having received a grant of authority from the state, they in turn delegate the responsibility for implementation to administrators or representatives, who may or may not be members of the class of recipients of authority (staff members of professional licensing boards or trade associations). As self-interested individuals, these agents may behave opportunistically to advance their own interess at the expense of the association members.

Implications for Public Policy

During the mid-1960s to the mid-1980s, public policies in the United States have undergone historic changes. We have witnessed, on the one hand, an enormous increase in the degree and extent of social regulation such as equal employment, environmental and consumer protection, occupational and product safety, financial disclosure, and civil rights. On the other hand, deregulation of whole industries has occurred in trucking, airlines, telephone equipment, intercity telecommunications, and securities brokerage. What accounts for these seemingly contradictory trends, and what do they tell us about public policies toward business and business-government relations?

There seem to be four general forces at work. First, as the structure of markets changes, so does the structure of regulation. Regulations that were once well-suited for a given market failure no longer fit the situation well. This clearly happened in the deregulation of airlines, trucking, and intercity telecommunications. Airlines and trucking were, when first regulated, infant industries subject to problems of excessive competition. By the 1970s, though, both were mature industries with well-developed route systems serving every corner of the nation. The costs of price controls far exceed the benefits, as the results of deregulation have demonstrated. When telecommunications was first regulated, the basic technology was wires and poles, with substantial economies of scale, making the industry a natural monopoly. With the development of microwave communications in the 1950s, and its widespread adoption by the 1970s, the industry was no longer a natural monopoly. Again, a change in economic conditions justified a shift in public policy. The same is true of social regulation, but with a resulting increase, rather than decrease, in regulation.

A second force underlying regulatory change is changing public attitudes about what constitutes market failures. Neither environmental pollution nor racial employment discrimination were new problems in the 1960s, yet neither had occupied prominent positions on the public-policy agenda. Led perhaps by populist journalism and mass communications media, public perceptions of the social harms caused by these and other market failures increased dramatically. Legislative hearings shed the search light of political attention and public opinion on these problems, new laws were enacted, and whole new regulatory agencies created. It may well be that, as a body politic, we over-reacted to the problems, weighing the costs of market failures while discounting the costs of regulatory intervention. But the point here is that changing public values and attitudes do cause changes in public policies toward business.

The third force affecting regulatory change is the growth of knowledge regarding the consequences of production and consumption activities. There have been many cases of externalities, for example, that simply were not known, sometimes for decades. The long-term health effects of workplace environments and consumer products have become much better understood with recent advances in medical knowledge. We did not regulate in the past because we literally did not know of, or understand the sources of, harms to public health and safety. As our knowledge improves, we can change the mix of markets and regulations to better achieve efficiency and equity objectives. Many changes in occupational safety, product safety, and related regulations exemplify the application of new knowledge in the policy-making process.

Increasing knowledge of political, social, and economic institutions, and their consequences represents a fourth major factor affecting regulatory change. As we learn more about regulation and markets and the costs and benefits of using these institutions as methods of economic organization, we use that knowledge to increase, decrease, or modify regulation to improve social performance. Many of the important regulatory changes of the past few years embody innovative techniques or institutional forms. As with all forms of innovation, the development of better ways of regulating can reduce the costs, and increase the effectiveness of regulation.

Finally, regulatory change is driven by shifts in the general conditions of the economy. While market failures can be costly in human terms, regulation can be costly in economic terms. As a society, we are continually confronted with the choice of whether to regulate, but, more fundamentally, how much can we afford to regulate. As the United States has declined from its former position of a dominant world economic power, we have had to confront the ultimate economic choice: of deciding how much public provision of goods, and how much public protection from bads, we are willing to pay for. That is a central source of the tension and the vitality of a democratic society.

Notes

1. For this view of the legal framework of markets, we owe intellectual debts to Commons (1959) and Samuels (1966). For full bibliographic references, see the bibliography of the preceding article in this book.
2. Schelling (1971) presents an insightful analysis of the use of laws or other instruments of authority in cases involving congestion or free riders.
3. For an excellent set of essays on product quality regulation, see Caves and Roberts (1975).
4. Hemenway (1975) is a thorough analysis of voluntary product standards, with several case studies.
5. Hawley (1981) presents a very interesting discussion of associationalism: the use of public authority to promote social control by private associations.
6. Schmalansee (1979) offers a comprehensive review of the rationale for, and implementation of natural monopoly regulation, and an excellent bibliography of recent theoretical and empirical research in that field.
7. For an excellent synthesis and survey of the public choice literature, see Mueller (1979).
8. Weidenbaum (1981) has estimated compliance costs to be a large multiple of government expenditures on regulation.
9. For a discussion of the role of information and knowledge in regulation, see Hays, Samuel P., "Political Choice in Regulatory Administration," in McCraw (1981).

The Fight Against Government Waste

George S. Goldberger

In campaigning for the presidency before the 1980 election, Ronald Reagan vowed to reduce the intrusion of the federal government into the lives of the American people. In June 1982, he created the President's Private Sector Survey on Cost Control (PPSS) to search for waste and inefficiency in the federal government.

Under the leadership of J. Peter Grace, chief executive officer and chairman of W.R. Grace & Co., and 160 other top business executives, more than 2,000 volunteers were recruited to work on this eighteen-month study. They came up with 2,478 ways to cut waste and enhance revenues, thereby reducing the federal deficit. The proposals, in forty-seven reports and a two-volume summary to the president, are supported by 1.5 million pages of documentation. The PPSS cost taxpayers nothing; it was completely funded by the private sector donating $76 million in people, services, travel, and supplies. If Congress and the Executive Branch would act on the Survey's recommendations, they would save the government—and the taxpayers—$424.4 billion over a three-year period once fully implemented, or about $140 billion a year.

The president's idea was not to change the functions of government. It was simply to have expert businessmen take a close-up look at those functions that were comparable in both the public and private sectors. The federal government does run like a business; it just runs like a poor business. Government hires and fires people, keeps accounting books; uses computers, manages bank accounts, borrows and lends money (lends money it does not have to people who cannot afford to borrow), buys and sells materials (when the government sells something it usually winds up costing the taxpayers money), produces reports (it does a lot of that), and performs dozens of the same functions that a private corporation does.

While many of the functions performed by business and government are comparable, there is an important difference between them. Business has to perform functions efficiently and profitably if it is to survive. That is the discipline of the marketplace. Competition ensures that an individual company simply cannot afford to maintain a bloated payroll, or mismanage its cash, or pay more than it has to for the goods and services it purchases. The federal government, in contrast, does not have to make a profit. It does not even have to keep score since it cannot lose. It can print or borrow money to offset its losses (deficits) and it has no competitors. The government has no incentive to efficiently and effectively perform its functions. According to Peter Grace:

> If the American people realized how rapidly federal government spending is likely to grow under existing legislated programs, I am convinced they would compel their elected representatives to get the government off their backs.[1]

In the past, U.S. taxpayers have allowed government to escape the discipline of the marketplace, giving government a free hand to mismanage the nation's affairs. But, recently, the American people have become concerned about the way government has been spending their tax dollars, and their elected representatives are feeling the pressure to cut wasteful spending practices. Taxpayers have awakened to the fact that, once government has spent their money, they ultimately have to pay up, whether it's now or later—whether it's them or their children and grandchildren.

The President's Private Sector Survey

PPSS was established in 1982 to review government operations and make recommendations for reducing and eliminating federal waste and inefficiency. When President Reagan called to ask Peter Grace to head the new cost study commission, he agreed, considering it a personal honor and a duty to serve the President and our country. Like many, Grace had watched and criticized increased federal spending for years; the President provided Grace with an opportunity to substitute action for words.

Grace certainly had some qualms about the task. Just how much could realistically be accomplished by this sort of project? Would this be another commission report to be filed away and gather dust? How could he ask some of the highest-ranking and busiest executives in the United States to put so much time and effort into a deficit-cutting study when everybody knew the budget could not be cut? There was another consideration: President Reagan said he wanted this to be entirely a volunteer effort. The government would not contribute a cent. He asked that civic-minded corporations donate money and materials and, most important, their best managerial talent. How many millions would have to be raised? What would the contributors have to show for their donations? Would the commission do any good?

Grace's first task was to recruit 160 of the best and brightest of American corporate talent—the chief executives of the nation's leading corporations—to serve on the PPSS Executive Committee. His main criteria for selecting the members was expertise in sound management of large enterprises, as evidenced by their own performances in business. He signed up business leaders like Frank Cary, chairman, executive committee of IBM; Armory Houghton, chairman, Corning Glass Works; Willard C. Butcher, chairman, Chase Manhattan Bank; Professor Lawrence Fouraker, Harvard Business School; Robert Beck, chairman, Prudential Insurance Company; Clifton Galvin, chief executive officer, Exxon; Robert Galvan, chairman, Motorola; and Donald Keough, president, Coca-Cola. The list of those who served on the PPSS Executive Committee reads like an honor roll of American business leadership.

No consideration was given to politics in putting together the commission. The desire to reduce federal spending and eliminate the deficit cut across all political lines. A management office was established in Washington to oversee survey operations. The chief operating officer was J.P. Bolduc, a former vice-president and partner with Booz, Allen and Hamilton, a management consulting firm, and now a vice-chairman at W.R. Grace & Co. The deputy director was Janet Colson, who was special assistant to the president and served as liaison between the White House and the survey.

A dozen senior management consultants and executives, at considerable cost, set aside their professional practices to join the management office and work on the survey. They directed the day-to-day work of more than 2,000 corporate volunteers who served on thirty-six task forces—these volunteers were accountants, line officers, and management and financial experts on loan from large corporations. Twenty-two task forces focused on single departments or agencies, and fourteen focused on major functions cutting across all departments and agencies, on topics such as personnel management and procurement.

Using the Treasury Task Force, for example, the project managers and core staff people were thoroughly briefed on the workings of the government, especially the Treasury Department. This stage included initial interviews with top Treasury officials and the preparation of a bibliography of reports and materials to study. Department spending and income trends over the past twenty years were examined.

All the task forces were amazed to learn that the federal government keeps no historical record of its spending by line item. Expense records such as utility costs, phone bills, and travel were not kept, so PPSS had to compile this data by itself. Historical spending data is essential to identify excesses in any cost-cutting analysis. Thus, it is no wonder that past attempts at cutting costs have been less than successful. Hundreds of General Accounting Office (GAO), Office of Management and Budget (OMB), and Inspectors General reports were reviewed and analyzed to determine the spending track record.

Next, the Treasury Task Force conducted extensive interviews with senior Treasury officials, studying all relevant information to identify which specific issues to analyze in depth. Once the issues were identified, task force members surveyed the various areas looking for targets where cost-cutting measures would be most effective in providing important long-term savings.

The task force avoided recommending only short-term solutions to problems. The entire appropriations process suffers from a short-term perspective ensuring that politically palatable compromises, often with costly, unnecessary long-term results, will be adopted. Finally, the task force spent weeks verifying its facts and analyses, preparing a plan for putting its recommendations into effect, and writing up its recommendations. Once all the task force recommendations were in and the reports were written (around December 1983), they were condensed into a two-volume final report to the president.

The PPSS labors, which extended over almost two years, produced forty-seven in-depth reports, which, including the final report, totaled more than 21,000 pages, with an additional 1.5 million pages of supporting documentation. Three-year savings of $424.4 billion in spending cuts and revenue enhancements were recommended, ranging in size from about $500,000 to $58.9 billion. All this work was done at a donated cost of $76 million in manpower, equipment, and materials. The federal government only paid for Ms. Colson's salary; the rest came from the private sector.

From the start, PPSS was concerned with avoiding even the appearance of a conflict of interest. All members of the executive committee were cleared by the White House Office of Legal Counsel. Then, those members of the executive committee who were assigned to serve as task force chairpersons were also cleared for conflicts of interest by the departments and agencies they would be investigating.

Everybody else who worked for the commission was subject to strict internal rules against conflict of interest.

None of those checks and balances stopped congressional critics from accusing PPSS of conflict of interest. Representative John Dingell of Michigan, "patron saint" of the Environmental Protection Agency, claimed that the Treasury Task Force should be locked out of its offices. Representative William Ford, also of Michigan, was even more vociferous; he was particularly distressed that PPSS uncovered excesses in the Civil Service system. Ford is chairman of the House Post Office and Civil Service Committee—the committee responsible for correcting government-spending excesses. When it came to protecting the respective "turf" of a representative, congressional criticism grew in proportion to the PPSS recommendations perceived to be endangering that representative's special interests.

Rigid rules sometimes prevented PPSS from making the best use of the corporate leaders who volunteered for the executive committee. For instance, Frank Cary, chairman of the Executive Committee of IBM, is a computer expert. However, government officials said that if he headed the Data Processing Task Force, there might be the appearance of a conflict of interest. Somehow IBM might get a special advantage. That possibility seemed pretty remote, but, in the end, Frank Cary had to be assigned to the task force on the Department of Housing and Urban Development.

The policy versus management issue was another problem for the Survey. Congress seems to look on almost any administrative change in the federal government as a "policy matter." But policy was not the interest at all. PPSS did not pretend to say how the government should use its resources in defense, education, welfare, highways, and other matters of national interest. The survey did look at how well policy was executed, but it was only concerned with efficiency. As an example, the decision of government to give out food stamps was not PPSS's concern. The purpose was to see how well the government was performing in getting those stamps out at the least cost.

It is, admittedly, difficult to draw the line between operations and policy. If there is a gray area in operations, in either the public or private sector, it is the difference between policy and management. For example, the PPSS report on subsidized programs recommended that the government poverty figures be revised to include in-kind income such as food stamps and housing subsidies. That recommendation makes good management sense. If someone's income is counted as, say, $4,800 a year, but that person gets $200 worth of food stamps a month and a housing subsidy of $250 a month, then it makes sense to consider that person's income as being $10,200 a year, including $5,400 in food stamps and housing subsidies. If that is the process, that person may be ineligible for some other kind of aid, for instance, a subsidized loan or free dental care. Perhaps that person should be disqualified from one or both programs, but whether he should be or not is a policy question.

PPSS learned the government does not know how much any one particular individual or business is receiving in subsidies. This lack of a tracking system results in government being unable to determine what policy to choose. PPSS recommendations were to provide that information. PPSS also has been accused of having exaggerated savings estimates. It has been charged that the commission's estimated savings of $424 billion is 50 percent off the mark. The GAO did a six-month review of the work of the commission. In this review, the first time GAO examined PPSS work, it concluded that about 25 percent of what PPSS recommended made sense and ought to be implemented. What GAO failed to mention in that report, however, was that any PPSS recommendations where the savings were estimated to be less than $1 billion were not reviewed. Nor did GAO review any recommendations that had been implemented in 1983, 1984, or any that would require implementation beyond 1987. These were quite restrictive parameters, but even with these restrictions, GAO determined that about 25 percent of the PPSS recommendations warranted action.

A year later, at the request of a couple of senators, the GAO examined the recommendations again. This time the GAO spent nine months reviewing the commission's recommendations and then reported that 80 percent made sense for implementation. Why the change? We do not know. Nonetheless, whether the GAO's 25 percent or 80 percent figure is accepted, there is merit to the survey findings.

A Harvard professor extensively criticized PPSS on the basis of a one-page fact sheet distributed at public presentations. On this particular occasion, J. Peter Grace distributed a fact sheet with ten key points. One of these dealt with the General Services Administration (GSA), and the overlap and duplication of effort between the GSA and other federal agencies. The professor attended this presentation and took the commission to task on the subject of the GSA. Without contacting PPSS and without looking at the supporting material, he wrote a twenty-six-page critique based on the one-page hand out. PPSS responded with a fifty-page rebuttal that we sent to the professor, the media, and every member of Congress. PPSS has not heard any more about the professor's criticism.

The charge of exaggerated savings has supposedly been substantiated by the emergence of different figures. There are major differences between the numbers PPSS derived and the numbers federal agencies and Congressional committees are trying to use as actual numbers. An example can be found in Margaret Heckler's office, the former secretary of Health and Human Services. Secretary Heckler had 5,023 people in her immediate office. PPSS recommended a cutback to 2,017. Heckler cut the personnel level to 3,000, and PPSS was then accused in the media of exaggerating numbers. But the difference, in this example, was a function of judgment, different assumptions, and the agencies' interpretations of the Survey recommendations.

Another major criticism PPSS encountered was an engrained belief that since the Survey recommended turning over a number of government functions to nongovernmental bodies, there would be opportunities for tremendous profits on behalf of the private-sector parties who would provide these functions. Privatization critics failed to see that the federal government would save money by turning over some functions to private enterprises.

In each of these cases—and there are others—PPSS has stood up to the criticisms, making its members available every time PPSS has been invited to testify before Congress to demonstrate its case. PPSS has rebutted attacks on its own behalf. While PPSS members have some differences about the interpretation and implementation of the survey recommendations, no one has substantiated that PPSS lied, cheated, distorted, or exaggerated the truth.

Ten Points No One Should Argue Against

As a starting point, many of the PPSS recommendations can be summarized into ten broad principles on which there should be general agreement as cost-saving measures.

1. PPSS believed that the government's commercial activities should be contracted out or privatized to fully recover their costs. They should not be subsidized at taxpayer expense. The users of those services should pay for them. An overall review of federal user-charge policies is needed because current pricing practices are inconsistent both within and across agencies. The GAO supported this recommendation.

PPSS further recommended specific steps to improve the management of the government's commercial activities. The survey recommended the establishment of a separate and centralized organization within agencies to manage user-charge programs and to implement a management reporting system to professionalize the management of those programs. While many of the recommendations on user-charge programs could be accomplished under presidential authority, both PPSS and the GAO recognized the absolute necessity of congressional involvement and support to achieve meaningful program improvements and cost savings.

The U.S. government spends $3 million a day to operate, maintain, and improve the nation's commercial navigation system but recovers only $120,000 a day—4¢ on the dollar—in user charges. The federal government subsidizes grazing fees, but charges only about one-fifth the comparable charges assessed on nonpublic lands. The program covers about 40 percent of its costs. Even if grazing fees were increased to fully recover the cost to the government, they still would be only about one-half of what is charged on public lands. Similarly, yacht owners whose engines die are towed to shore free, courtesy of the U.S. Coast Guard. No user fees are charged. Rather than focus on specific actions, the adoption of a consistent government policy of full cost recovery for commercial activities would save $10.9 billion over three years.

2. Government lending programs need revision. All too frequently the government lends money it does not have to people who cannot afford to borrow. Not surprisingly, the government does not get back much of the money it lends. PPSS recommended that federal lending practices parallel the policies and procedures adhered to in the private sector. This means establishing origination and application fees sufficient to cover the associated government costs. The government should charge interest and penalties on late loan payments and centralize to the maximum extent possible a debt collection staff with clear-cut standards and objectives. Further, since the government's credit programs are so heavily oriented toward loan origination rather than loan servicing, PPSS recommended a transition from direct to guaranteed lending wherever possible.

3. The government's procurement practices are neither efficient nor cost-effective; they're mired in excessive and inconsistent regulations, limited and inaccurate information, and uncoordinated, poorly planned acquisitions. They fail to take full advantage of competition to reduce costs and they have imposed an impressive array of disincentives to professional procurement program management.

PPSS recommended actions to enhance the role, responsibility, authority, and accountability of program managers, while strengthening the role of the Office of Federal Procurement Policy by its integration into the overall budget process. PPSS procurement-related recommendations were heavily oriented toward increasing competition to control costs. Spare parts should be purchased competitively and from the actual manufacturer, yet in 1982 the Navy only purchased 16 percent of its spare parts on a competitive basis. With Department of Defense (DOD) spare-parts purchases totaling $22.6 billion in fiscal year (FY) 1984, the potential for savings is significant.

If Congress truly is serious about controlling waste and inefficiency in military spending, a good place to start would be with legislative obstacles and impediments to efficient procurement. According to DOD Assistant Secretary Laurence Korb, simply eliminating from the defense budget "pork barrel" costs for things the military neither wants nor needs would save taxpayers $10 billion a year. PPSS estimated that procurement reforms could save the government $34.5 billion over three years.

4. Any commercial or industrial function currently performed by the government, which could more economically be performed by the private sector, should be turned over to the private sector either by contracting the function out or by privatization. OMB estimates potential annual savings of $5 billion, and the Congressional Budget Office (CBO) stated that vigorously pursuing a policy of contracting-out could shift 140,000 federal jobs to the private sector. However, Congress historically and all too frequently obstructs agencies' cost-reduction initiatives.

For example, the Veterans Administration, which accounts for about 20 percent of all civilian workers outside the Defense Department, is exempt from contracting-out provisions. Congress, in fact, has even included specific language in appropriations bills that prohibits the expenditure of federal funds to even investigate the possibility of contracting-out.

In regard to privatization, clearly the government is engaging in many activities that would be best left to the private sector or other levels of government, for example, providing electric power through the Power Marketing Administrations. Getting the government out of many of these businesses by contracting-out or privatization could save the taxpayers $37.0 billion over a three-year period. PPSS concluded that effective implementation of a policy of reliance on the private sector is not likely to occur unless Congress legislates a national policy and further acts to remove legislative obstacles to contracting-out.

5. The government's procedures for managing and compensating its employees should be consistent with those of the private sector. The need to increase work-force productivity and establish incentives for effective management is clearly evident. For example, current compensation practices relate a federal manager's salary to the size of both the work force and the work load managed. Obviously, the incentive to increase efficiency and productivity while reducing personnel requirements is limited or nonexistent.

PPSS recommended that the government develop an adequate work-force policy to determine the number of people and the skills necessary to accomplish objectives. The Survey also recommended that the government's pay-comparability surveys be adjusted so they accurately reflect what they purport to measure—private-sector salaries—and that retirement, sick leave, and vacation costs be reduced so they are comparable to those in the private sector.

The GAO supported the PPSS recommendations to reform the pay-setting systems for federal white- and blue-collar workers. In addition, the GAO supported the survey's recommendations regarding productivity and work-force planning, with the GAO noting that historical constraints on work-force planning—for example, personnel ceilings and hiring and promotion freezes—are barriers to effective personnel management that should be eliminated. In total, the PPSS recommendations related to federal compensation, fringe benefits, and work-force management would save $90.9 billion in three years following full implementation.

6. A recurring deficiency in the structuring of government programs is their failure to direct benefits to the intended recipients. For example, while the government might establish as a national priority insuring the nutritional requirements of all poor children, it seems incapable of targeting those benefits to those actually in need. Thus, our tax dollars go to subsidize the school lunches of children whose families have $100,000 incomes. Even the intended recipients receive their benefits under a myriad of overlapping and duplicated programs. In the case of child nutrition programs, the taxpayer can be subsidizing six meals each day for the same child.

On a larger scale, despite expenditures of $124 billion in 1982 on means-tested programs for the poor—such as Aid to Families with Dependent Children, food stamps, and Medicaid—the poverty gap was reduced by only $37 billion, from $50 billion before means-tested transfer payments to $13 billion after all these transfer payments had been made. In theory $124 billion should have brought all households out of poverty and should have been sufficient to bring all households to 125 percent of the poverty level with $47.5 billion left over. Despite the magnitude of the dollars expended for subsidies ($462 billion in 1982), adequate information does not exist to determine the degree to which the intended recipients of these subsidy programs are receiving sufficient benefits or the degree to which benefits are being bestowed upon undeserving recipients to the detriment of all taxpayers.

PPSS recommended that agencies be required to develop annual evaluation plans, improve their program-evaluation data, and use this data on a consistent basis in establishing budget requirements. Fundamental to many improvements in government operation is tying this evaluation process to the budget process. PPSS also recommended consolidating administrative functions of the federal subsidy program. As a specific action, PPSS recommended that a form, similar to a W-2 form issued to wage-earners, be issued by each federal department or agency to recipients of federal subsidies. This would enable the government to determine for the first time who is getting how much from which federal subsidy programs, and to determine whether or not the programs are fulfilling their intended purpose. In total, PPSS estimated that $58.9 billion could be saved over three years through the improved targeting of benefit programs.

7. Congressional encroachment in what should be straightforward executive-branch operating decisions is a major obstacle to efficient and cost-effective management of the government. Over and over, PPSS witnessed congressional intervention to ensure that unneeded employees are retained, that unneeded facilities are kept open, that duplicated benefits are paid through overlapping subsidy programs, and that taxpayer dollars are wasted through inefficient procurement practices. For example, Congress repeatedly has acted to prevent the closing of obsolete and/or unnecessary military installations throughout the United States. Congress still appropriates funds to operate a military facility in Virginia surrounded by an eight-foot moat. Another fort in Utah still protects the overland stagecoach route from Indians. These facilities would make better museums than military bases and would result in sizable dollar savings to the taxpayers. Because these facilities are in the "turf" of influential members of Congress, however, they are not closed. The OMB estimates that a thorough realignment of military bases could lower defense expenditures by $2 to $5 billion annually. PPSS-specific recommendations on congressional involvement in day-to-day executive-branch operations would, if implemented, save $8.8 billion over three years.

8. Government should balance the wants of certain segments of society against the needs of the taxpayer when it evaluates legislation. The failure to carry out this philosophy can be seen clearly in the evolution of federal health-care programs. While it was recognized that all Americans have a justifiable right to the health care they need, programs were designed to provide them with the health care they want without regard to cost. For example, those who need medical care want to get that care from the doctor of their choice, even if that doctor charges unreasonably high fees. Unfortunately, it is the taxpayers who pay for this.

Federally subsidized power sells at one-third the market rate, costing industrial users in the Northwest only 2.45 cents per kilowatt hour. The Power Marketing Association, which provides these subsidized rates, is funded by the U.S. government. By contrast, industries in San Diego, California, pay 12.08 cents per kilowatt hour for power generated by private utilities.

9. No single department or agency is responsible for overall executive-branch administrative direction and policy setting. Responsibilities for property, financial management, human resources and computer management are distributed among many agencies. The impact of this fragmentation is a lack of attention to significant opportunities for cost reductions and management improvements.

The reporting relationship between central agency staffs (OMB, Office of Personnel Management (OPM), GSA, and Treasury) is generally ill-defined and incomplete. PPSS recommended the creation of an office of federal management within the executive office of the president to provide centralized leadership and policy direction. The absence of the right information, at the right time to make the right decision, renders the government incapable of effectively assessing its strengths and weaknesses and makes it difficult for government to maintain managerial efficiency.

10. The government needs to adopt a businesslike approach in managing its finances. PPSS found that the acquisition and implementation of common computer systems would save substantial resources and would improve management information overall.

Federal financial-management procedures have little in common with accepted private-sector accounting principles. Budgeting, accounting, cash, and loan and debt management, as well as auditing functions are conducted in the government largely independent of one another. As a result, there are opportunities for waste, fraud, and abuse. To correct these deficiencies, PPSS recommended that the proposed Office of Federal Management (OFM) take responsibility for formulating and coordinating financial management policies and practices throughout the government.

The responsibilities of the OFM would be similar to those of a private-sector corporate headquarters financial staff: directing and coordinating the government's overall accounting and financial reporting policies and activities, and developing a program to identify and implement government-wide financial improvements on an on-going basis.

Citizens Against Government Waste

In August 1984, syndicated columnist Jack Anderson and J. Peter Grace cofounded Citizens Against Government Waste (CAGW). CAGW is a nonprofit, bipartisan, national membership foundation working to educate the American people and members of Congress about the many opportunities for eliminating waste and inefficiency in government as identified by the Grace Commission, congressional committees, federal employees, and other sources.

To achieve these objectives, CAGW is conducting a number of programs to educate the public. Among them, CAGW continues to mount a national drive to acquire millions of signatures on a petition calling for an end to the excesses and unnecessary squandering of government funds for foolish projects, wasteful programs, and inefficient operations. CAGW recruits members daily to show the skeptics in Washington that Americans from all walks of life are extremely concerned about deficit spending.

The CAGW petition drive is being aided by businesses nationwide. One corporate supporter, Wal-Mart Stores, Inc., the second largest discount chain in the nation, participated in the CAGW drive by soliciting signatures from vendors, associates, employees, and customers. Their drive yielded over 300,000 signatures that were collected at over 750 stores.

CAGW is supplying information to the two congressional "Grace Caucuses," one in the U.S. House of Representatives, cochaired by Congressmen Beau Boulter (R.-TX) and Buddy Roemer (D.-LA), and the U.S. Senate Grace Caucus cochaired by Senators Gordon Humphrey (R.-NH) and Dennis DeConcini (D.-AZ). Total membership in the two caucuses has topped 25 percent of the entire U.S. Congress. Both the House and Senate caucuses were formed during summer 1985, in a bipartisan effort to study and implement the best of the 2,478 recommendations proposed in the PPSS report.

In a Rose Garden ceremony addressing members of both caucuses, President Reagan agreed to seek implementation of over 80 percent of the recommendations, over a three-year period at a cost savings of more than $240 billion. Over 70 percent of these agreed-to recommendations, however, require congressional approval before they can be enacted and the savings realized.

It is in this spirit that members of the House and Senate decided to act on the recommendations and formed the caucuses. As members of Congress, they are in a position to legislate their beliefs. Unlike hundreds of special interest and lobbying groups around Washington, D.C., who approach Congress from outside the chambers, caucus members can directly propose legislation to implement their recommendations.

There are fourteen task forces in the House caucus. Each group is assigned to consider a specific portion of the recommendations. Task-force participation is divided among the caucus members by virtue of each member's field of interest and expertise. The task forces regularly hold hearings and study the testimony of experts who offer suggestions for increasing the efficiency of the federal government.

Before a hearing of the House Grace Caucus Task Force on Contracting Out and Privatization, OMB Director James Miller walked into the room with a copy of the PPSS Privatization Report and agreed with Grace recommendations calling privatization opportunities a "major untapped potential for savings." He agreed with a number of Grace proposals, including the philosophical point that "government need not produce the services which it elects to provide." CAGW officials are regularly called on to testify at hearings that address wasteful, fraudulent, and inefficient government practices.

Recognizing the tremendous potential of utilizing U.S. trade associations and professional societies as a vehicle to spread the word about waste and inefficiency in government, CAGW has enlisted their assistance. Over 1,500 trade associations and businesses have joined CAGW's "War On Waste" and CAGW is expanding its national program to gain the endorsement and active participation of others. National trade and business associations have joined CAGW's Associations United to Cut Federal Spending (AUCFS), a federation of trade and business associations that support the implementation of the Grace Commission's recommendations and other cost-saving measures.

Member organizations have participated by using CAGW's educational materials and PPSS's specific recommendation to prepare their own legislative initiatives to help the cause. Each AUCFS member organization has its own legislative network within its membership. Thus, the CAGW message is transmitted to thousands of businesses across the country and, subsequently, passed on to individual members of Congress indicating the emerging ground-swell of demand for political reforms. AUCFS represents over 3,200,000 American families when the associations' membership is totaled.

The U.S. Jaycees, a 268,000-member organization, received a $25,000 grant to develop a program to educate the public about the PPSS findings. Working with CAGW, the Jaycees' program focuses on grass roots educational projects, such as seminars, petition drives, and letter-writing campaigns. CAGW hopes that the Jaycees' program can be continued and sustained by further support from foundations.

Furthering the momentum of CAGW are forty-four state coordinators in two-thirds of the states from Maine to Hawaii, and from Minnesota to Texas. The coordinators help CAGW achieve objectives of eliminating federal waste and inefficiency by working at the local level and organizing functions that require local direction. They oversee signature petition drives throughout their state, conduct local media interviews, set up steering groups and other support organizations, and accept speaking engagements on CAGW's behalf.

Adding to CAGW's "War On Waste" at the state level are a number of state initiatives to reduce waste and inefficiency in government spending. Florida has a citizens group called TAXWATCH, Inc. Michigan's Governor Blanchard helped create a group called the Executive Corps, made up of fifteen private-sector executives to serve as efficiency watchdogs and consultants. In New York, Governor Cuomo launched a Management and Productivity Program that achieved over 92 million in cost saving in 1985. Utah has established a Commission of Economy and Efficiency. California has the Assembly Committee on Governmental Efficiency.

The trend is becoming clearer every day. People are upset about the wasteful, fraudulent, and inefficient practices of government, whether local, state, or federal. In the past year, Virginia and Texas have set up their own mini–Grace Commissions to study and implement legislative and policy decisions to cut back a top-heavy and burdensome government.

A CAGW Speakers Bureau also is operational and includes over 200 experts from across the country, including many of the nation's chief executive officers who served on the PPSS team. In 1985, CAGW speakers went out to thousands of organizations across the nation, reaching hundreds of thousands with its message. CAGW speakers give the inside story on the Grace Commission, relate their experiences with the survey, and move their audiences to take up the fight. Speakers Bureau participants are available for radio and television appearances, grant newspaper and magazine interviews, and will speak to large and small groups interested in learning more about the Grace Commission and its recommendations.

Recently, CAGW launched a $50 million, multimedia advertising campaign through the New York-based Advertising Council. The campaign included public-service announcements for television, radio, magazine, newspapers, business press, and outdoor posters for bus and transit companies. With the message of "our country can't afford government waste, and neither can you," CAGW urges citizens to call the toll-free hotline (1-800-USA-DEBT) to learn more about the PPSS recommendations and the "war on waste."

All along, the CAGW approach has been to focus on a massive, grass roots educational effort that reaches out to Americans in every walk of life. By promoting a greater understanding of the problems and solutions, CAGW aims to create and sustain a "climate for change," which will call for a new direction—a direction that will put the United States back on the road to fiscal stability. CAGW's most basic assumption is simply that an educated electorate is the first and most vital step in effecting change. In its first year, over 100,000 phone calls were received on CAGW's toll-free hotline as well as thousands of letters, postcards, and signatures on its petition. Today about 100 calls a day are received on the hotline requesting additional information.

Grace Recommendations Today

If you watched the State of the Union Address in 1986, you know that the president once again publicly appealed to the Congress to act on the Grace Commission recommendations. He asked Congress to grant him a line-item veto, an early PPSS recommendation, to achieve the deficit target mandated by Gramm-Rudman-Hollings legislation. (All three Senators are Grace Caucus members.)

On the following day, the president submitted his budget and the OMB's *Management of the United States Government Fiscal Year 1987* report. The report contained some very good news on the Grace Commission findings. It stated that completed recommendations will save taxpayers $30.6 billion in 1986. It also listed nearly 600 recommendations as having been implemented in prior years including measures to:

offset delinquent loans against income tax refunds,

develop a modern payroll system with electronic funds technology,

speed the collection of government receipts,

charge interest and penalties on delinquent debts,

increase use of automated data processing,

reduce commodity distribution and warehousing costs,

implement dual sourcing for weapons systems and components,

require the use of common parts in weapons systems,

expand the use of contracted services,

improve agency printing and production,

expand multi-year procurement.

The progress to date in Congress has been slow but steady. The 99th Congress enacted eighty PPSS recommendations with government estimated savings of $33.2 billion over the next three fiscal years. The tempo of activity in Congress vis-à-vis the PPSS recommendations will certainly pick up in the 100th Congress as both House and Senate Grace caucuses introduce new packages of recommendations advocated by the Grace Commission to reach the mandatory deficit reduction targets for the next four fiscal years as mandated by the Gramm-Rudman-Hollings deficit-reduction act. Given this target and the legislative agenda packages provided by the Grace caucuses, Congress can be expected to show an enhanced interest in the opportunities for reducing wasteful and inefficient government spending.

Note

1. J. Peter Grace, *War on Waste* (New York: MacMillan, 1984), p. v.

Operating in a New Competitive Environment: The Reagan Administration's Approach to Antitrust Proposals

U.S. Department of Justice

On February 19, 1986, the administration sent five legislative proposals to Congress for important improvements in U.S. antitrust laws. The five bills are entitled the Merger Modernization Act of 1986; the Interlocking Directorate Act of 1986; the Antitrust Remedies Improvements Act of 1986; the Foreign Trade Antitrust Improvements Act of 1982; and the Promoting Competition in Distressed Industries Act. (The Merger Modernization Act, the Interlocking Directorate Act, and the Antitrust Remedies Improvements Act are discussed here.) The administration's proposed reforms will greatly benefit U.S. industries, workers, and consumers. The antitrust laws are critical aspects of our free-market economy, but some of their key provisions, enacted in 1890 and 1914, need prompt revision.

Many Americans now compete in global markets, and cannot afford to be shackled by outmoded, unduly restrictive antitrust rules. The time has come to improve and modernize the antitrust laws. During the past twenty years, advances in economic theory have shown that the antitrust laws should protect consumer welfare and promote economic efficiency. Unfortunately, current antitrust laws have instead been applied at times in a way that inhibits innovative business activities that would benefit consumers.

The proposals deal with mergers, treble damages and other antitrust remedies, interlocking directorates, jurisdiction in cases involving international commerce, and alternative antitrust relief under the Trade Act of 1974. This legislation will strengthen the ability of American business to maintain a position of leadership in world trade, and allow U.S. consumers to reap the benefits of free trade and fair competition.

Excerpts from the Merger Modernization Act of 1986

A Bill

To clarify and improve the analysis of mergers under the antitrust laws.

Be it enacted by the Senate and House of Representatives of the United States of America in Congress assembled, That this Act may be cited as the "Merger Modernization Act of 1986."

Sec. 2. Section 7 of the Clayton Act (15 U.S.C. 18) amended by

(a) in the first paragraph—
(1) striking out "the effect of" and inserting in lieu thereof "there is a significant probability that";
(2) striking out "may be" and inserting in lieu thereof "will"; and
(3) striking out "to lessen competition, or to tend to create a monopoly" and inserting in lieu thereof "increase the ability to exercise market power";

(b) in the second paragraph—
(1) striking out "the effect of" and inserting in lieu thereof "there is a significant probability that";
(2) striking out "may be" and inserting in lieu thereof "will"; and
(3) striking out "to lessen competition, or to tend to create a monopoly" and inserting in lieu thereof "increase the ability to exercise market power"; and

(c) in the third paragraph—
(1) striking out "the substantial lessening of competition" in the first sentence and inserting in lieu thereof "a substantial increase in the ability to exercise market power"; and
(2) striking out "lessen competition" in the second sentence and inserting in lieu thereof "increase the ability to exercise market power"; and

(d) inserting immediately after the third paragraph the following new paragraph:

"For purposes of this section, the ability to exercise market power is defined as the ability of one or more firms profitably to maintain prices above competitive levels for a significant period of time. In determining whether there is a significant probability that any acquisition will substantially increase the ability to exercise market power, the court shall duly consider all economic factors relevant to the effect of the acquisition in the affected markets, including (i) the number and size distribution of firms and the effect of the acquisition thereon; (ii) ease or difficulty of entry by foreign or domestic firms; (iii) the ability of smaller firms in the market to increase production in response to an attempt to exercise market power; (iv) the nature of the product and terms of sale; (v) conduct of firms in the market; (vi) efficiencies deriving from the acquisition; and (vii) any other evidence indicating whether the acquisition will or will not substantially increase the ability, unilaterally or collectively, to exercise market power."

Analysis of the Merger Modernization Act of 1986

It is widely recognized that mergers, in general, have important procompetitive and efficiency-enhancing effects. On occasion, however, particular mergers can be anticompetitive. While such mergers should be prevented before they occur, it is extremely important that the effort to interdict anticompetitive mergers not interfere with the ability of U.S. firms to reorganize freely through mergers and acquisitions that enhance productivity, innovation, and worldwide competitiveness. Inappropriate restraints on efficiency-enhancing mergers impose heavy costs on society. Businesses and consumers suffer alike when companies are unable to combine to better meet competitive challenges, both foreign and domestic.

Today, U.S. industries face increasing competition from their foreign counterparts. If U.S. firms are to compete vigorously in world markets, they must be free to restructure their operations to take advantage of opportunities to increase their efficiency and respond to changing market conditions and technology. Thus, it is vital that merger law today be as clear as possible in distinguishing procompetitive from anticompetitive mergers.

As our understanding of the economics of free markets grows, it sometimes becomes necessary to fine tune the antitrust laws to ensure that they remain properly focused on enhancing competition. Thus, for example, the Foreign Trade Antitrust Improvements Act of 1982 clarified the application of the antitrust laws to export commerce and the National Cooperative Research Act of 1984 guaranteed the application of the antitrust rule-of-reason standard to the analysis of competition-enhancing research and development joint ventures.

In the more than seventy years since section 7 of the Clayton Act was enacted in 1914, the body of economic learning on which antitrust enforcement policy and judicial doctrine regarding mergers is based has changed substantially. The uncertainty surrounding merger analysis in 1914, and even in 1950 when section 7 was last revised substantially, can be seen in the vague wording of section 7, which prohibits mergers the effect of which "may be substantially to lessen competition, or to tend to create a monopoly." Until the late 1960s, courts lacked a sophisticated analytical framework for merger analysis. They therefore relied primarily on the size of merging firms and crude measures of concentration in the affected markets to gauge the competitive effects of mergers, giving little, if any, consideration to equally relevant factors.

Modern merger analysis, exemplified by the 1984 Department of Justice *Merger Guidelines*, is more refined and takes into full consideration foreign competition, entry conditions, and efficiencies. This more refined analysis is increasingly being adopted by the federal courts in Clayton Act section 7 cases.

Unfortunately, refining and modernizing outdated merger standards and analysis through the issuance of enforcement guidelines and case-by-case adjudication is slow and can result in an inconsistent body of case law. Efforts to establish a modern and consistent merger standard are complicated by the fact that the current language of section 7 carries the baggage of decades of inconsistent and economically unsophisticated merger analysis. Both Congress and the Supreme Court have construed this language to mean that before a merger may be condemned, it must be shown that there exists a reasonable probability or likelihood that it will substantially lessen competition. Notwithstanding this construction, however, and explicit acknowledgment that section 7 is not concerned with ephemeral possibilities, section 7 has been applied in the past in an overly restrictive manner that is patently inconsistent with proper merger-enforcement policy. In consequence, the confusion surrounding the existing language in section 7 is slowing the pace at which the modernization of merger analysis under the antitrust laws can proceed.

In an economy facing increasing competitive pressures from foreign firms, unnecessary delay in the modernization of merger analysis should not be countenanced. Revising the language of section 7 to incorporate the advances in merger learning that have been made since the mid-1960s will provide a new, state-of-the-art foundation on which future refinemenents and improvements can be built, while at the same time finally laying to rest outmoded economic and legal analysis of mergers that can be found in older court decisions. This is the purpose of the Merger Modernization Act of 1986.

The act achieves its goals in three basic ways. First, the act amends the first two paragraphs of section 7 to state more precisely the degree of certainty regarding anticompetitive effects that is legally required to prohibit a merger. The act replaces the "may be" and "tend to" language in section 7 with the requirement that there be a "significant probability" that a merger will be harmful before it will be prohibited. This new standard more accurately reflects current case law and enforcement policy interpreting section 7. In particular, it makes clear that section 7 is not intended to prohibit mergers on the mere possibility, rather than the significant probability, that anticompetitive effects will follow.

Second, the act makes clear that section 7 is directed against mergers that threaten to increase consumer prices. Specifically, it replaces the existing "lessen competition" or "create a monopoly" language with a more precisely defined standard that is in keeping with modern economic analysis, namely, that anticompetitive mergers are those that "substantially increase the ability to exercise market power." Market power is defined in the act as "the ability of one or more firms profitably to maintain prices above competitive levels for a significant period of time." The act thus affirms that section 7 is intended to preserve competition, rather than competitors per se. It does so by focusing merger analysis on the increased ability of firms to raise prices to consumers as a consequence of a merger and away from the mere fact that one or more firms will be eliminated from the market by acquisition. While this principle is increasingly accepted by courts interpreting section 7, the new language is clearer and less likely to be misapplied.

Third, the act establishes a sound framework for determining the likely effects of mergers by clearly directing courts to consider the important economic factors that bear on that analysis. It thus assures that no one factor will be determinative of a merger's legality, to the exclusion of other probative economic evidence.

Whether a proposed merger will give rise to an increased ability to exercise market power within clearly defined product and geographic markets is the central issue under section 7. Section 7 has always required and will continue to require that the anticompetitive effects of a merger or acquisition be evaluated "in any line of commerce . . . in any section of the country." Thus, the first step in any merger analysis is to determine relevant product and geographic markets, because it is only within the confines of meaningful economic markets that the competitive effects of a proposed merger can be accurately evaluated.

In order to define relevant markets, it is necessary to evaluate the probable future responses of both purchasers and foreign and domestic producers in an attempt to exercise market power. Market power is the ability profitably to institute and sustain a price increase above the competitive level. The availability of close substitutes for the product in question and the ability of other firms to enter into or expand production are the major constraints on market power. Thus, a market can be defined as a product or group of products and a geographic area such that a profit-maximizing firm that was the only seller of those products in the area would impose a significant and nontransitory price increase above prevailing or likely future levels. Relevant markets only can be determined in the context of specific mergers, but accuracy in their definition is crucial.

Once the relevant market (or markets) has been correctly defined, it is possible to evaluate the probable effect of a merger on the ability of one or more firms in the market profitably to maintain prices above competitive levels. The Act identifies six specific factors that courts should consider in assessing that effect. It also directs the courts to consider any other relevant evidence.

The first of the six factors is "the number and size distribution of firms and the effect of the acquisition thereon." The more concentrated the market, the greater the likelihood is that one dominant firm, or two or more firms acting collectively, could exercise market power. The greater the percentage of the market supplied by a dominant firm, the easier it would be for that firm profitably to restrict output sufficiently to effect a price increase. Where collective action is needed to restrict output and raise prices, the costs of achieving and maintaining such action will be less, the chances for success will be greater, and a smaller number of firms cooperating will be needed. Of course, it is not the number of firms in the market alone that must be considered. The relative size of the firms in the market is also relevant to the likelihood that collusion would be successful. For this reason, a concentration measure such as the Herfindahl-Hirschman Index (HHI), which takes into account both the number and size distribution of firms in the market, is generally the starting point for merger analysis. Factors indicating that future concentration in the relevant market is not accurately reflected by current circumstances—for example, changing market conditions or the weakness of particular firms—also must be taken into account in the analysis.

Second, the act requires courts to consider the "ease or difficulty of entry by foreign or domestic firms" into the market. If firms not presently in the market could profitably enter in response to a price increase, it is less likely that firms presently in the market could profitably maintain prices above competitive levels for a significant period of time. Conversely, if entry into the market is unlikely, significant market concentration reflects more accurately the risk of a price increase following a merger.

The third factor to be considered is "the ability of smaller firms in the market to increase production in response to an attempt to exercise market power." The effect of this factor is similar to ease of entry. An attempt by larger firms acting alone or in concert to exercise market power would be undercut if smaller firms in the market had the ability to increase their output significantly in response to a price increase.

Fourth, the act requires courts to consider "the nature of the product and terms of sale." First, the homogeneity/heterogeneity of the product is relevant in assessing the likelihood of collusion. When the product in the market being analyzed is relatively undifferentiated, agreements among producers to raise prices should generally be easier to reach than they are with respect to products that are more complex, heterogeneous, and subject to options. Also relevant is the degree of difference between the products and sellers considered to be in the market and the next-best substitutes. The larger the gap at the edge of the product and geographic markets, the more likely are effects that can be predicted on the basis of market concentration data. Finally, some sellers may be more effective rivals of particular firms than other sellers, as a result of proximity or the public perception that they produce a superior product, or for some other reason. If such rivals merge, there is a greater chance for the exercise of market power.

The fifth factor identified in the act as relevant to the analysis of a merger is the "conduct of firms in the market." If the firms in the market have a history of violating the antitrust laws, and market characteristics basically have not changed, increasing the degree of concentration in the market will be of greater concern than it would be if the firms had no such history. If the relevant market has not been operating competitively in recent years, increased concentration resulting from a merger could further strengthen any existing potential for the exercise of market power.

Sixth, the act directs courts to consider "efficiencies deriving from the acquisition." In cases where the factors just discussed indicate that the merger would result in a significant risk of market power, the courts should consider probative evidence of efficiencies achievable by the merger. Such efficiencies might derive from economies of scale, better integration of production facilities, plant specialization, lower transportation costs, and similar savings relating to specific manufacturing, servicing, or distribution operations of the merging firms. Other efficiencies also can be considered where they can be sufficiently demonstrated to be achievable.

It should not be the burden of firms to establish an affirmative case for the existence of efficiencies when the analysis does not indicate that the merger otherwise would result in a significant probability that market power could be exercised. Where it is necessary to consider efficiencies, however, the courts should also consider whether similar efficiencies could be achieved by the firms without merging.

Finally, the act requires the consideration of "any other evidence indicating whether the acquisition will or will not substantially increase the ability, unilaterally or collectively, to exercise market power." This catchall provision ensures that the courts will not ignore any significant economic evidence regarding the likely effects of a merger. This provision also builds into section 7 additional flexibility to take proper account of further advances in economic learning with respect to the effects of mergers and acquisitions in a market economy.

Excerpts from the Interlocking Directorate Act of 1986

A Bill

To make necessary and appropriate amendments to the antitrust laws governing service as a director of competing corporations.

Be it enacted by the Senate and House of Representatives of the United States of America in Congress assembled, That this Act may be cited as the "Interlocking Directorate Act of 1986."

Sec. 2. The fourth paragraph of section 8 of the Clayton Act (15 U.S.C. 19) is amended by—

(a) striking out "any one" and inserting in lieu thereof "each";

(b) striking out "$1,000,000" and inserting in lieu thereof "$10,000,000";

(c) striking out the period after "laws" and inserting in lieu thereof the following:

"provided, that service as a director in two or more corporations shall not be prohibited by this section if the sales, determined on the basis of annual average gross revenues over the preceding two completed calendar or fiscal years, as may be appropriate in the circumstances, of each such corporation of each product or service sold by such corporations in competition with one another (1) are less than 5 percent of such corporation's total sales, unless the sales of all such products or services by such corporation exceed 25 percent of such corporation's total sales; (2) together with such corporation's sales of all other such products or services are less than $1,000,000; or (3) are less than 3 percent of the total sales in each line of commerce in each section of the country in which such corporations compete"; and

(d) adding at the end the following:

"For each fiscal year commencing after September 30, 1986, the $10,000,000 and $1,000,000 thresholds in this paragraph shall be increased as of October 1 each year by an amount equal to the percentage increase in the Gross National Product, as published by the Department of Commerce or its successor, for the year then ended over the level so established for the year ending September 30, 1985."

Analysis of the Interlocking Directorate Act of 1986

The Interlocking Directorate Act of 1986 makes several important and timely changes in section 8 of the Clayton Act, which generally prohibits service by any person as a director of two or more competing corporations engaged in interstate commerce if any one of those corporations has capital, surplus, and undivided profits of more than $1,000,000. The act provides exceptions to section 8's prohibition where competition between two or more firms is *de minimis,* and thus where their sharing of a common director poses no threat to competition generally. The act also amends and updates section 8's jurisdictional threshold to confine its coverage to larger firms.

Section 2 of the act makes four amendments to section 8. First, section 2 requires each corporation sharing a common director to exceed section 8's capital, surplus, and undivided profits jurisdictional threshold in order for the prohibition of that section to be applicable. This requirement will confine section 8's application to interlocks among large firms, thus freeing smaller businesses of federal antitrust oversight of the make-up of their boards. Competitive concerns raised by interlocks involving smaller businesses are not significant, and do not warrant such oversight.

Second, section 2 of the act raises the $1 million capital, surplus, and undivided profits threshold in section 8 to $10 million. This dollar threshold, established in 1914 and never changed, is badly out of date. Third, section 2 of the act establishes explicit *de minimis* exceptions to section 8's prohibition of interlocks among competing corporations. Courts interpreting section 8 strictly have declined to recognize any implicit *de minimis* exception. Thus, minor competitive overlaps that raise no significant competitive concerns are hindering the selection of the best-qualified directors, especially by diversified firms.

There is little competitive risk presented by an interlocking directorate where competition between the affected firms is no more than *de minimis*. Where the competitive overlap is a very small part of each firm's business, active consideration of the details of the overlapping business by the boards of directors is most unlikely. Where the competitive overlap affects no more than a very small part of any relevant market, it is no cause for concern about harm to competition. In these situations, and where the competitive overlap involves commercial activities very small in absolute dollar amounts, the prophylactic rule of section 8 clearly is overly restrictive.

Section 2 addresses this problem by defining three "safe harbors" that would exempt certain interlocks between competitors from the coverage of section 8. The first safe harbor generally protects interlocks between firms, each of whose sales of any competing product are less than 5 percent of its total sales—a fact within the certain knowledge of the firms themselves. The second safe harbor protects interlocks where the total competitive overlap amounts to less than $1 million of each firm's business—again a simple fact known to the firms. The third safe harbor protects interlocks between firms, each of whose sales of any competing product are less than 3 percent of any relevant market in which they compete. These safe harbors will make it much easier for corporations to select qualified directors with no real possibility of competitive harm and no uncertainty regarding the lawfulness of their decisions.

Finally, section 2 indexes the new $10 million jurisdictional threshold and the new $1 million *de minimis* "safe harbor" to the gross national product, in order to prevent distortion of their effects by the passage of time.

Excerpts from the Antitrust Remedies Improvements Act of 1986

A Bill

To promote and improve efficient and effective enforcement of the antitrust laws.

Be it enacted by the Senate and House of Representatives of the United States of America in Congress assembled, That this Act may be cited as the "Antitrust Remedies Improvements Act of 1986."

Title II—Treble Damage Reform

Sec. 201. Subsection (a) of section 4 of the Clayton Act (15 U.S.C. 15(a)) is amended to read as follows:

"(a) Any person who shall be injured in his business or property by reason of anything forbidden in the antitrust laws may sue therefore in any district court of the United States in the district in which the defendant resides or is found or has an agent, without respect to the amount in controversy, and shall recover actual damages by him sustained, interest calculated at the rate specified in section 1961 of title 28, United States Code, or at such other rate as the court finds to be fair to fully compensate such person for the injury sustained, on such actual damages for the period beginning on the earliest date for which injury can be established and ending on the date of judgment, unless the court finds that the award of all or part of such interest is unjust in the circumstances, and the cost of suit, including a reasonable attorney's fee; provided, that except as provided in subsection (b), damages sustained by reason of such person having been overcharged or underpaid by any person subject to liability under the antitrust laws for such damages shall be trebled; and provided further, that prejudgment interest under this section on actual damages that are trebled shall be recovered only if, pursuant to a motion by the injured person promptly made, the court finds that the award of all or part of such interest is just in the circumstances, taking into consideration only—

(1) whether such person or the opposing party, or either party's representative, made motions or asserted claims or defenses so lacking in merit as to show that such party or representative acted intentionally for delay, or otherwise acted in bad faith;

(2) whether, in the course of the action involved, such person or the opposing party, or either party's representative, violated any applicable rule, statute, or court order providing for sanctions for dilatory behavior or otherwise providing for expeditious proceedings; and

(3) whether such person or the opposing party, or either party's representative, engaged in conduct primarily for the purpose of delaying the litigation or increasing the cost thereof.

Sec. 202. Section 4A of the Clayton Act (15 U.S.C. 15a) is amended to read as follows:

"Sec. 4A. Whenever the United States is injured in its business or property by reason of anything forbidden in the antitrust laws it may sue therefor in the United States district court for the district in which the defendant resides or is found or has an agent, without respect to the amount in controversy, and shall recover actual damages by it sustained, interest calculated at the rate specified in section 1961 of title 28, United States Code, or at such other rate as the court finds to be fair to fully compensate the United States for the injury sustained, on such actual damages for the period beginning on the earliest date for which injury can be established and ending on the date of judgment, unless the court finds that the award of all or part of such interest is unjust in the circumstances, and the cost of suit; provided, that damages sustained by reason of the United States having been overcharged or underpaid by any person subject to liability under the antitrust laws for such damages shall be trebled; and provided further, that prejudgment interest under this section on actual damages that are trebled shall be recovered only if, pursuant to a motion by the United States promptly made, the court finds that the award of all or part of such interest is just in the circumstances, taking into consideration only—

(1) whether the United States or the opposing party, or either party's representative, made motions or asserted claims or defenses so lacking in merit as to show that such party or representative acted intentionally for delay, or otherwise acted in bad faith;

(2) whether, in the course of the action involved, the United States or the opposing party, or either party's representative, violated any applicable rule, statute, or court order providing for sanctions for dilatory behavior or otherwise providing for expeditious proceedings; and

(3) whether the United States or the opposing party, or either party's representative, engaged in conduct primarily for the purpose of delaying the litigation or increasing the cost thereof."

Sec. 203. Paragraph (a)(2) of section 4C of the Clayton Act (15 U.S.C. 15c(a)(2)) is amended by striking the second sentence and inserting in lieu thereof the following:

"The court may award under this paragraph, pursuant to a motion by such State promptly made, interest calculated at the rate specified in section 1961 of title 28, United States Code, or at such other rate as the court finds to be fair to compensate natural persons in such State for the injury sustained, on such total damage for the period beginning on the earliest date for which injury can be established and ending on the date of judgment, if the court finds that the award of all or part of such interest is just in the circumstances."

Title III—Defendants' Attorneys' Fees

Sec. 301. Section 4 of the Clayton Act (15 U.S.C. 15) is amended by adding after subsection (c) the following new subsection:

"(d) In any action under this section, the court shall award the cost of suit, including a reasonable attorney's fee, to a substantially prevailing defendant upon a finding that the plaintiff's conduct was frivolous, unreasonable, without foundation, or in bad faith."

Sec. 302. Section 16 of the Clayton Act (15 U.S.C. 26) is amended by adding at the end thereof the following:

"In any action under this section in which the defendant substantially prevails, the court shall award to such defendant the cost of suit, including a reasonable attorney's fee, upon a finding that the plaintiff's conduct was frivolous, unreasonable, without foundation, or in bad faith."

Title IV—Claim Reduction

Sec. 401. The Clayton Act (15 U.S.C. 12 et seq.) is amended by inserting immediately after section 4H the following new section:

"Sec. 4I. (a) The court shall reduce the claim under section 4, 4A, or 4C of this Act of any claimant releasing any person from liability or potential liability for such claim by the greatest of: (1) any amount stipulated for this purpose; (2) the consideration paid for the release; or (3) the actual damages fairly allocable to the person being released from liability or potential liability (or treble such actual damages to the extent such claim is for treble damages) and any interest on such actual damages under section 4, 4A, or 4C of this Act.

(b) For purposes of subsection (a):

(1) Where the claim is based upon a contract, combination, or conspiracy among competitors and damages are sustained by reason of overcharges or underpayments resulting from such contract, combination, or conspiracy, damages shall be allocated on the basis of each such competitors' proportionate share of the total of all such competitor's overcharges or underpayments in the market affected, unless the court determines that a more equitable result would be achieved by allocating damages according to paragraph (b)(2).

(2) With respect to all other claims, damages shall be allocated on the basis of relative responsibility for the origination or perpetration of the violation for which damages are being awarded and the benefits derived therefrom, unless the court determines that a more equitable result would be achieved by allocating damages according to paragraph (b)(1).

(c) Nothing in this section shall affect the joint and several liability of any person for any claim under the antitrust laws."

Title V—Effective Date

Sec. 501. The provisions of this Act shall apply to all actions commenced after the date of enactment of this Act.

Analysis of the Antitrust Remedies Improvements Act of 1986

The first (unnumbered) section of the bill provides that the act may be cited as the Antitrust Remedies Improvements Act of 1986.

Title II—Treble Damage Reform

Title II amends sections 4, 4A, and 4C of the Clayton Act to make timely and important reforms in the recovery of antitrust damages by private parties, the United States, and state attorneys general as *parens patriae*. Congress has recently addressed treble damages and other remedies issues in connection with particular activities in the Export Trading Company Act of 1982 and the National Cooperative Research Act of 1984. Title II recognizes and endorses the rationale of such reforms by making necessary changes in antitrust remedies as they apply across the board.

Section 201 amends section 4 of the Clayton Act, which governs recoveries by private parties, to provide for the recovery of treble damages only for those injuries sustained by reason of the plaintiff "having been overcharged or underpaid by any person subject to liability under the antitrust laws for such damages." Actual damages would be recoverable in all other cases.

With few exceptions, plaintiffs' recoveries in all private antitrust damage actions are currently trebled automatically. Trebling is intended to provide potential plaintiffs with additional incentives to complement public enforcement with private actions, and to help deter anticompetitive conduct. Where clearly harmful conduct such as unlawful horizontal price-fixing or bid-rigging is involved, trebling is entirely appropriate. Such conduct is unquestionably detrimental to the economy and cannot be overdeterred. Suits to challenge price-fixing or bid-rigging are usually brought by the victims of overcharges or underpayments caused by these practices.

Where potentially procompetitive practices such as aggressive low pricing or innovative distributional practices are involved, however, trebling can have serious anticompetitive side effects. Overdeterrence is a major concern here—trebling can cause firms to shy away from such conduct, even though it may have significant economic benefits. Moreover, competitively beneficial practices often are challenged by competitors or potential competitors with perverse motivations to sue. Competitors may use the threat of treble damages to coerce a successful rival into abandoning or restricting conduct or arrangements that enhance efficiency and lower prices to consumers.

An optimal antitrust penalty would take into account the likely harm from the conduct to society, and the probability that the conduct will be detected, prosecuted, and punished. Where such harm is obvious, and the chance of its discovery relatively low, the penalty must be high to deter violations. Conversely, where harm is uncertain, and the conduct is open and notorious, the penalty should be low. The risks of mistakenly classifying beneficial conduct as anticompetitive must also be recognized in constructing an optimal penalty system. Unfortunately, the current universal treble-damage rule in antitrust cases bears little resemblance to such a system.

Increasingly recognized by courts, Congress, and legal and economic scholars in the 1980s, these problems now warrant a general modification of the automatic trebling rule in antitrust cases. Section 201 responds to these concerns by modifying the treble-damage rule in private antitrust damage actions under section 4 of the Clayton Act to obtain a closer approximation of an optimal penalty. It first establishes a fully compensatory, actual-damages remedy, and then provides for the trebling of damages sustained "by reason of [the plaintiff] having been overcharged or underpaid by any person subject to liability under the antitrust laws for such damages." As thus amended, section 4 would continue strongly to deter clearly anticompetitive conduct, while avoiding overdeterrence of conduct that may actually benefit consumers and the economy.

Practices such as price-fixing and bid-rigging that result in overcharges to customers or underpayments to suppliers are unequivocally anticompetitive and are likely to be concealed. Section 201 continues to award treble damages to persons who have been injured by reason of such overcharges or underpayments, and thus properly focuses the full deterrent force of private treble-damage enforcement on unambiguously anticompetitive practices. Under section 201, victims of these practices, often consumers or small businesses, will retain the needed incentive to discover and challenge clearly harmful behavior.

Under section 201, however, antitrust claims brought by competitors or would-be competitors of the defendants usually will be limited to full compensation—actual damages plus prejudgment interest (discussed *infra*), costs, and attorneys' fees. These plaintiffs generally seek lost profits rather than recoupment of over-charges. Limiting such recoveries to full compensation (including attorneys' fees) is appropriate for several reasons. First, such damages are less clearly related to the social cost of a violation and may actually overstate the harm. Second, business competitors are likely to be in a position to observe the conduct that is the basis for such claims. Third, and perhaps most important, claims brought by competitors are precisely those that often challenge potentially procompetitive behavior. These cases frequently are brought to frustrate hard competition rather than promote it. Limiting recovery to full compensation addresses the overdeterrence problem created by such cases, but does not deprive a plaintiff with a just cause of a complete recovery. Thus, section 201 would continue strongly to deter covert cartel behavior, while avoiding deterrence, that is, inhibition, of business conduct that generally benefits consumers and the economy.

In order to establish a fully compensatory, actual-damages remedy, section 201 provides for automatic prejudgment interest in actual damage cases under section 4 of the Clayton Act. The rationale for awarding prejudgment interest to a plaintiff is that the plaintiff's injury is suffered long before the damages are recovered. In addition to receiving its damages, the plaintiff should be paid interest for the lost use of its money during the period from commencement of the injury to entry of judgment.

Prejudgment interest on antitrust damages is available under existing law, but only in very limited circumstances. In 1980, Congress authorized limited prejudgment interest in response to concerns that the courts' inability to award such interest created incentives for defendants to delay resolution of antitrust cases. The 1980 legislation provided that, in general, prejudgment interest is to be awarded in antitrust cases only where the opposing party has litigated in bad faith, has violated a rule or order providing for sanctions for dilatory behavior, or has engaged in conduct intended to delay the litigation or increase its cost.

Whatever the justification for the limitations on the award of prejudgment interest in present law, where antitrust recoveries have been limited recently to actual damages (as in the National Cooperative Research Act (NCRA) of 1984), it has been deemed necessary to award prejudgment interest on such damages as a matter of course if the plaintiff is to be made whole. Thus, amendments to de-treble antitrust damages should also provide automatic prejudgment interest on actual damages to plaintiffs.

Under section 201, prejudgment interest on actual damages is to be calculated at the rate specified in section 1961 of title 28 of the United States Code, or at such other rate as the court finds to be fair to compensate injured persons for the injury they have sustained, and covers the period from the earliest date for which injury can be established through the date of judgment. This rate of interest and the period for which interest is to be granted are similar to those provided in the NCRA.

Recovery of interest from the date of injury will provide full compensation for victims of antitrust violations. In connection with passage of the NCRA, it was recognized that it may be difficult or inequitable in certain circumstances to provide interest in accordance with this rule. Where the date of the onset of injury cannot be precisely determined, the plaintiff may prove that the injury began prior to a certain date and receive interest from that date. Where prejudgment interest would result in duplicative damages (for example, where loss of use of lost profits has already been factored into the damage award) or where litigation has been unreasonably delayed by the plaintiff, section 201, like the NCRA, gives the court flexibility to limit or withhold prejudgment interest. The ability of the court to vary the rate of interest from that set forth in 28 U.S.C. § 1961 (the coupon yield equivalent of the average accepted auction price for the last auction of fifty-two-week U.S. Treasury bills settled immediately prior to the date of judgment) is a new feature of this legislation, and reflects the fact that, in antitrust cases, damages may be recovered for injuries sustained many years prior to the date of judgment, during which interest rates may have been substantially lower (or higher) than current Treasury bill yields.

Section 201 does not change the circumstances in which prejudgment interest may be awarded in cases in which damages are trebled, as established by Congress in 1980. Where such interest is awarded, however, it will be calculated as set forth above. Section 201's reform of the treble-damage remedy does not affect the current rules for determining standing, injury, or liability in private antitrust damage actions under section 4 of the Clayton Act. The phrase "damages sustained by reason of" added to section 4 by section 201 uses key language already contained in section 4 to clearly signal this intent.

Section 202 of the bill amends section 4A of the Clayton Act to permit the United States to recover treble damages when it is injured by reason of having been overcharged or underpaid by an antitrust violator. Under existing law, the United States can never recover more than actual damages under the antitrust laws. Section 202 would provide the United States, as an overcharged purchaser, with a treble-damage remedy against price-fixers and bid-riggers. This change would result in increased deterrence of particularly onerous violations that constitute theft from taxpayers, and would put the United States in the same position as private plaintiffs with respect to damages. Section 202 also provides for prejudgment interest on actual damages in actions by the United States under section 4A, under the same terms as such interest may be awarded to private plaintiffs under section 4 as it would be amended by section 201.

Section 203 amends section 4C of the Clayton Act, under which state attorneys general as *parens patriae* may recover treble damages for antitrust injuries sustained by natural persons residing within their states. Section 203 does not change the current rule under which all such recoveries are trebled, because damages sought on behalf of consumers in *parens* cases are always the kind of damages that would be trebled under section 4 of the Clayton Act as it would be amended by section 201. Thus, section 203 only conforms the provisions governing prejudgment interest awards in *parens* cases under section 4C of the Clayton Act to the provisions governing such awards under sections 4 and 4A as those sections would be amended by sections 201 and 202.

Title III—Defendants' Attorneys' Fees

Title III addresses concerns that the current imbalance in antitrust law regarding the award of attorneys' fees facilitates the potential abuse of antitrust remedies. Section 301 adds a new paragraph (d) to section 4 of the Clayton Act to provide for the award of costs, including a reasonable attorney's fee, to a substantially prevailing antitrust defendant on a finding that the plaintiff's conduct was "frivolous, unreasonable, without foundation, or in bad faith." Section 302 provides the same relief for defendants in injunction actions under section 16 of the Clayton Act.

Currently, sections 4 and 16 of the Clayton Act entitle only prevailing plaintiffs to reasonable attorneys' fees. With certain exceptions, including cases governed by two recent antitrust-related statutes—the NCRA and the Export Trading Company Act of 1982—the general rule is to deny attorneys' fees to prevailing defendants.

Private enforcement of the antitrust laws is an important supplement to government prosecution. Some plaintiffs may abuse the process, however. This abuse may take the form of strike suits filed primarily to extract a settlement from a defendant for something less than the defendant's anticipated litigation costs. It may also arise when a competitor, fearing innovative procompetitive conduct by a rival, files a potentially lengthy injunctive action to convince the defendant to abandon his or her plans rather than bear high litigation costs. This type of conduct undermines the purposes of private enforcement and generally increases the costs that litigation imposes on society.

Title III recognizes the possibility of such abuse by awarding costs, including attorneys' fees, to substantially prevailing defendants if the plaintiff's conduct has been "frivolous, unreasonable, without foundation or in bad faith." This standard, used as the model for the defendants' attorneys' fees provision in the NCRA, derives from the Supreme Court's decision in *Christiansburg Garment v. EEOC*, 434 U.S. 412 (1978), a case involving prevailing parties' attorneys' fees under § 706(k) of Title VII of the Civil Rights Act of 1964.

As was recognized during consideration of the NCRA, each element of this standard has an independent meaning and is to be analyzed and applied separately. The determination of whether a plaintiff's conduct has been unreasonable must be based on an evaluation of the factual and legal merits of the case. Conduct may be judged to be unreasonable even though it might not be considered frivolous, without foundation, or in bad faith. Also, the standards are to be applied to conduct throughout the litigation of a case. Although the initial filing of an action may be warranted, discovery can bring to light information that makes continued prosecution of that action unreasonable. Attorneys' fees incurred by a prevailing defendant subsequent to such discovery should be recovered.

The defendants' attorneys' fees provisions of Title III complement other provisions of federal law that seek to prevent abuse of the judicial system. But because there is a strong public interest in preventing groundless antitrust actions that may harm the economy by deterring procompetitive conduct, these provisions for defendants' attorneys' fees are to be given broader interpretation than comparable provisions applied to civil actions in general (for example, Rule 11, Federal Rules of Civil Procedure).

It may be noted that the standard under which defendants may seek attorneys' fees in *parens patriae* cases under section 4C of the Clayton Act—that the state attorney general has acted "in bad faith, vexatiously, wantonly, or for oppressive reasons"—differs somewhat from the *Christiansburg Garment* standard to be incorporated in section 4. Because the incentives of state attorneys general differ from those of purely private plaintiffs, however, Title III does not modify the defendants' attorneys' fees provision in section 4C. Nor does it modify the attorneys' fees rules in antitrust damage cases brought by the United States under section 4A. The United States is not entitled to attorneys' fees as plaintiff in such cases, but may be liable for defendants' attorneys' fees under the standards of the recently reenacted Equal Access to Justice Act and under rules of general application in civil cases. These provisions appropriately address the conduct of actions by the United States and should continue to govern in government antitrust cases.

Title IV—Claim Reduction

Section 401 creates a new section of the Clayton Act—section 4I. New section 4I provides that when a plaintiff settles with one or more defendants in an action under section 4, 4A, or 4C of the Clayton Act, or releases in any way a potential defendant from liability without filing a suit, that plaintiff's claim against the remaining defendants shall be appropriately reduced.

Under current law, all defendants found liable for damages in antitrust cases are jointly and severally responsible for the plaintiff's entire, trebled recovery. Under the joint and several liability system, defendants typically expect to share that liability among themselves, perhaps through formal agreements, perhaps through seriatim or universal settlements with plaintiffs. Should the plaintiff settle with any liable or potentially liable party, however, the plaintiff's remaining claim is reduced only by the amount the plaintiff receives for the settlement. Thus, a nonsettling defendant facing what is already very substantial real liability can see that liability magnified if the plaintiff settles with other liable persons for nominal or relatively small amounts, particularly if such settlements are with those responsible for a major portion of the plaintiff's damages. This "whipsaw" effect may force a defendant to abandon its factual claims and legal defenses, whatever their merits.

New section 4I addresses this problem directly. Paragraph (a) reduces the plaintiff's claim (which, under other proposed amendments, will include all damages and interest on actual damages from the date of injury to the date of judgment) by at least the proportionate share of that claim fairly allocable to any person being released from liability. Such proportionate share would include a fair share of the plaintiff's actual (or, where appropriate, trebled) damages plus interest on such actual damages from the date of injury to the date of judgment, as will be provided in amended sections 4, 4A, and 4C. Thus, the effect of claim reduction will be to relieve nonsettling defendants from all liability arising from the conduct of persons receiving releases.

Paragraph (b) provides the method for determining fair shares of damages for the purpose of claim reduction. Where proscribed concerted conduct has resulted in overcharges or underpayments, the amount of damages allocable to a person receiving a release from liability is that person's proportionate share of all the participants' overcharges or underpayments in the market affected. For all other claims, the damages allocable to the settling person shall be determined by its relative responsibility for the violation and by the benefits it derived from the violation. Appropriate discretion is reserved for courts to adjust these rules where necessary to achieve a more equitable result. For example, in a bid-rigging case, market shares may not be an appropriate measure of either culpability or benefits derived from the conspiracy. In the manner of claim reduction legislation previously reported by the Senate Judiciary Committee (S. 995, 97th Cong., 2nd Sess.), paragraph (c) of new section 4I makes clear that claim reduction for settlements does not affect the joint and several liability of the remaining defendants.

Under new section 4I, whipsaw settlement tactics will no longer be possible since no defendant will see its potential real liability increased by another person's settlement. Therefore, defendants are not likely to be denied the opportunity to test their liability in court. Furthermore, plaintiffs will no longer have any incentive to release the most culpable persons for nomimal amounts. Since the amounts the plaintiff can recover from the remaining defendants will be reduced by the share of the plaintiff's claim attributable to settling persons' conduct, the amount a plaintiff would accept from a person being released from liability will be correlated to that person's culpability. Larger, more culpable persons will be less likely to receive early and attractive settlements with claim reduction than under the current system. In sum, claim reduction should preserve incentives for plaintiffs to challenge anticompetitive conduct and thus will maintain deterrence while providing a more equitable system for the settlement of claims.

Title V—Effective Date

Section 501 makes the provisions of Title II through Title IV effective in all actions commenced after the date of enactment of the act.

Note

Excerpted and adapted from the legislative package prepared by the Justice Department and submitted to Congress on February 19, 1986. The package was introduced by Senator Strom Thurmond and Representative Hamilton Fish in the Ninety-Ninth Congress, Second Session.

The Assault on Antitrust: The Reagan Administration's New Antitrust Proposals
Eddie Correia

The antitrust laws represent the basic national policy favoring competition in the U.S. economy. The original antitrust law, the Sherman Act, was enacted in 1890 as part of a broad national reform movement to stop monopolistic business abuses. Three years earlier the Interstate Commerce Act, aimed at abuses by the railroads, was passed driven by the same political currents.

The Clayton Act and the Federal Trade Commission (FTC) Act, both enacted in 1914, were intended to strengthen the basic prohibitions of the Sherman Act. The two statutes took different approaches—the Clayton Act proscribing specific types of business conduct, and the FTC Act empowering a Commission with a broad mandate to enforce a general prohibition on "unfair methods of competition." In 1936, Congress passed the Robinson-Patman Act, which revised provisions prohibiting price discrimination in the Clayton Act. Finally, the Cellar-Kefauver Act in 1950 created a stricter prohibition on mergers that could harm competition. Except for essentially procedural changes, these remain the basic antitrust laws today.

The antitrust laws are aimed fundamentally at preventing a single firm, or firms acting together, from raising prices above competitive levels or restricting competition in some other way. The most classic form of antitrust violation is price-fixing by competitors. The oil industry, for example, has historically responded to periods of high production and resulting low prices by attempting to achieve agreement among competitors to raise prices or reduce output. The Organization of Petroleum Exporting Countries (OPEC) cartel is the latest and, at least for a while, most successful example of this tradition.

In general, there was a bipartisan consensus about the need for vigorous enforcement of the antitrust laws through the late 1970s. Since then, however, there has been a heated dispute within the legal and academic community about the importance of antitrust principles and about how they should be enforced. In particular, a group of scholars, led by Frank Easterbrook, Richard Posner, and Robert Bork (all of whom are now on the federal bench), forcefully argued that the antitrust policies had become counterproductive. The principal theme of this "Chicago school" has been that the antitrust laws have gone too far in restricting business behavior and that many antitrust rules prevented harmless or even positively procompetitive behavior. They advanced a number of basic propositions: that very high levels of market concentration are required for industries to exhibit reduced competitive performance; that agreements between companies at different levels of the production and distribution chain (vertical agreements or combinations) are virtually never anticompetitive; and that the relevant market in which to assess competitive effects is much broader than has traditionally been assumed.

The Reagan administration has borrowed heavily from the Chicago school in devising its own antitrust policies. Its first appointments as heads of the Justice Department's Antitrust Division and the FTC, William Baxter and James C. Miller III, made no secret of their opposition to much of the antitrust laws and the enforcement policies of previous administrations. If anything, other officials within the administration have been even more hostile to the antitrust laws. In February 1985, Secretary of Commerce Malcolm Balridge proposed repealing the basic statutory provision used to challenge anticompetitive mergers, the 1950 Cellar-Kefauver Act. In February 1986, the administration submitted to Congress proposals to make basic revisions in the antitrust laws.[1] Secretary Balridge was clearly influential in determining the shape of these proposals and has been one of the principal administration advocates for them. Most of these proposals are fundamentally misguided. They undercut much of the deterrent effect and antitrust rules and allow anticompetitive mergers while failing to promote efficiency.

Antitrust and Foreign Competition

At the heart of the administration's recent proposals is the idea that the antitrust laws are the real villain behind our poor showing in international competition. Administration representatives argue that U.S. firms could do better against international competition if they were allowed to combine. The secretary of commerce points to the rise of large international firms in Europe and Japan as models to emulate.

This notion that U.S. firms can become more competitive internationally if the big get bigger is the rationale behind a proposed new antitrust exemption from the basic prohibition of mergers that may harm competition. Under the proposed bill, the president would be authorized to order an exemption for industries determined by the International Trade Commission to be hurt by foreign competition. For a temporary period, perhaps five years, the president could make it easy for firms to merge in electronics, automobiles, textiles, shoes, steel, and other high-import industries.

There is virtually no empirical support for the administration's argument that a more permissive antitrust policy will improve our international competitiveness. For example, if antitrust enforcement leads to higher trade deficits, why have the deficits soared during the Reagan administration as antitrust enforcement has declined? If bigness would make us more competitive internationally, why is it that U.S. firms do not overwhelm foreign competition since we have the largest manufacturing firms in the world in automobiles, electrical equipment, steel, and textiles? Japan has nine companies manufacturing automobiles, forty-four making textiles, over thirty making steel products, and over ninety making electrical equipment in a domestic economy less than half the size of the United States. Yet the Japanese remain the symbol of strong international competition.

The fact is that vigorous antitrust enforcement has nothing to do with increasing trade deficits. However, the absence of vigorous competition in the domestic market can certainly harm international competitiveness. American steel and autos developed in a domestic market that did not force consistent capital investment and improvement to keep up with state-of-the-art technology. Oligopolies grown sluggish by a lack of vigorous competition were suddenly faced with cheap imported steel and cars from technologically advanced Japanese plants. The result: a painful loss of American jobs and a push for protection from foreign competition.

The same scenario is predictable if the president allows one industry after another to consolidate in order to compete internationally. Industries taking a beating from imports will come to the White House arguing their salvation is in joining up with their largest competitor. With a fanfare of promises and high expectations, the president will bless the merger. A few years down the road—with higher costs, less efficient operation, and a less competitive domestic market—the same industry will come back complaining about the unfair tactics of foreign firms who want to sell their higher quality product at a lower price. Meanwhile, the American consumer will be the big loser.

A recent study by FTC economists concluded:

A policy liberalizing the antitrust laws specifically for declining industries would be ill-advised. Such a move would open the way for anticompetitive mergers for which there is no efficiency justification. Some have argued that such a liberalization might be justified to save jobs in areas hard hit by declining employment and/or to improve the balance of trade. However, there is no persuasive reason to believe that the mergers that would be allowed under the liberalization in question would increase employment or improve the trade balance. Indeed, anticompetitive mergers that do not improve efficiency could reduce U.S. employment and U.S. firms' ability to compete with foreign firms as domestic prices rise and output falls. As a result, changes in merger policy that allow anticompetitive mergers are not a solution to the problem of industrial decline.[2]

Ironically, the administration is promoting a policy that will increase prices and make us less competitive in the world, not more. Allowing our major manufacturing industries to consolidate during a five-year merger spree will do permanent competitive harm to the U.S. economy. Moreover, mergers allowed during a five-year permissive window will almost certainly become permanent. Very few large mergers have been reversed by government divestiture decrees long after they were consummated.

The element of truth in the administration's argument is that the antitrust laws should consider foreign competition when appropriate. As U.S. firms face more competition from foreign imports, it does not make sense to say that a proposed merger only should be evaluated based on competition from domestic companies. Making sure that foreign competition should be considered when appropriate, however, is a very different proposition from creating a more permissive across-the-board merger standard for industries facing foreign competition. The law is flexible enough to consider foreign competition now. In order to make sure courts consider this factor, Senator Howard Metzenbaum of Ohio has introduced legislation requiring it to be included in the legal analysis.[3] The administration's point that foreign competition should be an appropriate case is unobjectionable. However, its basic policy proposal—promoting mergers to help U.S. firms become more efficient—should be rejected.

Changing the Standard for Illegal Mergers

The administration has also proposed to change the standard for illegal mergers. Under current law, mergers are prohibited if the effect "may be substantially to lessen competition, or to tend to create a monopoly."[4] The Reagan proposal would require proof that "there is a significant probability that such acquisition will substantially increase the ability to exercise market power." The administration bill also lists a series of factors required to be considered in evaluating a merger, including the number of firms in the market, the difficulty of entering the market, and the ability of existing competitors to increase production; and other factors, including a catchall category for "any other evidence" indicating the statutory standard would be violated.

Neither the current standard nor the one the administration proposes, provides much clarity about what mergers are illegal. However, even if the list of factors the administration proposes were to be enacted, the statutory language would give no real additional guidance in complying with the law. The Justice Department, since 1968, has published detailed guidelines to determine what mergers would be considered suspect. These guidelines were revised in 1982 and again in 1984. In addition, the courts have issued hundreds of opinions dealing with various fact situations, creating a rich and complex body of law regarding mergers. Compared to this well-developed body of law, a vague new standard and a cryptic listing of factors to consider (about which there is general agreement now) will not add any significant element of certainty to the current legal framework.

One thing is clear, however. The administration intends their standard to be much tougher to meet than the current one. Just how much tougher would depend on the nuances of legislative history and years of court decisions interpreting the new law. The courts will undoubtedly presume that the Congress did not take the trouble to revise fundamentally a statute existing since 1950 unless it intended to make a basic change in the current legal standard. While it is impossible to predict precisely what mergers would be allowed that are now prohibited, it is safe to assume it would be easier for large competitors to combine. To evaluate this kind of change, it is useful to consider two issues: (1) how do the antitrust agencies and the courts now determine whether a merger is illegal? and (2) has the law been too strict in forbidding mergers, thus preventing efficient and productive business combinations?

The basic problem in evaluating mergers is predicting the future effect of a complex business transaction when our understanding of how markets work remains unclear. Most economists agree that a market with a handful of competitors will be less competitively vigorous than one with dozens. But, exactly how concentrated the market must be before prices begin to rise because of reduced competition is unknown. There is also general agreement that concentration is a greater problem if new competitors cannot enter the market easily, if the competitors tend to share information frequently, and if other factors make coordinating prices easy to do. Nevertheless, despite general agreement about the basic economic theory, there is enormous disagreement about the likely effect of any specific merger. Applying the law against harmful mergers means predicting the future, and thus a fair amount of educated guesswork is inevitable. Anyone who says we need to be certain before prohibiting a merger is really advocating a policy that allows all mergers to proceed unimpeded.

The courts have long struggled with how to apply the very general legal standards against harmful mergers. By 1960, merger cases had become confused undertakings with issue upon issue presented to the courts for an analysis that the courts were ill-prepared to make. In an influential law review article in 1960, Professor Derek Bok, now president of Harvard University, argued that the courts should focus primarily on the combined market shares of the merging firms and presume competitive harm if the market shares exceeded some threshold level.[5] This kind of approach was adopted by the Supreme Court in 1963 in the *Philadelphia National Bank* case[6] and reached a high point in 1966 in the *Von's Grocery*[7] opinion. In the latter case, the Court decided that a merger that would lead to a firm with 7.5 percent of the market was unlawful. The Court probably went too far in the *Von's Grocery* case, and this example would not be followed today. Since 1966, the courts have become more sophisticated in their analysis of mergers. The clear trend in the law has been to make it more complex and more difficult to prove a merger violates the law. During the 1970s, the courts and the antitrust agencies required more solid economic proof that a merger was likely to harm competition before deciding it was unlawful.

Then, the Reagan administration entered the scene with a clear bias that virtually every merger was beneficial. In 1982, the Justice Department issued merger guidelines, setting its own interpretation of the requirements of an illegal merger. These included: (1) raising the combined market shares for which any question would even be raised; (2) raising the standard for a concentrated market; and (3) requiring proof of a series of other factors, including the fact that new firms could not easily enter the market and that existing firms were not likely to increase production to offset price increases resulting from a merger. In addition, the department has tended to define the market very broadly, making it hard to show the companies that have a significant market share. Further, the analysis takes into account the possibility that firms can convert current production capacity to make the products of the merging firms, that foreign competition will increase, and the the merger will reduce costs.

The economic analysis for each of the Justice Department's guidelines can become enormously complex and burdensome. In 1984, the Justice Department came up with yet another version of the guidelines, making proof of an illegal merger more difficult. This increased burden-of-proof requirement, combined with an administration that is biased in favor of mergers, has led to a laissez faire merger climate and infrequent enforcement for illegal mergers. During the mid-1980s, the number of mergers has gone steadily upward. The number of mergers over $100 million in value was 94 in 1980, 113 in 1981, 116 in 1982, 137 in 1983, 200 in 1984, and 268 in 1985. The rate for mergers during the first half 1985 was the highest since 1974. The largest sixteen mergers in U.S. history have occurred during the last five years.[8]

One of the most striking facts is that as merger activity has gone up, merger enforcement has gone down. The number of merger cases filed by the Justice Department during FY 1981–1985 declined 25 percent from the average rate during FY 1976–1980. The FTC's pattern was similar. In addition, the antitrust agencies failed to even investigate proposed mergers at the rate of the previous administration. The rate at which the agencies asked merging firms for more information about their proposed combination declined 39 percent from 1979 to 1984.[9]

Any statutory change in the basic law against harmful mergers will enormously complicate the task of proving to a court that a merger should be prohibited. Some of the favorable early business reaction to the Reagan administration proposal was based on the argument that the new standard would be more understandable. It is doubtful that anyone knows what the new standard means precisely—only that it means it will be easier to merge. Has the U.S. economy been harmed because antitrust laws have been too strict on possible mergers? The answer is certainly no. While the administration continually argues that mergers promote efficiency, the tract record of acquisitions is poor.

Business Week reported in June 1985 that one out of three acquisitions in recent years has been undone.[10] Data published by W.T. Grimm & Co. showed that from 1980 to 1985 the number of divestitures jumped 35 percent—to 900, worth

$29.4 billion. In addition, *Business Week* cited a study by a management consulting firm, McKinsey & Co., which reviewed 58 major acquisitions between 1972 and 1983.[11] The study asked two questions: did the return on total amount invested exceed the cost of capital, and did the merger help the parent companies outperform the competition in the stock market. The study concluded that 28 of the 58 clearly failed both tests and six others failed one test.

A study by economists working with the International Institute of Management in West Berlin analyzed 765 mergers between 1962 and 1972 in the United States and Europe. They found that in the seven countries studied, mergers generally did not increase the profits of the companies, nor did they accelerate corporate growth.[12] Another study, by Dennis C. Mueller at the University of Maryland, investigated whether a series of mergers between 1952 and 1972 increased the companies' market share. It found companies acquired by conglomerates lost 42 percent of their original market share and companies acquired by competitors lost 20 percent.[13]

The point is not that all, or even most mergers, are harmful. Most are clearly competitively neutral and some no doubt improve efficiency and output. However, the claim by the Reagan administration that economic performance would be substantially improved with a much more permissive merger climate cannot be substantiated based on recent experience. The courts and the antitrust agencies have developed a high degree of sophistication in their evaluation of the likely effects of mergers. There is little doubt that the administration's efforts to promote even more combinations has far greater potential for reducing competition than for promoting efficiency.

Weakening Remedies

The final attack by the administration on the current antitrust framework is the proposal to limit the damages that a successful plaintiff can obtain. Under current law, plaintiffs who win antitrust cases are awarded three times their actual losses, plus a reasonable attorney's fee. In addition, a plaintiff can recover his entire damages from any single defendant who was a part of an antitrust conspiracy (though he cannot recover twice). This principle of "joint and several liability" is the same as the standard rule for intentional injuries under state law. A person who is intentionally injured by three people can recover his damages from all three proportionally or from any one of them or any combination.

These rules have had a number of very desirable results. First, they give an incentive to small businesses to take on giant corporations who have hurt their business through various anticompetitive practices. Antitrust litigation is notoriously long, complex, and expensive. In many, perhaps most cases, only the reward of substantial damages will encourage the small plaintiff to take the time and expense to vindicate his legal rights. Second, the threat of large damages is intended to deter people from breaking the law in the first place. Breaking the antitrust laws can be profitable beyond a corporation's wildest dreams. The OPEC countries made hundreds of billions of dollars on inflated oil prices until their cartel began to fall apart. A monopolist who drives everyone out of the market can multiply his profits tenfold. It takes a stiff penalty to discourage such lucrative conduct, particularly when it is not easy to prove the violation. Finally, the "joint and several liability" rule, allowing recovery of all of one's damages from a single defendant encourages early settlement of cases and prevents a small plaintiff with little money from having to win major lawsuits against a large number of giant defendants.

The administration wants to undercut the treble-damage remedy by reducing the category of cases in which trebel damages are available and by forcing the plaintiff to sue each defendant to recover his entire award. The principal provision would limit treble damages to persons "overcharged or underpaid by any person subject to liability under the antitrust laws for such damages."[14] The intent of this provision is primarily to limit claims for lost profits to actual damages.[15]

The effect of this provision would be to reduce substantially the damages available in any case where the harm to the plaintiff has been lost business. Such cases include a small company driven out of business unfairly by a monopolist, a retailer who is terminated from a distribution arrangement by a manufacturer for discounting below list prices, and a company driven out of business by an agreement among its competitors (for example, a discount real estate broker who is denied access to listings of available property). Each of these cases presents serious anticompetitive risks. There is no persuasive reason for seriously undercutting the incentive for these injured parties to bring antitrust actions.

The fundamental problem in undercutting private remedies is that private enforcement of the antitrust laws plays a much greater role than public enforcement in deterring anticompetitive behavior. In 1984, there were 1,100 private antitrust actions compared to only 101 brought by the federal government.[16] Only in the merger area does the government shoulder most of the responsibility for enforcing the law.

Conclusion

The Reagan administration has made no secret of its general hostility toward the antitrust laws. Its proposals and new direction in enforcement policy have generated a debate about antitrust and its usefulness to U.S. consumers. To some extent, this debate has been a productive one. Some applications of antitrust laws, particularly in the 1960s, did not really promote competition. However, over the past decade, the courts and the antitrust agencies have focused on business conduct that has significant anticompetitive potential with little promise for increasing efficiency. The danger in the current administration effort is that it would undercut the core of antitrust principles on the false assumption that antitrust has been a bar to desirable business conduct. The result would be a less competitive economy—bad for business as well as consumers in the United States.

Notes

A modified version of this article appeared in *Multinational Monitor*, Feb. 15, 1986.

1. Introduced as Senate bills 2160 through 2164. See *Congressional Record*, Mar. 7, 1986, pp. S2280–S2289.
2. Frankena and Pautler, "Antitrust Policy for Declining Industries," Federal Trade Commission, Oct. 1985, pp. xii–xiii.
3. S. 2022, introduced Jan. 27, 1986; see *Congressional Record*, Jan. 27, 1986, pp. S335–S340.
4. Section 7 of the Clayton Act of 1914, as amended by the Cellar-Kefauver Antimerger Act of 1950, 15 U.S.C. Section 18.
5. Bok, "Section 7 of the Clayton Act and the Merging of Law and Economics," *Harvard Law Review* **74**:226 (1960).
6. *United States* v. *Philadelphia National Bank*, 374 U.S. 321 (1963).
7. *United States* v. *Von's Grocery Co.*, 384 U.S. 270 (1966).
8. Merger data are from W.T. Grimm & Co., Chicago, Illinois.
9. Based on the rate at which filings of proposed mergers under the Hart-Scott-Rodino Act, 15 U.S.C. Section 18a, are followed by a request for additional information by the Justice Department or the Federal Trade Commission. See Annual Report to Congress Pursuant to Section 201 of the Hart-Scott-Rodino Antitrust Improvements Act of 1976, Federal Trade Commission.
10. *Business Week*, June 3, 1985, p. 88.
11. Ibid.
12. *The Los Angeles Times*, Mar. 20, 1984, p. 11.
13. Ibid.
14. See Section 201 of S. 2162.
15. Testimony of Douglas H. Ginsburg, assistant attorney general, Antitrust Division, Department of Justice, before Senate Committee on the Judiciary, Mar. 21, 1986, p. 9.
16. Salop and White, "Private Antitrust Litigation: an Introduction and Framework," presented at Georgetown Conference on Private Antitrust Litigation, Nov. 8–9, 1985, table 1.

The Securities and Exchange Commission and the Regulatory Process

Robert Chatov

The creation of the Securities and Exchange Commission (SEC) is a classic example of the market failure theory of government regulation. The consensus in the early 1930s when the securities laws and the SEC were created was that the free market, insofar as the capital markets were concerned, had failed, and that federal regulation was required to put them back in order. Extremely broad and powerful authorizations for commission action were included in the initial securities acts. There could be no claim that commission powers were inadequate. Actions taken would be at the commission's option, free of serious legal constraints.

What began as a classic example of government intervention ended as a classic example of government regulatory behavior. Major commission powers were transferred to the SEC's regulatees. Important legal issues were left unresolved. Prime effort was placed on pursuing individual malfeasors under the acts, as opposed to strengthening the structural conditions under which the capital markets functioned. To be sure, the structural conditions of the capital markets today are better than they were before the SEC's advent, but measured against the SEC's potential contribution, the job in large part remains incomplete. This article examines the SEC as an example of the regulatory process through commissions. Particular focus is on corporate financial rule making and the SEC's central role within a typical regulatory-commission consensus network.

The designation "Blue Sky Laws" refers to state legislation passed initially around the turn of the twentieth century to regulate the issuance and sale of corporate securities. Most states passed some regulatory measures in this area, but few of the acts were effective. Few provided for coordination with other states. Implementation and enforcement was hampered by lack of funds, experience, and adequate collection and dissemination of information. Sale of securities from outside states proved almost impossible to control. "Boiler rooms" and "bucket shops" operated almost unhindered. As the dollar value of equity securities passed that of bonds in the mid-1920s, mass public participation in the capital markets reached unprecedented levels. The stock market crash of 1929 and its aftermath ended the old era of capital market regulation only by the states.

The Stock Market Crash of 1929 and Its Aftermath

In the late 1920s, serious financial abuses occurred in the sale of securities. Investment trusts—which were organizations issuing securities that represented interests in other securities—and holding companies were great contributors to the speculations characterizing the boom years of the late 1920s. Many stock purchasers were misled into unwise investments by questionable sales practices abetted by financial reports inadequately revealing sources of income and other accounts. Before 1933, the corporations themselves were the final arbiters of what appeared in their published financial reports. The New York Stock Exchange's powers to influence corporate financial reporting was minimal. The independent accounting fraternity as well had little power in this regard. After all, independent accountants were employees of the corporations. Accounting technique was still in a relatively early stage of development. Uniformity in accounting reporting was not mandatory, although accounting standards were claimed to exist. However, the claim had little substance; nonedifying consolidated financial statements were the norm, and accounting training and testing varied considerably among the different state societies. Neither of the two national accounting practitioner organizations did much in the way of financial standard-setting activities.[1]

The Senate Banking and Currency Committee hearings of 1932–1934 (popularly known as the Pecora hearings) demonstrated that basic problems behind the stock market crash were to be found in the deliberate manipulations of some institutions in the financial section and in the way many corporations had been governed. Directors and officers of financial institutions and corporations had manipulated their organizations to the disadvantage of the public, in general, and to shareholders, in particular. These allegations were not new. Harvard economics professor William Z. Ripley[2] and Columbia law professor Adolf A. Berle, Jr., had written on the subject during the 1920s.[3] Berle exposed, in a series of articles, many of the manipulative devices used by managers to attack shareholders' interest. Berle's catalog of abuses included managerial manipulations of different types of stocks, of holding companies, of partly owned subsidiaries, and so forth. Whereas the common law held that someone had to rely on information in a specific way before they could sue on the basis of having been misled, Berle took a broader view of the matter. He concluded that shareholders relied on the accuracy of disseminated information whether or not they saw it because it affected market values! He argued that accounting devices were used by management in depriving shareholders of their rights. Furthermore, he understood that when the courts used accounting concepts as part of their decisions, they were essentially giving them the force of law. Many of Berle's ideas subsequently were included in the securities acts.

The stock market crash of 1929 was a financial calamity that turned into an unprecedented economic disaster. Optimism had continued throughout the summer of 1929 and into the early fall, when the market hit its peak on September 3. The market was unsettled after that date, sliding downward somewhat, when it reached the breaking point on October 24—a date known thereafter as "Black Thursday." October 28 and 29 saw precipitous declines in stock values, which soon affected the commodity markets as well. The slide continued, with a temporary rally in April 1930, reaching a bottom in the summer of 1932. By then the economy had staggered into a depression of a magnitude unseen since the depression of the 1870s that had followed the panic of 1873.[4]

The Pecora hearings began in April 1932. The most prestigious people in the financial community were brought in as witnesses, including Charles Mitchell, A.H. Wiggin, Clarence Dillon, Winthrop Aldrich, Thomas W. Lamont, J.P. Morgan, George Whitney, and Richard Whitney. The admissions extracted from the hearings were very serious, and set the stage for the federal legislation that would follow. The hearings continued into 1934. Among the revelations were the dissemination of deliberate misinformation, and speculative activity based on questionable ethics, including the use of preferred lists of customers who could purchase stocks at below-market prices, and the use of rigged stock market pools.[5]

The conclusions drawn from the hearings helped determine the content of the securities acts. It was believed that complete financial disclosure would cure securities misrepresentation; that commercial banks ought not to engage in stock jobbing; that private banks ought not to be allowed to float securities and accept deposits at the same time. A mdoel was available in the British Companies Act, and in the presidential campaign of 1932, Franklin Delano Roosevelt committed himself to passage of a remedial act upon his election.[6]

The Securities Act of 1933

The goals of the 1933 and 1934 Acts were to ameliorate the abuses that had occurred in the stock market. Authority over corporate financial reporting and new corporate issues was intended to prevent dissemination of false corporate financial information. The 1933 Act dealt with new corporate issues. Authority to administer the act was given to the Federal Trade Commission, creating a new registration division to do the job. The 1933 act covered corporate securities already on the market. Problems in drafting the legislation prevented achieving the original objective of including old and new securities as well as the exchanges under the same act. New issues and the exchanges would not be dealt with until 1934.

The preamble of the Securities Act of 1933 stated that its aim was "to provide full and fair disclosure of the character of securities sold . . . and to prevent frauds . . . and for other purposes." The act specified the government's right to determine the information content in the required registration statements, and defined the personal legal liability in section 11 of those signing the registration statement. Liability was changed from the common law concept of the obligation of the reasonable man to a new concept that imposed a fiduciary relation on those signing the prospectus. A material misstatement or omission from the prospectus gave the purchaser the right to rescind the contract and to recover the difference between what he had paid and what the stock was then worth in the market, whether or not the purchaser had relied on the prospectus. The reaction to this particular provision was violent. It generated the most concentrated assault of the private sector on government seen in the twentieth century, referred to at the time as the "Wall Street Strike" of 1934.[7] The new law, however, contained the basic legal and administrative element of modern securities law—government responsibility to specify the necessary operational rules and regulations, to carry on investigations, and to bring civil actions and recommend prosecutions.[8]

The Securities and Exchange Act of 1934

The private sector pressed for a separate commission that would understand the problems of the industry. It obtained one—the SEC—in the 1934 act, which also brought all previously issued securities and the exchanges under regulation. In addition, the law returned Section 11's provisions back to common law standards. The power of the private sector's wishes in the matter was too strong to resist.[9] This time the Congress took a more expansive look at what the securities laws were to accomplish. Section 2 established effectiveness and fairness as the two essential criteria. Effectiveness was couched in terms of the dependence of the national economy, and federal taxation on the integrity and untampered operation of the capital markets. Fairness was expressed in a matter of the markets being honest. Powers of the commission were spelled out. The SEC was given the opportunity to set whatever rules it deemed necessary for compliance with the acts.

The SEC's range of operation potentially was enormous. Standards of financial reporting could have been entirely generated by the SEC itself under Section 13. Section 2's provisions with respect to "transactions by officers, directors, and principal security holders . . . " also provided ample opportunity to the commission to involve itself in a wide range of issues involving corporate governance. It seems clear from the wording of the 1934 act that the Congress was providing the basis for a proactive governmental unit, which would exert a new and influential leadership in the capital markets. After all, if Congress had wanted only a caretaker or minimal agency that was satisfied to collect information and be passive, several other governmental units could have processed the minimal level of rules and information required under the acts.

The 1934 act was a major victory for the private financial-industrial sector, nevertheless. It eliminated the Federal Trade Commission (FTC) because of the fear that the FTC, given its divided responsibilities, would be less sympathetic to the problems of financial-industrial constituency than would a separate agency. The second major achievement was having the liability provision under Section 11 revert to the "reasonable man" standard, and again put the burden of proof on the plaintiff, which minimized the danger of law suits by disgruntled shareholders.

The SEC's Powers

The Congress wrote in Section 2 that:

> National emergencies, which produce widespread unemployment and the disloca-
> tion of trade, transportation, and industry, and which burden interstate commerce
> and adversely affect the general welfare, are precipitated, intensified, and prolonged
> by manipulation and sudden and unreasonable fluctuations of security prices and
> by excessive speculation on such exchanges and markets, and to meet such emergen-
> cies, the federal government is put to great expense as to burden the national credit.

Thus a federal goal clearly was recognized—that excessive speculation was to be avoided since it was dysfunctional to the national interest.

The powers of the newly created SEC were reaffirmed. Section (13)a (1) gave the Commission power to require documents from registered corporations. Subsection (b) of Section 13 enabled the SEC to specify the form and methods of required reports, the details of balance sheets and earning statements, appraisal value, depreciation, recurring and nonrecurring income, and so forth. The SEC was given sufficient authority to administer and develop rules of corporate financial reporting. The interesting question is why the SEC did not exercise its authority? The events of the 1930s proved critical to the subsequent relations between the accounting profession, the rest of the financial-industrial sector, and the SEC.

The early commissioners had two alternatives in interpreting the securities acts: to actually oversee the operation of the financial capital markets to misuse their efficiency, or simply to pursue some vague standard for disclosure of financial information. The less controversial route was taken, with the securities acts interpreted primarily as disclosure statutes. In the Northern States Power case of 1935, by a 3–2 vote, the commission permitted an accounting treatment of which all of the commissioners disapproved on the grounds that the accounting convention had been disclosed in footnote. The commission thus demanded minimal performance rather than what was required for a fair statement of facts. Thereafter, the commissioners prevented the SEC from developing affirmative requirements for corporate financial reporting, thus setting the basis for the persisting disclosure mentality of the SEC.

Opposition toward the SEC by the accounting profession contributed to preventing the SEC from operating authoritatively and effectively in the corporate financial control area. In exasperation, Landis made a statement in a December 1936 speech that "the impact of almost daily tilts with accountants, some of them called leaders in their profession, often leaves little doubt that their loyalties to management are stronger than their responsibilities to the investors." The American Institute of Accountants (AIA) objected, pleading for a chance to handle the problems mentioned by Landis, who then suggested that an AIA representative contact the commission's chief accountant, Carman Blough. With Landis's approval, Blough agreed that the SEC would refer to the AIA all accounting questions with which the commission took issue, where accountants had signed the statement. Violation cases would also be turned over to the AIA Ethics Committee for action. In January 1937, Blough sent the AIA the first set of accounting questions, which led to institutionalizing the responsibility for accounting principles in the hands of the private sector. By mid-1937, the AIA indicated satisfaction with these arrangements. The SEC announced in 1937 that it would defer creating accounting standards to the accounting practitioners. The message was that the AIA could make the accounting rules, although if it did not, the SEC would. In 1937, at the fiftieth anniversary of the AIA, R.H. Montgomery made the presidential address entitled, "What Have We Done and How?" Montgomery indicated the AIA's satisfaction with the SEC authority abdication. He said, "We have survived the Securities and Exchange Commission, which has done a good job." Early in 1938, the AIA

Committee on Accounting Procedure (CAP) was reconstituted in order to undertake the task of making the accounting rules. The SEC's ASR No. 4 in 1938 made the policy official.[10]

The SEC's Failure to Retrieve Its Rule-Making Authorities

The SEC had retained its direct initiative in accounting and auditing standard rule making for only twenty-seven months, from its inception in October 1934 until December 1936. The SEC thereafter looked to the AIA as the source of accounting principles, regardless of how badly the private sector organizations did the standards-setting job. The SEC never tried to regain its authorities.

The AIA's CAP was reconstituted to develop accounting principles in 1938 with one full-time research assistant, one part-time research director (anti-academic Harvard Professor T.H. Sanders) and a committee of twenty-two, who were spread around the nation. Two-thirds had to approve a rule before it was released, even though the rule was to have only the AIA's moral authority (that is, members did not have to follow it). The CAP, to use Carman Blough's description, adopted the "put out the brush fires" approach, which lasted for twenty years until criticism from within the accounting profession and the financial sector—not from the SEC—caused its abandonment in 1959 for the Accounting Principles Board (APB). The CAP had issued fifty-one *Accounting Research Bulletins* (ARBs) (No. 43 was a restatement of the first 42), some standardization was accomplished, but ambiguously worded alternative accounting conventions characteristically were approved. ARB No. 48, for example, specified pooling of the interests as an acceptable alternative for purchase accounting when businesses were to be combined (purchase accounting could be abused and pooling was thought to correct the situation). However, the requirements for pooling to be acceptable were loose, and contained debilitating qualifiers and loopholes. Pooling became hopeless as a standard, and instead was used as the medium for some wild business-combination accounting in the 1960s, no doubt facilitating the conglomerate merger movement. In any event, the CAP failed, in part from criticism within the accounting profession and in part from outsiders—especially the Controller's Institute (later called the Financial Executives Institute, FEI), which felt it was having insufficient input into the ARBs.

The successor organization, the Accounting Principles Board (APB), magnified the ills of the CAP. Once again, the committee was too large and the staff was too small. The APB had eighteen members compared to twenty-two on the CAP. All APB members had to belong to the American Institute of Certified Public Accountants (AICPA). Of the twelve practicing public accountants' positions on the APB, the required affiliations were six "Big Eight" accounting firm members, three university professors, two financial executives, and one director of research. Up to eight analysts could be employed. APB recommendations, like the CAP before it, were not to be binding on the institute's members.

The role that accounting conventions played during the 1960s merger movement is debatable. At the time, many involved in the stock market observed the merger-active firms pursuing combinations and using the pooling of interest technique to produce instantaneous growth in earnings. These were assumed to create stock price increases. A good deal of trading occurred in the shares of firms like Gulf + Western and Boise-Cascade. The pooling device reduced the combined firms' outstanding shares while maintaining the earnings of both; earnings per share of the combined firm thus automatically increased above those of either of the two firms before combination. How many people were fooled, and under what circumstances, or how many were drawn into the market for these stocks, still remains a matter of argument and analysis. Pooling had the advantage of not providing the embarrassingly large good-will accounts associated with paying for a corporation in excess of its asset value. Pooling was not the only accounting device that was used during the conglomerate merger movement to produce illusory gains and earnings, but the controversy raging over the use of pooling caused abandonment of the APB, which was unable to act to stop the abuses.[11]

The SEC remained a spectator throughout. It remained content with issuing ritualized threats to the effect that if the accounting profession did not do something, the SEC might have to. The financial standards network understood the signal, which meant that the SEC was affirming the existing authority distribution. SEC Chairman Manuel F. Cohen's position in 1964 was typical: "from its inception, the commission had preferred cooperation with the profession to governmental action and has actively encouraged accountants to take the initiative in regulating their practices and in setting standards of conduct." Codification of the SEC's rules had been "accomplished in the spirit of cooperation and voluntary action" between the SEC and leading professional accountants.[12] "To the extent that the profession has been willing to move ahead we have been content to remain logically in the background, filling the vacuum when necessary and stimulating study and development of accounting and auditing principles on a continuing basis."[13] A new group of institutions, featuring the Financial Accounting Standards Board (FASB) as the standards-setting operation, was formed with the SEC's blessing to take over from the APB in 1972. The location of control over accounting principles determination thus remained constant within the existing network. No major structural changes in the composition of the groups were made, suggesting that FASB behavior would differ from its predecessors, the CAP, and the APB. FASB performance could be predicted to follow past private-sector patterns because SEC behavior, largely ceremonial, gave no indication of deviations from its past patterns.

A Retrospective Evaluation

The pattern of control over corporate financial reporting conventions is summarized in table 1. SEC relinquishment of control over corporate financial rule-making

Table 1

Institutional Control over Corporate Financial-Reporting Authority in the United States, 1887–1987

Private-Sector Control: Before June 1933	
1. 1887–June 1933	Financial-industrial system control, dominated by the corporate sector.
Public-Sector Control: June 1933–December 1936	
2. June 1933–October 1943 (17 months)	Federal Trade Commission Administration of the Securities Act of 1933 through the newly formed Registration Division headed by James M. Landis.
3. October 1934–December 1936 (27 months)	Securities and Exchange Commission Administration of corporate reporting rules.
Private-Sector Control: January 1937–1987	
4. 1937–1959	Primarily accountant-controlled through the Committee on Accounting Procedure (CAP), a committee of the American Institute of Accountants, later renamed the American Institute of Certified Public Accountants (AICPA).
5. 1959–1972	Primarily accountant-controlled plus some corporate representation, through the Accounting Principles Board, governed through the AICPA.
6. 1973–1987	Sharing of control by the AICPA and the Corporate sector, through the three-tiered organization composed of the AICPA-controlled Financial Accounting Foundation (FAF), its dependent Financial Accounting Standards Board (FASB), and its subsidiary advisory groups designated as the Financial Accounting Standards Advisory Council (FASAC).

standards development occurred within only twenty-seven months of its initial operations in October 1934. By December 1936, the SEC had declared its intention to permit the practicing accountants to develop corporate financial-reporting rules, and to permit the AIA to handle cases of ethics violations by its members.

Why did the commission initially choose to relinquish its authorities? There are several likely reasons. First, financial rule making is about as controversial an issue as one finds; whoever does the job will endure enormous hostility and abuse. A strong incentive is required to want the responsibility. From the SEC's point of view, transferring the heat—political, financial, business, and otherwise—was not a bad idea. Second, there are many different interests involved and many alternative ways of establishing rules that have different profit effects, so universal agreement on any rule is unlikely. Third, the SEC, before transferring its authority to the private sector, had taken the position that it would not specify the what and how of disclosure, but would put the responsibility on the reporting group to disclose what was material. Given this initial ambiguous position by the SEC, transferring standards setting to the private sector was an easy, next step. Fourth, the private sector, particularly the practicing accountants, had maintained constant recalcitrance and hostility toward the SEC. The pressure had taken its toll, particularly on Chief Commissioner Landis. Fifth, it is likely that some of the commissioners believed comprehensive rules establishment was a technical impossibility. The vote to transfer the authorities, however, was not unanimous by any means. Associate justice of the Supreme Court William O. Douglas, an SEC commissioner at the time the decision was made, indicated that he and Commissioner Healy wanted the SEC to retain its authority and to develop accounting principles, but they were outvoted by Commissioners Landis, Mathews, and Ross. It was a close decision.[14]

Rule-Making Decisions from 1977–1986

The Metcalf Hearings of 1977

In 1977, the Senate Subcommittee on Reports, Accounting and Management, of the Committee on Governmental Affairs, conducted hearings on the operation of accounting firms and the performance of the accounting function in the United States.[15] The subcommittee staff had already published an extensive report in 1976, *The Accounting Establishment*, which had been highly critical of the accounting industry.[16] The study's conclusions included a series of judgments alleging that the "Big Eight" accounting firms controlled the AICPA, which in turn controlled the FASB through its appointment of Financial Accounting Foundation (FAF) members; that combining Management Advisory Services (MAS) with auditing had compromised the accounting firms; that accounting conventions developed by the accounting establishment with the SEC's approval had resulted in unreliable information and overly flexible reporting methods.

The study recommended major changes in existing structural relations between the SEC and its constituents, and in the development and implementation of accounting rules and auditing standards. Federal standards and surveillance were to be developed and applied to auditors and audits; auditing and accounting operations were to be divorced from management consulting activities, thus preventing conflicts of interests; a reduction in the dominance of the Big Eight accounting firms was recommended. A federal group was recommended as a new rule-making authority, but the study suggested that the SEC was so sufficiently compromised by past performance and existing relations with their constituents that rule making should be given to a Cost Accounting Standards Board (CASB) type group, or to the General Accounting Office.

The Metcalf committee addressed a set of major problems including securities acts violations involving bribery of foreign officials, money laundering, and independent auditors' inability to uncover (or if they were uncovered, to reveal) those abuses. Endemic creation of alternative accounting treatments by the SEC-legitimated private sector were criticized, as were the accounting combination techniques involved in the conglomerate merger movement. The Metcalf committee's recommendations, however, were mild indeed, compared to the staff reports. New legislation, structural changes, and power reallocations among the pivotal institutions were not recommended. Instead, the recommendations suggested a series of behavioral reforms designed to improve auditing, accounting, and standard setting.

Some private-sector changes were made in response to the committee's recommendations. Accounting firm peer reviews were instituted (the reviewing accounting firms, oddly enough, found little at fault with brother accounting firms). Responding to the conflict-of-interest problem, the SEC issued ASR No. 250 requiring proxy statements to indicate when MAS and auditing was performed by the same accounting firm. The requirement was dropped within a few years, the SEC having concluded that the information was of little investor value. The SEC included the obligatory ceremonial caution that it might have to reconsider the issue if things did not go well.[17] The crucial conflict-of-interest potential thus remained; clients could be counseled on how to run parts of their business by the same accounting firm hired to report on the client's performance. The SEC and its constituents had resumed their usual patterns very quickly after the Metcalf hearings closed. It was to be expected. When institutions develop an established interactive mode over half a century, polite requests for behavioral changes are unlikely to alter their performance.

The Dingell Hearings of 1985–1986

The Dingell committee (Subcommittee on Oversight and Investigations, Committee on Energy and Commerce, U.S. House of Representatives) examining the operations of the SEC and the accounting industry started its hearings in 1985, indicating that the improvements in financial reporting and auditing looked for by the Metcalf committee had not been forthcoming. Besides the unresolved issues left over from the Metcalf hearings, several new events sparked the reopening of congressional hearings.

Accounting firms had continued to operate and expand their substantial management advisory service operations. Commissioner Shad reported that for the eleven firms having more than one hundred SEC clients, the contribution of MAS activities to total fees ranged from 5 percent to 28 percent. One firm received more than 20 percent.[18] Withdrawal of ASR No. 250 may have encouraged the expansion of MAS operations. The SEC report did not mention the dollar implications, which are impressive. Peat Marwick's U.S. billings for the year ending June 30, 1984 was estimated at $890 million, and at $909 million for the following fiscal year—a time when Arthur Andersen & Co., the largest firm, had revenues estimated at over $1 billion.[19] The implication is that MAS revenues may have been between $100 and $200 million for either of the two firms. Whatever the actual amounts, the revenue contributed is large enough to be a matter of policy concern, particularly since MAS may be the most important area of business growth for accounting firms.

Furthermore, several spectacular auditing failures occurred where nationally important firms received auditors' clean bills of health. Shortly afterward, it was learned that the firms were insolvent at the time of the audits. The SEC had remained aloof from re-examining auditing procedures, which alarmed Congressman Dingell and others. These incidents underscored, at least for Representative Dingell, the questionable relationship of the SEC and the accounting practitioners. Where the Metcalf hearings had limited prospects and objectives, the Dingell hearings had the potential of producing legislation that altered the existing financial reporting network's structure and power allocations. Congressman Dingell's comments in the *New York Times* before the opening of the hearings were pointed:

> Through its oversight function, the subcommittee seeks to determine whether the SEC's delegation of its statutory authority to self-interested private parties has adequately fulfilled the commission's mandate to protect the public interest. The investigation will be fair, but if problems are revealed that need resolution—either by more effective SEC regulations or by the industry itself—changes will doubtless be recommended.[20]

Not since the 1930s had the disagreements among the principals been stated so clearly. Chief SEC Commissioner Shad defended the status quo in the face of the committee challenge.[21] The committee-SEC confrontation crystallized over the appropriateness of management advisory services being offered by accounting firms because of the conflict-of-interest potential. The issue is extremely important because of what it indicates about the SEC's role. Defenders of the MAS-auditing combination assert that no reason exists to prohibit the practice because no cases have been uncovered where a conflict arose and the public interest suffered. Critics claim that cases have arisen, and furthermore, that sub-rosa arrangements seldom leave documented traces. Those deliberately engaging in wrong-doing take pains to conceal it. Others unconsciously involved will rationalize away the action.

In the midst of the controversy, the SEC cited the Cohen Commission as its authority for believing that there was an absence of incriminating or circumstantial evidence of MAS-auditing conflict; Chief Commissioner Shad described it as an "*independent Commission . . . established by the American Institute of Certified Public Accountants . . . in 1974 to study the role and responsibilities of independent accounts*" (italics in original).[22] It long had been the practice of the existing financial accounting-auditing system in the United States to selectively appoint subgroups to investigate themselves, with the predictable results. Those named to the investigative bodies have established track records, and are unlikely to contain individuals critical of the system appointing them. What was striking, however, was the SEC's acceptance of the Committee as independent when it had been appointed by a group with a built-in financial interest in the matter.

Consensus Networks and SEC Behavior

Several central disputes appeared in the Dingell hearings: the effectiveness of auditing, the role of the SEC, and the appropriateness of vesting in the private-sector functions assigned by Congress to the government agency. The SEC and the private-sector groups performing the public roles testified according to form, the SEC defending the system's organization and outputs, and the private sector groups doing the same, claiming that the conflict-of-interest problem was an illusion.

The testimony by the SEC and others indicated the degree to which the financial reporting network had solidified its role allocations. Extensive descriptions were supplied of operations and functions stressing group interactions. The overall picture was that of a mature, firmly established, interactive network, in which it became unclear at times which institution—the SEC, the FASB, or the AICPA—was the centerpiece, so closely had grown the alliances between them. The interaction appeared so firmly established that upsetting the balance of powers would be difficult. After some fifty years, it becomes easier to argue the legitimacy of de facto arrangements.

The key to SEC behavior is in the nature of independent regulatory commissions as political creatures. Their origin on the federal level was in the creation of the Interstate Commerce Commission in 1887. Independent commissions were created thereafter in two waves: one group before World War I, and the other group, which includes the SEC, during the Depression of the 1930s. The predominant mission of these commissions was to oversee some specific areas of economic activity usually dealing with matters of price and entry, that is, the prices that regulatees could charge for their products, or the numbers and identities of those who would be permitted to compete, and under what circumstances. Examples of these commissions include the Federal Trade Commission (antitrust, trade practices, packaging), the Federal Communications Commission (radio, television, interstate and international wire cable and radio), the Civil Aeronautics Board (airlines, terminated in 1984), and the Federal Maritime Commission (shipping).

Unlike the executive agencies—for example, the Environmental Protection Agency (air, water, and pollution standards), the Federal Highway Administration (highway safety standards), and the Occupational Health and Safety Administration (workplace health and safety)—that report to the president and therefore are much more vulnerable to the political process, the independent commissions are more isolated from direct political control. This was intentional. Independence of the commissioners was considered the key to effective administration at the time that the commission form of government was adapted to the federal regulatory process. Therefore, the commissioners were appointed for a period of years greater than the president's term, and once appointed, could not be removed except for cause—simply displeasing the president was not enough.

Both the executive agencies and the independent commissions have fundamental governing flaws. Presidents have a variety of ways of curtailing agency administrative action to which they are hostile; these ways include reducing budgets, sabotaging the operational efficiency of agencies, and refusing to enforce some laws. Independent commissions, however, have a pattern of becoming the creatures of the groups they are created to regulate. Why this becomes the case is a matter of debate. Some observers believe that the creation of the commissions was a conspiracy on the part of the regulatees to have a government agency created so that by controlling the agency they would be able to do legally what they were prevented from doing under the common law. Others see the matter as more of a fall from grace. That is, that the commissions were created to do a regulatory job, but because of their isolation from support groups fall into the regulatees' sphere of influence because of the latter's constant activism and aggressiveness and the prospect of future employment with the regulatees for key agency personnel.

On an institutional level, it is difficult to see if the commissions have alternatives other than to compromise with their regulatees, and at least to a degree, represent them. The prevailing mode of operation, among the commissions and the institutions dependent on them, is to proceed to consensus positions so that the networks' output can be achieved. That is why these institutions surrounding the regulatory commissions can be designated as consensus networks. There may be conflict from time to time, but the path of the actors within the networks is to achieve understandings about allocations of resources, authorities, and outputs. The greater the community of interest among the commissions' regulatees, the greater the pressure that can be brought against the commissions to make them conform to the networks' wishes. Multiple regulatee commissions like the FTC may become inefficient and ineffective at times, but the existence of diversified regulatees makes it difficult for the FTC to become predominantly a regulatees' advocate.[23]

Regulatory commissions can be recognized as the corporate staffs for their networks. Their functions reflect both complex situations and rational objectives. They plan, coordinate, and control. They maintain contact with all points of the network. They act as focal points for the dissemination of network information. Formal hearings provide forums for discussing issues of mutual concern and interest, which accounts for much of the networks' resilience. Where the commission fails to be able to provide an adaptive mode for the networks' institutions, it may be abandoned, like the CAB.

The operations of the SEC discussed here are best understood within the context of its characteristic functioning as part of a consensus network. The crucial institutions within the network are protected, for example, the accounting practitioners, the exchanges, the investment houses, and the corporations. Once having achieved a system that operates placidly, an independent commission like the SEC is either unwilling or unable to alter its operations since doing so would alienate powerful constituents. Those who threaten the system, and who have little power within it, receive the brunt of the agency's aggressiveness. For example, when insiders trade on secret information, they have an advantage over those without the information.

For that reason insider trading carries heavy penalties under the 1934 Securities and Exchange Act. Insider trading may distort capital market efficiency, and it certainly violates our notions of fairness. The SEC, quite understandably, carries on a continuing war against insider trading, but there is great question whether it manages to touch anything except the smallest proportion of the abuses that occur. In the long run, effective enforcement is likely to depend on more efficient ways of recording trades. The issue may be more a matter of technology than of law enforcement. Insider trading, nevertheless, apparently is a major dedication of the SEC, whereas the creation of financial reporting rules, as we have just observed, is not. Pursuit of individual violators is a safe activity, particularly when they have little power; challenging the interests of major constituents is not.

The perceived unevenness in SEC attitude causes a good deal of criticism at times, and gives rise to charges of political favoritism. When E.F. Hutton & Co. pleaded guilty to over 2,000 counts of mail and wire fraud in May 1985, the SEC found itself in a dilemma. Under the terms of the Investment Company Act of 1940, any company found guilty of criminal conduct in connection with investment advisory activities, securities trading, or underwriting is automatically debarred. However, the firm was one of the nation's most important brokerage houses, and putting it out of business would be bound to cause some disruption in the capital markets. Would Hutton be required to pay the penalty that the law demanded —a penalty one might assume would be required of a lesser firm?

E.F. Hutton was given a temporary exemption from the operation of this provision, with a hearing scheduled for the future on whether the exemption should be made permanent. Hutton agreed to cooperate with the SEC investigation, and consented to an injunction against future violations of the securities acts, without having to admit to past violations. This settled an SEC lawsuit against Hutton regarding violations of internal control and reporting requirements. The treatment of Hutton by the SEC was not harsh.

Contrast the treatment Hutton received with the famous Chiarella case. A "mark-up man" in a printer's employ correctly deduced the actual identities of five disguised takeover target firms that were mentioned in legal documents sent to the printer. By trading on the information, the defendant, Chiarella, made slightly more than $30,000 over fourteen months. Convicted of violating the prohibitions against insider trading in the 1934 act and sentenced to a lengthy jail term, Chiarella appealed his conviction to the U.S. Supreme Court where, fortunately for the petitioner, the conviction was overturned. The Supreme Court reasoned that since Chiarella did not fall under the classification of what constituted an insider, he could not be prosecuted under the terms of the act.[24] Chiarella was an outsider of little consequence but he had threatened the system, and the SEC would have made an example of him. In fairness, it ought to be recognized that the SEC doubtlessly wanted to establish that the 1934 act applied to a broad range of individuals, not only to those immediately associated with the corporations and financial institutions involved with the transactions.

The SEC's operations are best understood as typical of the species of government regulatory mechanisms known as the independent commissions. Long having had the reputation of being the best of the regulatory commissions, the recent experiences of the SEC have brought attention to whether or not the reputation is justified. Its functioning has been questioned in terms of whether it has accomplished the mandate placed on it in its organic acts. The SEC is open to challenge indeed, but the likelihood of affecting a change in its operations is slim, as is the chance that remedial legislation can be achieved. The case illustrates the lesson that once regulatory institutions are in place and operating in a consistent pattern, with the support of their constituent network institutions, outside shocks have little chance of affecting the old, appointed ways.

Notes

1. Chatov, Robert, *Corporate Financial Reporting: Public or Private Control?* New York: Free Press, 1975, pp. 38–54.

2. Ripley, William Z., "From Main Street to Wall Street," *The Atlantic Monthly* (January), **137**:94–112 (1926). "Stop. Look, Listen! The Shareholder's Right to Adequate Information," *The Atlantic Monthly* (September), **138**:389–399 (1926). "More Light!—And Power Too," *The Atlantic Monthly* (November), **138**:667–687 (1926). *Main Street and Wall Street.* Boston: Little, Brown and Co., 1927.

3. Chatov, Robert, "Adolph A. Berle, Jr.: Reformer or Reactionary? His Thoughts on Accounting and Its Relation to Corporate Legitimacy." Presented at the American Accounting Association Meeting, San Diego, August 18, 1982.

4. Chatov, *Corporate Financial Reporting*, pp. 13–22.

5. Schlesinger, Arthur M., Jr., *The Coming of the New Deal.* Boston: Houghton Mifflin, 1958, pp. 434–437.

6. Ibid., pp. 437–440.

7. Chatov, *Corporate Financial Reporting*, pp. 75–80.

8. Ibid., pp. 33–36.

9. Ibid., pp. 55–70, *passim.*

10. Ibid., pp. 95–133, *passim.*

11. Ibid., pp. 185–231, *passim.*

12. Cohen, Manuel F., "Current Developments at the SEC," *The Accounting Review* (January), **40**:5–6 (1965).

13. Cohen, Manuel F., "The SEC and Accountants: Cooperative Efforts to Improve Financial Reporting," *Journal of Accountancy* (December), **12**:56–57 (1966).

14. Chatov, *Corporate Financial Reporting*, pp. 107–109.

15. Subcommittee on Reports, Accounting and Management, of the Committee on Government Operations (Affairs), U.S. Senate, 95th Congress, First Session, *Improving The Accountability of Publicly Owned Corporations and Their Auditors*, Washington, D.C.: U.S. Government Printing Office, November 1977.

16. Subcommittee on Reports, Accounting and Management, of the Committee on Government Operations (Affairs), U.S. Senate, 94th Congress, Second Session, *The Accounting Establishment*, Washington, D.C.: U.S. Government Printing Office, December 1976.

17. Securities and Exchange Commission, Accounting Series Releases No. 264, 296 and 304, the latter of which was issued on January 28, 1982, and contained the final rules on the matter.

18. Shad, John S.R., Statement Before the House Subcommittee on Oversight and Investigations of the Committee on Energy and Commerce, 99th Congress, First Session, March 6, 1985.

19. Berton, Lee, "Peat Marwick Asks 65 Partners in U.S. to Leave," *The Wall Street Journal*, February 22, 1985, p. 6; "Peat Marwick Departures Indicate Firm's Chief Isn't Leading Merely a Routine Efficiency Drive," *The Wall Street Journal*, March 21, 1985.

20. Dingell, John D., "Who Audits the Auditors?" *New York Times*, March 13, 1985, p. B-3.

21. Shad, 99th Congress, First Session.

22. Ibid., p. C-8, footnote.

23. Chatov, Robert, "Cooperation Between Government and Business," in *Handbook of Organizational Design, Vol. I, Adapting Organizations to their Environments*, Paul C. Nystrom and William H. Starbuck, eds. London: Oxford University Press, 1981.

24. *Chiarella v. United States*, 445 U.S. 222 (1980).

Privatization

E.S. Savas

Privatization is an awkward name for a concept that is having a far-reaching effect on the role of government. Opponents deride privatization as a primitive and simplistic call to turn government functions over to private business. In fact, it has come to symbolize a new way of looking at society's wants and needs, and a rethinking of the role of government in fulfilling them. It means relying more on private institutions and less on government to satisfy society's needs. To define it more precisely, privatization is the act of reducing governmental involvement, or increasing private-sector involvement, in an activity or in the ownership of assets.

Contracting with private firms to finance, construct, and operate waterworks or prisons, or to sweep the streets, prune trees, or repair ships, is a form of privatization; so is contracting with a not-for-profit agency to deliver "meals on wheels" to elderly shut-ins, or to operate a half-way house. Issuing food stamps and housing vouchers to the poor is an example of privatization, and can be contrasted to having government-run farms and grocery stores, and public-housing ghettos. Urban dwellers practice privatization when they form neighborhood security patrols, and so do suburbanites who join volunteer fire departments. Selling off a state-owned airline, hospital, or coal mine is privatization, and it is also privatization when government gets out of the business of insuring home mortgages or running commuter buses and lets the marketplace provide those services.

The very distinction between *public* and *private* is elusive. We speak of a park or a government office building as being publicly owned, but we use the same term to describe IBM, because it has many stockholders and any member of the public is free to buy part of the company; it is a private firm that is publicly owned. In the same way, a public restaurant is one that is open to the public at large, although it may be owned by a sole proprietor. Confusingly, we use the word *public* to describe three very different circumstances: government ownership, widespread ownership, and widespread access. This semantic confusion is nevertheless instructive, for it implies that government ownership—and by extension, government action—is not necessary to achieve widespread (that is, public) benefits. Privatization capitalizes on this underappreciated truism and takes advantage of the full array of ownership and operating relations to serve the public interest by satisfying people's wants and needs.

Pressures for Privatization

There are two types of major forces behind the privatization movement: pragmatic and philosophical. The goal of the pragmatists is better government, in the sense of a more cost-effective one. The goal of those who approach the matter from a philosophical perspective is less government, one that plays a smaller role vis-à-vis private institutions.

The Pragmatic Viewpoint

When governments face severe fiscal stress, that is, when the cost of government activities is rising but the public's resistance to higher taxes is also rising, public officials seek any promising solution to their quandary. Typically, they first resort to borrowing to close the gap between revenues and expenditures, whether openly by issuing bonds and notes, or covertly by creative bookkeeping that masks the magnitude of the disparity. But public antipathy to more government spending leads to voter rejection of bond referenda, and the growing adoption of generally accepted accounting principles in government forecloses the surreptitious option.

The remaining choices for public officials are narrowed to reduced services or greater productivity. Naturally, reducing or cutting back services is unpopular among beneficiaries of the service, and so greater productivity is often seen as more attractive politically. The problem with increasing productivity, however, is that it is difficult to do, and it often creates resentment among the affected public employees. The history of modern government is replete with sequential or simultaneous efforts to improve government by centralization, decentralization, reorganization, performance budgeting, planning-programming-budgeting systems (PPBS), zero-based budgeting (ZBB), management by objectives (MBO), management training, sensitivity training, organization development, worker incentives, shared savings, labor-management committees, productivity councils, computerization, management science, operations research, and numerous other ways. Their combined impact, however, has been disappointingly modest. A more fundamental, strategic approach is needed.

Privatization is a strategic approach to improving the productivity of government agencies. As will be shown, there is overwhelming evidence that privatization, when carried out prudently, generally leads to large increases in efficiency while improving or at least maintaining the level and quality of service. For this reason, cost-conscious public officials, spurred by good-government groups and by others who favor privatization for other reasons, are turning to privatization as an important tool for better public management and as the ultimate key to more cost-effective government.

The Philosophical Viewpoint

The role of government differs in different societies, and even within a single society it changes over time, waxing and waning over decades and centuries. In the United States, in the last sixty years, there has been a lot of waxing but little waning of government. Many view this trend with alarm because it poses a danger to democracy. Their reasoning is based on political philosophy. As more and more of the people's earnings are taken by government, as decisions about the disposition of these moneys are made by increasingly distant and unresponsive organs of government, and as government's presence pervades more and more areas of human activity, there is a loss of freedom. In drawing up the Constitution and the Bill of Rights, America's founding fathers took great pains to protect citizens from their government. The history of civilization showed that government could be a serious threat to the individual rights they cherished. Even in a democratic society, government institutions could become instruments of tyranny; those who mobilize majority support could use government's coercive sanctions to deprive those in the minority. Therefore, the framers of the Constitution designed a system that imposed the minimal level of collective coercion necessary to secure the blessings of liberty. At each turn the power of government was circumscribed by checks and balances.

Those who favor privatization on these grounds of political philosophy feel that government has become too big, too costly, too inefficient, and overly intrusive and dominant in the lives of Americans. Of course, collective action is necessary in our complex world, even more than in simpler communities. But the United States has gone astray in recent years, these proponents argue, behaving as though government were the only institution available to society for acting collectively. In fact, there are many different and versatile institutions that can act at least as effectively: civic and neighborhood associations, religious institutions, charitable and fraternal organizations, ethnic clubs, businesses, and unions, to name a few. All of these are private societal institutions that express collective choice and take action for the benefit of many people. One should not neglect the most important private institution in society: the family. After all, the family is the original department of health, education, welfare, housing, and human services!

Government Monopolies

We begin by comparing the basic features of the way government and private groups provide services. A government service is paid for by taxes, user charges, or a combination of the two, and the work is done by government employees. The critical weakness of this traditional public-sector approach is that it relies on government monopoly. Considering how vigorously we oppose monopolies in the private sector, it is remarkably perverse that in the public sector we have done just the opposite. We suffer under the delusion that total reliance on a single supplier is the best way to assure satisfactory delivery of public services—if the supplier is the government. Yet we know how difficult it is to make any monopoly—public or private—serve the interests of its customers rather than the interests of its owners or employees. It is a long-discredited fiction that government agencies exist solely to serve the public; as in all human organizations, other less lofty, but understandable, goals are pursued as well.

How do we justify government monopoly? Often, we hear the assertion that government can do it cheaper because it does not make a profit. But there is a growing body of empirical evidence that refutes this simple-minded generality: the gains to the public from greater efficiency far offset the small amounts that go to profit. This rationalization of government monopoly is thus no more than a myth, and a dangerous myth at that. Total and permanent dependence on one supplier, whether a government agency or a private organization, can be ecomically and politically hazardous to the public interest. Without effective freedom of choice, the citizen-consumer of public services can be exploited. Citizens need alternatives, because when choice is replaced by compulsion, there is no such thing as a public servant. Anyone who has been in the Soviet Union and dealt with officious bureaucrats, surly waiters, or rude retail clerks—all government employees—has experienced this problem in its most endemic form. In a less extreme way, U.S. citizens may feel the same bureaucratic indifference in post offices, welfare agencies, and drivers' license bureaus. The problem is manifest. The questions are: How to privatize? What government functions lend themselves to competition? What functions are best performed by government monopolies despite the potential hazards?

What to Privatize. To begin with, there are some obvious functions that ought to continue in the hands of government, even if there is some waste and inefficiency. For example, no one would want the nation defended by Joe's Fighter Squadron: "Planes Intercepted While-U-Wait." Nevertheless, there are many ancillary defense functions that could be handled by contractors or franchises, including base and equipment maintenance, office chores, and many of the activities involved in feeding, housing, and providing for the daily needs of military personnel and their families.

Aside from national defense, however, there are few functions that could not be privatized, at least partly. For example, police protection is the local analog of national defense. While the police themselves should remain government employees, there is ample room to back them up and support them with private guards, private alarm services, and voluntary neighborhood patrols, as well as private custodial services for precinct station houses and private repair shops for police cars and radios.

How to Privatize. In reality, the tough question is not whether a service should be privatized, but what form the private delivery of the service should utilize. Under privatization, there are five possible methods of service delivery:

1. Government contracts with private organizations, in which case government picks the contractor and foots the bill.
2. Government awards franchises to private organizations, and the organizations charge their customers.
3. Government issues vouchers to eligible citizens, who then choose the service supplier but the government ultimately pays the bill.
4. Voluntary organizations, recognizing a need, undertake a job through volunteers or fundraising.
5. Entrepreneurs see and fill a need through the marketplace.

Looking at each of these five delivery methods in turn, we can see that there are many examples of services that have already been privatized in one or another American community. In the first category, almost two hundred municipal functions are currently contracted out to private organizations (both for-profit and not-for-profit). These are listed in table 1.

Franchises are the second method of delivery. Although in some communities local governments supply the majority of utilities, in others franchises are awarded to provide electric power, gas, water, bus service, taxis, cable television, and hot dogs in municipal stadiums. Increasingly, franchises are granted to operators of recreational facilities on public property, such as tennis courts, golf courses, swimming pools, and skating rinks.

In the third category, vouchers have been used successfully to provide food, rent, medical care, cultural events, and education. Compelling proposals have been offered to use vouchers for elementary and secondary education, for vocational training, to replace wasteful and degrading forms of housing assistance, and as a form of unemployment insurance, where the job-seeker has a valuable voucher to offer potential employers.

The fourth method, voluntarism, has also been a growing form of privatization. Voluntary service spans the gamut from neighborhood organizations that clean streets, maintain parks, and run Little Leagues, to labor unions that distribute surplus food and fix up the homes of retirees, to charities that rehabilitate addicts and

Table 1
City and County Services Provided Contractually by Private Firms

Adoption, air pollution abatement, airport operation, airport services, alarm system maintenance, ambulance, animal control, appraisals, architectural auditing, auditorium management;

Beach management, billing and collection, bridge (construction, inspection, and maintenance), building demolition, building rehabilitation, buildings and grounds (janitorial, maintenance, security), building and mechanical inspection, burial of indigents, bus operation, bus shelter maintenance;

Cafeteria and restaurant operation, catch-basin cleaning, cemetery administration, child protection, civil defense communications, clerical, communications maintenance, community center operation, computer operations, consultant services, convention center management, crime laboratory, crime prevention and patrol, custodial;

Data entry, data processing, day care, document preparation, drug and alcohol programs;

Economic development, election administration, electrical inspection, electric power, elevator inspection, emergency maintenance, environmental services;

Family counseling, financial services, fire communications, fire-hydrant maintenance, fire prevention and suppression, flood control planning, foster-home care;

Golf course operation, graphic arts, guard service;

Health inspection, health services, homemaker service, hospital management, hospital services, housing inspection and code enforcement, housing management;

Industrial development, insect and rodent control, institutional care, insurance administration, irrigation;

Jail and detention, janitorial, juvenile delinquency programs;

Labor relations, laboratory, landscaping, laundry, lawn maintenance, leaf collection, legal aid, legal library operation, licensing;

Management consulting, mapping, marina services, median strip maintenance, mosquito control, moving and storage, museum and cultural;

Noise abatement, nursing, nutrition;

Office machine maintenance, opinion polling;

Paratransit system operation, park maintenance, parking enforcement, parking lot and garage operation, parking lot clearing, parking meter servicing, parking ticket processing, patrol, payroll processing, personal services, photographic services, physician services, planning, plumbing inspection, police communications, port and harbor management, printing, prisoner transportation, probation, property acquisition, public administrator services, public health, public relations and information, public works;

Records maintenance, recreation services and facility operation, rehabilitation, resource recovery, risk management;

School bus, secretarial, security, sewage treatment, sewer maintenance, sidewalk repair, snow (plowing, sanding, removal), social services, soil conservation, solid waste (collection, transfer, disposal), street lighting (construction and maintenance), street services (construction, maintenance, sweeping), surveying;

Tax collection (assessing, bill processing, receipts), tennis court maintenance, test scoring, traffic control (markings, signs, and signal installation and maintenance), training (of government employees), transit management, transportation of elderly and disabled, treasury functions, tree services (planting, pruning, removal);

Utility billing, utility meter reading;

Vehicle fleet management, vehicle maintenance, vehicle towing and storage, voter registration;

Water meter reading and maintenance, water pollution abatement, water supply and distribution, water treatment, weed abatement, welfare;

Zoning and subdivision control.

help the handicapped. Corporations have been leaders in encouraging voluntary activities on the part of their employees—even giving them time off work to do so.

The fifth method of service delivery is the free market. Most Americans rely on the marketplace to provide food, clothing, shelter, and most other daily needs, as well as health care, recreation, transportation, and so forth. In addition, as the demand for social services has grown, the market has been quick to respond with child-care centers, adult education, nursing homes, senior-citizen communities, and even singles bars and dating services. Moreover, private mail and parcel delivery is thriving in competition with the U.S. Postal Service.

Principles of Privatization

It is clear from this brief review that most so-called public services can be provided either by government or by one or more of the five forms of privatization just discussed. How, then, does one sort through the myriad goods and services necessary in modern society and decide which ones should be handled in which manner? Clearly some general principles are needed.

Two characteristics of goods and services—access and consumption—provide enough distinctions to sort all goods and services into useful categories. Access refers to the ease or difficulty of denying someone a particular good. For instance, it is easy to prevent someone from taking a fish from the supermarket, unless he pays, but it is almost impossible to stop him from taking a fish from the sea. Consumption can be exclusive at one extreme or common at the other. For example, consuming a slice of bread is an exclusive act (for the bread is no longer available to anyone else), but a television broadcast is consumed in common (for no matter how many television sets are tuned to a particular program, that program still remains available for everyone else's use).

These two concepts can be combined to define four classes of goods, as shown in figure 1. Private goods are consumed exclusively and can be denied to anyone who does not pay for them (most store-bought goods and services are in this category). Toll goods, such as telephone services, are consumed in common (the more subscribers, the better), but someone who does not pay can be denied access to the network. Because access can be denied to private and toll goods, the market

	Easy to Deny Access	Difficult to Deny Access
Individual Consumption	private goods	common-pool goods
Joint Consumption	toll goods	collective goods

Figure 1. Summary Chart Defining Goods in Terms of Their Intrinsic Characteristics

will readily supply them, and government involvement is generally not needed except to establish ground rules for market transactions, safety assurance, and regulation of those toll goods that are so-called natural monopolies. In distinction are those goods and services that allow unlimited access. Common-pool goods, like the fish in the sea, are consumed on an exclusive basis, as just defined, but access to them cannot readily be denied to anyone. They are virtually free for the taking. As a result, they can be squandered and destroyed. Since the market will not supply such goods, collective action is needed to protect the supply.

The most problematic of all are collective goods, for their consumption is common and ready access is available to all. National defense is a classic collective good (as were city walls in earlier days), and so are lighthouses, city streets, and common grazing grounds. Many citizens avail themselves of such goods, but users do not pay directly to benefit from them. Obviously, the goods would not exist for long, or at all, without collective action. Hence, coercion (in the form of taxes) is needed to make everyone pay a fair share. Collective action is also needed to provide those private and toll goods that society decides are to be subsidized and provided as though they were collective goods, such as education.

Comparing the Privatization Arrangements

Now we can join the discussions about types of service delivery and types of goods. Table 2 shows the arrangements that can be used to provide each type of good. Note that not all types of service can be used to supply all types of goods. For example, collective goods can be provided only by government, contract, or voluntary arrangements.

We can complete the picture by noting that each method of delivery has distinctive features. No one arrangement is universally best; each has a unique combination of attributes that make it better or worse for a particular activity. Table 3 describes each of the different methods of service delivery in terms of ten important characterics, namely, the extent to which the arrangement promotes competition; responds to consumer preferences; relates costs to benefits, which induces

Table 2
Types of Goods and the Arrangements That Can Be Used to Supply Them

Arrangement	Private Goods	Toll Goods	Common-pool Goods	Collective Goods
Government agency	+	+	+	+
Contract	+	+	+	+
Franchise	+	+		
Voucher	+	+		
Market	+	+		
Voluntary	+	+	+	+

Table 3
Characteristics of Different Institutional Arrangements

Characteristics	Government Agency	Contract	Franchise	Voucher	Market	Voluntary
Promotes competition		+ +	+	+ +	+ +	+
Is responsive to consumer preferences				+ +	+ +	+ +
Relates costs to benefits			+ +	+ +	+ +	+ +
Achieves economies of scale		+ +	+ +	+ +	+ +	
Permits redistribution of wealth	+ +	+ +	+ +	+ +		
Can further other purposes	+ +	+	+	+		
Handles poorly specified services	+ +			+ +	+ +	+ +
Requires multiple suppliers		+ +		+ +	+ +	
Is relatively invulnerable to fraud						+ +
Limits the number of government employees		+ +	+ +	+ +	+ +	+ +

Note: + characteristic is present to some degree.
        + + characteristic is present to a great degree.

efficiency; achieves economy of scale; permits redistribution of wealth to the extent desired, as determined by democratic means; can be used to further other public purposes; can handle services for which clear specifications cannot be written; requires that there be more than one supplier or potential supplier of the service; is relatively invulnerable to fraud; and limits the number of government employees.

Close inspection of this table should dispel concerns that privatization inevitably imposes a greater burden on the poor. Many who oppose privatization on the grounds that it is unfair to the poor assume incorrectly that privatization requires a pure market arrangement, and they conjure up the vision of every family, rich and poor alike, having to pay individually for their children's basic schooling. That is not the case at all. Contracts, vouchers, and subsidized franchises (for example, subsidized private bus lines) permit as much redistribution of wealth as direct government service does, and as much as the public desires (because in each case the government sets the terms and pays the bill).

Monopoly versus Competition

In summary, most so-called public services can be privatized through one arrangement or another, but each service has to be considered individually to determine which arrangement, if any, is likely to be an improvement. Significantly, more often than not, the real issue is monopoly versus competition rather than public versus private, as it is so often posed for rhetorical purposes. The public-private dichotomy is too simplistic a formulation, as all methods of providing services involve some role for government. Even free markets require governments to establish weights and measures, control the value of currency, and enforce contracts. Progress toward more efficient, effective, and equitable provision of so-called public services will be most rapid if we avoid ideology and focus instead on finding the most appropriate arrangements for providing the services we want and need. As to the relative merits of the different arrangements, this is an empirical question that is answered in the next section.

The Evidence on Privatization

A growing body of evidence attests to the superiority of one form of privatization—contracting—over conventional in-house government work. Careful studies involving hundreds of communities, in the United States and abroad, compared the relative efficiency and effectiveness of municipal agencies and private contractors in providing identical services. For example, Los Angeles County reviewed the cumulative results of its privatization program between 1979 and 1984. It concluded that its 434 separate contracts cost only $108 million, whereas if county agencies had done the work directly, the cost would have been $167 million, or 55 percent more.[1]

A detailed analysis sponsored by the Department of Housing and Urban Development found that the cost of street construction by city agencies was 96 percent greater than similar work by contractors, and that municipal costs were greater by 43 percent for street cleaning, 73 percent for janitorial services, 56 percent for traffic-signal maintenance, and 37 percent for tree pruning. In each case there were no differences in quality. Only in payroll preparation were the costs equal.[2]

The most studied municipal service is refuse collection. Nine independent, large-scale studies have been conducted by academics and by government agencies in the United States, Canada, West Germany, Japan, and Switzerland. All concluded that municipal collection is significantly more costly than contract collection, by anywhere from 15 percent to 124 percent.[3] Moreover, a citizen survey covering more than eight thousand randomly selected households in eighty-two randomly selected cities showed greater satisfaction with private companies than with municipal agencies, for the same level of collection service.[4]

International studies comparing public and private bus operations show the former to be 67 percent to 100 percent costlier than the latter, but no better or safer. (The public bus agency in Calcutta, India, employed a whopping fifty employees per bus, far more than the private bus lines in the same city.)[5] In the United States, an exhaustive review of 249 transit systems by researchers at the University of California at Irvine concluded that privately owned and managed bus systems were the most efficient.[6]

Early results indicate that the private sector can do better in constructing and operating prisons, waste-water treatment plants, street lights, and resource-recovery facilities. In support functions such as data processing, food service, and audio-visual services, an analysis of 235 federal-agency contracts reported by the Office of Federal Procurement Policy showed that the cost of such work by government had been 38 percent higher than contract work.[7]

A clear trend toward privatization is under way. A 1984 survey of fifty-five state and local highway officials by *Roads* magazine disclosed that, by a two-to-one ratio, the officials would be relying more on contractors and less on their own forces for road construction and maintenance because they "are convinced that the private contractor can do the job more cost-effectively than public crews and equipment can."[8] More than one hundred different municipal activities are now being provided by contract, ranging from adoption services to zoning control.

Public officials believe that contracting costs less and provides the same or better quality of service. Surveys of county and municipal officials in a random sample of 117 jurisdictions show that about 60 percent of the officials consider contracting to be less or equal in cost to in-house service, and about 80 percent say it provides better or equal service.[9]

Discussion

Simple pragmatism, not ideology, is the driving force that leads public officials to contract out state and local services. The officials are learning that they can maintain and even improve services while reducing costs significantly, and today this is important for reelection (at least as important for reelection), at least as important as patronage and swollen public payrolls were in earlier days.

The reason why privatization works so well is not that the people employed by government are somehow inferior to those employed by the private sector; they are not. It works because privatization offers choice, and choice fosters competition, which leads to more cost-effective performance. Contracting out means dissolving unnecessary government monopolies and introducing competition in the delivery of public services. The public benefits from this competition—provided that sound bidding, contracting, and performance-monitoring procedures are employed.

Governments are responsible for deciding which services are to be paid for by the public, but they do not have to produce and deliver the services using government employees. In effect, privatization elevates each government agency to the same commanding position as a manufacturer who can decide whether to make or buy a component for the product he is assembling. The efficient manufacturer will maintain a competitive balance among his suppliers, including his own plant, to assure the best possible overall results. Predictably, public-employee unions oppose contracting out because they see an end to their monopolies and a loss of jobs to their new competitors in the private sector. Ironically, these private workers are themselves often unionized.

The advantages of prudent privatization have been demonstrated beyond reasonable doubt. The question is one of political will, and of following sound practices in contracting out and in monitoring the performance of contractors. Privatization leads to a better division of responsibilities between the public and private sectors, which takes advantage of the strengths of each sector and overcomes the limitations of the other. The result is better and less costly services to the public.

Notes

This article is based on E.S. Savas, *Privatization: The Key to Less But Better Government.* Chatham, N.J.: Chatham House Publishers, 1986.

1. Letter report from the Chief Administrative Officer, County of Los Angeles, to County Board of Supervisors, January 23, 1985.
2. Barbara J. Stevens, *Delivering Municipal Services Efficiently: A Comparison of Municipal and Private Service Delivery.* Washington, D.C.: U.S. Department of Housing and Urban Development, June 1984.
3. For example, see E.S. Savas, "Public vs. Private Refuse Collection: A Critical Review of the Evidence," *Journal of Urban Analysis* **6**:1–13 (1979).
4. "Customers Rate Refuse Service," *Waste Age* **12**:82–88 (1981).
5. Charles Feibel, and A.A. Walters, "Ownership and Efficiency in Urban Buses," Staff Working Paper No. 371. Washington, D.C.: World Bank, 1980.
6. James L. Perry, and Timlynn T. Babitsky, "Comparative Performance in Urban Bus Transit: Assessing Privatization Strategies," *Public Administration Review* **46**:57–66 (1986).
7. Office of Federal Procurement Policy, "Enhancing Governmental Productivity Through Competition: Targeting for Annual Savings of One Billion Dollars by 1988." Washington, D.C.: Office of Management and Budget, March 1984.
8. "ROADS Public Fleet Survey," *Roads* **22**:16–19, No. 12 (December 1984).
9. Patricia S. Florestano, and Stephen B. Gordon, "Public vs. Private: Small Government Contracting with the Private Sector," *Public Administration Review* **40**:29–34 (January/February 1980). "Private Provision of Public Services: Contracting by Large Local Governments," *International Journal of Public Administration* **1**:307–327, No. 3 (1979).

5

Corporations and Stakeholders

The Whistleblower and the Law
Kenneth D. Walters

A perpetual problem for managers is how to deal with an employee who "blows the whistle" on the company's alleged illegal acts, unethical practices, or any conduct that may be publicly embarrassing. The immediate reaction of the manager is likely to be one of frustration—how could an employee be so disloyal as to embarrass his boss and the company in public? What happened to team play? Doesn't the management have any authority to stop this nonsense? After all—who is in charge?

Before the manager leaps to any conclusions or takes strong actions, he or she would be best advised to consult the company's legal counsel. The law may give the whistleblower legal rights to say what has been said. Even if the manager can legally discharge the employee, would it be wise to do so? Or the dilemma should be considered from the standpoint of the employee. The whistleblower sees something in the company that seems to be immoral, illegal, or unethical. What should the employee do? Is it any of the employee's business? Should he or she just keep quiet? Before the employee "goes public," it is wise to analyze the situation very carefully. While one may have some legal rights to blow the whistle, the way in which one proceeds could be critical to remedying the wrong and also to protecting future job prospects.

This article shows that the legal status of the whistleblowing employee remains somewhat precarious. And even if the whistleblower eventually wins a legal case, the victory may be more moral than financial. Advancement in the business world can be difficult when a disloyal or litigious label is attached to an employee.

In 1975, I wrote in the *Harvard Business Review* that whistleblowers were likely to gain new legal rights and to assert those rights vigorously in the years ahead.[1] Little did I anticipate the avalanche of lawsuits that would bury us. A new breed of employees, nurtured on Vietnam War protests, Ralph Nader's muck-raking, and Watergate, were taught that most institutions do not deserve the loyalty that their parents invested in them. The whistleblower phenomenon of the past fifteen years thus reflects the growing willingness of today's employees to "bite the hand that feeds them." Whistleblowing is done under the guise of serving the public interest ahead of private interest, but while this lofty motive is clearly present in some cases, in other cases the whistleblower is a publicity-seeking egomaniac who masquerades as one possessing superior moral instincts.

To document the tremendous growth and interest in whistleblowing, several books have emphasized the prevalence of whistleblowing and the developments affecting the whistleblower's legal status. David Ewing's excellent book, *Freedom Inside the Organization*,[2] is a general call for more corporate tolerance and legal protection for whistleblowers. Ewing describes many cases of employers who got rid of troublemakers—only to discover that the companies would have benefitted by paying attention to the prophetic messages of the whistleblowers.

Alan F. Westin's book, *Whistleblowing*,[3] also views the corporate policies that stifle the whistleblower as being misdirected and unwise, purely from the standpoint of the corporation's own best interests. The Ford Motor Company engineers who raised questions about the design of the Pinto should have been listened to from the beginning. Westin encourages companies to develop more tolerant policies toward whistleblowers, but he also advocates tougher laws to allow investigations of an employee's allegations against an employer.

Leslie Chapman's book, aptly titled *Your Disobedient Servant*,[4] tells how civil servants in Great Britain have had such difficulty revealing featherbedding and waste in government and in state-owned companies. His book is a long litany of mostly discouraging reports on the vast waste of resources in government bureaucracies and the formidable task a whistleblower has in getting the message out that the waste is greater than anyone had suspected. On the positive side, he shows how one conscientious and persistent person can make a difference in controlling costs, yet the personal price that must be paid in order to get results in a bureaucracy can be quite staggering and even debilitating to the whistleblower.

The most dramatic development in whistleblowing since the mid-1970s has not been the new books written about whistleblowers, but the new legal rights that whistleblowers have acquired. Little-known clauses in numerous pieces of federal legislation can be used to give some legal protection to whistleblowers, among them clauses in the Safe Drinking Water Act, the Toxic Substances Control Act, the Occupational Safety and Health Act, and the Clean Air Act amendments. The employee can file under these statutes whether he or she works for a private or a public organization, as long as the organization's activities are affected by one of these laws. But the federal laws are of limited help to the whistleblower. The most significant change has come in the creation of new exceptions to the time-honored employment at will rule.

The Employment at Will Rule

Until recent years it has been firmly established that when a private-sector employer hires an employee to work for an indefinite period of time (employment at will) and there is no formal employment contract limiting the circumstances justifying dicharge, either the employer or the employee may terminate the relationship at any time, and for any reason or for no reason. A legal encyclopedia states the rule clearly:

> Few legal principles would seem to be better settled than the broad generality that an employment for an indefinite term is regarded as an employment at will which may be terminated at any time by either party for any reason or for no reason at all.[5]

Occasionally, discharged employees could persuade a court to make an exception to the rule. For example, they might argue that their employment contracts contained express or implied provisions that they would be employed as long as they performed satisfactorily. Some employees have contended that their employers promised that they could only be discharged for "just cause." Finally, other terminated workers have successfully alleged that their employment contracts stipulated certain procedures for discharge that were not followed. But these limitations on the rule have been few and far between. The number of exceptions to the traditional employment at will rule gave cold comfort to most employees who informally agreed to work for a specified wage, without any negotiations or agreements on job security.

In recent years some courts have created new exceptions to the rule, holding that discharging an employee with a motive based on bad faith, malice, or retaliation may constitute legal grounds for a wrongful discharge claim by the employee. Another theory being adopted by the courts is that employers may not be permitted to discharge employees for reasons that violate public policy.

Public Policy

The rationale increasingly cited by the courts in their trend to modify the employment at will rule is that employers may not discharge employees for reasons that are against public policy. "As a general exception to the rule . . . an employee may claim damages for wrongful discharge when the motivation for the firing contravenes public policy."[6] But what actions by employers are against public policy? An examination of the specific cases shows how difficult this question is to answer.

In *Petermann v. International Brotherhood of Teamsters*[7] an employee was fired for testifying against his employer (a labor union) at a legislative hearing. The firing was held to be unlawful since it was against public policy to commit perjury. The court held that it would violate public policy to permit an employer to discharge a worker for refusing to commit perjury.

In *Frampton* v. *Central Indiana Gas Co.*,[8] the Supreme Court of Indiana ruled that a discharged employee who contended that she was fired after she filed a workmen's compensation claim could sue for retaliation. The court stated:

> If employers are permitted to penalize employees for filing workmen's compensation claims, a most important public policy will be undermined. The fear of being discharged would have a deleterious effect on the exercise of a statutory right. Employees will not file claims for justly deserved compensation—opting, instead, to continue their employment without incident. The end result, of course, is that the employer is effectively relieved of his obligation.[9]

The courts also have been willing to find civil remedies for wrongful discharges where state legislatures have not clearly authorized them. In addition, they have even approved wrongful discharge claims where state statutes give an administrative agency exclusive jurisdiction over such unlawful employment practices. In *Raden* v. *City of Azusa*,[10] even though the California legislature had restricted the damages available to employees discharged for filing workmen's compensation claims to 50 percent of the benefit amount, the court held that the worker discharged could bring a wrongful discharge suit for compensatory and punitive damages in excess of the statutory limitation.

In summary, the public policy exception to the general employment at will rule has grown up around certain categories of cases, especially workmen's compensation claims. Other categories include firings for union activity or jury duty. The courts have found that employer policies that abrogate these "compelling public rights and interests" may create private rights to sue for unlawful discharge.

But what are the limits to the public policy exception? There is nothing to prohibit terminated workers from using their imaginations to raise any number of public policies that would be undermined by their discharges. In the Petermann case just discussed, the California court defined public policy as "the principles under which freedom of contract or private dealing is restricted by law for the good of the community. . . . Whatever contravenes good morals or any established interests of society is against public policy."[11] This definition appears to invite almost any claim of conscience or preference being raised against an employer in a dispute over the employee's discharge. Can an employee safely criticize the employer's product if he or she believes superior products are available? Must Chevrolet dealers keep employees who say that Hondas are better, since there are public policies in favor of consumer protection and free speech? These are questions that have not yet been fully explored by the courts, but they could seriously affect a whistleblower's case.

Bad Faith or Malice

In 1974, the New Hampshire Supreme Court in *Monge* v. *Beebe Rubber Co.*,[12] ruled that a married employee with three children could recover damages when she claimed that she was fired because she refused to go on a date with her foreman. The court declared:

> We hold that a termination by the employer of a contract of employment at will which is motivated by bad faith or malice or based on retaliation is not in the best interest of the economic system or the public good and constitutes a breach of the employment contract.[13]

The decision in the *Monge* case does not seem revolutionary given the facts involved, but the basic rationale of the decision meant that courts would increasingly examine the circumstances surrounding discharges of employees—an inquiry that the courts previously avoided. Thus, the *Monge* case opened up the whole question of which firings were motivated by bad faith or malice. Bad faith and malice are open-ended concepts, and discharged employees have a strong incentive to try to show that the employer was unreasonable or unfair in personnel decisions.

One way of showing bad faith or malice is to argue that an employee was fired because he or she was trying to promote the public interest over the employer's selfish interests (blowing the whistle). This allows an employee to claim the high moral ground and, by comparison, call into question the motives of the employer.

Employers should bear in mind that whether a particular firing was for bad faith or malice will be decided by juries, who are more likely to sympathize with a wounded and idealistic employee rather than a hard-nosed boss who is trying to protect the company. Recent cases have held that discharged employees may recover punitive damages and compensatory damages, including damages for mental anguish, and pain and suffering. When the employer is perceived to have been unreasonable or unfair, the cost can be high.

Rights of Whistleblowers

How have the public policy and bad faith and malice exceptions affected whistleblowers? A number of cases have specifically considered the rights of whistleblowers. For example, in *Tameny* v. *Atlantic Richfield Co.*,[14] the Supreme Court of California ruled that a plantiff could sue for wrongful discharge when he was fired after fifteen years of satisfactory performance on the job because he refused to take part in an alleged price-fixing violation. The court recognized that a growing number of cases were recognizing wrongful discharges of employees where "the termination contravenes public policy."[15]

In a similar case, *McNulty* v. *Borden, Inc.*,[16] a former employee charged that his district manager gave special pricing concessions to some customers but not to others, which constituted unlawful price discrimination under the Clayton Act. When the employee refused to participate in the special pricing scheme, he was discharged. The court ruled that if his discharge was in furtherance of a price-fixing scheme that violated the Clayton Act, public policy would be defeated if the discharge remained unredressed.

Whistleblowers have not restricted their voices to protesting antitrust law violations. In *Harless* v. *First National Bank in Fairmont*,[17] a manager of a bank credit department charged that his employer had intentionally overcharged customers on the prepayment of their installment loans and did not make proper rebates to customers. The bank manager contended that he complained about these unlawful practices to bank vice-presidents, and was subsequently discharged when he disclosed incriminating files to auditors. The court said: "Where the employer's motivation for the discharge contravenes some substantial public-policy principle, then the employer may be liable to the employee for damages occasioned by the discharge."[18]

In *O'Sullivan* v. *Mallon*,[19] an x-ray technician was fired after refusing to perform catheterizations, her objection being that state law only permitted licensed nurses and physicians to perform this task. The court ruled that her dismissal was improper because employers should not be able to fire a worker for refusing to perform an illegal act.

In these cases just discussed, the whistleblowers won. They are considered to be somewhat controversial cases, however, for a number of reasons. First, did the legislatures that enacted antitrust laws, consumer protection laws, and laws regulating the medical and nursing professions, ever intend to give employees a specific right to sue for wrongful discharge? If the answer to this question is "no," what are the limits to the public-policy exception? A second concern of employers is the well-recognized legal rule that employees have a duty of loyalty to their employers. Third, are there clear limits to the concepts of bad faith and malice? When is a discharge for a compelling economic reason likely to be called into question merely because an employee was fired for what some might see as an unfair reason? These are some of the concerns that have led many courts to reject or severely limit the exceptions to the employment at will rule, a subject to which we now turn.

When Whistleblowers Lose

The cases cited show that the courts have expanded the rights of employees by finding new exceptions to the employment at will rule. But it would be a mistake to assume that courts in all states have followed this path. In fact, many courts have unequivocally rejected the public policy and malice and bad faith exceptions— even where essentially the same facts were presented where other state courts found exceptions to the rule.

In *Christy* v. *Petrus*,[20] the Supreme Court of Missouri rejected the employee's claim that he could sue for wrongful discharge since he had been dismissed for seeking workmen's compensation. The court held that the legislature had not provided for a civil remedy for such a discharge.

Bender Ship Repair, Inc. v. *Stevens*[21] involved an employee who alleged that he had been fired for serving on a grand jury against his employer's wishes and was therefore entitled to a wrongful discharge claim. The court ruled that at will employees can be discharged with or without cause, and that the public-policy argument was not opposite.

Many courts have refused to protect whistleblowers who refused to participate in, or who blew the whistle on, their employer's business practices that they felt to be unethical or illegal. In *Hinrichs* v. *Tranquilaire Hospital*,[22] an employee charged that she was discharged because she would not falsify certain medical records as her employer had instructed. The court stated that under the employment at will rule, an employee can be terminated for "a good reason, a wrong reason, or no reason."[23] The public-policy exception, said the court, "would abrogate the inherent right of contract between employer and employee" and is "too vague a concept" to create a new right against unjust dismissal. "Such creations are best left to the legislature," the court concluded.[24]

A similar finding was reached in *Martin* v. *Platt*,[25] where employees revealed that their immediate supervisor was soliciting and receiving kickbacks from suppliers. The company terminated the employees. The court rejected the employees' claim, ruling that it would not create a new right of unjust dismissal where no right was explicitly authorized by the legislature. Other courts have taken the same position.

As well as the public-policy exception, the bad faith and malice exceptions also have been rejected by the courts in a number of states. In *Pirre* v. *Printing Developments, Inc.*,[26] an employee charged that when his company got new management, the new people had very poor ideas about innovations. He spoke out against the innovations, and in fact they subsequently failed. He further charged that the new management began to unfairly criticize his work prior to discharging him. The court rejected his claim that management was held to a standard of behaving in good faith and without malice.

A whistleblower in *Lampe* v. *Presbyterian Medical Center* learned the hard way that her disobedience would be punished, even though it was based on the best of motives.[27] The employee, a head nurse, refused to obey the employer's instructions to reduce the overtime given to nurses. Her reason for disobeying was her conviction that patient care would deteriorate if fewer hours were worked. The court held that general public policies in favor of protecting public health did not give her the right to disobey her employer.

In *Percival* v. *General Motors Corp.*,[28] an employee contended that he was fired for refusing to give the government false information as urged by the company in what he called an "Industrial Watergate." The court found that the employee, who was the head of the mechanical development department, had failed to show the violation of a compelling public policy:

> It should be kept in mind that, as far as an employment relationship is concerned, an employer as well as an employee has rights; a large corporate employer such as General Motors must be accorded wide latitude in determining whom it will employ and retain in employment in high and sensitive managerial positions.[29]

Some cases have ruled that the whistleblower was not the person to raise the objection about the company's policy. In *Geary* v. *United States Steel Corp.*,[30] a salesman of steel tubes complained that the company's tubes had been insufficiently tested and were dangerous. When he was fired he sought damages, arguing that his discharge was in retaliation for his protests and therefore violated a public policy favoring safety. The court ruled that the salesman was responsible only for the sale of the company's products, not the safety of the products. The *Geary* case seems to suggest that employees cannot complain about issues that may be outside of their areas of responsibility, whatever their motivation or intention may be.

A particularly interesting case, *Pierce v. Ortho Pharmaceutical Corp.,*[31] involved an employee who was director of medical research for Ortho, a position responsible for the research of a new medication, Loperamide. The early work on Loperamide showed that it contained forty-four times the amount of saccharin permitted by the Food and Drug Administration (FDA) in a twelve-ounce serving of a diet soft drink. The FDA at that time had not issued standards for acceptable levels of saccharin in drugs.

The Medical Research unit of Ortho had to decide whether the company should seek FDA approval to conduct human testing of Loperamide. Pierce, the employee, recommended that the company not seek FDA permission for further testing since she believed that high levels of saccharin could cause cancer and hence the company should drop further development and testing of Loperamide. When the company decided to go against her recommendation and to seek FDA permission to conduct further testing, she vehemently protested the decision, which ultimately resulted in her discharge.

Pierce claimed that she was discharged in violation of a strong public policy to promote public health and safety. The New Jersey Supreme Court ruled for the employer, stating that the employee's discharge did not violate her code of professional ethics because she was not the one making the final decision as to the propriety of human testing of the drug. Her role was simply to evaluate whether the drug should be subject to FDA review. She was not placed in a situation where she was forced to choose between her job or compliance with her own code of ethics, said the court, but was merely refusing to accept a contrary medical opinion. "An employee at will who refuses to work for an employer in answer to a call of conscience should recognize that other employees and their employer might heed a different call."[32]

If the test suggested in the *Pierce* case is followed by other courts, a whistleblower, in order to be successful in a wrongful discharge suit, must show that he or she was personally charged with stopping the illegal or unethical activity and was fired specifically for an attempt to fulfill this responsibility.

Suggestions for Managers and Employees

The general picture that emerges from the legal developments affecting whistleblowers is not very clear. In some states the whistleblower is more likely to benefit from exceptions to the employment at will rule than in other states that have not created these exceptions. But even if the law is on the whistleblower's side, a legal victory may take many years to achieve. Ernest Fitzgerald, the civil servant who was originally dismissed for revealing Air Force weapons cost over-runs in 1969, eventually was reinstated to his job after thirteen years of lawsuits. Fitzgerald remarked that for most federal employees, reporting abuses is "extremely dangerous to their careers."[33]

Fitzgerald's comment is even more pertinent to the employee who blows the whistle on a private-sector employer. Even when the employee has a good case for unlawful discharge, the machinery available to enforce it is immensely costly and time-consuming. Most people have neither the heart nor the pocketbook to begin a fight that may last for many years.

The fact is that almost all people in organizations want and expect their own subordinates to be loyal. Just as no family with servants would tolerate a housekeeper who spread the word that the homeowners were terribly messy, so no manager is charmed by a subordinate who is vocal with criticisms of the boss's policies. Furthermore, the mentality that attaches to many whistleblowers is that of complete belief in their own righteousness. Whistleblowers can be an intolerant and insufferable lot; they also can be convinced that it is their personal mission to right the many wrongs they see in society. The difficult question becomes what is an employee's business, and what is none of the employee's business?

The whistleblower became a folk hero in the 1960s when it was fashionable to question authority and to promote the public interest over selfish business interests. As a result of widely publicized examples of employees who heroically put their necks and jobs on the line when they blew the whistle, many laws have been enacted to give whistleblowers added legal protection from reprisals. The anomalous result is that these new legal rights have made the whistleblower less heroic. If a whistleblower does not stand to lose his job for his act of courage, then what is heroic about his act?

Thus, I view the new legal path that the courts have embarked on with skepticism and sadness. To protect whistleblowers, a new maze of judicial elaborations will arise to differentiate between legitimate whistleblowing and unprotected whistleblowing. As we have seen, the law on the whistleblower's rights may become so complex, voluminous, and contradictory that few employees can have any realistic idea of what they can be fired for saying and what they can say safely. But one thing is sure: they will vigorously assert their legal right to blow the whistle.

The more we rely on the courts to protect whistleblowers, the more elaborate the legal machinery for enforcing rights must become, and the more resources society will need to pour into the processes of litigation and adjudication. We should not pass laws or make judicial decisions to give whistleblowers new rights without recognizing that this process costs money, and does in fact carry significant costs to employers and to society. The Japanese somehow have managed to settle their employer-employee disputes without the full-blown legal combat that Americans seem so determined to engage in to resolve every disagreement and ethical dilemma.

Notes

1. Kenneth D. Walters, "Your Employees' Right to Blow the Whistle," *Harvard Business Review*, July–August, 1975.

2. David Ewing, *Freedom Inside the Organization*, New York: E.P. Dutton, 1979.

3. Alan F. Westin, *Whistle Blowing*. New York: McGraw-Hill, 1980.

4. Leslie Chapman, *Your Disobedient Servant*. London: Chatto and Windus, 1978.

5. 62 A.L.R. 3d 271 (1975).

6. *Jackson* v. *Minidoka Irrigation District*, 98 Idaho 330, 563 P.2d 54, 57 (1977).

7. 174 Cal. App. 2d 184, 344 P.2d 25 (1959).

8. 260 Ind. 249, 297 N.E.2d 425 (1973).

9. Ibid., p. 427.

10. 97 Cal. App. 3d 336, 158 Cal. Rptr. 689 (1979).

11. 174 Cal. App. 2d 184, 344 P.2d 25, 27 (1959).

12. 316 A.2d 549 (1974).

13. Ibid.

14. 27 Cal. 3d 167, 164 Cal. Rptr. 839, 610 P.2d 1330 (1980).

15. Ibid., p. 1336.

16. 474 F. Supp. 1111 (E.D. Pa. 1979).

17. 246 S.E.2d 270 (W. Va. 1978).

18. Ibid., p. 275.

19. 160 N.J. Super. 416, 390 A.2d 149 (1978).

20. 365 Mo. 1187, 295 S.W.2d 122 (1956).

21. 379 So. 2d 594 (Ala. 1980).

22. 352 So. 2d 1130 (Ala. 1977).

23. Ibid., p. 1131.

24. Ibid., p. 1131.

25. 386 N.E.2d 1026 (Ind. App. 1979).

26. 432 F. Supp. 840 (S.D. N.Y. 1977).

27. 590 P.2d 513 (Colo. App. 1978).

28. 539 F.2d 1126 (8th Cir. 1976), *aff'd* 400 F. Supp. 1322 (E.D. Mo. 1975).

29. Ibid., p. 1130.

30. 456 Pa. 171, 319 A.2d 174 (1974).

31. 166 N.J. Super. 335, 399 A.2d 1023 (1979), *rev'd* 84 N.J. 58, 417 A.2d 505 (1980).

32. Ibid., p. 514.

33. "Light Still Yellow for Whistle Blowers," *U.S. News & World Report*, June 28, 1982, p. 7.

Work-Related Ethical Attitudes: A Key to Profitability?

Thomas W. Dunfee

Two hypothetical firms are identical in every respect (for example, age and condition of capital equipment, cost of money, managerial talent and experience) except that the employees of one firm possess significantly more positive ethical attitudes than their counterparts at the other firm. What impact, if any, would this difference in ethical attitudes have on the two firms? Should one firm be expected to be more profitable than the other? If so, which one, and what is the process by which workforce ethical attitudes affect profitability?

Comparatively little attention has been given to the role of employee effort and attitudes in the profitability equation. The role that employee ethical attitudes might play has been essentially ignored. Yet, it is reasonable to hypothesize that, as the economy becomes more heavily service-oriented and therefore more dominated by job tasks having more discretionary elements, employee effort and commitment become increasingly important factors in the real rate of economic growth. This article will discuss various ways in which the work-related ethical attitudes of a firm's employees may influence that firm's productivity and, as a result, its profitability. After identifying several areas of possible impact, the article will then discuss ways in which managers can influence the quality of work-related ethical attitudes held by the firm's employees.

Work-Related Ethical Attitudes Defined

As a starting point, it is necessary to define the somewhat illusive concepts of values and attitudes. A value may be thought of as a person's general orientation toward a mode of conduct. It constitutes a mental weighing system, based on general principles, pertaining to the desirability of a particular class action, for example, truthtelling or the use of violence. Values translate into action through the development of attitudes. Thus, an attitude may be defined as a persistent disposition to act in a certain way in a given situation or environment. The formation of particular attitudes arises from the intersection of individual values and environmental factors. Attitudes form over time as decisions are made and repeated. They become hardened through a process of personal precedent analogous to that followed by common-law court systems.

For example, an individual beginning a new job may suddenly confront previously unexperienced situations, such as pressure to accept gifts associated with potential purchases in contravention of company rules. Required to make a decision, the individual makes a conscious choice influenced by personal values. The outcome is then evaluated. A short time later the individual again confronts the decision of whether to accept a gift. Again a conscious decision will be made, this time influenced by the evaluation made as to whether or not the first outcome was efficient. As the individual continues to confront similar decisions over time, a pattern of behavior evolves that does not require critical thinking to determine how to act. This reflexive pattern of learned behavior relates to specific situations and is accompanied by a concomitant attitude toward that type of situation. The process of attitude formation is represented in table 1.

The composite of the values that an individual holds constitutes a private utility function that incorporates all personal preferences and desires. The subgroup of

Table 1
Attitude Formation

How Decision Is Made	Decision	Outcome
Conscious analysis Use of values	Situation A Decision X	Positive
Conscious analysis Use of values	Situation A Decision Y	Negative
Conscious analysis Use of values and past experience	Situation A Decision X	Positive
Unconscious reaction	Situation A Decision X	Crystallization of attitude toward Situation A

values pertaining to actions that have an impact on others constitutes one's personal moral code. Religious beliefs and training, educational background, political and economic philosophy, socialization through family and peer-group influences, and work experience all come together to produce a personal moral code of ethical values with associated attitudes.

Because attitudes are context-specific, the same individual may develop somewhat inconsistent attitudes for different situations. For example, an individual may hold values giving great weight to honesty as a goal of proper behavior. That person would never cheat at cards or dissemble with spouse or children. The high value given to honesty also could be reflected in the workplace, where the individual would be scrupulously honest in dealings with his employer. Yet the same person might regularly cheat on income tax returns, because other countervailing values (for example, strong views concerning the proper role of government, objections as to how tax revenues are spent) might influence the development of an attitude toward tax compliance.

Presumably, most adults have reasonably well-formed sets of values. A major, sudden change in a mature individual's basic values is unlikely except under extraordinary circumstances. However, most ethical attitudes are presumed to be comparatively malleable, and thus likely to be influenced by the environment in which decisions will be made. This is particularly the case when an individual confronts an unfamiliar environment, such as a new job. The different environment may result in the individual developing a number of new attitudes in a short period of time. Because the environment is different, the existing attitudes that the individual has may be seen as inappropriate and, as a consequence, new ones may develop. It is particularly during this time that an individual employee's attitude may be influenced by factors within the control of the firm.

Individuals beginning a new job may suddenly confront previously unexperienced ethical questions, such as whether to give or accept gifts associated with potential purchases or sales, or whether to follow a superior's instructions to ignore formal company rules. In forming attitudes toward these questions, the individual may emphasize values relating to conformity and efficiency and decide that, although those kinds of actions are not proper in one's personal life, they can be rationalized as appropriate in the commercial world. The development of special ethical attitudes for business decisions would find support in the views of Albert Carr (1968), Milton Friedman (1962), and Theodore Levitt (1958), among others, who argue that social considerations are antithetical to the proper role of business.

This tendency to think of ethical attitudes and commercial activity as existing on different planes of life is both common and unfortunate. In this view, ethics and business appear as two distinctly separate, unrelated factors that should be kept apart—in the same manner as religious belief and theoretical mathematics. There is concern that careless mixture of the two dissimilar substances may produce a volatile compound of conflict and stress that will result in many unintended inefficiencies. This view underlies the rash of current jokes to the effect that *business ethics* is an oxymoron. The view that ethical attitudes are unimportant, or even worse, inappropriate, ignores the real costs that negative attitudes can impose on all types of business activities. In fact, the presence of positive ethical attitudes is central to the efficient operation of a business.

Examples of Work-Related Ethical Attitudes

Are there, then, certain types of ethical attitudes that may, in and of themselves, influence the productivity of employees? As a starting point, it seems clear that only certain kinds of ethical attitudes would be likely to influence an employee's productivity. (The word *employee* is used to designate all types of corporate employees including senior and middle managers, blue-collar employees, and clerical, technical, and professional staff.) Whether an employee tithes in charitable or religious donations, or believes that it is immoral to eat red meat, is not likely to affect productivity in most circumstances. This section focuses on three ethical attitudes illustrative of those that are likely to make a difference in the workplace.

Honesty. An employee's attitude toward honesty will determine whether, among other things, he or she will behave with integrity in regard to truth-telling, respecting property rights, and disclosing pertinent information within the context of the job. The worker with a predisposition toward honest behavior will not act in an opportunistic manner (opportunism, as used in this article, assumes guile and deceit) toward the employing firm or toward business colleagues.

Loyalty. Attitudes toward loyalty will determine whether an employee has a predisposition to form commitments to an entity, either the firm or specific individuals within it. An individual predisposed toward loyalty will consider the interests of the object of the loyalty in making personal decisions. For example, when faced with an opportunity to take another job, a loyal employee will consider the consequences of the decision on his/her employer in deciding whether to make the change. The degree of loyalty an employee feels will determine the weight given to the present employer's interests in his or her personal utility function.

Responsibility. An ethical attitude toward responsibility will determine whether employees put themselves on the line concerning assigned tasks, attempt to shift blame when things go wrong, accept undeserved accolades, or seek to avoid obligations wherever possible. Citizenship (in the sense of undertaking the full scope of related functions) is often a component of responsibility. A worker with a predisposition toward accepting responsibility also will be likely to participate as a good citizen in activities that contribute to the betterment of the job and workplace, but do not fall precisely within the basic job description. For example, a manager might spend time after hours helping staff with personal problems or a favored extramural project.

Characteristics of Work-Related Ethical Attitudes

The three work-related ethical attitudes (WREAs) identified in the previous section overlap with the popular concept of the work ethic. Basically, the work ethic denotes the fundamental values that workers associate with the role of work in their lives. A common question asked in surveys concerned with trends in the work ethic is whether or not the interviewee would continue to work if such an effort was not financially required. Presumably those answering positively see work as having an intrinsic value providing its own noneconomic satisfactions.

It is commonly asserted that the work ethic has been declining in the United States and that the decline has contributed significantly to lackluster economic performance in the face of intense foreign competition. Such a charge is easily asserted but difficult to prove. Anecdotal evidence goes in both directions: some managers decry lack of commitment and concern on the part of their employees, while others cite instances of improved quality control, and so on. The survey data that exist (Yankelovich and Immerwahr 1983) indicate that a majority of Americans still see work as having significant intrinsic worth.

However, the work ethic, as commonly defined, is not perfectly synonymous with the examples of WREAs discussed in this article. A general orientation toward the role of work in one's life does not necessarily correlate closely with attitudes concerning honesty, loyalty, and responsibility. Interestingly, Yankelovich and Immerwahr recently found that a general acceptance of the work ethic by a majority of U.S. workers did not necessarily translate into productive behavior. The workers they surveyed simultaneously rated the value of work high, yet indicated that they did not currently work nearly as hard as they were capable of doing.

Not much is known about the present level of WREAs or how they have changed over time. The many recent assertions of increased tax cheating (a phenomenon obviously hard to measure) carry the inference that honesty in that context is declining. The estimates made of losses that firms incur through employee theft indicate that negative attitudes about honesty and loyalty are not restricted to dealings with the public sector. Similarly, the finding that significant numbers of workers are holding back in their efforts infers relatively negative attitudes toward loyalty and responsibility. Definitive analysis will have to await the compilation and evaluation of time series surveys of WREAs. In the absence of hard data, the following hypotheses are offered as reasonable.

1. WREAs vary widely across the population. This should be expected in a society as heterogeneous as that of the United States. A study conducted by George England (1974) and others at the Industrial Relations Center of the University of Minnesota of values held by managers from five nations found that there were "large individual differences in personal values within every group . . . studied." The same is presumably true for each of the WREAs. For example, some individuals will tend to be scrupulously honest under all circumstances. At the opposite extreme, others will be totally opportunistic. Across the U.S. work force as a whole, most individuals are probably between the two extremes regarding their propensity to hold positive WREAs. For each separate attitude, the curve would presumably be slightly different, that is, there may be a tendency for the national work force to have, in the aggregate, a more positive orientation toward one WREA than another.

2. Individual WREAs do not correlate perfectly. An individual having a very positive attitude toward honesty will not necessarily have a positive attitude toward loyalty or responsibility. An extremely independent individual may be very honest and yet not develop strong commitments to others. A responsible person may be very conscientious about his or her specific job function and yet fail to translate that into loyalty to the business firm as an entity. Thus, some individuals will have positive attitudes toward only one or two of the important individual WREAs.

3. WREAs can be modified. It was assumed earlier that WREAs will be influenced by their environment, particularly when an individual first encounters the work environment of a firm. By modifying that environment and by giving weight to WREAs in the employment process, management has the capacity to influence the nature of the aggregate WREAs held by the firm's work force. As a corollary, the degree to which WREAs can be modified will vary from individual to individual, and personal values and pre-existing attitudes are important determinants of the extent to which WREAS will change.

WREAs and Business Productivity

Let us now return to the hypothetical that began this article. Assume that there are two car rental firms identical in every relevant economic factor except that the employees of one firm have, on average, a far more positive orientation toward WREAs. Is that difference alone likely to make the more ethical firm more profitable?

As noted earlier, the argument has occasionally been made that positive ethical attitudes are dysfunctional and get in the way of efficient business decisions. In this view, business is seen as a game with its own rules operating outside of the social niceties. The manager-players who do not follow the special rules, perhaps because of ethical considerations, are thought to be at a significant disadvantage. This view, invoking a Gresham's law of business ethics, was advocated nearly twenty years ago by Albert Carr (1968) in his controversial *Harvard Business Review* article entitled "Is Business Bluffing Ethical?" Under the business-as-a-game analysis the firm with the more ethical work force is expected to be less profitable.

The negative view is often supported by anecdotal evidence pertaining to sales lost because of high-minded ethical stands and other similar occurrences. Advocates of the negative view have paid little attention to the effect of negative ethical attitudes on the efficiency of administrative and contracting functions performed by business firms.

Employee Effort

The move toward a service economy, coupled with the increasing complexity of certain business functions, has greatly increased the discretion that many employees may exercise over how a job is performed. As job tasks move away from the standardized and the routine, performance becomes more and more difficult to measure and monitor. A work force that has more positive attitudes toward responsibility and pride will be less likely to take advantage of any inherent limitations in the system of evaluating job performance. A positive orientation to all three of the identified WREAs should result in fewer instances of time theft, where employees take excessive sick leaves, or personal days, or long coffee and lunch breaks. Output quality may often be influenced by employee attitudes toward loyalty and responsibility. For instance, the employees of the auto rental firm in our hypothetical case might often find themselves able to exercise discretion as to how they approach their jobs. WREAs would determine whether a counter clerk makes a special effort to work faster when confronting a line of waiting customers, or whether maintenance personnel preparing vehicles for reuse do those little extras that may be noticeable to the discerning car renter.

Worker Turnover

Many U.S. corporations have experienced a high degree of employee turnover at all levels of operations. In manufacturing, monthly turnover rates in excess of 2 percent of the work force are not uncommon. Although some turnover is both normal and constructive, there are many costs imposed by excessive turnover. Employees who leave often take with them firm-specific skills that can be replaced only by incurring substantial training costs. In addition, there are invariably little efficiencies that come from knowing the particular people and procedures associated with a firm. Although these may be fairly quickly replaced, they may add up to a significant cost when a large number of people leave within a short period of time.

Turnover should be marginally less with a more loyal work force. Loyal workers would consider their relationship with the firm as a positive attribute of their present jobs. They would also be more likely to incorporate the needs of the firm into their own personal calculations when considering a competing job offer. As a consequence, they would, on average, require a higher price before they would be willing to switch to a job with another firm.

Opportunism

Employees with negative WREAs pertaining to honesty and loyalty would be more likely to engage in opportunistic behavior against their own firms. Examples of opportunistic behavior include embezzlement of funds, pilferage of office supplies, billing personal phone calls to the firm, and so on. A National Institute of Justice study (Clark and Hollinger 1983) identified the massive scope of this problem. The study's authors estimated annual losses to employee theft in the range of $5 billion to $10 billion. Of even greater significance is the fact that one-third of the workers surveyed admitted that they had stolen property from their firms during the prior year. That much of this loss is due to an attitudinal problem is suggested by research indicating that many of the workers taking property do not see it as theft but instead as extra compensation to which they consider themselves entitled. Further support for the conclusion that employee theft is an attitudinal problem is the fact that in the NIJ study there was no identifiable correlation between economic and local conditions and employee theft (Clark and Hollinger 1983, pp. 32–33). Thus, internal and personal factors appear to be more significant determinants of employee theft than external factors. And, there are many other ways in which employees may directly harm their own firms. For example, some employees surreptitiously compete with their own employers: they take trade secrets and use them, or they overtly moonlight, skimming some accounts away from their employers. Or, when leaving, they take critical proprietary information with them to enhance their personal value in their new jobs.

Presumably, the more positive the WREAs that a firm's work force holds toward honesty and loyalty, the lower the likely losses to opportunistic acts. Opportunistic acts may occur across the full spectrum of the work force. Production-line employees may have access to parts and tools. Sales employees may misdocument transactions or engage in various scams against their employers. Middle- and upper-level managers generally have access to valuable firm information that can be used to the substantial detriment of the firm. Attitudes toward honesty and loyalty thus influence the likelihood of opportunism in regard to the full range of business firm activities.

Our hypothetical auto rental firms could be victimized by a wide range of opportunistic actions. Give-away merchandise, gasoline, replacement parts, tires, and similar items could be pilfered. Purchasing agents could accept gratuities in return for making less efficient purchases on behalf of their firms. Prospective clients could be referred to competition with a kickback for the disloyal employee. It does not require a vivid imagination to realize that employee WREAs could make a difference in the cost of opportunism incurred by the two firms.

The firm with the work force possessing negative WREAs should be less profitable because of losses directly incurred by and costs of monitoring against opportunistic behavior. Many firms today are giving greater attention to controlling losses to employees. They have installed surveillance systems and have set up elaborate procedures to deal with miscreants. These actions clearly document the significant costs that may be associated with negative WREAs. Although policing systems are typically cost-justified, they may be faulted for dealing more with the symptoms than with underlying disease. A better long-run solution is to find a way to deal with the propensity of employees who commit such acts—a propensity determined in part by the aggregate WREAs held by the firm's work force.

Good Will

The reputation of a firm will develop over time through the evolution of outsiders' perceptions. Dishonest or uncaring employees can engender a significant amount of negative perception. In an important sense, employees are their firm when they interact with outsiders. If these employees consistently reflect negative WREAs, the general reputation of the firm will ultimately be affected.

This factor would be of particular importance to the car rental firm. The speed, accuracy, and cordiality with which employees provide service is critically important in a competitive environment. The importance of employee attitudes is reflected in the advertisements used by car rental firms, which often stress the friendliness and pride of their employees. Yet, cordiality is clearly discretionary with employees. Thus, over time, intangible factors within employee control may have a significant impact on the competitive status of a firm.

Causes of Negative WREAs

The level of WREAs is likely to vary from firm to firm, with the employees of some firms having on average more positive WREAs than those of other firms. There are several possible causes of negative WREAs. For example, a firm may be totally indifferent to WREAs in the hiring process. A firm that chooses employees solely on the basis of grade point averages or schools attended would, at best, produce a work force exhibiting an average cross section of preexisting WREAs. Failure to signal in the interviewing process that the firm considers WREAs to be important may cause prospective employees who are concerned about the ethical environment of a prospective employer to accept employment elsewhere.

The corporate culture or environment may also have a negative effect on employee WREAs. The corporate culture is comprised of the shared values of the members of the organization. These values often appear to new employees to be firmly set and may greatly affect the development of firm-specific WREAs on the part of new employees. Employees who encounter superiors who are dishonest or who have minimal loyalty to the firm may ultimately begin to modify their own WREAs. Managers of Japanese firms that have operated U.S. subsidiaries have expressed surprise and concern regarding the low level of loyalty evidenced by American middle managers, who would often quickly move on to another job. The Japanese senior executives were particularly perturbed by the fact that such action was likely to affect the attitudes of the employees who had been supervised by the departed managers.

Employees of firms that have encountered widely publicized ethical problems (for instance, Lockheed, E.F. Hutton, General Dynamics) may be affected in several ways. They may find it difficult to take pride in their association with such a firm and to develop a true sense of loyalty. Or, they may consider such incidents as representative of their company's employees and may, as a consequence, make some changes in their personal WREAs. Such snowballing effects can ultimately have the effect of significantly lowering the aggregate level of WREAs held by the firm's work force.

Conflicts between individual WREAs and the corporate culture may produce considerable dissonance, which hampers employee efficiency. Individual employees who attach great significance to their WREAs may feel substantially compromised when the corporate climate requires involvement with actions the individual considers unethical. The stress will be even greater if an employee finds it necessary to perform directly what he or she considers an unethical act. The reality of such conflicts is emphasized by a *Wall Street Journal*-Gallup survey of middle managers, stating that 10 percent had been pressured by their superiors to commit an illegal act and 40 percent had been asked to do something they considered unethical (Ricklefs 1983). An employee required to break a government procedure (for instance, violate designated payment rates to consultants, or ignore restrictions on hiring a certain category of prospective employees) either may develop negative attitudes toward the firm or may shift his or her own standards, thus contributing to a general decline of WREAs at the firm.

Management Strategies Influencing WREAs

The argument has developed that WREAs may be an important component of overall firm productivity. In order to maximize return a firm must encourage the development of positive WREAs on the part of all employees. Providing a well-organized and equipped workplace is not enough; neither is providing a pleasant work environment. One thing that can make a difference is the level of WREAs in the work force: employees with positive WREAs will be more likely to respond to the challenges of the workplace. Although this factor may be critically important, it has been neglected by many business firms. A New York Stock Exchange study (1982) entitled *People and Productivity: A Challenge to Corporate America* indicated that only a distinct minority of corporations have human resource programs designed to stimulate productivity. Most existing programs are of recent vintage, and they are much more common among the largest corporations. Human resource programs have consistently received high marks from the firms employing them, and many of the programs have components that may influence WREAs. In fact, the most common improvements reported from the use of such programs is enhanced employee attitudes and morale. (Sixty-seven percent of corporations implementing human resource programs report such improvements.) Yet, human resource programs only partially solve the problem of raising employee WREAs.

How, then, can management influence the level of employee WREAs? As a starting point, a firm must identify the ethical attitudes that are critically important to its operation. A high technology firm may value loyalty in order to maintain the security of its scientific know-how; a securities firm may stress honesty; and a drug manufacturer may conclude that responsibility is critical to ensure a high degree of product quality. After making such a determination, a company can stimulate the development of positive WREAs in many ways.

Hiring Criteria

The existing WREAs that individuals possess will often give clues to the types of job attitudes they will develop. Thus, once the important WREAs for the organization have been identified, they should be incorporated directly into the firm's hiring procedures. For example, a series of standardized interviewing questions can be developed that will allow the interviewer to draw a sense of the job candidates' WREAs. Questions pertaining to attitudes about tax compliance could be asked to ascertain ethical attitudes toward honesty. Similarly, questions relating to affiliations with other organizations could produce information about attitudes regarding loyalty. Dunfee and Robertson (1984) have proposed prototype questions that could be used to identify WREAs.

A very effective device would be to cross-check information provided on job applications and resumes. Dishonest responses reveal attitudes that may well carry over into other aspects of a person's job performance. David Begelman, who set up fraudulent schemes at Columbia Pictures, and Janet Cooke, who made up sources for a *Washington Post* story, were both found to have used false resumes.

Many firms already use objective tests designed to produce psychological profiles of prospective employees. These tests may assess the honesty of individuals who will personally handle large sums of money or valuable commodities. Test scores regarding general attitudes may allow for a relative comparison of people applying for the same position. However, such tests do not allow for in-depth probing regarding critical WREAs. A combination of interviews and objective tests, although more costly, may work best to isolate critical WREAs.

Realistic job previews coupled with a serious probationary period may also help to identify desired WREAs. By fully describing the position, the interviewer can obtain the candidate's reactions to various aspects of the job. Then the candidate could actually be put into the work environment for a probationary period before a final decision is made to offer a permanent position. The candidate can thus make an accurate assessment concerning the requirements of the job, and can also develop a rough impression as to whether his or her personal values are compatible with the employer's corporate culture. Concurrently, the supervisor can judge the candidate.

Several firms have reported improved employee productivity after they changed their hiring procedures and gave some attention to positive WREAs in their selection process. North American Tool & Die was reported to have cut down greatly on its percentage of rejected products by emphasizing hiring "good human beings." Because it is a small company, the president, Tom Melohn, was able to conduct personal interviews with each prospective employee and look for "caring personalities." Such personal attributes were given greater weight in the hiring procedure than technical background and experience. Once emphasis was placed on desired WREAs, the company became more profitable and quality control problems significantly decreased. Similarly, Morgan Stanley reported good results from changing the credentials it required of individuals hired to handle back office work. The firm found that the very technically oriented people it had hired in the past related poorly with the other employees of the firm because they did not share basic attitudes. In response, Morgan Stanley sought to hire general liberal arts graduates who would be more likely to fulfill the citizenship dimensions of their jobs. The new approach was considered to be a success.

The use of interviews, tests, and probationary periods to evaluate WREAs of prospective employees will unavoidably raise questions of invasion of privacy and of possible illegal discrimination. Privacy is justly treasured by U.S. workers. Some prospective employees may object on the basis of principle to a more personalized selection process and may refuse to answer questions pertaining to WREAs. If a large number of people object on such grounds, the universe of prospective employees available to a firm evaluating WREAs may be greatly circumscribed. However, because WREAs are so obviously related to job performance, it would be surprising if very many people did object. Evaluating WREAs differs from considering truly personal factors such as sexual preferences or political and religious beliefs.

A current controversy surrounds mandating drug testing of employees. Some employees welcome it; others object very strongly. Taking drugs can have an extremely detrimental effect on job performance, yet many employees resent the idea of testing on principle. Although the publicity given to drug testing might make employees resistant to responding to questions designed to probe WREAs, there are several important differences between drug testing and WREA questioning. The testing for drugs requires some form of physical invasion; testing for WREAs does not. Drugs may be used in private so that they do not have an impact on work. WREAs by definition affect work. The type of WREAs discussed in this article go to the heart of job performance. Properly used, a selection process based on WREAs should not breach any legal rights of privacy.

The question of discrimination raises thornier problems. Employers may not discriminate on the basis of race, religion, or sex in hiring and in other important conditions of employment. A focus on WREAs will necessarily require that subjective judgments be made. Further, it may well be the case that certain WREAs may vary among the population in relation to one or more of the prohibited discriminatory factors. A hiring system that relied on a prohibited factor as a proxy for desired WREAs (for instance, whether the candidate was a Mormon) would clearly violate various state and local laws pertaining to discrimination. Hiring by giving weight to WREAs in a manner entirely independent of the prohibited discriminatory factors would not.

In his discussion of the special game-based rules of the marketplace. Carr (1968) suggested that the good business game player should lie on a psychological profile test in order to provide the answer that the employer was looking for. That would presumably increase the chance of getting a good job. Such an action would in and of itself represent negative attitudes toward honesty and loyalty. If attitudes of this sort should become endemic to the U.S. work force, they would have the effect of greatly reducing business efficiency. Sophisticated interviewing and testing techniques should be able to identify blatantly dishonest answers. A game player following Carr's suggestions would clearly reveal negative WREAs toward honesty and might, ironically, be turned down for a job with a company placing significant weight on that criterion.

Job Evaluation Criteria

Employee WREAs may be influenced by the criteria a firm uses to evaluate job performance. If basic ethical values are reflected unequivocally in work evaluation, that may influence the development of preferred WREAs. For example, many corporations have adopted codes of ethics that contain provisions detailing parameters of expected ethical behavior. Rules and standards are set for accepting or giving gifts, competing with the corporation, complying with the antitrust laws, and so on. Incorporating compliance with ethically based code provisions into the standard job evaluation framework may improve the WREAs of the firm's overall work force. Breaches of such provisions should not be treated as exogenous to the basic job expectations—as something to be dealt with through specialized enforcement mechanisms set up under the code. Instead, opportunistic behavior should be subject to sanction through the usual job evaluation processes in order to reinforce preferred WREAs.

Establish Reinforcing Corporate Culture

Corporate culture is the integrated pattern of human behavior that is transmitted to each generation of employees. The corporate culture at any given time consists of the shared values of the members of the corporate organization. It both shapes and is shaped by the WREAs held by individual employees. Managers can take steps to mold a corporate culture in a particular direction. Corporate culture is not limited to spontaneous evolution but, instead, may be significantly influenced by discretionary managerial decisions. The nature of the corporate culture is a critical element of the socialization process that will influence the development of WREAs on the part of new employees. Introductory training and educational programs provide a good point at which to identify values and attitudes that the corporation considers important. Explicit discussions of important WREAs may have a major influence on employees at this point, when they are just starting to form a group of attitudes toward the firm.

On a long-term basis, the characteristics of the company's corporate culture will have a deeper, more lasting effect on employee WREAs. For example, assume that a company strongly prefers that its work force develop WREAs concerning loyalty to the firm. How might a firm modify its corporate culture to encourage loyalty? A basic starting point would be recognition that reciprocity is a critical dimension of loyalty in most circumstances. An employee should not be expected to develop strong feelings of loyalty in response to an organizational climate that fails to evidence any reciprocal commitment. Concerns about employee heaith, job safety, or social life represent reciprocal commitments likely to reinforce WREAs pertaining to loyalty.

The New York Stock Exchange report on *People and Productivity* summarized the various studies comparing Japanese-managed U.S. subsidiaries with similar U.S. companies. The Japanese-U.S. subsidiaries were found to differ primarily by their adoption of practices likely to influence the development of loyalty-related WREAs. For example, the Japanese-U.S. subsidiaries took every step possible to avoid laying off workers. They would employ a mix of strategies, such as using temporaries (who could be let go), implementing across-the-board wage reductions, and giving preference to existing company employees in filling jobs in growing parts of the company. As a consequence, the Japanese-U.S. subsidiaries were far less likely to lay off workers during economic downturns than were their U.S. competition.

Similarly, the Japanese-U.S. subsidiaries were more likely to provide company-sponsored recreation, which showed a concern for the whole employee. Such programs would likely reinforce loyalty-related WREAs of employees. The company would be seen as more central to the employee's life and therefore as fitting within the context in which the employee applies personal values without modification. Delta Airlines, consistently one of the most profitable members of the airline industry, follows similar practices. Delta officials speak of a sense of family at the firm, which helps to build attitudes toward responsibility and loyalty.

A company that fails to take steps to produce a climate conducive to positive WREAs may create a vacuum in which employees so predisposed may foster a frontier-style, everyone-for-themselves mentality. Thus, a district manager may give an incompetent underling a very positive recommendation in order to foist the unproductive worker off on another unit of the company. Or, perhaps worse, G. Gordon Liddy-type individuals may read between the lines for directions to take illegal or unethical actions because they assume that the company implicitly values unethical behavior.

Employee Ownership

There have been a number of reported instances in which employees have taken over an unprofitable firm or plant and almost immediately made it more productive. Apparently the change of environment—giving employees a piece of the action—has resulted in rapid and significant changes in employee WREAs. That WREAs would shift in such a circumstance seems highly plausible. The focus of work attitudes has changed dramatically: it is now a question of being loyal to or honest with oneself rather than a remote, distinctly separate entity. Also, such a change in relationship means that the employee will directly bear the consequences of the company's failure. The risk-sharing involved with total employee ownership is likely to be a very strong motivator.

The instances of total ownership by employees are rare. As far as the former management is concerned, a sale of the business to employees is, of course, only a defeatist action of last resort. But there are many forms of partial employee ownership. Thousands of companies have employee stock ownership plans (ESOPs) that provide for some form of employee ownership. Plans vary as to the numbers of employees covered, payment of dividends, voting rights, and required participant investment. ESOPs usually work like retirement plans, with trustees holding the stock and maintaining an account for each employee, which constitutes deferred compensation. ESOP plans typically apportion stock among covered employees on the basis of salary levels. The standard stock option plans, however, require investment by the employee and can be targeted to an individual's own job performance. Stock option plans have long been used to provide incentive compensation for senior executives and, at the same time, to strengthen the executive's commitment to the firm. An ESOP can spread these same benefits to all the employees of a firm.

The effect of an ESOP on participating employee WREAs is likely to depend on the extent of employee ownership (very low levels of participation are not likely to have much impact), and whether employees are treated as full stockholders with rights to vote, receive dividends, and even sell the stock. A real financial asset is more interesting than an annual report from a retirement plan. Ultimately, the effect on WREAs will be determined by the extent to which the ESOP narrows the distance felt between the employee and the firm. In a survey reported by March and McAllister (1981) in the *Journal of Corporation Law*, two-thirds of the companies using ESOPs reported that contributions to the plan exceeded 5 percent of total annual compensation accounted for the participating employees, and 31 percent of the companies reported contributions of 15 percent or more. If the percentage of compensation accounted for by an ESOP is considered significant by many employees, they would develop strong interest in the performance of their company's stock, a factor reinforcing positive attitudes toward loyalty. However, most ESOPs do not allow their employees to directly vote the stock—a decision limiting the employees' involvement with the company and therefore the opportunity to modify WREAs. The *Journal of Corporation Law* survey found that only 5 percent of the companies operating ESOPs paid dividends directly to the participating employees. Direct payment of dividends would also correlate the firm's profitability to employee performance, thus modifying WREAs.

Empirical evidence indicates that providing employees some form of ownership interest does indeed improve performance and productivity. The 1982 New York Stock Exchange report reviewed the various studies evaluating gain sharing and concluded that "*All* of the studies have shown positive results." The *Journal of Corporation Law* study found that employee turnover declined and work improved significantly in firms using ESOPs, and that employee grievances, absenteeism, and tardiness declined, but relatively less. The survey also compared the overall productivity of ESOP companies with the national productivity average, and found that the ESOP companies performed significantly better in every time period considered. The survey did find, contrary to the argument advanced above, that the granting or not granting of voting rights to ESOP-held stock did not affect productivity.

Compensation Plans

Incentive plans that correlate employee performance and compensation are likely to have a positive effect on the development of desired WREAs. Again, the employee gains a sense of working for his or her own self, as opposed to working solely for a separate entity, and is thus more likely to develop desired attitudes.

Incentive plans can be keyed to group or to individual performance. A properly designed group plan will tend to reinforce cooperative behavior and encourage interpersonal loyalty. However, group plans are always subject to the danger that more productive members will become irritated that their less productive colleagues benefit equally. Such feelings may degenerate into undersirable WREAs.

Individual incentive plans can range from a sales commission to a piece-rate system. These systems tend to create quite disparate compensation rates within the same firm, and if they are improperly designed they may also reward counterproductive behavior. But, properly set up, they may enhance responsibility and loyalty-related WREAs. Such systems may have a self-reporting dimension and, if so, they are then highly dependent on the honesty of the employees. Loyalty to the firm also may be a factor when a system could deteriorate into destructive competition among the firm's own employees as, for example, when salespeople co-opt contacts and leads from their colleagues. Concurrent measures to encourage development of honesty- and loyalty-related WREAs would have to be employed in order for the system to work effectively.

The existence of a possible correlation between the nature of employee WREAs and the compensation rates offered by a firm raises several interesting questions. Do higher compensation levels tend to ensure that employees develop desired WREAs? Or vice versa? For example, would employees aware that their firm is paying below the industry average be more likely to be opportunistic in regard to their employer? Would they feel that they were entitled to whatever they could take from the company? Or might the correlation work in the opposite direction? Could a firm that had carefully selected employees with high personal values of loyalty and honesty, and then encouraged their development into desired attitudes, pay lower wages than the industry average and still have a productive work force? Empirical research is needed to answer these and similar intriguing questions.

Employee Participation

Employees may see the work environment differently depending on whether they have some personal involvement in relevant business decisions. Different (and more positive from the firm's viewpoint) WREAs may come into play when the employee has a say. Recognition of this dimension would account in part for the great current popularity of quality circles and other quality-of-work-life programs. These programs have been highly rated by many of the companies that have tried them. Part of their success may be due to bringing out previously untapped knowledge and insights; however, changed WREAs also may be a significant part of the success story. Most people act differently when they have a stake in a decision, both as to how they approach the decision-making process and how they support the decision after the fact.

Real involvement in a decision-making process will reduce the perceived distance between the individual and the firm. The overlapping of the individual's and the firm's interest in that decision may result in development of very positive WREAs. At the 1983 Wharton-Reliance Symposium, Thomas J. Murrin of Westinghouse described how that company directly involved the clerical staff who used word-processing systems in the decision of how best to standardize the many systems in use throughout the company. Once convinced that they had a genuine role, the users put a great deal of high-quality effort into the decision. And once it was made, they were very supportive. It should be noted, however, that giving employees only a sham involvement in a decision process is likely to produce intensely negative WREAs.

Conclusion

Little attention has been paid to date to the relationship between WREAs and business productivity. This article has argued that certain WREAs (for instance, honesty, loyalty, and responsibility) significantly influence employee productivity. WREAs are seen as contributing to diminished employee opportunism and to increased work effort. Managers may influence the level of WREAs held by a firm's work force by selecting employees with desired pre-existing WREAs; considering desired WREAs in job evaluations; reinforcing desired qualities by modifying the organizational climate; providing some degree of employee ownership; providing incentives in compensation plans; and involving employees in relevant decision making.

Note

Revised and updated version of "Employee Ethical Attitudes and Business Firm Productivity," published in *8 The Wharton Annual 75-86* (1983). The valuable contributions of Diana C. Robertson are gratefully acknowledged.

References

Carr, A., 1968. "Is Business Bluffing Ethical?" *Harvard Business Review* **46**(I):I43–153.

Clark, J.P., and Hollinger, R.C., 1983. *Theft by Employees in Work Organizations—Executive Summary*. Washington, D.C.: National Institute of Justice, U.S. Dept. of Justice.

Dunfee, T., and Robertson, D., 1984, "Work-Related Ethical Attitudes: Impact on Business Profitability," *Business and Professional Ethics Journal* **3**:25–41.

England, G.W., 1974. "Personal Value Systems of Managers and Administrators," in *Academy of Management Proceedings, 33rd Annual Meeting*, Boston, August 19–22, 1973, p. 83.

Fishbein, M., and Ajzen, I., 1975. *Belief, Attitude, Intention and Behavior: An Introduction to Theory and Research*. Reading: Addison-Wesley.

Friedman, M., 1962. *Capitalism and Freedom*. Chicago: University of Chicago Press.

Levitt, T., 1958. "The Dangers of Social Responsibility," *Harvard Business Review*, Sept.–Oct. 1968.

March, T., and McAllister, D., 1981, "ESOPs Tables: A Survey of Companies with Employee Stock Ownership Plans," *Journal of Corporation Law* **6**:551–623.

People and Productivity: A Challenge to Corporate America, 1982. The New York Stock Exchange Office of Economic Research.

Ricklefs, R., 1983. "Ethics in America," a four-part series in the *Wall Street Journal*, Oct. 31, 1983–Nov. 3, 1983.

Rokeach, M., 1973. *The Nature of Human Values.* New York: Free Press.
Yankelovich, D., and Immerwahr, J., 1983. *The Work Ethic and Economic Vitality,* The Public Agenda Foundation, New York.

Updating the Corporate Board

Murray L. Weidenbaum

Discussions of that venerable institution, the corporate board of directors, are moving from the financial pages and the learned journals to the front pages and the nightly television news. It is becoming apparent that in a period of dramatic takeover battles the role of the board can be crucial.

The Business Roundtable, in its proposals on responding to hostile takeovers, states that first consideration should be given to three factors: the fundamental values of the free market, the rights of shareholders, and the judgment of corporate boards of directors. On the positive side, the Roundtable endorses mergers and acquisitions approved by boards of directors of acquired companies. In contrast, it criticizes corporate raiders proceeding "without appropriate involvement of directors."[1] The Roundtable is referring to acquisitions that are made by buying large amounts of the company's stock from existing shareholders.

On the legislative front, Senator John H. Chaffee of Rhode Island has introduced a bill to regulate takeovers, which provides a special role for the boards of directors of both the bidding and the target companies. In the case of the bidders, a majority of the company's outside directors would have to approve takeover attempts when the value of the transaction amounts to less than 20 percent of the target company's net book value; above 20 percent, the effort would require shareholder approval. For the target company, majority approval by outside disinterested directors would be needed on any offer for over 20 percent of the company's outstanding shares.

Some companies have enacted "poison pill" provisions, which put the board of directors squarely in the middle of these merger and acquisition battles. The directors adopt such a measure to discourage unwanted takeovers. The "pill" is in the form of new rights to shareholders to acquire, at a marked discount, a large equity stake in any successful suitor whose offer has not been approved by the company's board. This provision is being contested in the courts on the grounds that it effectively usurps the voting rights of the stockholders. Simultaneously with these efforts to expand the role of corporate directors, criticism of the board has become pervasive. One retired board chiarman of a successful company describes the board of directors as the "Achilles heel of the American corporation."[2] A leading scholar refers to the corporate board as an "impotent legal fiction."[3] "Rubber stamp" seems the kindest description that critics offer.

The new burst of public attention to the corporate board, from friend and foe alike, is matched by widespread ignorance—both of how that important economic institution functions and how it has been changing on its own in recent years. Thus, it is appropriate to examine the evolving role of boards of directors, with special attention to strengthening the board at a time when it is often the focal point of corporate response to external threats. Although I present my own viewpoint, developed in part from my service as a corporate director, much of the material is a distillation of many studies in law, economics, and business administration.

Criticisms of the Board

Three major criticisms have been leveled at the institution of the corporate board of directors.

"The Board Is a Rubber Stamp"

The most frequently made criticism of the corporate board of directors is that it is ceremonial, rubber-stamping the views of management. This belief comes from many sources. In his 1948 classic study of large companies, R.A. Gordon concluded that directors are closer to top management than to the stockholders, and that ratification of management proposals by the board is largely a formality.[4] He also reported that, as a result of its control of the proxy machinery, it is more common for management to select directors than vice versa.

Myles L. Mace, in his authoritative study of corporate boards in the late 1960s, reported that the role of directors is largely advisory and not of a decision-making nature. He quotes one company president as saying, "The board of directors serves as a sounding board. . . . The decision is not made by the board."[5]

An account of the bankruptcy of the Penn Central reached an even stronger conclusion:

> Penn Central's directors seem to have done very little to earn the $200 each received each time he attended a board meeting. . . . With few exceptions, they appeared to be blind to the on-rushing events that sent the Penn Central hurtling off the tracks.[6]

Frederick D. Sturdivant concludes that most research lends credence to the critics' notion that the board of directors is a weak, ineffectual body in providing accountability for corporate actions. In this view, the corporate board is seen as a cozy group of insiders: "members of top management, an attorney from the corporation's outside law firm, the president from the company's bank, and a few of the chief executive officer's (CEO) personal friends."[7]

"The Board Is Dominated by the CEO"

A closely related criticism is that the board's deliberations are dominated by the CEO, who typically also serves as chairman. When the same person controls the agenda and conduct of boardroom proceedings as well as the day-to-day performance of the company, the power of the individual director may indeed become attenuated. One recent study revealed that, in the case of 77 percent of the corporations surveyed in 1984, the chairman of the board is also the chief executive officer. Moreover, 42 percent reported that their CEO is also the chief operating officer.[8]

Management consultants report that too many directors act as part of top management, rather than as monitors able and willing to reward and penalize management's performance.[9] A long-time board member states that the ambiguity of the role of the corporate board begins with the prevailing combination of management leadership and board leadership in the same person.[10]

"The Board Is Plagued with Conflicts of Interest"

Corporate directors often are criticized for conflicts of interest and for showing greater concern for the welfare of other companies. Many outside directors of corporations do business with the companies on whose board they serve. The literature contains a number of cases of apparent wrongdoing on the part of outside directors who also were officers of companies that supplied services to the corporation.[11]

In the case of the Penn Central, a staff report of the Committee on Banking and Currency of the U.S. House of Representatives censured the company's board members for their excessive involvement in other corporate boards. The Committee staff noted the subservience of many of the outside directors to the interests of the financial institutions of which they were officers. As corporate boards shift to a larger percentage of outside directors, the likelihood of such corporate "interlocks" will increase.[12]

In the case of the larger firms, a problem is emerging in the form of opportunity for "backscratching" when setting management compensation. The board's compensation committee is typically a group dominated by outside directors. What's wrong with that? Frequently those outside directors are senior officers of other firms, who are very sympathetic to motions for generous treatment of their counterparts. Aside from the intrinsic merits of the matter, their self-interest dictates such a stand. After all, the compensation committees of their own boards are often similarly composed of CEOs of peer firms. Moreover, the management consultants advising those committees take full account of such peer-group action by the other boards. The ratchet effect that results is quite obvious.

Other nominally independent outside directors, in practice, may represent another set of special interests—those of the local community. Senior officers of local firms that primarily sell goods and services to the surrounding area may see great value in the company donating lavishly to local causes, even if its markets are national or international. Another serious concern is the relationship of the inside directors to the chairman CEO. After all, he is their day-to-day supervisor, usually with the effective authority to radically change the directors' role in the company and even to fire or demote them. It is rare to see a subordinate officer serving on a board dissent from the position taken by the CEO.

Voluntary Changes in the Boardroom

While the criticism by writers on corporate governance continues unabated, important changes in the boardroom are being made on a voluntary basis. These adaptive adjustments have resulted from significant shifts in the environment in which corporations and their boards function—increased government regulation and the threat of further intervention, heightened activity by citizen groups, greater foreign competition, rising levels of litigation by shareholders, and criticism from the press. In part, these changes deflect or reduce the pressures for new statutes or regulations requiring compulsory modifications in corporate governance. Also, the increased liability of corporate directors for their actions is reinforcing the trend toward their greater involvement in company decision making.

According to the head of a major consulting firm, "Passive ceremonial directors are fast becoming an endangered species." A recent survey of the boards of directors of large U.S. corporations concluded that "the days of the 'rubber stamp' board are over." Clearly, many boards are taking on a more active role. Eight basic voluntary changes in the boardroom can be identified.

1. Outside directors have become a majority of most boards of large companies in the United States, and the move toward more outside directors continues. The proportion of industrial corporations in the United States with majorities of outsiders on their boards increased from 50 percent in 1938 to 83 percent in 1979.[13] A 1984 study reported that the typical board of the larger corporations contained nine outside directors and four inside directors, or a ratio of 69 to 31 percent. The prevalence of "dependent" outside directors is diminishing. In 1974, commercial bankers served on slightly more than half of all corporate boards and only on 31 percent in 1984. Similarly, attorneys providing legal services for the company served on 28 percent of corporate boards in 1984, down from 40 percent in 1974.[14]

2. A broader diversity of backgrounds is evident in the type of persons serving on corporate boards. Increased numbers of directors have public service, academic, and scientific experience. Boards also include rising percentages of women and minorities. One comprehensive survey shows that 45 percent of the boards examined had women directors in 1984 compared to 11 percent in 1974. During the same period, the percentage of boards with ethnic minority members rose from 11 percent to 26 percent, those with academics from 36 percent to 52 percent, and those with former government officials from 12 percent to 31 percent (see figure 1).

3. Auditing committees have become a nearly universal phenomenon. Typically, these financial oversight bodies are composed entirely of independent outside directors (an absolute requirement for firms listed on the New York Stock Exchange). The audit comittees have direct access to both outside and inside auditors and usually review the financial aspects of company operations in great detail. As recently as 1973, only one-half of large U.S. corporations had auditing committees. In 1984, the proportion was 98 percent.

4. In many companies, nominating committees propose both candidates for the board and senior officers. These committees usually have a strong majority of outside directors (typically, four out of five). A 1984 study reported that 48 percent of the companies surveyed had nominating committees, compared to 7 percent in 1973.

5. In most large companies, compensation committees evaluate the performance of top executives and determine the terms and conditions of their employment. These committees are composed largely or entirely of outside directors. In 1983, 88 percent of the large companies surveyed had compensation committees. In practice, many of these committees rely extensively on outside consultants whose compensation surveys often set the framework for committee deliberations.

6. Since 1970, about 100 major companies have established public-policy committees of their boards. These committees give board-level attention to company policies and performance on subjects of special public concern. Topics with which public-policy committees often deal include affirmative action and equal employment opportunity, employee health and safety, company impact on the environment, corporate political activities, consumer affairs, and ethics.

7. Internal management and accounting control systems have been strengthened. In part, the impetus has come from the need to comply with the provisions of the Foreign Corrupt Practices Act. The activities of the audit committees surely are a reinforcing factor. As a result, the flow of information to board members has been upgraded and expanded.

8. Recruiting directors has become more difficult. Increasing the role and the remuneration of directors has helped make board service more attractive.

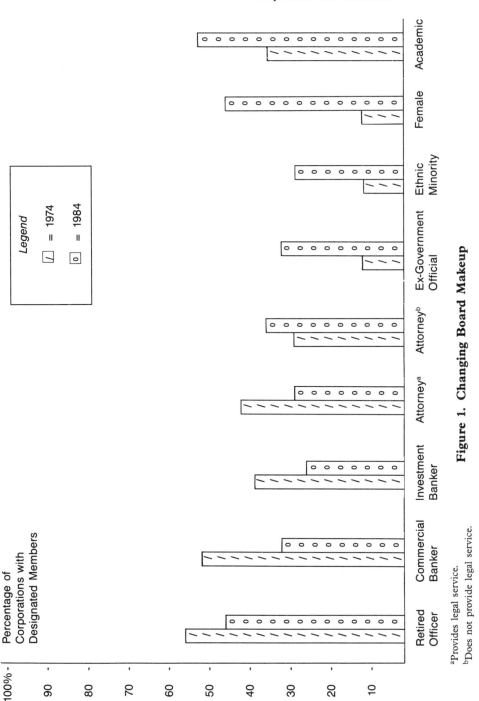

Percentage of
Corporations with
Designated Members

Legend

☐ = 1974

☐ = 1984

Figure 1. Changing Board Makeup

[a]Provides legal service.
[b]Does not provide legal service.

However, these positive factors are on occasion offset by a change in the narrow, technical area of directors' liability insurance. In recent years, courts have narrowed the scope of the business judgment rule, which provides broad discretion to board members in carrying out their functions. The resultant acceleration of lawsuits against corporate boards has increased the costs of the insurance companies that have previously covered the bulk of such expenses. In turn, this has led to a marked decline in the willingness of carriers to write directors' and officers' liability insurance policies. As a consequence, some directors have reduced the number of boards on which they serve in order to concentrate on their responsibilities on the remaining boards. As yet, there is only anecdotal evidence on the unwillingness of otherwise qualified individuals to serve as corporate directors in view of the rising litigation and declining insurance coverage.[15]

Recommendations for Strengthening the Board

Despite the progress that has been made in recent years, most writers on the role of the corporate board reach some variation of the same conclusion: the board of directors is a vital part of the business firm, but it often does an inadequate job of carrying out its responsibility to represent the shareholders.

The result can be a policy vacuum, which provides opportunity for those outside of the corporation. Dramatic moves have been made to take advantage of the fundamental shortcoming of corporate boards. These responses have come from the so-called predatory raiders who attempt to take advantage of the latent support of shareholders for changes in the status quo. Of course, corporate managements view this phenomenon differently. A spokesman for the Business Roundtable describes the strategy of "professional raiders" as waging "blitzkrieg warfare" devised to "outflank the corporate board of directors and stampede the stockholders." There is no need to glamorize the activities or the motives of the raiders. One of the most successful takeover specialists describes his efforts as "acting in pursuit of personal financial gain and not out of altruism. . . . I do it to make money."

We must recognize the extent to which takeover battles have occurred because of the cumulative inaction of some boards of directors. It is easy enough to denounce the current crop of financial entrepreneurs who have little interest in the production of goods and services, but who profit—often in the form of "greenmail"—merely from making unsolicited takeover bids. But if they are opportunists, we must ask whether existing board and management practices have created these opportunities. A clue is given, perhaps inadvertently, by the Roundtable's lament that a successful corporate defense may involve drastic restructuring to maximize share value in the short run. Without endorsing the desirability of such a change, we can wonder whether it does reflect the true desires of many shareholders to indeed want to maximize share value in the short run.

Despite their attraction to defending managements, legislative proposals to make unfriendly takeovers more difficult do not deal with the fundamental need to respond to the desires of the shareholders. That is both the basic responsibility of the board and the key to its potential power. Corporate officials, both board members and officers, may forget that shareholders continually vote with their dollars. The less frequently key issues are presented to the shareholders, the more likely they are to resort to their ultimate weapon.

It is ironic that some of the problems of the takeover targets may have arisen from the desire to be more socially responsible. Much of the modern management literature refers to the need for top management to balance the desires of employees, customers, suppliers, public-interest groups, and shareholders. For example, the Committee for Economic Development, in its widely circulated report on the social responsibility of business, stated that the modern professional manager regards himself as a trustee balancing the interests of many diverse participants and constituents in the enterprise (shareholders are only listed as one among many worthy groups):

> The chief executive of a large corporation has the problem of reconciling the demands of employees for more wages and improved benefit plans, customers for lower prices and greater values, vendors for higher prices, government for more taxes, stockholders for higher dividends and greater capital appreciation.

The corporate responsibility approach has fostered dissatisfaction of shareholders and thereby undermined the support for management. A 1982 survey by the National Association of Corporate Directors revealed that only 53 percent of shareholders believe that directors consider stockholder interests in acting on mergers and acquisitions. That is not an overwhelming vote of confidence.

The heart of a positive response to unsolicited takeover efforts is for directors to act more fully as fiduciaries of the shareholders, as the law requires. The same authorities who are almost universally critical of the way in which corporate boards operate are unanimous in their belief that a well-functioning governing board is essential to the future of the modern corporation. Virtually no one has concluded that the board of directors has outlived its usefulness. Even such business critics as Ralph Nader would lodge majority responsibility for governing the corporation in a revitalized board of directors.

The most fundamental need in corporate governance is educational—to get senior corporate officers to understand their high stake in enhancing the role of the board of directors. There would be fewer challenges to the existing managements of their companies if more boards acted from a day-to-day concern with the interests of their shareholders. The benefits of a more active board will not be attained without costs. Achieving a stronger and more effective board means sharing the authority now lodged in the CEO—and at times reaching somewhat different decisions. But that does not require the establishment of a competitive power center. It does mean being more conscious of the desires of shareholders, and of the need to keep them more fully informed. Only one person—the chief executive—can guide the corporation's day-to-day activities. That function cannot be performed by a committee.

Successful directors learn to monitor and question while creating an atmosphere of confidence in the management. Simultaneously, a truly secure CEO will not attempt to stifle criticism by individual directors. The legendary Alfred P. Sloan reportedly made the following statement at a General Motors board meeting:

> Gentlemen, I take it we are all in complete agreement on the decision here. . . .
> Then I propose we postpone further discussion of this matter until our next meeting
> to give ourselves time to develop disagreement and perhaps gain some understanding of what the decision is all about.[16]

What about the composition of the board? Experience teaches us to be leary of simple solutions. An example is the popular proposition that only outside directors should serve on a corporate board, with the possible exception of the CEO. Diversity of talent is a strength in the management of an economic organization.

Corporate boards should consist primarily of independent outsiders. Outside directors should not represent banks, law firms, customers, or the community in which the corporation happens to have its headquarters. Such actual or potential conflicts of interest should be avoided. A strong but minority representation of knowledgeable insiders should continue. Nominating committees would do well to bear in mind the advice of S. Prakash Sethi that a board of directors is not a debating society: "While it is normal to have different viewpoints and expertise represented on the board, it is illogical to represent special interests on the board."[17]

Retired officers of a company do not belong on its board. It is enough to have independent outside directors looking over the shoulders of the management, without the previous generation of management also doing so. The outsiders have less stake in defending the status quo than do the retirees who may have created existing conditions. There are advantages in retired corporate officers serving as directors of other companies, so long as they are not competitors of or suppliers to the company from which they have retired.

Opinions differ sharply on whether the CEO should also serve as chairman of the board. In my personal view, the board chairman should be an outside director in order to assure the independence of the board. It would be helpful if the presiding officer had relevent experience—the recently retired CEO of another firm or of a large non-profit institution, for instance. Other senior members of the management also can be useful board members. One or more vice-chairmen would be appropriate. Usually, these are people of considerable experience who hold primarily a counsel or advisory relationship to the CEO, and who served in major operating positions earlier in their careers. Their presence on the board does not give rise to the problems that occur when operating officials are made board members—when they participate in reviewing their own operations and those of their colleagues. Because of the crucial relationship of financial reporting to the monitoring function, the chief financial officer probably also should be a board member. None of these inside directors can be expected to differ frequently with the CEO, thus emphasizing the need for a substantial representation of outside, independent directors.

The board chairmanship should be a private role whereas the CEO represents the firm to the public. Only the CEO and his subordinates can truly represent the firm in public arenas since they bear the responsibility and possess the authority to conduct the business of the company. This approach requires a high degree of good will on the part of both outside directors and corporate officers. The indispensable factor in ensuring an effective board is that directors and management be committed to making the board work. A great deal of effort and discretion is required on the part of outside directors to carry on an active and constructive role that is simultaneously probing and supportive.

The points just made for board service apply with equal force to committee work. Compared to board meetings, directors are more likely to take the initiative in committees. Some institutional protections of the independence of board comittees are necessary and are now often in place. Specifically, the audit committee—even if the corporation is not listed on the New York Stock Exchange—should consist entirely of independent outside directors. The compensation committee, which passes on the pay and fringe benefits of top management, should be similarly constituted. Also, the nominating committee, with a key role in selecting directors and senior executives, should be comprised of independent outside members.

In contrast, the finance and public-policy committees can benefit from a balance between insiders and outsiders. The management directors bring a special institutional knowledge, while the outside directors hopefully operate with a wider framework. Another reason for the mixed finance committee is that is provides a built-in opportunity to balance the pressures for dividends and retained earnings. Often many shareholders emphasize the short-run benefits of increased income, whereas management is more concerned about investing in the company's future growth. Also, the officers may simply find it easier or at least more satisfactory to use retained earnings rather than going to the credit markets. For the typical business firm, this is not an either-or choice, but a case of balancing two important and basic considerations.

CEOs and other busy professionals will have to ration more carefully the number of boards on which they serve, and boards should be more selective in their new appointments. Outside directors should be truly independent. They should not also simultaneously be paid consultants or advisors to the management. They should not have their own interests in mind, be it supporting the local community or advocating more generous treatment of corporate executives generally. Outside directors need to bear in mind that, in a very special way, the future of the corporation is in their hands—so long as they serve the desires of the shareholders.

The subject of board turnover is often a painful matter. A directorship is not a type of civil-service appointment, but it is not easy to dislodge a long-term director. Long-time directors become so accustomed to the existing way of doing business that they viscerally oppose innovation on the oldest bureaucratic grounds: "We have never done it that way."

A Look to the Future

A growing array of external forces impinges on the contemporary corporation. Some of these factors are financial and economic, focusing on the traditional functions of business enterprise. Others are social and political, dealing with business responses to other issues. Together, these influences will likely produce significant further changes in the composition of corporate boards of directors and in the conduct of the boardroom.

Looking ahead, researchers and practitioners alike in the twenty-first century probably still will be speculating about the needed changes in the roles and activities of corporate directors. Fundamentally, this will reflect the fact that the corporation is a continually evolving institution in the U.S. economy and, as external requirements change, key elements such as the board of directors continue to adapt and modify their actions. These factors help to explain the fundamental strength and long-term resiliency of private enterprise institutions in the United States.

Notes

This is a revised version of the author's article, "Updating the Corporate Board," *Journal of Business Strategy* (forthcoming). It draws heavily on the author's study, *Strengthening the Corporate Board* (St. Louis: Washington University, Center for Study of American Business, 1985).

1. "Free Market, Shareholder Rights, Director's Judgment are Key to Takeover Solution," *Roundtable Report,* April 1985, pp. 3–4.

2. Kenneth N. Dayton, "Corporate Governance: The Other Side of the Coin," *Harvard Business Review,* January/February 1984, p. 34.

3. Peter Drucker, "The Bored Board," *Wharton Magazine,* Fall 1976, p. 19.

4. R.A. Gordon, *Business Leadership In the Large Corporation* (Berkeley: University of California Press, 1948), pp. viii, 131.

5. Myles L. Mace, *Directors: Myth and Reality* (Boston: Harvard University, Graduate School of Business Administration, 1971), p. 13.

6. J.R. Daughen and P. Binzel, *The Wreck of the Penn Central* (Boston: Little Brown, 1971), p. 12.

7. Frederick D. Sturdivant, *Business and Society* (Homewood, Ill.: Richard D. Irwin, 1981), p. 341.

8. Lester B. Korn and Richard M. Ferry, *Twelfth Annual Board of Directors Study* (New York: Korn/Ferry International, 1985), p. 4.

9. Arch Patton, "Why Corporations Overpay Their Underachieving Bosses," *Washington Post,* March 3, 1985, p. C-2.

10. Courtney C. Brown, *Putting the Corporate Board to Work* (New York: Macmillan, 1976), p. 15.

11. Edward S. Herman, *Corporate Control, Corporate Power* (New York: Cambridge University Press, 1981), pp. 41, 136.

12. S. Prakash Sethi, Bernard Cunningham, and Carl Swanson, "The Catch-22 in Reform Proposals for Restructuring Corporate Boards," *Management Review*, January 1979, p. 28.

13. Herman, *Corporate Control*, p. 36; *The New Director* (New York: Arthur Young & Co., 1981), p. 6; Edwin S. Mruk and James A. Giardina, *Organization and Compensation of Boards of Directors* (New York: Arthur Young & Co., 1983), p. 11.

14. Lester B. Korn and Richard M. Ferry, *Twelfth Annual Board of Directors Study* (New York: Korn/Ferry International, 1985).

15. David B. Hilder, "Liability Insurance is Difficult to Find Now for Directors, Officers," *The Wall Street Journal*, July 10, 1985, p. 1.

16. Quoted in Robert J. Haft, "Business Decisions By The New Board," *Michigan Law Review*, November 1981, p. 35.

17. Sethi et al., "The Catch-22," p. 39.

Golden Parachutes: Good for Management and Society?

Philip L. Cochran
Steven L. Wartick

Golden parachutes (GPs), a relatively new and controversial management perquisite, are continuing to increase both in number and in controversy. In 1981, only 11 percent of the *Fortune* 500 firms had GPs.[1] With the passage of the Deficit Reduction Act of 1984 (DEFRA) (which severely restricted GPs), most analysts believed that GPs would fade away. Just the opposite seems to have happened. Examination of their 1985 proxy statements indicates that over 18 percent of the 1985 *Fortune* 500 firms had GPs.

Golden parachutes once again have begun to receive a great deal of unfavorable press. For example, in November 1985, just months prior to Beatrice's acquisiton by Kohlberg, Kravis, Roberts, and Company, the Board of Directors of the Beatrice Corporation awarded $24 million in GPs to six of the firm's managers. This award will grant William W. Granger $7 million for his four-month tenure as chairman of Beatrice.[2] Another GP receiving some notoriety was the package granted to Michael J. Bergerac of Revlon. After Pantry Pride acquired Revlon, Mr. Bergerac left Revlon with a total severance package of $35 million, $21 million of which represented his GP. Such severance packages represent abnormal returns even for well-paid senior executives.

Although GPs appear entrenched in corporate circles, the press's response to GPs has been less than favorable. The *Washington Post* once described GPs as "executive incompetence insurance."[3] *Business Week* referred to GPs as "the gilded ripoff" and argued that the ethical differences between GPs and theft are "hard to discern."[4] Editorials and articles that criticize GPs have also appeared in *Forbes* and *Fortune*.[5] Likewise shareholders seem to be reacting negatively to GPs. There are currently shareholder lawsuits filed against Beatrice, City Investing, RCA, and Revlon over the granting of GPs to their executives.[6] Beatrice is dealing with eighteen lawsuits. Prior to its merger with Allied, Signal Co. had granted its executives $42 million in parachutes, but settled a shareholder lawsuit out of court by agreeing to reduce the value of the payouts to about $25 million.[7]

Even though there has been a significant growth in GPs, business reaction has not been uniformly supportive. In a number of recent takeovers the acquiring companies are refusing to pay the GPs to the executives of the acquired companies. For example, after Minstar acquired AMF Inc., it refused to pay Tom York, AMF's previous chairman, his $5.2 million parachute. Irwin Jacobs, Minstar's chief executive officer (CEO), contends that since "Tom York's record was not good; why should the AMF directors give him that?"[8]

In this article we argue that GPs are bad for corporate stockholders and for the business system in general. We contend that GPs represent an unwarranted raid on stockholders' funds. GPs are, in effect, a reward for mismanagement. The public seems to view GPs as an example of managerial excess. This, in turn, could lead to increased levels of regulation.

What Is a Golden Parachute?

Golden parachutes are defined by Section 280G of the Internal Revenue Code to be contracts in which a corporation agrees to make payments to certain key officers in the event of a change in control of the corporation. In common usage they also include a provision that GPs are effective only after termination of the covered individual. What distinguishes GP contracts from other forms of employment contracts is that they generally apply to voluntary termination as well as to involuntary termination. However, not all GP contracts explicitly cover voluntary termination. They might instead go into effect for one of several reasons after a change in control. Among these reasons are a change in job title, a change in responsibilities, and a change in job location. In short, the ability "to pull the ripcord" is the distinguishing factor in our definition of a GP.

Another point that may be considerd pertains to guaranteed employment. A guaranteed employment provision in an executive's contract says that after a change in control, the executive is guaranteed a specified position for a given number of years. In some cases the guarantee goes on to say that if the executive's position is changed, the executive may choose to resign and collect the compensation that he or she would earn through the remainder of the guarantee period. The determination of whether a position has changed is most often left with the affected executive. In many cases, however, it is not specified what would happen if the executive chooses to leave the company or if the executive chooses to minimize his or her activity within the company and maximize activity in other endeavors. Because of the clear control the executive has in the first case, and the ambiguity existing in the second case, contracts that guarantee an executive continued employment after a change in control appear to fit within the definition of a golden parachute. In summary, GPs may be defined as provisions that allow for corporate executives to receive severance compensation if they voluntarily or involuntarily leave the corporation after a change of control. Guaranteed employment provisions are a particular type of GP.

Who Has Golden Parachutes?

Estimates of the percentage of major firms that offer their managers golden parachutes vary widely. The *New York Times* recently reported a Hewitt Associates study stating that 33 percent of the 250 largest industrial corporations now offer their executives GPs. This was up from 15 percent in 1981.[9] Our study found that 18 percent of the 1985 *Fortune* 500 firms had golden parachutes versus 11 percent in 1981. The differences between these two sets of figures may be the result of differences in the definition of GPs as well as differences in the sample populations.

Golden parachutes do not seem to be concentrated in any particular industries with the possible exceptions of the chemicals and miscellaneous manufacturing industries.[10] However, in a 1985 study, Cochran, Wood, and Jones discovered that within the *Fortune* 500 firms, smaller and financially weaker firms had a greater probability of granting their executives golden parachute contracts.[11] These results are consistent with the hypothesis that golden parachutes are sought by managers of firms that are more likely to be takeover targets.

What Is Included in a Golden Parachute?

The precise contents of a GP are impossible to determine without having access to the employment contracts of the executives who have GPs. From examination of the proxy statements, however, a general picture of what is included in a GP can be drawn. For example, the number of executives covered by GPs ranges from one to all officers. Lambert and Larcker report in their study of 90 firms that implemented GPs from 1975 through 1982 that 26 percent of the officers and directors are typically covered by golden parachute contracts.[12] Since change of control is a key variable in distinguishing GPs from severance pay, it is important in relation to the contents of GPs. However, in the proxy statements, only 31 percent of the sample defined what the firm meant by change of control. In approximately half of the proxy statements where change of control was not defined, it was noted that the definition of the term could be found in the executives' employment contracts. Of those companies defining change of control in their proxy statements, the definition centered on change in the majority of the board, accumulated ownership by one entity, or a combination of both factors.

A change of over half the directors in a short time period appears to be a nearly universal GP trigger. However, some firms also are basing the trigger on changes in accumulated ownership. Often these clauses allow executives to collect their GPs if any single entity accumulates more than a given threshold percentage of the firm's outstanding stock. These thresholds range from 20 to 50 percent. Given this rather liberal definition of change of control, GPs could be triggered inadvertently. In fact, "when Gulf & Western's stake in Mohasco, an interior furnishings company, went over the magic 20 percent mark, four executives bailed out with some $800,000 among them."[13]

The total costs of GPs for any particular firm are difficult to measure accurately since, in most cases, the proxy statements do not disclose all the details of the GPs for all covered executives, and often simply refer to provisions in the employment contracts. Few firms estimated a total dollar liability for their GPs. Ametek, for example, estimated its costs at $3.9 million for thirteen covered executives. Baxter Travenol Laboratories estimated its costs at $30.3 million for twenty-two executives.

Lambert and Larcker attempted to estimate the cost of GPs for the firms in their sample. By making some broad assumptions they found that the cost of GPs as a function of total annual earnings is 12.1 percent and as a function of market value is 1.7 percent.[14] Thus, the total cost of these new perquisites is not insignificant even when compared to the firm's profits or market value.

DEFRA set a cap on GPs at three times average annual compensation for the last five years. Any payments above this level will result in a 20 percent excise tax for the individual receiving the payment and the corporation will not be able to deduct any of the payment as a business expense. This law caused most firms offering GPs to limit them to just less than the cap. For example, Aiken sets GP payments at 299 percent of the average annual compensation for the last five years.[15]

Besides compensation based on salaries, many GPs also include provisions for accelerating stock options and long-term incentive compensation. Bonuses also are estimated and paid, and fringe benefits (most often, insurance and pension) are included as well. The total compensation received by an individual is therefore a function of several variables and is difficult to determine prior to the execution of the GP.

A final area of interest concerning the contents of GPs relates to limitations. In some companies with GPs there is a specified time limit in which the executive can take advantage of a GP. With the guaranteed employment provisions, that time limit centers around a date. For the lump-sum type of GPs, this limitation involves a time period from six months to five years after a change of control. The most frequent time limitation is two years.

Even though it is impossible to predict the exact contents of a GP, it is still possible to describe the contents of a typical GP. A typical agreement contains the following:

1. Coverage for 25 percent of the officers and directors;
2. Change of control, being defined as a change in the majority of the board or the acquisition of over 20 percent of the outstanding stock by some distinguishable party;
3. Compensation consisting of two to three years salary plus accelerated stock options, bonuses, and long-term incentive compensation;
4. Insurance benefits for two to three years after a change of control and pension or retirement provisions;
5. A two year time frame after a change of control in which to activate the GP.

Criticisms of Golden Parachutes

In general, the concern about GPs centers around four criticisms: the managerial performance criticism, the "arms length" criticism, the fiduciary responsibility criticism, and the public relations criticism. Most of these criticisms stem from the suspicion that GPs are implemented in order to benefit existing management, and not, necessarily, shareholders. Criticisms of GPs, therefore, fall within the general concerns of corporate governance, that is, the relationship between management and shareholders.

The *managerial performance* criticism has two dimensions. The first dimension suggests that GPs are providing special compensation for managers to perform duties that they are already responsible to perform. This criticism is based on agency theory, that is, management serves as an agent for the shareholders and is therefore already charged with maximizing shareholder wealth. To the extent that GPs provide additional compensation in order to get managers to objectively represent shareholder interests in takeover, offers of GPs are tantamount "double dipping."

A second element of managerial performance criticism relates to the relationship between managerial performance and takeovers. Takeovers generally occur only when some external group believes that they can manage the firm's assets more efficiently than current management. This argument suggests that GPs are nothing more than multi-million dollar rewards to executives who have mismanaged a company, so that the company's stock price is depressed to the extent that an outside group is willing to pay a considerable sum in order to gain control of the target's assets. Recent evidence suggests that successful takeovers result in gains to the stockholders ranging from 20 percent to 30 percent.[16] This could lead to the conclusion that firms that become takeover targets do so because their current management has been very inefficient.

The *arms length* criticism focuses on the relationship between executives and their boards of directors. The central premise of this criticism is that executives, through control of their boards, give themselves the golden parachutes. If so, then GPs would be yet another manifestation of the effects on a firm when control shifts from stockholders to managers—a phenomenon first discussed by Berle and Means in 1929 and thoroughly documented in the past two decades.[17]

Cochran, Wood, and Jones tested the hypothesis that boards of directors with higher percentages of employee directors would have a greater likelihood of granting their executives golden parachutes. They found just the opposite.[18] This may be evidence that the criticism is invalid. However, it may simply indicate that the mere presence of outside directors on a firm's board of directors does not, in itself, assure that the firm will be managed in the shareholders' interests. Cochran, Woods, and Jones's article on the selection of members of corporate boards is replete with examples of CEOs choosing outside board members who are likely to be sympathetic with their views.

The *fiduciary responsibility* criticism is based on the relationship between management and stockholders. This argument equates GPs with theft. For example, given that a raiding firm is willing to pay only so much to acquire a target firm, and given that the target successfully pumps up the costs that the raider must pay, then the target is worth correspondingly less. For every additional million dollars that a raider must pay in GPs, a million dollars is taken from the target's shareholders.

The *public relations* criticism suggests that GPs are irresponsible. In a time of economic hardship and union givebacks, news of GPs can prove, at best, to be a serious embarrassment. In an era in which most firms fight any legislation that will force them to give advance notice of plant closings and fight special severance pay to workers thrown out of jobs when facilities close, it is ironic that management gives itself such lavish severance benefits. Even if GPs can be justified economically or ethically, one must ask whether or not the existence of GPs compensates for the various costs associated with the negative publicity they arouse—costs that may eventually include additional government regulation.

Responses to the Critics: An Assessment

Although there has been extensive criticism of GPs, some have tried to defend them. Examination of the proxy statements of the *Fortune* 500 firms with golden parachute agreements shows four broad defenses for GPs. Although offered as counterpoints to the criticisms, we see the defenses as flawed in several ways.

Objectivity. This defense suggests that without assurances about their futures, executives might be more concerned about their own interests than those of the shareholders. Presumably, executives would therefore be more concerned about being viewed favorably by their future boards than viewed favorably by their current boards. GPs eliminate this potential problem because the executive knows, at least at a minimum, what the future holds.

In their study of the effects of GPs on stock prices, Lambert and Larcker refer to their theory as the "incentive alignment argument." They say that if their theory is correct, then the stock market should react favorably whenever a firm adopts a GP.[19] They tested this hypothesis and concluded that indeed the market price of a firm's stock did tend to rise following public disclosure of golden parachute contracts with its managers. However, in another study, using a different methodology and sample, Cochran, Wood, and Woolridge found no significant relationship between disclosure of GPs and changes in stock price.[20]

Even if the stock market did react favorably to news that management had received GPs, this is not necessarily an argument for GPs. For example, the stock market may be reacting to additional information that the firm may be a takeover target. And even if the stock market did react favorably to news of GPs, because GPs make executives more disposed to accepting a merger that would benefit the stockholders, the payment might be considered very similar to payment of an extortion demand. Aren't there better public-policy mechanisms that also could accomplish this goal of less management resistance to mergers?

Easterbrook and Fischel, for example, have presented a powerful case for total managerial passivity in the face of a takeover; they contend that any managerial resistance ultimately decreases shareholder wealth.[21] They argue that stockholders would be better served if management stayed neutral with respect to any takeover attempt. Perhaps legislation or regulation limiting management's responses to a takeover bid would be better public policy than would encouraging golden parachutes.

Another troubling possibility is that a GP might actually create an incentive for management to seek an inferior bargain for the firm's stockholders in the event of takeover activity. For example, if a firm's management is dealing with two or more potential buyers and there is uncertainty about whether or not the GP agreement is easily enforceable, then it is reasonable to assume that the management will be more disposed toward the buyer most likely to pay the GP, and less disposed toward the buyer who will fight the GP. One also could assume that certain corporate raiders would recognize this loophole and attempt to exploit it by offering management more (for example, by promising not to question their parachutes) and stockholders less. Thus GPs, rather than aligning managements' incentives with those of the stockholders, could actually establish incentives that run counter to those of the stockholders.

Loyalty. The loyalty defense implies that GPs are justified on the basis of reward for past service. Managers may have spent many years developing knowledge and expertise relevant to a specific firm. This investment of their human capital may result in returns to the firm in future years. Managers may see their later years of service as a reward for that investment. A successful takeover resulting in their dismissal would thus rob them of the fruits of this investment. A firm is a takeover target (generally at a significant premium over recent market price) because some other company believes that it can manage the firm's resources considerably more efficiently than can existing management. Why would shareholders want to reward that management group with golden parachutes?

Retention. The retention defense is probably the one most commonly used to defend GPs. The suggestion is that GPs encourage executives to stay with their firms, both during a takeover attempt and after the completed takeover. This defense presupposes that without GPs the uncertainties surrounding a takeover might be sufficient to cause a number of key executives to leave at a time of severe organizational trial. GPs therefore buy the continued leadership of senior management. As such, GPs are merely another form of executive compensation similar to bonuses, stock options, and so forth. In fact, they could be viewed as just another facet of a total executive compensation package. This defense of GPs is questionable since most takeover specialists scoff at the notion that management is likely to depart during a takeover attempt. They note that there is virtually no evidence of managers bailing out in a time of crisis. Rather, the group dynamics of senior management are such that to do so would seem disloyal and the person bailing out would lose face.[22]

Cost. This defense proposes that GPs add to the acquisition cost of a takeover, thus becoming a legitimate means of forcing the acquirer to re-evaluate his intentions. Since GPs go into effect only in the event of a successful takeover, they can be used as a device for raising the price to the "raider" but not to a compatible "white knight." A second aspect of this defense is that the cost of GPs is actually borne by the stockholders of the acquiring firm and not the stockholders of the executives' firm. Issues of fiduciary responsibility are therefore irrelevant to the GP contract.

The total cost of GPs, though significant, is rather small compared to corporate profits and market value. Further, since the market determines the value of a target in a takeover attempt, driving the cost up for a raider but not for a white knight serves only one interest—management's. Do shareholders really care whether their stock is acquired by a raider or a white knight? More than likely they do not—but management does. What then, besides a possible transfer of funds from shareholders to managers, does a GP accomplish?

Legal and Ethical Perspectives

The preceding section assessed GPs from mostly a managerial/economic perspective. In addition to these concerns, GPs must be considered from both legal and ethical perspectives. When Congress passed the Deficit Reduction Act in 1984, it specifically recognized and placed limits on GP contracts. For GPs enacted after June 14, 1984, DEFRA levies a 20 percent excise tax on top of regular income tax if the GP is defined as "excessive" by the Internal Revenue Code Section 280G. Excessive GPs are those whose remuneration is in excess of three times average annual compensation for the last five years. In addition, DEFRA made payments of excessive GPs no longer tax deductible for business, thus considerably increasing their costs.

DEFRA not withstanding, the reaction of courts to GPs seems to be increasingly hostile. In Wisconsin, for example, a court struck down a GP because it had no provision for offsetting the GP with money earned at another firm after the manager "pulled the ripcord." In several other cases, parachutists have agreed to reduced benefits in order to avoid potentially hostile court decisions.[23]

The legality of GPs has rested on the business judgment rule. The business judgment rule can be interpreted to suggest that "management has the right, and even the duty, to oppose a tender offer it determines contrary to the firm's best interest."[24] To the extent that management can successfully claim that GPs aid opposition to hostile tender offers, the courts are likely to uphold these agreements. The business judgment rule has served as an effective shield against virtually all suits that question management decisions—decisions including the implementation of GPs.

Unanswered legal questions center on management's relationship to the members of the board. More specifically, the concern is with the separation of senior-level management decision making and decision making by the board. For example, at Gulf Resources the role of Robert H. Ailen was at issue. The new board controlling Gulf Resources has refused to pay Allen's GP because Allen was both chairman of the board and CEO of Gulf Resources prior to its acquisition. The new board claims that "as chairman he [Allen] ratified the decision to cover him and his fellow officers with the severance plan, which reportedly amounted to some $13 million."[25] Thus, the old board "did not have the degree of independence and disinterestedness necessary to authorize the [parachute] agreement."[26]

The question of management and board decision making is further complicated when, as in the case of the Brunswick Corporation, directors as well as managers receive GPs. At Brunswick, any outside director over 55 years of age with more than five years service may quit after a hostile takeover and continue receiving an annual retainer of $22,000 for life.[27] Given such circumstances as those in Gulf Resources and those in Brunswick, there is a finite possibility that the courts may actually set a new precedent in the area of GPs.

Still, the legal community is strongly divided over GPs.[28] Some attorneys see GPs as nothing more than common-law fraud. Others view GPs as no different than other executive perquisites. The more moderate view of GPs and perhaps the most likely view for the future is that GPs will be considered on a case-by-case basis and no precedent will be established. In rendering their decisions, the courts will examine the time at which a GP was enacted and whether or not the board provided due consideration.

Even if GPs are legal, they are not necessarily ethical. In fact, it is difficult to find any ethical justification for them. This is not to suggest that high compensation in itself is unethical since fortunes of a major company often turn on the judgment of senior management. Income differentials are a necessary element of a market economy, helping to drive the economy toward efficiency. Rather, the ethical validity of GPs hinges on considerations of management's responsibilities to its shareholders during takeover attempts. In its role as agents of the stockholders, management has responsibilities to its shareholders that should supersede its own interests.

From the shareholders' perspective, GPs are of little value and probably are harmful. GPs serve management's interests by reducing the uncertainty and costs resulting from management performance, but GPs do little for shareholders. We see GPs as a direct and unjustified transfer of wealth from shareholders to managers without any benefits to any other stakeholder groups. This violation of the agency relationship between management and stockholders makes GPs unethical.

Conclusion

During the 1980s, GPs have provoked a major controversy both in the popular and business press over abuses of managerial perquisites. Although there have been a few notable instances of golden parachutes being refused by senior management,[29] the trend appears to be toward even greater use of this perquisite. The widespread public perception that the mere existence of GPs is fundamentally perverse is fueled by the fact that they reward the captains of the losing side. In July 1984, these negative public perceptions led to the inclusion of a section in the Deficit Reduction Act that specifically discusses and places limits on golden parachutes.

Our concern here is that GPs are giving U.S. business another "black eye." The existence of GPs today is similar to the existence of insider trading prior to 1933; insider trading amounted to theft, even before it was made illegal. As Sethi has noted, "corporate interests must emanate from the public interest and cannot be inconsistent."[30] Not only is it in the public interest and shareholder interest to eliminate GPs, but it is also in the interest of the U.S. business community.

Notes

Portions of the work appeared in "Golden Parachutes: A Closer Look" *California Management Review* **26**(4):111–125.

1. Philip L. Cochran, and Steven L. Wartick, "Golden Parachutes: A Closer Look" *California Management Review* **26**(4):113.
2. Steven Greenhouse, "Golden Chutes Under Attack," *New York Times*, December 10, 1985, p. D2.
3. Jerry Knight, "Golden Parachutes Reward Corporate Failure," *Washington Post*, September 13, 1982, p. 1.
4. "The Gilded Ripoff," *Business Week*, October 4, 1982, p. 136.
5. "Pulling the Golden Ripcord," *Forbes*, May 24, 1982, p. 31; Ann M. Morrison, "Those Executive Bailout Deals," *Fortune*, December 13, 1982, p. 84.
6. Steven E. Prokesh, "Too Much Gold in the Parachute?" *New York Times*, January 26, 1986, section 3, p. 1.
7. Eleanor Johnson Tracey, "Parachutes A-Popping," *Fortune*, March 31, 1986, p. 66.
8. Prokesh, "Too Much Gold," p. 1.
9. Ibid.
10. Cochran and Wartick, "Golden Parachutes," p. 115.

11. Philip L. Cochran, Robert A. Wood, and Thomas B. Jones, "The Composition of Boards of Directors and the Incidence of Golden Parachutes," *Academy of Management Journal* 28(3):664–671 (Sept. 1985).

12. Richard A. Lambert, and David F. Larcker, "Golden Parachutes, Executive Decision Making, and Shareholder Wealth," *Journal of Accounting and Economics* 7:179–203. (1985)

13. Morrison, "Bailout Deals," p. 85.

14. Lambert and Larcker, "Golden Parachutes," p. 182.

15. "Collins Aiken 1985 Proxy Statement," p. 9.

16. M. Jensen, and R. Ruback, "The Market for Corporate Control: The Scientific Evidence," *Journal of Financial Economics* 11:5–50.

17. R. Joseph Monsen, and Anthony Downs, "A Theory of Large Managerial Firms," *Journal of Political Economy*, June 1963, pp. 221–236; Robert Larner, *Management Control and the Large Corporation* (New York: Dunellen, 1971).

18. Cochran, Wood, and Jones, "Boards of Directors," p. 670.

19. Lambert and Larcker, "Golden Parachutes," p. 185.

20. Philip L. Cochran, Robert A. Wood, and J. Randall Woolridge, "Effects of Golden Parachute Agreements on Shareholder Wealth," *Center for Issues Management Research Working Paper 86-3.*

21. Frank H. Easterbrook, and David H. Fischel, "The Proper Role of a Target's Management in Responding to a Tender Offer," *Harvard Law Review*, April 1981, pp. 1161–1204.

22. David J. McLaughlin, "The Myth of the Golden Parachutes," *Mergers and Acquisitions*, Summer 1982, p. 48.

23. Greenhouse, "Golden Chutes Under Attack," p. D2.

24. Easterbrook and Fischel, "Proper Role of a Target's Management," p. 1163.

25. Frederick C. Klein, "A Golden Parachute Protects Executives, But Does it Hinder or Foster Takeovers?", *Wall Street Journal*, December 8, 1982, p. 56.

26. Ibid., p. 56.

27. N.R. Kleinfield, "Golden Parachutes for Ousted," *New York Times*, April 6, 1982, p. D17.

28. John Moore, "Congress Takes a Dim View of Golden Parachutes," *Legal Times*, October 25, 1985, p. 5.

29. Tim Mertz, "Texas Gas Golden Parachutes Rejected by Aides, Two Days After Board Voted Pacts," *Wall Street Journal*, June 13, 1983, p. 7.

30. S. Prakash Sethi, "Corporate Political Activism," *California Management Review*, 24:34 (Spring 1982).

A Strategic Framework for Dealing with the Schism between Business and Academe

S. Prakash Sethi

Members of the business community, especially large corporations, are among the major financial supporters of institutions of higher learning in the United States, devoting substantial portions of their charitable contributions to private and public universities. Between 1970 and 1981 direct corporate support of colleges and universities increased from approximately $230 million to $870 million.[1] As social institutions, the business and academic communities provide the ideological and economic resources that are the bulwarks of individual freedom and democracy. Moreover, each institution provides services and products needed by the other.

Nevertheless, the business and academic communities live in an environment of uneasy peace often disrupted by periods of intense mutual distrust and hostility, as when students demonstrated on campus against U.S. weapons manufacturers during the Vietnam war.[2] More recently, a number of well-known universities have publicly expressed their displeasure against U.S. corporate investments in South Africa. They have voted their stocks against management and boycotted other corporations' products and services.[3]

It is true that many U.S. universities, squeezed for funds, are entering into joint agreements with business corporations to benefit from commercial development of products based on university research in such areas as electronics, microcomputers, and genetic engineering.[4] However, a study of university-industry relations by Peat, Marwick, Mitchell & Co., shows that it is unlikely that industry will become a major source of research and development funds for the universities any time soon. Compared to a current estimate of about 3.5 percent from industry, the federal government supplies about 68 percent of R&D funds to U.S. universities,[5] but this fact alone is not likely to ameliorate the situation. On the contrary, unless a systematic effort is made to understand the sources of conflict between business and academic institutions, closer collaboration between universities and corporations would exacerbate some of the existing issues and create certain others, further increasing the tension.

An important element for business and its sociopolitical environment during the 1960s and 1970s was the emergence of numerous new social activist groups in the United States. Often concerned chiefly with single issues or ideas, these groups employ primarily judicial and political means to achieve their goals, and use the news media to develop constituencies and societal legitimacy for their causes. They feel that a free-market economy and a competitive system are generally unable to protect their interests or improve general societal conditions in directions they consider desirable. These groups almost invariably advocate means that require income transfer among various segments of the population, allocation of resources through nonmarket channels, and creation of entitlements—without reciprocal obligations—for their constituents.

An Increase in Pressures on the Business Community

The social activist groups have been quite successful. One has but to look at the plethora of income transfer and entitlement programs, and at the vast body of governmental regulation of private enterprise, to grasp the magnitude of changes they have helped effect in the U.S. economic and sociopolitical systems. It is unlikely that the trend toward conservatism in the United States will have a significant effect on the activities of new groups or reduce their pressures on the business community. While the public may have become disillusioned with government-imposed solutions, the nature of today's problems has not changed, nor has people's perception of the inadequacy of response by private enterprise and market forces. The highly successful efforts by the conservationists' lobby in thwarting Reagan Administration efforts to relax environmental controls and regulations represent but one example.[6] Thus, with every contraction in the government's role, one can anticipate a corresponding increase in pressures on the business community. The new constituencies will be active in ensuring that business is held accountable and delivers on the promise of public welfare through market-based solutions.

An important reason why the business community has been largely unable to deal effectively with new social activist groups lies in the failure of the business community to recognize the importance of the academic community both as the core group and as a prime source of ideas that later become causes célèbres for various new constituencies and are elevated to major public concerns.

When the business community responds to government initiatives for new regulations, media charges of unethical or antisocial behavior, or social activists' demands for greater public accountability for their actions, it is in fact reacting to ideas that originally were sprouted in academe and later became institutionalized into concrete policy objectives and programs. The business community has had minimal input during the idea formulation stage because it has lacked adequate and reliable access to the academic community.

History tells us that a preponderance of new approaches to action emanate from ideas that are nurtured by academicians and scholars whose primary goal is to question the status quo—to search for what could be rather than to accept what is, and to challenge established values and institutions in spite of the fact that they work, not because of it.

Business, then, must have three types of rationale—economic, political, and intellectual—to seek and maintain societal legitimacy for its survival and growth. Historically, business has been quite successful in maintaining its economic basis for societal support. It has also maintained a satisfactory political rationale for societal legitimacy. This has been possible through a strategy of creative adaptation to changing societal needs and expectations and has included an assiduous cultivation of relevant constituency groups. Unfortunately, business has not yet succeeded in building a sustained level of interaction with the academic community and has suffered a severe erosion in its intellectual support for societal legitimacy.

Business's Approach to the Academic Community

It is the contention of the author that business must develop a new approach to dealing with the academic community—an approach based not only on what business expects of the academic community but, equally important, on how the academic community perceives itself and its expectations of the business community. Business has a critical need for support by the academic community to stem the steady erosion of its societal and intellectual legitimacy, and to play a more effective role in the formation of the public agenda by gaining entrance into the academic community during the idea-formulation stage.

A conceptual framework is presented in this article to analyze the differences between the business and academic communities on three dimensions—core values, objectives and goals, and organizational structures—that give rise to particular strategies pursued by the two institutions. Also provided here is a set of criteria by which to classify various academic groups along the dimensions of their relative importance to the issue life-cycle and their responsiveness to the types of strategies available to the business community. And finally, issue-strategy matrixes are developed to help business select those strategies that are most likely to evoke effective responses from the relevant academic groups.

It must be noted here that no amount of concept development and strategy selection criteria is likely to be effective if the business community views this exercise as getting the academic community to do its bidding. Instead, the ultimate objectives of building effective academic community relations for business should be:

To gain entrance into the academic community as a source of ideas and viewpoints that deserve equal hearing and consideration on their own merits, rather than as a quid pro quo for providing financial support or other substantive considerations.

To convert a relationship from an essentially dormant and mutually suspicious mode to a primarily active mode with the promise of raising the threshold of trust.

To build bridges between business and various segments of the academic community through facilitation and encouragement of an open exchange of ideas, attitudes, and experiences between the two groups. It is hoped that this process will create a lasting understanding and respect for each other's value set, modus operandi, and achievement criteria. This would make it possible for the institutions to work together toward their mutual gain, and for the common good.

Before discussing the new conceptual framework and strategic approaches to managing business-academic community relations, it may be beneficial to analyze briefly the relative strengths and shortcomings of some of the traditional business approaches to the academic community.

Recruitment-Related Activities

Corporate executives establish contacts with those universities and professors that are sources of potential employees—especially professional and managerial-level employees. Contacts are maintained both at the staff level and by line executives, through formal and informal channels.

There is generally a good follow-up system. Corporate recruiting officers build long-term relationships with college placement executives and important faculty members. University people, in turn, are able to bring together students and potential employers in an environment of mutual respect and trust, thereby making the recruitment effort quite positive, amiable, and efficient. The recruitment effort is supported and reinforced by such corporate philanthropic activities as scholarships and funding for program development and curriculum enrichment.

The practice of industry support for universities, confined largely to activities keyed to direct-measurable benefits, has a major drawback in that cost-benefit analyses either by the universities or by the business community cannot always be taken for granted. Business support is not always sustained on an enlightened basis. For example, U.S. universities have been experiencing severe shortages of faculty and specialized equipment, and there is a decline in Ph.D. enrollments in such fields as engineering, computer sciences, and business. The universities do not have adequate funds to purchase modern equipment and hire and retain talented individuals for research and teaching. Although some highly ambitious and innovative efforts have recently been announced by individual corporations and industry groups, the situation is still quite precarious, and is not likely to improve significantly in the foreseeable future.[7]

Sponsored or Contract Research and Specialized Program Support

Business may provide special grants to sponsor research in areas offering promise of significant impact on a company or industry's activities. The university may enter into a contractual arrangement under which one or more corporations will undertake to finance research in return for the exclusive right to commercial exploitation of products resulting from such research. The tobacco industry may support a research effort to discover potentially hazardous links between smoking and tobacco. Pharmaceutical and cosmetics industries may sponsor research in genetics, molecular biology, or toxic side-effects of certain chemicals. Engineering and electronics industries may support research in the properties of various structures and even in theoretical physics, assuming possible future industrial applications.[8]

The quid pro quo between corporate support and an academic institution's response in such cases is direct and measurable. The avowed corporate objective is to support basic research that would help resolve some of the major questions pertaining to public health and safety when an industry's products and services are involved. This goal in itself is eminently worthwhile and member corporations in the industry concerned rightly deserve credit for pursuing the goal.

Problems sometimes arise even in this category of business-academic community relations and must be handled with care. Where research is narrowly based and primarily concerned with alternative ways of solving a practical problem, the relationship is mutually rewarding and highly satisfactory. Questions of academic freedom, however, arise when (a) the findings of contracted research are kept secret, and (b) the research scientists demand faculty status with all its attendant rights, knowing they cannot or will not fulfill some of the obligations normally mandatory with the acquisition of status.[9] Moreover, academic research seldom comes neatly packaged from a single source. Instead, discoveries are built on knowledge painfully gained but freely dispersed and shared. The process of discovery itself may be slowed if it is fractionated and if potentially important links in the building blocks of scientific inquiry are kept secret because of contractual constraints imposed by a funding source.

Other problems may arise when different parts of the academic community act quite independently of each other in apparent disregard of the interests of the universities to which they belong. Thus, while MIT and Harvard were receiving funds from major corporations for their nuclear engineering research, some of their scientists were publicly denouncing the growth of nuclear power production.

Institutional Support of High Public Visibility

A third area of corporate support of the academic community has been through participation in programs that meet some long-term needs of an institution and may also generate highly visible publicity and good will for the corporation. Broadly defined, these programs include those involving contributions in building construction, establishment of endowed chairs in various academic/professional fields, and funding of research centers that advocate certain philosophies and viewpoints, and do not merely concentrate their activities within specific areas of academic inquiry. These programs help an academic institution's long-term interests but provide those outside the institution very limited scope for influencing program quality or direction, thus causing many corporate executives to question the desirability of contributions.[10]

Summary of Business Approaches

Basic approaches to building business-academic community relations are highly laudable and can be very useful in specific circumstances. However, they have three drawbacks:

1. They reach only a small part of the academic community as defined in earlier sections of this article.

2. They are primarily institution-centered. Thus, their impact on specific programs is at best indirect and at worst minimal.

3. Educational support programs of most corporations are indistinguishable from one another. They lack elements of innovativeness and flexibility, the two necessary ingredients for making such programs instruments of effective corporate strategy.

A Strategic Framework to Improve Business-Academic Relationships

Having discussed the relative strengths and weaknesses of traditional business approaches to dealing with the academic community, we turn now to the development of a new framework that can:

Delineate and define the sources of business-academic community tensions and conflicts.

Provide a systematic approach to ameliorate tensions and generate more timely and effective corporate responses.

One important fact must be noted. While the framework, in its generalized form, can be utilized in developing effective strategies for more conventional aspects of industry-academic community relations, its prime significance lies in its usage (a) in analyzing those emerging issues of public policy that lie outside the domain of traditional areas of industrial-university relations, and (b) in those rare instances where the business community has no effective means of entrance into the academic community, or, for some other reason, has little or no influence during the idea-formulation stage.

The components of this framework are:

1. An understanding of the differences in the nature of the two institutions. It incorporates such elements as the intellectual core or value set of the institution, and the institution's mission, goals, leadership style, and organizational structure and dynamics.

2. A system of categorizing the academic community into segments that have both greater identity with particular corporate goals and closer correspondence with specific public-policy issues of particular concern to individual corporations and industry groups.

3. Development of a system of issue-strategy matrixes that analyzes the growth of an issue on a life-cycle spectrum, and identifies and evaluates various corporate strategies in terms of their effectiveness in reaching targeted segments of the academic community.

Nature of the Corporation

The intellectual core and value set of the corporate entity lie in the basic right of individuals to combine their resources to produce goods and services that society needs and at prices competitively determined in the marketplace. The success of a corporation is determined in direct proportion to its ability to serve public needs. Profits are a measure of a corporation's reward for doing a job well. In the strict sense of the word, the most profitable corporation is also the most socially responsible corporation, for it has satisfied the needs of a larger segment of society.

This is, however, a very narrow construction of the social role of capitalism in general, and of corporations in particular. As noted earlier, the market system is not a perfect mechanism; it requires at least a certain degree of state supervision to enforce the rules of the game. Moreover, as Irving Kristol points out, the virtue of capitalism lies not so much in its ability to create wealth and allow men to be selfish, as in its ability to provide a system of social rewards and benefits that people consider just, fair, and equitable.[11]

A corporation's goals are reasonably well defined both from the perspective of the corporation's traditional external constituencies (current and potential investors) and its internal constituencies (management and employees). One of the most important characteristics of these goals is that they are embodied in the institution of the corporation itself. Thus, while there may be marginal differences between various constituencies as to the magnitude and rate of goal achievement, the overall identity with the institution's goals remains unchallenged. This monolithic intensity demanded by the corporation of its employees provides the corporation with the power to shape to its own ends the outlook of those who serve it.

Corporate goals also are defined in specific terms measurable both in terms of quantity and over time. Rewards for individual performance are closely tied to the achievement of corporate goals. One consequence is that managers may emphasize the development of those qualities that require narrow specialization and have a high degree of relevance to corporate functions.[12]

The organizational structure of the corporation is essentially hierarchical in character. Increased authority for action runs parallel to an ever enlarging responsibility for performance and rests in successively fewer hands. Although entry into the system by individual employees is voluntary, there are high exit barriers created through a system of rewards and penalties that increase with length of tenure, and dissuade an employee from leaving the corporation and from acting counter to its interests. Thus, within broad limits, the top management and especially the chief executive officer set not only the rhythm and work-style for the corporation, but also the moral tone and how the company relates to its external constituencies and responds to changing societal expectations.

Nature of the Academic Community

The institution of our concern has been defined here as the academic community and not the university. This distinction is fundamental to an understanding of the problems that exist in dealing with this amorphous constituency. Unlike a corporation in which the institutional entity and those who work for it share a commonality of purpose, a university and academic community are not one and the same. Failure to recognize this crucial difference will most likely lead to an erroneous understanding of the institution, the development of wrong strategies to deal with it, and a faulty analysis and interpretation of probable outcomes.

The intellectual core and value set of the academic community consist of two elements: the discovery of new knowledge or unfettered search for inquiry, and the efficient transmission of knowledge or accumulated experience of earlier genera-tions to the present one.

There is considerable confusion and misunderstanding among large segments of the population, including members of the business community, the news media, and politicians, about the proper role of a university. This stems in part from equating teaching only with the transmission of accumulated knowledge, and not with crea-tion of new knowledge. The teacher-scholar is criticized, especially in major "elite" universities, for not spending enough time teaching in the classroom. This criticism overlooks the more fundamental issue of the quality of knowledge being transmitted. The argument of balance between the two functions is somewhat spurious because it implies a priori understanding of how much time it would or should take to pur-sue a given line of inquiry, and when the inquiry should be considered completed.

Another major problem has to do with the measurement of performance. While it is relatively easy to count the number of students graduated or the degrees awarded by a university, the quality of education imparted can be measured only indirectly and after a long period of time.

The research and scholarship aspects of a university are even more difficult to measure. Those of us in the academic community take just pride in a multitude of medical discoveries, scientific inventions, or engineering breakthroughs, but we recognize them only at their fruition stage. In this process, the work of hundreds of scholars carried out over many years is often unknown to all but those researchers and scholars who build their work on the earlier findings of other scholars. For example, today's management practices would not have been possible without the contributions of social scientists from various disciplines such as economics, social psychology, computer sciences, mathematics, and so forth.

The contribution of social sciences to society can be judged only in historical terms. Harvard University's president, Derek Bok, contends that the pursuit of knowledge and understanding is in itself of greatest value. "Research and scholar-ship," he says, "offer us a continuing critique of our values, our behavior, our in-stitutions, and our social practices with benefits that eventually touch the lives and learning of all students at all levels of education, and indeed of all human beings who seek to broaden their understanding."[13]

The similarity of a university to a corporation, however, is far greater in style and structure than in substance. The university has two products or services to offer the community:

1. *The training of students and the quality of education they receive.* The cost of this product or service, however, is not related to its market worth; the students do not pay fees based on their potential earnings nor do the employers con-tribute to the welfare of the university in a way directly attributable to the benefits they receive from the university.

2. *The creation and discovery of new knowledge.* By its very nature, all basic research produced by scholars becomes public property. In their pursuit of knowledge, scholars publish their research soon after it is completed so that others can

build on it. No financial benefits that accrue to society are captured by the creators of the new ideas. Thus, the university is in an unusual position. It internalizes most of its costs while it externalizes most of its gains. The process is exactly the reverse of that used by private economic institutions.

The goals of the university are not easily defined in precise and measurable terms. In abstract terms, the goals of the university are (a) the pursuit of knowledge and excellence, and (b) the transmission of that knowledge to society without outside or inside interference. These facts underscore the importance of a number of issues in terms of the business community's ability and effectiveness in dealing with the academic community.

1. The organizational structure of a university is collegial. Decisions are made through a collectivity of individuals. The locus points for decision making are scattered among various groups. University administrators have only limited scope to channel the intellectual resources of a university in a particular direction. The university and its administrators see their self-worth in providing a hospitable environment in which the scholars may work and impart knowledge to students. Even the criteria for quality of research are established and judged by the faculty.

2. The abstract nature of the goal set also implies that various faculty members within the same university espouse ideas, advance theories, and offer solutions to a given set of research problems that would be quite different form each other. In a corporate entity, such a state of affairs would be considered inimical to the corporation's best interests. In an academic community, however, it would be considered quite normal and healthy.

3. In the corporate community, the prestige, social status, and sense of professional achievement of an executive are closely identified with those of his firm, and the executive's success is associated with the growth and prosperity of the firm. For an academician, however, work is the primary focal point of self-worth and the institution merely a place to carry it out.

4. In the academic community, a scholar-teacher identifies his goals primarily with those of professional peers and only secondarily with the university where he works. He achieves recognition and stature largely through his peers' acceptance of the quality of his research. Even his reward system at the university of his employment, and indeed the stature of the university where he works, are determined by the degree of his recognition among his peers.

5. A scholar's stature and influence among his peers increase in direct proportion to his success in discovering the truth as he sees it and his ability to offer new answers to unsolved problems. The few who reach this pinnacle of success exercise influence that is out of all proportion to their numbers. The vast majority of other academicians who follow these researcher-scholars do so not because the latter offer reinforcement for established values, but because they have successfully questioned conventional wisdom.

6. The spheres of influence and communication networks in the academic community are not confined to institutional boundaries, but overlap institutional and even professional affiliations. Therefore, an academic institution is not an appropriate unit of analysis in developing corporate strategies for building networks with the academic community.

Segmentation of the Academic Community

The next stage in the development of our strategic framework is to redefine major segments of the academic community so as to form internally cohesive and separately identifiable groups, which must be reached via different types of corporate strategies. As noted earlier, members of the academic community pursue different sets of goals, operate on different principles, and measure their performance from both the institutional and the individual perspective. They employ criteria different than those used by members of the corporate community. Thus, an exclusive or even major reliance on universities as the primary units for our attention and program-focusing would be highly inefficient in terms of resource utilization. We must, therefore, classify the relevant academic community into segments that are clearly identifiable and internally cohesive—those that have minimum within-group variability and maximum between-group variability. They should have similar programmatic and information needs, and should be reachable through similar communication networks. This is accomplished through the application of two principles: (1) community of interest, and (2) concentric circles of influence.

The community of interest principle implies that membership is based on organizational and informational needs of the group (see figure 1). The group is identified through its institutional boundaries, which are facilitative in character. A member may belong to more than one group at any given time. Group membership requires some action on the part of a member. Interaction between different groups is primarily at the institutional level. Organization of the group is generally quite structured and leadership is formalized. Top leaders have an important and active role in the functioning of the group. Examples of groups based on the community of interest principle are universities and colleges, professional and trade associations, and economic institutions such as corporations and banks.

The concentric circles of influence principle divides relevant segments of a group in terms of their common core (see figure 2). From that core, influence spreads in waves through a ripple effect. The institutional boundaries of the group are amorphous. Group membership is not based on what a member does, but on how his or her actions influence members of other relevant groups. The leadership of the group is not formalized and is constantly changing. Group members are bound together more through a community of purpose than a commonality of outcome.

The application of the principle of concentric circles of influence will yield academic community segments that are most relevant for our purposes. In some cases, however, the community of interest principle may provide us with segments that are particularly suited for a given locality or region, or that may offer significant communication economies for reaching multiple groups developed under the concentric circles of influence principle.

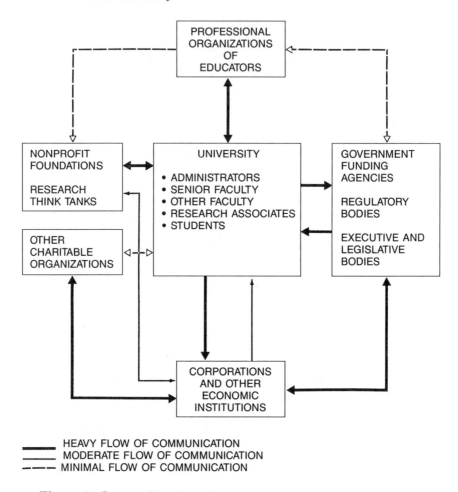

Figure 1. Groups Based on "Community of Interest" Principle

Based on the two principles, we can divide the entire academic community into four generalized segment-types that can be more efficiently reached and cultivated by the business community. Each corporation and industry group, however, must develop custom-made segments in response to specific issues of public policy or corporate needs. These segment-types are:

Intellectual Elites and Thought Leaders (INTELIT).

Emulators and Disseminators of Ideas (EDIS).

Young Turks and Budding Scholars (YOBUD).

University and College Administrators (UNIADMIN).

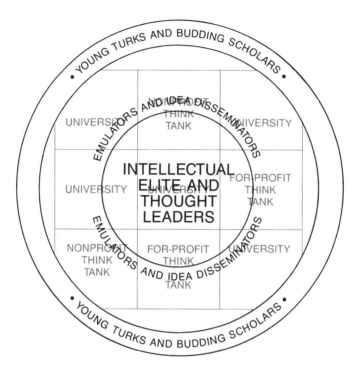

Figure 2. Groups Based on "Concentric Circle of Influence" Principle

Intellectual Elites and Thought Leaders (INTELIT). The inability to reach this group lies at the heart of most of the difficulties experienced by the business community in having its views become an integral part of the idea-development process in American society. It may also account for a large measure of the business community's difficulty in playing an appropriately important role in the determination of the nation's public agenda. Therefore, this group must be the primary focus of our inquiry and attention.

This category includes top academicians, scholars and researchers widely recognized for ideas and influence through their writings and public speaking. In terms of the long-term objective of the business-academic community relations specified earlier, it should be clear that intellectual elites are not limited to the areas of business and economics. Instead, we must also include scholars in the humanities, social sciences, and physical sciences who are concerned with similar issues. In the humanities, for example, scholars in such disciplines as philosophy, religion, history, and literature, have had notable impacts on our understanding of values, social ordering, and relative roles of public and private institutions in social organization. In the social sciences, certain other relevant disciplines, in addition to economics, are sociology and political science.

A simplified description of the process whereby ideas are generated among the intellectual elites and thought leaders is found in figure 3. It shows the diffusion of ideas until they are integrated into the public lexicon and become accepted parts of the national political and public agendas. Stage 1 describes the process of idea formulation and definition. Ideas are floated in terms of theories that are constantly debated, repeatedly tested against other probable scenarios, and refined and retried until a consensus is reached, only for the cycle to be repeated. Finally, the idea becomes a viable theory and moves into the broader public domain.

At this critical stage of theory generation, corporations and their spokespersons, as shown in figure 3, have little or minimal inputs into the system. This has occurred both by design and default. Pespectives on economic rationality or capitalism that may be introduced into the system emanate largely from the business and economic scholars who are part of the intellectual elite. Either that, or the perspectives are acquired via the news media. In the case of business and economic scholars, these perspectives may represent idealized and abstract versions of capitalism and market economy. In the case of other scholars, they may represent stereotypes. The situation is highly unsatisfactory. In each case, it leaves a large void in terms of informational inputs that should be integral parts of theory formulation.

Figure 3 also shows that business scanning processes do become aware of new ideas as they move from Idea Creation Stage to Limited Diffusion and Adoption Stage. At this juncture, however, most of the information remains with the technical or planning staff people within the organizations concerned. It is not transmitted to line executives or management. Corporate management generally becomes aware of these new ideas once they (a) have passed the Limited Diffusion and Adoption Stage, (b) have become part of the political agenda, and (c) are on their way to becoming part of the public agenda. The elapsed time in the process may be extended to three years or even more. By then, management's choices have become limited to reactive or defensive responses.

Emulators and Disseminators of Ideas (EDIS). This group consists of a majority of all other educators who influence vast bodies of students through classroom teachings and who espouse, articulate, and synthesize ideas developed by members of the first group—intellectual elites and thought leaders.

Young Turks and Budding Scholars (YOBUD). In this group are two types of persons: (a) research-oriented junior faculty members spotted as up-and-coming scholars, and (b) graduate students with high potential.

University and College Administrators (UNIADMIN). This group is made up of college and university administrators. Their administrative positions lend them stature and credibility at the local or national level, depending on the prestige of the university. Many of these administrators are also researchers and scholars, and command much public attention when they speak out on issues of public policy. The primary concerns of the members of this group are those of brick and mortar,

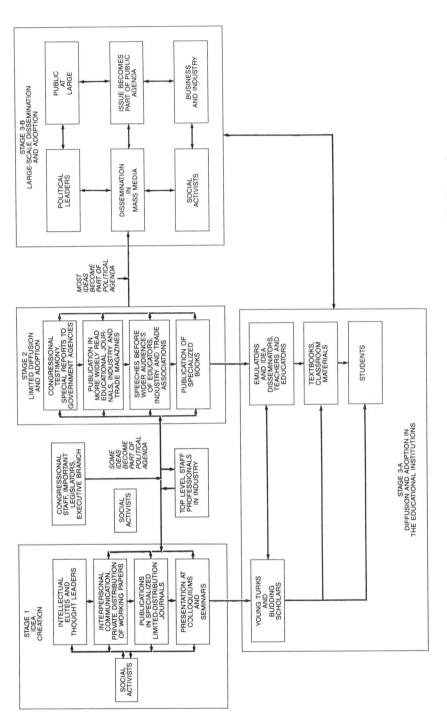

Figure 3. Process of Diffusion and Adoption of Ideas in the Public Domain

operating budgets, and program quality. However, the members also play signifi-cant roles in raising issues pertaining to higher education and national policy.

Issue-Strategy Matrixes

The impact of a constituency group's activities on a corporation's policies and opera-tions must depend, to a large extent, on the nature of the issue under contention and review. To be relevant, a strategic plan for academic community relations, or any other constituency relations, must be developed within the context of a specific time horizon and relate to a particular social issue of concern to the special consti-tuency in question.

Developing an effective issue-strategy mix requires two components: the issue-environment matrix and the issue-management matrix.

The Issue-Environment Matrix

The first aspect of this matrix[14] deals with the definition of the external environ-ment or the context within which the corporate response is made and evaluated. The second aspect deals with the categorization of the types of corporate responses.

The impact of the external environment on a problem and the effectiveness of a corporate response can best be evaluated in terms of the life cycle of that prob-lem. This is accomplished by dividing the elapsed time between the emergence of a problem and its solution and ultimate elimination into four stages: (a) pre-problem, (b) identification, (c) remedy and relief, and (d) prevention. During the pre-problem stage, the social effects of market externalities or second-order effects are highly diffused and, taken individually, are not significant in terms of their impact on either the corporation or the affected parties. However, when similar acts are performed by a large number of companies and are continued over a long period, their cumulative effect is substantial. When that happens, a problem is born.

The elapsed time at the pre-problem stage is probably the longest of all the four steps, although there is a tendency for the time span to become narrower with increasing industrialization. Most individuals and institutions respond to the prob-lem passively. Their efforts are aimed at adaptation, and the problem is treated as given.

Once the impact of a problem has become significant enough, there is a drive among the affected groups to define it, identify its causes, and relate it to the source. This is one of the most difficult stages in the entire process. The changing state of technology, the compound effect of multiple factors on the occurrence of a prob-lem, and the lack of adequate data—plus the possibly delayed emergence of symp-toms when the causes have long gone—all combine to make problem identification difficult. The definition of the problem may also involve the vested interest or value-orientation of a particlar group.

This period is characterized by intense social conflict between contending groups in terms of where to assign blame for the problem. Public perception of corporate behavior during the pre-problem and problem-identification stages determines the extent of flexibility available to corporations in later stages.

Conflict and Cooperation

Once a causal linkage has been established, the question of compensatory and/or punitive damages to the affected parties must be considered. The remedy and relief stage is often marked by both conflict and cooperation between opposing groups as they seek to maximize the protection available to injured parties while passing the burden for payment to "those" who can most afford to pay—the government. The roles played by the courts, legislatures, and executive and administrative agencies of government assume greater importance here than in other stages.

The prevention stage is not sequential, but generally overlaps with the problem-identification and remedy and relief stages. The prevention stage involves a large measure of uncertainty and difficulty in making an accurate appraisal of potential costs and benefits. It is not uncommon to find a high degree of self-righteousness in the pronouncements of various groups—pronouncements that may be long on rhetoric but short on substance. Groups tend to advocate solutions that favor their particular viewpoints. They also tend to understate the potential costs to other groups with opposing viewpoints.

There are three types of corporate responses to nonmarket societal factors. These responses emerge because (a) there is pressure for the business to minimize the second-order effects of its activities; (b) there is the desire to become a good corporate citizen; and (c) the sociopolitical environment calls for greater corporate participation in the determination of the national agenda. The three patterns can be defined as social obligation, social responsibility, and social responsiveness.

Corporate behavior in response to market forces or legal constraints is defined as social obligation. The criteria for legitimacy in this arena are economic and legal only. A social obligation response is essentially defensive in character, and is generally used in the pre-problem stage. When used in other stages of the issue life cycle, it leaves little flexibility for the corporation to modify its behavior without paying high economic and social costs.

A social responsibility pattern of corporate response implies bringing corporate behavior up to a level where it is in congruence with currently prevailing social norms, values, and performance expectations. It does not require a radical departure from normal patterns of corporate activities or behavior. While the concept of social obligation is proscriptive in nature, the concept of social responsibility is prescriptive and interactive.

The third stage of the adaptation of corporate behavior to societal needs is in terms of social responsiveness. The corporation is expected to anticipate the changes that may be the result of the corporation's current activities, or that may be due to the emergence of social problems in which the corporation must play an important role. Again, while activities related to social responsibility are prescriptive in nature, activities related to social responsiveness are proactive.

The appropriateness of a given corporate response pattern will depend, to a large extent, on the stage of the issue life cycle, the patterns of responses adopted by other corporations and industry groups similarly placed, the nature of constituency groups and the intensity of their advocacy, and prior public expectations based on a corporation's behavior in similar situations in the past.

Figure 4 presents a grid pattern showing the relationship between the intensity of an issue and the corporate response pattern through the stages or life cycle of issue evolution. It is important to note that the speed with which an issue moves from an emerging to a critical stage is, from the corporation's viewpoint, largely determined through an interaction between external environmental forces and patterns of corporate responses.

When an issue is in the pre-problem stage, there is, of course, little public awareness of it, let alone an intensity of public concern. If the corporate response is either that of social responsibility or social responsiveness, the public's attitude

INTENSITY OF THE ISSUE →

STAGES OF ISSUE EVOLUTION

DIMENSIONS OF CORPORATE BEHAVIOR	PRE-PROBLEM STAGE	IDENTIFI- CATION STAGE	REMEDY & RELIEF STAGE	PREVENTION STAGE
SOCIAL OBLIGATION				X CRITICAL ISSUE
SOCIAL RESPONSI- BILITY				
SOCIAL RESPONSIVE- NESS	X EMERGING ISSUE			

INTENSITY OF CORPORATE RESPONSE

Figure 4. Grid Pattern for Determining the Life Cycle of an Issue from "Emerging" to "Critical"

toward the corporation will likely be highly positive. It is then unlikely that the issue will subsequently create social conflict, regardless of the efforts of groups that might wish otherwise. A failure to accurately perceive the intensity of an issue, and thereby develop a suitable response, will most likely contribute to a loss of trust in business by influential thought leaders and eventually by large segments of the public.

The Issue-Management Matrix

The final stage in our analysis brings together the elements of issue identification, selection of appropriate academic community segments, and development of corporate strategies that will generate positive responses from the targeted academics. Once a sociopolitical issue has reached the critical stage, it is obviously much too late for the business community to develop long-term strategies. Instead, all attention must be devoted to containing the extent of damage. An issue may reach the critical stage because the entire business community or individual corporations have failed to develop appropriate responses during the early stages of the issue's life cycle.

The best strategy for the business community is to develop coalitions with the academic community when an issue is still in the pre-problem stage. Other things being equal, the societal life cycle of an issue generally parallels the growth of a product or an industry. Thus, the expansion of the chemical industry would go hand in hand with the problem of toxic waste disposal. Therefore, planning for the amelioration of second-order effects must begin at the same time. It should be an integral part of the corporation's growth strategy. At this stage, the role of intellectual elites and thought leaders (INTELIT) becomes critical. The following process can facilitate the development of an effective strategy to reach an INTELIT group:

1. *There is a specific INTELIT group for a given class of issues.* Members of the group can be identified through their writings in scholarly journals and books, testimony at congressional hearings, professorships in top universities, and peer-group references. INTELIT groups for specific issues are likely to be fairly small, generally ranging between fifty and two hundred members, and must be carefully identified and tracked.

2. *The corporation should try to learn as much as possible about the research interests of INTELIT members.* The objective is to build a higher threshold of trust between the INTELIT members and the corporation. The expectation is that, during the idea formulation stage, INTELIT members will seek out and evaluate business viewpoints with the same degree of objectivity and care as they give to other sources of information. This trust can only be built over a long period of time. The corporation must respect the researcher-scholar's academic integrity and freedom of inquiry. It must be prepared to continue its cooperation even when an individual INTELIT scholar's conclusions turn out to be contrary to the corporation's interests.

3. *Programs can be developed to establish and sustain contacts with the members of the appropriate INTELIT groups.* Once a company learns of a scholar's interest in a research project, it can offer to provide information, which has been collected through corporate sources and would not otherwise be available to the scholar. This should be a continuing process and should start long before the company has any reason to seek the scholar's help in a particular case. In addition, corporations can organize specific programs that facilitate cross-fertilization and exchanges of ideas among INTELIT members.

The types of individual programs will depend on the needs of the INTELIT group, the resources of the corporation, and the nature of the issue. It should be kept in mind, however, that no strategy for reaching an INTELIT group is likely to be successful if (a) the corporation's general response mode is that of "social obligation"—reactive and defensive; (b) its commitment is intermittent and based on ad hoc considerations; and (c) the company is unwilling to change its position despite new findings or overwhelming consensus in the INTELIT group.

When contacts with the INTELIT group are established in the pre-problem stage, the INTELIT group can be most helpful to the corporation in the identification, and remedy and relief stages of the issue life cycle, providing credibility to the corporate viewpoint. The corporation, however, must be seen in the social responsibility mode. In the prevention stage of the issue life cycle, when new solutions are being developed, INTELIT group support cannot be taken for granted. A great deal of uncertainty will exist at this stage as to costs, technical feasibility, and perceived equity and fairness, or political viability, of various solutions. The corporation is likely to achieve greater understanding of its viewpoint if its strategies are in the social responsive mode—that is, if they are anticipatory and proactive.

Figure 5 presents a strategic grid for issues management. The INTELIT group is most important when an issue is in cells 3 and 7. The establishment of effective contact with the INTELIT group is a prerequisite for a sustained relationship with two other groups—the Emulators and Disseminators of Ideas (EDIS) and the Young Turks and Budding Scholars (YOBUD).

EDIS is by far the largest group in the academic community and is most useful when an issue is in cells 2, 4, and 5. The objective is to keep the issue from reaching a critical stage by moving to cells 1 and 7. The effective strategy for servicing this group is to provide it with good material that group members can use in their roles as teachers. The strategies must fall within the social responsibility mode. The corporation must be seen as striving to meet legitimate societal expectations when the issue has reached the problem identification and remedy and relief stages.

The Young Turks and Budding Scholars (YOBUD) respond to the same approaches as established intellectual elites. They also are identified and reached through the same channels as the INTELIT group members. The YOBUD group, however, is more amorphous and requires special handling. The corporation can encourage this group to choose research projects where there may be a mutuality

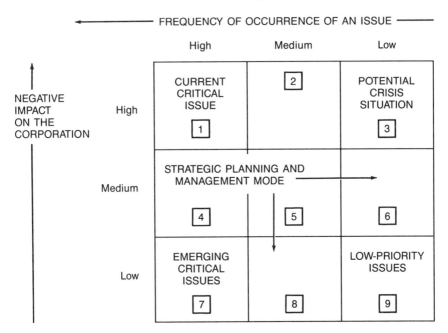

Figure 5. Strategic Grid for Social Issues Management

of interest. These projects will fall in cells 6, 8, and 9. At the same time, group members may be particularly sensitive to corporate contacts and may construe any offer of help as an effort at buy-out. Where possible, members of the YOBUD group should be contacted through INTELIT members who will often act as mentors and associates of the young scholars.

The UNIADMIN group responds to the strategies that most corporations use in their existing university relations programs. It should be apparent that strategies developed for the INTELIT group have a spillover effect on all other groups. Furthermore, strategies designed for each segment of the academic community must be mutually consistent and respond equally both to the needs of the corporaticn and those of the targeted groups in the academic community.

Notes

Reprinted from the *Public Affairs Review*, 1983. Copyright © 1983 by the Public Affairs Council.

1. Council for Financial Aid to Education, New York. Clifton R. Wharton, Jr., "Corporate Giving and the Public University." *The Corporate Director* (July–August 1982), pp. 12–16.

2. "Dow Shalt Not Kill" in S. Prakash Sethi, *Up Against the Corporate Wall: Modern Corporations and Social Issues of the Seventies,* 1st edition (Englewood Cliffs, N.J.: Prentice-Hall, 1971), pp. 236–266.

3. "Harvard Sells Citicorp Issues in Apartheid Protest," *New York Times,* February 19, 1981, p. 37. Roger M. Williams, "American Business Should Stay in South Africa," *Saturday Review,* March 30, 1978, pp. 14–21. *General Motors Interest Report 1980.* U.S. Congress, *United States Private Investments in South Africa,* Hearings before the Subcommittee on Africa and on International Economic Policy and Trade of the Committee on International Relations, 95th Congress, 2nd Session, 1978. Derek C. Bok, "Reflections on the Ethical Responsibilities of the University in Society: An Open Letter to the Harvard Community"; "Reflections on Divestment of Stock: An Open Letter to the Harvard Community"; "Reflections on Boycotts: An Open Letter to the Harvard Community," Supplements to the Harvard University *Gazette,* March 9, April 6, and May 18, 1979.

4. Numerous examples of recent corporate-university agreements would indicate that such cooperative arrangements are likely to continue in the future. See for example: "Business and Universities: A New Partnership," *Business Week,* December 20, 1982; Ann Crittenden, "Universities' Accord Called Research Aid," *New York Times,* September 12, 1981, p. 32; "W.R. Grace to Fund Research by MIT on Biotechnology," *The Wall Street Journal,* August 3, 1982; David P. Garino, "Monsanto Slowly But Deliberately Shifts Emphasis to Research, Patented Products," *The Wall Street Journal,* January 13, 1983, p. 25.

5. Peat, Marwick, Mitchell & Co., *The University-Industry Relationship in Perspective— Report to the Corporate Liaison Committee of Cornell University,* New York, October 1981.

6. William Symonds, "Washington in the Grip of the Green Giant," *Fortune,* October 4, 1982, p. 136.

7. Carolyn Phillips, "Universities in U.S. Are Losing Ground in Computer Education," *The Wall Street Journal,* January 14, 1983, p. 1. Examples of some recently announced programs for enhanced university support are those of Exxon, IBM, SOHIO, and the semiconductor industry.

8. *Business Week,* December 20, 1982.

9. See for example, Stanley Klein, "A Fracas Over Funds Roils M.I.T.," *New York Times,* November 15, 1981, p. F1; Ann Crittenden, "Industry Role in the Academia," *New York Times,* July 22, 1981, p. 25; Paul E. Gray, "M.I.T. Wants Closer Ties With Business," *New York Times,* September 27, 1981, p. F2.

10. For two discussions of the issue of industry support of education, see Paul L. Montgomery, "Why Corporations Fund Study of Big Business," *New York Times,* March 3, 1981, pp. 15, 17; Rochelle L. Stanfield, "Campuses and Corporations: Industry Offers Money, But Not Without Strings," *National Affairs,* November 29, 1980, pp. 2021–2024.

11. Irving Kristol, "When Virtue Loses All Her Loveliness: Some Reflections on Capitalism and the 'Free Society'," *The Public Interest* (Fall 1970), pp. 3–16.

12. Robert H. Hayes and William J. Abernathy, "Managing Our Way to Economic Decline," *Harvard Business Review* (July–August 1980), pp. 67–77.

13. Derek Bok, "Reflections on the Ethical Responsibilities of the University in Society: An Open Letter to the Harvard Community," supplement to the Harvard University *Gazette,* March 9, 1979.

14. For a more detailed explanation of this model see S. Prakash Sethi, "A Conceptual Framework for Environmental Analysis of Social Issues and Evaluation of Business Response Patterns," *Academy of Mangement Review,* January 1979, pp. 63–74.

6

Sources of Public Pressures

Citizen Activism and Corporate Political Strategies:
Evolution from 1970–1985
John M. Holcomb

While the formal institutions of government—the Congress, the presidency, and the courts—are the arenas of power in U.S. politics, it is now widely accepted that interest groups are pivotal political actors. They participate at every stage in the public-policy cycle. Through the studies they produce, the visibility of their leaders, and their access to reporters and the news media, they can often place issues on the public-policy agenda. Through their direct and grassroots lobbying activities, they influence the legislative process and policy formulation. Through their litigation activities and participation in regulatory agency proceedings, they play a major role in policy implementation. They can legitimate or undermine public policy through their monitoring and publicity efforts. Finally, through their own research efforts, and outreach to their members and the grassroots, they can assess the impact of public-policy measures. Although informal actors in the policy-making process, political interest groups are critical ones.

Interest groups are so central in the U.S. political process that a group theory of politics has emerged[1] and is the foundation for American political pluralism. Pluralists have concluded that the will of the majority often does not determine public policy, but that minority interests, or coalitions of minorities, often shape the policy outcome. Although most of the interest group literature stresses the importance of occupationally defined groups and other economic interests, recent literature has focused on the importance of noneconomic groups.[2] These studies demonstrate the importance of a group's noneconomic resources as well, reinforcing a conclusion of the earlier interest group literature.

Such noneconomic groups include a wide variety of citizen groups, which will be the focus of this article. They have proliferated at the national, state, and local levels, although national groups have been the most scrutinized in the literature. The first part of this article traces the rise of citizen activism, describes its attributes, and explains the political strategies that citizen organizations have used to advance a host of political issues.

Citizen groups have affected corporations both directly and indirectly. In a direct sense, they have initiated lawsuits against companies, sponsored shareholder resolutions on a host of issues, and launched boycotts and demonstrations. Perhaps their most profound effect on the business community, however, has been accomplished indirectly through their influence on public policy-making. Citizen groups of different types were largely responsible for a laundry list of social regulations that affect industry—on equal employment, environmental protection, employee health, and product safety. Hence, business was forced to deal with citizen activism, in one way or another. The range of responses has been wide, and the typical posture that business has assumed toward its critics has changed dramatically over time. The second section of this article analyzes the various response modes. Finally, future trends and prospects for citizen activism are examined and future research needs are assessed.

Scope and Origin

Ever since James Madison warned of the rising power of factions, political observers have appreciated the power that interest groups wield in our political system. What is unusual about the period since 1960, however, is the growth and prominence of organizations promoting collective benefits for society in general, not just selective benefits for their own constituents or a narrow segment of society. From civil rights and antiwar protests, to citizen action against nuclear power and toxic hazards, the last two decades have witnessed the steady development of new forms of political activity and a resurgence of traditional forms of citizen activism.

The accelerated pace of interest group activity is certainly compatible with our pluralistic political system and what one authority lables "interest group liberalism."[3] However, the wide scope of such activity is new and impressive. One survey, for example, found that there are 53 lobbies for minority groups in Washington, D.C., 33 lobbies for women, 31 environmental lobbies, 15 lobbies representing older Americans, and 6 lobbies advocating population control. Other studies have found the existence of 350 environmental organizations in the country and 8,000 grassroots neighborhood groups.[4] Many interest groups, especially those that have recently formed, view themselves as adversaries of the corporate world or are viewed as such by business.

The reasons for the rapid increase in citizen-organizing are numerous. Certainly the models provided by the civil rights and antiwar movements of the 1960s, and the alienation generated toward large institutions, remain foremost. However, other causes include the failure of the major political parties to perform their traditional functions, the rising power of the media in communicating issues of public concern, the leadership that intellectuals and other activists played in the formation of many interest groups, and the financial support provided by leading foundations and other patrons. The impact of such interest groups is felt both by the government and by business directly. Economist Mancur Olson concludes that the growth of interest groups, especially those connected to business and labor, has contributed to our inflation and economic stagnation.[5] John Gardner, founder of Common Cause, sees a special-interest state that has created paralysis in government decision making. In 1978, so-called single-issue groups began to be the target of much criticism, as both *Time* and *Newsweek* magazines produced cover articles on the phenomenon. Politicians joined the clamor, complaining about the impact of single-issue groups on their decision-making responsibilities and on their re-election campaigns.[6]

Structure and Political Resources

The groups seen as adversaries of business possess a variety of organizational structures. Although most groups have memberships or constituencies, 30 percent in one sample were membership groups.[7] Such organizations usually exist on the financial support of foundations or wealthy donors. Moreover, many groups, even including membership groups, are oligarchic in structure, with organization policy determined by staff members rather than by the mass membership or even the board of directors. Groups like Common Cause and the Sierra Club, however, do stress accountability to their memberships. The ability of organization entrepreneurs to remain fairly independent of membership influence is accentuated by their increasingly diversified funding strategies. Beyond the support derived from wealthy patrons, staff leaders have typically generated other sources of funds—sales of group services or publications, government contracts, and even industry support for conferences or other special projects. Even when national citizen groups have memberships, they are usually drawn from the upper-middle income sector, with a disproportionate share of members having advanced educational degrees. Surveys of the memberships of Common Cause, the League of Women Voters, and several environmental groups verify this conclusion.

There recently has been a rapid growth, however, in groups more democratic in nature, with low-income members, and less dominated by either staff or certainly upper-income members. Whereas many of the older consumer and environmental groups are oligarchic in structure and traditional in function, grassroots neighborhood and local groups are more democratic in structure and novel in their strategies and functions. Such groups may be separate neighborhood organizations, chapters in statewide groups, or components of regional and even national coalitions.[8] Staff functions are provided by many of the community organizers of the 1960s, and memberships of such groups have grown dramatically in the past decade.

While most of the traditional groups seen as adversaries to business developed through the initiative of their leaders rather than spontaneously in response to specific events,[9] the more democratic grassroots groups seem to have evolved in reaction to events and appear to be less dependent on their leaders.

It is important to realize that members and leaders of activist groups are not necessarily advocates of growth in government functions, nor are they by any means traditional socialists in outlook. Those operating at the national level often cannot even be considered radical. Studies of the political opinion and ideology of public-interest group leaders show them to be antistatist and even libertarian in outlook.[10] They are far more interested in having citizens, rather than bureaucrats, exercise power. In this sense, they resemble progressives much more than "New Deal" Democrats.

The political resources that can be tapped by such organizations are typical of the resources of traditional interest groups. *Money* and *membership size* are certainly two traditional political resources. Many of the leading cause-oriented groups are doing quite well in this respect. In 1984, the American Civil Liberties Union (ACLU) had a budget of over $10 million, while the budget of Common Cause, the primary government reform and campaign finance lobby in the country, almost reached that level. The major environmental groups led the way in generating revenue. The National Wildlife Federation had a $41 million budget, while the Audubon Society and the Sierra Club each had over $22 million. The major public-policy think tanks—the American Enterprise Institute, the Heritage Foundation, and the Brookings Institution—also were doing well financially, each having budgets in the $10–15 million range. Some of the cause-oriented groups, especially those of a liberal orientation, grew in membership during the early 1980s, partially in response to policies of the Reagan administration. Environmental groups experienced steady grains in membership while peace and arms control groups grew even more rapidly.[11]

The *grassroots structure* of groups, and their ability to mobilize their members, is a political resource. Common Cause and the Sierra Club, for example, have organizations in virtually every state, and can activate their members on either statewide or national issues. Groups that are seen as part of the "New Right" are flexing similar organizational muscle. Computer tapes of Richard Viguerie, dubbed the direct mail king of the New Right, reportedly contain the names of 20 million Americans that can be mobilized on conservative causes. The Conservative Caucus now has members in over 360 congressional districts. In response to conservative forces and to the growing activism of state legislatures, environmental and consumer groups have attempted to strengthen their grassroots presence in the 1980s. Both the Sierra Club and the National Audubon Society are devoting more resources to their state chapters, while Ralph Nader's Congress Watch has organized a state office in Texas and plans to organize one in Georgia.

Leadership quality and expertise is another important political asset. Among corporate adversary groups, Nader's name is of course foremost. Beyond Nader, however, are a host of other skilled tacticians and experts. In the energy field, Amory

Lovins of Friends of the Earth authored *Soft Energy Paths*, a blueprint for non-nuclear energy alternatives. Jeremy Rifkin is an author and issue entrepreneur whose opposition to genetic engineering in the 1980s has made it a controversial issue. Finally, Lois Gibbs, who led the fight against chemical hazards at Love Canal as head of the Love Canal Homeowners Association, has used her fame and credibility to help victims of toxic waste dumps throughout the country by organizing a Citizens Clearinghouse on Toxic Waste.

The *credibility* or prestige of an organization can be a tremendous political asset. Opinion polls reveal that Nader's credibility remains high with the public, and such organizations as the Sierra Club and Common Cause receive positive reactions as well.[12] The sense of *moral authority* that a group brings to its cause is an important political resource. Members of the Moral Majority, for instance, bring a sense of self-righteousness to their political beliefs, leading them to feel more intensely than others about issues like abortion or prayer in school. Likewise, members of other religious organizations exert a moral authority on issues like global peace and arms control, leading them to be more committed to their political beliefs and more responsive to the calls for action issued by their group leaders.

Another political resource that sometimes benefits advocate groups is their close *working relationships* with legislative and agency staff, and with enterprising and investigative reporters. One writer, for instance, contends that "entrepreneurial staffs" of legislators often play an "intermediary role" between public interest lobbies and congressional output.[13] Ralph Nader, for instance, supposedly enjoyed such a relationship with Michael Pertschuk when he was a top aide on the Senate Commerce Committee.

A political resource often cited as a source of strength for citizen groups is the member of group leaders appointed to important *government positions*. President Carter, for instance, appointed a number of environmental group staff members, especially from the National Resources Defense Council, to key positions in the Environmental Protection Agency (EPA) and other government agencies. Meanwhile, public interest lawyers moved up in important advisory positions in the executive office of the president, and a top Nader staff member, Joan Claybrook, was appointed director of the National Highway Traffic Safety Administration. President Reagan likewise appointed key personnel from conservative citizen groups and think tanks to important government positions. The infamous James Watt, Reagan's first secretary of the interior, had been director of the Mountain States Legal Defense Fund, a conservative legal foundation that battles environmental groups in court. Reagan also appointed James Miller of the American Enterprise Institute to be chairman of the Federal Trade Commission and later director of his Office of Management and Budget. Representatives of other think tanks, like the Hoover Institution, were also prominent among Reagan appointees.

Strategies and Issues

The political strategies pursued by groups perceived as adversaries by business vary with the character and mission of the group. National organizations with a goal of influencing government policy rely on the traditional political strategies—lobbying, litigation, policy research, coalition building, and support for elected officials. Grassroots organizations more frequently resort to boycotts and demonstrations, and church bodies and university investors bring shareholder resolutions against companies.

Activist groups are pursuing their political strategies through the increasing use of two other political tools as well—ballot measures and electoral support activities. In the 1982 and 1984 elections, over two hundred measures were qualified for the ballot in all fifty states during each election year. Initiative campaigns have become a major industry, as more than $65 million was spent by the proponents and opponents of the most important initiatives in the 1982 elections, and three national reporting services on ballot campaigns have been launched. Initiatives often related to such issues as the tax structure, utility rates, public morality, nuclear power and nuclear waste, and consumer protection. Initiatives expert David Magleby predicts that, "the 1980s will be the decade of the greatest initiative action yet."[14]

Activist groups are increasingly involved in candidate recruitment and electoral support, at both the national and state levels. In 1980, activist leaders organized the ill-fated Citizens Party, to run Barry Commoner for president. In the wake of Reagan's victory, activist groups became more pragmatic and focused on supporting sympathetic candidates running for state and federal offices in later elections. Five national environmental groups organized political action committees in 1982 and endorsed more than one hundred and fifty Senate and House candidates. They spent close to $2 million on these campaigns, mobilized thousands of voters around the country, and over two-thirds of the candidates they supported were successful. Environmental groups also were active at the state level, forming thirty political activist committees (PACs) for the 1982 races. For the 1984 elections, environmental PACs spent another $3 million.[15]

Grassroots political groups affiliated with the Citizen Action Network were also notably effective in 1982 and 1984. Their 2,500 staff and canvassers raised $12 million in 1982, knocking on 50,000 doors a night throughout the year. In all, 70 percent of the candidates they supported at the federal, state, and local levels were elected.[16] Having briefly examined the political importance of the initiative device and electoral support activities, the importance of the more typical political strategies will emerge as various issues involving the corporate community are examined.

Environment

Traditional political strategies have been utilized to enact and implement environmental measures. Antipollution efforts and wilderness preservation have resulted from traditional lobbying and research campaigns of groups like the Sierra Club, the Environmental Policy Center, Friends of the Earth, the National Audubon Society, and the Wilderness Society. One observer concludes that the dozen largest environmental lobbies rival the sophistication of most corporate lobbies in Washington.[17]

The environmental campaign also has benefitted from the existence of coalitions. Amendments to the 1970 Clean Air Act were enacted and implemented under the pressure of the Clean Air Coalition, which includes the major environmental groups, as well as Common Cause, the League of Women Voters, and the Oil, Chemical and Atomic Workers Union. In the late 1970s, the Alaska Coalition was active in protecting the maximum acreage of wilderness in that state from development. It was composed of over a dozen environmental groups. The Superfund Coalition was organized by the National Audubon Society to lobby for passage of the Chemical Superfund law and to advocate improvements in the law as well. The coalition includes the major environmental groups and Ralph Nader's Congress Watch.

Litigation has been a major strategic weapon for environmentalists, reinforced by the legal expertise and resources that reside in the environmental sector. They easily overshadow those possessed by other citizen groups. The three major litigating arms of the environmental movement are the Natural Resources Defense Council, the Environmental Defense Fund, and the Sierra Club Legal Defense Fund. Litigation has been useful to delay or prevent the construction of nuclear power plants and other industrial development projects. In the 1980s, litigation was particularly-useful to force the EPA and other recalcitrant agencies to enforce the law. In 1984, J. Michael McCloskey, executive director of the Sierra Club, claimed, "I think the Sierra Club has more enforcement actions going than the government has now, and we're a private citizens group with a fraction of their budget."[18]

Thorough research and publicity is always a useful political tool, especially as the media uses that information to help shape public opinion. In this regard, the Conservation Foundation has been a major voice on environmental policy. Considered unusually detached in its analysis, it made an impact with its sharp attack on Reagan administration policies in its report, *State of the Environment 1982*.[19]

The growing concern over toxic waste also has led to the spontaneous use of numerous direct-action groups at the local level, supported and served by such national groups as Environmental Action and the Citizens Clearinghouse on Toxic Waste. Meanwhile, on wilderness and animal protection issues, Greenpeace and Earth First have pursued militant tactics. The growing prominence of direct-action groups has prompted some observers to comment on a split within the environmental community, between the mainstream and more radical groups.[20]

Energy

The energy issue has been the focus of perhaps the most comprehensive array of interest group strategies. On the natural gas deregulation bill alone, 117 lobbies were enlisted in the fight, with the Energy Action Committee as one of the primary opponents of deregulation. Energy Action also campaigned in vain for oil company divestiture legislation. A number of groups also have lobbied against nuclear power, including Nader's Critical Mass and Congress Watch organizations and Friends of the Earth.

Research against nuclear power has been produced by the Union of Concerned Scientists, while research on behalf of utility rate reform has been conducted by both Environmental Action and the now defunct Public Interest Economics Center (PIEC). PIEC, in fact, assisted grassroots organizations in writing testimony to present before state public service commissions overseeing rate increase requests. Meanwhile, litigation to halt the spread of nuclear power has been primarily advanced by the Natural Resources Defense Council.

Demonstrations against nuclear power have been launched by the Clamshell Alliance and over a dozen similar organizations across the country. The Mobilization for Survival is a coalition of eighty organizations that has demonstrated against both nuclear power plants and nuclear proliferation. Grassroots activity against utility rates has emerged within the past few years. Associated Community Organizations for Reform Now (ACORN) has organized in many states against utility rate hikes, and such statewide organizations as Massachusetts Fair Share and Illinois Public Action have followed the same agenda.

Shareholder resolutions favoring nonnuclear energy alternatives have been introduced before utility companies. Meanwhile, coalitions formed on the energy front. Over sixty grassroots, environmental, and labor organizations formed the Citizen/Labor/Energy Coalition in 1978, to fight utility shutoffs, rate hikes, and nuclear power. Coalitions with conservative interests also are appearing with increasing frequency. The Coalition against Clinch River, for example, opposing federal support for the breeder reactor, brought together such environmental groups as the Sierra Club, the Natural Resources Defense Council, and Friends of the Earth with such conservative groups as the Heritage Foundation and the National Taxpayers Union. The conservative groups, brought into the coalition by the market-oriented Competitive Enterprise Institute, opposed both the expense entailed by the federal subsidy and the interference with market principles. Liberal/conservative coalitions also have formed to oppose federal synthetic fuels programs.[21]

Health and Safety

Nader's Congress Watch is increasingly lobbying with the unions on issues of employee health and safety. In 1984, Nader's Health Research Group criticized the Health and Human Services Department for failing to notify 200,000 workers of halth risks from exposure to toxic substances, a danger discovered in a series of government studies.[22] In the early 1980s, the Sierra Club was highly critical of the Occupational Safety and Health Administration's (OSHA) nonenforcement policies, exposing them in a report titled, *Poisons on the Job: The Reagan Administration and American Workers*. Hence, publicity and policy research have been typical tools used by citizen groups on worker health issues. The Environmental Defense Fund has been the major litigating organization on issues of employee health, while feminist groups have organized on worker health rules unique to women and the unborn.

Grassroots organizing at the local level on chemical and toxics issues became more important in the 1980s, especially after the Union Carbide disaster in Bhopal,

India, in December 1984. Local coalitions of environmental, labor, and community groups aggressively promoted right-to-know laws, and twenty states now require employees to inform workers and the community about dangerous materials used in a plant. Beset by stringent state regulations, business responded by lobbying for federal preemption and the passage of a uniform and more lenient federal standard.

A heightened concern over the harmful impacts of smoking on health, and over nonsmokers' rights also developed in the 1980s. Local groups successfully lobbied for public health measures to control smoking in 36 states and many cities. In the wake of a series of unsuccessful attempts to pass a statewide "Clean Indoor Air" initiative in California, citizen groups successfully lobbied for laws segregating smokers in the workplace in 21 cities and counties in the state.[23] Antismoking initiatives have been promoted by a national citizen group, Action on Smoking and Health, and by such mainstream organizations as the American Cancer Society and the American Lung Association.

Corporate Accountability

An evolving range of political strategies also has been evident on various dimensions of the corporate accountability issue, including corporate governance and disclosure of information. For instance, lobbying at the national level on issues of corporate governance is pursued by Nader, while grassroots strategies to promote public control of corporate decisions is pursued by organizations like the Campaign for Economic Democracy in California. Research on the issue is pursued by a growing number of organizations. Nader's Corporate Accountability Research Group was responsible for the much-publicized federal chartering proposal in the 1970s. Corporate Data Exchange is studying institutional shareholdings and corporate directorships in a number of industries. The Peoples Business Commission has suggested that unions direct their pension fund investments to companies in distressed communities.[24] The Council on Economic Priorities is promoting disclosure of corporate information on subjects like equal employment, pollution emissions, and cost of nuclear power for the purpose of rating corporate performance. INFORM is serving a similar function, while even Common Cause is promoting disclosure of corporate communications with federal agencies and decision makers.

Various litigation approaches are being utilized on this issue. The Center for Law in the Public Interest sued companies guilty of illegal political payments, resulting in court-imposed outside directors on the corporate boards of Northrup Corporation, Phillips Petroleum, and Mattel. Shareholder resolutions calling for disclosure of corporate social impacts, as well as disclosure of illegal corporate behavior, executive compensation, and directorship ties have been sponsored by institutional investors such as the Interfaith Center for Corporate Responsibility. The issues of disclosure, corporate governance, and employee rights motivated a wide spectrum of citizen groups to organize a series of protests, teach-ins, and mock trials of corporations on Big Business Day, April 17, 1980.

Employment Opportunity

Lobbying, research, and litigation to promote the enactment and implementation of equal employment laws have been the focus of such traditional groups as the National Association for the Advancement of Colored People (NAACP), National Organization for Women (NOW), and the ACLU. Lesser-known public interest law firms, however, like Public Advocates and Equal Rights Advocates, have also been active on this issue. Shareholder resolutions, demanding disclosure of data showing the hiring and promotion patterns of women and minorities, also have been introduced by church groups and women's organizations.

Demonstrations have meanwhile been launched by local women's groups, such as 9 to 5 in Boston and Women Employed in Chicago, protesting discrimination against female clerical workers. Another organization, the Working Women's Institute, has exposed sexual harassment of women at work, and the Coalition of Labor Union Women is attempting to organize more women into unions. Comparable worth, rewarding traditionally female jobs at levels equivalent to those of male jobs of comparable value, has become the most important employment issue to women's organizations in the 1980s. While NOW pressures the Supreme Court and Congress to accept the concept, seven states have adopted equity pay as a result of legislation or labor negotiations, and twenty-five others are studying their pay scales to determine if they discriminate against women.[25]

Consumerism

The traditional consumer organizations lobbied in the 1970s for labelling and other consumer protection laws. In the 1980s, they have more typically petitioned the Food and Drug Administration (FDA) and other government agencies to rule on product hazards, or have sued the government to enforce the law. Nader's Health Research Group often files petitions with the FDA to rule against dangerous drugs or food additives, and then the Public Citizen Litigation Group will file suit if the FDA does not respond. The Center for Science in the Public Interest (CSPI) also is concerned about dangerous or unhealthful foods, and produces studies and publications for the general public. CSPI sues the government for nonenforcement of the law. In 1985, for instance, it sued the FDA for failing to ban potentially dangerous food dyes, in violation of the Delaney Clause.[26] The Community Nutrition Institute (CNI) meanwhile, is suing the FDA in 1986, for failing to ban aspartame, an artificial sweetener that CNI claims is dangerous.

Consumer groups have successfully overturned in court various agency decisions made during the Reagan era to rescind previous regulations. Decisions by the National Highway Traffic Safety Administration to rescind the passive restraint standard and the tire treadwear standard were both overturned by courts as "arbitrary and capricious." The CSPI sued the Treasury Department's Bureau of Alcohol, Tobacco and Firearms for rescinding on the ingredient labelling standard, also overturned in court.

Consumer groups are monitoring the impact of economic deregulation, and lobbying at both the national and state levels to prevent higher costs or lower quality services to low-income consumers. The Consumer Federation of America (CFA) has been actively following both banking and telecommunications deregulation in the 1980s, joined on the latter issue by the Telecommunications Research and Action Center (TRAC).

Consumer groups often form coalitions to pursue their lobbying. In the 1980s, coalitions most often have formed to block Reagan administration initiatives. In 1981, for instance, a wide range of consumer, environmental, and labor groups formed the Coalition for Safe Foods, to prevent repeal of the Delaney Amendment. In the early 1980s, CSPI formed a coalition of groups called SMART (Stop Marketing Alcohol on Radio and Television), which includes the Consumer Federation of America, the National PTA, the National Women's Health Network, Action for Children's Television, and the American Medical Student Association. The coalition has called for a series of restrictions on the marketing and advertising of alcoholic beverages.

Multinational Corporations and Foreign Policy

Research on the practices of multinational corporations (MNCs) has been produced by scholars at traditional think tanks like the Brookings Institution, but also by experts like Richard Barnet, coauthor of *Global Reach*, based at the Institute for Policy Studies. The Council on Economic Priorities has studied the production of major defense contractors. Other groups, like the Center for Defense Information and the Project on Military Procurement, have criticized the defense budget and specific weapons systems. The nuclear freeze campaign resulted in resolutions passed in hundreds of town meetings and advisory resolutions passed in the 1982 elections in nine states and twenty-four cities. Litigation on the overseas impact of U.S.-made goods has also been initiated by the Natural Resources Defense Council, demanding that an environmental impact statement be generated for goods financed by the Export-Import Bank.

The Kennedy-Hatch bill, which would loosen existing restrictions on the export of potentially hazardous products to Third World countries, has generated opposition lobbying and coalitions among environmental and church groups. The Union Carbide disaster in India has further politicized the chemical and pesticide issue, and has led to the formation of the Pesticides Coalition among religious, environmental, and health groups.

Shareholder resolutions are frequently used, particularly by the Interfaith Center on Corporate Responsibility (ICCR), to publicize or protest policies by MNCs. Illegal foreign political payments by U.S. companies and the international marketing practices of infant formula producers were the subjects of numerous shareholder resolutions. The Nestle boycott was the most visible aspect of the infant formula fight and reinforced the leverage that was being exercised on U.S. companies through shareholder resolutions. On the issue of investment in South Africa, shareholder resolutions introduced by ICCR have likewise joined with direct action tactics to advance the issue. Beyond the demonstrations that have been conducted before the South African embassy, civil rights groups like TransAfrica and the NAACP, along with religious organizations, have promoted divestment laws in states and localities. At least five states and several cities have prohibited investment of employee pension funds in companies that operate in South Africa or in firms that fail to comply with the Sullivan Principles (a voluntary code of various affirmative action policies).[27]

Economic Structure/Tax Policy

Some organizations, such as the Institute for Policy Studies and the National Center for Economic Alternatives, are involved in broad-gauged research, calling for public or community control over economic decisions otherwise made at the discretion of large corporations. The National Center for Economic Alternatives, for instance, engaged in research examining community ownership of a steel plant abandoned by Youngstown Sheet and Tube Company.

In the 1980s, the tax reform and deficit control fights have spawned widespread citizen group activity. Conservative groups like the National Taxpayers Union (NTU) and the National Tax Limitation Committee (NTLC), along with the Libertarian Cato Institute, have campaigned for federal spending cuts rather than tax increases to close the deficit. These organizations have supported the Gramm-Rudman-Hollings Deficit Control Act and the Balanced Budget Amendment to the constitution, while NTU and NTLC previously influenced the passage of tax limitations measures in over half the states since 1978. Meanwhile, at the opposite end of the spectrum, social spending lobbies have maintained that the deficit should be controlled through cuts in only defense spending and through tax increases. Such social spending lobbies include the Children's Defense Fund and the Center on Budget and Policy Priorities, antihunger groups like the Food Research and Action Center and Bread for the World, and religious groups like the National Council of Churches and the Friends Committee on National Legislation. Citizen groups that have formed specifically to address the budget deficit, like the Bipartisan Budget Appeal and the Committee for a Responsible Federal Budget, have meanwhile argued for a comprehensive approach to deficit reduction, including tax increases and spending cuts in all areas.[28]

Corporate Political Activities

Research and lobbying to control access to the political process, either through political contributions or lobbying activities, have been the key functions of Common Cause. Initiatives enacting lobbying disclosure have been successfully pursued in states such as California. Moreover, litigation initiated by the Media

Access Project and other groups has attempted to limit the political messages that corporations can communicate, either through the media or in the form of bill inserts to customers. In three major cases, however, the Supreme Court has struck down restrictions on corporate political expression to customers and the public.

Business Response

The response of the business community to activist pressure has ranged along five dimensions—confrontation, imitation, cooperation, participation, and negotiation. Each of these responses will be explained in detail.

Confrontation

Unfortunately, the typical business response to citizen groups is a hardline approach. Firestone Tire and Rubber Company, for example, showed no willingness to cooperate with either the National Highway Traffic Safety Administration or the Center for Auto Safety over the recall of unsafe radial tires. Meanwhile, Hooker Chemical Company still disclaims any responsibility for the toxic waste disaster at Love Canal. And an article in *Barron's* (see note 32 at end of article), commenting on the corporate response to shareholder resolutions, states, "Management generally has welcomed the critics as warmly as it would a Leninist brigade mounting the ramparts." Such hardline approaches often include resort to inflammatory rhetoric and outright name-calling. For example, William Simon, former Treasury secretary, labels corporate critics and intellectuals as "moral and economic despots," and energy spokesman Llewellyn King has accused corporate critics of attempting to halt economic growth in America.[29] Such rhetoric is now standard fare in some chief executive speeches. One utility company executive, for instance, in a widely reprinted speech, spoke of a band of "coercive utopians" bent on bringing America to its knees, affording them the opportunity to seize positions of power and design the country's future.[30] Another utility company once composed a lengthy volume, *The Counter-Establishment*, outlining the cast of characters and strategies being used to undermine our industrial society. It is the portrait of interlocking directorates and a neat conspiracy theory.

Unfortunately, the nation's leading business press often resorts to the same inflammatory descriptions in its exposes of corporate adversaries. *Fortune Magazine*, for instance, labeled such critics "the corporation haters" in an article that focused on the infant formula controversy.[31] And *Barron's*, in a discussion of the protest against the U.S. Steel mill closing in Youngstown, Ohio, referred to the "Marxist" values of the protest leaders, some of whom were "avowed socialists."[32] Such use of ad hominem attack is, of course, no response to the merits of the case being made by corporate critics.

The rigid and negative posture assumed by many corporations and business representatives is reinforced by a somewhat respectable social theory, that of the "New Class." Irving Kristol, among others, has popularized the notion of an anti-capitalist class, opposed to the consumption ethic, highly educated, and working predominantly in the public sector. As just one example of the attractiveness of this theory, a scientific advisor to the Westinghouse Electric Corporation, in addressing a meeting of the Atomic Industrial Forum, characterized antinuclear activists as "a new class of highly educated, secure and relatively affluent Americans who had found jobs on legislative staffs, in foundations, academic institutions, the media and public interest groups."[33] That is almost precisely the description used by Kristol. Whatever the scientific merit or methodological validity of the New Class theory, however, it is unfortunate that it often serves as the foundation for confrontation politics, a "we/them" view of the world. Rather than attempting to understand issues, and separate legitimate from illegitimate grievances, executives often become preoccupied with the nature of their adversaries.

Another typical confrontation response from the business community is a direct attack on a group's funding, or an attempt to undermine the legitimacy of its funding sources. Top executives, angered by lawsuits brought by public-interest law firms, have urged supporting foundations to drop their backing. In many states, universities that support Public Interest Research Groups through student fees, especially through so-called negative checkoff schemes, have received complaints from business representatives, local chambers of commerce, and statewide organizations supported by business. Some of the complaints have escalated into lawsuits or legislative proposals to terminate the funding mechanism. In 1985, the Supreme Court upheld an appeals court decision ruling the negative checkoff scheme on invasion of First Amendment rights. In North Carolina, where antiunion sentiment is especially strong, the business community was able to defeat a proposal for state support of a Labor Education Center to be based at a state university. Even to study the issue of worker organizing was considered abhorrent. Moreover, business figures like David Packard and William Simon have called for a halt to unrestricted corporate grants to universities where scholars have advocated values contrary to a free-market system. Dow Chemical Company terminated its support for Central Michigan University when it invited Jane Fonda to speak on campus.

Such attacks on the financial base of activist expression are heavy-handed and short-sighted. They constitute a frontal assault on our pluralistic political system by implicitly questioning the legitimacy of any political values at odds with our business system. Moreover, such attacks confirm the view of many that the business system is autocratic and cannot tolerate any dissident viewpoints.

The corporate community has embellished its attack on the financial base of advocate groups when it comes to the issue of taxpayer funding. Here, business is on theoretically firmer ground as it exhorts legislators to protect the public purse from exploitation by corporation critics. Business leaders have been agitated for a long time by lobbying and litigation conducted by tax-exempt adversaries, and are even more outraged by the prospect of public subsidies for citizen groups to intervene in agency proceedings. The National Chamber Litigation Center and the Consumer Alert Council, a conservative group, have both sued to prevent agency fee reimbursement to organizations like the Consumer Federation of America. During the 1980s, the Reagan administration generally has stopped implementing the agency fee program, so business concern has abated.

While the idea of government support for lobbying or litigation may seem puzzling at first glance, the business opposition fails to address the issue in its larger context. First, corporations themselves can deduct from their income taxes contributions for direct lobbying activities as ordinary and necessary business expenses under section 162(e) of the Internal Revenue Code. Those who oppose public subvention of lobbying activities also must realize that the government spends millions of dollars a year to lobby itself, in the form of "congressional liaison" activities by executive agencies and departments. Moreover, the idea of subsidizing the "otherwise unrepresented," a key criterion in agency fee programs, conforms once again to pluralistic political theory, and is sounder conceptually than simply distributing government largesse to any business group or government agency that chooses to influence policy.

The final, and most reprehensible, hardline response by the business sector is surveillance of its critics. The days of General Motors hiring private detectives to investigate Ralph Nader are apparently not over for many companies. Georgia Power Company spent $750,000 a few years ago to infiltrate consumer organizations and spy on their members. Other utilities, and indeed companies in other industries, support private research organizations that compile dossiers on individuals and "terrorist" organizations that in some cases fall short of being violent.[34]

Imitation

If the confrontation approach pursued by some companies is self-defeating and damaging to the system, the imitation of strategies developed by corporate adversaries is at least a natural and understandable reaction. The tendency to emulate the successful tactics of one's opposition can hardly be faulted, even though it is not clear that the policy results have been uniformly positive.

Such imitation has developed rapidly since the mid-1970s, and business has reaped the rewards in the form of favorable policy outcomes. The heavy grassroots lobbying by business and the National Right to Work Committee, for example, is given credit for the defeat of labor law reform and common situs picketing legislation in the Ninety-Fifth Congress.[35] The American Bankers Association and member banks alerted customers in 1981 to a legislative proposal to withhold taxes from interest payments, and orchestrated a flood of opposing mail on Capitol Hill.

Not only has business itself become more involved in grassroots lobbying, and in high-level direct lobbying through such organizations as the Business Roundtable, but it also has given support to new citizen groups lobbying on behalf of business concerns. The Consumer Alert Council, for example, was established in 1977 by Barbara Keating, a Conservative party candidate for the Senate from New York in 1974. The council has lobbied for industry deregulation and against such measures as the automobile airbag. Americans for Energy Independence, founded in 1975 by individuals committed to promoting energy self-sufficiency through all available means, has enjoyed the financial support of electric utilities, electric equipment manufacturers, labor unions, small oil companies, and major ones like Atlantic Richfield Company and Mobil Oil. The American Council on Science and Health (ACSH) has provided scientific corroboration for many of the positions endorsed by industry. It has refuted various cancer scares and alleged product dangers, and argued for the relaxation of food safety laws. ACSH has a million dollar budget and enjoys the support of such companies as Alcoa, DuPont, Exxon, Eli Lilly, Rockwell International, and Westinghouse.

To counter the publicity orientation of citizen groups, and the allegedly favorable treatment given such groups by the media, the business community is responding with a different sort of publicity orientation—the paid variety. It is spending more and more each year on political issue advertising in the print media. The efficacy of such advertising is subject to much dispute but the growing tendency for corporations to utilize the capability is not.

Beyond its grassroots lobbying activities and support for other lobby groups, business has been more heavily involved in political campaign contributions since the mid-1970s. Based on the successful models of AFL-CIO's Committee on Political Education, and the liberal National Committee for an Effective Congress, and based furthermore on the legal facilitation and encouragement of political action committees, business rapidly escalated its participation in campaign funding. Whereas there were only eighty-nine business-related PACs in 1974, there were over three thousand in 1984. Moreover, there is great potential for a further growth in the number of business PACs, and an emerging trend in business-giving to support Republican challengers who favor an adherence to free-market principles.[36]

Having been stung in the past by some of the studies sponsored by the Nader network, especially the Center for the Study of Responsive Law and the Corporate Accountability Research Group, along with many other policy think tanks, business now recognizes the value of policy research. As a result, many neoconservative think tanks have gained financial strength through corporate donations. The resources of the American Enterprise Institute (AEI), for example, have rapidly grown to equal those of the Brookings Institution. AEI has a Center for the Study of Government Regulation chaired by a favorite neoconservative—Irving Kristol. The Hoover Institution and the Institute for Contemporary Studies (ICS), both on the west coast, are growing with business support. ICS has published books critical of affirmative action, energy conservation, and government regulation of business and academia. The Center for the Study of American Business at Washington University specializes in studies critical of government regulation as does the Law and Economics Center at Emory University. Both centers exist with substantial support from the business sector. Even policy centers of a more conservative stripe are attracting business backing. The Heritage Foundation, for example, the leading think tank of the New Right, founded in 1974 with seed money from Joseph Coors, now has a budget exceeding $10 million and rivals the older think tanks, AEI and Brookings, in both resources and influence.[37]

Finally, in response to the numerous lawsuits against corporate America and the proliferation of public-interest law firms, the business community has sponsored its own constellation of litigation centers. The model for all of them is the Pacific Legal Foundation (PLF), organized in 1973 with substantial help from the Fluor Corporation. PLF supports twenty-four lawyers on a budget of $3 million, and has initiated litigation to challenge environmental regulation, land use limitations, and pesticide controls. In 1975, the National Legal Center for the Public Interest, actually a business-supported entity, launched a successful drive to organize six similar litigation centers in each region of the country. Lawsuits initiated by such centers have demanded search warrants for OSHA inspections, cost-benefit calculations for government regulations, and more latitude for political contributions by trade associations. The boards of trustees of PLF and all the other litigation centers are dominated by corporate executives and corporate lawyers. Additionally, the U.S. Chamber of Commerce has organized its own litigation arm.

Cooperation

The seriousness with which corporations view their adversaries, however, is perhaps best exemplified by their efforts to coalesce with their critics on issues when they hold common views. For example, the U.S. Chamber of Commerce has fought with Nader's Congress Watch and the Sierra Club against disclosure of grassroots lobbying activities. Allstate Insurance Company cooperated with Ralph Nader in the campaign to make airbags mandatory in automobiles while they still opposed each other on no-fault insurance. Oil company officials worked with the NAACP to formulate a statement endorsing deregulation of natural gas. No-fault auto insurance was supported by consumer groups and by some leading insurance companies, because they anticipated lower costs from the measure. Moreover, Ford Motor Company and the National Auto Dealers Association joined the coalition as well. Airline deregulation was promoted by the Ad Hoc Committee for Airline Regulatory Reform, composed of consumer groups and such business interests as Sears Roebuck, United Airlines, and the National Association of Manufacturers. Meanwhile, the U.S. Chamber of Commerce and oil companies joined Common Cause and Nader's Congress Watch to defeat labor interests on the cargo preference bill in 1977.

On environmental and fuel economy measures, moreover, business is finding that its best ally is labor unions. The 1977 amendments to the Clean Air Act, for example, were softened for the auto industry with the help of the United Auto Workers (UAW).[38] Furthermore, Chrysler Corporation was aided substantially by the UAW in securing passage of the bailout legislation.[39]

In a fight for barge tollway legislation in 1978, the railroads found their competitive interests coincided with the economic and environmental interests of public interest groups. Hence, the railroads established the Council for a Sound Waterways Policy that funded activities of the Public Interest Economics Center and the Environmental Policy Center.[40] Such ad hoc alliances are simply good pragmatic politics but they may be inhibited where corporate paranoia prevents such working relationships. In 1985, forty-one environmental and health groups joined with the National Agricultural Chemicals Association and such companies as Shell to reach common agreement on amendments to pesticide control legislation. Since there was relative equality in bargaining power among the parties, and each side had something to lose if the negotiation failed, agreement on a compromise was reached.[41]

Participation

One of the most positive and progressive steps corporations might take in response to pressure groups is to include them in the corporate planning process. A panel of the American Assembly has suggested as one change in corporate governance that companies establish citizen advisory committees composed of constituencies especially affected by corporate policy, those who are the victims of corporate externalities. Beyond structuring such constituency input into corporate policy-making in the form of advisory committees, or possible designated outside directors, corporations might solicit the advice of outside constituencies on an ad hoc basis. For example, before designing a new financing proposal for directory assistance calls, New England Telephone company attempted to accommodate the advice and interests of senior citizen and handicapped groups.[42] Likewise, Pacific Power and Light Company hosted representatives of the Gray Panthers and Common Cause to give the company advice on new utility rate structures.[43] Half of all utilities have established consumer advisory panels, and major food companies have also adopted the structure. In an issue advertising campaign, Aetna Life and Casualty explains that it is taking steps to combat insurance redlining in four major cities as a result of talks with leaders of National People's Action, one of the foremost coalitions of grassroots neighborhood groups in the country. Such collaboration is the most positive demonstration that a company genuinely intends to interact with its environment, not simply react to it.

Co-optation is the key danger to avoid for any group that becomes involved in a participative planning venture. Similarly, the urge to co-opt must be resisted by the sponsoring corporation. For example, one of the Roman Catholic representatives working on the infant formula controversy became persuaded that she could have an impact through a dialogue with Abbott Labs company, that produces infant formula. As a result of the dialogue, the company adopted new precautions against marketing abuses, basically involving new labels and warnings. Viewing this measure as an inadequate response to the problem, other members of the infant formula movement believed the nun to have been co-opted.

Negotiation

Obviously, conflict cannot always be prevented through participative planning. Without conflict, there would never be any real progress. However, when conflict does arise, it is likely to be in no one's interest for the conflict to escalate into confrontation. Name calling and questioning the values or motives of one's adversary is likely to be self-defeating. Some companies are recognizing this fact in the context of dealing with shareholder resolutions. More and more companies have negotiated over the years with the Interfaith Center for Corporate Responsibility to amicable settlements. The resolutions are usually withdrawn in exchange for some positive steps taken by the corporation.[44] Hence, the company minimizes the adverse publicity it might have otherwise received.

Beyond the ad hoc, one-on-one negotiations, that companies pursue with groups like the Interfaith Center, more structured negotiation or mediation efforts are occurring involving a number of parties. One of the first was the National Coal Policy Project. Organized by an executive of Dow Chemical Company and a former Sierra Club president in 1976, almost one hundred persons from industry and the environmental community participated on Project task forces. Observers have been impressed that the participants were able to reach agreement on over two hundred separate issues. For example, the environmentalists agreed to a so-called one-stop siting process that would replace the current multiple permit process for utility plant construction, while industry representatives agreed to a proposal for intervenor funding for environmental representatives appearing before government agencies.[45] In the wake of the Coal Policy Project, other mediation efforts have developed, especially on environmental issues. The Conservation Foundation launched a mediation panel on toxic substances, and is now the leading sponsor of such efforts. The Institute for Resource Management in Utah and the Keystone Center in Colorado are also pursuing mediation efforts, and all claim a high level of success.

Of the five response modes assumed by business, the confrontation mode is the most unfortunate and damaging. Imitation and cooperation are shrewd, sensible, and inevitable defensive responses. However, they do little to prevent needless conflict or advance positive change. The most desirable modes for business to consider are those of participation and negotiation. Through them, business may adjust corporate policy to the needs of multiple constituencies and see how it can contribute to sound public policy.

Future Trends

Shifting focus once again back to the activist groups and corporate critics, it is appropriate that we determine what lies in the future. Will they wither or prosper? Is the present concern that business and other institutions share over group pressures likely to fade from the scene? If the phenomenon is transitory, is it not advisable to avoid expending much effort on structured responses?

Some take the position that corporate critics and liberal lobbies are waning. Economic theorist Mancur Olson adheres to the position that their success must inevitably be temporary. Since the benefits provided by such groups are collective rather than selective, Olson maintains that there are no long-term incentives for citizens to join and support such groups.[46] However, the theory is not only contradicted by reality, but it presumes that people are guided mainly by economic rationality. Meanwhile, other research validates the theory that people are driven by quality of life concerns, by ideology, and by systematic biases in their decisions to join groups, and that they lack the information to make membership decisions based solely on rationality.[47]

For a number of reasons, citizen groups seem to have reached the state of healthy middle age and are not yet ready to die. First, many of the factors giving rise to the proliferation of interest groups will likely continue to have an influence on the future. Mass education and the issue consciousness it generates is not dramatically receding. The decaying political parties do not appear to be on the verge of recapturing their historic functions. And the influence of the media does not seem to be dissipating. In fact, even if the mainstream coverage of the major media give way to the strength of special-interest publications and cable television, advocacy and issues content is likely to be sharpened rather than blunted. Especially in an unregulated environment, we are liable to see environmental or consumer broadcasts developing, just as we have religious and minority stations today. Indeed, Ralph Nader is already taping a series of programs for cable television.

Second, as groups have matured and weathered the storms of cutbacks in federal funding, they have become more savvy and diversified their funding strategies. Nonmembership groups are developing memberships through direct mail campaigns; some are rediscovering the role in door-to-door canvassing campaigns; and others are finding larger markets for their publications and services. Successful groups must regularly adjust to the shifting priorities and fads of major foundations and other donors, and environmental groups are certainly doing so. Based on interviews with environmental leaders, one observer predicted in 1985 that this sector will be "bigger, richer, more pragmatic, and more part of the political mainstream."[48]

Third, despite burnout among some staff leaders, and a growth of material and selfish motivations among the young, an infusion of some new talent continues to staff activist organizations. While much of that young talent was attracted to conservative political organizations in the early 1980s, campus protests against apartheid in South Africa indicate there is still a core of concerned and progressive students who may be attracted to citizen activism. Surveys of student attitudes also demonstrate that the tide may be slowly turning in a liberal direction. Moreover, with the rapid proliferation of grassroots community groups, particularly to protest toxic waste dumps, local leadership talent seems to emerge where no one thought it existed.

Some contend that groups have proliferated too rapidly and now endanger their own base of support. As a result of conflicting demands for support and membership, people are not responding as positively to direct mail campaigns as they once did. However, groups may be passing through the phase of competition for members and on to cooperative efforts through coalitions. While business and labor fight in tandem against certain government regulations, environmentalists are building stronger ties to other factions within the labor community, and farm organizations are working together with labor unions to battle the economic crisis besetting the agricultural sector. Such coalition building may ultimately stabilize the citizen group movement while also strengthening it. Meanwhile, the growth of grassroots community groups does not yet seem to have reached the saturation point.

Finally, citizen groups will continue to form in reaction to new problems, and society continues to leave us with no dearth of problems. The impact of new technologies will continue to generate unforeseen problems. Who, for example, ten years ago might have predicted the current scope of chemical waste dumps, along with their consequences? Or who might have predicted the rise of genetic engineering and its attending problems? Once some of these problems develop, they may be no less intractable than poverty or threats to civil liberties, and the ACLU is not soon in danger of disappearing. If new problems generate groups that live as long as the problems they fight, the movement of corporate critics is unlikely to wither and die.

While problems will continue to intrude, and citizen groups will continue to live long lives, the mosaic of issues will not be the same from one period of time to the next. Hence, some groups may contract while others expand. Simply because civil rights organizations have lost money and members in recent years, as civil rights issues meet stronger resistance, corporations should not think the pressure is off. Employee health issues and the impact of new technologies have more than filled the breach of public concern.

Not only do issues change, but groups shift their tactics and strategies to meet changing conditions. Just as the end of protest politics is publicized, and the sophisticated tactics of public interest groups are lauded, another period of protest politics may be dawning. Civil rights forces demonstrate against apartheid. Victims of toxic waste dumps protest their plight, and right-to-life groups and feminist organizations march for their respective positions on the abortion controversy. In fact, the new wave of protest in the 1980s is creating division between citizen groups, especially within the environmental sector. Grassroots protest groups disagree with some of the positions of the major environmental groups, and accuse the staff members of those groups of joining the political establishment. While the political pendulum swung to the right in the late 1970s and early 1980s, it appears to be swinging back somewhat in the mid-1980s. Politics is turning more to the activist side while also returning to the grassroots. Due to federal spending limits, and the fact that the states are providing a more hospitable climate for business regulation in a host of areas, citizen groups are adjusting and turning their attentions to the states and localities. There is also a heightened concern, among environmental, health, and church groups for international issues.

374 • Business and Society

As citizen activism evolves into a new stage, there is evidence that business has matured in its response to group pressures. While participative mechanisms such as consumer advisory panels have not grown rapidly in most industries, mediation efforts have received more attention, especially with the growing concerns of executives over the costs of litigation. How business handles a new wave of more militant protest remains to be seen.

Future Research

The rise of citizen groups, the business response, and the interaction between the two forces suggest an agenda of research questions that have yet to be investigated. Much work remains to be done by both political scientists and management experts, and they are both ignoring areas ripe for exploration. The areas are suggested here.

Case Studies

Case studies on business/group conflict have been conducted but not to the extent necessary for comparisons or for development of valid generalizations. Sethi set the pace in an earlier work, but few others have followed the lead.[49] David Vogel has written a useful analysis of business/group conflict on shareholder resolutions,[50] and this approach should be used with a focus on other group strategies as well. Political scientists have investigated case studies of interest group conflict, but largely in the context of legislative struggles rather than direct action against corporations.[51] Another genre of case studies might focus on a specific constellation of groups. For example, *Balancing the Scales of Justice* is a survey of public interest law firms. Such studies that focused on organizations specializing in international politics, women's issues, or media reform issues would undoubtedly shed new light on the issues of concern and strategies pursued. Studies by those with a background in organizational behavior might help explain how specific citizen groups really function and why they succeed or fail. Jeffrey Berry made some strides in the case study chapters of his book *Lobbying for the People*, but many major citizen groups and sectors are yet to be examined. Think tanks are just beginning to be studied. Case studies on business/international group conflict would be valuable, as well as case studies that focus solely on group activities in other countries. U.S. experts on comparative politics are gradually meeting this challenge.

Longitudinal Studies

Since the rise of citizen activism stemmed primarily from the 1960s, it is perhaps not surprising that few studies have been conducted that trace the changes over time. The evolution of issues, political strategies, and participation levels would be valuable information and knowledge. In a series called *Public Interest Profiles*, the Foundation for Public Affairs in Washington, D.C. has composed detailed descriptions of citizen groups that have made some impact on the corporate community. Over two hundred fifty organizations have been summarized, and the data included reveals certain patterns in the evolution of issues and the extent of participation. The Foundation also attempts to track the emergence of new groups and adds at least ten a week to its files. Lobbying disclosure laws at the state and federal levels would generate useful data on lobbying activities for scholars to examine in the future.

Although there is an abundance of studies on political power and the power structure, little work has been done that specifically compares the power of business with the power of citizen groups, whether it be according to resources, policy outcomes, or real benefits accrued. Furthermore, little of the work in political theory, whether it arrives at pluralist or elitist conclusions, takes account of the rise of citizen groups.

Some useful research has been contributed, however. Theoretical and empirical work has been completed that attempts to explain why poeple join citizen groups, and much of it is quite sophisticated. Moreover, some impact studies are being pursued that assess the effect of laws or regulations specifically relating to citizen groups. The impact of public participation provisions in existing laws has been assessed. More could be done, however, to assess the impact that a specific group or constellation of groups has had on public policy. One conceivable study, for instance, might examine the impact of energy litigation. A start has been made in this direction in a useful study of public-interest law and in another of conservative legal foundations,[52] but impact studies could be pursued much more vigorously.

Despite the progress made so far, much fertile territory remains. Furthermore, since citizen activism is pervasive and a real concern to policy makers, we should begin to focus on the pertinent questions soon. It is likely that the needs and demands for good research in this field will expand rapidly as citizen groups have more policy consequences.

Notes

This article is updated from an article by John M. Holcomb in *Private Enterprise and Public Purpose*, S.P. Sethi and Carl L. Swanson, eds. (New York: Wiley, 1981).

1. David B. Truman, *The Governmental Process* (New York: Alfred A. Knopf, 1951); Edward C. Banfield, *Political Influence* (Glencoe, Ill.: The Free Press, 1961).
2. Jeffrey Berry, *Lobbying for the People* (Princeton, N.J.: Princeton University Press, 1977); Andrew S. McFarland, *Public Interest Lobbies: Decision-making on Energy* (Washington, D.C.: American Enterprise Institute, 1976); Andrew S. McFarland, *Common Cause* (Chatham, N.J.: Chatham House Publishers, 1984); Joyce Gelb and Marian Lief Palley, *Women and Public Policies* (Princeton, N.J.: Princeton University Press, 1982); Allan J. Cigler and Burdett A. Loomis, eds., *Interest Group Politics* (Washington, D.C.: Congressional

Quarterly, Inc., 1983); Norman J. Ornstein and Shirley Elder, *Interest Groups, Lobbying and Policy-making* (Washington, D.C.: Congressional Quarterly, Inc., 1978); Henry J. Pratt, *The Gray Lobby* (Chicago: The University of Chicago Press, 1976); Frences Fox Riven and Richard A. Cloward, *Poor People's Movement* (New York: Random House, 1977).

3. Theodore, J. Lowi, *The End of Liberalism: The Second Republic of the United States* (New York: W.W. Norton & Co., 1979).

4. Stuart Langton, "Citizen Participation in America: Current Reflections on the State of the Art," in *Citizen Participation in America,* ed. Stuart Langton (Lexington, Mass.: D.C. Heath & Co., 1978). See also "Single-issue Politics," *Newsweek,* November 6, 1978, pp. 48–60.

5. Olson, *The Rise and Decline of Nations* (New Haven, Conn.: Yale University Press, 1982).

6. Rep. David Obey stated, "Everyone who wants to get re-elected has to take 21 single-issue groups worth 2.5 percent each to build a majority," as quoted in "Single-issue Politics," *Newsweek,* November 6, 1978, p. 60.

7. Jeffrey M. Berry, *Lobbying for the People* (Princeton, N.J.: Princeton University Press, 1977).

8. Representative groups include Massachusetts Fair Share, California's Citizens Action League, Connecticut Citizen Action Group, Illinois Public Action, National People's Action and Associated Community Organizations for Reform Now (ACORN). Each has grown dramatically in recent years.

9. Berry, *Lobbying for the People.*

10. James O'Toole, "What's Ahead for the Business-Government Relationship," *Harvard Business Review,* March/April 1979, pp. 94–105.

11. Kathleen Teltsch, "Philanthropies Focus Concern on Arms Race," *New York Times,* March 25, 1984, pp. 1, 42.

12. Eric A. Weiss, "The Future Public Opinion of Business," *Management Review,* March 1978, pp. 8–15.

13. Michael J. Malbin, "Congressional Committee Staffs: Who's in Charge Here," *The Public Interest,* Spring 1977, pp. 16–40.

14. Jay Mathews, "New Forces Take Political Initiative," *The Washington Post,* July 3, 1984, pp. A1, A10; Austin Ranney, "Referendums and Initiatives 1984," *Public Opinion,* December/January, 1985, pp. 15–17.

15. Philip Shabecoff, " 'Green Vote' Cited as Factor in Races," *New York Times,* November 7, 1982, p. 36; and Andy Pasztor, "Environmentalists Switch Tactics," *Wall Street Journal,* April 13, 1984, p. 62.

16. John Herbers, "Grass-Roots Groups Go National," *New York Times,* September 4, 1983, p. 46.

17. Margot Hornblower, "Environmental Movement Has Grown a Sharp Set of Teeth," *Washington Post,* June 2, 1979, p. 2.

18. Norman J. Ornstein and Shirley Elder, "Clean Air Legislation: Traditional Foes Align," *Interest Groups, Lobbying and Policymaking* (Washington, D.C.: Congressional Quarterly, Inc., 1978).

19. Rochelle L. Stanfield, "Rvokelshavsand Clark Seeks to Blunt Environmental Lobby's Political Swords," *National Journal,* June 30, 1984, p. 1259.

20. Philip Shabecoff, "New Leaders and a New Era for Environmentalists," *New York Times,* November 29, 1985, p. D28.

21. Christopher Madison, "Federal Subsidy Programs Under Attack by Unlikely Marriage of Left and Right," *National Journal,* December 31, 1983, pp. 2682–2684.

22. Cass Peterson, "U.S. Won't Notify Workers of Hazards, Nader Charges," *Washington Post,* October 23, 1984, p. A17.

23. Jane E. Brody, "The Growing Militance of the Nation's Nonsmokers," *New York Times,* January 15, 1984, p. 6E.

24. Jeremy Rifkin and Randy Barber, *The North Will Rise Again: Pensions, Politics and Power in the 1980s* (Boston: Beacon Press, 1978).

25. Carol Lawson, "Women in State Jobs Gain in Equity Pay," *New York Times,* May 20, 1985, p. 22.

26. Julie Kasterlitz, "Reagan Is Leaving His Marks on the Food and Drug Administration," *National Journal,* July 6, 1985, pp. 1568–1572.

27. Thomas W. Lippman, "Growing Number of States, Localities Barring Investments in South Africa," *New York Times,* January 23, 1983, p. F5; Karvin Barker, "Cities Act Against Apartheid," *Washington Post,* February 8, 1985, pp. A1, A6.

28. Robert Kuttner, "Revenge of the Democratic Nerds," *The New Republic,* October 22, 1984, pp. 14–17.

29. William Simon, *A Time for Truth* (New York: Readers Digest Press, 1978); Llewellyn King, "Nuclear Power in Crisis: The New Class Assault," delivered at the Uranium Institute, London, England, July 12, 1978.

30. H. Peter Metzger, "The Coercive Utopians: Their Hidden Agenda," delivered at the American Nuclear Society, Albuquerque, New Mexico, December 1, 1978.

31. Herman Nickel, "The Corporation Haters," *Fortune,* June 16, 1980, pp. 126–136.

32. John C. Boland, "Unholy Alliance," *Barron's,* June 2, 1980, pp. 9, 20–25, 31.

33. David Burnham, "Nuclear Power Backers and Critics to Mark 3 Mile Island Anniversary," *New York Times,* March 18, 1980, p. A13.

34. Richard P. Pollock, "The Shifty Eye of Reddy Kilowatt," *Mother Jones,* May, 1978, pp. 13–14; Joanne Omang, "Area Power Firms Keep File on Critics," *Washington Post,* November 21, 1977, p. A2; Vasil Pappas, "Utilities Generate Sparks by Keeping Close Eye on Critics," *Wall Street Journal,* January 11, 1979, pp. 1, 32; Phil McCombs, "Activists Monitored by Vepco," *Washington Post,* September 7, 1978, p. C1.

35. Ornstein and Elder, "Common-Site Picketing: Major Defeat for Labor," *Interest Groups, Lobbying and Policymaking.*

36. Edwin M. Epstein, "Business and Labor under the Federal Election Campaign Act of 1971" in *Parties, Interest Groups, and Campaign Finance Laws,* ed. Michael J. Malbin (Washington, D.C.: American Enterprise Institute, 1980); Larry J. Sabato, *PAC Power: Inside the World of Political Action Committees* (New York: W.W. Norton & Company, 1984).

37. Peter H. Stone, "Businesses Wider Role in Conservatives' 'War of Ideas,' " *Washington Post,* May 12, 1985, pp. F4, F5.

38. Ornstein and Elder, "Clean Air Legislation: Traditional Foes Align," *Interest Groups, Lobbying and Policymaking.*

39. Alan Berlow, "Chrysler Aid Speeded by Broad Lobby Effort," *Congressional Quarterly Weekly Report,* November 17, 1979, pp. 2581–2583.

40. T.R. Reid, *Congressional Odessey: The Saga of a Senate Bill* (San Francisco: W.H. Freeman and Company, 1980).

41. Rochelle L. Stanfield, "Politics Pushes Pesticide Manufacturers and Environmentalists Closer Together," *National Journal,* December 14, 1985, p. 2846–2851.

42. James R. Emshoff and R. Edward Freeman, "Who's Butting Into Your Business?" *The Wharton Magazine*, Fall 1979, pp. 44–48, 58–59.

43. Presentation by Jack McIsaac before a conference sponsored by the Foundation for Public Affairs on *The New Politics* in Washington, D.C., April 18, 1979.

44. David Vogel, *Lobbying the Corporation: Citizen Challenges to Business Authority* (New York: Basic Book, Inc., 1978).

45. Luther J. Carter, "Sweetness and Light from Industry and Environmentalists on Coal," *Science*, (March 1978, pp. 958–959.

46. Mancur Olson, *The Logic of Collective Action: Public Goods and the Theory of Groups* (Cambridge, Mass.: Harvard University Press, 1971).

47. Terry M. Moe, *The Organization of Interests: Incentives and Internal Dynamics of Political Interest Groups* (Chicago: The University of Chicago Press, 1980).

48. Shabecoff, "New Leaders," p. D28.

49. S. Prakash Sethi, *Up Against the Corporate Wall: Modern Corporations and Social Issues in the Seventies* (Englewood Cliffs, N.J.: Prentice-Hall, Inc., 3rd edition, 1977).

50. Vogel, *Lobbying the Corporation*.

51. Ornstein and Elder, *Interest Groups, Lobbying and Policymaking*.

52. Burton A. Weisbrod, Joel F. Handler, and Neil K. Komesar, *Public Interest Law: An Economic and Institutional Analysis* (Berkeley: University of California Press, 1978); Lee Epstein, *Conservatives in Court* (Knoxville, Tenn.: University of Tennessee Press, 1985).

Business and Church Activism in America

Oliver F. Williams

Religion has been considered an important force in the shaping of American life. The Frenchman Alexis de Tocqueville, writing some one hundred fifty years ago, observed that religion played an essential role in America by shaping citizens who valued just and wholesome communities; he saw religion as crucial to the fabric of the nation.[1] Max Weber, in his famous *The Protestant Ethic and the Spirit of Capitalism*, argues that capitalism would have never developed without the religious influence; some of the core virtues of religion—honesty, industry, frugality, and thrift—formed communities of men and women who were the most productive and creative in their work.

Today many mainline Protestant and Catholic churches, rather than foster "the spirit of capitalism," often appear to be its harshest critics. Through proxy resolutions, boycotts, removal of funds from banks with objectionable policies, and other strategies, church groups are increasingly applying direct pressure to business corporations. What sorts of religious convictions motivate church groups in their dealings with business? Are the churches intent on creating a culture adverse to business, or can corporate managers forge a more cooperative relationship with these powerful institutions? This article will examine the historical evolution of church involvement in the economic life of the nation and analyze the various strategies used today by church groups in addressing business. It will conclude by considering the future of church activism and its likely influence in our society in the years ahead.

The Manager's Dilemma: Living between the Times

Jewish and Christian religions offer a vision of the way God intends the world to be. Churches that are critical of business ultimately attribute their opposition to their interest in advancing a more humane society; their protests are a tangible way of moving toward this vision. Yet is was not so long ago that there was a strong social consensus that the best way for business to advance a humane society was to compete efficiently in the market. Providing quality goods and services at the best price was taken to be business's contribution to the common good. Executives in the 1980s are living between the times; that is, they are caught between the time when there was a strong social consensus that the market mechanism was the best way to control business activity, and some possible future time when society has a clear consensus about how business institutions ought to advance human welfare.

We are living in a time when this new consensus is in the making. What is clear is that economic language—the language that traditionally often provided the sole rationale for corporate decisions—is not in itself acceptable to religious activists and many other socially concerned persons. Listening to many discussions between management and corporate critics, one is struck by the fact that they are often speaking different languages: management defends decisions in the economic language of profit and loss, and critics question the same decisions in the ethical language of justice and rights. The parties of such discussions usually pass like ships in the night; in the end, these conversations generate much heat and little light.

The implications of living between the times are far-reaching and affect how managers come to think of themselves. Most people want to be decent and moral, and they would like their efforts in business to reflect these characteristics. Under the former consensus on values in the social environment, managers could have some confidence that they were meeting their obligation to human welfare by participating in the market. Today, business executives are often caught in the middle. While most would acknowledge that they must consider the social costs of economic decisions, it is seldom clear where the moral person should draw the line in assessing the social and economic values at issue. We know business corporations are not the Red Cross, but what should they be? It is here that constructive dialogue with church activists may be helpful.

Christian Beliefs and the Business World

Many business leaders are puzzled as to why mainline Protestant and Catholic churches are often critical of business corporations. Understanding the religious convictions of these church leaders is essential. A core conviction of Christians is that the ministry of Jesus was to proclaim the coming Kingdom of God. While this conviction has been unchanging, the way in which the term *Kingdom of God* has been understood in the Christian community has changed radically at various periods. A new meaning of *Kingdom of God* today has resulted in a self-understanding that often prompts Christians to oppose business corporations vigorously.

The first generation of Christians understood themselves as a special community chosen by God to prepare for the sudden arrival of his kingdom. They thought that the world as they knew it was about to end, and that they would be part of a transcendent Kingdom of God, a new world somehow discontinuous with the present one. Later generations came to believe that the church was to be that community that strives for and points toward the Kingdom of God, a kingdom that would finally arrive in God's good time. The notion of a coming kingdom finds reasonance in the human heart, for people have always been restless for a land of peace and happiness, of "milk and honey." In the Hebrew Scriptures the prophets speak of a time of the kingdom when the lion will lie peaceably with the lamb. Christian Scriptures record the teaching of Jesus and portray a vision of the qualities of the kingdom—peace, justice, harmony, and brotherhood. Throughout the history of Christian communities there have been a variety of ways of relating the kingdom to the times. While the notion of the kingdom provides a vision of the sort of life we ought to have, the question is whether one should try to realize the kingdom here and now, approximate it, or anticipate it?

For most of Christian history the Kingdom of God was thought to be present in the institutional church in a small way, only to be fully realized by God at the end of time. In the church communities' men and women, in the spirit of Christ, could grow in charity, compassion, generosity, and so on. They could live virtuous lives and anticipate the final coming of God's kingdom where his rule of love would finally reign. The intellectual giant who fashioned the theological synthesis that shaped the Catholic Church for over seven hundred years is Thomas Aquinas (1225–1274).[2] Aquinas, as a man of his time, was not primarily concerned with changing social structures or making the world a better place to live. For him, the whole purpose of life in this world was to become virtuous and thereby to prepare for eternal happiness in the next world. Focusing on the virtues highlighted in the Bible—faith, hope, and charity—and Aristotle's four cardinal virtues—wisdom, justice, fortitude, and temperance—Aquinas encouraged Christians to lead lives and to form societies that would accent growth in virtue.

Life as Aquinas knew it, in the thirteenth century, was based on an agricultural economy and, by contemporary standards, almost everyone was poor. Society was understood to be static, on a model ordained by God, where the ideal was for all to have sufficient goods for their particular state in life. Lords, peasants, craftsmen, and merchants were taken to be in their role according to the divine plan. Upward mobility was foreign to this world, and for one to strive to accrue wealth beyond one's level was thought to be sinful—the sin of avarice. Aquinas and other theologians of the time supplied much practical guidance on just prices, usury, and trade in order to promote and protect the virtuous character of Christians, but they would never go so far as to encourage the creation of wealth. Trade and all forms of wealth creation were suspect, for making money cultivates greed in the merchant's heart and greed corrupts the life of the community. In the Thomist perspective, honor ought to be given to virtuous persons, yet if some citizens are particularly ingenious at making money, honor will likely be bestowed on them for their riches; this will slowly erode the high moral quality of the community.

Until recent times the vision of life's purpose espoused by Aquinas was the dominant one of the churches. Today, however, the proclamation of the kingdom is understood to entail working for sociopolitical changes that are likely to alleviate the plight of the poor. While Christians have always been taught to be concerned for the poor, the traditional response was personal charity. Although the sixteenth-century reformers, following Martin Luther, championed structural changes in society to eliminate the causes of poverty, this emphasis was short-lived. Only in our own time do we hear the loud call from the churches for systemic changes in institutions so that wealth might be more equitably distributed.

The efforts toward systemic change and reform of business corporations are understood to be mandated by that belief that the church is the "budding and beginning of the Kingdom," and that this future kingdom, the one that God will finally bring about, lights up the visions of Christians and spurs them on to work for political forms of justice and peace here and now. The new role of the churches is to labor for the values of the Kingdom of God—justice, love, peace, brotherhood, and so on—in the sociopolitical order. To be sure, the churches never intended to de-emphasize in any way their spiritual mission, but rather sought to draw out and make explicit the implications in the social order of living the Gospel. This new perspective is fully incorporated into the teachings of the churches.

The Sources of Conflict

In its basic thrust, the new church's emphasis on making the world a better place is quite congruent with the ideals of many business persons and organizations. To be sure, there will always be some tension, for the church perspective highlights God's intentions to have a world of peace and justice, and speaks in terms of ultimates that are only to be realized in eternity. The business perspective focuses on more proximate objectives and must always calculate the trade-offs involved in employing resources efficiently; freedom is a key value for corporate managers, for the wider the scope of management prerogatives, the more likely the goal in question will be achieved.

The trick is to keep the inherent tension between business and the churches on a creative track rather than a destructive one. For example, where liberation theology dominates the church discussion, there has seldom been fruitful dialogue with the business community. Some discussion of the origin and aims of liberation theology may be helpful, since this theology is often influential in the churches of developing countries.

Liberation versus Gradualism: A Contemporary Debate

In 1970, the World Council of Churches founded the Commission for the Churches Participation in Development (CCPD); this commission has championed structural changes in society and advocated a liberation style of change in preference to the traditional gradualist approach. The World Council is presently dominated by Third World countries and its statements are sometimes militant and decidedly anticapitalist. John C. Bennett, noted Protestant social ethicist and leader in ecumenical affairs, comments that the "World Council . . . no longer reflects the older and more disciplined ethical thinking of the First World."[3] While critical, he is sympathetic to the Third World intellectuals; he goes on to say that "the First World theologians can be criticized for provincialism and complacency."

The liberation style of doing theology has its roots in the Catholic Church of Latin America, and is intended to be a direct challenge to Christians who seem all too comfortable with suffering and deprivation in this present world. The writings of these Latin American theologians are characterized by a concern to see the world from the viewpoint of poor persons, and by an all-pervasive call to realize justice and liberation from poverty, and to realize this vision soon. The dominant motif is the people's participation in overcoming their oppression. It is an emphasis on a rapid change in social structures—a quick fix for the ailments of society—that is characteristic of the liberation approach. Not surprisingly, liberation theology is often marked by strong anticapitalist and anti-American rhetoric; from a liberationist perspective, the United States and its economic system hold little promise for Third World development. Some church leaders, although they may not fully espouse liberation theology, often speak from its militant posture. For example, in an interview in *Forbes* magazine, Paulo Evaristo Cardinal Arns, Catholic archbishop of São Paulo, Brazil, when asked about the problems of inflation and unemployment in Brazil, responded: "These problems (are) consequences of the installation of the multinational corporations and of a savage capitalism that can produce these ills in order to reap greater profits later."[4] Many detailed studies by economists and scholars most sympathetic to the terrible plight of the poor in Brazil offer a much different analysis. In fact, many argue that multinationals and capitalism, with appropriate government regulation, are the only hope for the poor in Brazil.

Although there is agreement within the churches that the plight of the poor must be alleviated, there is debate over the appropriateness of liberation theology. Many are concerned with its affinity with leftist political movements. Some accuse it of too easily advocating violence as a means of social change. There are others, however, who consider it as one of the valid means of transforming society. Persons espousing this theology are sensitive people who have been deeply touched by the condition of the poor and want transformations now. There is little appetite to wait a century and a half—the time it took to fashion such wealth-producing capabilities in the West. There is scant mention of the cultivation of habits of industry and other virtues. From a liberation perspective, the key issues are not these. Rather, the focus in proclaiming the Kingdom of God is on a positive strategy to overcome "oppression of the poor by the rich" and a great optimism that together humankind can fashion a different sort of world. Gustavo Gutierrez, a pioneer in this theology, makes the point well in his *A Theology of Liberation.*[5]

From the point of view of today's corporate leaders, a key feature of this theology is that it has little patience in its crusade to make the world a better place. The champions of this theology are strident in their condemnation of multinationals and corporate capitalism. However, an important point here is that church leaders who espouse the more extreme forms of liberation theology are not typical, and that it would be a mistake to characterize mainline Protestant and Catholic leaders in the United States in this militant mold.

Strategies of Church Activists in the United States

As two of the world's largest multinational institutions, the church and the corporation have a pervasive influence throughout the world. While churches have always highlighted the essential connection between personal and social ethics, it is only in the last fifteen years that they have formulated strategies designed to influence the social impact of business corporations. The initial concern of churches was that their own considerable economic resources be invested with an eye toward social responsibility. Stemming from the doctrine of private property, church teaching stressed that ownership entails responsibility, and the churches tried to be models of what good economic stewardship might be.

To assist church bodies in their judgments on investments, the National Council of Churches established the Corporate Information Center (CIC) in 1971. In 1974, the CIC merged with an ad hoc group of Catholic religious orders and Protestant denominations that had formed to protest a proposed corporate mining venture in Puerto Rico. This new coalition, housed in the New York City headquarters of the National Council of Churches, is known as the Interfaith Center on Corporate Responsibility (ICCR). The staff of the center provides research on corporate social performance, and coordinates and formulates church activist strategies.

A good argument can be made that church critics are capitalism's best friend. The professional staffs of churches link the local congregations with national structures through a vast network. Activists from the church staffs and ICCR provide one channel for business leaders to keep informed of the fresh ideas of public concern. Social concern shareholder proposals, even if only representative of a minority, serve as an important safety valve. Many of the reforms enacted in business and government first surfaced in the writings and activities of church critics. Business's ability to respond to public concern is one reason it is still accepted as a vital part of our society.

In a typical year, church proponents file over one hundred shareholder proposals but withdraw about 30 percent of these after dialogue and negotiation with the companies in question. The point here is that the church activists can be thought of as providing a service by surfacing issues of public concern such as equal employment opportunity, loans to South Africa, and plant closings, and that many of the apparent conflicts are settled in a spirit of mutual respect by communication and discussion.

For the most part, religious social teaching has always accepted the American economic vision of growth with equity. On balance, however, there have been many more words said about justice than growth. Often religious documents do not exhibit a clear understanding of the inevitable trade-offs necessary in any economic system. The point of most mainline religious criticism of Western capitalism has been that the virtues of entrepreneurship, productivity, creativity, and individual achievement have been stressed at the expense of concern for the fairness of the results. Most of the activities of church critics can be seen as a counterbalance, trying to ensure that the benefits and burdens of corporate activity are equitably distributed, and that the rights of the least advantaged are not neglected. From my experience with a number of business leaders, it is my impression that many see a genuine value in church activist groups. Sensitive leaders understand that the legitimacy of their institution depends on public approval and support. Insofar as activists mirror the convictions of thoughtful members of the society, their work ensures that business, with social approval, will continue to perform its vital function of providing goods and services.

Church groups have come to assume that dialogue with business groups without pressure or the threat of pressure will not be effective in resolving injustices under discussion. While there is clearly some truth to this premise, many observers, both within and outside of the churches, have cautioned activists about the unintended consequences of such a strategy. For example, consider the widely reported infant formula controversy.

The substantive issue underlying the controversy was the extremely high infant mortality rates in developing countries; corporation leaders and their critics agree on this. While no one is claiming that infant formula is the sole cause of these deaths, the critics have argued that the aggressive marketing practices have persuaded many women to shift from breastfeeding to bottlefeeding. The use of infant formula and bottlefeeding has two adverse consequences: (1) the loss of protective antibodies from breast milk and (2) the potential to misuse the formula either by using impure water or by diluting the formula to make it last longer. There is also the problem of illiteracy in many areas so that often the product's instructions cannot be properly understood. In addition, refrigeration was not available for most users. With this sort of analysis, in 1970, Dr. Derrick B. Jelliffe, then head of the Caribbean Food and Nutrition Institute in Jamaica, recommended that all commercial formulas be withdrawn from the market in developing countries. Needless to say, his recommendation was not without controversy. In 1975, the ICCR, along with some of its member groups, presented shareholder resolutions requesting information on marketing practices in the Third World to two of the major formula companies, Bristol-Myers and American Home Products. Abbott Laboratories, through its Ross Laboratories division, also was challenged in a shareholder resolution by church groups to examine its overseas marketing practices.

In 1977, the University of Minnesota Catholic Newman Center founded the Infant Formula Action Coalition (INFACT). This organization, along with the ICCR, organized a national boycott against the Swiss-based Nestle S.A., the largest supplier of commercial formula in the Third World. This consumer boycott continued for 6 1/2 years and was the subject of much media attention and conflict before it was suspended in late January 1984. More than seventy American organizations representing churches, doctors, nurses, teachers, and other professionals had joined the boycott.

Drawing support largely from church organizations, the Nestle boycott leaders mounted a major campaign on the premise that a serious problem could be remedied by changing objectionable marketing practices in the Third World. In 1981, the coalition's efforts to have an international code on the marketing of infant formula adopted by the World Health Organization (WHO) were successful. The voluntary code suggests that free samples, mass advertising to consumers, and a number of other sales lures should be suspended. The focus of the boycotting groups was now to pressure the industry to implement the International Code. All Nestle products and services, from Nestle Crunch candy bars to Stouffer hotels and restaurants, were under the boycott.

Throughout the conflict, charges were traded by both sides. For example, before a U.S. Senate hearing on the issue in 1978, a Nestle's spokesman argued that the protest was directed by "a worldwide church organization, with the stated purpose of undermining the free enterprise system." A June 1983 newsletter of INFACT reported a typical statement of boycott leaders: "Malnutrition, the pain of diarrhea and disease, and the constant threat of death are not the natural birthright of a child, but the result of a social system informed and directed by powerful corporations working for their own selfish interests."

Although Nestle agreed in 1982 to abide by the WHO code, it was not until 1984, after much hostility, that the church groups finally suspended the boycott. Because some multinational corporations (MNCs) have changed the way they market infant formula in the less-developed countries (LDCs), church groups may have a claim to some success. But the length of the Nestle boycott and the seeming intractability of its leaders, even in the face of Nestle's acquiescence, caused some damage both to the company and to the cohesiveness of the church groups.[6]

A senior official of Nestle said the boycott's principal cost was employee morale. When religious groups engage in protracted conflict with business, in this case to "save starving babies," it is difficult to gauge the damage to both esprit de corps and the public perception of the legitimacy of business and the economic system. Experience from this conflict between industry and religious activists would seem to indicate two sorts of serious errors. On the one hand, industry should not assume all critics are Marxist and are seeking a revolutionary socialistic system. Critics should be listened to and their remarks carefully assessed. On the other hand, critics should be straightforward with the goals they are seeking. No matter how good the end, a less than forthright means is beneath the dignity of church representatives. The church as a moral leader ought to ensure that its representatives are beyond reproach. In this light, consider the strategy on infant formula summarized by James Post in a recent article.

> Societies often have difficulties in shaping "sensible" policy solutions to complex policy issues. The reason that children die in developing nations is not because infant formula is a bad product. Rather, there is an environment of poverty, illiteracy, inadequate sanitation, unhealthy water, and limited health services that create dangerous conditions for the use of formula. Marketing did not create these conditions, but marketing was a more *actionable* aspect of the problem than poverty, water, or education. . . . Because business corporations are responsive to external pressure, action targeted at them has a better chance of producing change than actions aimed at such underlying conditions as poverty and illiteracy. A marketing code will not alleviate the problems of poverty, illiteracy, and poor sanitation, but it can help to ensure that companies do not exploit such conditions to their own advantage.[7]

While this may be acceptable strategy for some consumer groups, is it the most appropriate one for the church—the model of what human community ought to be like? The church indeed must be concerned to better the lot of the poor, but are not straightforward attempts to influence public policy much more fruitful? Should not the churches' major effort be directed at securing public policy aimed at improving the underlying conditions of poverty, illiteracy, and so on? Is settling for a marketing code, settling for too little? To be sure, the churches must be involved on both levels, criticizing injustices in business as well as initiating discussion of just public policy. Too much energy spent on the former, however, may leave little for the latter. The prospect of collaborative efforts with corporations to solve poverty problems will be unlikely if churches are alienated from business.

A Managerial Perspective

Reviewing the role of business in society in the last fifty years, it is surprising how the responsibilities of business have dramatically increased. Clearly, capitalism is not static but is what some have called a moving target. Business is part of a dynamic social system, and as new social and political problems have been identified, society has repeatedly turned to business for solution. Business is perceived as being powerful and effective. However, business is also mistrusted. Bigness has always been suspect in America. Corporations often have appeared insensitive to human values; some clearly have been. Many still think that profit maximization is the sole motive of business, even though a careful analysis of many corporations would yield a much more complex pattern.

The Nestle case illustrates an instance where a multinational assumed additional responsibilities for the complex sociocultural and environmental systems within which it was operating. However, the assumption of this responsibility was accompanied by protests, largely from religious organizations that applied pressure directly to the corporations. More prompt action may have avoided such coalitions. In the case of Nestle, there is still a protest organization with staff members ready to continue boycott and other activities, even though many of the original supporters have judged the founding problem to have been solved. The most effective business response may be to have managers who are adept at responding promptly to those societal expectations that are feasible and judged appropriate. Some way of institutionalizing this process may be helpful.

Church leaders too must scrutinize their "prophets." Moral language, especially when used by church personnel, is powerful. It has a remarkable ability to arouse passions and motivate persons of religious conviction. However, moral language can be abused when it is used without careful analysis. The churches could dilute an essential part of their heritage, should they fail to exercise diligence in the use of moral language. Business leaders who are church members could perform a great service for the religious community by offering their perspective to the church. As a matter of course, top management of the future would do well to know moral language and ethical analysis, not only to protect themselves but, more importantly, to consciously expand the horizon for decision making. Knee-jerk responses, either from the left or the right, ill-serve organizations and society in general.

The Churches, Public-Policy Initiatives, and the Business Community

The dilemma of an increasingly activist church is illustrated well by considering the response to the first draft of the U.S. Catholic bishops' letter on the economy: "Catholic Social Teaching and the U.S. Economy." The original schedule called for the first draft in November 1984 and then, on the basis of responses, a second draft in June 1985. The final version was projected for November 1985. As it turned out, there was such an overwhelming response to the first draft—largely negative from the business community—that the second draft has been postponed until November 1985. The final draft, it is hoped, will be ready in November 1986.

What this postponement reveals is that the bishops do intend to listen to their critics. They understand themselves to be part of a teaching and learning church, and this is a learning phase. That the bishops are seeking advice from leaders in the private and public sectors is not only a tribute to their political skills but, perhaps more important, it is a reflection of their conviction that God speaks to the entire community of faith. Authority in the Catholic church can be understood with the analogy of a lens. As a lens focuses light, so the role of the bishops is to gather together the best insights of the community for the matter in question and teach them to the people. While fundamental moral principles (for example, concern for the poor) are never in dispute, the concrete applications of these principles in specific policies are subject to much debate.

Over Their Heads?

The first draft of the pastoral letter on the economy has detailed policy applications for welfare reform, the crisis in farming communities, unemployment, collaboration in shaping the economy, and international economic concerns. The basic intent of the letter is to remind and to teach that there is a moral dimension to the economy, yet this message may be lost in the debate over particular applications. For example, consider the remarks of a sympathetic critic, Joseph A. Califano, Jr., secretary of Health, Education and Welfare from 1977 to 1979.

> When the bishops move to what they call "policy applications," they sound more like one of the great society legislative messages I helped draft for Lyndon Johnson than a group of clerics calling attention to the moral, religious and ethical dimensions of the society they are trying to reshape. Here the bishops bring much of the criticism on themselves. . . . My concern is that by dipping its toes too deeply in the waters of detailed federal programs, the bishops' message may be drowned.[8]

While the bishops are careful to point out in their "Policy Applications" section that the moral authority of applications is much less than that of universal moral principles, Califano offers a telling criticism. In the judgment of many, the bishops are simply in over their heads in discussing concrete policies. Whether critics are right or wrong, the authority of the bishops never again will be the same. However, the document has stimulated intense debate and hopefully will result in a general raising of the level of awareness of the moral dimension of economic decisions.

Edward L. Hennessy, Jr., chairman of Allied Corporation, brings to light a penetrating critique of the bishops' economic ethics:

> It seems to me that intelligent discussion of the pastoral's recommendations requires that we put a price on them. Then, the bishops and everyone else can make a judgment about whether the cost might merely inconvenience the well-to-do,

or whether it might reduce incentive, lessen the capital investment which creates jobs, slow the economy and seriously interfere with the goals of balancing the budget, cutting interest rates and making the United States competitive again with foreign producers.

No one I know questions the need to provide adequate social services for the poor in our society. But the draft pastoral, in its apparent determination to redistribute a significant part of our society's wealth, risks damaging the most productive economic system yet devised. It is a risk the bishops of the American church should, I think, hesitate to take.[9]

Is Hennessy correct in his judgment? There is nothing near a consensus on the issues in question. When the church speaks in the area of medical or sexual ethics, it has a long tradition to draw from. The problem is that there is not an established body of literature and a tradition of economic ethics that is commonly accepted by the relevant academic and professional communities. To be sure, the bishops' document itself has stimulated the development of such literature, but the field needs much plowing. There is much to be done. Understanding the trade-offs and conflict in values is essential for the future agenda in economic ethics.

Toward the Future

It may be that the social activist movement is only a phase in the church life as it moves toward a genuine ministry to managers of our public and private institutions. Today people are running corporate America often without any guidance or support from their churches. Business executives are often treated by their churches as either robber barons—with open hostility—or as rich benefactors—with undue deference. It is time for the churches to relate to managers as persons—persons who often have substantial power and influence to shape communities and lives, and who need the support of their religious community.

The church has been relatively successful in providing ministry to the medical community. Men and women trained in theology and ethics also learned the medical sciences, and on this basis offer their insight and guidance. A movement parallel to the one that produced medical ethics is long overdue for the management community. Managers ought to seek out their church leaders and offer their time and talent to advance this endeavor in economic ethics. It could yield high dividends for all.

Conclusion

It is safe to say that, one way or another, religious organizations will continue to have an impact on corporate and public policy. The tension inherent in this interaction can be creative and not destructive if managers are prepared both institutionally and personally. Corporate managers are schooled to produce goods and sevices in the most efficient manner at the best possible prices. Religious leaders, because of their commitments, often single-mindedly focus on the just distribution of what is produced, and give little attention to the producing segments of society. Each group displays little understanding of the other's position. Church leaders might come to see that in a finite world there are limitations to what can be done, and when it can be done. Corporate managers might be aided in developing a sensitivity to the many constituencies who are affected by economic decisions of business. To be sure, religious activists of the radical sort will never acknowledge the legitimacy of economic language. Just as surely, there are hard-nosed business types who are tone deaf to the compelling quality of some ethical arguments. Our hope for the future resides in those leaders in both the worlds of business and religion who together will forge a new and more humane consensus.

Notes

1. Alexis de Tocqueville, *Democracy in America*, ed. Phillips Bradley (New York: Vintage Books, 1945), vol. I, p. 316. This chapter appeared in earlier articles: "Religion: The Spirit or the Enemy of Capitalism," *Business Horizons* 26(6):6–13 (1983); "Catholic Bishops Take on Economics," *Business and Society Review* S4(3):21–26 (1985).

2. For further elaborations of many of the points in this article see *The Judeo-Christian Vision and the Modern Corporation*, ed. Oliver F. Williams and John W. Houck (Notre Dame, Ind.: University of Notre Dame Press, 1982).

3. John C. Bennett, "Protestantism and Corporations," in *The Judeo-Christian Vision and the Modern Corporation*, p. 88.

4. Norman Gall, "When Capitalism and Christianity Clash," *Forbes*, September 1, 1980, pp 100–101.

5. Gustavo Gutierrez, *A Theology of Liberation*, trans. Sister Caridad Inda and John Eagleston (Maryknoll, N.Y.: Orbis Books, 1973).

6. The Nestle case is discussed in more detail in my article, "Who Cast the First Stone," *Harvard Business Review* 62(5):151–160 (1984).

7. James E. Post, "Assessing the Nestle Boycott: Corporate Accountability and Human Rights," *California Management Review* 27(2):127 (1985).

8. Joseph A. Califano, Jr., "The Prophets and the Profiters," *America*, January 12, 1985, p. 6. Califano was responding to the first draft, although the issues he questions are essentially the same in the second draft.

9. Edward L. Hennessy, Jr., "A Pastoral for the Poor, Not the Economy," *America*, January 12, 1985, p. 17. For an analysis of the underlying economic and ethical issues of the U.S. bishops' letter on the economy, see John W. Houck and Oliver F. Williams, eds., *Catholic Social Teaching and the U.S. Economy: Working Papers for a Bishops' Pastoral* (Washington, D.C.: University Press of America, 1984).

7
Corporate Responses to External Pressures

Why Good Companies Get into Trouble
James O'Toole

In 1983, I concluded some four years of research about a group of companies that I was convinced were among the best managed in the United States. I called them the "vanguard" because I then believed that they could serve as future models for all large, publicly held corporations. These were companies that were both highly profitable and socially responsible. In fact, they did well by doing good. But, before the ink was dry on the book,[1] the exemplary list of corporations I had cited therein had begun to read more like a litany of has-beens than the roll-call from the business hall of fame I had intended. Several critics leapt on a number of my less-fortunate corporate examples (Atlantic Richfield, Levi Strauss, and Control Data, to name just an embarrassing trio) and offered these as "proof" that the principles espoused in the book were misguided. Setting aside the point that one cannot logically disprove a proposition simply by discrediting the examples used to illustrate it, I nevertheless, must admit that the curmudgeons of the business world raised an interesting point: specifically, that none of the authors of the many recent books on managerial excellence has been able to produce a list of good companies that is enduring. (*In Search of Excellence*'s list had a half-life of about six months.)[2]

This fact has led me to undertake some considerable headscratching about why is it so many good companies these days suddenly find themselves up to their collective crotches in crocodiles and the crocodiles win. The most cynical explanation is that the employee-centered, "humanistic" philosophies practiced by many so-called excellent companies ultimately backfire and lead to their financial ruin. There is, alas, a *prima facie* case to be made against the once-fabled "right brain" style of management that favors intuition, informality, hugging, white wine busts, and the like. Recall that during the era when the personal computer and semiconductor businesses were booming, such high-tech idols as Atari, Apple, D.E.C., H.P., Osborne, and Intel appeared to all the world to be captained by managerial geniuses.

In hindsight, we now see that their hot-tubs-and-sabbaticals approach was more a consequence than a cause of their being on the ascent side of a product cycle during which demand for computers temporarily exceeded supply. It is instructive in this regard to travel the length of the Silicon Valley today. With only a few remarkable exceptions, the fabled "progressive" managers of yesterday have turned into get-tough, left-brained clones of the old-fashioned tyrants who manage in the Monongohela Valley. *Sic transit humanitas!*

Still, this doesn't mean that humanistic management *caused* the current high-tech decline any more than it was responsible for the boom period in Silicon Valley's recent past. The truth is that all companies go through periods of boom and bust. Given a highly dynamic competitive environment, how could it be otherwise? What company hasn't had a bad quarter (or a bad year) in recent times? Even those who have topped *Fortune*'s annual list of "most prestigious" corporations have stumbled of late—witness IBM's PCjr, HP's struggles with personal computers, and Dow-Jones's embarrassing "Heard on the Street" column fiasco. The lesson here is that there are no perfect companies (as there are no men or women without faults). Moreover, simplistic theories about the cause of managerial failure—like simplistic theories about the source of managerial excellence—won't wash on careful analysis.

Since all companies get into trouble from time to time, perfection is thus not a valid criteria for excellence. A truer test of a company's greatness is how its managers behave during bad times. In this regard, consider a high-tech company that has topped no one's list of great companies, but has nonetheless weathered the vicissitudes of the computer market with far greater stability than have its glitzy Silicon Valley rivals. Motorola is not a denizen of lotus land; in fact, it is headquartered in the suburbs of that quintessentially smokestack town, Chicago. Motorola is not led by the kind of charismatic, splashy, larger-than-life, obsessive characters who spend twelve-hour-days walking around their Silicon Valley plants telling every employee how to do his or her job. In contrast, Motorola's leaders are thoughtful, careful, analytical types who are dedicated to institutionalizing the structures, systems, and habits that empower all employees to do their own jobs without constant coercion and direction.

Recall that in Silicon Valley's good old days managers attempted to manipulate their employees with public manifestations of love—celebrations in which productive workers received praise (and hugs) for their efforts. In contrast, all Motorola's 60,000 domestic employees are part of self-managing work teams, and all are eligible for up to a 41 percent monthly bonus based on their team's performance. While Motorola's managers believe that there is never any excuse for failing to give productive employees recognition for their efforts, they also recognize that the real currencies of organizational life are money and power—two things that the egotistical stars of many high-tech companies appear to have trouble sharing.

In the heyday of Silicon Valley, there was tons of talk about "culture" and oodles of effort dedicated to contriving symbolic actions and fabricated myths to communicate corporate affection for employees (one would have believed that high-tech workers were entitled to a hot-tub break whenever they became stressed-out from more than two hours of straight work). But these same companies undercut whatever value they derived from their symbols and rhetoric when they engaged in massive layoffs at the onset of each of the recent semiconductor recessions. In distinction, Motorola plans ahead and is often—but not always—able to utilize reduced work weeks in lieu of morale-destroying layoffs. Most important, when recessions hit Motorola they respond in a fashion alien to the inhabitants of Silicon Valley: they do *nothing* fundamentally different than in good times. Of course, they respond by making appropriate strategic, tactical, and product changes, but the company's fundamental principles—including employee participation in decision making, sharing of productivity gains, "open and complete argument on controversial issues," honesty, integrity, and the goal of "zero product defects"—are never compromised. Contrast this to the crisis management that occurred at such high-tech companies as Atari and Osborne.

What Motorola's managers understand—and what allows them to cope with the effects of recessions better than their Aquarian competitors—is that management is basically a *moral undertaking*. Am I saying that viewing business as a moral undertaking will guarantee success, or that failure to do so will cause a good company to go bad? Sorry, life isn't that simple. I'm merely asserting that no company has ever gotten into financial hot water by taking the high road. No company has ever produced red ink *because* it behaved ethically, *because* it obeyed the law, *because* it provided high-quality goods, *because* it invested for the long term, *because* it treated employees with respect or *because* it put something back into host communities. Of course, companies that do none of these things succeed, too. Yet, the low road is fraught with risk. For it is often the case that corporations who play fast and loose end by alienating customers, vendors, employees, and stockholders—witness Texaco, E.F. Hutton, General Dynamics, A.H. Robbins, and J.P. Stevens.

Indeed, all I am claiming is that managers have a *choice*. As there are no rules that free managers from the terrible responsibility of choosing what products to market and what strategies to pursue, managers must also choose whether to treat employees well or to treat them poorly, and choose whether to produce safe, high-quality goods or shoddy ones. There is no guarantee what the financial consequences of such choices will be: corporations that mistreat employees and peddle inferior products may either succeed or fail; the same can be predicted for those that show respect for employees and customers. Nonetheless, that this choice *even exists* comes as news to most managers, for they have been led to believe that success is only possible by taking the low road, by pursuing the quick buck. Heretofore, they have believed that doing good was inimical to doing well.

But there is now evidence that managers are free to make a choice that few had thought open to them: they can choose to conduct their work lives with the same high principles with which they conduct their private lives. The companies I have studied, including Motorola, Dayton Hudson, Deere, Herman Miller, and W.T. Gore, dispel the myth that the only way to succeed in business is at the expense of employees, customers, and society. The high road these companies pursue is *not* one of altruism, it is *not* pious or trendy "social responsibility," and it is *not* do-goodism. Much as an individual can lead a moral life without being a social worker or a Mother Teresa, a corporation can behave morally by leading a principled existence—what Aristotle called a "good life" in the individual context.

From an organizational perspective, leading a good life entails balancing the legitimate claims of all the corporation's constituencies—suppliers, dealers, employees, host communities, as well as shareowners and managers. For example, Deere has a policy it calls "mutual advantage" that it extends to all its various constituencies. When this principle is applied to dealer relations, it means that the company won't dump unsaleable inventory on their tractor dealers in order to make corporate books look good in the short run (as is the practice, for instance, in the auto industry). A few years back, Levi Strauss executives behaved similarly when they cancelled all white-collar and executive raises immediately after gaining a significant wage give-back from their unionized employees. Contrast this to the attitude displayed at GM a few months later when executives voted themselves sizeable bonuses hard on the heels of winning significant concessions from the UAW. When Deere and Levi practice such "moral symmetry" they are *not* engaged in altruism; they simply see that treating employees, unions, and dealers with respect is in the best interest of investors in the long term. The real question is why auto executives continually choose to shoot themselves in the foot by acting expediently.

Dedication to high purpose is another moral precept that guides great companies. Again, this is a principle that GM violated in the 1970s when it proudly echoed Alfred Sloan's famous line that "We are in the business of making money, not cars." That worked fine until GM ran into competition from Toyota and Nissan executives who said, in sharp contrast, that *they* were in the business of making high-quality cars in order to bring jobs to their resource-poor island nation. Now, which company is most likely to attract, maintain, and motivate the most dedicated and productive employees—one that offers them a noble vision or one that shows contempt for the quality of its own product? In Johnson & Johnson's famous Credo, in Deere's Green Bulletin, and in the other "constitutions" of great companies, the stated purpose of business is to provide society with the high-quality goods and services it needs in order to generate the profits necessary to maintain employment and to improve the nation's standard of living. Profits are an obvious necessity in this view—the more profit the better, in fact. But profits are seen as means, *not* as ends—an important moral distinction that not only builds employee commitment, but addresses head-on the criticisms of antibusiness legislators who seek excuses for increased corporate taxation and regulation.

Continuous learning is another principle that is religiously adhered to in great companies. Again, using GM in the 1970s as an example of a good company that got into trouble, we see what happens when a corporation becomes complacent and arrogantly believes that it has "solved" the problem of management. For decades, GM's managers repeated over and over the once-successful policies developed by Alfred Sloan in the 1920s until they finally hit upon an environment in which these concepts were no longer valid. High-priced gas, changed consumer preferences, Japanese competition, new worker values, and government regulation brought home to GM in the late 1970s the lesson that nothing fails like success. In the best companies, in distinction, everyone is constantly challenging past premises and *un*learning the things that once led to success but promise failure in the future. On a visit to Motorola, I was surprised when a young manager buttonholed CEO Robert Galvin: "I heard what you had to say at this morning's meeting, Bob, and I'm going to prove you wrong; I'm going to shoot you down!" I thought the kid's career was kaput, but there was Galvin, beaming proudly as he explained to your bewildered correspondent, "That's how we became the nation's leading producer of semiconductors." Indeed, it's through such listening to *all* of their constituencies that great companies stay flexible and are thus able to meet ever-changing competitive challenges.

The final principle I'll mention is high aim. Contrast GM's satisfaction in the 1970s with being the world's *biggest* auto manufacturer to the quite opposite aspirations of Lee Iacocca that Chrysler should become "the *best* at everything we do." It is a sad commentary on the state of American business that an executive can become a national hero merely by dedicating himself to what ought to have been a given. If the old goal at Chrysler (and at GM, at U.S. Steel, and so forth) wasn't to be the best, good Lord, what *were* they aiming for? Fortunately, a few corporations have had high aim for decades. Dayton Hudson—America's fastest growing retailer, the retail industry leader in customer service, and the leader of all American business in terms of community service—has as its goal "to be premier in every aspect of our business." Significantly, when I visited DH's headquarters I found healthy dissatisfaction with the fact that they were not yet nunmber one in tapping their human resources. If one wishes to avoid failure, better a dissatisfied management than a complacent one.

If eminent companies succeed through commitment to such moral principles, why is it that some such companies nonetheless go bad? Having observed the precipitous recent decline of three of the corporations I featured in *Vanguard Management*, I think I've begun to understand the process by which they did themselves in. First hand, I observed the tragedy of ARCO (the amazing shrinking oil company). For nearly a decade, ARCO had been a paradigm of the values just described, yet it self-destructed with meteoric determination. When the price of oil plummeted, ARCO's immediate reaction was to abandon the very characteristics that had led to its distinction. Formerly, ARCO had been a statesmanlike leader of its industry, master at flexible, long-term planning, gloriously entrepreneurial, and always careful to assess the impact of its activities on host communities. But, almost overnight, the company reverted to the "tough-minded" practices of its least-imaginative competitors (and, in so doing, not only added to the depth of its fall, but may have destroyed corporate morale to the extent that a full recovery is problematic). How could this have occurred? In corporation after corporation, the pattern repeats itself: when times get rough, the guys in the black hats gain credibility because they offer this clear, unambiguous response to any crisis: "Cut out all the gooey malarky, and get tough!" In the absence of confident leadership, such calls for expedient behavior carry the day because they promise immediate results. ARCO had been made particularly vulnerable to such expedience because the architect of their old culture, Thornton Bradshaw, had recently left the company (and was off saving RCA when the price of oil collapsed). Now, Lod Cook, recently appointed CEO, is faced with the Herculean task of cleaning out the stables befouled by the expedient behavior of his confused predecessor.

Control Data Corporation's fall has been even more precipitous . . . and tragic. Perhaps no other corporation had a better fix on what business must do to avoid further governmental interference in the economy. But CDC then violated the very principles on which its philosophy rested. It arrogantly ignored the needs of stockholders, treating customers in a cavalier fashion, and dealing with partners in their community-based joint ventures with contempt. CDC also became a nonlearning organization, too slow to tailor its fine educational software for use in personal computers, and failing to develop a competitive next generation of peripherals for that same home market. Significantly, CDC did not fail (as some on Wall Street claim) *because* of its efforts "to find profitable ways of meeting society's unmet needs." Instead, it failed *in spite* of this enterprising orientation.

Levi Strauss presents the most instructive case of why the good go bad—and of the heavy toll that must inevitably be paid as a consequence of succumbing to short-term amorality. In a headlong rush to achieve the insatiable levels of growth demanded by stock speculators, Levi aborted its principles—mistreating the very dealers who had participated in its earlier success, cutting corners here and there to look good *now,* and ultimately laying off long-term employees for the first time in Levi's history. Having failed to meet the desires of Wall Street, while in the process losing the traits that had once made the company special, the heirs of Levi Strauss then realized they had made the wrong choice. Significantly, they have now chosen to take the company private (at great expense) in order to return to the time-consuming path of building lasting business relationships and allowing entrepreneural ideas time to develop—activities that the investing community was too impatient to endure.

In each of these three cases cynics have drawn the wrong conclusion: they have claimed that ARCO, CDC, and Levi slipped *because* they were intent on doing well by doing good. In fact, these companies got into trouble when, faced with difficult external challenges, they betrayed their principles instead of staying the course. This is not to say that these three companies ended up with any choice other than to lay off employees; my argument is that prior, expedient decisions led them to the sad point where they had no other choice. Moreover, the examples of Motorola and Dayton Hudson illustrate that the final chapters of the stories of good companies needn't be ones of moral transgression and economic failure.

The cynics are right of course, the low road is easier and, no doubt, can lead to success. But my point is this: if managers come to see that they can succeed by taking either the high or low road, won't many of them choose to pursue the higher course, even if it is more difficult? If some of these managers should then fail (as many must in a capitalist economy), won't they at least have the comfort of having known they gave the effort the *best* of everything that was in them.

Note

1. James O'Toole, *Vanguard Management* (New York: Doubleday, 1985).
2. Thomas J. Peters and Robert H. Waterman, Jr., *In Search of Excellence* (New York: Harper & Row, 1982).

Managing Stakeholder Relationships

R. Edward Freeman
Daniel R. Gilbert, Jr.

Since the post–World War II period the worldwide business scene has changed dramatically. However, business theorists and practicing managers still use the conceptual tools of the prewar era. As a consequence, various social and ethical issues appear as absolute anomalies to the theory and practice of management. Our conceptual apparatus, the lenses we use to look at the world, our worldview, our paradigms, and the way that we talk cannot process a Ralph Nader and Campaign GM, a Foreign Corrupt Practices Act, a "60 Minutes" story, the Tylenol poisonings, the Rely Tampon toxic shock scare, business executives being kidnapped, the Bhopal tragedy, and a host of other issues.

By focusing the understanding of business on the traditional relationships between customers, employees, suppliers, owners, and domestic competitors, managers are constantly surprised by governments, consumer advocates, environmentalists, terrorists, media, local communities, foreign competitors, and other groups who perceive that they have a stake in a business. There is a constant source of tension between business strategy, traditionally conceived as the appropriate means to an end of profitability, and the demands of society and ethics as seen through the eyes of other stakeholders in a business.

We need a new way to understand business, a new set of concepts that integrates the current reality of the global business environment with the simplistic truisms of managerial capitalism. We need a vocabulary that helps us to make sense of the real world of business today.[1] The concept of *stakeholders* and *stakeholder management* provides such a framework.[2] A stakeholder is any group or individual who can affect or is affected by a business. Thus, the stakeholder concept identifies the relevant set of actors in the environment of a business. Stakeholder management is the idea that the tasks of managers in a business are to manage the stakeholder relationships in a way that achieves the purpose of the business. Stakeholder management provides the tools by which we can connect strategy to social and ethical issues. Once a business is understood as a set of stakeholder relationships, there are a number of implications for the theory and practice of management. The purpose of this article is to articulate the stakeholder management framework.

Levels of Analysis

Any business needs to be understood at three levels of analysis.[3] The first is how does the business as a whole fit into its larger environment, or the *rational* level. The second is how does the business relate to its environment as a matter of standard operating procedures and routine management processes, or the *process* level. The third is how does the business execute actual *transactions*, or deal or contract with those individuals who have a stake.

An example of the rational level is to think of business strategy as a game played, for example, between IBM and AT&T. IBM does action X and AT&T responds with action Y. An example of what we mean by the process level would be to look internally and see how the performance and reward procedures work at both AT&T and IBM. An example of the transactions level would be to closely examine the behavior of IBM and AT&T salespersons to see how each treats customers, and to examine the terms of various contracts, deals, promises, and individual motivations of each player. Obviously these three levels of analysis are connected. In fact, we argue that in successful businesses they fit together in a coherent pattern.

The Rational Level

The rational level of the stakeholder framework must give an accurate picture of the place of a business in its larger environment. It must identify those groups who have a stake, and it must depict the nature of the relationship between stakeholder and firm.

Stakeholder Identification. Who are those groups and individuals who can affect and are affected by the achievement of an organization's purpose? How can we construct a stakeholder map of an organization? What are the problems in constructing such a map? Ideally, the starting point for constructing a map for a particular business is a historical analysis of the environment of that particular firm. In the absence of such a historical document, figure 1 can serve as a checkpoint for an initial generic stakeholder map.

Figure 1 depicts a stakeholder map around one major strategic issue for one very large organization, the *XYZ* Company, based primarily in the United States. Unfortunately, most attempts at stakeholder analysis end with the construction of figure 1. The primary use of the stakeholder concept has been as a tool for gathering information about generic stakeholders. General stakeholders refers to those categories of groups who can affect. While government is a category, it is the Environmental Protection Agency (EPA), the Occupational Safety and Health Administration (OSHA), the Federal Trade Commission (FTC), Congress, and so forth who can take actions to affect the achievement of an organization's purpose. Therefore, for stakeholder analysis to be meaningful, figure 1 must be taken one step further. Specific stakeholder groups must be identified. Table 1 is a chart of

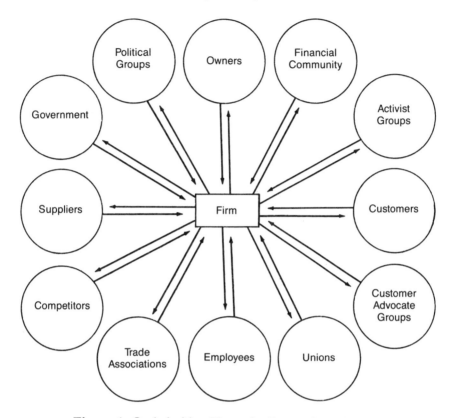

Figure 1. Stakeholder Map of a Large Organization

specific stakeholders to accompany figure 1 for the *XYZ* Company. Even in table 1 some groups are aggregated, in order to disguise the identity of the company. Thus, "Investment Banks" would be replaced by the names of those investment banks actually used by *XYZ*. Most very large organizations have a stakeholder map and accompanying stakeholder chart that are relatively similar to figure 1 and table 1. There will be variations among industries, companies, and geographies at the specific stakeholder level, but figure 1 and table 1 can be used as a checklist of stakeholder groups.

Table 2 is an analysis of the stakes of some of those specific stakeholder groups listed in table 1. Thus, the stake of Political Parties #1 and #2 is as a heavy user of *XYZ*'s product, as being able to influence the regulatory process to mandate change in *XYZ*'s operations, and as being able to elevate *XYZ* to national attention via the political process. The stake of *XYZ*'s owners varies among specific stakeholder groups. Those employees of *XYZ*, and the pension funds of *XYZ*'s unions are concerned with long-term growth of *XYZ*'s stock, as their retirement income will depend on the ability of *XYZ* to earn returns during their retirement

Table 1
Specific Stakeholders in a Large Organization

Owners	*Financial Community*	*Activist Groups*
Shareowners	Analysts	Safety and health groups
Bondholders	Investment banks	Environmental groups
Employees	Commercial banks	"Big business" groups
	Federal Reserve	Single-issue groups
Suppliers	*Government*	*Political Groups*
Firm #1	Congress	Political party #1
Firm #2	Courts	Political party #2
Firm #3	Cabinet departments	National League of Cities
etc.	Agency #1	National Council
	Agency #2	of Mayors
		etc.
	Customer	
Customers	*Advocate Groups*	*Unions*
Customer segment #1	Consumer Federation	Union of workers #1
Customer segment #2	of America	Union of workers #2
etc.	Consumer's Union	etc.
	Council of Consumers	Political action committees
	etc.	of unions
Employees	*Trade Associations*	*Competitors*
Employee segment #1	Business Roundtable	Domestic competitor #1
Employee segment #2	NAM	Domestic competitor #2
etc.	Customer trade	etc.
	organization #1	Foreign competitor #1
	Customer trade	etc.
	organization #2	
	etc.	

Note: The actual names of most stakeholder groups are disguised.

years. Other shareowner groups want current income, as *XYZ* has been known for steady but modest growth over time. Customer Segment #1 used a lot of *XYZ*'s product and was interested in how the product could be improved over time for a small incremental cost. Customer Segment #2 used only a small amount of *XYZ*'s product, but that small amount was a critical ingredient for Customer Segment #2, and there were no readily available substitutes. Thus, the stakes of the different customer segment stakeholders differed. One consumer advocate group was concerned about the effects of *XYZ*'s product decisions on the elderly, who were for the most part highly dependent on *XYZ*'s products. Another consumer advocate group was worried about other *XYZ* products in terms of safety.

As shown in figure 1 and tables 1 and 2 the construction of a rational stakeholder map is not an easy task in terms of identifying specific groups and the stakes of each. The figure and tables are enormously oversimplified, for they depict the stakeholders of *XYZ* as static, whereas in reality, they change over time, and their stakes change depending on the strategic issue under consideration.

Table 2
Stakes of Some Specific Stakeholders

Customer Segment #1	*Political Parties #1 and #2*
High users of product	High users of product
Improvement of product	Able to influence regulatory process
	Able to get media attention on a national scale
Customer Segment #2	*Consumer Advocate #1*
Low users of product	Effects of *XYZ* on the elderly
No available substitute	
Employees	*Consumer Advocate #2*
Jobs and job security	Safety of *XYZ*'s products
Pension benefits	
Owners	
Growth and income	
Stability of stock price and dividend	

Stakeholder Role Set. Many stakeholders wear multiple hats. Just as Merton (1957) identified the role set for individuals in society, and Evan (1966) generalized this notion for organizations to the organization set, we might combine these notions into a stakeholder role set, or the set of roles that an individual or group may play qua being a stakeholder in an organization. For example, an employee may be a customer for *XYZ*'s products, may belong to a union of *XYZ*, may be an owner of *XYZ*, may be a member of Political Party #1, and may even be a member of a consumer advocate group. Many members of certain stakeholder groups are also members of other stakeholder groups, and qua stakeholder in an organization may have to balance (or not balance) conflicting and competing roles. Conflict within each person and among group members may result. The role set of a particular stakeholder may well generate different and conflicting expectations of corporate action. Figure 2 is an example of the stakeholder role set of employees and a government official.

Stakeholder Interconnections: Networks and Coalitions. Stakeholders do not act in isolation, nor do they only interact with the firm, as shown in figure 1. In reality, each firm and each stakeholder is always enmeshed in a web of relationships. Figure 3 depicts the networks of relationships that can easily emerge.

XYZ Company found that one of their unions was also a large contributor to an adversarial consumer advocate group that was pressuring a key government agency to more closely regulate *XYZ*. Networks of stakeholder groups easily emerge on a particular issue and endure over time. Coalitions of groups form to help or oppose a company on a particular issue. Also, some firms are quite adept at

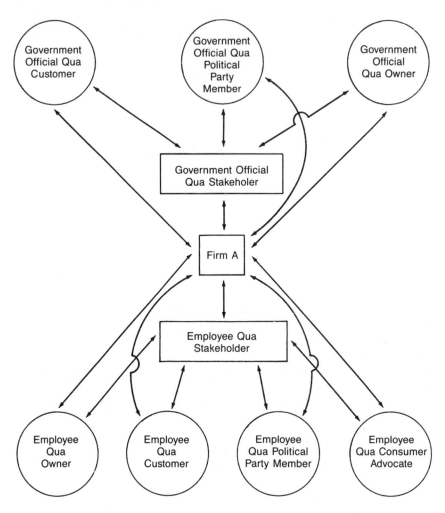

Figure 2. The Stakeholder Role Set: An Example

working indirectly, that is, at influencing Stakeholder A to influence Stakeholder B, to influence Stakeholder C.

More traditional examples include the emergence of the courts as a key stakeholder in takeover bids. Marathon Oil successfully used the courts and the agencies involved in antitrust to fend off a takeover bid from Mobil, while finding U.S. Steel to come to the rescue. AT&T recently marshalled the support of employees and stockholders to try to influence the Congress through a letter-writing campaign. While there is some research on power and influence networks, little is known in the way of formulating strategies for utilizing such networks in a positive and proactive fashion. Little is known, prescriptively, about what range of alternatives

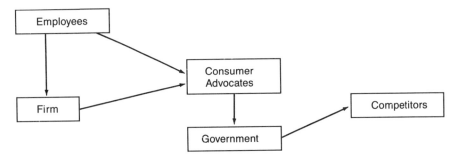

Figure 3. Stakeholder Networks

is open to managers who want to utilize such an indirect approach to dealing with stakeholders.

Stakeholders Are Multidimensional. The courts and some government agencies play a special role as part of the process by which groups interact. They have a special kind of stake, one of formal power. While they usually do not initiate action, they can serve as resolver of conflicts, or as guarantor of due process. If we generalize this notion we see the phenomenon of the differing kinds of stakes and the differing perceptions of stakes that various groups have. *Stake* is obviously multidimensional, and not measured solely in dollar terms. However, exactly what the dimensions of stake are is a more difficult question. Table 2 ranges across a broad spectrum of phenomena from more traditional dollar returns to stockholders to a call for voice in running the affairs of *XYZ* (Hirschman 1970). Clearly we need to understand stake in more detail.

One analytical device depicts an organization's stakeholders on a two-dimensional grid. The first dimension categories stakeholders by interest or stake. The idea is to look at the range of perceived stakes of multiple stakeholders. While there are no hard and fast criteria to apply here, one typical categorization is to classify stake from having an equity interest in the firm to being an influence, or in Dill's (1975) terms, "being a kibitzer, or someone who has an interest in what the firm does because it affects them in some way, even if not directly in marketplace terms." We might place a middle category between equity and kibitzer and call it having a *market* stake. These three categories of a continuum are meant to represent the more traditional theory of the firm's differing stakes of owners (equity stake), customers and suppliers (market stake), and government (kibitzer).

The second dimension of this classificatory grid can be understood in terms of power, or loosely speaking, the ability to use resources to make an event actually happen. The three points of interest on this continuum are voting power, economic power, and political power. Owners can expend resources in terms of voting power, by voting for directors or voting to support management, or even voting their shares in the marketplace in a takeover battle. Customers and suppliers can expend resources in terms of economic power, measured by dollars invested in R&D, switching to another firm, raising price, or withholding supply. Government can expend resources in terms of political power by passing legislation, writing new regulations, or bringing suit in the course.

Figure 4 represents this two-dimensional grid, with owners being the textbook case of an equity stake and voting power; customers and suppliers having a market stake and economic power; and government having an influencer stake and political power. The diagonal of figure 4 represents the development of classical management thought, and the prevailing world-view of the modern business firm. Management concepts and principles have evolved to treat the stakeholders along this diagonal. Managers learn how to handle stockholders and boards of directors via their ability to vote on certain key decisions, and conflicts are resolved by the procedures and processes written into the corporate charter or by methods that involve formal legal parameters. Strategic planners, marketing managers, financial analysts, and operations executives base their decisions on marketplace variables and a long tradition of wisdom and research based on an economic analysis of marketplace forces. Public relations and public affairs managers and lobbyists learn to deal in the political arena, to curry the favor of politicians, and to learn to strategically use PACs, "perks," and the regulatory process.

As long as the real world approximately fits this diagonal case of figure 4, there are few problems. Each set of managerial problems and issues has an established body of knowledge on which to draw in times of change. But the real world is often more complex, and the diagonal boxes of figure 4 are no longer the only ones to be filled in. For instance, in the auto industry one part of government has acquired formal power, the Chrysler Loan Guarantee Board, while in the steel industry some agencies have acquired economic power in terms of the imposition

Stake \ Power	Formal or Voting	Economic	Political
Equity	Stockholders Directors Minority Interests		Dissident Stockholders
Economic		Suppliers Debt Holders Customers Unions	Local Governments Foreign Governments Consumer Groups Unions
Influencers	Government SEC Outside Directors	EPA OSHA	Nader's Raiders Governments Trade Associations

Figure 4. The Power Stake Grid

of import quotas or the trigger-price mechanism. The Securities and Exchange Commission (SEC) might be viewed as a kibitzer with formal power in terms of disclosure and accounting rules. Outside directors, now, do not necessarily have an equity stake. This is especially true of women, minority group members, and academics who are becoming more normal for the boards of large corporations, even though it is far from certain that such directors are really effective and not merely symbolic. Some traditional kibitzer groups are buying stock and acquiring an equity stake. While they also acquire formal power, the yearly demonstration at the stockholders meeting or the proxy fight over social issues is built on their political power base. Witness the marshalling of the political process by church groups at the annual stockholders meeting in bringing up issues such as selling infant formula in the Third World or investing in South Africa. Unions are using political power, as well as their equity stake in terms of pension fund investing, to influence management decisions. Customers are being organized by consumer advocates to exercise the voice option and to politicize the marketplace.

Congruent Perceptions. Business and their stakeholders do not always agree on what is the appropriate stake of a group. In fact, there may be differing perceptions of both power and stake depending on one's point of view. An organization may not understand that a particular union has political power, and may treat the union as a purely economic entity, only to be surprised when the union gets a bill introduced in the legislature to prevent a proposed plant closing. The *ABC* Company completely misread the power and stake of a group of realtors who were upset over a proposed change in *ABC*'s product. The legislature in the state where *ABC* operates was composed of a number of realtors, who easily introduced a bill to prevent the proposed product changes. It was only by some tough eleventh-hour negotiations that *ABC* escaped some completely devastating legislation. The *DEF* Utility could not understand why a consumer advocate group was opposing it on a certain issue that had no economic effect on the group. Finally, *DEF* spoke to a consumer leader who told *DEF* that the only reason the group was opposing it was that *DEF* had not informed the group of the proposed rate change before the case was filed. In short, the consumer group perceived that they had a different stake than that perceived by the management of *DEF*. *DEF* managers naturally believed that as long as the proposed rate change was in the economic interest of the consumer group and its constituency, there would be no problem. The consumer group perceived things differently—they had a vital role to play as influencer or kibitzer.

Analyzing stakeholders in terms of the organization's perceptions of their power and stake is not enough. When these perceptions are out of line with the perceptions of the stakeholders, all the brilliant strategic thinking in the world will not work. There will be a problem of legitimacy. Each group will think that the other does not really care about its concerns, or bargains in bad faith, or is totally unresponsive. The congruence problem is a real one in most companies for there are few organizational processes to check the assumptions that managers make every day about their stakeholders. The rational analysis proposed here in terms of stakeholder maps must be tempered by a thorough understanding of the workings of the organization through an analysis of its strategic and operational processes.

The Process Level

Large complex organizations have many processes for accomplishing tasks. From routine applications of procedures and policies to the use of more sophisticated analytical tools, managers invent processes to accomplish routine tasks and to make complex tasks routine. To understand organizations and how they manage stakeholder relationships, it is necessary to look at the standard operating procedures—the organizational processes that are used to achieve some kind of fit with the external environment.

A good deal of research since the mid-1960s has gone into understanding how a corporation can be seen as a set or portfolio of businesses. Discrete business units are easier to manage, and factors for success may be easier to discern at the business level, than at the aggregated level of the corporation as a whole. The idea is to look at this set of businesses as stocks in a portfolio, with selection and nourishment given to winners and the door given to losers. Corporate planners and division managers (or strategic business unit managers) plot the firm's set of businesses on a matrix, which arrays an external against an internal dimension. The external dimension is usually labeled "Industry Attractiveness" and is usually measured by the growth rate of the industry under consideration. The internal dimension is usually labeled "Business Strengths" and is usually measured by market share. The corporate managers, after plotting the portfolio of businesses, seek to arrive at a balanced portfolio that maximizes returns (measured by return on equity, earnings per share, or return on investment, and so forth) and minimizes risks. Managers of particular businesses are then given a strategic mission based on their place in the portfolio and the potential of the business in question.

As a management process, portfolio analysis easily can be out of touch with the stakeholder maps of most firms, as depicted in earlier figures and tables. It simply looks at too narrow a range of stakeholders, and measures business performance on too narrow a dimension. An industry growth rate may be influenced by a number of nonmarketplace stakeholders; to rely solely on industry growth rate is to forego opportunities to influence stakeholders who may determine the future growth rate of the industry. For example, in the auto industry the following all have an influence on future growth rates in the industry: foreign competitors and governments, U.S. government agencies, the Congress, the courts, Ralph Nader and the Center for Auto Safety, environmental groups, and the United Auto Workers. However, if market share is relied on as the sole criterion to measure competitive strength, we will not necessarily invest resources to deal with all of the groups who can influence future market position. Market share is too broad a measure and an overreliance on it can be detrimental.

To illustrate, consider the fate of *JKL* Company after spending several million dollars in R&D to develop a new product that would serve as a substitute to a large established market. *JKL* believed that the product offered high growth potential, and in accordance with accepted theory, introduced the new product before getting approval from a key government agency that closely regulates the industry in which *JKL* would be competing. The product was later found to be carcinogenic and *JKL* took a large loss. Market share was not the sole indicator of success for *JKL*.

Or, consider Procter and Gamble's (P&G) experience with Rely Tampons. P&G had entered a mature market with a new product and spent heavily to gain market share. When reports linking Rely with toxic shock syndrome surfaced, P&G voluntarily removed Rely from the market rather than jeopardize future products and its corporate reputation. Industry attractiveness was not the sole criterion for the success of Rely. The future attractiveness of the market, together with the possibility of tarnishing P&G's excellent reputation, caused P&G to make a decision that was quite expensive. Even though it cannot be shown that use of Rely caused the disease, the mere possibility of a linkage was enough for P&G to recall the product.

Similarly, Johnson & Johnson acted quickly to recall the entire stock of Extra-Strength Tylenol after several deaths were reported as a result of criminal tampering with bottles of the product. Someone allegedly put cyanide capsules in bottles of the product after it was on retail store shelves. Johnson & Johnson's actions were lauded on "60 Minutes," a show sometimes critical of the actions of large corporations. The product has been reintroduced in "tamper proof" packages, and advertised heavily. Portfolio analysis simply cannot prepare the corporation to deal with issues such as those just discussed. Industry or market attractiveness analysis is not sophisticated enough to yield practical conclusions in areas where economics, social and political forces, and new technologies combine.

The point of this critique of portfolio analysis is not that managers must be certain of success before taking action, nor that since market share and industry attractiveness do not yield certainty they must be rejected. But, rather, the strategic processes that we use must, as a minimum, raise the right questions. Portfolio analysis processes are enormously useful in helping managers understand some of the factors for success in a business, yet for the most part they ignore non-marketplace stakeholders who can often, although not always, determine the success or failure of a business.

Organizational processes serve multiple purposes. One purpose is as a vehicle for communication, and as symbols for what the corporation represents. Standard operating procedures depict what activities are necessary for success in the organization. And, the activities necessary for success inside the organization must bear some relationship to the tasks that the external environment requires of the organization, if it is to be a successful and ongoing concern. Therefore, if the external environment is a rich multistakeholder one, the strategic processes of the organization must reflect this complexity. These processes need not be twenty-five-step rigid analytical devices, but rather existing strategic processes that work reasonably well must be enriched with a concern for multiple stakeholders.

Three such processes are illustrated in figures 5 and 6, and table 3. Figure 5 is an adaptation of Lorange's (1980) strategic planning process where specific questions dealing with stakeholders have been added. The language of strategic planning can be more useful if talk about stakeholders is included with talk about missions, programs, budgets, and control. Figure 6 is a process known as the *stakeholder audit*. Just as a financial audit depicts the financial roadmap of a firm, the stakeholder audit is a way of setting out a clear picture of the stakeholders in the firm, and the current strategies that a firm has for managing stakeholder relationships. Table 3 is a strategic review enriched by a concern for stakeholders. If division managers routinely have to answer questions about their stakeholders, then it is more likely that they will pay attention to managing stakeholder relationships.

The Transactional Level

The bottom line for stakeholder management has to be the set of transactions that managers in organization have with stakeholders. How do the organization and its managers interact with stakeholders? What resources are allocated to interact with which groups? There has been a lot of research in social psychology about the so-called transactional environment of individuals and organizations, and we shall not attempt to recapitulate that research here. Suffice it to say that the nature of the behavior of organizational members and the nature of the goods and services being exchanged are key ingredients in successful organizational transactions with stakeholders.

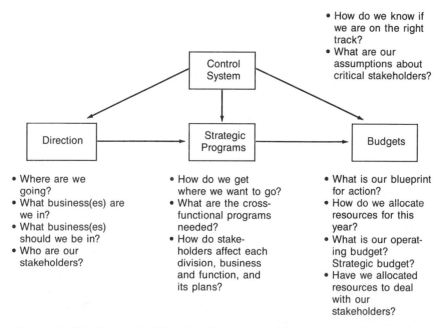

Figure 5. The Strategic Planning Process and Stakeholder Management

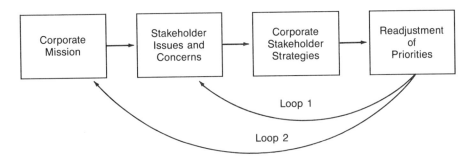

Figure 6. The Stakeholder Audit Process

Corporations have many daily transactions with stakeholder groups, such as selling things to customers and buying things from suppliers. Other transactions also are fairly ordinary and unexciting, such as paying dividends to stockholders and negotiating a new contract with the union. Yet when we move from this relatively comfortable zone of transactions to dealing with some of the changes that have occurred in traditional marketplace stakeholders and the emergence of new stakeholder groups, there is little wonder that transactions with the corporation's stakeholder map become a real source of discontent.

The *XAB* Company is an interesting study in how this lack of fit can be dysfunctional. *XAB* understood its stakeholder map and had some organizational processes to formulate and implement strategies with important nontraditional stakeholder groups. However, *XAB* sent some top executives out to talk with several of these groups who had little empathy with the causes of these groups. Needless to say, the company has made little progress with them. Perhaps the strategy and the processes are inappropriate given the objectives of the company. However, another interpretation is that the transactions between company and stakeholders have not given the strategy and processes a fair test.

Consumer complaints are an area where there is usually a noticeable breakdown in the organization's stakeholder transactions. Many large corporations simply ignore consumer complaints and dismiss them as that 5 percent of the market that they prefer someone else to serve. Large corporations have few successful processes for dealing with consumer complaints. One consumer leader commented that being told it was company policy to do things a certain way may well finish the incident for the manager, but it begins the incident for the consumer advocate. Several successful companies seem to overspend on handling consumer complaints. IBM's commitment to service, P&G's consumer complaint department, and the Sears philosophy of taking merchandise back with no questions asked, yield valuable lessons in understanding the nature of transactions with customers. These companies act as if consumer complaints yield an opportunity for understanding customer needs, which ultimately translates into a good bottom line and satisfied stakeholders.

Shareholder meetings have become rituals for most corporations, except for the occasional meaningful proxy fight. Rather than carry out meaningful transactions

Table 3
The Strategic Review Process

1. Do we know how each stakeholder will be affected by the strategy?
2. Do we know how each stakeholder can help us and hurt us?
3. Can we articulate a strategic program for each key stakeholder?
4. Who is responsible for implementation?
5. What assumptions are necessary for the strategies to be successful?
6. Are these assumptions realistic and valid?
7. What new strategies are needed?
8. Is the goal of this strategy still realistic?
9. What could cause us to fail?

with shareholders in accordance with a clearly thought out strategy and process, executives now treat stockholders to lunch and speeches (with the stockholders' money), and a round of abuse from corporate critics who have bought one share of stock in order to be heard.

Meetings with financial analysts are another opportunity for transactions, which can be made consistent with a firm's strategy and processes. Many executives understand that U.S. firms have underinvested in modern plant and equipment relative to foreign competition, and that they have lost sight of the marketing prowess of some of their competitors. How U.S. corporations can regain their competitive edge is a source of much debate in managerial and academic circles. Yet to regain competitive position is not easy or inexpensive. Many U.S. firms will have to "take a hit on earnings" for several years in a row to be truly competitive. Most financial analysts are by their nature short-term focused. If executives use meetings with analysts to tout earnings per share, which may be inflated in real terms, then analysts will continue to expect short-term results. Talk of an investment strategy to regain competitive edge will be just talk. The transaction that executives make with analysts must square with the strategy of the organization regardless of the pain. By taking a leadership position in this area, perhaps the thoughtful company can change the expectations of financial analysts.

Transactions with government officials often take place under adversarial conditions. Because government is a source of trouble for many companies, their transactions with government show their discontent. One company is reported to have rented a truck and dumped the requested documentation on the doorstep of the government agency that requested it. When stakeholder relationships are viewed on both sides as adversarial, it is a small wonder that anyone ever changes. The Business Roundtable, as a transactional organization for large businesses with the government, published a study decrying the cost of regulation and calling for regulatory reform. While it is clear that the regulatory process has gotten out of control in some areas, a more helpful transaction would have been to try to gain some formal input into the regulatory process. To gain such input would mean that a firm's transactions with the government could be made congruent with its organizational processes, and the firm could formulate strategies for influencing government in a positive way, breaking down the adversarial barriers of so many years and so many hard-fought battles.

If corporate managers ignore certain stakeholder groups at the rational and process level, then there is little to be done at the transactional level. Encounters between corporation and stakeholder will be, on the one hand, brief, episodic, and hostile, and, on the other hand, nonexistent, if another firm can supply stakeholders' needs. Successful transactions with stakeholders are built on understanding the legitimacy of the stakeholder and having processes to routinely surface their concerns. However, the transactions themselves must be executed by managers who understand the currencies in which the stakeholders are paid. There is simply no substitute for thinking through how a particular individual can win and how the organization can win at the same time.

Stakeholder Management and Ethical Issues

The stakeholder framework articulated in the previous section raises a number of ethical issues. If we decide to see business as a network of stakeholder relationships, then we can more clearly articulate the connection between business and ethics. Often managers and business commentators react to the phrase *business ethics* as if the term represents a contradiction. But *ethics* is not a mysterious word. To call an issue an ethical issue is merely to single it out as having to do with who is harmed or benefited by the issue, or whose personal projects are enhanced or stymied by the issue. Most business issues are ethical issues. Ethics is concerned with how various agents (individuals or organizations) interact on important matters. It deals with the distribution of benefits and burdens, rights and duties, and provides more fundamental reasons for the decisions that managers make.

Because the usual way that we talk about business in terms of technology, markets, profits, capital, and so forth does not always facilitate the identification of specific agents involved in a business decision, it obscures the ethical nature of business. The stakeholder framework and language is a better way to talk about business because it clearly shows us that many business decisions concern a number of parties, each of whom is harmed or benefited to some degree. We do not propose a specific ethical theory. There are many possible ones. We shall show how each level of analysis in the stakeholder management framework makes it possible to connect traditional business questions with social/ethical questions.

The Rational Level

At the rational level there are two kinds of ethical issues to be addressed. The first concerns the stakeholder map of the firm as a whole. A complete rational level of analysis, as depicted in figures 1 through 4, and tables 1 and 2, gives us a picture of a business not in isolation but in a particular social, cultural, and historical setting. We can more clearly see the relationships among institutions such as business, government, church, political groups, and so forth. And, to a certain degree each business has the choice of whether or not it wants to be a part of a particular institutional network. In short, each business can try to answer the question "What do we stand for?," thus delimiting the institutional settings in which it will choose to operate. At this macro-institutional level of analysis, a business will make decisions that determine whether or not it will do business in South Africa, Saudi Arabia, behind the Iron Curtain, and so forth.

A second ethical issue at the rational level is a determination of precisely what a business sees as the nature of the stake of each stakeholder. The resulting responses in terms of business strategy is at heart an ethical issue. If a firm decides that a particular group has no real stake, then it may act to ignore that group's claims, and either harm it or benefit it, respect its rights or not. In a sense, the firm can choose its stakeholders—those groups it wants to serve. This choice is known as *enterprise strategy* (Freeman and Gilbert 1987), and it involves setting the group rules for managing the entirety of stakeholders. A firm who chooses to serve stockholders exclusively will deal with government and other political groups in a radically different way than a firm who chooses to serve both stockholders and community. Since there are many different kinds of institutional settings and many different sets of stakeholders to serve within each setting, we point out that using the stakeholder vocabulary makes it easier to identify these choices at once as strategic and ethical.

The Process Level

At the process level there are two additional ethical issues that must be addressed in stakeholder terms. The first is the establishment of the rules and standard operating procedures for dealing with each stakeholder. The questions are those of corporate policy in routine decisions. What is the policy on consumer complaints, stockholder resolutions, purchasing contracts, labor negotiations, openers with the media, plant closings and openings, employee privacy, and other rights? Notice that answers to these questions will be partially determined by the choice of institutional settings and by the choice of which stakeholders to serve. But, these rational questions will not fully determine policy for dealing with each group.

A second issue at the process level is how does the firm handle routine matters, such as the emergence of new issues and stakeholders, new decision situations, and changes in institutional contexts. It is here that the development of an ethical code can be helpful, for such a code can serve to begin the reasoning process in a new and difficult situation. The process of developing an ethical code is a tricky one and should be undertaken with great care. Notice, also, that an ethical code cannot be radically different from the answers a firm gives to other ethical issues—it must be consistent with the values on which a firm decides to act in its institutional context and also with the guidelines by which a firm manages its day to day relationship with stakeholders.

The Transactional Level

The transactional level raises the most fundamental ethical issues, for it is here that individuals of the firm meet other individual stakeholders face to face. The most fundamental questions in ethics are "How should one treat one's fellow human beings? What rights does each person have in virtue of being a person?" Many ethical theorists argue that the answer to these questions starts with Kant's Principle of Respect for Persons. This principle says that each person deserves to be treated with respect, other things being equal, and should never be treated as a mere means to be used to further the ends of someone else.

The principle translates into "treat each stakeholder with respect and never as a mere means to an organization's or manager's end." The implications of this principle are vast. The projects of each stakeholder acquire prima facie legitimacy, and the organization's projects are likewise for stakeholders. The organization must learn to be responsive to determine whether or not there is ground for mutual benefit. Indeed, we believe that the principle needs a radical restructuring.

A second implication of this principle involves applying it inside the organization. The stakeholder vocabulary can be stretched to include the notion of internal stakeholders. There is a sense of stakeholder in which groups and individuals affecting a particular manager can be said to be stakeholders of that manager, even though these groups and individuals are internal members of the corporation. *Internal stakeholders* refers to those internal groups who may appear to a particular manager to be much more troublesome than external groups.

The manager responsible for carrying out a series of transactions with stakeholders does not and should not carry out the transactions alone. Other organizational members and units sometimes have the responsibility for a particular group and must be convinced of the need to go ahead with the program in question. Public relations must convince marketing that a program of image advertising is appropriate, so that the advertising experts in marketing can actually manage the implementation of the campaign with the ad agencies and media. Service representatives must convince sales persons that a new policy is in the customers' interests. R&D managers must convince manufacturing that materials can be bought from multiple sources to go ahead with new product plans. Planners must convince almost everyone that planning is important, and hence that the forms should be completed. Thus, as Kotter (1978) puts it, there are multiple dependencies inherent in the managerial job, for most managers. Since these dependencies exist over time to form lasting relationships, or the need for lasting relationships, the environment of a particular manager begins to look like that of the corporation as a whole, giving rise to the notion of internal stakeholders. Figure 7 is an example of the internal stakeholder in one particular managerial job. The same ethical question is crucial: How do I treat those other persons on whom I am dependent? Kant's Principle provides the start of an answer to this question. And, it is only by using the stakeholder vocabulary or some similar framework that we can see

Figure 7. Internal Stakeholders in a Manager's Job

these daily transactions as ethical in nature. Thus, the stakeholder management framework allows us to integrate traditional business strategy issues with the current anomalies of social and ethical issues. But, we have only started the process of learning to see the world in stakeholder terms.

Implications for Organization Structure

As the external environment of business has changed, structural remedies have been sought to cope with those changes by many large organizations. Classical, centralized functional structures have given way to decentralized business unit structures. In some cases, traditional functional disciplines have been merged with project or business unit organizations into a matrix structure (Galbraith 1973). But, the functional disciplines still exist and dominate the thinking of most managers and theorists.

If the arguments for coming to see a business in stakeholder terms are persuasive, then we must also come to see the functional disciplines themselves in stakeholder terms. Functional strategy understood as managing stakeholder relationships also is pervaded by ethical issues. We shall choose one function—public relations—traditionally conceived as the place to manage social and ethical issues, and sketch how the function can be better understood by using the stakeholder vocabulary. *Public Relations News* defines public relations as follows:

> Public Relations is the management function which evaluates public attitudes, identifies the policies and procedures of an individual or an organization with the public interest, and plans and executes a program of action to earn public understanding and acceptance.

Given such a definition, the function of the public relations manager is to be externally oriented, to make the company sensitive to the concerns of the external environment, and to convince the external environment (the public) of the worthiness of company positions. The stakeholder approach requires a redefinition of the public relations function, building on the communications skills of public relations (PR) professionals, yet is responsive to the real business environment of today. Figure 8 depicts the role of the traditional PR person as boundary spanner (Thompson 1967), having little credibility inside the organization (too identified with external groups) and little credibility outside the organization (too identified with the organization). In short, as figure 8 depicts, the PR manager is caught in the middle of environmental change.

As long as there is a small amount of change, then the PR manager can actually fulfill the role of defender of the corporation, and plan and execute a program of action to earn public understanding and acceptance. However, given the external and internal change that has occurred, this role is no longer realistic. Armed with the traditional weapons of the vitriolic press release, the annual report, a slick videotape, and corporate philanthropy, today's PR manager is a sacrificial lamb on the altar of multiple stakeholder dissatisfaction with corporate performance.

The stakeholder approach spreads the traditional PR role among every manager responsible for formulating strategic programs, where multiple stakeholders must be taken into account. The interactions among stakeholder programs, together with other factors, yield new and emerging issues that will affect the corporation. Thus, if managers merely balance current issues and negotiate with stakeholders, new issues and new stakeholder groups will not be managed until they can already have some tangible effect on the organization. It becomes the task of PR to not only participate in the strategic management processes just described, but additionally to scan the environment for new issues and new stakeholders and to bring these to the attention of the business unit managers responsible for unit performance. If managers can integrate issues and stakeholders, then a concern with the future as it affects the present can be realistically implemented. We might call the role of such an integrator of issues and stakeholders external affairs. Figure 9 illustrates the role of external affairs managers. There are five key tasks: (1) identifying new

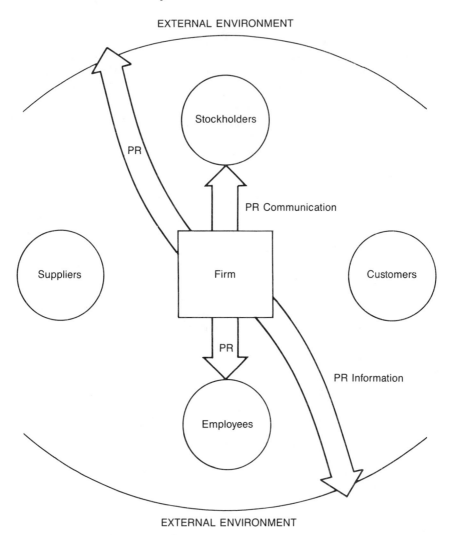

Figure 8. Model of Typical Conception of Public Relations

stakeholders, or calling attention to those stakeholders whom other managers have overlooked; (2) beginning the process of explicitly formulating strategies with these stakeholders; (3) helping to integrate the concerns of multiple stakeholders; (4) negotiating with key stakeholders on issues of mutual concern; and (5) searching for new issues and illuminating new concerns for other managers in the firm.

For the most part the task of identifying new stakeholder groups is an overlooked task in the corporation, and the task of creating the stakeholder map of the firm as a whole is never completed. Corporate planners scan the environment for a narrow

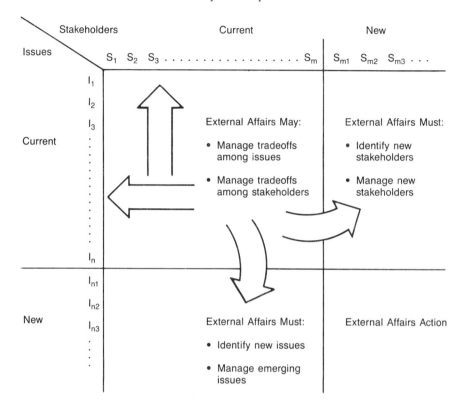

Figure 9. Public Relations Redefined as External Affairs

set of variables, namely those that affect the corporate plan, which all too often has nothing to do with the majority of the key stakeholders. External affairs (EA) managers are in the best possible position to know who really are the stakeholders in the firm, and to communicate this message internally to the general managers who are responsible for developing integrated business strategies.

Operating managers in marketing, production, finance, or other functions or profit centers are often too busy to worry about the effects of current issues on stakeholder groups over time. Therefore, someone needs to explicitly formulate a statement of the organization's objectives or mission in dealing with each stakeholder group. Such a statement becomes a guidepost for managers whose organizational units affect that stakeholder. It helps to make trade-offs among tough strategic issues that have differentiable effects on one stakeholder. It helps to give the organization and the stakeholder a sense of direction in terms of the overall stakeholder relationship. What is the overall corporate posture with respect to government? Are the actions of multiple organizational units consistent with that posture? What is the overall corporate posture with respect to consumer advocates? Are complaints handled, in every division, consistently with that posture? Is there an organized communication forum for managers and consumer leaders? These are only a few of the necessary questions that must get answered, and that are never asked, in the fragmented, day-to-day managerial world.

Rarely are trade-offs among multiple stakeholders considered. Managers stick to their functional knitting, and make decisions based on satisfying that external group with which they are most comfortable. EA managers must raise the bigger picture. How do we formulate policy or practice while taking multiple stakeholders into account? Their experience with thinking in big picture terms can be an invaluable resource to profit center managers caught up in the daily routine. The skills of EA managers must be considered, or else stakeholders will continue to multiply and put pressure on the firm through external means such as government, competitors, and so forth.

EA managers have communication skills. If stakeholder management is taken seriously, then these skills must be turned toward negotiation with stakeholders. Negotiation is a give and take process, a process of compromise, and of establishing "win-win" solutions. It is not identical with communication, but communication skills are a necessary ingredient in successful negotiation. EA managers cannot negotiate if they cannot make trade-offs and decisions. Therefore, negotiating depends on immersing the manager in the operations of the business. The EA manager must be seen as a valuable resource to the general manager, as a manager of vision and insight who can help the general manager decipher a complex external environment and one who can negotiate with a multiplicity of stakeholder groups.

Finally, the EA manager must think broadly and put together the pieces of figure 9 to identify new and emerging issues and stakeholders. The EA manager must be able to understand how the issues fit together and must be sensitive to the changes in the stakeholder environment. The EA manager in the current business environment must be willing to take risks and to manage these new issues and stakeholders before they are recognized and legitimated within the firm.

We could draw a stakeholder map and accompanying tasks for each functional specialty. Each manager has a certain set of stakeholders to whom he or she is responsible, and a set of internal stakeholders who see the manager as a conduit to the external environment. The picture that we have implicitly painted in the preceding pages is one of radical externalism, whereby every manager's work is either for the benefit of an external stakeholder group or as a conduit to an external stakeholder group. In the functional jobs described, every manager is a boundary spanner, and the resulting organization is a stakeholder-serving organization. Which stakeholders an organization chooses to serve is an important ethical question. However, regardless of the answer, we must address the issue of structuring the enterprise as a whole in a way to make it responsive to those stakeholders it serves.

In the modern, complex corporate structure that encompasses multiple SBUs, groups, sectors, divisions, corporate staffs, matrix configurations, and the like, it is too easy for the responsibility of stakeholders to become diffused. No one has a handle on the effects of the corporation on a particular category of stakeholders. Responsibility is necessarily decentralized, as work is differentiated. Integration occurs at the business or product level, but not necessarily at the level of summing up the impact of the corporation on a particular stakeholder group. If particular stakeholders have integrative processes of their own, then the possibility for misunderstanding increases. A customer who buys a great computer from IBM and a lousy photocopy machine may not understand what IBM is trying to accomplish with their customers. Likewise, a customer who buys superb private network service from AT&T and a lousy PBX may not understand the differences in the organization that result in such product differences. We are not claiming that absolutely everything an organization does with a stakeholder group has to be consistent with everything else. Only an incredibly responsive organization could fulfill that charge. We do argue for the existence of a manager responsible for bringing the needs of certain stakeholder groups to the constant attention of the other organizational units of the corporation.

By creating a skeletal stakeholder structure, an organization can get more closely in touch with the external environment. Such an organization should specialize in bringing stakeholder needs to the foreground, especially those needs that the organization is not currently fulfilling. These stakeholder managers would have no formal authority. Rather, they would gain authority through their expertise, and coming to be recognized by line managers as a group who could help. To become known for adding value these managers would have to treat the line operation as a client, and seek to serve both stakeholders and internal clients. One model is that of a lawyer who serves the court and his or her client. The lawyer is an advocate of the court to the client and an advocate of the client to the court. Figure 10 depicts one possible structure for such an organization. A manager for each important category of stakeholders would be appointed as customer manager, environmental group manager, media manager, government agency manager, or whatever, and would be responsible for several key tasks: (1) ensuring responsiveness to stakeholder concerns; (2) becoming a stakeholder expert; (3) keeping score between organization and stakeholder; (4) ensuring organizational program integration; and (5) serving as ombudsperson between organization and stakeholder.

The proposed organization could easily be overlaid onto an SBU-type organization, simply because the stakeholder managers would have little formal authority. They would be responsible for producing a charter that would state the goals and objectives of the organization with respect to a particular stakeholder. The goal of the stakeholder manager would be to produce a charter that coincides as closely as possible with the expectations of the stakeholders with respect to the organization, or to have a conscious program in mind to change these expectations. The charter would then serve as a guidepost for SBU managers, not as an ironclad policy. Deviations from the charter would be acceptable and even encouraged, especially when the deviations would better serve a stakeholder's needs. The stakeholder

Stakeholder Manager / Org. Unit	Customer	Consumer Advocate Groups	Environ- mental Groups	Government	. . .	S_{11}
SBU_1 SBU_2 SBU_3						
SBU_m						

Duties of stakeholder manager:
1. Insures responsiveness to stakeholder.
2. Becomes a stakeholder expert.
3. Keeps score.
4. Program integration.
5. Ombudsperson.

Figure 10. A Stakeholder Structure for Organizations

manager also would be responsible for a transactions audit for a particular group, to ensure (or at least assist in ensuring) that the transactions that members of the corporation execute with respect to a particular stakeholder are consistent with the stated strategic direction of the firm.

By carrying out these formal duties, the stakeholder manager would become an expert on his or her particular stakeholder, ensuring the organization of a knowledge base for future action. By continuous interaction with a particular stakeholder this base of knowledge would be constantly updated. Data files, newsletters, stakeholder reviews, and other mechanisms could serve as information dissemination processes to others who would be concerned with that stakeholder.

Stakeholder managers would be assigned the responsibility of formulating and implementing score-keeping mechanisms with their stakeholder groups. A scorecard could be developed and adapted for each particular stakeholder group, and measurements could be taken at the appropriate intervals, or original data collected where necessary. This score-keeping function would not replace, but would supplement, other methods developed by the strategic program implementers in the SBUs. The idea is that two separate measurements can give more useful information than one measurement alone. Personal bias and measurement errors can be minimized.

Stakeholder managers also would be responsible for achieving some sense of integration across multiple organizational units, and multiple strategic programs within an organizational unit. Formal responsibility for integration would still reside with the SBU manager. However, the stakeholder expert would be called on to advise on the interaction effects of certain strategic programs. Stakeholder experts would ideally operate as a profit center within the corporation, selling their services to SBU managers. Incentives for the stakeholder managers to be knowledgeable, responsive, and helpful to corporate strategists at all levels need to be formulated. We are biased towards a value-added approach whereby the SBU manager perceives enough value added to pay for the help that the stakeholder manager provides. The onus would be on the stakeholder expert to convince the SBU manager that he or she had a stakeholder problem that the expert could help to solve. Measuring value added at first would be a perception in the eyes of the client and the external stakeholder. However, as more experience is gained, more sophisticated and objective measures could be designed.

Finally, stakeholder managers would become ombudspersons, or places where stakeholders could go to have disputes listened to, and possibly resolved. The ombudsperson concept has great potential in the corporation, for there is a curious lack of processes that can be used to resolve disputes. Often, stakeholders who want voice in the affairs of the corporation must petition government at some level, with the result being onerous regulations, or unresponsiveness on the part of government. By cultivating a relationship with particular stakeholders, stakeholder managers could head off potential conflict in the government arena, which is costly to all parties.

While the structure briefly outlined here is quite speculative, some such mechanism needs to be put in place, especially with those stakeholders with whom the firm is currently experiencing negative results. An added feature of the organizational structure proposed here is that stakeholder experts could be pulled together to form a ready-made environmental scanning team, full of experts on concrete information about what the stakeholders of the corporations are likely to expect in the future. By structuring the organization to be super-responsive to its stakeholders, we see the final connection between strategy and social/ethical issues. If the organization is meeting the needs of its stakeholders on a daily basis, the atmosphere of moral crisis that pervades so much of current business can be set aside.

Agenda for Theory and Practice

There are a number of areas for further research and better practice using the stakeholder management framework. The first is the need for more experiments by managers in trying to better manage stakeholder relationships. We need new ideas and new ways to meet stakeholder needs. We need to apply the lessons from well-managed companies to nontraditional stakeholders. And, we need to continue to use the language of stakeholder management, especially the language of ethics to try to return the practice of management to a moral high ground. The second issue is that we need to more closely examine the connections between ethics and strategy in a systematic way.[4] We need a more complete set of the alternative ways to answer "what do you stand for?," and we need to know how a firm managed for stockholders will differ from one managed for other stakeholders. We need to more clearly formulate the ethical assumptions in current business vocabularies, especially those implicit moral assumptions in strategic management models.

The third issue is a broader one and asks whether or not a notion of management, implicit in these pages, can be articulated whereby managers bear a fiduciary duty to stakeholders.[5] Can we understand the firm as a set of voluntary self-governing transactions among those who have a stake in the firm, including a management responsible for the execution of these transactions? Such an application of the stakeholder concept would seek to articulate a Jeffersonian vision whereby the corporation becomes a major vehicle for the realization of democratic ideals.

Finally, we must understand management theory as a critical practice, seeking to interpret and reinterpret managerial action in terms that are essentially connected with human purpose. At least part of the reason that the current way of talking about business is not useful, is that business school professors, consultants, and other management intellectuals persist in seeing themselves as nineteenth-century scientists delineating an objective world by applying the scientific method. We have tried to show that such a vocabulary is optional, that there is another, better way to talk, using the stakeholder management framework, which will help to better cope with the world. To divorce the world of business from the matter of human agency and interests is like writing a novel with no characters. Such an interpretation will tell us very little about how to cope with our fellow human beings.

Notes

This article contains some ideas and passages that were originally developed in R.E. Freeman, *Strategic Management: A Stakeholder Approach.* Boston: Pitman, 1984. We are grateful to the publisher for permission to recast some of this material.

1. Throughout this article we sometimes focus on "a new vocabulary" or "a different way to talk." We believe that the words we use make a difference. Think of science as giving us some very useful words that enable us to do some very useful activities. The concepts and frameworks that we use in management are linguistic at heart, and saying that we need a better vocabulary is a way of saying that we need a better way of coping with the reality of the business world.

2. Freeman (1984, pp. 31–51) documents the intellectual development of the stakeholder concept. We claim no originality for the term, and instead see this present work as a descendant of the work of many others. See Freeman (1984) for a more complete bibliography.

3. In what follows we adapt Graham Allison's (1971) framework with the caveat that his three models, or levels of analysis, or lens can give one consistent explanation.

4. Such a systematic connection between ethics and strategy is the subject of a forthcoming book by Freeman and Gilbert (1987).

5. This is the subject of an ongoing research program. The initial arguments can be found in Freeman and Evan (1987).

References

Allison, G., 1971. *Essence of Decision.* Boston: Little, Brown.

Dill, W., 1975. "Public Participation in Corporate Planning: Strategic Management in a Kibitzer's World," *Long Range Planning* 8(1):57–63.

Evan, W., 1966. "The Organization Set: Toward A Theory of Inter-Organizational Relations," in W. Evan, ed., *Organization Theory: Structures, Systems, and Environments.* New York: Wiley.

Freeman, E., 1984. *Strategic Management: A Stakeholder Approach.* Boston: Pitman.

Freeman, E., and W. Evan, 1987. "Stakeholder Management and the Modern Corporation," in T. Beuchamp and N. Bowie, eds., *Ethical Theory and Business,* 3rd ed. Englewood Cliffs, N.J.: Prentice-Hall.

Freeman, E., and D. Gilbert, 1987. *Corporate Strategy and the Search for Ethics.* Englewood Cliffs, N.J.: Prentice-Hall.

Galbraith, J., 1973. *Designing Complex Organizations.* Reading, Mass.: Addison-Wesley.

Hirschman, A., 1970. *Exit, Voice and Loyalty.* Cambridge, Mass.: Harvard University Press.

Kotter, J., 1978. *Power in Management.* New York: AMACOM.

Lorange, P., 1980. *Corporate Planning: An Executive Viewpoint.* Englewood Cliffs, N.J.: Prentice-Hall.

Merton, R., 1957. *Social Theory and Social Structure.* Glencoe, Ill.: The Free Press.

Thompson, J., 1967. *Organizations In Action.* New York: McGraw-Hill.

Environmental Scanning and Tracking of Critical Issues: The Case of the Life Insurance Industry

Niels Christiansen
Sharon Meluso

Historical Roots

The Trend Analysis Program (TAP) of the American Council of Life Insurance (ACLI) was begun in 1970 out of concern for the impact of societal change on the future of the life insurance industry. It was born amidst the social turmoil of the late 1960s and early 1970s—the period of protest against the war in Vietnam, symbolized by the killing of four students by National Guardsmen at Kent State University in Ohio. It was the time of the youth movement—of hippies, yippies, and the "Greening of America." It was the time of violent political movements—the

Black Panthers, the SDS Weathermen, and the Symbionese Liberation Army. It was also the time of mass violence in our inner cities—the burning of Watts, the bombing of the Bank of America and other major corporate offices by radical groups. While a segment of the U.S. population was questioning the basic values and motives of the free enterprise system, in general, and corporate America, in particular, others during the 1960s began to focus their attention on the long-term implications of the societal changes taking place. It was a time of the flowering of *futurism*, of books such as Alvin Toffler's *Future Shock*, and the time of dire (Club of Rome) as well as utopian projections for the future.

The rash of societal changes and the growing attention to future implications of such changes in the late 1960s forced some within the life insurance business to begin considering how social change might affect the business. Of particular concern were changing patterns in marriage, childbearing, and home purchases— three key events at which time one typically purchases life insurance. Forward-looking leaders within the life insurance business commissioned the Institute of Life Insurance to study societal change and assess how these changes might affect the business in the years ahead. The genesis of the TAP program was from the 1967 *Future Outlook Study.*

The *Future Outlook Study* was developed by a task force comprised of over thirty senior life insurance executives charged with studying the future of the industry and examining the internal and external factors that could affect its growth. The study was a very pragmatic assessment of the future business environment for the life insurance industry and treated topics such as demographic trends and their implications; changing patterns in family life; changing dimensions of premature death, disability, and retirement; increased or decreased flow of savings; and the impact of computers on business practices.

The *Future Outlook Study* was very positively received within the industry as filling a clearly identifiable need. As a result, it was recommended that a permanent program be developed "to identify signs of long-term social, political, economic and technological change that might affect the life insurance business, and then, to bring these signs of change to the attention of decision makers in the business." Thus, TAP was launched as one of the first programs of its kind in any industry.

Why would such a program tracking social change develop in the life insurance business earlier than in other industries? The reason lies in the fundamental nature of the life insurance business itself. While typically classified in the financial services industry, the mutual aid societies and life assurance companies of the nineteenth century grew out of a preeminent social need, that is, to protect the widows and orphans of policy holders from being thrown into a life of poverty because of the premature death of the family breadwinner. Therefore, changes in the social bond of the individual to the family, his employer, and to public institutions have profound consequences for the development of the life insurance business.

It is obvious, however, that corporate leaders do not automatically recognize the effects of social change on their business. Fortunately, the insurance industry has had a number of enlightened leaders, including Blake Newton—ACLI's president from 1976 to 1980, and president of its forerunner, the Institute of Life Insurance—who did recognize the impact of social change on the life insurance industry. Indeed, Newton recognized not only the benefit of an early warning system to anticipate future societal change, but he saw the value of social research in general.

Concern within the business was directed both toward social characteristics that affect consumer needs in the marketplace and toward social issues that can result in legislation affecting the life insurance industry and the individual policy holder. It is doubtful that any other industry has surpassed the life insurance industry in its commitment to high quality social research and to studying changes in the environment that can affect the business.

How TAP Works

TAP Process and Participants

TAP relies on one of the most frequently used futures research methods to locate the first signs of social change: the scanning and systematic review of current literature. To do this, TAP utilizes a cadre of life insurance company volunteers, the *monitors*, to scan the print media for articles indicative of the changing environment. Monitors range from chief executive officers (CEOs) to research assistants, from actuaries to marketing specialists.

TAP scans publications ranging from relatively obscure quarterlies to weekly news magazines and daily newspapers for indicators of change in our social, political, economic, and technological environments. Once an item indicative of change is located, an abstract of the article is prepared by the monitor. Abstracts written by monitors are forwarded to the Abstract Analysis Committee (AAC), a group made up of senior ACLI staff and a consultant expert in trend identification. The AAC meets every two months to analyze TAP abstracts. The analysis conducted by the AAC is used in preparing two TAP publications, *Straws in the Wind* and the *TAP Report*.

TAP gauges the potential impact of fledgling trends by a variety of measures, such as tracking their time-lines, that is, the speed at which a trend finds its way from a little-known newsletter to feature coverage in *Newsweek* or the *Los Angeles Times*. The trend's speed at making its way to a feature article in a major periodical is one indicator of its importance to stakeholders. Trends are tracked in four separate areas:

Social—includes values, lifestyle, and demographic characteristics;

Economic—includes the causes and rates of change in production and distribution, factors such as inflation, recession, labor force descriptors, and taxation;

Political—includes policy making, regulatory and legislative behavior, international affairs, and public opinions and response;

Technological—includes those scientific systems by which society provides for the needs and wants of its members, as well as those scientific and technological developments that influence the way people live, work, and interact with themselves and their environment (such as new technologies in medicine, computers, and energy efficiency).

TAP's emphasis is on societal uncertainty, economic dislocations, political complexity, and technological change, and the potential questions they raise about the future, in general, and the life insurance business, in particular.

Straws in the Wind and the TAP Report

AAC members carefully review the abstracts in order to detect trends and issues, which may be inferred by the set of abstracts, and the conclusions are combined with those of other members of the AAC at its meetings. Out of this process comes a bimonthly newsletter, *Straws in the Wind*, which highlights the Committee's discussion of the abstracted items. It contains clusters of trends in selected areas that have not yet developed into a larger integrated issue and might later be treated in a *TAP Report*. Each issue of *Straws* is sent to all the monitors and company CEOs.

Monitors are invited to submit bylined articles for the "Monitor's Corner" section of *Straws*, dealing with trends they identify as important to the life insurance business, their company's in-house scanning programs, and other key areas of interest. *Straws* includes notices of upcoming meetings that may be of interest to monitors.

Once a year, the TAP Steering Committee reviews the issues developed in the analysis process and selects several trends and topics of major importance to the life insurance business to be analyzed in depth. For these topics, an outside expert is selected to review all of the TAP abstracts received on the topic and, based on that, to prepare a report on the future of the topic. This expert first presents his/her views to the monitors at the TAP conference, giving the monitors a chance to comment, question, and consider implications before the results of the study are published as *TAP Reports*. The reports are designed to give member companies additional tools for use in product development, market research, and strategic planning. Published approximately four times a year, *TAP Reports* are distributed to the monitors, company CEOs, insurance company staff, interested publics, the TAP Steering Committee, and, in special mailings, to key audiences such as the U.S. government—when the topics are relevant to the government.

TAP Conference

The annual TAP Conference is the focal point of the TAP program. It brings together the authors of the current *TAP Reports* with monitors before the writing of the final version of the publication occurs. Workshops and panel discussions held during the two-and-a-half day conference give monitors the opportunity to learn more about futures research and long-range forecasting techniques as they apply to the life insurance business. Individual sessions focus on the techniques of scanning, trend analysis, and abstract writing, as well as on applications of *Straws* and the *TAP Reports* to corporate strategic planning.

Computerized Data Base

TAP is presently developing a computer-based monitor network that will feature a data bank housing all TAP abstracts from 1982 forward. Abstracts will be indexed and cross-referenced based on both their subject and their implications for the life insurance business. As opposed to other computerized data bases, the monitor network will be specifically geared to life insurance business concerns.

The network also will serve as a clearinghouse for futures research information. It will list all publications in the field as well as other futures programs, and will offer a calendar of pertinent events such as training sessions, workshops, seminars, and college courses in the field. All of this information will be made available to monitors and their companies.

Utilization of TAP Information

Member Companies

TAP has attempted to monitor those trends that have the greatest potential for affecting the profitability and operation of life insurance companies. For example, in 1973, TAP identified the potential of sustained periods of double-digit inflation as threats to cash value life insurance and issued a report entitled *Life Insurance Companies and the Impact of Inflation.* The report concluded that high inflation would impact the industry in a number of highly negative ways:

> Traditional cash-value life insurance would not provide as much purchasing power for beneficiaries, even though policy holders might add to their coverage.

> There could be a massive drain on individual life insurance reserves and the underlying investments. Even if policies were not cashed in, policy loans might be used more heavily than ever before.

> There would be increased interest in policies offering benefits and premiums that were indexed.

The report advised: "If there is real danger of a major drain on life insurance reserves that will threaten solvency, perhaps we should start reducing dividends now to build up additional surplus." This report was instrumental in raising the issue of the threat of inflation to the business. Consequently, several life insurance companies began to seriously consider the development of interest-sensitive life insurance products, such as the variable life product.

Since TAP's inception, the program has matured from a little-known experiment to a system that is well-known both within and outside the life insurance business. Also during this time, social forecasting, futures research, issues management, and other future-oriented techniques have gained wider acceptance by the business community and the life insurance business. Indicative of this trend is the number of life insurance companies—American Family Life, John Hancock Life Insurance Company, New York Life Insurance Company, Northwestern Mutual Life Insurance Company, and Prudential Life Insurance Company, to name just a few—that have established or plan to establish programs that monitor trends and/or identify and analyze issues that may affect the business environment for life insurance companies. As a result, TAP-generated information has become a part of a formally defined process in many companies.

Some companies attach comments or summary sheets to the reports and circulate them to pertinent people. Others have formed task forces to follow and provide further analysis for their companies on issues raised by TAP. *TAP Reports* have been excerpted in company newsletters and magazines. Informally, *TAP Reports* have been used to train executives to understand the potential impact of social and technological changes on their company. Other uses of *TAP Reports* include:

Structured discussions. While merely reading the reports could in itself broaden management awareness, structured discussions about what the report means for individual companies have been used successfully by a number of ACLI member companies. Sometimes occurring within, sometimes occurring across individual company departments, such meetings typically deal with the issues raised in the reports. Specific suggestions for company operations or summaries of these structured discussions, issued as reports themselves, have resulted from these company meetings.

Boards of directors. The reports also have been valuable tools in discussions at company boards of directors meetings. The need for boards of directors to be aware of the forces that will affect their companies in the future is increasing. We have been told that several companies have already had the *TAP Reports* spark meaningful discussions at the board level.

Employee/management training programs. Since one purpose of any training program is to acquaint the employee with as many things as possible that could affect his/her role within the company, thus helping to maximize that role, TAP suggests the integration of its reports into companies' regular training curriculum, especially where management training is involved. We firmly believe that the managers of today and tomorrow will have to know more about the environment in which they conduct their business than about what is purely related to the title of their position.

Exposure to advertising agencies. TAP suggests that company advertising agencies be exposed to TAP. Since advertising is one of the main ways the life insurance business interacts with the public, communication professionals should be aware of the trends developing in the environment, and capitalize on this knowledge in the preparation of new campaigns.

Personnel policies and benefits. The reports could be of great value in dealing with company employees. Very often there are direct implications drawn between what is happening in society and its impact on the people in one's work force. TAP has suggested that companies encourage their personnel departments to review the reports on a periodic basis, especially when thought is being given to revising personnel policies and benefits.

Company research. TAP can be of tremendous value in suggesting research a company might wish to undertake, especially research related to new markets, new products, and investment opportunities. The implications of a particular *TAP Report* for new products and services are multifold, and companies might benefit from researching *TAP Report* hypotheses in light of their company's specific needs and goals.

Field force/communications. *TAP Reports* have been an important source of information for company field forces. The thoughtful agent is continually conducting a one-person analysis of his/her environment in order to aid client relationships. Exposure to TAP in field communications, agent conferences, and agency publications has helped agents to understand the general society better and even the various goals of individuals within the society, thus giving them a unique framework within which to develop client communications.

Use of TAP by the American Council of Life Insurance

TAP has primarily served the ACLI as an early warning system for emerging social issues having public policy and legislative implications. For instance, in the summer of 1977, TAP published a special report entitled "Freedom and Control in a Democratic Society: The Future of the Life Insurance Business/Government Interrelationships." Part of that report included a segment on "Equity vs. Equality," by W. Douglas Bell. In his piece, Mr. Bell asked, "What is going to happen in the field of risk clasification?" given the current tide toward "equality." The following is taken from that report.

> As a minimum, insurers will have to make certain they are dealing with objective criteria in the underwriting process and be better prepared to demonstrate the relationship of their underwriting criteria to the risk under evaluation. This could mean that truly objective criteria—age and sex—will continue to be valid for underwriting purposes, provided that they can be supported by reliable statistics.

In this instance, TAP was seven years early in identifying the unisex issue for the life insurance business. In 1984, insurance classification on the basis of sex became a legislative issue within Congress. Although the bill that would have prohibited the use of sex in the underwriting of insurance and annuity products did not pass, the broader issue of risk classification remains with the life insurance business today.

Issues identified by TAP that have public policy implications are fed into the ACLI Issues Management System through the ACLI Issue Strategy Group, a staff committee that reviews public policy issues of importance to the industry, ranks the issues according to their changing priority, and coordinates the development of industry position and strategy on each issue. This information is used not only by the ACLI as the industry trade association, but also by the individual companies to either keep abreast of current issues of concern or to plan corporate action in the area of public policy and government relations.

Challenges Experienced by TAP over Time

As with any program that exists over an extended period of time, TAP has had to contend with problems in the direction, focus, and operation of the program, which needs rethinking from time to time. The first of these is the time frame in which TAP operates. At various points in TAP's history, it has become very concentrated on futuristic topics. These have reached extremes, such as projected increases in the earth's temperature through the twenty-first century and the consequent melting of the polar ice caps. Obviously, such information has little immediate relevance for decision making in the life insurance business. At the other extreme, TAP monitors have at times focused on trends reported in the daily press or national business publications, reports that may have already been received by corporate executives. It has been a constant challenge to maintain a time frame that is neither too distant nor too short-range, and to communicate that need to TAP monitors.

A second challenge has been to separate the relevant from the irrelevant information in relation to the industry. Working in the area of futures research can have an intoxicating effect and requires a continual effort to maintain contact with present reality and with the bottom line. Also, the term *futurism* has received a somewhat pejorative connotation because of the number of practitioners who earn a handsome income by making astounding projections about the future and by creating the illusion that the future is going to be radically different from the past. The managers of programs such as TAP need to continually view the environment from the point of view of the CEO or the chief long-range planner in order to maintain perspective, as well as to keep analysis of future trends tied to the present and, in TAP's case, to the needs of the life insurance industry.

Maintaining the active participation of the monitors is also a constant challenge. Naturally, monitors vary considerably in level of participation. The challenge has been to effectively use the monitors who show a great deal of interest and not to expend valuable program resources on motivating those whose normal work duties preclude a more active involvement. In any event, effective management of the monitor network is a time-consuming endeavor.

Continuity also has been a constant challenge. The growth of issue management, environmental scanning, and long-range planning in life insurance companies has resulted in a number of TAP directors being recruited to major life insurance companies or starting their own consulting firms. Consequently, TAP has had five directors in its fifteen-year history. With the natural variation in individual orientation, the program has shown some shift in direction with each change of director. While the infusion of new blood into the program has had beneficial effects, it also has resulted in less attention being given to studying trends over time as opposed to the discovery of new issues and trends through the scanning process. This is an area being given increased attention in the future development of TAP.

The Future of TAP

The ACLI continues to strongly support the development of the TAP program. In a recent examination of the 1967 *Future Outlook Study*, it was found that many of the original topics and concerns of the industry regarding new products, the nature of the industry, and the effects of the social environment were virtually identical to those presently of highest priority to the industry. However, some change has naturally taken place. Three major changes are the following:

> The life insurance industry has become more complex. While some companies maintain their traditional position as being exclusively life insurance providers, others have broadened their activities to the wider financial services arena. This creates differing needs for the tracking of trends.

> The pace of environmental change and of new product innovation has rapidly accelerated. With the many changes in the family, longevity, health care, and employment that have occurred in the past fifteen years, and the need for new products to meet changing demands, the time frame for TAP scanning has been shortened to between five and eight years.

> A much more competitive business environment in the life insurance and financial services arena has reduced the cushion of comfort that allows the leisurely contemplation of broad issues. The demand for relevancy of TAP information has increased, as well as a demand to package information in a short, concise form to be absorbed quickly by executives without their having to wade through long reports. More attention is currently being paid to the packaging of TAP information to meet these needs.

Formal long-range planner positions have developed in companies and the overall concern for long-range planning has increased. In recognition of the need to anticipate future change and to plan accordingly, a new audience for long-range trend information has developed in the industry, which TAP is attempting to serve.

These and other changes have created greater demands for trend information, resulting in stronger involvement of the monitors in the interpretation of information produced from scanning, a larger commitment of ACLI staff time to synthesize and integrate information, and greater efforts to pinpoint specific relevant information and to target the appropriate decision makers in the industry. TAP's longevity is primarily due to practicing what it recommends to the industry itself: being sensitive to changes taking place in the life insurance industry and adapting to the changing demands for information that is crucial to business decision making.

Corporate Strategies for Effective Crisis Management: Corporate Decision Making and Corporate Public Policy Development

A Participant's Response

Rafael D. Pagan, Jr.

Never before in history has the corporate leader faced the danger of potential business catastrophe of the magnitude of the Nestle boycott, the Tylenol poisoning case, or the Bhopal tragedy. In such crises, both the corporation and the industry are put to the litmus tests of public opinion, law, and corporate survival. While these are cases where the companies involved can honestly claim that unforeseen circumstances or factors were involved, they unquestionably exemplify the fact that a modern corporation in crisis confronts not merely economic and technical issues but far-reaching political issues as well.

The notion of globalization is the warmed-over cliche used by some analysts—who see the disappearance of economic, political, religious, and trade borders—to explain the phenomenology of the modern corporation. However, the reality of global trade, business, politics, and religion has been with us for a long time. What is new is that never before have communication, transportation, and technological tools affected the speed, coverage, and general public awareness of a corporation's activity as they do now. In that sense, *Global Reach*—that oft-quoted textbook by Barnett and Mueller (1974) of the antilibertarian Institute for Policy Studies (IPS), whose factuality and intellectual discipline has frequently been challenged—

may have served its purpose well. It succeeded in encouraging U.S. consumers, academia, churches, and other such institutions to organize global mechanisms and networks to deal with the global reach of the avaricious and power-hungry transnationals or to influence public policy abroad.

Viewed historically, the decade of 1975 to 1985 was primarily a decade of vitriolic confrontation between the corporation and its critics. During this period, Howard Chase in particular, and Prakash Sethi, and other scholars developed the concept of issue management to deal with predictable or traceable potential problems for the corporation. Drawing on their established insights, this article represents a participant's perspective on how an external crisis (as opposed to domestic), confronting a major multinational corporation—Nestle—was creatively resolved to the satisfaction of both the company and its critics. To begin with, industrial crises may be specified as falling within one or several of the following three types:

1. *Sequential explosions.* Several events converge into a combination of foreseeable and unforeseen factors that create a critical mass leading to a catastrophe or accident. The Union Carbide Company tragedy in Bhopal, India in 1985 and the Three-Mile Island (domestic) accident are examples of this type of crisis.

2. *Unforeseen crises.* In these cases the image of the corporation is not in question but a key product or sales can be very seriously affected. Two recent examples of this kind of crisis are the Tylenol poisoning cases and the Gerber's tampering problem.

3. *Sociological factions.* This class of events concern safe products in a questionable sociological environment. Classic examples are the chemical, pharmaceutical, and food industries, which have been targeted for attacks by critics who claim that the promotional, marketing, advertising, and highly competitive practices of these industries clash with the sociological environment among the poor in the Third World.

This article discusses how Nestle, a nutrition and food company, managed the crisis created by the critics' attack on the infant formula industry where Nestle became the main target. Hence, it is of direct relevance to all third-type cases in the typology just discussed. The article first delineates the sequence of events leading up to the problem. It examines what happens to an issue when it festers too long and attains emergency status. Hence, it is of direct relevance to Type I cases as well. Second, it examines the strategy Nestle undertook to resolve the crisis. This may be of relevance to some Type II cases as well.

Background on the Nestle Crisis

From 1970 to 1984, Nestle, S.A., was the target of what one journalist called "an intense battle, the fiercest and most emotional ever waged against a multinational company" for its marketing of infant formula in poor countries. Nestle certainly was tempting prey for such a hunting expedition, since it was and still is, the world's largest developer and manufacturer of infant products. From 1976 to 1984, there persisted an organized boycott against the Swiss-based enterprise that was resolved—to the stated satisfaction of both sides and with expressions of mutual good will and trust—in October 1984.

It is possible to view the infant formula controversy as an issue of interest primarily to multinational businesses, scholars, and public relations professionals. But I believe that in future years it will be seen as a landmark in the development of a more assertive and productive attitude by business toward the larger world around it. The story of the boycott's resolution is also of interest to all who bear responsibility for the continued vitality of their businesses. The Nestle boycott teaches two lessons. The first, which we ignore at peril, is that potentially threatening issues are as likely to be sociopolitical as economic. No company, especially one as large and visible as Nestle, is exempt. Executives thus owe it to themselves and their firms to become as adept at managing political issues as they are at preparing annual reports.

The second lesson is that if a company commits itself and its employees to acquiring expertise in the socioeconomic arena, it can become as dynamic in shaping its political environment as it is in controlling its finances and marketing. In this connection, consider that American Telephone & Telegraph Co. (AT&T), one of the world's largest and most financially sound corporations, was not allowed to survive as a single entity. Why? It seems largely because the company failed to persuade federal policy makers that it could continue to operate without hobbling competition in emerging telecommunications fields. As a regulated utility, AT&T doubtless was aware of political considerations, but it proved unable in the crunch to respond effectively to changes in the political environment, which ultimately affected its demise.

Let us look at another case history, one that at first glance seems far less likely to yield a useful lesson. Chrysler Corporation, an auto manufacturer seemingly on the brink of bankruptcy, survived because a new chief executive, Lee Iacocca, persuaded Washington to lend his company the money that gave it a second chance. I consider Iacocca symbolic of a new executive breed that knows public policy is as important to a company's survival as are profits. Johnson & Johnson's handling of the two Tylenol poisoning scares furnishes still another example of creative corporate crisis management.

The Nestle experience also is interesting because its executives broke new ground by creating a self-sufficient subsidiary designed exclusively to deal with the infant formula marketing controversy. I was hired to organize just such a unit and to lead this effort, which will be examined in detail later. By way of background, it is important to realize that Nestle favored stable relations with nearly everyone it came in contact with—employees, customers, and host communities. It was renowned for nutrition research and for cooperating with health-care professionals in host countries. It chose not to own farms and plantations, the object being to avoid conflicts over land ownership. Instead, it worked with farmers and entrepreneurs to develop local enterprises.

Nestle initially adopted a passive strategy. This was understandable, considering that the company's headquarters were in Switzerland, a country long known for its political neutrality. Moreover, Nestle had a reputation in the international business community for Calvinist business ethics, noncontroversial nutrition products, and an unassertive corporate image. Nestle's low-key strategy served the company well for more than one hundred years, most occurring in a more innocent time than the present. Nestle was therefore unsure at first about how to conduct the guerrilla war in which it suddenly found itself.

Anatomy of the Issues: The Environment

The infant formula controversy began in December 1970, when a scientist at a United Nations-sponsored forum on nutrition claimed, quite inaccurately, that aggressive marketing of the product was responsible for a sharp decline in breast-feeding in underdeveloped countries. At that time, and for long afterward, neither Nestle nor any of its competitors had any mechanism in place for refuting such assertions. Had the company possessed such a capability, it would have included an information-gathering function to monitor the issue as it passed from scholarly journals, to church bulletins, to broadsheets, and then to the mass print and broadcast media. The company would have had at least two years to notice that the issue was growing, so that it could have prepared a strategy to deal with the issue at a formative stage. Nestle would have been paying attention to criticism as well as seeking to establish a rapport with its more responsible critics.

Instead, Nestle irritated its adversaries by denying the legitimacy of their concerns. It also made the mistake of treating an emotional matter as one in which the company knew what was best and would do what was right. Indeed, Nestle had unilaterally abandoned some outdated marketing practices, such as consumer advertising of infant formula in poor countries, but these facts were not effectively communicated. Around 1973, the issue changed from one affecting the infant formula industry, in general, to one spotlighting Nestle, in particular. As the leader in nutrition research, Nestle attempted to reply to critics on behalf of the industry. As the least politically sophisticated of the major companies in the field, however, it was less prepared to respond effectively to those who impugned its motives and aims. Nowhere was this more true than in the United States, where Nestle did not manufacture infant formula and its subsidiaries knew nothing about the issue aside from what they may have chanced to read. More politically minded critics targeted Nestle simply because of its position as the industry leader. Indeed, key officers of the boycott movement claimed they were urged by some of the company's competitors to focus on Nestle.

The Adversaries: David and Goliath

When a small antibusiness group in Switzerland accused Nestle in June 1974 of killing babies, the company sued for libel. This action—won by Nestle in a decision that many viewed as a Pyrrhic victory—gave the activists far more publicity than they otherwise would have received. Combined with Nestle's failure to establish a relationship with its more moderate critics, the court verdict also conferred leadership in the conflict on the company's more extreme adversaries, dimming prospects for an early agreement. At this juncture, an in-depth review of the ensuing developments is in order. On July 3, 1977, the Infant Formula Action Coalition (INFACT) announced the start of a consumer boycott of Nestle products sold in the United States. Because most of this merchandise did not actually bear the company's name, INFACT's boycott literature included an antishopper's guide, identifying both the targeted products and those from other manufacturers that could serve as substitutes.

Nestle's U.S. management hoped to counteract this effort by establishing contact with boycott sympathizers whose support might waver. A principal point was that the boycott threatened the jobs of 13,000 Nestle workers in the United States and that the U.S. Nestle companies did not manufacture or sell infant formula. Responding to these and similar arguments, Douglas Johnson, head of INFACT, stated in a letter to the president of Nestle's U.S. operations that the company's U.S. management was the "hand" of the multinational "body" and thus the vital link to the corporate "head" in Switzerland. Johnson proceeded to suggest that the U.S. branch of Nestle could assure its employees' jobs merely by persuading Swiss headquarters to accede to his group's demands. Because Johnson's letter seemed to hint that a settlement was possible, Nestle gave serious thought to his proposal for a meeting of company and INFACT representatives. This initial encounter took place in October 1977 and went surprisingly well. Although there was no agreement on ending the boycott, it was clear to the participants that the possibility remained open.

But any definitive decision on this point rested with INFACT's first national strategy conference, scheduled for November 1977. INFACT turned thumbs down on Nestle at this meeting. A second Nestle-INFACT meeting in February 1978 was no more successful. By this time, the coalition seemed less concerned with bringing about changes in Nestle marketing practices than in winning concessions that the company's foes could claim as victories. Moreover, Nestle managers were still smarting over an accident that had occurred at the October meeting. This was a mock funeral service of an infant formula victim, staged outside Nestle's Los Angeles office. Thereafter, relations between INFACT and Nestle cooled steadily.

The Adversaries: Political Phase

The controversy entered yet another phase with the opening of hearings before a congressional committee headed by Senator Edward M. Kennedy (D.-Mass.). Three main classes of witnesses were to testify—industry representatives, industry critics, and unaffiliated experts. Nestle chose as its spokesman Dr. Oswaldo Ballarin, chairman of the company's operations in Brazil and a consultant to the U.N. Protein-Calorie Advisory Group (PAG). Ballarin's chief adversary before the Kennedy panel was to be Dr. Derrick B. Jelliffe, a PAG expert who served also as director of the Caribbean Food and Nutrition Institute.

As the hearings approached in May 1978, Nestle concluded that the infant formula industry would be hard-pressed to make its case effectively. For one thing, each witness was to have only five minutes to present a prepared statement—not nearly enough time, in the company's view, to set forth the complexities of the problem. Nestle also felt that it was handicapped by Kennedy's known sympathy for the economically disadvantaged and his antipathy toward big business.

Kennedy began the proceedings with what impartial observers might well have regarded as a loaded question:

> Can a product which requires clean water, good sanitation, adequate family income, and a literate parent to follow printed instructions be properly and safely used in areas where water is contaminated, sewage runs in the streets, poverty is severe and illiteracy is high?

But worse, from Nestle's standpoint, was to come. Only a short way through his prepared statement, Ballarin asserted that the anti-industry campaign was led by "a worldwide church organization with the stated purpose of undermining the free-enterprise system." Kennedy interrupted to identify the offending "church organization" as the World Council of Churches and the National Council of Churches. Although Ballarin continued with his statement, the damage had been done.

The immediate effect of the Kennedy committee hearings, so far as Nestle was concerned, was to provide INFACT with an abundance of quotes to buttress its arguments. Among these was Jelliffe's claim that "some ten million cases of marasmus and diarrhea occur annually in infants in developing countries, related in part to inadequate bottle feeding." This was eventually hyped by INFACT into the assertion that "ten million Third World babies are starving because of the heartless, money-hungry actions of powerful multinational corporations." All the while, INFACT's boycott remained in force, although Nestle felt no significant impact on its sales.

Nestle's Counteraction

Nestle management now decided to try a new approach by going past the hand of INFACT and the Interfaith Center on Corporate Responsibility—a watchdog group founded by various religious orders and the National Council of Churches (NCC)—and dealing directly with the activist counterpart of the corporate head, namely, the NCC itself. Two meetings with council officials, in July and October

1978, produced only hostile confrontation, however. The church leaders apparently were still indignant about Ballarin's remarks at the Kennedy committee hearings. At the NCC's annual meeting in November 1978, delegates voted 280 to 2 to support the boycott.

Nestle next turned its attention to a scheduled October 1979 conference on infant feeding, cosponsored by the World Health Organization (WHO) and the United Nations International Children's Emergency Fund (UNICEF). The industry's aim at this gathering was to shift the discussion on infant formula marketing back to where it felt the responsibility for resolving the issue lay—with the government authorities, health professionals, and manufacturers' representatives who dealt with the issue on a daily basis. This strategy had the added advantage of reinforcing WHO's existing programs to promote better health for mothers and children and improve public hygiene in developing countries.

As the time for the meeting neared, corporate officials were disconcerted to learn that instead of the thirty or so nutrition and industry experts anticipated, over one hundred fifty participants would be on hand. These were to include some of the industry's more vocal critics, such as members of INFACT, War on Want, and the Third World Working Group. Nonetheless, Nestle was pleased on balance with the outcome of the conference. For one thing, many of the marketing reforms proposed in the consensus document issued at the end of the meeting, accorded with changes already implemented by the company. Even though some in industry were not in agreement with any form of code or guidelines, there was no quarrel with the conference's concluding commitment to formulate a more detailed WHO marketing code for developing countries.

International Involvement

The job of drafting the WHO code was entrusted to the organization's director general and secretariat by delegates to the May 1980 World Health Assembly. Over the next twelve months, the code went through four drafts. Nestle was encouraged that the final draft recognized the legitimacy of private industry's role in Third World infant feeding. For instance, Article I stated that the code's underlying aim was to provide safe and adequate nutrition for infants not only through the "protection and promotion of breast feeding" but also by the "proper use" of breastmilk substitutes, as assured through "adequate information" and "appropriate marketing and distribution."

Approval by the World Health Assembly in May 1981 was overwhelming: 118 votes for the code, 1 against, and 3 abstentions. The sole negative vote was cast by the American delegation, which cited apparent conflicts with the U.S. Constitution. The action was not unexpected, since the U.S. delegation had expressed reservations a year earlier about the precedent of delegating national policy-making prerogatives to international bodies.

Nestle Response: Organizing a Strategy Management Team

Four months earlier the concept of the Nestle Coordination Center for Nutrition (NCCN) as an organization that would serve in a dual role emerged from discussions with Mr. Ernest Saunders, who at the time headed Nestles' worldwide infant nutrition products (he is now head of Guinness, the London-based beverages-food company). He wanted Nestle to be known in the United States as a worldwide leader in nutrition research and development and for its nutrition products. We decided to combine that major function with the development and the implementation of a strategy to solve the anti-infant formula worldwide boycott.

The attack against Nestle had at that time spread to over seven hundred institutions including the World Council of Churches, the National Council of Churches, the Presbyterian Church, and several other major church denominations, as well as the National Education Association, and several other major unions, universities, and consumer's groups. The national media was almost totally against Nestle.

NCCN was organized and based in Washington, D.C., with a group of scientists who had extensive experience working for AID, and/or charitable organizations in charge of nutrition programs in many Third World countries. This team was combined with political strategists, sociologists, and ethicists. We made sure that this new Nestle organization had real science/nutrition functions as well as a public policy development function. NCCN was not a public relations unit. With the exception of one middle-level management woman, Carolyn Campion, NCCN had no other public relations experts nor functions as such. It was an entirely different approach to crisis management. It became a bridge between the company's critics and the most senior management at the Swiss and American Nestle headquarters, to whom I reported directly.

The establishment of the NCCN was the key step leading to the resolution of Nestle's international crisis and is now a much studied concept. I said in a speech delivered in 1983 that "The essential first step in resolving the infant feeding dilemma, was for Nestle to recognize that it was a political, as well as a nutritional issue and therefore to recognize the legitimacy of some of our critics' concerns and listen to them carefully." In the same speech, I also said that Nestle henceforth would "deal with the issue—not the activist critics. Nestle had wasted too much time trying to persuade, with scientific facts, hard-core activists whose motives were clouded by antibusiness biases." Furthermore, opposing viewpoints were to be treated with consideration and respect.

While harboring reservations about certain provisions of the WHO's International Code of Marketing of Breast-Milk Substitutes, Nestle was quick to endorse the document. The code established, after all, an internationally agreed-on set of procedures by which company policies and practices could be evaluated. The company's initial statement of policy on the code was expressed in testimony before Congress in June 1981. This included instructions to Nestle subsidiaries to cooperate with governments in developing national codes that would implement the WHO provisions in accordance with each country's social and economic traditions.

A gratifying development dating from this period was the dialogue that began to emerge between Nestle and the infant formula task force set up by the United Methodist Church (UMC) in the United States in 1980. These discussions were to prove crucial in removing the emotionalism from the infant formula controversy and ending the boycott of Nestle products in North America. For instance, NCCN made sure that the UMC task force was one of the groups receiving and reviewing the Nestle Instructions on implementing each of the WHO code provisions that were sent to company subsidiaries and agents in February 1982. Unfortunately, the instructions did nothing to alter the stance of INFACT, which charged that Nestle was trying to rewrite the code. Once the NCCN began its expanded interaction programs with the churches, the next step—a very crucial step in seizing the initiative away from the activists—was taken.

The Nestle Infant Formula Audit Commission

It was at this point that NCCN recommended to Nestle management in Switzerland that an independent body be established to monitor the company's code implementation record and to investigate complaints raised by concerned groups or individuals. This was a most difficult step for the Swiss management who always felt they had acted honorably and ethically, and some felt insulted with the idea of having such a group looking over their shoulders. Formation of the eight-member panel, composed of church leaders, medical experts, and scientists, was announced at a Washington news conference on May 3, 1982. Chosen as chairman of the Nestle Infant Formula Audit Commission (NIFAC) was Edmund S. Muskie, a former governor of and U.S. Senator from Maine, and a former U.S. secretary of state. Muskie also had been the Democratic vice-presidential nominee in 1968 and a candidate for the Democratic presidential nomination in 1972.

INFACT dismissed the Muskie Commission as a public relations ploy by Nestle and termed it an unacceptable vehicle for enforcing the WHO code. Muskie, however, insisted that the commission would be a truly independent entity even though it would be funded by Nestle. The initial refusal of leading supporters of the boycott to serve on NIFAC made it impossible for the critics to test Nestle's or the commission's good faith.

At the outset, NIFAC's primary task was to review the Nestle Instructions and to consult with WHO, UNICEF, and the scores of organizations and individuals caught up in the controversy. This process resulted in a set of recommendations by NIFAC aimed at clarifying and stengthening the original Nestle Instructions. Most of the resulting proposals were accepted by Nestle and were announced jointly with company and NIFAC representatives in October 1982. In NIFAC's first quarterly report, released at the same time, Muskie declared:

In the experience of the commission, Nestle has demonstrated a willingness to respond positively to the imperative of change in its marketing practices. In doing so, it has responded positively to the public interest as stated in the WHO code.

Significantly, the United Methodist task force recommended the same month that the church's ruling body refrain from joining the boycott. The task force went even further in a subsequent report, accusing the boycott organizers of attempting to obstruct and discredit NIFAC and giving currency to "substantial and sometimes gross misrepresentation" of Nestle policies and actions. Support for the Nestle boycott began to erode soon thereafter. In January 1983, the executive council of the American Federation of Teachers voted to rescind its participation, noting that "the Nestle Corp. has made substantial progress in changing its marketing procedures for infant formula."

The Media Reaction

Even earlier, the professional and general-circulation press had been voicing reservations about the supposed effects of infant formula marketing on the health of babies in developing countries. The American medical journal *Pediatrics* stated in its September 1981 issue,

> The crucial point for pediatricians to realize is that during more than five years of debate and hearings, no substantial, sound scientific data were ever set forth by the critics of industry or officials of the WHO to support the claim that marketing practices for infant formula have actually been a significant factor in decline in breastfeeding in the Third World or anywhere else.

In a similar vein, *The Washington Post* declared in a November 5, 1982, editorial, "Upon closer inspection, the data linking formula marketing and infant mortality turn out to be sketchy at best."

The boycott movement experienced additional defections in 1983, opening the way to a possible resolution of the controversy. Several church leaders at the National Council of Churches began to apply pressure on the boycott leadership to seek an agreement with Nestle. The activists narrowed their demands to four—educational materials, hazard warning on labels, gifts to health professionals, and free supplies to hospitals. These points raised genuine and complex issues with regard to implementing the code.

The Beginning of the End

Although NCCN had begun discreet contacts with the International Nestle Boycott Committee (INBC) in 1983 to establish a basis for discussions to end the boycott, and a chance encounter between an NCCN executive and a boycott leader in December 1983 led both to conclude that their differences had narrowed significantly, difficult procedural questions remained to be resolved. Like many international agreements, the WHO code had been deliberately left open to interpretation by governments so as to allow flexibility in applications. Nestle and INBC naturally had quite different ideas about the meaning of various code provisions, but negotiations to settle these differences would have been pointless. Both the company and the committee lacked credible standing among some in the public to decide how the code should be interpreted.

It was finally decided, at NCCN's suggestion, to seek guidance from WHO and UNICEF on the four areas of concern agreed on—gifts to health professionals, supplies, labels, and educational materials. Nestle outlined its position in a discussion paper, focusing on the four points. There followed a series of Nestle-INBC consultations with UNICEF in New York in January 1984, with members of the Muskie Commission present. UNICEF was asked to give its opinion on Nestle responses to each point, and on questions raised by INBC. WHO also was consulted throughout.

The end product of this process was a "statement of understanding," detailing Nestle's proposed method of dealing with the four points in line with its understanding of the spirit and letter of the WHO code. In view of this statement, which took into consideration WHO, UNICEF, and Muskie Commission views, INBC was able to accept that Nestle had responded positively to its concern. As a result, Nestle and INBC were able to announce in New York on January 24, 1984, that a decision had been reached to suspend the boycott for six months, pending final review of Nestle's compliance with the code. In the January 24 joint statement, INBC commended Nestle for assuming the role of leader in the infant formula industry's effort to put the WHO code into effect. Douglas Johnson, the head of INFACT, stated, "Nestle has moved forward to become a model for the whole industry, a model which created a new standard of corporate behavior."

The final, almost anticlimactic scene of the drama—announcement that the Nestle boycott was formally concluded—took place at a news conference in Washington, D.C., on October 4, 1984. Dr. Carl L. Angst, executive vice-president of Nestle, told the assembled news media and other interested parties, "This is not just a satisfactory, but a very happy moment. . . . Maternal and infant health have been a priority concern of Nestle for more than a century. They will continue to be so and Nestle can account for it."

We had promised Nestle management in Switzerland and in the United States that we would comply with their strict instructions regarding any action that would seem to our competitors, industry, and the public in general as a unilateral surrender to hard-line ideological activists, or that could be viewed as a negotiated embarrassing end for the company in this crisis. NCCN complied with this valid business concern in every detail. Even though some of the hard-line activist leaders were present at the announcement of the end of the boycott, their roles, participation, and direct discussion with NCCN had been minimal and always through a credible, visible third party—UNICEF, WHO, and the Muskie Commission.

The Strategy in Retrospect: The Muskie Commission

Looking back in 1985 at his role in helping to end the Nestle boycott, Muskie wrote:

> The commission [NIFAC] achieved its success in a controversy that was largely outside the legal domain—there were no judges to interpret the law, no police to enforce it and no legislators to amend it. . . .
> [A] company must recognize and understand that any use of an independent "commission" poses a risk, potentially grave, to the company. The commission might disagree with the company, or adoption of the commission's recommendations might place the company in a position in which its competitors can take advantage of it. . . . The commission may not have public authority and its conclusions may not be binding on governments, critics or even the company, but if it is endowed with independence and appropriate credentials, its conclusions can be persuasive and be accepted by the public.
> The company would be unable to disavow or to effectively discredit the commission, and the company's critics would make the most of the criticisms from "the company's own commission." The company would then be under considerable public pressure to conform to the findings of the commission, while it might also be under considerable competitive or cost pressure to reject the findings.

In going over the record of a conflict still vivid in my mind, I am struck, among other things, by the fact that the 118-to-1 vote on the WHO marketing code in 1981 showed that Nestle still lacked credibility ten years after the infant formula issue came to world attention. The company remained on the defensive, reacting to others' initiatives. It had no strategy for resolving the conflict on terms that would allow it to market infant formula in competitive fashion.

The Development of Corporate Public Policy in Response to Crisis

In the mid-1970s, some business strategists saw the need to define themselves in terms of broad political trends. They also saw that it would be advisable to include political thinking at every management level so that companies became aware of potentially troublesome issues early on and acted to defuse them. W. Howard Chase, a veteran business executive, coined the term *issue management* in 1976 and eight years later published a book with that title. Many of us with armed-forces experience saw similarities between military action and "corporate combat." One of our members, William E. Peacock, wrote a useful book with that name in 1984. The

Chase and Peacock books give business strategists brief overviews on the evolution of current thought on the need for businesses to develop high-level strategies in formulating public policy.

When Nestle offered me the task of dealing with its political problem, I accepted the assignment as the great challenge it was. The company and I agreed at the outset on two points that formed the basis of our strategy from that time forward. First, Nestle authorized me to resolve the conflict in a broad public policy context: to deal with the underlying attitudes so that the company not only would end the boycott, but also acquire more political awareness and confidence in its ability to map long-term public policy strategies. Second, we agreed that Nestle would empower me to organize an autonomous crisis-management unit, the entity that became the Nestle Coordination Center for Nutrition (NCCN).

I felt that settling the infant formula dispute might take years and that, while I needed the hands-on support of top management in Switzerland, strategy had to be given substance in the United States. This self-sufficient subsidiary was, to my knowledge, the first of its kind. As such, it represented a major step forward in the development of a political strategy capability for business. NCCN opened in temporary offices in Washington, D.C., in January 1981 with four senior executives and one secretary. We added a fifth senior executive in May and the five of us remained the entire senior staff until the boycott settlement in October 1984. NCCN built its support staff gradually and carefully, with little turnover despite four years of crisis conditions. We remained operationally lean, which helped us to carry out planned strategies with maximum speed, flexibility, economy of resources, and budgetary efficiency. Our budget was results-oriented, and we were always able to justify it to Nestle headquarters. We used specialized consultants on an as-needed basis, as well as specialized talents from Nestle itself. We kept open a constant two-way line of communication with Nestle, and had the full support and participation of senior management when the time came for meetings with church leaders involved in the boycott controversy.

Our first substantive decision was to stop the unproductive shouting match with Nestle's critics. We decided instead to listen, which served two purposes: (1) to gather information about the critics and their objectives, so we could develop appropriate ways of combatting them; and (2) to begin to earn the right to be listened to by them. Putting an end to the shouting freed Nestle from having to defend fixed positions; it also allowed for more mobility in trying to blunt the critics' thrusts.

Containment

While we organized our team and studied the problem and the corporate environment worldwide, we adopted a tactic of containment to gain time. We sent articulate spokespersons to meet with the news media, and with church and public-interest groups to answer the accusations against Nestle. In this initial phase of determining goals and plotting strategy, NCCN obviously also listened to Nestle. Our tasks were made easier by the fact that the company wanted to do the right thing and shared its critics' determination that infant formula be marketed responsibly.

On hearing out our adversaries, we found that while they were led by skillful political activists, the anti-Nestle campaign drew its moral authority and most of its support from people whose affiliations were with churches or groups founded on considerations of conscience. Our church-oriented critics were uncomfortable with profit-oriented multinational capitalism, especially as it bears on the development process in less dynamic, more traditional societies. However, they were willing to work with Nestle on behalf of the world's poor, and to see if multinational corporations were as useful and caring as Nestle claimed.

On the basis of our analysis of our key critics' motives, we established the goal of resolving the boycott through discussions designed to achieve what one boycott leader called a win-win result—an outcome satisfactory to both parties. We split our campaign into four phases: (1) to contain the critics' initiatives; (2) to work with moderate church and civic groups to see if we could satisfy their legitimate concerns; (3) to discuss with activist leaders ways of bringing the conflict to an end; (4) to create a corporate environment that would facilitate the realization of a public policy.

NCCN's timetable was determined by the fact that in May 1980, seven months before the center was established, the United Methodist Church formed a task force to examine Nestle's practices and recommend by October 1982 whether the Methodists should join the boycott—as many task force members were then inclined to do. The Episcopal Church and other religious denominations had appointed similar consultative bodies, some with different goals in mind.

In looking for a church group with which to establish a working relationship, we concluded that the Methodist task force was both knowledgeable and able to devote the time needed to explore the issue in depth. Its leader, Dr. Phillip Wogaman, then the dean of Wesley Seminary in Washington, D.C., was a respected administrator and ethical, creative, dialogue leader. Also, the task force was part of a religious denomination that influenced Nestle's other critics of conscience.

In May 1980, as NCCN and the Methodists were exploring a basis for dialogue, the World Health Assembly adopted its code on the marketing of infant formula. Some Nestle executives expressed reservations about this approach, but church groups took the position that the code at least could provide a framework within which to work for constructive change.

Nestle immediately issued a statement in Switzerland supporting the aim and principle of the code. The company repeated its support a month later in testimony before a congressional hearing in Washington at which U.S. infant formula manufacturers were taken to task for recommending that the Reagan administration cast the sole vote against the code. Nestle's statement in Switzerland had been lost in the rush by activists to attack the U.S. position, but its testimony in Washington enabled the company to begin seizing the initiative. Nestle, of course, had confrontationists of its own who wanted total victory over their adversaries, but when they saw that NCCN's approach was working, they cooperated with it fully.

Some boycott supporters began openly to question the moral basis for backing such an action against a Swiss company that enforced the code, rather than against other infant formula producers that opposed it. Many church people did not like the idea of being used for extraneous purposes by activists, or of being viewed as amoral political manipulators.

Interaction

Nestle's testimony was the catalyst for sixteen months of intense political give-and-take with the Methodists, during which NCCN brought together the new managing director of Nestle and the new head of the National Council of Churches, who until his election had been on the Methodist task force. But dialogue was not enough. At NCCN's recommendation, Nestle—using NCCN as a conduit—gave the Methodists sensitive internal documents that helped convince them of Nestle's sincerity and its longstanding efforts to respond to changing conditions in the Third World. The Methodists did not betray these confidences, so NCCN was able to contribute still more to Nestle's growing openness and political self-confidence.

At the same time, the Methodists were making highly useful contributions of their own. It was at their suggestion that Nestle, in March 1982, issue instructions to its operatives calling for compliance with the World Health Assembly code in Third World countries that had implemented no national codes of their own. In October 1982, as scheduled, the Methodist task force made its recommendation: that the church not join the boycott because Nestle had taken verifiable steps that met its critics' objections; its commitment was supported by genuine caring; and, not least, it was in better compliance with the code than were many of its competitors.

A Breakthrough Move

It cannot be doubted that putting together the impartial outside group of social auditors who served on the Muskie Commission also was a crucial step in building the credibility that Nestle drew on to bring the boycott to a close. Forming the commission was a chancy undertaking that threw the activist leadership off balance. Had Nestle rejected an audit commission as excessively risky, NCCN had other ways of achieving credibility. However, it was thought that such a body under a person as respected and prominent as Muskie had a high probability of success. As a result, anti-Nestle activists blunderd when they attacked NIFAC and tried to undermine the integrity of individual members.

NCCN's strategy called for meetings with influential groups, the news media being a high priority. In January 1983, the principal labor union supporting the boycott, the American Federation of Teachers, voted to withdraw. Later in the month Sister Regina Murphy, the head of the International Nestle Boycott Committee, was sufficiently impressed by testimony that Nestle was yielding market share to competitors in Third World countries where it was complying with the code (while some of its competitors were not), and she asked whether her own organization was keeping the boycott alive for its own sake.

The boycott could have ended in 1983, had it not been necessary for INBC to gain authorization for a settlement from groups in other countries, and had it not been desirable to gain the help of WHO and UNICEF staff in turning the code's ambiguous provisions into concrete instruction. Once this was accomplished, the path was clear for bringing the boycott to a conclusion in October 1984.

Some Final Observations

Aside from unforeseeable disasters such as Tylenol and Bhopal, it is certain that the Nestle boycott will not be the last crisis of its kind that major business firms will face. For example, in December 1984, the International Organization of Consumers Unions (IOCU) met in Bangkok to formulate a strategy for confronting business and to develop support for national and international regulation. That organization's stated goal is to have Third World regulatory capabilities—and consumer movements there—grow up along with business, rather than come along afterward and have to play catch-up.

All industries face the possibility of conflict, but IOCU placed special emphasis on those areas where what it calls "inappropriate technology" is being marketed or applied in the Third World, and where hazardous substances are involved. Among the industries singled out are pesticides and other agricultural chemicals, pharmaceuticals, fast and processed foods, beverages, tobacco, and nuclear power. IOCU is employing data banks to support Consumer Interpol, its extensive intelligence and monitoring network that exchanges information among national consumers' unions on business activities.

In addition, some of the more ideological Nestle boycott leaders have questioned the boycott settlement and have accused moderate churches of abandoning the people. This "people's movement"—of which the IOCU is a main arm—is confronting businesses, supposedly on behalf of people in the Third World. These activists are in earnest, and must be listened to. Our own information indicates that people remain highly sensitive to environmental and consumer issues—especially those involving cultural confrontations. Therefore, the ability to work with an affinity for political considerations has become essential for business, and during the past decade, business has begun to respond accordingly. Many companies have set up public-policy committees within their boards of directors. Others have created issue-management staff functions. Still others have hired management consultants to give their managers instruction in public-issue awareness.

The ability of business to define its mission broadly and to plan and implement public policy strategies is evolving at this very moment. The crisis management unit—either an autonomous subsidiary like NCCN or a consulting company with expertise in issue management—is an important step in this process. As yet, though, very few firms or think tanks are capable of developing plans to combat a concerted campaign against a multinational company. NCCN proved capable of adapting to Nestle's needs as the blueprint to end the boycott took final form. In retrospect, once Nestle seized upon the WHO code as the central point of its strategy and began a dialogue with the Methodists, there was little the activists could do to forestall a settlement.

Certainly, the specially tailored crisis management team had more freedom to act on Nestle's behalf than an off-the-shelf public relations unit would have had. NCCN was independent, not wedded to any fixed approach, and sufficiently decisive to change tactics as opportunities in the field seemed to dictate, while still keeping in mind the overriding goal of ending the boycott. It also provided Nestle with political security and expertise.

NCCN was able to keep skilled executives and consultants working together on a crisis basis for nearly four years. The boycott leaders proved to have less staying power. NCCN helped an internationally prominent company to establish a public-policy and issue-management capability that gave it the wherewithal to influence its political environment as well as the ability to operate confidently in the wider world.

In my advisory capacity and in developing and/or implementing crisis management strategies for a number of major transnationals and multinationals, who have been plagued by long-term crisis situations, in almost every case the corporation is caught ill-prepared or mostly unaware of the impending crisis. Conversely, corporate critics are alert to maximize on every opportunity that may weaken the operations and business opportunity of the targeted companies. They have developed excellent business intelligence and reporting networks. Their grassroots and public policy-oriented strategies are highly sophisticated and well tried through years of social guerrilla warfare. Matching or outclassing those capabilities is a challenge to any company whose policies isolate it from the grassroots and the public.

Corporations are learning to cope with these handicaps. They can be more than a match for radical social guerrillas. Issues can be redirected or channeled productively. Opening windows for responsible publics to participate in the joint development of a corporation's public policy can be a rewarding learning experience for both. Crisis can become the opportunity to reshape an obsolescent management structure or to streamline the decision-making process. It may sensitize and shock out of dormancy those concerned with foreign operations in the corporations. It forces the introspective examination of managements' ethics and the corporation's public personality.

I believe the Nestle case, as other such crises, are sensitizing corporations to look closer to the impact of their marketing practices and to the effects of new technologies in less advanced societies and environments. Thus, timely and sensitive development of a public-policy process is a most professional approach to corporate public relations, issue management, and crisis management. It provides tangible and measurable goals for the establishment of a mutually rewarding relationship between the corporation and its sociopolitical environment.

Note

1. Barnett, Richard J., and Ronald E. Muller. *Global Reach* (New York: Simon and Schuster, 1974.

The Integration of Corporate Social Policy into Strategic Management

Archie B. Carroll
Frank Hoy
John Hall

> "When *I* use a word," Humpty Dumpty said in a rather scornful tone, "it means just what I choose it to mean."
> "The question is," said Alice, "whether you *can* make words mean so many different things."
> "The question is," said Humpty Dumpty, "which is to be master—that's all."
>
> —Lewis Carroll,
> *Through the Looking Glass*

Those attempting to define the terms *strategy* and *strategic management* can sympathize with Alice's confusion. The meanings of these words shift and turn from author to author, and occasionally in the hands of a single author in different sections of the same work. A close examination of the literature shows that the lack of universally accepted definitions is more than just a matter of semantics. Depending on whose conceptualizations you accept, different factors are given quite different weight. This is especially true when consideration is given to the social environment and social responsibility issues and the role they play in corporate strategy.

It is our contention that most conceptualizations of strategic management pay scant attention to corporate social policy and its integration into corporate strategy. In this article, we pose a way of thinking about corporate social policy that (1) integrates it into strategic management/corporate strategy concepts, and (2) illustrates how social policy and goals can be operationalized into organizational practice. While this may not determine the question of mastery, it should aid in an understanding of the importance of corporate social policy in strategic planning.

Strategic Management and Social Policy

The impact of the social environment on business organizations is becoming more pronounced each year. It is an understatement to suggest that the social environment has become tumultuous, and a brief reminder of a few actual cases points out the validity of this claim quite dramatically. Such recent experiences as Procter & Gamble and the Rely Tampon recall, Firestone and its radial tire debacle, Ford Motor Company and its disastrous Pinto gas tank problem, and Johnson & Johnson and its Tylenol capsules are reminders of how social issues can directly affect a firm's product offerings (Gatewood and Carroll 1981).

In addition, there are many examples in which social issues have a major impact on firms at the general management level. Bank of Boston's alleged involvement in money laundering, E.F. Hutton's high-level check kiting scheme, and General Electric's and General Dynamics' fraudulent overcharges on defense contracts are a few examples where top managers escaped personal legal liability. Tennessee banker Jake Butcher and former deputy secretary of defense Paul Thayer were not as fortunate (Alexander 1985).

What started as an awareness of social issues and social responsibility in the 1960s, matured to a focus on the management of social responsiveness in the 1970s, and now looms on the horizon as an emphasis, if not preoccupation, with corporate social policy in the 1980s and beyond. The term *corporate social policy* has circulated since the mid-1970s. However, few writings have attempted to define it or to elaborate on how it meshes with the notion of corporate strategy or with the emerging nomenclature, strategic management. For the most part, when it has been used it has been employed in a rather general or collective fashion to refer to top management thinking about social issues and their impact and how management should respond to these social issues. Perhaps the most notable exceptions to this rather general usage are works by Sawyer (1973), Steiner and Steiner (1978), who conceptualized social policy as a specific part of business policy, Melvin Anshen (1980), and Edward Freeman (1984), who views social policy as a component of the stakeholder concept, which he then uses to formulate enterprise level strategy.

This article extends earlier general notions and proposes that social policy be fully integrated into the goal setting and implementation processes of the corporate structure. In addition, a brief discussion will be presented of operational social goals which, when combined with social policies, form the basis for achieving corporate social performance. The net result, it is anticipated, will be a more thorough comprehension of what corporate social policy is and how it relates to and meshes with evolving notions of strategic management.

The concern for corporate social policy has grown out of an orientation openly acknowledging that social and ethical concerns (consumerism, environment, product safety, discrimination, occupational safety, and so on) are facets of decision making that cannot be ignored (Carroll 1981). Decision processes, while varying among firms, may generally be described as responding to immediate social pressures and are labeled by Votaw and Sethi (1974) as pressure-response models. The responses may range from protective, defensive approaches to imaginative response approaches (Pearce and Robinson 1982).

From these reactive decision processes, Ackerman (1973) has concluded that two major deterrents exist that inhibit the complete integration of social policy into corporate strategy formulation. The first is the view that the social role of a firm is divorced from daily business activities and, therefore, should be treated as an appendage. The second deterrent is the notion that social goals represent a cost or reduction in profits to the firm. Ackerman, among others, has found, however, that some companies have been more proactive in their approach to the social environment and have employed more of a business policy model. This approach is one that moves the firms through a process of active social responsiveness. Using this approach, once a social issue has suggested a need for response, efforts are then directed toward articulating top management's overall posture and designing policy positions that reflect current management philosophy. Top management then becomes the design architect of corporate social policy.

Social Policy and the Strategy Levels

Various authors have found it useful to distinguish between those levels of an organization at which missions and policies are conceptualized and formulated, and those levels at which policies are operationalized and implemented. As there is no generally accepted paradigm for such a division, our approach here will be to ascertain a line of demarcation from a sample of recent paradigm that can aid in understanding corporate social policy.

Bates and Eldredge (1980) proposed three system levels for use in analyzing managerial activities and skills. At the *organizational* level, managers are involved with designing and formulating goals and strategies. High risk decisions are made by top level managers regarding the relationship of the organization with its environment. Managers' time horizon is relatively long term. *Coordinative* level managers coordinate and integrate activities across and among functional areas. While the risk level is moderate and time horizon of concern is short to mid-term, these managers are oriented to organizational goal achievement rather than the goal accomplishment of specific functional areas. At the *functional* level, emphasis is on implementation. The time horizon is short and the risk level is relatively low.

Harvey (1982) also has distinguished three levels of managerial concern. The highest level is labeled *strategic*. Its purpose, like that of Bates and Eldredge's organizational level, is to relate the organization to is environment. Harvey's two lower levels are differentiated by their concern for implementation of strategic plans and by their focus on units with a scope that is less than organization-wide. Middle management resides at the *coordinating* level and determines the functioning and control of operating units. Lower level managers make decisions on the *operating* level. Again corresponding to Bates and Eldredge's functional level, managers implement policies of lower risk and on a shorter time schedule.

Hofer and co-workers (1980) have developed four levels of strategy. The *societal* strategy level addresses the role the organization assumes in society and the processes by which the role is defined. Important social questions here include the nature of corporate governance, the composition and role of the board of directors, the firm's involvement in political activities, and trade-offs between economic and social objectives. The *corporate* strategy level addresses questions such as: "What business(es) should the company be in?" and "How should this set of businesses be managed to maximize the company's ability to achieve its objectives?" The *business* strategy level examines the question "How should a firm compete in a given business/industry?" Of particular importance here is an analysis of the macro-environments (social/cultural, economic, political/legal) in which the industry is located. The *functional* strategy level is the operational level and addresses the integration of the various subfunctional activities of the firm. It also assures that changes made at the societal, corporate, and business levels are integrated into the firm's everyday operations.

Pearce and Robinson's (1982) three levels of strategy are *corporate, business,* and *functional*. Strategic activities at the corporate level are conceptual in nature, involving high risks and potentially high returns. At the business level, decisions are more operational and less risky than at the corporate level, but are similar to the business level of Hofer and associates in that they focus on the firm's ability to compete within its industry. Typical business level decisions include plant location, distribution channels, and so forth. At lower management levels, strategy is operationalized. The functional level is characterized by lower risk, shorter range activities.

A four-level strategy is described by Thompson and Strickland (1981). *Corporate* "strategy is composed of two main elements: (1) the firm's scope of activities and (2) the priorities and patterns whereby internal resources will be allocated among these activities" (Thompson and Strickland 1981, p. 40). It is at the corporate level that policy is established positioning the firm relative to its external environment. The *business* strategy level also relates the firm to its environment, but in a more narrow sense, that is, to a single market or market segment. The two lower levels are concerned more with specifics. At the *functional* level, support strategies are devised for the management of a major support activity in order for that subactivity to contribute to the accomplishment of overall organizational goals. *Operating* level strategies are those guidelines that lower level managers follow in carrying out day-to-day responsibilities.

The last paradigm consists of four levels developed by Freeman (1984). The top level, *enterprise* strategy, focuses on social legitimacy concerns. The purpose of enterprise strategy is to integrate the firm with its environment, examining the role of the business in society. While not requiring a particular mode of social response on the part of the firm, enterprise strategy poses questions on the manner in which the firm will relate to society. Questions here include, "What is our role in society? What should our role be? What do we stand for as an organization?" The next level, *corporate* strategy, is limited to questions on which businesses the diversified corporation is to pursue. *Division* level strategy is concerned with synergy among divisions and the division's portfolio. The final level, *business* strategy, deals with questions of how to compete with specific businesses/products.

One concern in this article is in differentiating between what we term the *macro view* of corporate social policy, which would reside at higher levels of an organization, and the *micro view*, which would reside at the functional level. Table 1 portrays this distinction and its relationship to the six paradigms just described. From our review, we see that it is possible to draw a distinction between policy levels using the criteria of scope of goals, level of managerial decision making, conceptualization versus operationalization, level of risk, and time horizon.

Corporate Social Policy: The Macro View

The macro view of corporate social policy corresponds with the upper section of table 1, and deals with how top management perceives the concern for a social orientation and how much consideration is given to this social dimension as management frames its overall strategy or strategic posture. Corporate strategy refers to the top level decision process of determining basic organizational purpose. At this level, management is concerned with what *business the firm is in* and *what kind of company* it chooses or intends to be. At this level, commitments are made that will define the underlying character and identity the organization will have. Since top management has so much to do with establishing this basic character and identity, and setting the tone for everyone else and all decision making, it is also developing the company's fundamental posture on the degree to which social factors are going to be considered in company operations. One aspect of the company's strategy or strategic posture, therefore, will be its overall corporate social policy.

There are at least five major tasks in the strategic management process: (1) goal formulation; (2) strategy evaluation; (3) strategy formulation; (4) strategy implementation; and (5) strategy control (Schendel and Hofer 1979). It is in the first three tasks that (macro) corporate social policy is designed and articulated. In the fourth task—strategy implementation—micro or functional social policy is set or administered. Strategy control provides a feedback mechanism between the design and administration. Thus, the basic nature of the relationship of the two types of social policy is revealed: macro policy is first established and then micro policies are derived from it. Figure 1 depicts this relationship and illustrates how the control phase fits into the total scheme. Although the tasks are discussed sequentially, they are in fact interactive and do not progress in a neatly diagrammed pattern.

Table 1
Levels of Strategy in Business Organizations

	Bates and Eldredge, 1980	Harvey, 1982	Hofer et al., 1980	Pearce and Robinson, 1982	Thompson and Strickland, 1981	Freeman, 1984	Characteristics
Macro	Organizational	Strategy	Societal	Corporate	Corporate	Enterprise	Organizational goals
	Coordinative		Corporate			Corporate	Higher level decision making
			Business	Business	Business	Division	Concept formulation
						Business	Higher risk
							Longer time horizon
Micro		Coordinating					Functional goals
	Functional		Functional	Functional	Functional		Lower level decision making
		Operating			Operating		Operational implementation
							Lower risk
							Short time horizon

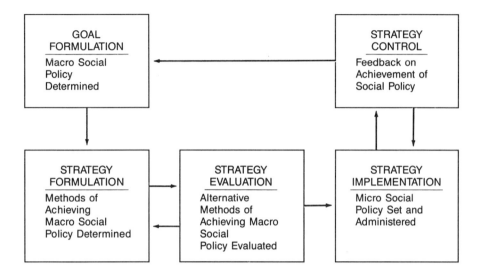

Figure 1. The Strategic Process and Corporate Social Policy

The complex task of goal formulation involves both establishing goals and setting priorities for those goals. Arguably, the most crucial step in the strategic process, goal formulation, is a politically charged process that involves the personal values, perceptions, attitudes, and power of the managers and owners involved in the process. It is at this stage that basic choices regarding the future of the organization are made. Social norms are one of the most general means of influence on the goal formulation process. The social norms that affect the participants in the goal formulation process come from many sources: parents, friends, teachers, church and civic organizations. These norms are in a constant state of transition and range from very broad ("Thou shalt not steal") to fairly specific guidelines (employees should be kept informed of corporate goals and objectives). Conflicts over social norms arise both because individuals have different social norms and because of conflicts in the norms: plant efficiency versus pollution, managerial efficiency versus enlightened management, obligations to society versus obligations to owners. At the goal formulation stage, the general framework and attitude of corporate social policy is established (Mintzberg 1979).

Strategy evaluation in an established organization involves both evaluating the organization's current strategy and evaluating a proposed strategy. There are at least six criteria for evaluating strategy: (1) internal consistency with the organization's goals, objectives, and functional policies; (2) environmental consistency with current and projected social forces; (3) the appropriateness of the strategy in view of the organization's available resources; (4) the degree of risk involved in the proposed strategy; (5) the time horizon involved; and (6) the strategy's workability (Tilles

1963). The second criterion, environmental consistency, requires at least an acknowledgement of social forces and issues.

Strategy formulation involves environmental, industrial, and competitor analysis, and occurs after the proposed strategy has been evaluated and found wanting in some aspect of goal achievement or is used when a new goal has been formulated. One way to look at corporate social policy—the macro view—is to consider it as just one of the crucial elements or factors that goes into the organization's choice of strategy. Several authorities have taken this approach as they have argued that strategy is a result of considering four aspects or factors that shape overall corporate policy—the company's decision as to what it is and is to be. They argue that the four aspects or factors are: (1) the company's competencies and resources; (2) market opportunities; (3) personal values and aspirations of the management group; and (4) acknowledged obligations to societal segments (Christensen et al., 1978). The first two of these are most fundamental—they have to do with what the organization *can* do and what market opportunities are in existence (what the organization *may* do). A third factor is what the organization *wants* to do—or more specifically, what top management or ownership wants to do as a statement of corporate strategy.

The fourth factor—acknowledged obligations to societal segments—is the corporate social policy element. It refers to what management and the organization *ought* to do, and thus refers to the question of how social responsibility meshes with, affects, and helps determine overall strategic choice. To some, the orderly, rational process of determining overall company direction and policy should not be subjected to such value-laden considerations as those bound to be represented by considering responsibilities that extend beyond legal obligations. It is certainly difficult, if not impossible, to quantitatively measure the cost/benefit trade-offs of social actions. For example, using the concept of sunk costs, Ford Motor Company may have made a financially astute decision to not recall some twenty-three million cars manufactured from 1968 to 1980 that are alleged to slip from "park" to "reverse" if the engine is left running. However, the Center for Auto Safety, a consumer group, estimates that faulty Ford transmissions have caused 234 deaths and Ford is involved in over one thousand lawsuits as a result of its decision (*Business Week*, 1984). In contrast, Johnson & Johnson won widespread approval for its actions in both Tylenol poisoning cases. While there definitely are problems involved, the business person who cares about social policy must examine the qualitative impact on the public good of the policy alternatives freely elected. Figure 2 illustrates the four factors as they impinge on the strategy decision of the firm.

It is straightforward to draw a diagram as presented in figure 2. It is far more complex and difficult to develop an overall business strategy that fairly takes into consideration all the diverse factors that merit attention in the decision process. Conflicts are inevitable. Regardless, social trends have been established and top-level managers must apply their management knowledge to the social realm, and devise corporate strategies embodying a corporate social policy that stakeholders of the firm consider acceptable.

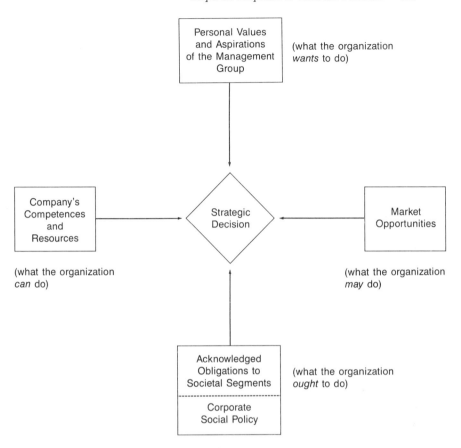

Figure 2. Factors Affecting Strategy: Role of Corporate Social Policy

As alluded to earlier, social responsibility has been frequently treated as an environmental factor to which corporations adapt. Bernstein (1981) presents a more recent view, one that we consider transitional, from which social responsibility is described as one of the "softer" strategic goals, to be pursued simultaneously with other goals. The approach in this article is more comprehensive and is consistent with the recommendation of Schendel and Hofer (1979) and Saunders and Thompson (1980). The strategy formulation process is incomplete without incorporating social issues and responsibility as one of the elements of the policy decision.

There are at least three basic reasons for managers to examine the impact of policy decisions on the public good. First, professional managers today realize their legitimacy depends on being responsive to the full range of their social responsibilities—economic, legal, ethical, and discretionary (Carroll 1979). Thus, there is a professional concern for legality, fairness, and decency developed as a result of their socialization and careful assimilation of all that has come to be expected of them by shareholders and the public. Second, there is the continuing and very real threat of increased government regulation. This regulation may be forthcoming if business behavior does not meet the standards that are being set for it by society. Third, it is becoming increasingly obvious that developing a responsive corporate social policy makes sound managerial sense. The variables that now affect business success exceed the simple (by comparison) and stable social, economic, political, and technological factors of the past.

Intricately intertwined into this third point is the question of business's success and, ultimately, its continued existence. At stake are opportunities which, if properly addressed, could mean added success. Social issues and forces can and should have an impact on corporate strategy, at least in those cases where management is able and perceptive. Sawyer (1973) suggests that as society changes, the resulting social forces should influence at least three types of near-term corporate strategic decisions: (1) marketplace decisions capitalizing on changing tastes and needs; (2) decisions based on protective reaction and, hopefully, on imaginative response to particular social issues; and (3) decisions anticipating fundamental change in our society. Through responses of these types, modern businesses today have the opportunity to "relate social issues to [their] ongoing flow of strategic decisions, and to benefit significantly as a result" (Sawyer 1973).

Corporate social policy, although it does not have a clearly accepted definition among those who write on and study these issues and among management practitioners, deals with managerial philosophy, thinking, and commitment at the highest reaches of the organization. The macro perspective assumes that once a social issue has been identified and acknowledged to be a social responsibility, efforts are energized toward integrating this perspective into the firm's overall strategy. Whether the issue becomes (1) just another factor that must be considered, or (2) a specific goal to be achieved along with others, turns out to be a function of managerial commitment, necessity, or corporate social policy. Corporate social policy, therefore, embraces management's highest order of commitment to the pursuit of social goals as well as economic goals. It mandates that management ask not just "What do we owe the shareholders?" but "What responsibilities do we have to consumers, environmentalists, minorities, government, employees, and other stakeholders while we pursue profits?"

Figure 3 illustrates the corporate social policy process depicted side-by-side with the strategic process. The social policy process is comprised of macro social policy, which includes societal/enterprise level strategy, corporate level strategy, business level strategy (as portrayed in table 1), and micro social policy, which includes functional social policies and operational social goals. Social action/implementation flows from the macro and micro policy levels. Feedback in the form of results and perceived successes and failures provides strategy control and information for the next goal/policy formulation stage.

Portrayed alongside the social policy process is the strategic process as depicted in figure 1. The stages of the strategic process have been aligned with the

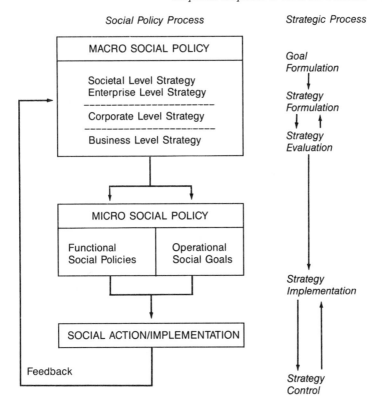

Figure 3. Social Policy Process and Strategic Process

corresponding elements in the social policy process to illustrate more clearly the interrelationship between the two processes. In reality, of course, the social policy process would become just one part of the strategic process, but we have isolated it in diagrammatical form for purposes of highlighting its features and correspondence with the strategic process elements.

Corporate Social Policy: The Micro View

Earlier, it was stated that functional or micro social policies were derived from the organization's larger statement of social policy or strategy. We have now traced how that larger view of social policy has been translated into corporate action through the development of a view of social performance and the social response process. Figure 3 summarized the essential elements in this process.

The notion of functional or operational social policies (at the micro level) refers to specific guides for decision making, which, when coupled with social goals, should facilitate corporate social action. Policies at this level are vehicles or guides for helping operational managers carry out the larger view of social policy held by the firm. Social policies as we are viewing them here would likely have been set at some middle management staff level, perhaps during the second phase of the corporate social response process. The purpose of such policies is to channel managerial decision making and, hence, company action, in desired directions. Such policies should provide for a more rational, systematic, and uniform company social performance.

Some of the best examples of social policies have been provided by George Steiner (1972). These serve as guides in providing a rational perspective to a company's social efforts. Several illustrations are worth examining.

It is the policy of this company to concentrate action programs on limited objectives. No company can take significant action in every area of social responsibility. It can achieve more if it selects areas in which to concentrate its efforts. The logic behind this policy is that a company can accomplish more if it identifies a few, good social objectives and concentrates on those. The alternative is to pursue many social objectives with the result being diluted effort and limited or superficial success with every activity pursued. By limiting the objectives pursued, particularly those in the philanthropic category, the organization can achieve a unity of effort that otherwise is impossible.

It is the policy of this company to concentrate action prorams on areas strategically related to the present and prospective economic functions of the business. The position taken here is that if a company is going to pursue social objectives, it might as well pursue those that are also in its strategic economic best interest. According to this policy, a bank would be more supportive of a United Way campaign that helps people in the community in which it exists rather than the environmental group "Friends of the Earth," which espouses causes more remote to the banking industry.

It is the policy of this company to begin action programs close at home before spreading out or acting in far distant regions. Since all companies have financial constraints on what they do, this policy only makes sense. It argues that companies should look to their own communities first in their selection of social programs. One illustration of this would be the large financial contributions the Coca Cola Company made to Emory University, both of which are located in the Atlanta area. Many firms have sufficient resources that they can pursue national efforts but this is frequently not the case.

It is the policy of this company to facilitate employee actions which can be taken as individuals rather than as representatives of the company. This policy places a high premium on employees pursuing programs of their own choosing. The policy takes the position that it is being socially active or responsive by facilitating or accommodating employee efforts. In this connection, a number of companies have given employees time off with pay to serve on community benefit committees, and have allowed managers to use company resources (for example, secretarial time, reproduction facilities, postage) while pursuing social objectives.

There are many other policies that could be mentioned, but these illustrate well the point that is being made. Companies can lend an added degree of rationality and uniform effort if they are simply willing to take the time to do so. The result can be a social program that is strategically related to the economic interests of the firm, and one that is undergirded by sound managerial judgment as to what is in the mutual interests of both the company and the recipient groups. The view taken here is that management should apply its judgment and knowledge to the social realm just as it does to the economic realm. If this is done, the company's corporate social response and performance can be the best for all affected.

Operational Social Goals

Side by side with functional social policies, as seen in figure 3, were operational social goals. Social goals, when combined with specific policies, work together to form the operational nucleus for implementing the social aspects of the firm's corporate strategy. All too often in the past, managers have not attempted to reduce their broad, platitudinous statements of social aspirations to goals that could be achieved as part of the organization's overall effort at implementing corporate social policy (Carroll 1978).

It is proposed here that management set specific operational goals that will serve as guides for business social action. These goals, patterned after operational goals that have been used for years in Management by Objectives (MBO) programs, should convert general goals into specific ones for which goal attainment is readily accomplishable, identifiable, and measurable. An MBO approach, with its emphasis on evaluation based on goal achievement, has the added advantage of implying that benefits accrue to the organization from the acocmplishment of social objectives. As Bates and Eldredge (1980) have suggested, cost-benefit analysis techniques can be applied to the social aspects just as easily as the economic aspects of corporate strategy. The productivity of a machine is expected to exceed the capital investment required over its useful life, although initial costs are almost certainly higher than immediate benefits. Social expenditures also are unlikely to provide an instantaneous return to the organization, but may be evaluated in terms of their longer-term implications.

Three illustrations for operationalizing social goals follow. The framework from which these examples are derived is provided by the three categories of social roles that enter the strategy system, as defined by Ackerman and Bauer (1976). The first category of social policy concerns issues not directly related to activities resulting from corporate strategies. An example might be urban blight. Provided here is a general objective, followed by a specific operational statement derived from the objective.

General Objective: To be a good community citizen by supporting urban renewal projects.

Operational Objective: To begin a program of urban improvement by holding the first meeting of the downtown revitalization committee at company headquarters on June 30, 1987, and provide initial financial support not exceeding $20,000.

The second social policy category relates to issues in which corporate strategies may have direct, external impacts in the course of regular economic activity. This case may be illustrated by the closing or moving of business operations from a locality that has been economically dependent on the enterprise.

General Objective: To minimize dysfunctional economic impacts on communities in which corporate operations are terminated.

Operational Objective: To establish a committee to assist displaced workers upon plant closings in transferring or finding comparable employment, and to donate $30,000 to the industrial development commission of the affected chamber(s) of commerce to aid in attracting new industry to the community.

The final social policy category is internal to the firm and results from normal business activities. Employment health and safety is an example.

General Objective: To ensure a safe working environment for all employees.

Operational Objective: To provide each employee with a written set of safety procedures relevant to job descriptions and require affidavit that procedures were read, and to conduct safety seminars twice a year with mandatory attendance.

To summarize, general objectives relating to corporate social policies can be developed as functional guidelines, but must be specified as operational objectives to be accomplished by middle and lower level managers. By so doing, the implementation of corporate social policy is enhanced.

Turning Social Intentions into Social Actions

No design, however grand, will aid the organization if the design is left on the drawing board. Translating social intentions into social actions is an administrative task that involves communicating the social policy component of the organization's strategy to the appropriate levels in the organization, and ensuring that the organization's structure and processes are arranged to accommodate the duties and jobs required by the social policy.

Corporate creeds and codes of ethics are two of the more obvious methods of communciating social policy to organization members. Johnson & Johnson's Credo, reproduced in figure 4, provides a clear, concise guide on the company's responsibilities to consumers, employees, communities, and stockholders. First given to employees in 1947, the Credo has been revised a number of times. While some may view it as mere platitudes, James Burke, the chairman of the board of Johnson & Johnson, notes that:

> All of us at McNeil Consumer Products and Johnson & Johnson truly believe that the guidance of the Credo played *the* most important role in our decision-making [in the first Tylenol poisoning case]. Ask yourselves, with a statement like that, if we had any alternative but to do what we did during the Tylenol tragedy. Ask yourselves how the Tylenol consumer, the Johnson & Johnson employee, the public, the stockholder would have felt. What would *your* attitude today be toward Johnson & Johnson if we hadn't behaved the way we did? (Peters and Austin, 1985, p. 331).

While the Johnson & Johnson Credo does not provide a specific plan of action for every situation, it does provide all employees with a framework for decision making within the social policy boundaries of the organization.

Elements of the organization's structure are important both in implementing social policy and in providing feedback for control and evaluation purposes. Boundary spanners—employees whose jobs meet at the boundary of the organization and its environment—include public affairs officers, issues managers, and customer service representatives. A powerful concept for understanding the nature and importance of boundary spanning roles in the organization is the stakeholder concept. An expansion of the notion that the stockholder group is the key group in an organization, a stakeholder is defined as: "Any group or individual who can affect or is affected by the achievement of the organization's objectives" (Freeman 1984, p. 46). A boundary spanner is thus any individual in the organization who conducts transactions with one or more of the organization's stakeholders.

Figure 5 is a stakeholder map for a single company or a single issue: Hooker Chemicals and the issue of Love Canal in the 1970s. The stakeholders on this issue varied both in their attitude toward the issue and in their potential impact on the firm. As a result, a variety of boundary spanners would be deployed by the organization to deal with the stakeholders. An interesting trend in boundary spanning roles is the emergence of a new kind of executive in organizations—the issues manager. The rationale behind this job is the concept of the issues life cycle: issues have a relatively predictable life cycle in that they tend to follow an S-shaped curve over time. In most instances, the initial indicators of an incipient issue are bits and pieces of data, such as isolated comments in speeches by leading experts or minor news stories. Some issues, such as the thalidomide drug case and the Bhopal tragedy, come to life slightly ahead of this point due to a catalytic event.

As the bits and pieces of information increase, activist groups form around the issue, and these groups attract both supporters and media attention. An example of

Our Credo

We believe our first responsibility is to the doctors, nurses and patients,
to mothers and all others who use our products and services.
In meeting their needs everything we do must be of high quality.
We must constantly strive to reduce our costs
in order to maintain reasonable prices.
Customers' orders must be serviced promptly and accurately.
Our suppliers and distributors must have an opportunity
to make a fair profit.

We are responsible to our employees,
the men and women who work with us throughout the world.
Everyone must be considered as an individual.
We must respect their dignity and recognize their merit.
They must have a sense of security in their jobs.
Compensation must be fair and adequate,
and working conditions clean, orderly and safe.
Employees must feel free to make suggestions and complaints.
There must be equal opportunity for employment, development
and advancement for those qualified.
We must provide competent management,
and their actions must be just and ethical.

We are responsible to the communities in which we live and work
and to the world community as well.
We must be good citizens — support good works and charities
and bear our fair share of taxes.
We must encourage civic improvements and better health and education.
We must maintain in good order
the property we are privileged to use,
protecting the environment and natural resources.

Our final responsibility is to our stockholders.
Business must make a sound profit.
We must experiment with new ideas.
Research must be carried on, innovative programs developed
and mistakes paid for.
New equipment must be purchased, new facilities provided
and new products launched.
Reserves must be created to provide for adverse times.
When we operate according to these principles,
the stockholders should realize a fair return.

Johnson & Johnson

Used with permission of Johnson & Johnson.

Figure 4. Johnson & Johnson Credo

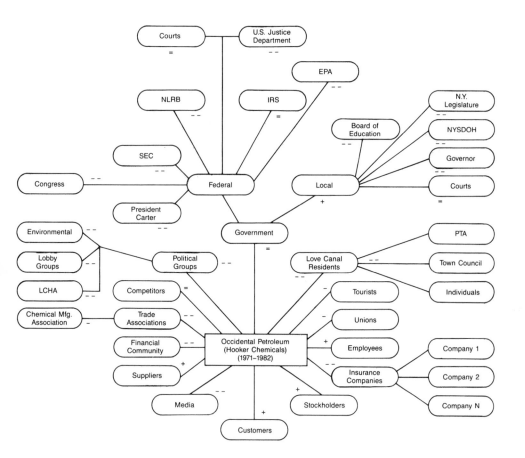

++ = very positive relationship
+ = positive relationship
= = neutral
− = negative relationships
− − = very negative relationship

Figure 5. Hooker Chemical's Stakeholders Issue: Love Canal (1971–1982)

how this stage develops is the issue of automobile safety and the efforts of activist groups, started by Ralph Nader, to bring the issue to the forefront during the mid-1960s. As more and more attention is drawn to the issue, politicians jump on the bandwagon. Once 20 to 40 percent of the population begins to see the issue as important, legislators, reflecting the views of their constituents, begin to take up the cause and the issue becomes the subject of government studies, legislation, and ultimately regulation (Molitor, 1977).

The job of the issues manager is to identify and track issues of concern to the firm and to integrate these concerns into an effective response pattern for the firm. Among the benefits of an effective issues management program are that it allows *management of* versus *reaction to* social issues; allows management to select issues that will have the greatest impact on the corporation; inserts relevant issues into the strategic management process; gives the company the ability to act in tune with society; protects the credibility of business in the public mind; and provides the organization with opportunities for leadership roles (Buchholz 1982).

Some of the payoffs that companies have experienced through issues management are worth briefly mentioning:

The S.C. Johnson Company removed fluorocarbons from its aerosol sprays three years before federal action forced others in the industry to do so.

Sears Roebuck spotted the flammable nightwear and Tris-treated fabric controversies early and removed the goods before government action.

Bank of America moved to change its lending policies two years before Congress required banks to disclose whether they were barring all loans in certain parts of a city ("redlining"). Early action cut the eventual cost of compliance and spared Bank of America public relations grief and antagonism from cities and activist groups.

Shortly after Ronald Reagan's election, Atlantic Richfield's issues management department accurately predicted that Reagan budget cuts would prompt states to compensate for lost federal money by taxing business. By lobbying early, they were able to head off tax proposals in a number of states (Gottschalk 1982).

Regardless of the methods or job positions used to communicate and implement social policy, a key aspect is commitment on the part of top management. Any organization can disseminate a corporate creed to its employees; living up to the statements in the creed, and ensuring that the actions of the organization and its top managers are within the framework of the creed requires more than mere words.

Crisis Management versus Corporate Social Policy

Regardless of how well the organization's corporate social policy has been developed, crises can occur. The Bhopal tragedy, the Tylenol poisonings, and the Three-Mile Island incidents hit the companies involved suddenly and catapulted them into national and world prominence. Poorly managed crises typically follow a predictable pattern. There are usually early warning signals of a potential crisis, but the warnings are either ignored or not regarded as particularly important. For example, internal reports at Union Carbide warned of potential problems at the company's Bhopal facility, but no action was taken.

The warnings can ultimately build to a climax of crisis proportions, but in a poorly managed situation the company may still try to down-play the issue's importance. When First National Bank of Boston pleaded guilty to failure to report $1.2 billion in transactions with international banks, it sent out its press release by mail and did not notify employees or customers immediately.

As pressure mounts, unprepared executives cannot cope effectively with the media attention and are overwhelmed by the clamor for information on the crisis. This can typically lead to two potential problems: clamming up, and looking for a quick fix to the crisis. In the 1985 "Tunagate" affair in Canada, the Canadian Broadcasting Company accused Star-Kist Foods Canadian subsidiary of shipping one million cans of spoiled tuna. On the advice of Star-Kist's parent company, H.J. Heinz, the Star-Kist general manager made no comment on the charges. As he kept silent, the media kept interest in the affair high. As a result of this siege mentality, Star-Kist's Canadian revenues declined by 90 percent. A poorly planned quick fix can have results that are equally disastrous, setting in motion a chain reaction that can destroy the company.

Because of the increasing possibility of a major disaster, the topic of crisis management is now on the front burner in many companies. If the crisis cannot be avoided, the organization can prepare for dealing with a crisis as effectively as possible. The steps in crisis management include:

1. Identifying areas of vulnerability. Some areas are fairly obvious, for example, chemical spills have been a major public concern for years. Less obvious areas, however, might need to be explored, such as a crisis by a competitor.

2. Developing plans for dealing with the most serious threats. While certain aspects of the company's response depend on the specific situation, an overall game plan can be developed. Advance planning on company communications and training executives on dealing with the media are both feasible and prudent.

3. Appointing crisis teams to deal with future crises. Not all executives work well under the kind of stress experienced during a crisis. At United Airlines, an executive vice-president heads a team in which the members carry beepers and are always on call. In the event of a United plane crash, the crisis team gathers at United's Chicago headquarters.

4. Simulating crisis drills. By simulating a crisis, crisis team members have the opportunity to learn from mistakes before the mistakes can seriously affect the company (Symonds 1985).

While crisis management techniques can be useful, it is imperative that they be imbedded in a sound corporate social policy and not be used as a faddish response to real, on-going problems. As noted earlier, Johnson & Johnson dealt effectively with the Tylenol incidents not because they were prepared to handle the media, but because they had a well-developed social policy and had communicated that policy throughout the organization. Citing its corporate credo that requires the company always to honor its commitments to consumers, J&J management promptly pulled all Tylenol everywhere off the shelves—a recall that cost about $100 million. In the second Tylenol scare, J&J announced that it would replace consumers' capsules with Tylenol caplets (tablets) and would no longer manufacture products in capsule form since it could not guarantee the safety of the capsules (Lee 1986, p. 38). In the Rely Tampon incident, Proctor & Gamble moved quickly to remove its product from stores and to inform the public of the potential dangers of its product. The actions of Proctor & Gamble, and the expenses they incurred in removing a product they spent twenty years developing, suggest that what happened was less a preparation for crisis than part of a larger picture of corporate social responsibility (Gatewood and Carroll 1981).

Conclusions

The accelerated evolution of strategic management in recent years has been underemphasizing one vital link: the area of social policy. Current practice is generally to treat social responsibility as a residual factor in the environment or as one criterion among many by which to evaluate organizational effectiveness. The purpose of this discussion has been to emphasize the need for incorporating social policy into strategic management processes and to prepare the means for affecting such a meshing of policy formulation and implementation.

It is at the macro level (to include the societal, corporate, and business levels of strategy) that a more proactive stance is needed for dealing with social policy. Corporate executives should be including social policy guidelines in their strategic plans from which functional policies can be derived and administered. Ultimately, much of the burden of actually achieving social goals must and should rest on middle and lower level managers. These managers cannot be expected, however, to achieve broad, abstract social objectives. There is a need to specify the objectives in the same way that economic objectives are specified. The ideas presented here are proposed as aids to those who seek to convert social responsibility platitudes into effective corporate social actions or to understand the vital role corporate social policy can assume in the strategic management process.

Note

An earlier version of this article appeared as "Integrating Corporate Social Policy Into Strategic Management," by Archie B. Carroll and Frank Hoy, *Journal of Business Strategy*, Winter, 1984 (vol. 4, no. 3), pp. 48–57.

References

Ackerman, Robert W., "How Companies Respond to Social Demands," *Harvard Business Review,* July–August 1973, pp. 88–98.

Ackerman, Robert W., and Raymond A. Bauer, *Corporate Social Responsiveness: The Modern Dilemma* (Reston, Va.: Reston Publishing, 1976).

Alexander, Charles P., "Crime in the Suites," *Time,* June 10, 1985, pp. 56–57.

Anshen, Melvin, *Corporate Strategies for Social Performance* (New York: Macmillan, 1980).

Bates, Donald L., and David L. Eldredge, *Strategy and Policy: Analysis, Formulation, and Implementation* (Dubuque, Iowa: William C. Brown, 1980).

Bernstein, Charles D., "Strategy and Action," *Interlink,* Winter 1981, Palo Alto, Calif.: Stanford GSB.

Buchholz, Rogene A., "Education for Public Issues Management: Key Insights from a Survey of Top Practitioners," *Public Affairs Review,* **3**:70 (1982).

Business Week, "Unsafe Products: The Great Debate over Blame and Punishment," April 30, 1984, pp. 96–104.

Carroll, Archie B., "Setting Operational Goals for Corporate Social Responsibility," *Long Range Planning,* April 1978, pp. 35–38.

Carroll, Archie B., "A Three-Dimensional Conceptual Model of Corporate Social Performance," *Academy of Management Review,* **4**(4):497–505 (1979).

Carroll, Archie B., *Business and Society: Managing Corporate Social Performance* (Boston: Little, Brown & Co., 1981).

Carroll, Peter J., "The Link Between Performance and Strategy," *Journal of Business Strategy,* Spring 1982, pp. 3–20.

Christensen, C. Roland, Kenneth R. Andrews, and Joseph L. Bower, *Business Policy: Text and Cases,* 4th ed. (Homewood, Ill.: Richard D. Irwin, 1978).

Freeman, R. Edward, *Strategic Management: A Stakeholder Approach* (Boston: Pitman, 1984).

Gatewood, Elizabeth, and Archie B. Carroll, "The Anatomy of Corporate Social Response: The Rely, Firestone 500, and Pinto Cases," *Business Horizons,* September/October 1981, pp. 9–16.

Gluck, Frederick, Stephen Kaufman, and A. Steven Wallick, "The Four Phases of Strategic Management," *Journal of Business Strategy,* Winter 1982, pp. 9–21.

Gottschalk, Earl C., Jr., "Firms Hiring New Type of Manager to Study Issues, Emerging Troubles," *Wall Street Journal,* June 10, 1982, p. 33.

Harvey, Don, *Business Policy and Strategic Management* (Columbus, Ohio: Charles E. Merrill, 1982).

Hofer, Charles W., Edwin A. Murray, Jr., Ram Charan, and Robert A. Pitts, *Strategic Management: A Casebook in Business Policy and Planning* (St. Paul, Minn.: West Publishing Co., 1980).

Lee, Chris, "Ethics Training: Facing the Tough Questions," *Training,* March 1986, pp. 30–41.

McCarthy, Daniel, Robert Minichiello, and Joseph Curran, *Business Policy and Strategy: Concepts and Readings* (Homewood, Ill.: Richard D. Irwin, 1975).

Mintzberg, Henry, "Organizational Power and Goals: A Skeletal Theory," in D.C. Schendel and C.W. Hofer (eds.), *Strategic Management: A New View of Business Policy and Planning* (Boston: Little, Brown & Co., 1979), pp. 64–80.

Molitor, Graham T.T., "How to Anticipate Public-Policy Changes," *S.A.M. Advanced Management Journal,* Summer 1977, pp. 4–13.

Pearce, John A. II, and Richard B. Robinson, Jr., *Strategic Management: Strategy Formulation and Implementation* (Homewood, Ill.: Richard D. Irwin, 1982).

Peters, Tom, and Nancy Austin, *A Passion for Excellence* (New York: Random House, 1985).

Saunders, Charles B., and John Clair Thompson, "A Survey of the Current State of Business Policy Research," *Strategic Management Journal*, 1:119–130 (1980).

Sawyer, George C., "Social Issues and Social Change: Impact on Strategic Decisions," *MSU Business Topics*, Summer 1973, pp. 15–20.

Schendel, Dan E., and Charles W. Hofer, *Strategic Management: A New View of Business Policy and Planning* (Boston: Little, Brown & Co., 1979).

Steiner, George A., "Social Policies for Business," *California Management Review*, Winter 1972, pp. 17–24.

Steiner, George A., and John F. Steiner, "Social Policy as Business Policy," in Lee E. Preston (ed.), *Research in Corporate Social Performance and Policy*, vol. 1 (Greenwich, Conn.: JAI Press, 1978), pp. 201–221.

Symonds, William C., "How Companies are Learning to Prepare for the Worst," *Business Week*, December 23, 1985, pp. 74–76.

Thompson, Arthur A., Jr. and A.J. Strickland III, *Strategy and Policy: Concepts and Cases* (Plano, Tex.: Business Publications, Inc., 1981).

Tilles, Seymour, "How to Evaluate Corporate Strategy," *Harvard Business Review*, July–August 1963, pp. 111–121.

Votaw, Dow, and S.P. Sethi, *The Corporate Dilemma* (Englewood Cliffs, N.J.: Prentice-Hall, 1974).

8
Corporate Law Violations and White-Collar Crime

The Expanding Scope of Executive Liability
(Criminal and Civil) for Corporate
Law Violations

S. Prakash Sethi

Ever since the emergence of large corporations, nations have attempted, with varying degrees of success, to come to grips with the problem of making these institutions adapt to changing societal expectations. Although public control and regulation of corporations have taken different forms in different societies, their aims have been essentially similar: (1) to improve efficiency in the production of socially desirable goods and services, (2) to ensure that the use of human and physical resources conforms to societal expectations, (3) to ensure equitable bargaining conditions and rights for various economic and social groups that must deal with corporations, either directly or indirectly, and (4) to ensure that social priorities and public policy alternatives are freely determined without being disproportionately influenced by large corporations.

A variety of incentives and penalties have been developed to ensure compliance. Incentives have included tax concessions, preference in the allocation of scarce material and human resources, greater discretion in managing corporate internal affairs, and increased economic rewards and social recognition for executives. The penalties have included withdrawal of tax benefits, nonavailability of resources, loss of discretion in management, personal and corporate economic penalties and loss of social status, and, in extreme cases, imprisonment for the offending executives.

In the recent past, top executives and corporate officers have only rarely faced imprisonment as a penalty for criminal violation of legal statutes, even where an executive was found to have direct complicity and/or involvement in the corporation's illegal acts. Prison sentences have been levied most often where a corporate executive was convicted of a law violation involving a company's stockholders. Otherwise, executives have almost invariably been protected by the corporate veil of secrecy. In the event the corporate veil was pierced and the executive found guilty, he was seldom imprisoned and his fines were invariably paid by the corporation. No significant social stigma ensued, and the offender received both moral and social support from his peer group, which considered such crimes to be "technical" violations of law and a misfortune for the offender who was caught.[1]

This situation has now changed rather drastically. There has been an enormous increase in the nature and extent of business activities subjected to governmental regulation or control. In addition to expansion of regulation of corporate activities in the traditional areas of securities, fraud, investment, financial abuse or misappropriation of funds, and market behavior, new activities such as product safety, environmental pollution, and hazardous working conditions or in-plant safety have become the concern of legislatures, regulators, and courts. This trend has come about with the growing realization that corporate law violations affecting public health and safety, called social welfare crimes, are more pervasive than originally perceived and more difficult to control.

The findings of a recent study of illegal corporate behavior conducted under the auspices of National Institute of Law Enforcement Assistance Administration (LEAA study) are worth noting.[2] The study analyzed data for the 582 largest publicly owned corporations (477 manufacturing, 18 wholesale, 66 retail, and 21 service) for "initiation of enforcement action" for law violation by 24 federal agencies during the years 1975 and 1976.[3] The LEAA study found that 60 percent of the corporations studied had at least one action initiated against them. Actions were classified into serious, moderate, and minor violations.

In the manufacturing sector, 300 parent corporations had an average of 4.8 actions taken against them. Almost half of the parent manufacturing corporations had one or more serious or moderate violations. More than 40 percent of the manufacturing corporations engaged in repeated violations. One parent corporation had 62 actions initiated against it.

Over three-fourths of all actions were in the manufacturing, environmental, and labor areas. About one-fourth of the corporations violated these regulations at least once. Illegal corporate behavior was found least often in the financial and trade areas, but even here 5 to 10 percent of the corporations did violate. Large corporations had a greater proportion of the violations than their share in the sample would indicate: over 70 percent of the actions were against them, and they had more than two-thirds of all serious or moderate violations.

Increased regulation has been accompanied by an expanded scope of personal civil and criminal liability on the part of corporate executives for law violations by subordinates. Two measures currently before the U.S. Senate and House committees illustrate this trend. The measure before Senator Edward Kennedy's Judiciary Committee[4] is the revision of part of the federal criminal code, called the *endangerment* provisions, and provides criminal penalties for any person who knowingly puts another person in imminent danger of health or bodily injury by violating a sweeping array of health and safety regulations. The House bill is Congressman George Miller's HR 4973[5] before Congressman John Conyer's Subcommittee on Crime. This bill carries an affirmative disclosure provision by which an executive is required to notify workers and appropriate government agencies, within a specified period, following discovery of a serious danger associated with a given product or manufacturing process.

Both the Senate and the House measures carry stiff fines for corporations and individual executives ranging from $25,000 to $200,000 per day, and minimum jail sentences of two years and over. The future of either of these measures being enacted is still uncertain, although the Senate measure was hammered out in consultation with the Business Roundtable.

This trend raises questions about the changing relationship between business and other social institutions, societal expectations of corporate executives, and the effect of expanding personal criminal liability on corporate decision making and performance and, by implication, on economic growth and social welfare. Even if one accepts the desirability of the social goals these means are intended to achieve, there is a question as to whether imposition of absolute and vicarious personal criminal liability on corporate executives is the best way to achieve these goals.

Expanding the Scope of Executive Criminal Liability

Four short case studies, from the United States, France, and Great Britain, provide a vivid picture of the increasing risk of exposure of a corporate executive to criminal prosecution in the course of managing the day-to-day affairs of a company.

The People of the State of New York
v. *Warner-Lambert Company et al.*

At 2:40 A.M. on Sunday morning November 21, 1976, a large section of a five-story manufacturing plant owned and operated by the American Chicle Division of the Warner-Lambert Corporation was destroyed by an explosion and fire that reached 1,000°F. The explosion originated in and involved the Freshen-Up gum department on the fourth floor. One hundred eighteen employees were working on the morning shift at the time of the explosion. Fifty-four received burns or other injuries; many required extended hospitalization. Six employees died as a direct consequence of second and third-degree burns over most of their bodies and from related complications.[6]

On August 1, 1977, the grand jury for Queens County returned a twelve-count indictment (six counts of manslaughter in the second degree and six counts of criminally negligent homicide) against two corporations, the Warner-Lambert Company and the American Chicle Division, and four individuals, all of whom were corporate officers of Warner-Lambert Company. The government accused the four American Chicle executives and Warner-Lambert for failure to take "precautionary measures to overcome or eliminate dust explosion hazard" in the plant. The six defendants were charged with "reckless manslaughter and criminally negligent homicide."

All six respondents entered pleas of not guilty on August 18, 1977, and subsequently argued there was insufficient evidence to support the indictment. The trial court, the Supreme Court of the State of New York for the County of Queens, agreed with the respondents and, on February 15, 1978, dismissed the indictments. The key to the court's decision is the requirement of the New York statute that the acts of omission or commission must involve a substantial and unjustifiable risk of death constituting a gross deviation from a reasonable person's standard of conduct. The court found no substantial or unjustifiable risk of death. First, there was an absence of data indicating that the inert materials might lend themselves to the danger of dust explosion. The defendants' due care (absence of a gross deviation from the "reasonable person" standard) was further evidenced by an insurance inspection two months prior to the explosion, which showed major reductions in dust concentrations of the inert materials and other corrective steps taken by the defendants to eliminate the dust. Nevertheless, the trial judge lauded the laborious and exhaustive efforts of the prosecution.

After considering further argument by the District Attorney of Queens County, the trial court reaffirmed its dismissal of the indictments on July 26, 1978. The District Attorney appealed to the Appellate Division, Second Judicial Department. On July 9, 1979, the Appellate Division reversed the order of the trial court, reinstated the indictments and directed that the trial proceed.

The Respondents. The Warner-Lambert Company and the American Chicle Division, maintain a manufacturing plant at 3030 Thompson Avenue, Long Island City, Queens County, New York. Several products are manufactured at this facility, including Freshen-Up chewing gum.

Arthur Kraft is Warner-Lambert's vice president in charge of manufacturing, with offices at Warner-Lambert's corporate headquarters in Morris Plains, New Jersey. Ed Harris is director of corporate safety and security for Warner-Lambert, with his office at the corporate headquarters in Morris Plains. While both men did visit the plant, neither was responsible for its day-to-day operations. James O'Mahoney is plant manager of the manufacturing facility in Long Island City where the explosion occurred. His offices are located on the fifth floor of the Thompson Avenue plant and he is involved in day-to-day operations. Mr. John O'Rourke is the plant engineeer at the Long Island City facility, with his office in that building. He worked in the Freshen-Up department on an almost daily basis.

The Introduction of Freshen-Up Gum into the American Market. In the latter part of 1969, the Research and Development Department at Warner-

Lambert's Long Island City factory began a market project to introduce a new chewing gum product to the American public. The product, subsequently to be sold as "Freshen-Up Gum," was unique because of its flavored liquid or jelly-filled center. The product had been previously introduced and successfully marketed in both Europe and Asia.

By 1972, experimentation and development had advanced sufficiently and a pilot or prototype manufacturing operation was established on the first floor to support limited production for the purpose of testing consumer interest and marketing potential. Consumer reaction was so favorable that in September 1974, full-scale production under the aegis of Warner-Lambert's manufacturing division was begun. The company invested $10 million in manufacturing equipment and expanded operations to include six processing lines on the fourth floor of the Long Island City plant operating 24-hours-a-day, six days a week. The fourth floor Freshen-Up Department had become fully operational by December 1975 and by the fall of 1976, production had risen to some two million packages of gum a day generating, at 20¢ per package, retail sales of over $400,000 per day. The new product sold better than any other chewing gum on the market, and Warner-Lambert found it could sell all it could produce. Efforts were made to reduce all "downtime," and supervisory personnel were promised bonuses for increased productivity.

Events Leading up to the Explosion. Whether the events that led up to the explosion demonstrate Warner-Lambert's failure or lack of failure to take appropriate action to protect its employees from a safety hazard are in dispute. The train of events began in February 1975, when the Freshen-Up operation was still located on the first floor of the Long Island City plant and the six processing lines on the fourth floor had not yet become operational.

The Freshen-Up Manufacturing Process. The manufacturing process developed by the corporation provided for slabs of basic gum product to be introduced into the processing line through a hopper located above a batch-forming complex called the "extractor/extruder." As the gum passed out of the extruder in the form of a "rope" approximately two inches in diameter, its center was injected with a variably flavored liquid or jelly filling. The product was then moved through a "rope sizer," wherein the gum strip was further reduced in diameter to a workable one-half inch. On leaving the sizer, the gum rope was drawn through an open transition plate at which point, among others, a powdered lubricant or metallic and organic compound known as magnesium stearate (MS) was applied to prevent stocking. The product was then introduced into a tablet-forming machine called the "Uniplast." The gum rope passed into a rotating die head furnished with plungers and guiding cams for the stamping and formation of 38 separate pieces of liquid-filled gum, each approximately three-eighths of an inch in thickness and five-eighths of an inch square. To facilitate release of the tablets and prevent adherence of the gum to the dies, the latter was sprayed with a cooling agent known as liquid nitrogen

(LN₂), which produced temperatures in and around the machinery sufficiently cold to form ice on the die head and base. On leaving the "Uniplast," the newly formed gum pieces were conveyed into a "cooling tunnel." From there they moved to the adjacent wrapping section for other processing and packaging.

The district attorney contended that the "Uniplast" machine, the centerpiece of the processing line, was designed by a German concern for the manufacture of hard candy at warm or room temperatures. It was not designed for gum production in the type of extreme cold and dust environment created by the manufacture of Freshen-Up gum. The "Uniplast" machine was made of cast iron and other brittle, low-alloy metals not suitable for use under the extreme cold produced by the application of liquid nitrogen. Nor was the machinery made to operate in a continuously cold environment 24 hours a day, six days a week. The district attorney argued that this extremely cold environment induced embrittlement or structural weakness of the metals and caused them to lose ductility or the capacity to withstand fracture when subjected to impact or temperature changes. The district attorney further contended that the machine's motor was not sealed to prevent electrical spark or arc emission or to prevent the emission of dust—features necessary in any process that generates industrial dust.

The 1975 Pilot Project. In February 1975, while the Freshen-Up operation was still a pilot project, an employee observed a small flash explosion of magnesium stearate (MS) produced from an electrical extension cord lying on the floor. When he reported the incident to the assistant production manager, he was told "yeah, well, it's one of the problems we have to work out." Based on what he had seen, the employee made an entry in a corporate journal as required under company rules, recommending discontinuance of the use of MS. Warner-Lambert contended that there was no explosion but "sort of a white flash, like similar to a small flashbulb going off" when another employee kicked a household electrical cord being used to operate a one-quarter inch drill with a brush on it to clean out the die punches. The corporate journal was, in reality, the employee's own logbook.

The problem of MS dust, however, was beginning to turn into a serious one. It was aggravated by the use of air hoses to blow away dust from the machinery. In June 1975, Warner-Lambert's manager of safety and fire protection, who worked directly under the supervision of Ed Harris, sent Warner-Lambert's own industrial hygienist to the Freshen-Up department to determine employee exposure to MS dust. Because the manufacture of Freshen-Up utilized large quantities of MS, concern arose regarding the nuisance level of the dust and the health problems that might arise from the workers' exposure to it. The hygienist issued a report in March 1976 recommending: (1) use of local exhaust systems, (2) substituting a vacuum unit for compressed air in the cleaning of machinery, (3) vacuuming, not sweeping, the floors, and (4) issuance of face masks until the above controls could be instituted by plant engineers. The face masks were issued, but the other recommendations were never implemented.

The Fourth-Floor Manufacturing Operation. In August 1975, the Freshen-Up project was moved to the fourth floor of the plant as Warner-Lambert began establishing the six production lines. In these operations, electrical contractors installing power lines and control panels were never informed that the operations would involve a combustible dust or that the equipment had to comply with standards and regulations for hazardous locations as set forth in the national and New York City electrical codes. Instead, emphasis was placed on establishing a production line that would satisfy the City Health Department regulations affecting food processing plants. The company's in-house electrician, who was aware of the amount of MS dust being generated on the first floor during the pilot project, specifically asked the plant engineer, John O'Rourke, whether he wanted a "dust proof" installation. He was told no because "there will be no dust."

In October 1975, Warner-Lambert's manager of safety and fire protection, who worked directly for Ed Harris, submitted a report to the Rockford, Illinois, plant warning of the explosive nature of MS and the proper venting ratios to be used to protect plant equipment in the event of an explosion. On February 24, 1975, Factory Mutual, a loss-prevention consultant employed by Warner-Lambert's insurance carrier (Arkwright-Boston Company) inspected the Freshen-Up department. It determined that "the magnesium stearate dust in the fourth story Freshen-Up gum manufacturing area presents a serious explosion hazard." The consultant recommended the installation of a central vacuum cleaning system, removal of accumulated dust, and modification of all electrical equipment to conform to national electric code standards for dusty locations. The implementation of these measures was necessary "to prevent a serious dust explosion." The consultant's findings and advice was relayed to the plant engineer, John O'Rourke, who assured the Factory Mutual consultant that Warner-Lambert would comply with the recommendations.

A written version of the report and advice was sent in writing to Ed Harris. When no reply was received, a follow-up letter was sent in June 1976, emphasizing once more "the possibility of a dust explosion due to the use of magnesium stearate powder." Under established corporate procedure, loss-prevention reports were distributed to Mr. Harris's department, the division of corporate safety, the corporation's insurance department, and the plant manager (James O'Mahoney). The plant manager had the responsibility to review recommendations, propose appropriate action to the division of corporate safety, and then initiate a proper request for action. The safety department was required to assist the plant manager in complying with the recommendations and then give the insurance company proper assurances that the recommendations had been instituted.

In April 1976, the New York City Fire Department inspected the Freshen-Up department. According to Warner-Lambert, the New York City Fire Department did not report any explosive conditions or the need for any action on the part of the corporation. In the following month, a compliance officer from the Occupational and Safety Health Administration (OSHA), of the U.S. Department of Labor visited the plant. According to Warner-Lambert, the OSHA inspection established that the air-borne dust was below the nuisance level of 15 milligrams per meter, and its only recommendation was to have a class A fire extinguisher on hand. The district attorney for Queens County disagreed and contended that the OSHA inspector discussed personally with defendants O'Rourke and O'Mahoney the dust problem and the need to eliminate its source. The plant's chief engineer also gave the same defendants, on May 5, 1976, a written report that MS use "continues to be our greatest problem."

On May 25, 1976, a formal proposal for the purchase of a central dust-removal system, at a cost of only $33,000 was submitted to O'Mahoney for transmittal to corporate headquarters. The request met with initial rejection from the corporation's engineering division as a short-term solution. Warner-Lambert continued to conduct tests in June of 1976 for the purpose of determining the nuisance level of dust in the department. According to the company, these tests established that the density of airborne dust was well below the explosive limit. On July 7, a meeting was held at Warner-Lambert's corporate headquarters for the purpose of considering the capital expense request of $33,000 to purchase a central dust-removal system. Present at this meeting were defendants Kraft and O'Rourke. The purchase request was determined to be "a waste of good money" and was therefore rejected. A decision was made to embark on a long-range solution to eliminate the use of MS altogether from the Freshen-Up production process. Arthur Kraft endorsed his hold on the written request and the topic of dust collection systems for the Freshen-Up gum operation was never again considered by top management. On July 13, 1976, the corporation's manager of safety and fire protection sent a brief note to O'Mahoney notifying him that the insurance carrier's February 1976 recommendation to eliminate the dust hazard would not be followed.

On August 10, 1976, O'Mahoney sent a memorandum to his staff recommending measures to cut down the use of MS because it was a "major problem— having a deleterious effect on employee health and safety." For the first two weeks of August 1976, production ceased and the entire department was cleaned. At the same time, strict procedures were promulgated concerning the control and use of MS to be observed on reopening of the department. These steps included tighter control over the amount of MS used in each shift, improved cleanup proceedings, and strict disciplinary measures for failure to conform with the guidelines. Coarser grade MS was utilized so that ambient dust levels would remain reduced. The cooling tunnel on processing line A was modified so that MS could be eliminated from the process altogether. Warner-Lambert would argue that these cleaning procedures and the decision to modify all the cooling tunnels to run without the need for MS obviated the necessity for the installation of either a dust collection or vacuum system.

On September 16, 1976, a second loss-prevention report was filed based on an inspection made by a representative of the insurance carrier, Factory Mutual. Warner-Lambert contended this report established that "the present dust concentration is well below the lower explosive limits." Thus, at the time of the accident, no risk of any kind could have been perceived by anyone familiar with the circumstances at the plant. The district attorney, however, challenged the report and established that while MS powder concentration had been reduced to 25 percent of the original, the inspector and author of the report knew nothing of the original concentration. The inspector had been told by corporate employees that present quantities were only 10 percent of the previous concentration, and added another 15 percent, not based on any facts, to insure the accuracy of her figures. She then "covered herself" by stating that the February 1976 recommendations would have to be followed should concentrations increase.

On November 15, 1976, the plant's chief engineer notified O'Mahoney and O'Rourke that the coarser grade of MS was still fouling up the fourth-floor air conditioning system and that concentration of ambient MS dust in the Freshen-Up department was substantial. While work had been begun to modify one of the processing lines to eliminate MS use (at a cost of some $40,000), no decision had been made to modify the other five lines. In fact, by the fall of 1976, public demand for Freshen-Up gum had forced production up to two million packages of gum per day and the six processing lines were operating twenty-four hours a day, six days a week.

The Causes of the Explosion. The cause or causes of explosion are a matter of controversy, and two versions have emerged: one offered by Warner-Lambert and its experts, and the other by the Queens County district attorney and his experts.

The district attorney contended that a dust explosion results when sufficient quantities of a combustible material, pulverized and suspended in a confined atmosphere, are ignited. The ignition is followed by the rapid propagation of flame (as the ambient material is consumed), intense heat, expansion of the air pressure, and finally a bursting effect. An explosion will occur when there are three essential elements: (1) a combustible fuel, (2) oxygen from the air, and (3) ignition sufficient to initiate combustion and reaction among the dust particles.

While MS dust will burn in a settled state, it is not regarded as explosive unless dispersed in the air in heavy enough concentrations to be rated as a severe, strong, or very strong explosive hazard. At the time of the explosion in question, the Freshen-Up gum department was using approximately 500 pounds of MS per day, six days a week, or about 1.5 tons per week. A minimum of 25 pounds of MS was allotted to and used by each of the six processing lines per eight-hour shift, with more being used on request.

According to the district attorney, the deaths, injuries, and physical damage resulted from the explosion of a heavy concentration of ambient (dispersed and moving about in the atmosphere) MS dust present in the Freshen-Up department during the early morning hours of November 21, 1976. Testimony was offered to the grand jury by employees as to the existence of a foglike atmosphere just prior to the explosion. A substantial residue of MS dust in the area involved was also reported after the explosion. Broken glass and contents of the plant's fourth floor were strewn all over the street and on the roofs of adjacent buildings. Some of these buildings were themselves damaged by flying debris and the force of the explosion. The windows on the fourth floor and elsewhere in the plant had been blown out and then in as the explosive pressure first vented itself out, creating a vacuum into which air from outside the building was then drawn. The Freshen-Up department was found to be in a shambles, with the interior walls pushed down; machinery and fixtures displaced, shattered, and twisted; and small pockets of fire in existence. These were all characteristics of a dust explosion. The ceilings, walls, and overhead areas showed charring or scorching, indicating not general fire damage, but the burning of ambient dust. Clothing had been blown off many of the employees, further evidence of the explosive quality of the ambient MS dust.

According to the district attorney's experts, there was a low-order detonation at the base of the D assembly line Uniplast machine, followed by a major dust explosion. The ignition or primary detonation was attributed to a mechanical sparking or heat-induced breakup of the parts of the Uniplast equipment on line D. The use of LN_2 had completely iced the rotating die head, which then jammed. The equipment, because it was not made to be used with liquid nitrogen, lost its ductility and became extremely brittle. The machine, operating under a tremendous strain just prior to explosion because of the jammed rotating die head, overloaded the motor as it drew more electrical current to meet the resistance of the slowed-up gears. The machinery began to break apart, due to the vibration or slippage of the components. The resulting heated metal, mechanical sparking, or friction ignited the settled or ambient MS dust at the base of the Uniplast equipment, causing a violent reaction or detonation in an oxygen-enriched atmosphere containing ambient MS dust in sufficient quantities for an explosion.

Warner-Lambert contended that liquid nitrogen is basically noncombustible and vaporizes quickly without dangerous effects when exposed to room temperatures. Because of its inherent stability, it is often used in fire extinguishers. MS, in bulk, inert, or settled form, does not create an explosive risk. If ignition is applied, it will only burn or smolder. If it is dispersed into the air at or above the lower explosive level (LEL), it will create a serious risk of explosion if ignited. Warner-Lambert contended that minimum combustible densities of cornstarch, flour dust, peanut hulls, and powdered sugar create a greater danger of explosion than MS dust.

Warner-Lambert's experts contended that the powerful primary detonation was actually caused by the "cryogenic phenomenon called liquefaction which results when volatile liquid oxygen is formed due to the exposure of the atmosphere at the base of the Uniplast machine to extreme cold—but otherwise harmless—liquid nitrogen." This, in turn, ignited settled MS dust at the bore of the Uniplast machine. The crucial point made by the experts for Warner-Lambert was that the explosion did not involve the two independent alleged "hazardous" elements, MS or liquid nitrogen. But for the unforeseen cryogenic phenomenon involving liquid nitrogen, the quantity of MS at the base of the Uniplast equipment actually presented no risk of fire or explosion.

Warner-Lambert's expert then testified that the creation of volatile liquid oxygen from the use of stable liquid nitrogen could not have reasonably been foreseen. Liquification is not regarded as a credible hazard in the use of liquid nitrogen. Warner-Lambert further argued that the company's supplier of liquid nitrogen, its insurance carrier, and the various governmental agencies such as the New York City Fire Department and OSHA never indicated, suggested, or warned of any risk associated with the use of liquid nitrogen. Consequently, the explosion and the resulting deaths occurred as a result of hazard that could not have been foreseen by Warner-Lambert, thus clearly indicating Warner-Lambert's lack of responsibility for the incident.

United States v. Park

On June 9, 1975, the U.S. Supreme Court upheld the conviction of John R. Park, president of Acme Products, Inc., Philadelphia, for rodent infestation found by the Food and Drug Administration (FDA) in the supermarket chain's Baltimore warehouse. The Court decided that the chief executive of a corporation can be found personally guilty of the criminal charges if unsanitary conditions anywhere in his company contaminate food or otherwise endanger health and/or safety.[7] The case thus greatly expanded the long-established Dotterweich doctrine,[8] under which corporate officers had been held personally liable for violations of the Food, Drug, and Cosmetic Act of 1938, although they had no direct involvement or actual knowledge of the violation.[9] Until Park, however, all convictions involved individual executives with immediate, close supervisory responsibilities over operations where violations occurred.

The facts are not in dispute. Acme is a national retail food chain with approximately 36,000 employees, 874 retail stores, and 16 warehouses in various parts of the United States. In November and December 1971, the company's Baltimore warehouse was investigated by an FDA investigator, who found extensive evidence of rodent infestation and other unsanitary conditions. In January 1972, the chief of compliance of the FDA's Baltimore office wrote to Park, informing him of the conditions in the Baltimore warehouse. A second investigation, in March 1972, revealed some improvement but still showed evidence of rodent infestation.

In March 1973, the United States filed a suit against Acme Markets and Park, charging them with five criminal counts of violations under the 1938 act. Acme pleaded guilty; Park moved for acquittal. The government offered no evidence that Park was guilty because he was aware of the problems in the Baltimore warehouse and was the corporate officer who bore general responsibility for all company activities that would subject him to criminal liability. Park testified that although he was responsible for all of Acme's employees and the general direction of the company, the size and complexity of Acme's operations demanded that he must delegate responsibility for different phases of operations to various line and staff subordinates. Furthermore, Park was told his vice-president in charge of the Baltimore division intended to take corrective action. Park did not believe that he could have taken any more constructive action.

The jury found Park guilty. In his appeal, Park contended, among other things, that the district court erred in its instructions to the jury in defining responsible relationship by stating that the statute makes individuals, as well as corporations, liable for violations when "the individual had a responsible relation to the situation, even though he may not have participated personally." The district court states the main issue in this case was whether "Park, by virtue of his position in the company, had a position of authority and responsibility in the situation out of which these charges arose." The court also indicated that the definition of the "responsible relationship was really a jury question and not even subject to being defined by the Court."

A divided court of appeals reversed and remanded the case for a new trial. The appeals court stated that although the *Dotterweich* doctrine dispensed with the need to prove "awareness of wrongdoing" by Park, it did not dispense with the need to prove that Park was in some way personally responsible for the act constituting the crime.

The Supreme Court reversed the appeals court, saying that (1) criminal liability under the Act does not turn on awareness of some wrongdoing or conscious fraud; (2) the Act permits conviction of responsible corporate officials who have the power to prevent or correct violations; (3) viewed as a whole, the jury instruction was adequate; and (4) the evidence that Park had previously been advised of unsanitary conditions at another warehouse was admissible since it served to rebut the official's defense that he had justifiably relied on subordinates to handle sanitation matters.

The Court recognized that because the act dispenses with the need to prove "consciousness of wrongdoing," it may result in hardship even as applied to those who share "responsibility in the business process resulting in" a violation. However, the act "in its criminal aspect does not require that which is objectively impossible," and a defendant is permitted to claim that he was powerless to prevent or correct the violations. The burden of proof in such cases, however, rests with the defendant.

The Court stated that a failure to exercise authority and supervisory responsibility was a sufficient basis for a responsible corporate executive's liability. Exact title or position in the corporate hierarchy was not relevant in determining responsibility; it was sufficient to show that by "virtue of the relationship he bore to the corporation, [the executive] had the power to prevent the act complained of." The act imposes not only a positive duty to seek out and remedy violations when they occur, but also, and primarily, a duty to implement measures that will ensure that violations will not occur. Thus, a level of *absolute liability* is imposed that permits no defense when the violation occurs.

Subsequent court decisions have further clarified the defense of "powerlessness on the part of corporate executives in preventing unlawful activities," suggesting and actually limiting its scope.[10] At present, the powerlessness defense is inapplicable when a defendant should have anticipated a problem and should have taken corrective action. There have been five such significant opinions since the Park decision. Three involved conviction of corporate officials for holding food in warehouses under unsanitary conditions. In each instance, the courts found that corporate officials failed to exercise the high standard of care imposed by the Act. Because of the criminal penalties now involved, corporate defendants argued for "Miranda" warnings—an argument the Court refused to accept. This defense raises an interesting possibility: that conduct previously considered under the less-demanding civil process may be subject to the criminal due process procedures recognized and embodied in the law.

Informal criteria have been identified as to when criminal prosecutions should be used by the FDA. In deciding whether or not to prosecute, the agency looks for that individual who knew or should have known of the circumstances, conditions, or actions surrounding a violation and who occupied a position with the authority to prevent, detect, or correct the violation. The FDA and the Department of Justice now favor including at least one responsible individual in all criminal prosecutions.

L'Affaire Chapron

On January 23, 1975, Roland Wuillaume was killed while trying to connect two railroad cars that were standing on an incline. One car rolled, crushing him. At the time of his death, Wuillaume was employed as a temporary worker in an asphalt plant of Huttes-Goudron et Dérivés (HGD), a subsidiary of the state-owned Carbonnages de France-Chimie (CDF). CDF has thirty-two subsidiaries and employs 6220 salaried workers, of whom 1645 are engineers and 2480 junior- and middle-level management personnel.

The subsequent investigation showed that at the accident the lighting in the area was defective. In addition, Wuillaume had a stiff hip and leg and was considered 67 percent incapacitated. Prior to the accident, he had been employed at the plant for seventeen days, four of which were devoted to training. Wuillaume had been hired as a store worker from a temporary employment agency, BIS, and was not qualified under the law or physically capable of performing the assigned task. Immediately following the accident, HGD improved the lighting and corrected the incline in the railroad bed. It also posted safety regulations and installed safety-related equipment.

Two unions, the Confederation Generale du Cadre (CGC) and the Confederation Federale du Travail (CFDT), filed a lawsuit charging that "the unions are enraged by the worker's death, and after suffering many deaths and poor and unsafe working conditions, they have decided to make an example of this case—perhaps, to force the judicial branch of the French government to take a stand." The unions also charged that HGD was using too many temporary workers and had too little regard for its employees' health and safety.

On September 29, 1975, eight months after the accident, M. Jean Chapron, executive director of HGD, was charged with cumulative negligence and involuntary homicide. The indictment read:

> By having a temporary worker doing the job of a specialized one, Chapron is directly responsible for the death of this worker. Considering that these facts have brought considerable disturbance to the public order, the detention of the accused is necessary to preserve public order from the disturbance caused by the transgression.

Chapron was imprisoned for five days. Georges Tredez, the director of the temporary employment agency, BIS, was also indicted for involuntary homicide but was not arrested.

Applicable French law specifies that a temporary worker must be hired under a written contract. However, Wuillaume, who was forty-eight years old at the time of the accident, did not receive any written job description and was not given a medical examination. HGD violated the law in terms of hiring and training policies. Because a temporary worker was ordered to perform a job of a specialized one, Chapron was considered directly responsible for the worker's death.

According to Patrice de Charette, the investigating magistrate, HGD had a record of safety violations. In March 1975, a work accident had killed one worker and injured five at the same factory. According to the CFDT, fourteen days before the accident a labor inspector had warned management about infractions in the hiring of temporary workers. Furthermore, since August 1970, there had been sixteen work-related accidents at the HGD plant, in which nine people were burned and three others killed. CGC and CFDT also accused CDF, the parent company of HGD, of general disregard for worker safety. In 1974 and 1975, three accidents in the company's other operations caused a total of fifty deaths.

The incident aroused tremendous controversy. Organized labor and workers in general were extremely unhappy about the relative lack of concern for industrial safety on the part of plant managements and even the government. The number of bodily injuries in work-related accidents exceeded one million a year, causing over three thousand casualties. In 1974, 592,390 safety-related law violations resulted in only 11,366 convictions and fines.

Chapron denied any negligence or culpability. His detention led to angry protests by the members of the CGC. The 170 members of this lower-level management union working at HGD decided to strike for forty-eight hours. Top management decided to close the plant. Throughout France, management in general was appalled by the manner in which the investigating magistrate, Charette, was handling the case, and charged that he was trying Chapron in the press and had proclaimed his guilt before the trial. CGC also charged political collusion among various prosecuting and investigating agencies. In addition to the union membership of the investigating judge and the prosecuting assistant district attorney, the work-safety inspector belonged to the CFDT, which is considered a left-leaning socialist union. One manager from the north of France stated "[T]he attitude of the judge was dictated by intention to do harm, but justice did come to these people [Chapron and Tredez]. There is no doubt that something should be done to review the limitless powers granted to an investigating judge."

According to the CGC, lower management was becoming more and more the scapegoat of society. In their responsibility for worker safety, they felt that they were between the hammer and the anvil. Faced with budgetary constraints, they were nevertheless accused of professional mistakes. They contended that it is impossible to institute 100 percent safety, as there is always a certain amount of risk in the workplace. Installing safety devices on machines tends to make workers less careful. Therefore, accidents will always occur.

Charette rationalized his decision to arrest Chapron by saying that his motives were the preservation of public order. (Article 144 of the Penal Code states that preventive detention can be imposed to preserve public order.) In detaining Chapron, Charette said, he used the same criteria he applied in the case of ordinary defendants. He also states that the workers' unions wanted him to bring to light the plight of the workers and that was what he was doing.

Over thirty-five thousand temporary detentions are ordered in France each year under the law, and few receive the kind of attention or scrutiny given to Chapron's case. Because of mounting unrest concerning Chapron's incarceration and the wide publicity given the trial proceedings, the minister of justice, M. Lecanuet, intervened and freed Chapron, who still remained under indictment.

The criminal court judge dismissed the charges against both Chapron and Tredez. CGT and CFDT were awarded 500 francs for damages; Chapron and Tredez were fined a total of 1000 francs. The judgment found that Chapron was not negligent and that the responsible party was the victim, Wuillaume. In addition, the suit filed by the victim's family was rejected. The grand jury stated that because a disturbance of public order must happen at the time of the violation, the detention of Chapron was not justified. Charette stated afterward that he still believed he was right, regretted nothing, and would do the same thing again.

The Houghton Main Prosecutions

In Great Britain, the three top officials (the manager, undermanager, and deputy) of the National Coal Board's mine at Houghton Main in Yorkshire were accused of failing to enforce safety procedures when five workers were killed in an explosion in June 1976. The British Health and Safety Act gives government inspectors the powers to hale accused managers into Crown courts, the lowest level of courts empowered to impose prison terms. The undermanager and deputy were charged with statutory breaches of duty, including failure to ensure that the auxiliary fan system was properly maintained, failure to ensure proper ventilation in a portion of the mine workings, and failure to make an adequate preshift inspection. The manager was charged with a breach of his duty to take necessary steps to ensure that staff under his supervision maintained adequate ventilation in the mine. All three officials pleaded not guilty. After lengthy hearings in July 1976, all were convicted and fined. The manager and undermanager appealed to the Crown court at Sheffield and were heard in September 1977. The conviction of the undermanager was upheld, but the conviction of the manager was dismissed.

The undermanager contended that he never knew of the failure and therefore could not have acted. The Crown court, however, found evidence of one oral communication, failure to examine safety reports, and failure to see that safety reports were signed. Of significance to the court was the failure of the undermanager to respond to directions by the manager to ventilate the mine seams even over the weekends, when workmen were not in the mine shafts, because the undermanager did not agree that it was necessary. The court concluded with the observation that while the duty of ventilation was laid squarely on the shoulders of the manager, the maintenance of the ventilation machinery was the responsibility of the undermanager.

The manager, however, was discharged. The court found that a reasonable system of reporting and supervision had been established by the manager and that he had appointed competent people to carry out the safety duties required by law. The court was unwilling to hold the manager personally responsible for the system's failure and for employees' failure to alert him to the safety danger.

The court's reluctance to hold the manager was inconsistent with its findings. First, the court held that a more stringent system of reporting and reading of safety reports would have impressed those responsible with the necessity of keeping the machinery running at all times. Second, the court held that it was satisfied that all the people to whom these duties were delegated were, in the normal usage of the word, competent. The court contended that the fact that some of them failed to use their competence in the expected manner was not the fault of the manager. The question then arose as to whose fault it was. The pertinence of the question becomes more obvious when it is recognized that the 1974 Act imposes on a workman a duty to exercise reasonable care, and if this duty is breached he may be prosecuted in a criminal court. A causal act of negligence now may result in a prison sentence by mandate of the legislature. Was the manager not negligent in his failure to establish a more stringent system of reporting? Was the manager not negligent in failing to see that his management team acted in a competent manner? The legislative mandate was clear. The court, however, was unwilling to go so far as holding top management criminally negligent.[11]

Other Examples

The seriousness of the situation is reinforced by the following examples. On November 13, 1978, Hudson Farms, Inc. (a composting firm) and its vice-president pleaded guilty in the U.S. District Court for the Eastern District of Pennsylvania, to charges of criminal violation of the Clean Water Act, resulting from a compost pile runoff into a nearby creek. Hudson Farms, Inc., was fined $50,000 on four counts of polluting White Clay Creek, and Clinton C. Rubie, Hudson's vice-president, was fined $5000 and given two years' probation. Hudson Farms and its vice-president sought dismissal of the indictment on the ground that EPA failed to issue an administrative compliance order before taking enforcement action. The court ruled that EPA was not required by Section 309(a) to issue an abatement order as a prerequisite to a criminal action.[12]

In November 1975, the owner-manager of a small French construction firm was convicted of negligent homicide when a worker died after falling nine stories when his scaffolding shook because of noise reverberations from a passing crane. The scaffolding did not have the required protective railing. Planche, the manager, argued that his firm had spent over $62,000 in the previous months on worker safety equipment, but there was no way he could "order people to respect their own safety." Planche was given a six-month suspended sentence and put on three-year parole. He resigned, saying, "I cannot live for three years with the sword of Damocles hanging over my head."

In June 1977, a court in Turin imposed three- to six-year prison sentences on five executives of a chemical plant, IPCA, and nicknamed it "the factory of cancer," for negligent homicide where thirty-two workers had died of cancer of the bladder in the last twenty years. The workers died from exposure to carcinogenic chemicals.

Other Areas of Expanded Executive Liability

These cases illustrate the nature of an executive's personal liability in certain specialized spheres of corporate activities, and the increasingly broad definition of this liability. However, they do not begin to show the whole new array of corporate activities where executives are to be held personally liable for corporate law violations without personal complicity. For example, in a study of twenty-seven health- and safety-related studies in the United States, O'Keefe and Shapiro found that a significant number of statutes that carried provision for civil and criminal penalties did not require prior knowledge or personal involvement on the part of the responsible executive.[13]

The Federal Water Pollution Control Act Amendments of 1972 stipulate personal liability for executives for organizational abuse of the environment and provide both civil and criminal penalties.[14] Another aspect of broadened personal liability for corporate officers is in the Occupational Safety and Health Act of 1970 (OSHA). OSHA provides for sanctions, including fines, against individuals who are responsible for, though unknowledgeable about, safety infractions. The constitutionality of administrative assessment of civil penalties that are tantamount to criminal sanctions has been upheld by the U.S. Supreme Court.[15]

The courts are also increasingly holding corporate directors and independent auditors, lawyers, investment bankers, and brokers responsible for exercising due care in the discharge of their duties.[16] The traditional defense that these groups used to present—that they depended on and trusted the information furnished them by management—is no longer considered sufficient.

The trend toward greater executive accountability and stiffer fines and prison sentences is also evident in such traditional areas of corporate crimes as antitrust and securities fraud. In 1977, 161 people were convicted of antitrust violations, compared with 175 in 1976. However, more violators are being sent to jail. And in April 1978, in an antitrust case in which several makers of electrical wiring devices were convicted of price fixing, 11 present and former officers received fines totaling $200,000 (in addition to the companies' fines of $705,000) and prison terms of one to three months. One person's sentence was suspended. The total time actually to be served—nineteen months with no parole—exceeds the total prison time previously served in the whole history of antitrust actions in the United States.[17]

The 1974 amendments to the Sherman Act increased the maximum penalties for individuals to a three-year jail term and $100,000 fine.[18] The Department of Justice guidelines for sentencing recommended that the prison sentences should be adjusted upward according to the managerial level of the convicted offender. The Foreign Corrupt Practices Act of 1977, designed to curb overseas illegal payoffs, provides for maximum penalties upon conviction of up to $1,000,000 for corporations, and $10,000 in fines and five years in jail for officers and directors.[19]

Why the Expanding Scope of Executive Criminal Liability?

At the heart of the movement toward holding managers personally responsible for corporate law violations lies the struggle of individuals and societies to come to grips with the reality of the corporation and to subject it to effective societal controls. It reflects the failure of more traditional means of correcting corporate abuses, both conventional and unconventional. Corporate legal infractions and their control must therefore be studied in the context of the relationships among socioeconomic structure, criminal law, penal sanctions, and the individual's role and expectations in society.

Failure of Market Institutions

Under the assumptions of a competitive market system, social control over economic organizations is exercised through the nature of a company's output. Most individual corporations are small enough that, taken individually, their actions do not significantly affect the economic, sociopolitical, and physical environment. When a corporation's products or services do not meet society's needs, they are not purchased; the corporation's ability to acquire and pay for physical and human resources is thereby restricted, and eventually it ceases to exist. Under this system, it is assumed that all needs for change will be communicated to the corporation via the external environment's response to its output. Changes in the character of the corporation's output will be carried out by the organization and will be internally generated (figure 1, Stage 1).

As companies become large and diversified, they become increasingly immune to market discipline. The signals for change are weak and diffuse and do not always seem relevant when viewed in the context of the dominance of positive signals whose significance is reinforced when the decision maker may then become subject to the tyranny of small decisions. Environmental signals for change are inadequately communicated through the market link, and members of the organization are either unwilling or unable to initiate changes within the organization that would enable it to meet societal expectations. When such changes become difficult to effect through market link, an attempt is made to control production process and decision-making structure—that is, to modify the internal environment that brings about the undesirable behavior. Thus, elements of the decision-making structure and process that were previously internal to the organization become subject to outside pressure, scrutiny, and control. A regulatory framework develops to achieve this end (figure 1, Stage 2).

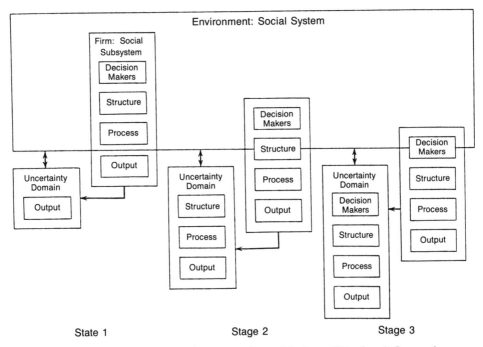

Figure 1. Business-Society Interface: Modes of Societal Control

Failure of Existing Enforcement Structures

Government interference in the corporate organizational process ranges over a wide spectrum. The Securities and Exchange Commission announced on April 28, 1977, that it would conduct a broad reexamination of its rules relating to shareholder communications in order to increase shareholder participation in the corporate electoral process and in the government of the corporation.[20] The use of outside consultants to devise ways in which corporate board members can better meet their responsibilities has been proposed as a shield for directors from outside societal and legal pressures.[21] The use of such outside consultants, however, would permit greater use of outside directors with a greater sense of social accountability.

Process Controls. In the traditional areas of government regulation of economic activities, process controls have included types of marketing practices considered unfair and therefore illegal. New social legislation in such diverse areas as pollution controls and environmental safeguards, in-plant worker safety, and protection of employees from job discrimination based on sex, color, age, or ethnic origin have imposed new process controls—for example, installation of scrubbers on smokestacks, affirmative action programs, and justification of such corporate practices as preemployment aptitude testing, minimum education requirements, designation of certain jobs as suitable for males or females, and age-based mandatory retirement policies.

Experience has shown that process controls tend to produce a great deal of regulatory delay and red tape. When viewed externally, a given corporate activity—the synergistic output of all individuals within the corporation—may be considered undesirable and even illegal. When viewed from within, however, such behavior is considered normal and, in economic terms, rational. Governmental institutions shift their emphasis to compliance with the letter of the law or regulations without regard to the substantive changes that necessitate these regulations. Specificity of regulatory requirements becomes paramount in an effort to minimize the scope of management ingenuity in getting around the law. Yet such efforts are doomed to failure. The regulators can never have the necessary expertise to anticipate developments in technology or to understand the organizational labyrinths through which management can work in fulfilling legal requirements without making any substantive changes. Government is always a step behind the corporation. Thus, the carrot-and-stick approach may evoke a more reliable response in the short run, but this advantage is bought at the cost of an additional, and perhaps faster growing, need for policing. It may also retard potential technological innovation and result in greater social costs.

Controls on Persons. The failure to change corporate behavior through regulations of output or modification of decision makers (figure 1, Stage 3). The assumption here is that imposing penalties on managers will divert the same ingenuity and resourcefulness that had previously been employed to further corporate growth and subvert legal requirements toward directions considered socially more desirable. By imposing performance criteria on managers, government obviates the need to demonstrate how a given objective might be accomplished and shifts the burden of explaining why it has not been achieved.

Prison sentences come after public officials have concluded that fines alone do not work. The assumption underlying prison sentences is that the threat of punishment will lead the top-ranking executives of a corporation to exert pressure on their aides, who will in turn exert pressure on their aides—a kind of trickle-down theory of ethics.

One reported study of 275 shoe-manufacturing firms in New England tends to support this assumption. A statistical sampling of business records established that recidivism is infrequent. The experience of conviction, it appears, leads to more law-abiding behavior.[22] A government campaign to bring selected prosecutions, together with attendant publicity, the spectacle of frequent conviction, and severe punishment, may play a role in shaping community attitudes toward business conduct considered unlawful. Creating a climate of moral revulsion toward certain types of business activity by labeling the conduct criminal, and imposing prison sentences may help to decrease recidivism.[23]

Public admission of sins as an additional sanction may also aid in creating a moral climate. Tax violators in Germany are required to publish a newspaper advertisement confessing their tax fraud, stating the penalty imposed and promising not to do it again. This procedure, known as positive repentance, might be useful in inhibiting corporate offenses but might also narrow the distinction between immoral conduct and unlawful conduct.[24]

As corporations have grown in size, complexity, and economic power, it has become necessary to consider the type, degree, and magnitude of corporate accountability to society. Legislators, regulators, and judges have chosen a shortcut approach that provides short-term relief but creates long-term problems. By treating the corporation as a person, all the laws developed by society over the centuries to define relationships between society and individuals (persons) could be applied with few, if any, modifications to corporations ("persons"). Laws specifically adapted to corporations needed to be developed only in areas peculiar to corporate activity, that is, shareholder-management relationships. All other societal relationships could be resolved by viewing this artificial, intangible organization, known as the corporation, as though it were a real, live, flesh-and-blood person. Time has shown, however, that a square peg was fitted into a round hole. The amazing fact is that the momentous and far-reaching decision to treat corporations as persons was made without argument by the Supreme Court in 1886, almost as an afterthought in an otherwise obscure railroad regulation case.[25] When individuals violate society's laws, they can be fined or imprisoned. How can a corporation be jailed? If the corporation is fined, is this not a hardship on innocent shareholders? If the costs are passed on to the public through higher prices, who is paying the penalty, the corporation or the public? The complexity of corporate organization creates further

problems of identification and assignment of responsibility. How does one identify the individuals within the corporate structure who unlawfully acted on the
firm's behalf, particularly when specialization of tasks frustrates the identification
of these individuals?[26]

It is no secret that corporate executives, regardless of their culpability, have
not suffered the fate of common criminals in terms of incarceration for economic
crimes. While the "law in books" pertaining to corporate crimes is not dissimilar
to the laws regarding other types of crimes, enforcement is characterized in the
case of corporate crimes by slow, inefficient, and highly differential implementation. Historically, there have been a variety of reasons for this phenomenon.

Status of Executives. Most of the laws dealing with corporate crimes and their
enforcement are aimed at people with a high socioeconomic status who share an
affinity through schools, clubs, professional backgrounds, religious affiliation, and
a variety of other social institutions with the groups responsible for making laws
and enforcing them—legislators, judges, and prosecutors. The difference between
the common law offenders and the law-violating executives is that the latter group
often has an elaborate and widely accepted ideological rationalization for the offenses, and possesses great social significance and considerable economic and political power. Crimes involving physical violence against individuals are sternly dealt
with, but economic crimes are considered social aberrations and are dealt with quite
differently. Imprisonment is deemed unnecessary, as these individuals are not considered a threat to society. Rehabilitation through a prison sentence is also uncalled
for, because economic criminal behavior is not treated as habitual but as a one-
time occurrence, and recidivism is believed unlikely. Fines are often quite nominal,
invariably paid by the corporations, and therefore carry little economic hardship.
More often than not, the executive continues to work at his old job and often finds
himself an even better job with former competitors. This is true even when the
executive has had to serve a prison sentence. Organizational structure and pressure
to achieve personal as well as organizational goals generate circumstances under
which infringement of legal statutes and social codes constitutes a normal response.

A total of 16 officers of 582 corporations were sentenced to a total of 597 days
imprisonment (not suspended sentences); 360 days (60.6 percent) were accounted
for by 2 officers who received 6 months each in one case. Of the remaining 234
days, 1 officer received a 60-day sentence, another was sentenced to 45 days, and
another received 30 days. The average for all imprisoned executives was 37.1 days;
excluding the two 6-month sentences, the remaining 14 averaged 16.7 days; and
excluding the 60-, 45-, and 30-day sentences, the remaining 11 averaged 9.0 days.
The 14 executives who received 60 days or less were all involved in a price-fixing
conspiracy. The other case involved tax fraud. The sentences were often suspended after some parts of them were served.[27]

The group orientation of corporate crimes depersonalizes business leadership.
Thus, while the impact of corporate crime may be quite serious for the society

and often more violent in its consequences than a multiplicity of individually committed street crimes, the corporate personality diffuses the individual burden of guilt. Through a battery of accountants, lawyers, scientists, and other experts, management can demonstrate the bureaucratic imperatives of shared responsibility, thereby denying or seriously weakening the notion of personal obligation.

Conflict with Social Mores. The laws against corporate crimes are not in apparent harmony with social mores. The notion of differential association is relevant here. It seems likely that a manager who is imbued with the folklore of rugged individualism is more likely to be a law violator if he associates with those who view violation of corporate laws with indifference or are themselves law violators.

The impact of violations in social welfare crimes is highly diffuse and indirect, while the cost of compliance can be shown to have immediate and direct effect on certain identifiable constituencies that exert constant pressure on management to minimize the impact of these costs on those groups. The manager's group norms do not consider a violation of these laws to be antisocial. The statutes are considered nuisances or regulations imposed by overzealous bureaucrats. Support from group norms for the manager's behavior tends to break down further his self-perception as a law violator. Fines are of little value either as specific or as general deterrents. One evidence of this tendency can be seen in the fact that antitrust violations have continued to increase despite the threat of triple damages and criminal fines. Studies by Sutherland and other legal scholars have shown that large corporations have been guilty of repeated violations.[28] A recent study by a public interest group showed that more than half the corporate members of the Business Roundtable were involved in illegal political briberies at home and payoffs abroad.[29]

Recognizing that business practices that depart from legal norms do not necessarily violate other, nonlegal societal norms has resulted in a distinction between crimes and criminally deviant behavior. Many of the more recent laws and regulations are not part of the normative occupational structure, having been imposed by outsiders, that is, government bureaucrats. A law may have been violated, but an occupational norm has not been affected. Thus, the violator may identify himself as a lawbreaker but not a criminal. Kadish calls it the problem of moral neutrality and questions the criminalization of morally neutral conduct.[30] The problem is dramatized by a study in the mid-1930s that showed that prevailing opinion in Akron, Ohio, did not feel that coal miners' stealing of coal from inoperative mines was wrong. The act became wrong if the theft was for resale for profit. It was overwhelmingly recognized that the law was violated in both instances, but only one theft was considered wrong. The same population thought it was wrong for a corporation to close its plant and move to another community because of labor unrest. It was recognized, however, that the wrongful conduct by the corporation was, in fact, lawful.[31]

What a community and its members consider wrong may not be unlawful. What society calls unlawful may not be thought morally wrong in a given community at a given time. A crime is more than a statement of a societal moral code; it is the product of a societal mechanism administered by highly organized institutions designed to impart societal policy to the activities of the accused. The cost of punishing a criminal is borne by society as a whole—a major distinction between criminal and other forms of law. Designating a given activity as a criminal offense does not always demonstrate society's labeling of that activity as immoral, but often is a societal recognition that civil enforcement has failed.[32]

Post Hoc Character of Many Corporate Crimes. It would be inaccurate to assume that an increase in the highly visible types of corporate law violations indicates widespread flouting of laws by corporations. An important segment of corporate crimes is highly technical in nature, and it is only after the courts have spoken that one can say whether or not a law was broken. It is often difficult to distinguish, without benefit of hindsight, between innovations in business practice that will eventually be approved and those that will eventually be stigmatized and punished as crimes. The landmark cases may indicate a propensity to probe the law's farthest limits—quite a different practice from deliberate infraction of a known law.[33]

The vagueness of many of the more recent statutory violations creates still additional compliance problems. Because of the difficulty of defining proscribed conduct, courts are reluctant to impose penalties of any kind for conduct whose specific illegality is in doubt. The problem of legal vagueness is partially resolved by a statutory prohibition that specifically defines the unlawful behavior or by administrative clarification of mandatory corporate conduct through rules and regulations. The requirement of knowledge of the act by the alleged violator can overcome the vagueness problem in the substantive law that is due to technicalities or uncharted areas of developing law.[34] Furthermore, in many situations, such a course may be socially desirable. Where a law is aimed at broadening the scope of social-welfare crimes or assigning individual responsibility—which in the given scheme of things must be done somewhat arbitrarily—it is important that careful judicial review precede any imposition of penalties, both to prevent abuse of executive power and to protect individual rights. Most corporate crimes remain noncriminal for a long time because of the inability of the criminal law and enforcement agencies to keep pace with corporate practices.

The entrenched position of senior management in corporations, lack of effective means of social accountability, support for illegal actions from group norms and mores, and differential enforcement of laws against corporate crimes have all combined to provide corporate executives with an irresistible temptation to violate the law.

Inadequacy of Existing Legal Philosophy

A traditional Anglo-American concept of criminal law, namely, *mens rea*, postulates that there must be a guilty mind or wrongful purpose for a criminal offense to be punishable.[35] *Mens rea* is a societal decision, a legal principle embodied in our system of jurisprudence, that an individual is not responsible for a wrong he or she has committed and should not be punished unless, in some way, his or her mind or will can be implicated in the offense. In determining the presence or absence of *mens rea*, three elements must be considered: (1) Did the individual make a choice to commit a wrongful act? (2) Was this choice freely made? (3) Did the individual know or could he have recognized the wrongfulness of his act? An individual who is insane is incapable of making a choice to commit a wrongful act (element 1). An individual acting under duress is not freely making a choice (element 2). An infant is not capable of knowing that a choice is wrong (element 3). *Mens rea*, in the context of these three elements, recognizes the ethical need for awareness of wrongdoing to establish criminal responsibility.[36]

Large corporations employing thousands of people and making millions of decisions impose impossible burdens on society to isolate a particular decision and identify a particular individual to be held responsible where only the last link in the long decision chain is visible. Thus, transplanting laws to corporations by treating them as legal persons has not been wholly successful. The corporation has no individual will of its own, legal assumptions notwithstanding, nor can it be sent to jail. Even if the entire corporate decision process were exposed to public scrutiny, it might still be impossible to isolate and identify the guilty person because of the collectivity of the actions that resulted in law violation and the lack of intent or knowledge on the part of thousands of people who may have contributed in some sense to that decision. For example, the black smoke billowing from a chemical plant is clearly in violation of environmental law. Who is to blame? The worker who failed to check a meter? The maintenance crew? The purchasing agent? The design engineer? Or the company president?

Overcoming the necessity of proving *mens rea* has been approached in one of three ways. There has been a tendency by the courts to infer the presence of *mens rea*, thus relieving public prosecutors of the need to prove this element by direct evidence.[37] A second, more popular approach has been the establishment of strict liability by statute.[38] In such instances, the need to establish *mens rea* is eliminated as an element of establishing a criminal offense. This public policy has been articulated in legislation that eliminates criminal intent as a large element of establishing criminal liability, that is, public-welfare offenses. The third approach revolves around the growing concept of criminal negligence. The philosophical base for the vicarious liability arising out of criminal negligence is that every sane person intends the natural and probable consequences of his or her actions. Conduct is negligent where harm could have been anticipated by a reasonably prudent person. The positive element of this concept is reasonable precautions against causing harm, and the negative element is failure to exercise this duty.[39]

The problem of *mens rea* has been of more concern in common law than in European jurisdictions. Common law courts have traditionally been more conservative and more oriented toward individual rights. They have also traditionally been reluctant to impose duties arising out of negligent conduct. Comfortable with the concept of *mens rea*, they have imposed criminal sanctions on a strict liability basis, because of a legislative mandate, or accepted certain legal presumptions in order to ease the burden of proving *mens rea*.[40]

European jurisdictions, however, have had no philosophical problem with punishing negligent behavior. They are not convinced of the need to establish *mens rea*. The result is an absence of (1) criminal sanctions imposed on a strict liability basis and (2) legal approaches to get around the burden of proving the presence of *mens rea*. It has been suggested that part of the difficulty in assessing liability for criminal negligence is a failure on the part of common law jurisdictions to distinguish between the concepts of legality and culpability. Legality is concerned with a risk that is substantial and unjustifiable. Culpability is concerned with the failure to perceive that this risk involves a gross deviation from standards of care that reasonable persons would observe under similar circumstances.[41]

The willingness of society to experiment with the notions of vicarious liability in a widening area of corporate misconduct suggests that a changed sociopolitical structure is beginning to come to grips with the issue of greater corporate accountability. The rationale lies in the realization that the legal fiction of management accountability is no longer tenable, as managements are largely self-perpetuating, with little control from stockholders. Furthermore, even if such accountability were effective, it would no longer be socially adequate, given the pervasive impact of modern large corporations on every aspect of our lives. Thus, society has a right to demand from corporate executives and to require that executives be held responsible for the actions of their subordinates and the corporations they manage. The critical element in the new situation is not the fact of personal criminal liability, but that, in proving guilt, it is no longer necessary to show criminal intent. Instead, a manager's criminal liability accrues from the fact that he or she holds a position in the corporation that makes him or her responsible for the operations where the violations occurred. It is irrelevant whether he or she was directly involved in the illegal activity or was merely negligent, careless, or incompetent.

Reform Proposals and Some Policy Options

Implications for the Future

The trend toward harsher penalties for corporate executives comes just when opinion polls indicate that business credibility in the public eye is extraordinarily low. Since it may satisfy the public desire that rich and poor be punished equally for their crimes, increased attention is being paid to white-collar crime. Broader participation in the political process by the poor, women, and members of minority groups has also altered the composition of power elites in legislative and judicial circles, and access to higher education by these groups has changed the character of other professional groups, thereby eroding the support base of corporations and business leaders and making them more vulnerable to individual criminal penalties. Thus, broadening of the definition of corporate crimes and stiffening of penalties against violators may be seen as a partial manifestation of the ascendancy to political power of groups that perceive themselves as victims of the established economic order but were previously helpless to seek satisfactory redress.

A society has a right to use criminal penalties and imprisonment of executives to deter corporate misdeeds. There may indeed be circumstances under which corporate executives are held to higher standards of accountability than those imposed on individuals acting in their personal capacities. It was suggested earlier that *mens rea* was a societal criterion for assigning responsibility. Under the notion of vicarious liability, society seems to be replacing the concept of *intent* to do harm with that of *capacity* to do harm. Thus, a failure to use this capacity of authority carries with it a penalty for nonperformance. Plato said that the only difference between the criminal and the honest is the act. The converse of the innocent is not the guilty one, but the harmful one.

Imposition of a criminal penalty, including jail, under conditions of vicarious liability is, however, an extreme punishment that could result in otherwise unintended and socially undesirable consequences. It introduces a new element of uncertainty into a chief executive's discretion in dealing with internal affairs and creates further strains on the interaction between corporations and other social groups, including government agencies. The following are issues that suggest themselves for further study.

1. What are the economic, social, and political implications of broad expansion of the personal liability of corporate officers for the activities of their subordinates? In particular, how would they affect the behavior of top executives and their responses to society's demand for more products, services, and employment?

2. What are the reasonable and realistic limits on the extent to which a corporate officer can be held personally liable for the acts of subordinates? How can these be ascertained, given the complexity of modern large-scale organizations?

3. In terms of corporate organizational behavior, how would increased liability affect product innovation, risk taking, market development, organizational structures, decision-making processes, and incentives and rewards systems?

4. Are certain types of activities particularly likely to expose top executives to personal liability? Given that corporations are likely to make efforts and develop procedures to minimize the impact of such activities, how would they affect the overall social goal of deterring real or alleged corporate law violations?

One of the explanations for resorting to prison sentences for corporate executives can be found in their supposed deterrent effect. The support for this underlying belief can be found in numerous statements made by U.S. Department of Justice officials and also in the pronouncements of various judges when imposing sentences. Recent sentencing guidelines from the Department of Justice recommend that the severity of the punishment rise with the defendant's relative position in the management hierarchy. Such an assertion, however, is not backed by good evidence or by systematic theoretical analysis. Indiscriminate use of such penalties, therefore, could cause considerable damage to the social fabric by aggravating conflicts between business and other social groups. It could also adversely effect economic well-being through restriction of corporate performance and hence of economic growth.

The first step should be the development of a theoretical framework to link sociopolitical conditions that would support imprisonment as a penalty for corporate executives, identify corporate activities that are susceptible to modification through imprisonment and other criminal penalties, and ascertain the degree of severity of various penalties that would be effective. Among the environmental variables are societal consensus, congruity with general social mores and specific (peer) group norms and codes of behavior, and moral and philosophical tenets setting standards for individual behavior and exceptions to such behavior that would be subjected to sanctions.

Another consideration is the sheer impossibility of one chief executive personally monitoring all employees' activities. The Supreme Court stated in the *Park* case that the law did not require what was impossible in terms of an executive's responsibility must be left to the judgement of prosecutors, juries, and judges. This, however, is a cumbersome process and likely to be inefficient. One alternative would be to specify by statute the management level and the individual who would be held responsible for various legal infractions. Some steps in this direction have been taken by such agencies as the Federal Communications Commission and the Food and Drug Administration. This avenue, however, must be systematically explored. A careful analysis of corporate structure must precede a designation of responsible officer or institution by statute.

A corporate chief executive cannot personally monitor even a small area of a large corporation's product-related activities—corporate bylaws notwithstanding. Consider, for example, the problem of canning firms. In an *amicus curiae* brief filed before the Supreme Court in the *Park* case, the National Canners Association alluded to the increasingly complex technical requirements imposed by the Food and Drug Administration, which now fill six volumes of the Code of Federal Regulations. The regulations prescribe virtually every step of the canning process and are so technical and complex that they are literally unintelligible to those who lack technological training in these areas.

The current labeling requirements for certain medical diagnostic devices are another example. Among the most detailed of the FDA's labeling schemes, these regulations require four pages to list required interpretation by different people with expertise in such diverse fields as medicine, engineering, and statistics. Since no company president can be expected to develop the requisite expertise in each of these fields, he must rely on technically trained subordinates. Top management is equally dependent on these qualified persons for information on any problems that might arise with respect to compliance.

Increased personal liability may make executives reluctant to introduce new products and services in the marketplace. Not only would this be likely to have an adverse effect on corporate growth, but it could also restrict consumer choice. Furthermore, the increased uncertainty, risk, cost of testing, and quality assurance would raise the cost of doing business, which would fall disproportionately heavily on smaller companies, thereby reducing market competition and injuring society.

There is some evidence that increased regulatory requirements have adversely affected business investment in research and new product development. The increased regulatory requirements of disclosure, product safety, effectiveness, and truth in advertising, coupled with potential liability suits for indeterminable injuries, have led many a company to withhold new products from the market, leading to greater homogeneity and standardization of products and thereby reducing consumer choice.

Potential criminal liability or exposure to civil assessment will, in all likelihood, lead executives to take steps to ensure that they have knowledge of and control over activities that could lead to the imposition of sanctions. Thus, higher management may be reluctant to decentralize operations or delegate responsibility. The lower-echelon manager will feel the close scrutiny of the responsible officer. This could limit initiative and stifle innovation. Because of a desire to maintain close supervision and control over company operations, growth may be sacrificed. This could lead to consumers being denied the fruits of economies of size, nearby availability of producers, and access to information. However, it could be argued that by compelling the executive to maintain closer supervision and control, the company will be more responsible to societal needs and demands, and thus expansion and growth will be undertaken only with clear and reasoned justification.

It seems clear that the movement toward increased criminal liability of executives has not been given the kind of public exposure and discussion it deserves in view of its unknown and potentially significant effects. Since the notion of punishing a wrongdoer in the traditional sense is inappropriate here, the applicable criterion is that of social welfare or public interest to be derived from controlling corporate misconduct. A careful balancing of competing interests is therefore in order. Companies, for their part, must initiate new procedures and develop new safeguards to ensure their economic survival and well-being as well as to protect their top executives from exposure to personal liability for goodfaith efforts made on a company's behalf during the normal course of business.

Legislative Proposals for Reform: H.R. 4973

An analysis of the H.R. 4973[42] currently before the Subcommittee on Crime of the House Judiciary Committee is instructive because it illustrates the various philosophical and political underpinnings of approaches to corporate crime and the measures that might be used to deter them.

The text of H.R. 4973 reads as follows:

A bill to amend title 18 of the United States Code to impose penalties with respect to certain nondisclosure by business entities as to dangerous products.

Be it enacted by the Senate and House of Representatives of the United States of America in Congress assembled, that chapter 89 of title 18 of the United States Code is amended by adding at the end of the following new section:

1822. Nondisclosure of certain matter by certain business entities and personnel

(a) Whoever—

(1) is an appropriate manager with respect to a product or business practice:

(2) discovers in the course of business as such manager a serious danger associated with such product (or a component of that product) or business practice; and

(3) knowingly fails to so inform each appropriate Federal agency in writing, if such agency has not been otherwise so informed, and warn affected employees in writing, if such employees have not been so warned, before the end of 30 days after such discovery is made; shall be fined not less than $50,000 or imprisoned not less than 2 years, or both, but if the convicted defendant is a corporation, such fine shall be not less than $100,000.

(b) As used in this section—

(1) the term "appropriate manager" means a person having management authority in or as a business entity with respect to a particular product or business practice, if such authority extends to informing Federal agencies and such business entity's personnel about serious dangers associated with such product (or any component of such product) or such business practice;

(3) the term "product" means a product of the business entity with respect to which the relevant accused person is the appropriate manager;

(4) the term "discovers," used with respect to a serious danger, means obtains information that would convince a reasonable person in the circumstances in which the discoverer is situated that it is probable the serious danger exists;

(5) the term "serious danger," used with respect to a product or business practice, means that the normal or reasonably foreseeable use of, or the exposure of human beings to, such product or such business practice will cause death or serious bodily injury to an individual;

(6) the term "serious bodily injury" means an impairment of physical condition, including physical pain, that creates a substantial risk of death or which causes serious permanent disfigurement, unconsciousness, extreme pain, or permanent or protracted loss or impairment of the function of any bodily member or organ;

(7) the term "warn affected employees," used with respect to a serious danger, means give sufficient description of the danger to all individuals working for or in the business entity who are likely to be subject to the serious danger in the course of that work; and

(8) the term "appropriate Federal agency" means a Federal agency having regulatory authority with respect to the product or business practice and dangers of the sort discovered.

SEC. 2. The table of sections for chapter 89 of title 18 of the United States code is amended by adding at the end the following new item: 1822. Nondisclosure of certain matters by certain business entity personnel.[43]

The bill severely limits the scope of its application by restricting the liability of an executive to nondisclosure pursuant to discovery of a potential danger associated with a product or business activity.

1. There is no provision in this bill for the situation in which an executive does not "discover" the existence of a dangerous situation. The "knowledge requirement" offers the least amount of deterrence to senior executives who have the most power to affect corporate policies and procedures because of their ability to isolate themselves from day-to-day operational details.

2. The knowledge requirement does not prevent crimes due to reckless and negligent supervision.

3. The reckless and negligent supervision requirement poses certain problems of evaluating the quality of management after the fact. Even honest judgements of error may then appear to be reckless decisions. In order that the law be applied effectively and equitably, it would be important to show that the functional area where the illegal act occurred was within the domain of the executive charged, and that he had the authority to prevent its occurrence.

4. Two approaches are possible to accomplish the goals of maximum prevention of harmful acts, easy determination of responsibility of executives committing these acts, and fairness in the imposition of penalties.

    (a) Every law that proscribes certain activities in health, safety, and environmental areas should require that the corporation designate an executive who will be responsible for ensuring corporate compliance with that law. Since this would be tantamount to prewarning, the executive so designated could now offer a "lack of knowledge" defense. Since compliance would be this excutive's sole responsibility, any violation would become a prima facie case for reckless and negligent supervision. This approach may have certain limitations in that more than one law may have a bearing on a specific corporate activity, or more than one corporate activity may be covered by a single law, thereby raising the problem of overlapping areas of responsibility and supervision.

    (b) Corporations might develop "social accountability centers" similar in purpose and goals to profit centers. Profit centers are organized on a rational basis since the performance has to be isolated and measured. Top management rewards a manager on the basis of a profit center's performance.

With a "social accountability center," all harmful and dangerous acts would be charged to the manager of that center. This approach might cause responsibility for compliance with certain laws to be distributed among more than one person within a corporation. However, it has the distinct advantage of segmenting areas of corporate activities so that an executive's responsibility is clearly established.

The second important aspect of H.R. 4973 has to do with types of penalties that could be imposed on corporations and individuals for corporate crimes. One of the primary reasons for resorting to prison sentences for corporate executives is their supposedly deterrent effect. Since corporate activity is normally undertaken in order to reap some economic benefit, corporate decision makers choose courses of action based on a calculation of potential costs and benefits, among them the risk of punitive sanctions. In order for this system to be effective, it must meet two criteria:

1. The proportion of violations discovered and convictions obtained should be large enough to increase the odds in favor of discovery of a crime and conviction.

2. The penalty must bear a realistic relation to the severity of the crime.

H.R. 4973 would not be likely to create an effective deterrence mechanism for the following reasons:

1. In the case of corporations, a small fine is not likely to deter violations when significant economics gains can be obtained by ignoring the law. In fact, inadequate penalties might become a license to violate the law. However, if a fine is large, it is also likely to be counterproductive. A company could pass the fine on to the consumer in terms of higher prices. A large fine could also result in significant tax savings so that society is, in fact, paying part of the fine through reduced tax revenues. A large fine could reduce a firm's profits and might adversely affect its ability to raise additional capital and correct alleged violations.

2. Fines levied against individual executives are likely to be paid by the company, in one form or another, because the gains to the corporation from law violations would be greater than the cost of fines.

3. Imprisonment penalties that are quite severe are also unlikely to be very effective. Experience has shown that both juries and judges are unwilling to impose long prison sentences for corporate crimes because there is no general societal awareness of the seriousness of these crimes and consequently no social climate of moral revulsion against the wrongdoers.

Alternative Proposals

In order to provide maximum deterrence against corporate crimes, personal criminal penalties should be made an integral part of a prevention package. Such penalties should be used in moderation and in conjunction with other measures, rather than as the last element in a sequential chain starting with censure and ending with imprisonment.

1. The frequency and incidence of prison sentences should be increased significantly so that they convey to the public a true picture of the widespread nature of corporate crimes, if that is the case. The sentences should bear a close relationship to the severity of the crime so that juries would not be reluctant to impose them.

2. To create a societal consensus on the undesirability of corporate crimes, prison sentences could be accompanied by a public apology from the corporation and the executive, together with a description of their deeds. Such apologies are common in both Germany and Japan and seem to have been effective in bringing public attention—and public condemnation—to violators.

3. The prison sentence should be combined with a probationary period. An executive who is convicted of criminal wrongdoing should be barred from holding an executive level position in a publicly held company for a prescribed number of years following release from prison.

4. Corporations and individuals should be denied of all benefits—direct and indirect—accrued to them as a result of an illegal activity, following the pattern codified in 18 U.S.C. sections 1961–1965. This would be in addition to the usual fines or jail sentences.

5. Firms convicted of violations should be prohibited from doing business with other firms whose executives had been convicted of similar violations. Such restrictions are already imposed on Nevada's gambling industry, where firms known to have been associated with mob-tied businesses are barred from operating in the state.

6. Corporations whose operations have been in violation of criminal laws should be subjected to special reporting requirements. The company or its officers could, for example, be required to make regular periodic statements to the court stating that no violations existed. If violations were later proved, the firm or individual could be convicted of perjury as well as the violation, and the penalties naturally would be harsher.

Notes

The author gratefully acknowledges the assistance of the following people in the research leading to this article: Dr. Keith MacMillan, the Administrative Staff College, Henley-on-Themes, England, and Mr. Rene Dougin, directeur general, Gloria, S.A., France. Mr. Roland Zier, vice-president public relations, Warner-Lambert Co., and Mr. Charles N. Walsh, assistant district attorney, Queens County, New York, provided invaluable assistance in collecting material relating to various case studies described in this article. Mrs. Catherine Carpenter and Diane Bagot of UTD, and Mrs. Anita Bertoncini of Gloria, S.A. France, assisted in the English translation of French language documents. Mr. Carl Swanson, counsel with the law firm of Seay, Gwinn, Crawford, Mebus, and Blakeney, assisted in the research for the project.

1. Harry V. Ball and Lawrence M. Friedman, "The Use of Criminal Sanctions in the Enforcement of Economic Legislation," 318–336; Sanford H. Kadish, "Some Observations on the Use of Criminal Sanctions in the Enforcement of Economic Legislation," 296–317, in *White Collar Crime: Offenses in Business Politics and the Professions* (Geis and Meier, eds., 1977).

2. Marshall B. Clinard, Illegal Corporate Behavior, National Institute of Law Enforcement and Criminal Justice, Law Enforcement Assistance Administration, U.S. Department of Justice, Washington, D.C., October 1979 (hereafter referred to as LEAA study). U.S. Congress, "White Collar Crime: The Problem and the Federal Response." Subcommittee on Crime of the Committee on the Judiciary, U.S. Congress, 95th Congress, 2nd Session, Washington, D.C., 1978.

3. LEAA Study, 19–20.

4. S. 1722 Sections 1617 "Endangerment" and Section 1853 "Environmental Pollution."

5. H.R. 4973.

6. *The People of the State of New York* v. *Warner-Lambert et al.,* indictment No. 915–977; Memorandum Opinion, S. Ct. Queens County, Criminal term, Part VIII, (February 15, 1978); Record on Appeal, Vol. 1, *The People of the State of New York* v. *Warner-Lambert et al.,* indictment No. 915–977; Appellants' Brief of *The People of the State of New York* v. *Warner-Lambert et al.,* filed September 1978; Brief of Defendant-Respondent Warner-Lambert Company, *The People of the State of New York* v. *Warner-Lambert et al.,* indictment No. 915–977; Opinion of the Appellate Division Supreme Court, Second Judicial Department, July 9, 1979, *The People of the State of New York* v. *Warner-Lambert et al.,* indictment No. 915–977.

7. *United States* v. *Park,* 421 U.S. 658, 95 S. Ct. 1903, 44 L. Ed. 2nd 789 (1975). For a detailed analysis of the case, see S. Prakash Sethi and Robert N. Katz, "The Expanding Scope of Personal Criminal Liability of Corporate Executives—Some Implications of *United States* v. *Park,*" 32, Food, Drug, Cosm. L.J. 544–70 (1977).

8. *United States* v. *Dotterweich,* 320 U.S. 277, 64 S. Ct. 134, 88 L. Ed. 48 (1943).

9. For a brief history of the evolution of the concept of absolute and vicarious criminal liability of corporate executives under the Act and the Dotterweich doctrine, see Daniel O'Keefe, Jr. and Marc H. Shapiro, "Personal Criminal Liability Under the Federal Food, Drug, and Cosmetic Act: the Dotterweich Doctrine," 30, Food, Drug, Cosm. L.J., 5 (1975).

10. Daniel F. O'Keefe, *"Criminal Liability: Park Update,"* 32, Food, Drug, Cosm. L.J., 392–404 (1977).

11. Letter addressed to Dr. Keith MacMillan from F.J. Youngman, Deputy Legal Advisor, National Coal Board, dated February 8, 1978, including statement by Judge of the Crown Court at Sheffield, dated September 2, 1977.

12. *U.S.* v. *Hudson Farms, Inc.,* criminal indictment No. 78–222, U.S. District Court for the Eastern District of Pennsylvania, Environmental Reporter, November 24, 1978, 12 ERC 1944; *U.S.* v. *Frezzo Brothers, Inc.,* criminal No. 78–218, November 24, 1978. U.S. District Court, Eastern District of Pennsylvania, Environmental Reporter, 12 ERC 1481.

13. O'Keefe and Shapiro, supra n. 9, at 33–38.

14. 33 U.S.C. 1319 (b), (c), (d).

15. *Atlas Roofing Co.* v. *Occupational Safety Commission,* 430 U.S. 442.

16. "The War on White-Collar Crime," *Business Week,* June 13, 1977, at 66; "The Liabilities of Sitting in a Bank's Board," *Business Week,* September 26, 1966, 26; "U.S. Currency Comptroller Seeks to Force Restitution to Banks for Insiders' Abuses," *Wall Street Journal,* December 7, 1977, p. 13.

17. "Jail Terms, Fines May Be Toughest in Antitrust History," *Dallas Times Herald,* p. 8, Feb. 6, 1978, at 8.

18. P.L. 93–528, December 21, 1974, 88 Stat. 1706.

19. 15 U.S.A. $ 78 dd-2; see "The Foreign Payoff Law is a Necessity," *New York Times,* February 5, 1978.

20. Lewis S. Black, Jr., "Shareholder Democracy and Corporate Governance," 5, Sec. Reg. L.J., 291–317 (Winter 1978).

21. Wallace Forbes and Arthur R. Rosenbloom, "A Shield for Directors: The Outside Consultant," *Management Rev.,* December 1977, at 26–28, 37–39.

22. Robert E. Lane, "Why Businessmen Violate the Law," in Geis and Meir, supra n.1 at 102–116.

23. Ball and Friedman, supra n.1, at 333–334; Kadish, supra n.1, at 304–308.

24. Gilbert Egis, "Deterring Corporate Crime," in Nader and Green, *Corporate Power in America* (1973) at 182–197.

25. Arthur S. Miller, "Courts and Corporate Accountability," in Nader and Green, supra n.20, at 198–214.

26. Christopher D. Stone, "Controlling Corporate Misconduct," 38, *Public Interest,* Summer 1977, at 55–71.

27. LEAA Study, xxii.

28. Edwin H. Sutherland, "Crime of Corporations," in Geis and Meier, supra n.1, at 71–84; "Stiffer Sentences for Price-Fixers?" *Wall Street Journal,* December 17, 1976. CF Lane, supra n.22, at 111–112.

29. Judith Miller, "Study of Questionable Payments Accents Involvement of Officers," *New York Times,* February 25, 1978, at 27.

30. Kadish, supra n.1, 304–315.

31. Ball and Friedman, supra n.1, at 325.

32. Ibid., at 327–329.

33. Kadish, supra n.1, at 299–301.

34. Kadish, supra n.1, at 300.

35. R.J. Urowsky, "Negligence and the General Problem of Criminal Responsibility," 81, *Yale Law Journal,* 949–979 (1972).

36. Jerome Hall, "Negligent Behavior Should Be Excluded From Penal Liability," 63, *Columbia Law Review,* 632–644 (1963).

37. Gerard O. Mueller, "The Devil May Care—Or Should We? A Reexamination of Criminal Negligence," 55, *Kentucky Law Journal,* 29–49 (1966).

38. Idl: Richard A. Wasserstrum, "Strict Liability in the Criminal Law," 12, *Stanford Law Review,* 731–745 (1960).

39. Mueller, supra n.37; Frances Bowes Sayre, "Public Welfare Offenses," *Columbia Law Journal,* 55–88 (1933); George P. Fletcher, "The Theory of Criminal Negligence: A Comparative Analysis," 119, *University of Pennsylvania Law Review,* 401–438 (1971).

40. Fletcher, supra n.39, at 401–405.

41. *Id.* at 401–405, 423–431.

42. S. Prakash Sethi, "Corporate Law Violations and Executive Liability," Testimony on H.R. 4973 before the Subcommittee on Crime of the House Judiciary Committee, December

13, 1979. For additional reading on various approaches to analysis of corporate illegal behavior and proposals for regulating and deterring such behavior see: "Developments in the Laws— Corporate Crime: Regulating Corporate Behavior Through Criminal Sanctions," *Harvard Law Review*, 92, No. 6 (April 1979), 1227; "Reflections in White-Collar Sentencing," *The Yale Law Journal*, 86, No. 4, (March 1977), 589; George P. Fletcher, "The Theory of Criminal Negligence: A Comparative Analysis," *University of Pennsylvania Law Review*, 119, No. 3 (January 1971), 401; "Comments: Criminal Sanctions for Corporate Illegality," *The Journal of Criminal Law and Criminology*, 69, No. 1 (Spring 1978), 40; "Toward a Rational Theory of Criminal Liability for the Corporate Executive," *The Journal of Criminal Law and Criminology*, 60, No. 1 (Spring 1978), 75.

    43. *Congressional Record*, July 27, 1979, E-3923.

The Racketeer Influenced and Corrupt Organizations Act (RICO): Constraint on Corporate Crime or Unfair Business Weapon?

Anthony J. Celebrezze, Jr.
Steven J. Twist

The Racketeer Influenced and Corrupt Organization Act (RICO), passed by Congress in 1970,[1] is the subject of a debate centering on, first, the purpose of the law as intended by Congress and, second, the need for substantial changes in provisions of the law. The law specifically prohibits: investing in an enterprise with the proceeds of a pattern of racketeering; acquiring an enterprise by a pattern of racketeering; and operating an enterprise by a pattern of racketeering. Under RICO, *pattern of racketeering* is defined broadly as two or more instances of criminal activity in a ten-year period and includes offenses dealing with personal violence, the provision of illegal goods and services, corruption in private or public life, and various forms of criminal fraud. A range of activities including white-collar crimes such as mail and securities fraud, tax evasion, bribery, and industrial espionage, as well as crimes involving elements of organized crime, for example, murder, extortion, gambling, loan-sharking, and political corruption, have been considered under RICO suits.

    The statute imposes criminal sanctions on violations of its substantive prohibitions that include imprisonment and fine (twenty years and $25,000), and criminal forfeiture of the proceeds of transactions and of bases of power. In light of the Criminal Fine Enforcement Act of 1984, the fine may also be $250,000, if an individual is convicted, $500,000 if other than an individual is convicted, or twice the loss or twice the gain. The rights of innocent parties—that is, those without knowledge—and victims are explicitly protected.

Since 1970, similar legislation has been enacted in twenty-three states. While an important purpose of the law was to aid prosecutors, individuals and corporations have the right under RICO to file civil suits for triple damages. Suits filed under RICO include government cases against organized crime and tax fraud, as well as civil suits of individuals against recognized firms, and of legitimate businesses against other legitimate firms. Increasingly, the civil provisions have been successfully used at the federal and state level by the federal govenment as well as by state and local units of governments victimized by conduct prohibited by RICO.[2]

Proponents of change argue that Congress intended the bill as a protection against attempts by organized crime to infiltrate legitimate businesses, and that the broad interpretation of the law is having unintended consequences. John Shad, Chairman of the Securities and Exchange Commission, noted that in the case of federal securities suits, "RICO is altering the balance of rights and remedies established over the last fifty years by Congress, the courts, and the Securities and Exchange Commission" by considering securities fraud as racketeering and by allowing for triple damages rather than actual damages as provided for in federal securities laws.[3]

Business Criticism of RICO and Efforts to Dilute Its Application to Legitimate Business Enterprises

Since 1980, a number of large corporations have been sued both by private parties and public agencies under the RICO Statutes. Many leading business commentators have argued strongly against the application of RICO to legitimate business enterprises. Currently, there are three bills pending in Congress aimed at modifying the application of RICO to legitimate business enterprises. These are:

1. *H.R. 2517*, introduced on May 15, 1985, by Congressman Conyers, which would: (a) strike the term "racketeer" from the statute; (b) strike person from the definition of "enterprise"; (c) limit "pattern" to acts within five years of the indictment; (d) limit "pattern" by a "fraud plus" requirement; and (e) limit "pattern" by a common scheme requirement.

2. *H.R. 2943*, introduced on July 10, 1985, by Congressman Boucher for himself and Mr. Fish, Mr. Gekas, and Mr. Hyde, which would: (a) impose a criminal conviction limitation on the civil right of recovery; and (b) impose a one year statute of limitations on the civil right of recovery.

3. *S. 1521*, introduced on July 29, 1985, by Senator Hatch, which would: (a) limit the right of civil recovery to competitive, investment, or other business injury; and (b) limit "pattern" by a "fraud plus" requirement.

Advocates of RICO as it stands presently argue that changes are not necessary. The National Association of Attorneys General and the National District Attorneys

Association support the basic RICO concept. Both the National Association of Attorneys General and the National District Attorneys Association have passed resolutions dealing with RICO (see appendixes A and B). The two associations support efforts to clarify or strengthen the RICO concept, while at the same time opposing the principal provisions of the three previously mentioned major bills now pending before Congress.

A major motivating force behind a number of efforts to amend RICO is a concern with the propriety of the use of RICO in the business fraud context. The concern is expressed that RICO is being used unfairly as a business weapon. We share that concern, but do not believe that the evidence bears it out. In addition, we believe that present remedies against the possibility of vexatious litigation are adequate to curtail abuse. Nevertheless, we make suggestions for fine-tuning RICO and creating a treble damage remedy for victims of improper RICO litigation.

In the main, the current controversy over RICO has not centered on its criminal provisions or its possible civil application in the areas of violence, the provision of illicit goods and services, or the corruption of governmental entities or unions. Instead, the controversy has focused almost exclusively on private suits brought in the commercial fraud area. Special pleas, particularly by segments of the accounting and securities industries, are now being heard suggesting that it is outrageous to bring racketeering charges against legitimate business people.

The dictionary, however, defines a *racket* as a business run by fraud or extortion, and a *racketeer* as one who runs a racket. If legitimate business people violate RICO's terms, they ought to be called *racketeers*. No justification can be offered for limiting the term *racketeer*—or RICO—to those whose names end in vowels. *Racket* and *racketeer* have never been words limited to organized crime in the classic mobster sense. Murray I. Gurfein wrote:

> Racketeering, a term loosely applied to a variety of criminal schemes has not yet received exact legal definition. . . . It . . .applies to the operation of an illegal business as well as to the illegal operation of a legal business. . . . The word gained currency in the 1920s, but its origin remains obscure. . . . The most plausible [theory notes that the] word racket has been used to describe a loud noise and hence a spree or party or "good time." In the 1890s social clubs of young men in New York City, under the auspices of political leaders, gave affairs called rackets; since among their number there were members of neighborhood gangs, it was found easy to coerce local tradesman to buy tickets.[4]

Hence, obtaining money by coercion or fraud became racketeering.

RICO, of course, follows this common usage by terming its predicate offenses racketeering activity, and making, for example, the operation of an enterprise through a pattern of racketeering activity that affects commerce, the gravamen of one of its standards of unlawful conduct. If the suggestion of those who would take "racketeering" out of RICO were carried to its logical conclusion, the Congress should also rename federally cognizable *murder, rape,* and *robbery* with less perjorative terms. These people have forgotten the proper role of social opprobrium in the administration of justice, criminal and civil (see, for example, J. Feinberg, *Doing and Deserving* **98**:100–105, 115–116, 1970.) At its best, in civilized and democratic countries, punishment surely expresses the community's strong disapproval of what the criminal did. "Most white-collar crime is not at all morally neutral."[5]

Congress faces a test of its will in the proposal to take "racketeering" out of RICO. Will it adopt a double standard of labelling for white-collar offenders? It is not just that businessmen have a reckless disregard for the law. Also significant is the fact that they have a powerful voice in determining what the law shall be, how it shall be interpreted and enforced. Dire predictions also are being made of an unjustified flood of new federal litigation, as if litigation of any proportion would be unjustified if the victims could establish their allegations. Voices cry out most stridently that RICO is antibusiness. Nothing could be more self-serving or further from the truth. Former Treasury Secretary W. Michael Blumenthal put it well, "The misbehavior of a large corporation makes news because the majority do not misbehave [but those who are] ethically strong and morally clean [should be the first to denounce those who are not for they] threaten the survival of the free-enterprise system."[6]

That major corporations do engage in illegal practices, however, cannot be seriously questioned. A survey of 1,043 major corporations between 1970 and 1980 indicated that 117 had significant convictions or consent decrees for 98 antitrust violations; 28 cases of kickbacks, bribery, or illegal rebates; 21 instances of illegal political contributions; 11 cases of fraud; and 5 cases of tax evasion.

Legitimate business people, in fact, have little to fear from federal or state RICO legislation. Neither makes criminal that conduct that is not now already criminal under its predicate offenses. Both merely provide enhanced sanctions and new civil enforcement mechanisms. Legitimate business people do not perpetrate fraud; they are victimized by it. Good faith commercial disputes, moreover, do not constitute criminal fraud. Nothing in RICO provides to the contrary.

While it may be that some RICO suits have been brought by unethical plaintiff's lawyers hoping to obtain quick settlements by the filing of strike suits, that characterization may not be made of all, or most, RICO litigation. Major corporations that have sued under RICO, for example, include IBM, Crocker National Bank, Standard Oil of Indiana, Armco Steel, Pepsi Cola Bottling Company, Banker's Trust Co., Aetna Casualty and Security Co., Allstate Insurance Co., and State Farm Fire and Casualty Co. IBM sued Hitachi, Ltd., under RICO for the theft of computer software; the suit was settled for upward of $200 million. Similarly, the Crocker National Bank litigation against Lehman Brothers, Rockwell International, and Singer, Hunter, and partners, (a law firm) involved $225 million in computer leasing fraud; the case was settled for $65 million.

No one knows how much fraud is practiced against the federal government in the defense contract and procurement area. A generally accepted estimate does not even exist. That the figure must be enormous, however, is underlined by the recent guilty plea of the General Electric Co. (GE) to defrauding the Pentagon on its Minuteman missile contract. Other investigations involving GE are pending. Similarly, the General Dynamics Corporation, another of the nation's largest defense contractors, has acknowledged giving Admiral Hyman Rickover over $67,000 in gratuities between 1961 and 1977. In addition, the Inspector General of the Pentagon recently informed Congress that forty-five defense contracting firms are under investigation. The allegations against nine of the top ten largest defense contractors include cost mischarging, labor mischarging, subcontractor kickbacks, product substitution, security compromise, defective pricing, cost duplication, false claims, supply accountability, gratuities, bid-rigging, and bribery (see appendix C).

A general estimate of fraud—both by insiders in the government and recipients of benefits—in other government benefit programs is, however, put at $2.5 to $25 billion. Specialized estimates of individual programs make the higher figure more likely. Medicaid beneficiary fraud, for example, is put at $1.2 billion; medicaid provider fraud amounts to $715 million. Medicare fraud amounts to $1.5 billion.

More generally, fraud is estimated to cost the nation's business and individuals more than $100 billion each year. Securities theft and fraud costs $8 billion. Movie piracy costs $1 billion. Records and tape piracy costs $400 million. Commodities investment fraud costs $200 million. Recent investigations indicate that as much as $100 million may have been bilked from buyers of mobile homes, many of which were federally insured. Bank fraud, particularly by insiders, is also deeply disturbing. In the 1980 to 1981 period, the failure of 105 banks and savings and loans cost $1 billion. Roughly one-half of the bank failures and one-quarter of the savings and loan collapses had as a major contributing factor the criminal activities by insiders, few of whom, according to the findings of a study by the Barnard Committee, were adequately sanctioned, criminally or civilly. Last year that committee noted:

> Despite such enormous losses, neither the banking nor the criminal justice systems impose effective sanctions or punishment to deter white-collar bank fraud. The few insiders who are singled out for civil sanctions by the banking agencies are usually either fined de minimis amounts or simply urged to resign. The few who are criminally prosecuted usually serve little, if any, time in prison for thefts that often cost millions of dollars.[7]

Ultimately, many of these costs of fraud are passed on to the rest of us. Insurance fraud, for example, annually costs $11 billion, and since the typical insurance company must generate $1.25 in premiums for every dollar it pays out, the bill that the nation must meet amounts to $13.75 billion. Much insurance fraud is also systematic. In southern California alone, it is estimated that some forty insurance fraud rings, run by crooked lawyers and doctors, bilk the insurance industry out of $200 million a year. While the costs of vexatious litigation are also generally spread throughout society by directors and officers liability insurance, too often the costs of fraud are not shared through various kinds of insurance, and they rest on the shoulders of the victims who can ill-afford to carry or sustain them. Indeed, in light of Ohio's experience with the failure of ESM Government Securities, Inc.—including a paid-for false audit report, and the repercussions in the savings and loan industry and on the gold market—no one ought seriously to contend that such fraud is a "garden variety" problem that may be "weeded" with business-as-usual legal techniques.

It is for these reasons that we oppose the "fraud plus" requirement that Congressman Conyers' bill (H.R. 2517) and Senator Hatch's bill (S. 1521) would impose on RICO. Congressman Conyers' bill would mistakenly, but at least consistently, impose it on both criminal prosecutions and civil actions; Senator Hatch's bill would, inconsistently, impose it only on civil suits. Under either bill, criminal fraud alone would not be enough to make up a pattern of racketeering; it would be required that "fraud plus" some other offense—murder, kidnapping, gambling, and so forth—be shown.

No valid reason exists to give organized crime offenders or white-collar crime offenders such a free ride under RICO if they confine their criminal activities to fraud. Victims of crime are injured just as surely whether or not another predicate offense accompanies the fraudulent scheme. If the amendment is justified, as a method to curtail abusive fraud litigation, the complete answer to it is that it overshoots its mark. Remedies should be tailored to the character of the abusive fraud suits, if that is the objective. But all members of a class of RICO suits should not be eliminated because some members may have been improperly brought. That remedy is worse than the abuse. It ought not, therefore, be adopted.

Similarly, we see no valid reason why Congress should adopt the provisions of Senator Hatch's bill (S. 1521), which would limit the class of compensable injuries under RICO to competitive, investment, or business injuries. Why should business people alone be given a treble damage claim against organized or white-collar offenders? That would turn RICO into a piece of special-interest legislation. What about individuals injured when they are not engaged in a commercial relationship? What about consumers who are not in business, but are still participating in the marketplace? What about unions that cannot be injured competitively, through investment, and have no business? Unions, particularly, have been taken over by organized crime figures. Union treasuries have been victimized by embezzlement; their welfare funds have been exploited by corrupt lending practices. Why exclude unions from the Act's protections at this late date? What about union members? Why should they be excluded? What about other noncommercial entities, like charities, which have no business? What of governmental units? They seldom have competition, can be invested in, or have, strictly speaking, a business. Why should we exclude general injury to governmental property by criminal activities under RICO? Congress did not adopt Senator Hatch's approach in 1970, as the Supreme Court held in *Sedima*. We can see no valid reason to adopt it now. Finally, we see no valid reason why Congress should adopt the provisions of Congressman Conyers' bill (H.R. 2517) that would exclude individuals from the definition of enterprise. We agree with the RICO Cases Committee of the American Bar Association.[8]

The second circuit in its *Sedima* opinion suggested that it was "extraordinary if not outrageous" to bring a civil RICO suit against legitimate businesses; the court cited among its examples of such legitimate businesses, E.F. Hutton & Co.[9] The guilty plea of E.F. Hutton to illegally overdrawing its bank accounts by more than $10 billion (obtaining a free ride averaging $150 million a day) indicates how unwise the Circuit Court's illustration was. Justice White in the Supreme Court's *Sedima* decision (105 S. Ct. at 3287) put it well: " 'Legitimate' . . . enterprises . . . enjoy neither inherent incapacity for criminal activity nor immunity from its consequences."[10]

Treble damage suits under RICO promise remedial relief against such outrageous conduct that will be swift, sure, and severe—characteristics deemed essential by modern economic analysis. Professor (now Judge) Posner suggests that modern economic analysis supports private enforcement mechanisms of more than actual damages against deliberate antisocial conduct, particularly where the factor of concealment is present. If our society authorizes the recovery of only actual damages for deliberate antisocial conduct engaged in for profit, it lets the perpetrator know that if he is caught, he need only return the misappropriated sums. If he is not caught, he may keep his ill-gotten gains, and even if he is caught and sued, he knows that he may be able to defeat part of the damage claims or at least compromise. In short, the balance of risk under traditional simple damage recovery provides little disincentive to those who engage in such conduct.[11] Similarly, studies of the antitrust statutes show that most antitrust suits are settled now at close to actual damages. Ironically, it may be necessary to authorize *treble* damages to assure that deserving victims receive *actual* damages in the RICO area.

Public enforcement with its principal reliance on the criminal law cannot be relied on to do the whole job of policing fraud. We must be candid about the limitations of the criminal justice system in the white-collar area. Resources available for investigation and prosecution are scarce. The common law criminal trial is ponderous. The cases are complex. Offenders will most often be treated as first offenders even if they had actually engaged in a pattern of behavior over a substantial period of time. A few convictions will yield only a minimal deterrent effect. J. Conklin rightly concludes:

> The criminal justice system treats business offenders with leniency. Prosecution is uncommon, conviction is rare, and harsh sentences almost nonexistent. At most, a businessman or corporation is fined; few individuals are imprisoned and those who are serve very short sentences. Many reasons exist for this leniency. The wealth and prestige of businessmen, their influence over the media, the trend toward more lenient punishment for all offenders, the complexity and invisibility of many business crimes, the existence of regulatory agencies and inspectors who seek compliance with the law rather than punishment of violators all help explain why the criminal justice system rarely deals harshly with businessmen. This failure to punish

business offenders may encourage feelings of mistrust toward community morality, and general social disorganization in the general population. Discriminatory
justice may also provide political radicals with a desire to replace a corrupt system
in which equal justice is little more than a spoken ideal.[12] (citations omitted)

The funding of the Securities and Exchange Commission, for example, has
increased since 1979, but its staffing has decreased, and its pending investigations
are down. Yet the number of shares traded on the New York Stock Exchange has
shot up 300 percent since 1977; the number of first-time registrants has increased
by 260 percent. Even among legitimate brokerage firms, the incentive structure
for commissions encourages a fraud known as *churning,* trading stock without regard
for investment objectives. Similarly, the futures industry in the United States has
grown tremendously in recent years. The 139.9 million future contracts traded in
1983 represents a level of trading activity fifteen times greater than that reached
in 1968. The value of contracts traded exceeds $5 trillion a year. Nevertheless,
the resources of the Commodities Futures Trading Commission have remained
relatively constant. Some would suggest that the industry is a scandal waiting to
happen, for the commission "is thoroughly out-gunned in the ongoing battle against
commodity fraud."[13] In addition, accounting firms, once thought to play the role
of outside watchdogs, are under heavy competitive pressure to go along with questionable annual reports, and they are increasingly losing their independence, since
they also offer management consulting advice, as the testimomy before the Dingle
Committee so amply shows. The need for more effective deterrent to fraud in the
world of legitimate business is, therefore, manifest.

The perspective of history in the area of antitrust and securities regulation
is enlightening. Congress passed the Sherman Act in 1890, principally to attack
the oil, tobacco, and sugar trusts, but it is applied to all contracts in restraint of
trade, not just those entered into by the Rockefeller family in connection with the
founding of the Standard Oil Company. Today, if our markets are free, it is principally because of that private enforcement mechanism. Indeed, between 1960 and
1980, of the 22,585 civil and criminal antitrust cases, 84 percent were instituted
by private plaintiffs. Nevertheless, the promise of the 1890 statute was only slowly
redeemed. It took until 1910 for the government to bring and the Supreme Court
to uphold the breakup of the Standard Oil monopoly, and it took almost a half
century to bring the private enforcement mechanism into play.

Fortunately, the Supreme Court and the business community have now come
to see the Sherman Act as "the Magna Carta of free enterprise" as "important
to the preservation of economic freedom and our free-enterprise system as the Bill
of Rights is to the protection of our fundamental personal freedoms."[14] Hopefully,
the judiciary will come to see that RICO, too, serves important public policies.
RICO and the antitrust statutes are, for example, well-integrated. Former Assistant
Attorney General for Antitrust Donald Turner observed, "There are three possible kinds of force which a firm can resort to: violence (or the threat of it), deception,

or market power."[15] RICO focuses on the first two; antitrust focuses on the third. Society needs them both, if its markets are to be not only free, but honest.

Civil RICO builds on the experience of the last half century in the antitrust and securities areas and generalizes it across the marketplace. As the antitrust acts seek to maintain economic freedom in the marketplace, RICO seeks, in the fraud area, to promote integrity in the marketplace. RICO is, therefore, neither antibusiness nor pro-business. It is pro-victim.

Those who express a concern with frivolous suits under civil RICO have the burden of proving that a substantial number have been filed, that existing safeguards against such suits are not adequate to remedy them, that new safeguards against such suits that are adequate cannot be designed, and that the detriment from these suits outweighs the benefit from leigtimate suits. None of these burdens has been met. In fact, a study of the United States Judicial Conference in 1983 concluded that "the existing tools [were] sufficient [although] not fully understood or utilized." It is the experience of a majority of seasoned litigators in the RICO area that adding a RICO claim to a suit does not facilitate settlement; it inhibits it, particularly when a legitimate business is involved. Generally, such business wrongfully accused of racketeering will not settle suits—even those that should be compromised—as long as the racketeer label is in the litigation. Indeed, it is difficult to understand how a suit with "no merit" faces a defendant with "ruinous exposure." If the plaintiff's suit has no merit, his chance of success is zero, and zero multiplied by three (or any other number) is still zero. It is doubtful that you will find that the litigation was meritless. It is doubtful, in short, that responsible corporate or other defendants are paying off strike suits in the RICO—or any other area—at more than their settlement value, no matter what the theory of the complaint is. Neither the racketeer label nor the threat of treble damages will convince prudent managers lightly to surrender scarce resources merely because another files a suit. No matter how colorfully it is phrased, the claim that such managers act against their own interests is not credible.

If unethical attorneys have brought some frivolous suits under RICO falsely alleging fraud, they should be disciplined and, if necessary, additional remedies should be designed to deal with frivolous litigation. Current law already authorizes the award of actual fees to defendants where actions are brought frivolously, unreasonably, or without foundation. What is needed, therefore, is a provision that authorizes treble actual costs, including attorney's fees. We should not, however, compound our injury from such frivolous litigation by denying all victims of racketeering rooted in fraud their day in court under RICO. Fraud is a national problem in our society that requires stronger, not weaker, legislative efforts to curtail it.

Nor can it be persuasively argued that private RICO suits threaten unjustifiably to flood the federal courts. RICO was not discovered by the private bar until about 1979. Studies by the Department of Justice indicate, however, that less than 500 civil RICO suits have been brought to date and that 65 percent of them have had an independent basis for federal jurisdiction. The litigation, accordingly, is neither wholly new nor of flood proportions. It is most likely that RICO suits will eventually fall somewhere between the present antitrust (1,200 civil, 75 criminal) and securities and commodities (3,000 civil, 26 criminal) litigation. This would place RICO cases well below the major areas of current federal litigation: overpayments and enforcement of judgments (41,000), prisoner petitions (26,000), social security (20,000), civil rights (20,000), and labor (11,000).

A point must be made, too, about the fact of litigation. Litigation itself is not an evil. "Over the course of centuries," the Court noted, "our society has settled upon civil litigation as a means for redressing grievances, resolving disputes, and vindicating rights when other means fail." "That our citizens have access to their civil court," the Court concluded, "is not an evil to be regretted; rather, it is an attribute of a system of justice in which we ought to take pride." We agree. Accordingly, it ought to be recognized that the mere fact of RICO suits is not a matter to be decried or deplored.[16]

The concept in RICO of a private enforcement mechanism reflects ideas found in the antitrust laws. Similarly, the RICO civil suit in the area of commercial fraud promises to serve as a like guarantee of the integrity of the market place. Much of what the Supreme Court has said about the antitrust laws may be said of the RICO private civil suit concept. RICO creates "a private enforcement mechanism that . . .deter[s] violators . . . and . . . provide[s] ample compensation to . . . victims."[17] Such "private . . . litigation is one of the surest weapons for effective enforcement."[18] A private "treble-damage remedy [is needed] . . . precisely for the purpose of encouraging *private* challenges to violations."[19] Such suits "provide a significant supplement to the limited sources available to the government."[20]

Professor Edelhertz rightly observed:

> White-collar crime, like common crime, can have a serious influence on the social fabric, and on the freedom of commercial and interpersonal transactions. Every stock market fraud lessens confidence in the securities market. Every commercial bribe or kickback debases the level of business competition, often forcing other suppliers to join in the practice if they are to survive. . . . The pharmaceutical company which markets a new drug based on fraudulent test results undercuts its competitors who are still marketing the properly tested drugs, and may cause them to adopt similar methods. Competitors who join in a conspiracy to freeze out their competition, or to fix prices, may gravely influence the course of our economy, in addition to harming their competitors and customers.[21]

It has been suggested that RICO ought to be limited to organized crime. We believe it should not be so limited. First, no generally accepted definition of *organized crime*—or for that matter, *white-collar crime* or *garden-variety fraud*—exists. But if it did, it ought not be employed to limit the ability of victims of racketeering activity to seek relief under RICO. Our deepest legal traditions run against writing different laws for different people. Victims of crime rightly care little that their life savings were taken by mobsters wearing black suits and white ties or crooked accountants wearing business suits and white collars. Ask the victims in Ohio of the fraudulent audit report that led to the demise of EMS Government Securities, Inc. and Ohio's savings and loan industry whether they were more harmed last year by fraud or drugs coming out of Florida, and enforcement priority of the federal government. Ask, too, the victims of the collapse of the savings and loan industry in Maryland. Second, the problem of proof, no matter how the phrase is defined, would be virtually insurmountable for the private civil plaintiff. If such a showing were required in a criminal case, even the government, with its extraordinary evidence-gathering techniques, would have a difficult time showing organized crime.

Third, proof of such a requirement, if it were limited to the private civil side, would create an anomalous result. The complaining witness in a criminal RICO prosecution would find himself saddled with an extra element not required of the government, one that he probably could not prove. He would be, therefore, a RICO victim in the criminal case, but would not be entitled to a RICO remedy in the civil suit. His recovery would be stymied by the additional element. No law ought to foster such results. Fourth, the requirement would be unprecedented in federal law. Congress has enacted a number of specific statutes since the 1930s designed to deal with aspects of the organized crime problem. Yet it has never limited those statutes in application to organized crime figures or organized crime groups. The Supreme Court in a number of decisions has refused to limit the statutes to organized crime or any similar designation, despite the motivation that might have led to the statutes' adoption.[22]

It also has been questioned whether or not RICO ought to contain equitable as well as legal relief for private plaintiffs. We believe that equitable relief for private plaintiffs is already authorized under law.[23] We believe that the equitable remedies provided in Section 1964(a) of 18 U.S.C. (1982) are essential to the realization of RICO's remedial goals. Those goals include the elimination of substantial profits and economic power bases obtained through corrupt practices. In light of these goals, equitable remedies are equally effective whether civil RICO actions are initiated by the United States or by private parties.

Section 1964(a) is directed at dismantling illicit and corrupted enterprises, forcing defendants to disgorge ill-gotten gains, and preventing defendants from using their unlawfully acquired economic power as leverage in the marketplace. No logical or principled reason exists to permit such equitable relief in U.S.-initiated civil RICO actions, but not in private-party suits. We can think of no reason why Congress in 1970—or now—would have circumscribed the federal courts' exercise of equitable powers.

Congressman Boucher's bill (H.R. 2943) would make private claims for relief under RICO subject to a criminal conviction limitation. That requirement was, of course, rejected by the Supreme Court under RICO in *Sedima*.[24] The committee should consider the issue, however, on its merits apart from the Supreme Court's decision. When the issue is examined on its merits, we believe that the conclusion is inescapable: a criminal conviction under criminal RICO or its predicate offenses ought not be a requirement for bringing a civil RICO claim.

RICO was, of course, modeled by its sponsors on the antitrust laws, which do not require proof of a criminal conviction to bring a civil action.[25] A prior criminal conviction requirement would unduly restrict access to the courts by those private attorneys general and would in effect discard the private attorney general function. We see no valid reason for applying a different rule under RICO. Such a change, some critics urge, is needed to prevent frivolous RICO suits and to keep the workload of the federal judiciary manageable. These two concerns have already been discussed. Neither is valid. Other substantial policy reasons exist that make the prior criminal conviction limitation unwise.

First, the requirement of a prior criminal conviction would drastically restrict the private plaintiff's access to the courts. This result is illustrated by considering the number of civil and criminal actions filed in federal court in the areas of antitrust and securities. As noted, in the antitrust areas, 1,200 civil actions are filed each year, while only 74 criminal cases are brought to court. Under securities and related laws, 3,000 civil actions are filed each year, while only 26 criminal actions are brought to court. Requiring a prior criminal conviction in either of these areas would castrate the civil remedies available under these statutes. A similar result would be obtained under RICO. Indeed, that is the not-too-well-hidden purpose of those who recommend the criminal conviction limitation. It would turn RICO's promise of remedial relief for victims of crime into a sham. Congress ought not be a party to that kind of legislative fraud.

Second, if this change was adopted, matters wholly unrelated to the merits of the plaintiff's RICO claim would determine who could recover, or even who could file a suit. When a federal prosecutor, for example, decides not to bring a RICO case, he would, therefore, completely foreclose any possibility for any RICO victim to have his day in court under RICO. A federal prosecutor might, for example, decide to grant a defendant immunity, or permit the defendant to plead to another offense, or agree to turn state's evidence. In that case, a civil plaintiff, either an individual, or a state or local unit of government, would be totally barred from recovery under RICO. Even more troubling would be a denial of access to the court where no conviction was obtained because of a procedural flaw at the grand jury stage or at the criminal trial not related to guilt or innocence.

Third, a prior RICO conviction requirement would prejudice the criminal justice system as a whole. By requiring a conviction on the RICO count, a defendant's incentive to plea bargain to a non-RICO offense would be dramatically raised. By avoiding a RICO conviction, the defendant would shield himself against all civil claims, leaving the victim without RICO recourse. Fourth, beyond its impact on a defendant's incentive to plea bargain and the credibility of witnesses, requiring a prior criminal conviction would place unwarranted political pressure on prosecutors, since the opportunity for a RICO victim to recover would depend on the institution and success of the government's case.

Congressman Boucher's bill also would provide for a statute of limitations for private claims for relief. RICO presently does not contain a statute of limitations. This lack has created a great diversity of results in the courts. We agree that Congress ought to act to provide greater guidance in this area. We suggest, however, that the statute of limitations for RICO should be modeled on antitrust law.

It has been suggested that RICO be limited by imposing a burden of proof higher than preponderance of the evidence. A call has been made, in the absence of requiring a prior RICO criminal conviction as a prerequisite to bringing a civil suit, to change the burden of proof by which the civil RICO plaintiff must establish his case. Some suggestions would raise the burden of the plaintiff's proof from a preponderance of the evidence, the civil standard, to "beyond a reasonable doubt," the criminal standard. Others advise a change in the proof of the predicate offenses to the criminal standard, while leaving the remainder of the plaintiff's case to be proved by a preponderance.

As noted before, RICO was modeled on antitrust statutes, which only require proof by a preponderance of the evidence.[27] We see no valid reason for imposing a higher burden on RICO. A majority of the state statutes that explicitly deal with the issue set the standard at a preponderance.

Civil RICO is explicitly remedial, not penal. As such, the preponderance standard should apply. When the purpose of a statute is penal, and life and liberty interests are at stake, then the proof required for the government to prevail must be beyond a reasonable doubt. When the interests in issue are primarily pecuniary, then the higher standard is not demanded, and the risk of error should be shared by the parties.

One challenge often made to the present burden of proof is based on the possibly stigmatizing effect of a RICO verdict. By changing the burden of proof, RICO critics hope to shift the "risk of opprobrium." This concern, however, is not enough to warrant the heightened standard. In analogous civil actions, which impute equally stigmatic labels as that of racketeer, the standard remains a preponderance of the evidence.

The Supreme Court in *Sedima* (105 S. Ct. at 3283) observed: "As for stigma, a civil RICO proceeding leaves no greater stain than do a number of other civil proceedings."[28] A major factor in enactment of the federal securities statutes was, in fact, a desire by Congress to correct deficiencies in the common law protections against fraud developed in the nineteenth century. The Supreme Court in *Herman* v. *MacLean* considered the applicable standard of proof in a private action under the Securities Exchange Act of 1934. Mindful that common law fraud under nineteenth century jurisprudence—with its emphasis on a philosophy of laissez faire—required a clear and convincing standard, the Court, nevertheless, labeled reference to common law practices, "misleading . . . since the historical considerations underlying the imposition of a higher standard of proof (has) questionable pertinence here." The Court found the preponderance of the evidence standard applicable in a Section 10(b) (5) case. This standard, the Court found, "allows both parties to 'share the risk of error in roughly equal fashion.' (cite omitted) Any other standard expresses a preference for one side's interests" (103 S. Ct. at 692) despite the "risk of opprobrium that may result from a finding of fraudulent conduct," not to express a preference for either side. This committee should not express a preference in favor of an alleged RICO perpetrator as opposed to an alleged RICO victim. How can Congress put its thumb on the scales of justice in favor of the perpetrator?

In conclusion, we express our firm support for all efforts to clarify or strengthen RICO and express our firm opposition to any effort to curtail or weaken it, particularly in the fraud area. Specifically, we oppose any effort:

1. to strike "racketeer" from RICO or to add an "organized crime" limitation to RICO;

2. to strike person from "pattern";

3. to limit "pattern" to acts within five years of the indictment;

4. to exclude criminal fraud from RICO, either directly, or indirectly, by the adoption of a "fraud plus" limitation;

5. to limit "pattern" by a common scheme requirement;

6. to add a criminal conviction limitation to RICO or to place an unreasonably short statute of limitation on RICO;

7. to limit civil recovery to competitive, investment, or business injury;

8. to make the burden of proof for private civil plaintiffs under RICO higher than preponderance of the evidence.

Specifically, we support any effort:

1. to clarify RICO to guarantee that private civil plaintiffs will be able to secure full equity relief;

2. to clarify RICO to make more specific the offenses incorporated in it and to add appropriate offenses to the statute, particularly in light of comprehensive recent congressional legislation.

In addition, we would support the adoption of:

1. an express claim for treble damage relief for the federal government;

2. the clarification of the provisions for attorneys fees, where suits are settled;

3. the addition of an appropriate statute of limitations;

4. the addition of an express right on the part of the attorney general to intervene in private civil RICO litigation.

Notes

Attorney J. Celebrezze, Jr., attorney general of Ohio, and Steven J. Twist, chief assistant attorney general of Arizona. Testimony before U.S. House Judiciary Subcommittee on Criminal Justice, October 9, 1985.

1. 18 U.S.C. S 1962 (1982).

2. See, for example, *Federal Deposit Insurance Corp.* v. *Hardin,* 608 F. Supp. 348 (N.D. Tenn. 1985) (bank fraud); *State of Okla. ex. rel. Department of Human Services* v. *Children's Shelter, Inc.,* 604 F. Supp. 867, 870–871 (W.D. Okla. 1985) (medicaid fraud); *Comm'n.* v. *Cianfrani,* 600 F. Supp. 1364, 1368–1369 (E.D. Pa. 1985) (treble damage award against state senator for "ghost" workers); *Anchorage* v. *Hitachi Cable Ltd.,* 547 F. Supp. 633 (D. Alaska 1982) (bribery of purchasing agent). At the state level, RICO has been most successfully implemented in Florida, Arizona, Oregon, and New Mexico.

3. Shad, John. "Why RICO Needs Reforming," *Fortune,* March 3, 1986, p. 109.

4. G. Tyler, ed. *Organized Crime in America* (Ann Arbor, Mich.: University of Michigan Press, 1962), pp. 181–182.

5. See *Task Force Report: Crime and Its Impact—An Assessment: Task Force on Assessment,* President's Commission on Law Enforcement and Administration of Justice, pp. 104–108 (1967). U.S. GPO #J-98-2.

6. Subcommittee on Crime, House Judiciary Comm., 95th Cong., 2d Sess., *White Collar Crime: The Problem and the Federal Response* 15 (Comm. Print 1978).

7. Committee on Government Operations, *Federal Response to Criminal Misconduct and Insider Abuse in the Nation's Financial Institutions,* H.R. Rep. No. 1137, 98th Cong., 2d Sess. at 5 (1984).

8. See *A Comprehensive Perspective on Civil and Criminal RICO Legislation and Litigation.* A report of the RICO Cases Committee, ABA, Criminal Justice Section, Washington, D.C., 1985.

9. 741 F. 2d 482, 487 (2d Cir. 1984).

10. *Sedima, S.P.R.L.* v. *Imrex Co., Inc.,* 102 S. Ct. 3275 (1985); *American National Bank and Trust Co. of Chicago* v. *Haroco, Inc.,* 105 S. Ct. 3291 (1985).

11. By adding to the settlement value of such valid claims in certain cases clearly involving criminal conduct, RICO may arguably promote more complete satisfaction of plaintiffs claims without facilitating indefensible windfalls. In fact, if suits are settled at too low a figure, the deterrent impact of the damage claim will be undermined.

12. John E. Conklin, *Illegal But Not Criminal: Business Crime in America* (Englewood Cliffs, N.J.: Spectrum Books, Prentice-Hall, 1977), p. 129.

13. Senate Comm. on Governmental Affairs, *Commodity Investment Fraud,* S. Rep. No. 97-495, 97th Cong., 2d Sess. 10 (1983).

14. *United States* v. *Topco Associates, Inc.,* 405 U.S. 596, 610 (1972).

15. C. Kaysen and D.F. Turner, *Anti-Trust Policy: An Economic and Legal Analysis* (Cambridge, Mass.: Harvard University Press, 1959), p. 17.

16. *Zauderer* v. *Office of Disciplinary Counsel of the Supreme Court of Ohio,* 105 S. Ct. 2265, 2278 (1985).

17. *Blue Shield of Virginia* v. *McCready,* 457 U.S. 465, 472 (1982).

18. *Leh* v. *General Petroleum Corp.,* 382 U.S. 54, 59 (1965).

19. *Reiter* v. *Sonotone Corp.,* 442 U.S. 330, 344 (1979) (emphasis in original).

20. Ibid.

21. H. Edelhertz, *The Nature, Impact, and Prosecution of White Collar Crime* (Washington, D.C.: National Institute of Justice, 1970), pp. 6–9.

22. The Supreme Court in *Sedima* specifically held that RICO applies to " 'any person'—not just mobsters." We see no reason to depart from that ruling.

23. Professor Johnson's able piece, "Predators Rights: Multiple Remedies for Wall Street Sharks and the Securities Laws and RICO," *Journal of Corp. Law* **10**:3 (1984). See also, "The Availability of Equitable Relief in Civil Cause of Action in RICO," *Notre Dame Law Rev.* **59**:945 (1984).

24. *Sedima, S.P.R.L.* v. *Imrex Co., Inc.,* 102 S. Ct. 3275 (1985); *American National Bank and Trust Co. of Chicago* v. *Haroco, Inc.,* 105 S. Ct. 3291 (1985).

25. *Standard Sanitary Mfg.* v. *United States,* 226 U.S. 20, 52 (1912). (A conviction would "take from the statute a great deal of its power.")

26. *Ramsey* v. *UMW,* 401 U.S. 302, 307–311 (1971).

27. *Sedima, S.P.R.L.* v. *Imrex Co., Inc.,* 102 S. Ct. 3275 (1985); *American National Bank and Trust Co. of Chicago* v. *Haroco, Inc.,* 105 S. Ct. 3291 (1985).

Appendix A:
The Racketeer Influenced and Corrupt Organizations Statute

WHEREAS, Congress enacted in 1970 the Racketeer Influenced and Corrupt Organization provisions (Title IX) of the Organized Crime Control Act; and

WHEREAS, Title IX is applicable to patterns of racketeering activity involving:

1. personal violence;
2. provision of illegal goods and services;
3. corruption in private or public life; and
4. various forms of fraud; and

WHEREAS, Title IX provides important new criminal and civil sanctions to protect victims of patterns of racketeering activity, including:

1. criminal forfeiture of proceeds of racketeering activity;
2. criminal forfeiture of interests in enterprises;
3. equitable relief for the government;
4. equitable relief for victims of racketeering activity; and
5. treble damages, costs, and attorney's fees for victims of racketeering activity; and

WHEREAS, twenty-two states have enacted legislation patterned after Title IX; and

WHEREAS, other states are actively considering the passage of legislation patterned after Title IX; and

WHEREAS, states and local units of government have begun to make effective use of Title IX and state legislation patterned after it; and

WHEREAS, Title IX provides important new sanctions in the area of fraud against state and local units of government; and

WHEREAS, fraud against state and local government has a multi-billion dollar annual import; and

WHEREAS, state and local units of government have found that Title IX and state legislation patterned after it are effective and essential means of redressing wrongs;

NOW, THEREFORE, BE IT RESOLVED, that the National Association of Attorneys General supports efforts by states to enact legislation patterned after Title IX and to strengthen the criminal and civil provisions of Title IX, particularly in their application to public and private civil sanctions in the area of fraud against the government; and

BE IT FURTHER RESOLVED, that the National Association of Attorneys General opposes efforts to repeal or modify, in whole or in part, the provisions of Title IX, particularly in their application to public and private civil sanctions in the area of fraud against the government; and

BE IT FURTHER RESOLVED, that the Executive Director and General Counsel of the National Association of Attorneys General is authorized to transmit this Resolution to appropriate committees of Congress, the Administration, and other appropriate individuals and associations.

Appendix B:
The Racketeer Influenced and
Corrupt Organizations Statute

WHEREAS, Congress enacted in 1970 the Racketeer Influenced and Corrupt Organization provisions (Title IX) of the Organized Crime Control Act; and

WHEREAS, Title IX is applicable to patterns of racketeering activity involving:

1. personal violence;
2. provision of illegal goods and services;
3. corruption in private or public life; and
4. various forms of fraud; and

WHEREAS, Title IX provides important new criminal and civil sanctions to protect victims of patterns of racketeering activity, including:

1. criminal forfeiture of proceeds of racketeering activity;
2. criminal forfeiture of interests in enterprises;
3. equitable relief for the government;
4. equitable relief for victims of racketeering activity; and
5. treble damages, costs, and attorney's fees for victims of racketeering activity; and

WHEREAS, twenty-two states have enacted legislation patterned after Title IX; and

WHEREAS, other states are actively considering the passage of legislation patterned after Title IX; and

WHEREAS, states and local units of government have begun to make effective use of Title IX and state legislation patterned after it; and

WHEREAS, Title IX provides important new sanctions in the area of fraud against state and local units of government; and

WHEREAS, fraud against state and local government has a multi-billion dollar annual import; and

WHEREAS, state and local units of government have found that Title IX and state legislation patterned after it are effective and essential means of redressing wrongs;

NOW, THEREFORE, BE IT RESOLVED, that the National District Attorneys Association supports efforts by states to enact legislation patterned after Title IX and to strengthen the criminal and civil provisions of Title IX, particularly in their application to public and private civil sanctions in the area of fraud against the government; and

BE IT FURTHER RESOLVED, that the National District Attorneys Association opposes efforts to repeal or modify, in whole or in part, the provisions of Title IX, particularly in their application to public and private civil sanctions in the area of fraud against the government; and

BE IT FURTHER RESOLVED, that the Executive Director and General Counsel of the National District Attorneys Association are authorized to transmit this Resolution to appropriate committees of Congress, the Administration, and other appropriate individuals and associations.

Appendix C:
Defense Contractors under Investigation by the Pentagon and the Allegations Involved

1. McDonnell Douglas Corporation, cost mischarging.
2. Rockwell International Corporation, cost and labor mischarging.
3. General Dynamics Corporation, cost mischarging, subcontractor kickbacks, labor mischarging, product substitution, security compromise, defective pricing, cost duplication, false claims.
4. Lockheed Corporation, labor mischarging.
5. Boeing Company, cost mischarging, supply accountability, labor mischarging.
6. General Electric Company, false claims, defective pricing, labor-cost mischarging, product substitution.
7. United Technologies Corporation, gratuities, subcontractor kickbacks, cost mischarging, bribery, defective pricing.
8. Raytheon Company, labor mischarging, product substitution.
9. Litton Industries, bribery and subcontractors kickbacks, labor mischarging, false claims, bid-rigging, cost mischarging.
10. Grumman Corporation, cost mischarging.
11. Martin Marietta Corporation, subcontractor kickbacks, cost mischarging.
12. Westinghouse Electric Corporation, cost mischarging.
13. Sperry Corporation, labor mischarging, cost mischarging, defective pricing.
14. Honeywell, Inc., diversion of government property, bid rigging.
15. Ford Motor Company, defective pricing, labor mischarging, falsification of performance records.
16. Eaton Corporation, conflict-of-interest gratuities, cost mischarging.
17. TRW, Inc., defective pricing, cost mischarging.
18. Texas Instrument, Inc., product substitution.
19. Northrop Corporation, labor mischarging, false progress payments.

20. Avco Corporation, subcontractor kickbacks, cost mischarging.

21. Textron, Inc., cost mischarging.

22. Allied Corporation, conflict of interest.

23. Tenneco, Inc., cost mischarging.

24. GTE Corporation, unauthorized acquisition and utilization of classified data, labor mischarging.

25. Sanders Associates, Inc., unauthorized release of contract information.

26. Motorola, Inc., labor mischarging.

27. Congoleum Corporation, mischarging, gratuities theft.

28. Harris Corporation, defective pricing.

29. Gould, Inc., cost mischarging.

30. Emerson Electric Company, cost mischarging, gratuities cost mischarging.

31. Johns Hopkins University, civilian health and medical program of the uniformed services fraud.

32. Tracor, Inc., product substitution.

33. Lear Siegler, Inc., product substitution.

34. Fairchild Industries, gratuities, production substitution, cost mischarging, false statements.

35. Dynalectron Corporation, cost mischarging.

36. Todd Shipyard Corporation, noncompliance with contract.

Note: The names of the remaining nine defense firms under investigation were not released because they had not been informed of the investigation. *New York Times,* June 22, 1985, p. 25.

9
Corporate Political Involvement

Corporate Political Activism
S. Prakash Sethi

Political involvement can be broadly defined as participation in the formulation and execution of public policy at various levels of government. It has been and must always be a necessary and important activity for any private interest group in our pluralistic society. To the extent that the locus of the public policy agenda—the decisions about the future shape of society and the role of the private sector in that future—shifts from the marketplace to the political arena, it is imperative that corporations increase their political involvement. They can thus insure that public policy choices are influenced by the views of the private sector in general and by the corporate sector in particular.

Political involvement and political power are inextricably linked. Therefore, where political participation might be viewed by one group as a positive act in a democratic system, another group might construe such participation as abuse of power and an attempt to subvert democratic processes. A survey of business people might show a greater desire for political activism, whereas public opinion polls show a desire on the part of the public for business to be politically less active. The issue is not whether business should or should not be politically involved but what the nature and objective of such involvement should be. The paramount issue is that of legitimacy or societal acceptance of corporate political actions and their underlying motives.

Challenge of the Eighties

The sociopolitical environment in the United States and the Western world is poised for a significant change in the 1980s. There is a precipitous shift in public sentiment toward conservatism in political philosophy, an aversion to reliance on government to solve every real and imagined social problem, and a growing willingness to accept the discipline of the marketplace in developing social choices and in allocating the nation's physical and human resources. The 1980s offer the corporate community a tremendous opportunity to take public positions on current social, political, and economic issues and to play an active role in the formulation and implementation of the national agenda and public choices.

This opportunity carries with it an equally enormous responsibility. The current antigovernment public sentiment is not necessarily pro business or pro big business. The public distrust of big business and business leaders is not any less than its distrust of government bureaucracies and political leaders. The style and substance of corporate political involvement and the contributions of business to the public interest will largely determine the degree of public acceptance of the corporation as a political participant and whether or not the corporation becomes a positive influence for social change. Failure to accept this challenge will leave the corporation a beleaguered giant constantly fighting elusive enemies to protect its natural turf but gradually giving way before changing social tides.

The purpose of this article is to describe briefly a conceptual approach by which corporations may engage in political activities and some of the consequences that might ensue. My goal is to demonstrate that political involvement should ideally be developed in terms of strategic choices to meet carefully defined policy objectives. Positive political activism carries with it certain risks that must be evaluated before selecting among the various strategies. Certain strategies of political intervention may yield short-run gains but may have serious, adverse, long-term consequences.

Environmental Factors

Development of meaningful corporate political strategies must take into account three environmental factors.

Past Corporate Activities

Historical antecedents provide a set of criteria against which current business practices, both political and nonpolitical, are likely to be evaluated by the body politic. Past corporate abuses color the public's judgment of current corporate motives and create a perceptual stranglehold on the public's acceptance of a legitimate corporate role in the public policy process. Corporate efforts to change these perceptions will require an enormous expenditure of resources in terms of positive reinforcement and public education. Any inconsistencies in current corporate behavior and rhetoric, or the perception that the corporation is not acting in the public interest, will have a disproportionate impact on the future political role of the corporation and reinforce the negative perceptions created in the past.

Current Corporate Environment

Today's problems create pressures for devoting corporate resources to short-term business and political objectives. However, an astute, timely political strategy is typified by a "good fit" between a corporation's business objectives, its political objectives, its internal skills and capabilities to operate effectively in the political arena, and its leadership role and management style in recognizing and responding to societal issues and to the external political environment it confronts. A careful analysis of current societal needs and responses can provide a learning curve in which the potential impact of various long-term business and political strategies can be simulated and evaluated.

Future Environment

The greatest challenge facing corporations is an understanding of the societal needs of the future in developing political as well as business strategies. It would be a grievous error to extrapolate the future as if it were simply an extension of current conditions and the recent past. In a constantly changing society, such an approach will leave the corporation in an untenable position. To an extent, this future environment is influenced by current corporate activities and those of other private sector groups (economic and noneconomic). Accordingly, the synergistic effect of the confluence of the political activities of these groups is hard to predict. Thus, a strategy that is implemented by a defensive or reactive response is not likely to be effective as one enforced by a set of normative goals of what should be the nature of our society in the future and how we might achieve it.

The essence of corporate political activism is for the corporation to develop a cogent view of the public interest and, then, political positions and strategies that embody this notion. The rationale for business's developing a positive notion of the public interest is best described by Paul Weaver.[1] He states that what business needs is to develop the ability to take positions that embody a clear notion of the public interest and to employ language in stating a public position that is perceived by the public as embodying such a notion. Weaver contends that what business lacks is not only a position but the habits of thinking and talking about the ways in which companies and products contribute to our way of life and help people to realize their personal objectives.

Business people cannot participate effectively in the political process until they can articulate who and what they are socially, what role their products and services play culturally, and what difference it really all makes. This demands positive political strategies, not ad hoc responses to immediate crises. Then the public interest will not be in conflict with the corporate interest. But the corporate interest must emanate from the public interest and cannot be inconsistent with it. The public interest must not be perceived, prescribed, or acted on by the corporate community as if it were the secondary effect of corporate actions whose degree and magnitude depend on the extent to which corporate self-interest can conveniently accommodate the general interests of society.

A Schematic Framework

Public policy is formulated through elected representatives who pass laws and through regulatory and administrative agencies that promulgate rules and regulations to interpret and enforce those laws. Private groups influence the public policy process through their electoral activities and intervention and pleadings before the regulatory bodies. Corporate political activism could be analyzed within the context of three stages. Contained within each stage are proposed or hypothesized external environmental and internal corporate conditions and anticipated political risks.

Stage I: The Defensive Mode

The corporation perceives its objectives to be totally legitimate, considers anyone opposing those objectives to be an adversary, and generally operates by itself in the political arena. The primary corporate goal is to maintain the status quo in terms of political climate, legislative makeup, and regulatory environment. The strategies of implementation are essentially ad hoc, contextual, proscriptive, and reactive. The external or environmental conditions conducive to the defensive mode include:

An apathetic and relatively uninformed voting populace;

A hierarchical leadership in legislative bodies with leaders exercising great power and in which incumbency is very important;

Voting based on party lines and loyalty to individual candidates;

A regulatory process subservient to the elected political leadership, highly legalistic in deliberations and rule-making processes, and susceptible to high-powered lobbying;

Succession to elective positions primarily through the political party hierarchy; and

Nontraditional political challengers who are relatively unknown and who have no broad-based public support and little prior media exposure.

Working hypotheses suggest that the internal corporate conditions that provide the impetus for a defensive political posture are these:

The corporation is part of an industry that is old and relatively noncompetitive. It has a long and proud tradition and has set ways of doing things.

The corporation has a large asset base and a dominant market position in a given industry or geographical region.

Corporate leadership has a significant amount of discretionary funds—from political action committees or individuals—that can be used for political campaign funding.

The corporation has an autocratic or strong-willed chief executive officer with long tenure in office. Succession to top management is primarily from within the corporate hierarchy.

Corporate products and services are sensitive to economic cycles or adversely affect the physical environment. The company may have a monopoly or near monopoly in the marketplace.

There is a lack of emphasis on long-range or strategic planning. Growth is more dependent on market size (geographical expansion or acquisition) than on new products and research and development.

Unforeseen and unpredictable emergencies require strong, immediate action. A crisis, such as the accident at the Three Mile Island nuclear facility or the phenomenal increase in the number of imported cars, so threatens corporate survival that all long-run considerations or ideological beliefs must be suspended to achieve short-run goals and avert an immediate crisis.

The conceptual model further suggests that the political risks for the corporation for staying in the defensive mode are these:

Different corporate political activities may be mutually inconsistent, may give contradictory signals to other groups, and may have little or no long-term payoffs.

Exclusive dependence on key elected officials for achieving corporate goals may leave the corporation exposed to future risks should there be a change in the political fortunes of these officials.

Excessive direct lobbying of legislative committees and regulatory bodies may make the corporation appear as a manipulator and a power broker in the public's eyes.

Other groups will be less willing to give in to corporate interests when their influence increases in political organizations.

Too many crises indicate lack of planning.

The general public has little awareness and understanding of a corporation's position and rationale on various political issues. This leads to low public credibility and denies the corporation a broad base of public support regardless of the legitimacy of its position on a given issue.

Stage II: The Accommodative Mode

The corporation perceives the achievement of its political objectives as dependent on its ability to co-opt other groups to its viewpoint and is thus willing to notify, to a limited extent, its corporate objectives in furtherance of coalition or industry-wide goals. Temporary compromises and coalitions are the norm rather than the exception. They involve bringing corporate behavior into congruence with currently prevailing societal norms, values, and performance expectations, particularly those of sympathetic groups or institutions. The accommodative mode does not require a radical departure from traditional political goals and strategies. It is simply more responsive and adaptive to a changing political structure that would bring constraints if the corporation did not alter its traditional response. Thus, this response mode is prescriptive and conciliatory. The external or environmental conditions conducive to the accommodative mode generally include the following characteristics:

There is a constantly growing number of voters, diluting the potential impact of each individual vote. (There is increasing voter apathy toward electoral participation.)

There is a phenomenal increase in the cost of reaching potential voters and persuading them to vote.

A situation arises in which issues become more complex, explanations more obtuse, and decisions more difficult. When confronted with difficult choices and the declining influence of the individual vote, voters are more likely to remain "rationally ignorant," to refuse to weigh issues carefully and instead to rely on superficial impressions received through the media. Voter sentiment records constant changes in opinion polls based on contrived political events, and the election of candidates depends more on advertising campaigns than on the quality of the programs offered.

Elections are decided by a minority of voters (a 40 percent turnout would mean that 21 percent of all eligible voters could determine the outcome of an issue). Those who vote are generally organized around a single or a few selected issues and are not concerned with the broad social agenda. Voter sentiment differs from general public sentiment on a given issue, such as gun control. Group coalitions and accommodations are important.

There is a fragmented political party structure with weak leadership control. Reelection is more dependent on serving a narrow constituency than on loyalty to the party's agenda.

Legislative and regulatory processes are more open and subject to public scrutiny.

There is a mass media, especially the electronic media, with a voracious appetite for news and events. Minor incidents, human errors, or instances of poor judgment escalate into national scandals with high emotional content.

A large number of special interest groups and social activists exploit the mass media for their own purposes and influence public opinion.

Positions of power in legislative bodies and regulatory agencies are acquired by social activists, who make these bodies into adversaries of business rather than impartial regulators working in the public interest.

There is growth in the number of single-issue public interest groups that maintain excellent surveillance of corporate activities and thereby reduce a corporation's flexibility to undertake programs and activities without undue external pressure.

The internal corporate conditions that provide an impetus for an accommodative political posture are these:

The corporation is of more recent origin and has not yet settled into a relatively stable, noncompetitive market environment. It is still in the process of establishing its managerial systems and organizational structure and is thus prepared to make minor modifications in its way of doing business.

The corporation has not yet established a large asset base and dominant market position in a given industry, geographic location, or product market.

While the corporation may have a strong leader at the helm, professional management is being recruited from outside the organization, and tenure within the organization is no longer a guarantee of promotion to the top ranks of the organization.

Management is more sensitive to social issues and public interest groups. It has been the target of such groups or public concern about the gap between corporate and public interests and found that adversarial confrontation is not always the most effective and successful way of responding to society's needs.

The corporation has become sensitive to the need for strategic planning. It has begun to plan on the functional or business level but has not yet engaged in long-range corporate planning at top management levels. There is a growing management concern about crisis management of social issues and demand for greater use of planning concepts in responding to social needs.

The political risks for the corporation for staying in the accommodative mode are less severe than those in the defensive mode. In many cases, it is more a a question of degree than substance. For example:

Different corporate political activities and positions may be mutually inconsistent, leading to a loss in long-run payoff in terms of building a loyal constituency for the corporate position.

The corporation may form coalitions with groups who enjoy short-term, but not long-term, public acceptance as acting in the public interest and thereby risk being labeled as opportunistic and losing its public credibility.

The connection between support for various political positions and immediate corporate interests may be less direct and obvious, making such programs difficult to sell to senior management and operating managers.

Corporations may exploit the "rationally ignorant" voter by launching mass media campaigns where issues are peddled like bars of soap in jingles and slogans in thirty-second commercials. While this technique may win an immediate campaign, in the long run it increases voter alienation and thus the power of single-purpose groups.

Stage III: Positive Activism

The process of adaptation is only partially served if corporations develop their political strategies in response to external factors and other groups. While this mode improves the congruence between corporate strategies and societal expectations, much more is called for. The issue in terms of the positive activism mode is not how corporations respond to external pressures but what role they play in the initiation and development of a national agenda and in the public policy process. In this mode, corporations become active in leading political change rather than responding to it. Political activism calls for the exercise of power in a manner that is in congruence with a normative and publicly defensible notion of public power. This mode is proactive in character; that is, corporate political programs anticipate the shape of things to come and develop strategies to increase the probability of the occurrence of socially desirable outcomes and prevent undesirable outcomes. The external or environmental conditions conducive to the positive activism mode are these:

> a growing public acceptance of the legitimacy of corporate political activism based on responsible exercise of corporate power in the accommodative phase;

> increased trust in corporations and their leaders, thereby allowing corporations greater discretion in undertaking programs and activities, and more activities under the scope of self-regulation;

> an increasingly informed public less swayed by demagoguery of either the left or the right;

> an open environment of public debate and communication where corporate leaders are willing to disagree publicly with each other as to what is best for society and are willing to speak out against positions advocated by other groups;

> other external conditions that are the same as those in the accommodative mode.

The internal corporate conditions that provide impetus for a positive activism mode are these:

> The corporation is part of an industry that is growing, has a high technology base, and is competitive in the marketplace.

> The corporation is quite profitable, innovative, and aggressive, with global markets and international orientation.

Management is professional and seasoned, not young and impetuous. The top executive is decisive, has control of the organization, is respected by other managers for ability and competence rather than feared for an authoritarian management style.

Management views the corporate role in the broader sense of serving society's needs and recognizes the political interests and power of other groups in a democratic society.

Long-range planning and environmental analysis are an integral part of the corporate decision-making process.

Top management seeks to build a broader public constituency for its activities, is interested in projecting the corporation as a responsible citizen, and is willing to carry its share of responsibility in solving society's problems.

Management encourages internal dialogue and discussion before settling on political choices and strategies.

The political risks for the corporation in the positive activism mode are these:

A corporation may become too wedded to a given public agenda, particularly one that it initiated and helped to develop, and may be reluctant to change its position when such a change is called for. This risk is not different from the one a corporation faces when it stays tied to a particular product line or market strategy with which it is associated long after it has outlived its usefulness.

Cost and benefits are more widely separated, thereby making rational analysis of alternative strategies difficult. Such a situation sometimes provides a strong executive with an opportunity to commit the corporation to his or her vision of the public interest, which may not stand rigorous analysis and debate.

All other risks are similar to those in the accommodative mode.

The political activities a corporation can undertake are classified in four categories: campaign financing, direct lobbying, coalition building, and indirect lobbying and advocacy advertising. Table 1 briefly summarizes the form such activities are likely to take under the three behavioral modes.

Guides for Corporate Action

In today's pluralistic society, political participation is not a luxury but a necessity, and must receive top management attention and corporate resources to do it right and do it well. The cost of being wrong can be very high. However, political

Table 1
A Three-Stage Schema for Classifying Corporate Political Activities

Type of Political Activity	Modes of Corporate Behavior		
	Defensive Mode	*Accommodative Mode*	*Positive Activism Mode*
Campaign financing	Incumbent legislators in key decision-making positions with direct impact on corporate interests; little consideration to political party, philosophy, principles, long-term legislative goals	Support of candidates and challengers with compatible political philosophy and legislative programs; short-run or direct corporate interests important but not dominant considerations	Support or active opposition of candidates, even at the cost of short-run corporate interests, on the basis of a normative concept of public interest and policy agenda supported by the corporation
Lobbying	Informal and secretive lobbying of key legislators to support legislation considered beneficial to the corporation; use of professional lobbyists, generally former legislators or bureaucrats; locus of activity primarily in Washington and state capitals; senior management with low visibility	Emphasis on participatory approach and industrywide solutions; emphasis on professional management with public affairs/public relations background; strong support staff in corporate headquarters; greater public visibility of senior management; public posture as responsible corporate citizen and corporate statesman; use of social issues management concepts to identify with and respond to groups and issues that might adversely affect business interests	Direct lobbying aimed at broad programs and policies based on a cogent notion of the public agenda; issues transcending immediate corporate and even business interests; where compatible with normative and positive notions of public interest, support of legislative programs opposed by other business and industry groups; highly visible senior management, speaking out on public issues and offering advice and assistance to executive and legislative branches

Coalition building	Resistance to any accommodation to other groups' viewpoints or interests; community affairs activities and corporate contributions that are primarily for conventional, noncontroversial programs, highly diffused but centered in regions or locations with corporate plants or significant activities	Support of business-oriented interest groups; where necessary and imperative, temporary coalitions set up with erstwhile opponents to develop broader support for specific programs; community affairs and contributions activities with a discretionary element; new programs and groups supported on the basis of perceived need and corporate expertise	Development of new groups and support of existing groups to develop broad coalitions in support of a national policy agenda; when necessary, taking stands that may not be of short-term benefit to the organization but which have future long-term advantages; community affairs and contributions activities forming an integral part of the overall corporate approach to social issues management; emphasis on the development of third sector as bulwark against increasing government encroachment in the social arena; programs with a future orientation, with emphasis on identifying special areas of need and making maximum impact through early start and research and development
Indirect lobbying (grassroots lobbying through mass media aimed at large segments of population or members of specific groups)	Little use of indirect lobbying; advocacy advertising, when used, projects sponsor as self-righteous, defends corporation's position, or attacks not only opponent's positions but also its motives	Grassroots lobbying to specific groups sympathetic to corporate interests (stockholders, employees, pensioners); stockholder management and environmental scanning integral parts of public affairs management; extensive use of mass media to advocate public acceptance of corporate positions by projecting them to be in the public interest	Active use of mass media and special corporate publications; external communications to improve the quality and quantity of information available to the general public on complex social issues; public education in addition to advocacy of specific policies and programs

participation simply to defend a corporate position on a given social issue, to support a candidate considered friendly to the firm, or to sell the free enterprise system is not sufficient. Effective political participation demands the advancement of a coherent political position, something most business people do not have today. What they offer are positions in support of immediate, short-term commercial interests. Take the case of the automotive industry. On one hand, there is a call for less government intervention in the name of highway safety and environmental protection. On the other hand, there are requests for government loans to shore up a failing corporation and for protectionist import quotas to isolate the U.S. automotive industry from foreign competition. It adds up to a giant contradiction that destroys public credibility in the allegiance of the business community to free enterprise concepts.

A good example of business advocating its position in terms of the public interest is the policy positions taken by the drug industry on the so-called thalidomide amendments to the Food, Drug, and Cosmetic Act. Manufacturers are required to prove the efficacy of new drugs and to evaluate adverse side effects through exhaustive, time-consuming, and costly tests before marketing them. The industry contends that overzealous implementation of the law discourages drug development and prevents the use of some drugs by patients who would benefit from them. While the amendments have been costly to the industry, a growing body of studies indicates that the amendments have caused more deaths than saved lives by preventing or delaying the approval of a number of drugs now in use in other countries. The drug industry has drawn on these findings to define its public policy position and done so in terms of the public's interest in improving health care rather than in terms of its private interest in avoiding government regulation. Presumably, it is at least as strongly motivated by the latter as by the former, but the industry has been successful in stating its position in terms of the public interest and as a bona fide effort to address public needs.

This is not to suggest that the defensive mode of political participation may not be advisable in specific circumstances in which the firm is faced with an immediate legislative proposal that may have adverse effects upon the firm with little, if any, long-term benefits to the firm or to the public. Nor does it mean that accommodation with opposing interest groups may not be politically desirable, as illustrated by the current joint efforts of business and consumer activists to prevent further legislative curtailment of their lobbying activities at the federal level. What it does mean is that there is a need to develop a series of step-by-step strategies designed to let corporations participate in the political arena in a positive active mode.

A corporation desiring a successful political action program must take a number of preliminary steps and develop some essential mechanisms before it can determine the appropriate mode of behavior or the political activities that would be most appropriate.

Step one: corporations need an effective environmental scanning process designed to identify the scope and magnitude of the social problems as well as the nature, extent and source of the societal pressures confronting the corporation—an early warning system, using both inside and outside experts, to identify and monitor trends and emerging issues and to alert the corporation to present and potential problems in the social area.

Step two: corporations need a communications network programmed to disseminate the data developed by the early warning system to appropriate individuals and organizational units within the corporation who have the authority to respond in a meaningful manner consistent with corporate and public interests.

Step three: corporations need an internal organizational structure and decision-making processes that will develop relevant and effective responses to these external societal pressures and problems. Such responses must be proactive rather than reactive and designed to present the corporate position in a manner that embodies the notion of the public interest.

The suggestions for strategies presented below are organized into the four classifications of corporate political activities: campaign financing, direct lobbying, coalition building, and indirect lobbying (grassroots lobbying and advocacy advertising).

Campaign Financing

Financing of candidates for public office is the form of political participation most familiar to corporations. It is a time-honored method of influencing the formulation and implementation of public policy. It is also a mechanism for political participation that has been grossly abused in the past and that has destroyed public acceptance of the corporation as a political participant and resulted in extensive federal control of campaign financing. Political Action Committees (PACs) are now the mechanism by which corporations can channel monies to candidates for public office. Shortly after the passage of the Federal Campaign Act of 1971, corporate PACs followed their traditional patterns of campaign contributions by largely financing incumbents holding key legislative positions regardless of party affiliation or political philosophy—the defensive mode. More recently, some PACs have adopted the accommodation mode and have shown a willingness to give support to challengers who are perceived as more supportive of the values associated with the free enterprise system and to take the risk of offending an incumbent legislator who, if reelected, might act in a manner contrary to the best interests of the corporation.

Of greater significance is the movement toward positive political activism by using the legislative distinction between contributions and expenditures, a distinction that received constitutional blessing from the U.S. Supreme Court in *Valeo Rom v. Buckley*. There is a growing trend for PACs to advertise their stand on public policy issues or for candidates through the expenditure route rather than make a contribution to a candidate or party without further thought as to how that money is spent, what message is publicized, or whether the policy position as advertised is consistent with that of the corporation.

There is a danger, however, that PAC expenditures will be used primarily to avoid the legal constraints imposed on the amounts of money a PAC can contribute to a given candidate or party rather than to enhance the public debate on issues and candidates. If PAC expenditures are utilized to support the corporate position on issues and candidates that embody a notion of the public interest, then the public policy process can be enhanced and the vitality of the nation's social, political, and economic systems can be safeguarded. If expenditures by PACs are viewed as a means of selling a corporate viewpoint and not of improving the quality of public information through an intelligent discussion of issues, public acceptance of a corporate role in the political arena will be limited and largely adversarial in nature.

The PAC mechanism also can be used as a device for developing a corporate public policy position. There is a strong indication that many PACs are run by and for the benefit of a few top officers. Yet evidence is developing that many lower-echelon personnel, frustrated with the current political process, have renewed their interest in the political system through participation in PAC activities. By broadening PAC membership to include all individuals eligible to join, including the biannual solicitation of employees permitted by law, rather than limiting PAC membership to a few top officers, the PAC can become a means of developing a public policy position on social issues that will embody a notion of the public interest as viewed by the corporate constituency as a whole rather than by a few key corporate officers who may or may not be speaking for their employees or the shareholders.

Lobbying

Business people have historically concentrated their political activities on lobbying and have achieved their most notable successes with this form of political action. But until recently, lobbying was in the defensive mode, limited to informal and secretive lobbying of key legislators using professional lobbyists who were former legislators or government officials. The democratization of the political parties, the growing independence of legislators, and the constant turnover in government officials has made this lobbying mode somewhat obsolete. Corporations are increasingly turning to an industry approach. The Business Roundtable is an excellent example of the accommodative mode. Senior management, working together, have been successful in defeating the establishment of another government agency, the proposed Consumer Protection Agency, and in turning aside legislation that might strengthen the union movement. The growth of public affairs professionals is illustrative of the greater involvement of corporations in public policy issues in the prescriptive and conciliatory mode.

The current trend is toward direct lobbying, supported by grassroots lobbying, utilizing corporate personnel who can put forward an intelligent case on a complex issue, are comfortable in shirt-sleeve sessions with senatorial staffs, are prepared to answer rapid-fire questions from Capitol Hill and corporate headquarters, and can ensure that important information gets to the right people at the right time. As one long-time Washington lobbyist has observed, "My job used to be booze, broads, and golf at Burning Tree. Now it is organizing coalitions and keeping information flowing."[2]

Coalition Building

In the past, corporations resisted the accommodation of any views in opposition to those held by a few key officials. Support of external organizations and groups tended to be for noncontroversial activities and centered largely in geographical areas where the corporation was doing business. But as the Washington lobbyist observed, organizing coalitions has now become a new political way of life. The success of such coalition building can be seen in recent business campaigns against measures to authorize common-situs picketing, establish a consumer protection agency, and expand union power through labor law reform. Such success has not been without its costs. Persuaded that corporate efforts to rouse public opinion helped tilt the voting on these and other issues, some legislators are trying to stifle corporate efforts to influence public policy. Their success may depend, in large part, on whether corporate coalition building is viewed as a prescriptive response to a societal problem. Moreover, it should be undertaken as a constructive approach toward accomplishing a goal rather than a naked power play to deprive other groups of the possibility of developing reasonable compromises. The corporation should be viewed as ready and willing to develop broad coalitions in support of a national policy agenda, including working with interest groups that may not be business oriented.

Indirect Lobbying

This is one area where the corporations can have a maximum impact but so far have not done so. Unions early recognized the value of being directly involved in the electoral process and pioneered many of the grassroots lobbying techniques now used by corporations. This is changing, however. Businesses are making greater use of the Government Key Contact program and the Congressional District Identification System. The former utilizes selected individuals within the company to serve as a communication link with public officials with whom the company needs or chooses to communicate. This individual not only has a grasp of company operations and a sense of the political process, but works or lives in the district of the legislator who is to be contacted. The Congressional District Identification System is a computerized approach to organizing and targeting constituents and legislators according to defined political units. Indirect lobbying is done in political units where the corporation has its greatest constituency, statistical strength, or presence. Both techniques are a practical response to the growing sensitivity of legislators to their constituencies. As one lobbyist noted, he increasingly hears members of Congress say, "Yes, I hear you, professional lobbyist, but what do the folks back home say?"[3] Grassroots lobbying is a response to the realization by interest groups that public opinion has a greater influence over most policymakers in the post-Watergate era. More important, members of Congress appear to be more responsive to the demands of their constituencies than to the wishes of party or congressional leaders.

In establishing grassroots lobbying programs, the literature emphasizes techniques—how to reach as many people as possible in the most cost-effective manner. There is little concern about the message content or whether the utilization of external communications will further the public policy position adopted by the corporation. One can anticipate public rejection of grassroots lobbying and further efforts by corporate critics to silence the business community if grassroots lobbying is viewed from the narrow perspective of means rather than as an end that will further public debate on issues and candidates.

Advocacy advertising is another facet of indirect lobbying, and it has raised important questions of public policy and corporate strategy that have generated controversy and debate.[4] Advocacy advertising is a double-edged instrument. When properly employed it can contribute to a greater understanding on the part of the public of what can be reasonably expected of corporations in meeting societal expectations. When employed as a substitute for positive corporate action, it can lead to greater public hostility and a demand for further governmental control of management processes.

Advocacy advertising should be an integral part of the total corporate communication program and designed to communicate the firm's public policy positions. This communication must bear a close relationship to the activities of the corporation, the vision of society and its role that the corporation wishes to project, and societal expectations regarding corporate performance. Too often, advocacy advertising is confined to what the corporation wants the world to hear rather than what the world wants the corporation to talk about.

As presently constituted, the public relations department is the window of the corporation that shows the world an image the corporation has of itself. The typical public relations officer is not an expert in the company's primary activities and does not have any line responsibility or experience. More often than not, the public relations officer is reduced to the role of corporate apologist. The first change should be in the area of information dissemination. The public relations window should both project an image and take one in. The public relations officer should communicate to corporate management what the rest of the world thinks of the company and why. The public relations officer can use his or her knowledge to sensitize management to changes in the external environment and what they mean for the corporation, can become part of the environment scanning process.

It is imperative that all external communications be credible to their intended audience, given the adversary character of advocacy advertising and the low public acceptance of corporate communications. One element of credibility would be the clear identification of the sponsoring corporation and willingness to state the nature and purpose of such advertising. Many companies have been hiding their advertising under such innocuous sounding sponsorships as "Citizens for Better Economic Environment" or "Group for Clean Nuclear Energy." There is a further need to ensure the truthfulness, accuracy, and completeness of the communication. The use of outside experts to comment on the communication would go a long way toward improving the credibility of corporate public communications and the viewpoint they support.

The cause of business is poorly served when corporate spokespeople concentrate their fire on corporate critics but refuse to speak out against business people and business practices that are illegal or socially irresponsible. By refusing to take a public position against wrong-doing, they invite criticism against all business and convey the image of business as unresponsive to the public interest. Finally, no amount of advocacy advertising is likely to yield results if there is a large gap between the image business is trying to promote and what business is actually doing. Effective advocacy advertising demands the development of public policy positions and a meaningful commitment by the corporation at all levels of management to conduct the affairs of the corporation in the public interest.

Notes

1. Paul Weaver, "Corporations Are Defending Themselves with the Wrong Weapon," *Fortune* (June 1977), pp. 186–196.
2. "New Ways to Lobby a Recalcitrant Congress," *Business Week* (September 1979), pp. 140–149.
3. Ibid.
4. S. Prakash Sethi, *Advocacy Advertising and Large Corporations* (Lexington, Massachusetts: D.C. Heath & Co., 1977).

Ethical Rules for Corporate PAC-Men

Steven Markowitz

Like democracy itself, the current system of financing U.S. political campaigns is not nearly perfect. But, as has been said about democracy, it is nevertheless far superior to any of the alternatives. Most in the business community do not want to turn back the clock to the era of secretive, virtually unlimited contributions by a few wealthy, influential individuals. Equally unpopular would be a system of government control of campaign funding. Therefore, the supporters of current practice have a strong stake in protecting the present system. Furthermore, political action committees (PACs) can play an important and positive role in this system and can be justified and defended in terms of ethics, democracy, openness, efficiency, and effectiveness.

Some aspects of the current system, however, including the real and apparent behavior of political action committees could stand some scrutiny. The attack on PACs, particularly business PACs, is familiar to any student of U.S. politics and corporate public affairs. The major public concern about PACs is that they are nothing more than a "vehicle for buying influence." Or as Citizens Against PACs says: "To officeholders and candidates hungry for campaign funds, PAC money talks louder than votes." The truth of the matter is that any system of private campaign financing lends itself to the perception and occasional reality of influence seeking and bribery.

The issue becomes sharper with the rise of the PACs because the size and number of contributions are so much greater—and they are out there in the open for everyone to see. The public also sees some contribution practices and patterns that are almost shameless, shameless on the part of the contributing PAC and shameless on the part of the candidate soliciting the contribution. How can even the most objective observer not be swayed by reports of powerful committee chairmen with no opposition raising record-breaking PAC contributions? What should the public think when Washington lobbyists flock to fundraising events almost eliminating the need for local fundraising? What of PACs supporting one candidate in an election and then after he or she loses, helping the opponent pay off campaign debts? How can that be justified on the basis of ideology or good government? Finally, does it make sense to contribute to candidates who have no need for funds or who run their campaigns in an irresponsible or unethical manner?

Much of the criticism of PACs is warranted but many of the objections are based on selection and manipulation of data to prove preconceived notions and to support preferred alternatives. Critics often ignore the activities of nonbusiness PACs and generally lose their objectivity in their analysis of alternate systems of campaign finance.

There is considerable public confusion regarding the level, impact, identity, and operation of corporate PACs. For instance, many people fail to distinguish between the corporation and its PAC. Few know that corporate PACs contributed less than 10 percent of total contributions to congressional candidates in 1982. Most importantly, many critics have assumed the existence of a business monolith with all corporate PACs acting in lockstep. This monolith provides an easy target and raises the specter of big, bad business. The reality is that corporations frequently find themselves competing with other corporations in the public policy area. Often the impact of corporate PAC contributions balances them out—and this does not even consider the enormous counterbalancing effect of trade, union, and ideological PACs. Professor Amitai Etzioni of George Washington University, and a severe critic of PACs, recently noted in *The Wall Street Journal* that "as PACs multiply, they tend to neutralize one another. Only in radical literature does 'Wall Street' act in unison."

The Pros and Cons

If there is a real concern about PACs in general it is that they have contributed to the divisiveness of the American body politic and have enhanced the role and influence of the special- or single-interest groups. The recent report of the Twentieth Century Fund Task Force on Political Action Committees noted: "Not only do PACs and interest groups, by definition, fail to attend to the larger public good, but they also limit the vision of many Americans, focusing their attention on a narrow—and often distorted—agenda of issues." Common Cause and others view PACs as a grave threat to democracy.

However, little attention is paid to the role PACs have played in developing greater public awareness of and participation in the political system. Regardless of one's views on PACs, it would be hard to argue against more people registering, voting, contributing to candidates, working in campaigns, and generally being more informed and interested in candidates and issues. If anything, it can be argued that PACs are a boon to democracy.

But the attack on PACs is seldom on these philosophical levels. The common denominator in the attacks is that in essence they are all fundamentally emotionally based. Anyone involved in public policy development as it affects business knows that this is not uncommon. The general public reacts viscerally to oversimplified media reports of corporate wrongdoing and generally does not have the patience or the knowledge on which to base more reasoned judgment, particularly when a superficial, snap judgment is easier to understand and emotionally satisfying. There are unnumbered instances of companies and industries trying to respond to attacks or trying to make their case on an issue on a strictly substantive, rational, argument-for-argument basis—and failing miserably in the process.

PAC Perception

With respect to business PACs, there is widespread perception that they totally dominate the political and legislative scene. Despite the absence of any evidence, one is led to believe that employees of corporations fear for their jobs and careers if they do not contribute to their companies' PACs. It is widely believed that business PACs are run by a few corporate moguls for the sole benefit of big business and are anti-consumer, anti-environment, and partial to the Republicans. And it's all too easy to accept the argument that companies form PACs only as a means of directly influencing legislative decisionmaking and all that righteous stuff about contributing to better government and participatory democracy is just fluff. Common Cause and other PAC critics are not likely to lose on this kind of battlefield, especially when the usual responses are learned dissertations and endless tabulations of precise, correct, and meaningful—but generally ignored—data on PAC activity.

The only thing that counts in an emotional battle is performance. If what the critics say about corporate PACs is unjustified, it is up to the business community to change public perceptions by demonstrating that what it claims to be the truth about PACs really is the truth. A strong case for PACs can be made, but the case must be based on a strategy of proving that PACs are not organized, administered, or acting as the critics charge they do. Their behavior and performance must meet the strictest standards of law and ethics. Safeguards must be developed as the public sees through mere window dressing.

Survival Strategy

One possible and positive strategy for the business community would be the development and adoption of a code of conduct or ethics for corporate PACs. Such a code would serve several very important purposes:

> It would provide a useful guideline for corporations to ensure that from both a philosophical and practical point of view they are operating their PACs in a recognized legally and ethically correct manner.

> It would help answer questions on PAC organization and procedures that are vague in the law.

> A code would provide a strong defense against those who question the integrity as well as the right of business PACs to exist. Adherence to an accepted and widely publicized code could become their Good Housekeeping Seal of Approval, particularly if PAC critics had some role in the formulation of the code.

> It could serve to deter companies or individuals who have or might be tempted to conduct themselves or their PACs in just the kind of ethically questionable way the critics charge all do.

> Finally, a code of conduct would be a shield to help business PACs collectively fend off pressures from candidates and influential office holders to engage in legal but nevertheless questionable activities.

A meaningful code would have to be specific, tough, and enforced if it is to be perceived to be anything more than a public relations gimmick to help counter the anti-PAC tirade. It would be helpful but not enough for each company to be able to include in its PAC brochures a statement that it subscribes to the Corporate PAC Code of Conduct. If supporters of business PACs truly see PACs as an avenue to good government and want them to survive, a realistic and enforced code of conduct must be an integral element of the strategy.

Drafting such a code will be an extremely difficult undertaking. No two companies and no two PACs are the same, and an overly narrow, rigid code would not be acceptable. However, broad generalities would leave too many loopholes to be helpful. Finding that middle ground of sufficient precision to be meaningful, and enough flexibility to accommodate a range of size and philosophy, is the challenge.

Code of Conduct

What follows is a suggested approach to a Corporate PAC Code of Conduct. Much of this would, of course, apply to noncorporate PACs as well. There are a variety of elements, comprehensive and possibly duplicative—and certainly subject to debate.

The PAC will abide by both the spirit and the letter of all applicable federal, state, and local law.

The PAC is just one element of a broad corporate political awareness and participation program.

The PAC is an entity separate and independent of corporate management.

The CEO and other senior executives of the corporation are encouraged to participate in the PAC but shall not manage or control it.

The major objectives of the PAC are to encourage employee participation in the political and legislative processes and to help elect candidates who best reflect the public policy philosophy of the employees of the corporation.

Every possible safeguard will be taken to ensure that contributions to the PAC are voluntary. The identity of contributors and noncontributors shall be confidential and an outside, disinterested third party shall handle the accounting and reporting functions. There will be no direct solicitation by superiors of their subordinates.

The PAC will conduct its candidate selection process in a democratic manner in order to give consideration to the political and public policy views of all interested employees.

The PAC will establish and publish the specific criteria by which it selects candidates for support.

The PAC will be bipartisan in all its activities and will consider contributions to candidates of all parties.

Employees will be allowed the option of designating or earmarking their contributions to the PAC for a specific candidate, committee or political party.

Employees will be encouraged to participate in the PAC by recommending candidates for support as well as by contributing financially.

No contributions will be made to candidates who are not running in the next upcoming election, or who have no opposition, or to candidates who clearly have no financial need. Also, no contributions will be made to pay off debts of past election campaigns, to specific fundraising events, or to candidates or committees that intend to use contributions for the support of other candidates.

The PAC will contribute only to candidates whose campaigns subscribe to accepted standards of accountability, fiscal responsibility, and ethics.

PAC contributions will not be contingent on the promise of a vote or action on a specific topic, issue, bill, or regulation. This principle will be stated orally or in writing at the time each contribution is made.

The PAC will report regularly to employees on its financial status and record of candidate contributions.

The PAC will undergo regular financial audits by an outside certified public accountant.

Undoubtedly some or all of these points are contentious and subject to question and interpretation. Compliance with many of them will require sacrifice and loss of discretion. Some may not view this loss of independence as acceptable. Furthermore, would other sponsors of PACs, such as unions and trade groups, similarly bound themselves?

If the corporate community does not collectively come up with something along these lines, one of three things will happen—and they might happen anyway. One possibility is that some organization or group might unilaterally devise its own code—which may or may not be acceptable—and back corporations into a corner. Another likelihood is that federal or state law or regulation might be tightened in ways that are even less acceptable in an effort to reform PACs. And last, the whole system could be lost as PACs continue to grow and the possibilities of abuse, greed, chicanery, poor judgment, or plain stupidity multiply. Business can seize the high ground and be statesmanlike and sensible while it still has the chance. Will it?

10
Corporate External Communications

Advocacy Advertising: A Novel Communications Approach to Building Effective Relations with External Constituencies

S. Prakash Sethi

In 1977, when I first published my book *Advocacy Advertising and Large Corporations,* the subject of advocacy, or idea-issue, advertising had begun to rise in the American consciousness. No doubt it was spurred in large measure by a spate of advocacy campaigns launched by oil companies, notably Mobil Oil, to explain and defend their large profits following the Arab oil boycott and the resultant skyrocketing of oil prices. The late 1960s and early 1970s also constituted the period when corporations were faced with broad public attacks and more intensive government regulation because of increased national concern for a cleaner environment, health and safety, and a better quality of life. It is not surprising that early entrants into the fracas, in addition to oil, were companies from such industries as chemicals, minerals, heavy (smokestack) industries, and forestry products.[1]

A great deal has happened in the interim. The sociopolitical environment of business in the United States has become far more receptive to the concept of paid political advertising by large corporations. There has been a tremendous increase in both the magnitude and the growth of advocacy advertising. The phenomenon has spread to many other countries, notably Canada, Great Britain, and to a lesser extent, the nations of Western Europe. The diversity of sponsorship also has increased, and is no longer confined to large corporations and industry groups. It now includes trade unions, ideologically oriented public-interest groups, religious organizations, political parties and candidates, and even state-owned corporations and government agencies. The types of issues covered have become more varied. This has had the unusual effect of creating combined sponsorships on specific issues among groups who otherwise do not share common goals and objectives.

An equally important element of change has been in the practice of advocacy advertising. Having analyzed over a hundred advocacy campaigns in depth, I have discerned a noticeable process of maturation. Sponsors have become more realistic about their expectations of what advocacy advertising can accomplish. They also have become more sophisticated about the use of this tool as an instrument of modifying public opinion and attitudes, and effecting change in national agendas and public policies.

A number of these elements have had a positive effect on the growing public acceptance of advocacy advertising. However, not all the changes have been constructive or in the right direction. Therefore, what we do with this important communication tool will influence not only the activities of its sponsors—notably the private corporate sector—but also, the nature of public policy debate. One has only to look at the onslaught of political commercials during an election campaign to appreciate how they have irrevocably changed the character of the electoral process, and indeed the political process, in the United States.

In the last analysis, advocacy advertising will not be judged solely or even primarily for its effectiveness as a communciation tool in achieving its sponsor's objectives. Advocacy advertising, ultimately, is an educational tool and a political tool designed to play an active role in influencing a society's priorities. Therefore, its legitimacy and effectiveness will also be judged in political terms, by the public's perception that its practitioners are using it responsibly and, in addition to their self-interest, also serving some larger public purpose.

What Is Advocacy Advertising?

Considerable confusion and misunderstanding exist as to what constitutes advocacy advertising because, in a sense, all advertising is advocacy. Moreover, even when we narrow the scope of advocacy advertising by excluding messages that promote a sponsor's products and services, there remains a vast area of institutional advertising where it must be distinguished from traditional public relations-good will advertising, public service messages, and public-interest "educational" advertising.

Advocacy advertising, including idea-issue advertising, is part of that genre of advertising known as corporate image or institutional advertising. It is concerned with the propagation of ideas and the elucidation of controversial social issues deemed important by its sponsor in terms of public policy. The managerial context of advocacy advertising is that of defending or promoting the sponsor's activities, modus operandi, and position on controversial issues of public policy. The behavioral and social context of advocacy advertising is that of changing public perception of the sponsor's actions and performance from skepticism and hostility to trust and acceptance, and/or to a more neutral position. The political context of advocacy advertising is that of the constitutional safeguards for freedom of speech; a sponsor is asserting its right to speak out on issues of public importance without any regulation or censorship on the part of other private groups or government agencies. The political context of advocacy advertising would thus encompass even otherwise allegedly purely educational messages where the issues raised involve important matters of public policy, may be of a controversial nature, and the sponsor's objective is to heighten public awareness of those issues or some preferred options for their resolution.

A Normative Framework for Understanding The Role of Advocacy Advertising

In a democratic society the primary tasks of the nation are carried out by the major private and public social institutions. The society at large exercises control over these institutions and holds them accountable through an evaluation of their activities. Freedom of speech, while fundamental to the notion of a free and democratic society, is not absolute. To operate in a reasonable, socially equitable, and politically acceptable manner, some restrictions are inevitable to curb the excess of one group while facilitating greater expression for other groups that would otherwise be squeezed out of the marketplace of ideas. Effective control is based on three elements: (1) the quality of the information provided by the institutions; (2) the capability of the news media to manage the public communications space to ensure adequate access for various viewpoints; and (3) the ability of the people to sift various ideas and select those that meet their expectations. Figure 1 provides a scheme for understanding these relationships.

It should be apparent that access to the public communication space is not unlimited and is constrained by a variety of factors. In general, monitors 1 and 2 are more flexible and offer substitution choices to the communicator in developing an effective entry into the public communication mix. Monitor 3 is much more rigid in character. It defines the boundaries of a communication, and also prescribes the exclusions in terms of the message and the medium that are proscribed. The constraints under monitor 3 are likely to be more onerous and penalties for noncompliance more burdensome, to the extent that monitors 1 and 2 are not used or a particular communicator can circumvent their working to the detriment of other groups so that the smooth working of the system is impeded.

The reception and interpretation of a communication by its recipient is subject to a variety of constraints, including source credibility, previously held beliefs, and peer group and opinion leader influences. The information is communicated back to different groups who then interact based on the intensity of beliefs expressed by the public and the likely effect on the future viability of the group if it does not conform to the wishes of the people.

Growth of Advocacy Advertising

Precise dollar estimates for advocacy advertising expenditures are not possible because of lack of a clear-cut definition. In the legal area, advocacy advertising

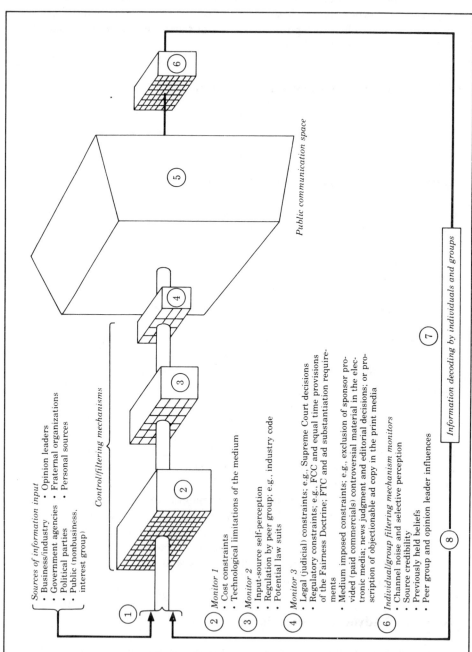

Sources of information input
• Business/industry   • Opinion leaders
• Government agencies   • Fraternal organizations
• Political parties   • Personal sources
• Public (nonbusiness, interest group)

Control/filtering mechanisms

Public communication space

Information decoding by individuals and groups

② Monitor 1
• Cost constraints
• Technological limitations of the medium

③ Monitor 2
• Input-source self-perception
• Regulation by peer group; e.g., industry code
• Potential law suits

④ Monitor 3
• Legal (judicial) constraints; e.g., Supreme Court decisions
• Regulatory constraints; e.g., FCC and equal time provisions of the Fairness Doctrine; FTC and ad substantiation requirements
• Medium imposed constraints; e.g., exclusion of sponsor provided (paid commercials) controversial material in the electronic media; news judgment and editorial decisions; or proscription of objectionable ad copy in the print media

⑥ Individual/group filtering mechanism monitors
• Channel noise and selective perception
• Source credibility
• Previously held beliefs
• Peer group and opinion leader influences

Figure 1

falls in the category of grassroots lobbying. Unfortunately, corporate tax returns do not provide adequate and systematic information on grassroots lobbying expenditures. The situation is further aggravated by the Internal Revenue Service's lack of precise guidelines and inadequate enforcement in the audit of business expenses for grassroots lobbying.[2]

Advocacy advertising in the mass media is only part of the broad range of grassroots lobbying. Even communications aimed at stockholders and employees, for example, legally would be considered grassroots lobbying when they concern legislative matters. Total advertising expenditures and grassroots lobbying by the business community were estimated to be about $1 billion per year in 1978. Assuming a conservative growth rate of 10 percent per year, I would estimate current business expenditures on all types of advocacy to have been approximately $1.6 billion in 1984.[3]

Diversity of Sponsorship

Another notable change from the mid-1970s to mid-1980s has been in the variety of new groups that have begun to use advocacy advertising. These include organized labor; voluntary private groups of all types and persuasions; governments and governmental agencies; and foreign governments and groups advertising in the United States to influence public opinion and political leaders.

Organized Labor

Organized labor unions have been taking tentative and somewhat cautious steps in the use of advocacy advertising. Among the many campaigns conducted by various labor groups during the last few years include those of the American Federation of State, County and Municipal Employees (AFSCME), the United Auto Workers (UAW), the AFL-CIO, the United Steel Workers of America, the Postal Workers, the Amalgamated Clothing and Textile Workers, and the International Ladies Garment Workers (figures 2 and 3). Some of the reasons for organized labor's engaging in advocacy advertising are similar to those of the business community, for example, loss of public trust. However, my analysis of most of the labor campaigns leads me to conclude that they lack a coherent long-term strategy and are not likely to be effective.

> The overwhelming emphasis is on rhetorical and emotional appeals delivered through thirty- and sixty-second television commercials. These commercials may warm the hearts of union members, but are likely to do little to improve their understanding of the issues involved or prepare them to discuss these issues with nonunion members or the general public.

BULLSEYE

Brazil is the latest country to propose sending hundreds of thousands of tons of subsidized steel slabs to the United States for finishing into steel products. The slabs would replace steel made in America, further reduce the steel-making capacity of this country, and throw additional thousands of steelworkers out of work.

The Brazilian deal, being promoted by the Wheeling-Pittsburgh Steel Corporation, mirrors the one new being negotiated between the British Steel Corporation and U.S. Steel.

In each case, a foreign, government-owned steel company would ship huge quantities of subsidized, semi-finished steel to companies in the U.S. American companies would close down steel making facilities and concentrate on turning the foreign steel into finished products.

Wheeling-Pittsburgh proposes to deal with a Brazilian military dictatorship which has "targeted" steel as a loss

Through targeting, a government gives preferred treatment to a chosen industry—subsidizing its development in many ways until its products can be dumped on foreign markets at prices which do not reflect the true cost of production.

Because of our high consumption and lack of a national industrial policy, the United States is a sitting duck for these practices. Look at what has happened in some other industries which have been targeted:

COMPUTERIZED MACHINE TOOLS: Japan's share of this market in the United States has increased from 5% to 50% since 1976. 24,000 American jobs have been lost.

COLOR TELEVISION: Japan targeted this industry in the 1960's. Since then, 13 American color television producers have dropped out, leaving only five. 27,364

leader in an effort to tap foreign trade markets. Brazil itself is in the midst of a massive debt crisis—owing $90 billion, more than any other nation.

The government-owned British Steel Corporation is faced with huge financial losses, and the proposed deal with U.S. Steel is widely described in Britain as a "bail-out".

If either or both of these deals should be finalized, we can expect a flood of similar schemes between other American steel companies and foreign governments.

Our country would lose its basic steel-making capacity and become dependent on foreign suppliers. This would seriously jeopardize our national security.

What is happening in the steel industry is a dramatic example of the problem of international targeting of selected industries.

American jobs have been lost. A total of 63,000 have been lost in related consumer electronics industries including radios, tape decks and phonographs.

AIRBUS: Western European countries targeted the world commercial aircraft market in the early 1970's with the creation of a joint venture called Airbus Industries—which now accounts for half of the free world market for widebodied aircraft. This rapid market penetration contributed to Lockheed's decision to stop production of the L1011, with a loss of 4,000 jobs.

This country, its industries, workers and stockholders suffer because of targeting by foreign governments. This situation will continue, and worsen, until we understand targeting and develop a national industrial policy to deal with it.

USA

Brazil Joins Britain In Attack On USA's Steel Independence

UNITED STEELWORKERS OF AMERICA

Lloyd McBride, President
Five Gateway Center
Pittsburgh, Pennsylvania 15222

Figure 2

THE NEW YORK TIMES, WEDNESDAY, APRIL 10, 1985

A17

UNCONTROLLED IMPORTS

They have taken nearly a million American jobs in apparel & textiles. They threaten the two million jobs that remain. We have one last chance. And it's in the Congress now.

S680/HR1562:

An urgent, rational bill that will put an end to uncontrolled imports of apparel & textiles, stop the erosion of our industry, save two million American jobs. And still give the nations of the world, poorer ones especially, legitimate access to our market.

THESE AREN'T JUST JOBS. WE'RE TALKING ABOUT TWO MILLION PEOPLE.

And look who they are: 7 out of 10, women. Sitting at sewing machines, standing on their feet in the mills. Supporting their families alone, or making the difference so that the family can live a little better, the kids get a little better chance.

These are people who desperately need work, they want to work and they don't have much choice about where they work.

When their plants close, they can't find jobs

YOU CAN SEE WHAT'S HAPPENING WITH YOUR OWN EYES.

In the stores, for example, look for a woman's blouse made here. Instead of there. See how long and hard you have to look. If you find it at all.

Or in those beautiful mail-order catalogs: page after page, see how much is import. How little, USA.

It ought to make us mad.

We are literally being imported out of existence—our mills, our fiber plants, our garment factories, and all the workers who depend on them for a living.

In the last 10 years: nearly a million jobs we had and could have had. Gone.

In state after state, hundreds of garment factories. Gone.

bringing the MFA back to its objectives of an open, orderly market fairly shared by everyone, and giving it the teeth to make it work.

S680/HR1562 doesn't break any new ground. It simply moves to correct the flaws that have damn near destroyed us.

THIS BILL IS EXTRAORDINARILY FAIR.

We're not saying, no more imports. We are saying, give us import levels we can deal with. Make it possible again for American industry and American workers to get a fair share of our own American market.

That's what this bill does. But it's not one-sided.

It recognizes the needs of the struggling economies, the impoverished peoples beyond our borders.

lucky to make $134 a week with a couple of kids to take care of.

More often, it's welfare. And bitterness. For them, dignity, pride, faith in America are wrapped up in paying their own way.

Two million jobs are slipping away.

It's not too late to save them.

WE'RE TALKING ABOUT TOWNS.

There are small towns all over this country where there's only one mill or one garment factory. The people depend on it for a living. And everything else in that town depends on those people: the local department store, the drug store, the movie house, the grocery, the gas station, the garage, the schools and services.

When the plant goes, the town goes. The other businesses fail, taxes disappear, the life of the town crumbles. A little bit of America dies.

It's already happening in many towns. And many more are hanging by a thread. We think that's urgent. Don't you?

WHY WE NEED THIS BILL RIGHT NOW.

The way things are going, by 1990 we won't have an apparel & textile industry in America at all. It's all here for everybody to see: today 1 out of every 2 garments sold in this country—men's, women's & kids'—is an import. Ten years ago, it was 1 out of 5. In category after category, imports up, up, up. And snowballing.

A FEW HORRENDOUS FACTS.

The Growth of Clothing Imports as a Percentage of the U.S. Market.

	1974	1979	1984
Women's & Children's Coats	22%	38%	52%
Men's & Boys' Shirts (woven, man-made fiber)	19%	42%	55%
Bras	29%	49%	58%
Sweaters (all)	44%	55%	68%

Imports have increased 123% in the past 10 years, 25% in 1983 alone, and a terrifying 32% over that just last year.

In 1984, in North & South Carolina alone: at least 61 textile plants. Gone.

Plant after plant, closing, and among them, just this year: our last remaining manufacturer of corduroy & velveteen, one of the oldest and most prestigious of our mills. Gone.

That's 1 out of 10 manufacturing jobs, more than steel & automobiles combined. And it's frightening.

THIS BILL IS NOT A BAIL-OUT.

Nobody's asking the government to foot the bills for us. Our American apparel & textile industry has become the most modern and productive in the world. It has spent on average a billion dollars a year on new plants and equipment. And it could hold its own against all comers, if those competitors were, like us, competing on their own.

But they're not. Our companies must compete with their governments. And their governments support them with financing, subsidies, tax-relief, and by keeping our goods out. And with workers at wages Americans find hard to believe: 16-cents-an-hour workers ·ag-cents-an-hour workers, 63-cents-an-hour workers, $1.18-cents-an-hour workers. Could you live on that? Neither could we.

We can compete in productivity, we can compete in quality. But there is no way American workers can compete with those pitifully, indecently low wages. And there is nobody who thinks we should.

NOT "PROTECTIONISM," FAIRNESS.

Since 1974 we've had a trade agreement, the Multi-Fiber Arrangement (MFA), which was supposed to keep imports in balance. But it's painfully obvious now that the loopholes are big enough to bring down our entire industry.

That's what this bill is all about. Plugging the loopholes which have distorted the MFA,

---

no longer flood us.

At the same time, it gives the smaller, poorer nations a greater opportunity in our market: more room for their goods, more room to grow. This is a bill that is not just fair, it is compassionate. A bill every American in good conscience can support.

AND THE SPONSORS SPAN THE POLITICAL SPECTRUM.

They are Republicans and Democrats, conservatives and liberals, moderates on both sides. In the Senate and in the House, they have rallied to this bill.

They have joined forces in common agreement that America cannot afford to lose another great industry, American workers cannot afford to lose one more job.

To date 227 representatives and senators have put their names on the bill.

Even so, we can't take passage for granted. Beyond that, we want the bill to do more than squeak through. We want overwhelming congressional support that will tell the world that we are determined to defend our home markets: they are welcome to come and trade with us, but we are no longer going to sit idly by while our industries are destroyed, our workers deprived of their right to earn a living at a decent American wage.

YOU CAN HELP. BACK S680/HR1562.

Write your representative. Write your senator. Let them know you want this bill. If they're sponsors, they'll know you support them. If they're undecided, they'll know how you want them to decide. If they oppose it, they'll know there is good reason to switch.

America needs this bill. We need this bill.

We're fighting for a fighting chance.

Amalgamated Clothing & Textile Workers' Union

International Ladies' Garment Workers' Union

RALLY: 12 NOON today, Wednesday, April 10, Herald Square.

(34th Street and Broadway)

Figure 3

These short television commercials are inappropriate as educational devices that could inform an increasingly skeptical public about the complexity of the issues, the shortcomings seen by the unions' detractors, and the substance of the unions' arguments. Although they may give instant gratification to their sponsors, they are unlikely to have any lasting impact on the public.

Campaigns by Foreign Government and Groups in the United States

The most prevalent form of advocacy campaigns by foreign governments in the United States are those of special advertising supplements that appear regularly in major national magazines and leading newspapers. They generally extol the stable political environment in these countries and the incentives for direct foreign investment.

A different approach to advocacy advertising campaigns is taken by nongovernmental foreign groups. Their aim is to reach the American public with their viewpoint on U.S. government policies they consider contrary to their interests. Such ads are generally one-time affairs, directed at a very specific group, and are timed to coincide with a specific legislative or public policy debate. Because of their ad hoc nature and poor reach and frequency, their effectiveness is questionable. Nevertheless, this type of advertising is on the increase and may become a significant phenomenon in the future.

Two recent examples of these ads are presented in figures 4 and 5. Figure 4 is an ad sponsored by a Japanese cooperative suggesting that Americans should not pressure the Japanese government to relax its import restrictions against U.S. citrus and beef. Figure 5 proclaimed that the Reagan administration's foreign policy constituted a gross violation of the fundamental principles of international law, and that the Reagan administration had substituted force for international law in its conduct of foreign policy around the world. The sponsor of the advertisement, the International Progress Organization, based in Vienna, Austria, did not provide enough information in the advertisement to enable the U.S. reader to judge its credentials and become informed about its representational character.

Voluntary Private Organizations

Advocacy advertisement sponsored by voluntary private organizations has been one of the fastest growing segments of this genre of advertising, yet as a group, voluntary private organizations have received little attention and their overall influence on public opinion remains largely undetermined. The sponsoring organizations can be classified into five groups:

1. Established nonsectarian organizations that engage in long-term advocacy campaigns on particular issues that are part of their organizational mandate, such as Planned Parenthood, the National Rifle Association, and Friends of Animals (figure 6).

A MESSAGE FROM THE FARMERS OF JAPAN TO THE PEOPLE OF THE UNITED STATES

urrent US-Japan agricultural talks aimed at import expansion will not ease the real problems in US-Japan trade relations. However, they could very well endanger the basis of farm life in Japan. Here's why.

DID YOU KNOW *that Japan is already the largest single importer of US agricultural products?*

Japan is the #1 market for US produced agricultural goods. Japan buys more than $10 billion worth of farm and fishery products annually.

DID YOU KNOW *that increasing beef and citrus imports will not significantly reduce the US-Japan trade imbalance?*

Expanding beef and citrus imports represent *at the most* an additional $500 million, but there is *no guarantee* that these imports will come from the US, since lower priced commodities from Australia, Argentina, Brazil and Israel are waiting to enter the market.

DID YOU KNOW *that beef and citrus represent major sources of income for Japan's small farmers?*

Beef and citrus imports have already reached 40% and 10% of its domestic production respectively. Japan is about the size of the state of Montana, with only 17% of its land arable. The average Japanese farm is 1/150th the size of the average US farm. If imports are allowed to increase, they will drive out domestically produced beef and citrus, which will mean the end of many small family farms in Japan.

DID YOU KNOW *that Japan's food self-sufficiency is the lowest of all the industrial countries—less than one-third its total requirements?*

Japan is the largest importer of agricultural and fishery products—a very risky situation for any country. A country should produce as much food at home as possible, relying on imports to meet unsatisfied demand. Japan learned this bitter lesson in 1973 when the US embargoed soybeans (for political reasons having nothing to do with Japan) and created tremendous economic difficulties.

DID YOU KNOW *that there are those in the US and Japan who seek a "cure" for trade problems in the industrial sector at the expense of the farmer?*

Increasing agricultural imports *cannot* erase the US trade deficit, which is due primarily to industrial goods (automobiles, steel and consumer products). This "quick fix" idea is a meaningless political gesture aimed at diverting attention from more basic economic difficulties.

DID YOU KNOW *that Japan has already established very liberal import policies on many agricultural products?*

Japan imposes no tariffs on imported feed grain, soybeans and wheat and has expanded imports of many other items. But no country can allow absolute free trade in its agricultural sector. As an example, the US protects its sugar, beef, dairy products and tobacco with import restrictions and subsidies. The farmer is an important part of the entire economic and social fabric of all countries, and must be protected.

We, the farmers of Japan, with our tradition of the family based farm, are the heart of our nation, just as the American farmer is the heart of your country. The Japanese farmer is not to blame for the current US-Japan trade frictions.

We must resist efforts on the part of any government, American or Japanese, to sacrifice the farmer for short term political goals.

The real answer to the current US-Japan trade issue lies in the economic revitalization of the US and a lessening of Japan's dependency on export growth—not in undermining the Japanese farmer.

This advertisement is sponsored by: **ZENCHU**

THE CENTRAL UNION OF AGRICULTURAL COOPERATIVES
Representing 6 million Japanese farming households.
8-3 Ohtemachi 1-chome, Chiyoda-ku, Tokyo 100, Japan
For further information write: ZENCHU, 1523 17th St. NW, Washington, DC 20036

Figure 4

The New York Times, Sunday, October 7, 1984

INTERNATIONAL PROGRESS ORGANIZATION

CONCLUSIONS AND JUDGEMENT OF THE BRUSSELS TRIBUNAL ON REAGAN'S FOREIGN POLICY

The International Conference on the Reagan Administration's Foreign Policy convened in Brussels from 28-30 September, 1984 under the auspices of the International Progress Organization. Reports were submitted by international jurists and foreign policy specialists on various aspects of the Reagan Administration's foreign policy. Among the participants of the conference were Seán MacBride (Nobel Laureate, Ireland), Prof. George Wald (Nobel Laureate, Harvard University), General Edgardo Mercado Jarrín (Peru), General Nino Pasti (former Deputy Supreme Commander of NATO) and Hortensia Bussi de Allende (Chile). The reports were presented before a Panel of Jurists consisting of Hon. Farouk Abu-Eissa (Sudan), Attorney, former Foreign Minister, Secretary-General of the Arab Lawyers Union; Prof. Francis A. Boyle (U.S.A.), Professor of International Law from the University of Illinois, Chairman; Dr. Hans Goeran Franck (Sweden), Attorney, Member of the Swedish Parliament; Hon. Mirza Gholam Hafiz (Bangladesh), Former Speaker of the Bangladesh Parliament and currently a Senior Advocate of the Bangladesh Supreme Court; Hon. Mary M. Kaufman (U.S.A.), Attorney-at-Law, prosecuting attorney at the Nuremberg War Crimes trial against I. G. Farben; Dr. Jean-Claude Njem (Cameroun), Assistant-Professor at the Faculty of Law, Uppsala University, and a Consultant of the Government; Prof. Alberto Ruiz-Eldredge (Peru), Professor of Law, former President of the National Council of Justice; and Dr. Muemiaz Soysal (Turkey), Professor of Constitutional Law, University of Ankara. An accusation against the international legality of the Reagan Administration's foreign policy was delivered by the Honorable Ramsey Clark, former U.S. Attorney General. The defense was presented by a legal expert of the Reagan Administration.

and consistent pattern of violations of the most fundamental human rights of the people of El Salvador.

5. Nicaragua. The Reagan Administration's policy of organizing and participating in military operations by opposition contra groups for the purpose of overthrowing the legitimate government of Nicaragua violates the terms of both the U.N. and O.A.S. Charters prohibiting independence of a state. The Reagan Administration has flouted its obligation to terminate immediately its support for the opposition contra groups in accordance with the Interim Order of Protection issued by the International Court of Justice on 10 May 1984.

6. International Court of Justice. The Panel denounces the patently bogus attempt by the Reagan Administration to withdraw from the compulsory jurisdiction of the International Court of Justice in the suit brought against it by Nicaragua for the purpose of avoiding a peaceful settlement of this dispute by the World Court in order to pursue instead a policy based upon military intervention, lawless violence and destabilization of the legitimate government of Nicaragua.

7. Mining Nicaraguan Harbors. The Reagan Administration's mining of Nicaraguan harbors violates the rules of international law set forth in the 1907 Hague Convention on the Laying of Submarine Mines, to which both Nicaragua and the United States are parties.

clear weapons system that can serve no legitimate defensive purpose under U.N. Charter article 51 and the international laws of humanitarian armed conflict.

11. No-first-use. In accordance with U.N. General Assembly Resolution 36/3 of 24 November 1981, the panel denounces the refusal by the Reagan Administration to adopt a policy mandating the no-first-use of nuclear weapons in the event of a conventional attack as required by the basic rule of international law dictating proportionality in the use of force even for the purposes of legitimate self-defense.

12. ASAT Treaty. The Panel calls upon both the United States and the Soviet Union to negotiate unconditionally over the conclusion of an anti-satellite weapons treaty.

D. Middle East

13. Lebanon. For the part it played in the planning, preparation and initiation of the 1982 Israeli invasion of Lebanon, the Reagan Administration has committed a Crime against Peace as defined by the Nuremberg Principles. Likewise, under the Nuremberg principles, the Reagan Administration becomes an accomplice to the Crimes against Humanity, War Crimes and Grave Breaches of the Third and Fourth Geneva Conventions of 1949 that have been committed or condoned by Israel and its allied Phalange and Haddad militia forces in Lebanon. Such complicity includes the savage massacre of genocidal character of hundreds of innocent Palestinian and Lebanese civilians by organized units of the Phalangist militia at the Sabra and Shatila refugee camps located in West Beirut that were then subject to the control of the occupying Israeli army. The Reagan Administration has totally failed to discharge its obligation to obtain Israel's complete and unconditional withdrawal from all parts of Lebanon as required by U.N. Security Council Resolutions 508 and 509 (1982), both of which are

Africa; it hampers effective action by the international community against apartheid, and facilitates aggressive conduct by the South African apartheid regime against neighbour states in violation of the U.N. Charter. As such, the Reagan Administration has become an accomplice to the commission of the international crime of apartheid as recognized by the universally accepted International Convention on the Suppression and Punishment of the Crime of Apartheid of 1973. The Panel also denounces the cooperation between the Reagan Administration and South Africa in military and nuclear matters.

18. Namibia. The Reagan Administration has refused to carry out its obligations under Security Council Resolution 435 (1978) providing for the independence of Namibia, as required by article 25 of the U.N. Charter. The right of the Namibian people to self-determination had been firmly established under international law long before the outbreak of the Angolan civil war. The Reagan Administration has no right to obstruct the achievement of Namibian independence by conditioning it upon or "linking" it to the withdrawal of Cuban troops from Angola in any way. Both the U.N. General Assembly and the Organization of the African Unity have recognized SWAPO as the legitimate representative of the Namibian people and the Reagan Administration is obligated to negotiate with it as such.

19. Angola. Cuban troops are in Angola at the request of the legitimate government of Angola in order to protect it from overt and covert aggression mounted by the South African apartheid regime from Namibia. There is absolutely no international legal justification for South African aggression against Angola in order to maintain and consolidate its reprehensible occupation of Namibia. The Angolan government has repeatedly stated that when South Africa leaves Namibia it will request the withdrawal of Cuban troops and Cuba has agreed

Based upon all the reports and documents submitted and the arguments by the advocates, the Brussels Panel of Jurists hereby renders the following conclusions concerning the compatibility of the Reagan Administration's foreign policy with the requirements of international law.

A. Introduction

1. General Introduction. The Reagan Administration's foreign policy constitutes a gross violation of the fundamental principles of international law enshrined in the Charter of the United Nations Organization, as well as of the basic rules of customary international law set forth in the U.N. General Assembly's Declaration on the Inadmissibility of Intervention in the Domestic Affairs of States and the Protection of Their Independence and Sovereignty (1965), its Declaration on Principles of International Law Concerning Friendly Relations and Cooperation Among States in Accordance with the Charter of the United Nations (1970), and its Definition of Aggression (1974), among others. In addition, the Reagan Administration is responsible for complicity in the commission of Crimes Against Peace, Crimes Against Humanity, War Crimes and Grave Breaches of the Third and Fourth Geneva Conventions of 1949.

B. Western Hemisphere

2. Grenada. The Reagan Administration's 1983 invasion of Grenada was a clearcut violation of U.N. Charter articles 2 (3), 2 (4), and 33 as well as articles 18, 20 and 21 of the Revised OAS Charter for which there was no valid excuse or justification under international law. As such, it constituted an act of aggression within the meaning of article 39 of the United Nations Charter.

3. Threat of U.S. Intervention. In direct violation of the basic requirement of international law mandating the peaceful settlement of international disputes, the Reagan Administration has implemented a foreign policy towards Central America that constitutes a great danger of escalation in military hostilities to the point of precipitating armed intervention by U.S. troops into combat against both the insurgents in El Salvador and the legitimate government of Nicaragua.

4. El Salvador. The Reagan Administration's illegal intervention in El Salvador's civil war contravenes the international legal right of self-determination of peoples as recognized by article 1 (2) of the United Nations Charter. The Reagan Administration has provided enormous amounts of military assistance to an oppressive regime that has used it to perpetrate a gross

Nobel Laureate Seán MacBride addressing the international conference on Reagan's Foreign Policy in Brussels (28 September 1984)

C. Nuclear Weapons Policies

8. Arms Control Treaties. The Reagan Administration has refused to support the ratification of the Threshold Test Ban Treaty of 1974, and the SALT II Treaty of 1979, in addition to renouncing the longstanding objective of the U.S. government to negotiate a comprehensive test ban treaty. As such the Reagan Administration has failed to pursue negotiations in good faith on effective measures relating to cessation of the nuclear arms race at an early date and to nuclear disarmament as required by article 6 of the Nuclear Non-Proliferation Treaty of 1968. Similarly, the Reagan Administration's "Strategic Defense Initiative", or 1983 threatens to breach the Anti-Ballistic Missile Systems Treaty of 1972.

9. Pershing 2 Missiles. The deployment of the offensive, first-strike, counterforce strategic nuclear weapons system known as the Pershing 2 missiles in the Federal Republic of Germany violates the Non-Circumvention Clause found in article 12 of the SALT II Treaty. The Reagan Administration is bound to obey this prohibition pursuant to the rule of customary international law enunciated in article 18 of the 1969 Vienna Convention on the Law of Treaties to the effect that a signatory to a treaty is obliged to refrain from acts that would defeat the object and purpose of a treaty until it has made its intention clear not to become a party.

10. MX missile. The MX missile is an offensive, first-strike, counterforce strategic nu-

legally binding on Israel and the United States under U.N. Charter article 25. This includes Israeli evacuation of Southern Lebanon.

14. The Palestinian Question. The Reagan Administration's policy towards the Palestinian people as well as the Reagan "Peace Plan" of 1 September 1982 violates the international legal right of the Palestinian people to self-determination as recognized by U.N. Charter article 1 (2). As recognized by numerous General Assembly Resolutions, the Palestinian people have an international legal right to create an independent and sovereign state. The Palestine Liberation Organization has been recognized as the legitimate representative of the Palestinian people by both the United Nations General Assembly and the League of Arab States. The Reagan Administration's nonrecognition of the PLO and its attempt to brand the PLO a "terrorist" group contravene the Palestinian people's right to liberation. The panel denounces the negative attitude of the Reagan Administration towards the call by the United Nations Secretary General for the convocation of an international conference under the auspices of the United Nations, with the participation of all parties involved in the conflict including the PLO, for the purpose of obtaining a just and lasting peace in the Middle East.

15. Israeli Settlements. The Reagan Administration's declared position that Israeli settlements in the Occupied Territories are "not illegal" is a violation of U.S. obligations under article 1 of the Fourth Geneva Convention of 1949 to ensure respect for the terms of the Convention (there article 49) by other High Contracting Parties such as Israel.

16. Libya. The Reagan Administration's dispatch of the U.S. Sixth Fleet into the Gulf of Sidra for the purpose of precipitating armed conflict with the Libyan government constitutes a breach of the peace under article 39 of the U.N. Charter. The Reagan Administration's policy to attempt to destabilize the government of Libya violates the terms of the United Nations Charter article 2 (4) prohibiting the threat or use of force directed against the political independence of a state.

E. Africa, Asia and the Indian Ocean

17. Apartheid. The Panel denounces the Reagan Administration's so-called policy of "constructive engagement" towards the apartheid regime in South Africa. This specious policy encourages discrimination and oppression against the majority of the people of South

to withdraw its troops whenever so requested by Angola. According to the relevant rules of international law, that is the proper sequence of events to be followed. The Reagan Administration's "linkage" of the presence of Cuban troops in Angola with the independence of Namibia encourages South African aggression against Angola, and thus it must share in the responsibility for South Africa's genocidal acts against the people of Angola.

20. Indian Ocean. The Reagan Administration's continued military occupation of the island of Diego Garcia violates the international legal right of self-determination for the people of Mauritius as recognized by the United Nations Charter. The Reagan Administration has accelerated the rapid militarization of the U.S. naval base on Diego Garcia as part of its plan to create a jumping-off point for intervention by the Rapid Deployment Force into the Persian Gulf. As such the Reagan Administration's foreign policy towards the Indian Ocean has violated the terms of the U.N. General Assembly's Declaration of the Indian Ocean as a Zone of Peace (1971).

F. Conclusion

21. United Nations Action. From the foregoing, it is clear that the Reagan Administration has substituted force for the rule of international law in its conduct of international affairs around the world. It has thus created a serious threat to the maintenance of international peace and security under article 39 of the United Nations Charter that calls for the imposition of enforcement measures by the U.N. Security Council under articles 41 and 42. In the event the Reagan Administration exercises its veto power against the adoption of such measures by the Security Council, the matter should be turned over to the U.N. General Assembly for action in accordance with the procedures set forth in the Uniting for Peace Resolution of 1950. In this way the Reagan Administration's grievous international transgressions could be effectively opposed by all members of the world community in a manner consistent with the requirements of international law.

Both the Security Council and the General Assembly should also take into account the numerous interventionist measures taken by the Reagan Administration, whether direct or indirect, seeking to impose financial and economic policies which are contrary to the sovereign independence of states, especially in the developing world, which severely damage the quality of life for all peoples.

Farouk Abu-Eissa

Mary Kaufman

Brussels, Belgium

Francis A. Boyle, Chairman

Jean-Claude Njem

Hans Goeran Franck

Alberto Ruiz-Eldredge

Mirza Gholam Hafiz

Muemtaz Soysal

30 September 1984

For more information please write to:

International Progress Organization A-1150 Vienna, Austria
Reindorfgasse 5, phone (222) 85 6112 Telex 136553.

Figure 5

PARENTAL NOTIFICATION? OR PARENTAL INVOLVEMENT?

FROM OUR PERSPECTIVE

Fourth, rather than encouraging free and open discussion between parents and teenagers about sexuality and reproduction, the regulations would merely inform parents, after the fact, that their daughters had received prescription contraceptives. Parental notification by mail, which may well result in recriminations and arguments, is a far cry from encouraging parental involvement in a teenager's decision-making about sexual behavior.

Government should not be allowed to intrude into the privacy of family relationships and the privacy of confidential relationships between doctor and patient. When such intrusion would worsen an already serious problem, it is even more reprehensible.

There are alternatives to government mandating parental *notification* as a means of reducing the problems outlined above, and they have proven to be effective in establishing parental *involvement* in teenage decisions about sexual activity.

With common sense, with realistic goals and programs, and with a 66-year history of service, Planned Parenthood helps parents and teenagers find a level of understanding

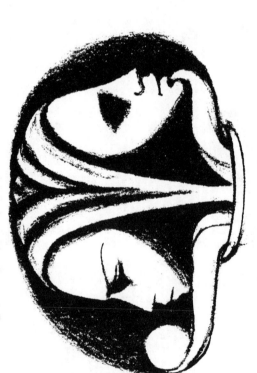

Art work by Ann Grifalconi.

On February 22, 1982, the Department of cies would increase, not decrease. One in

Health and Human Services published proposed regulations to govern family planning services funded under Title X of the Public Health Service Act. The regulations would require family planning providers to notify both parents of unemancipated minors under 18 who receive prescription birth control drugs and devices.

There is a 60-day comment period, ending April 23, during which individuals and organizations may make known their views on the proposed regulations and their potential effects. Comments should be submitted to Marjory Mecklenburg, Acting Deputy Assistant Secretary for Population Affairs, Room 725H, 200 Independence Avenue SW, Washington, D.C. 20201.

The obvious intent of the parental notification regulations proposed by the Secretary of Health and Human Services is to 1) reduce teenage pregnancies, 2) inhibit sexual activity among our nation's youth, 3) protect teenagers from the potential medical consequences of prescription contraceptives, and 4) increase the involvement of parents in young people's decisions about sexual activity.

First, the number of teenage pregnan-

four young people would stop attending family planning clinics if their parents had to be informed. A great majority would use "drugstore" methods or would use no birth control methods at all, greatly increasing the risk of unintended pregnancy. Fear of parental notification already is the most important reason teenagers delay obtaining contraceptives and is the cause of a large percentage of the more than one million teenage pregnancies that occur each year.

Second, sexual activity among teenagers would not decrease, primarily because most teenagers are sexually active for almost a year before they even seek contraception. In addition, only two percent of teenagers who attend family planning clinics would stop having sex if their parents had to be informed that they had received prescription contraceptives.

Third, the health risks for teenagers associated with pregnancy and childbirth are five times greater than the health risks associated with use of prescription contraceptives. In addition to the increased risks of mortality and morbidity among teenage mothers, their babies are much more likely to die in the first year of life than babies born to older women.

and discussion. We provide the facts. We offer guidance in bridging the generation gap. We offer programs parents and teenagers can attend together. And we provide information through publications. So that when teenagers are ready with the questions, their parents are ready with the answers.

The work of Planned Parenthood and other family planning service providers has helped parents and their teenagers voluntarily overcome the difficulty of talking together about personal matters. Right now, more than half of young teenagers who attend family planning clinics do so with the knowledge of their parents; one-fifth attend at their parents' suggestion. And the younger the teenager, the more likely the parent is to know about the visit.

All of this has been accomplished through parental involvement, not parental notification.

The statistics given were compiled by The Alan Guttmacher Institute, an independent corporation for research, policy analysis, and public education in family planning and population, and a special affiliate of the Planned Parenthood Federation of America.

Planned Parenthood®
Federation of America, Inc.

810 Seventh Avenue
New York, New York 10019
212/541-7800

This advertisement paid for by private contributions.

Figure 6

2. Established nonsectarian groups that use advocacy advertisements on an ad hoc basis, such as the National Organization of Women (NOW), the Izaak Walton League, the International Society for Animal Rights, the Animal Welfare Institute, the International Fund for Animal Welfare, and The Union of Concerned Scientists (figure 7).

3. Established sectarian groups that use advocacy advertising to promote their long-term policy positions, and also to speak out on current public controversies on an ad hoc basis. Examples are the Moral Majority, the Church League of America, Catholics for a Free Choice, and the Catholic Health Association (figure 8).

4. Ad hoc groups composed of well-known public personalities that join together to advocate public-policy positions on specific issues, such as the Coalition for a New Foreign and Military Policy, and the Bipartisan Budget Coalition (figure 9).

5. New advocacy groups that use advocacy advertisements to establish their identity, espouse their cause, and also raise funds from the public, such as Infant Formula Action Coalition (INFACT) and Common Cause (figure 10). It should be noted that groups classified in other categories may also make fundraising appeals as part of their advocacy advertisements.

A Conceptual Framework for Advocacy Advertising

Advocacy advertising can best be understood as a three-dimensional phenomenon: identification of sponsor's interest, intensity of advocacy, and specificity in identifying the adversary. Table 1 provides one attempt at classifying advertising campaigns within this framework. It should be helpful in understanding the broad range of activities that fall under the rubric of advocacy advertising.

Identification of Sponsor's Interest

This dimension measures the extent to which the sponsor is willing to identify its own interests with the contents of, and programs advocated in, the advertising message. There are five states of this dimension.

Disinterested Sponsor. The sponsor is clearly identified. Its interests are connected with the message only in a very general way. The advocacy is of broad ideological or philosophical nature. The sponsor hopes that the reader will identify the message with the sponsor and view the sponsor as a public-spirited and forward-looking organization. Illustrative of this approach is an advertisement by Internorth Corporation urging people to vote. A number of major corporate campaigns, notably those of LTV, fall in this group. Other advertisements sponsored

THE FISH WON'T BE BITING IN TWITCHELL CREEK TODAY,

OR TOMORROW, EITHER.

There was a time when with a little luck and a little patience, you could pull a fair-sized fish out of Twitchell Creek on Woods Lake in the Adirondacks.

But no more.

The fish are gone, along with the salamanders, ospreys, mayflies, swallows and myriad other creatures who once lived along the cool river banks.

They've been run off, or killed off by the rain, of all things. A deadly poisonous acid rain which has contaminated the water, choked the life out of the stream . . . and broken the delicate food chain on water and (we're finding out) on land as well.

All rain contains some acid, of course. But acid precipitation is different. And far more dangerous. Acid rain contains two killers: nitric acid and sulfuric acid which form when sulfur dioxide and nitrogen oxide mix with rain water. These two chemicals are being spewed by the ton-load into our air every day . . . emissions from the coal-burning power plants and industrial boilers our nation uses to keep going.

Fortunately, some lakes contain "buffers" . . . neutralizing agents which help lessen acid damage. But what of the others . . . in the Adirondack Mountains, in western Virginia, in the Great Smoky Mountains, throughout New England . . .

Who Will Stop The Rain?

The Izaak Walton League is working to do just that right now. The League was formed in 1922 by a handful of sportsmen who wanted to combat water pollution. And it endures today as a grassroots conservation organization composed of 50,000 fishermen, hikers, hunters and campers who speak out—and work hard —to protect wild America.

Congress passed a Clean Air Act in 1970—soon up for renewal—which set allowable limits for sulfur dioxide emissions from power plants. Some would like to relax those laws now . . . asserting the regulations will retard energy development. We disagree. We want stricter regulations to reduce these emissions still further. And we'll get them. Once and for all. Because there's something at stake here far greater than fishing. And that's life itself.

For more information on our activities, write:

THE IZAAK WALTON LEAGUE OF AMERICA

Izaak Walton League
1800 North Kent Street
Arlington, Virginia 22209

Figure 7

"They have labeled Moral Majority the Extreme Right because we speak out against Extreme Wrong!"

Jerry Falwell, President
Moral Majority Inc.

Why do Norman Lear, George McGovern, the ACLU, and others continually attack the philosophies and programs of movements like Moral Majority Inc?

The answer is simple — Moral Majority Inc. is made up of millions of Americans, including 72,000 ministers, priests, and rabbis, who are deeply concerned about the moral decline of our nation, and who are sick and tired of the way many amoral and secular humanists and other liberals are destroying the traditional family and moral values on which our nation was built.

We are Catholics, Jews, Protestants, Mormons, Fundamentalists — blacks and whites — farmers, housewives, businessmen. We are Americans from all walks of life, united by one central concern — to serve as a special interest group providing a voice for a return to moral sanity in these United States of America.

HERE IS HOW MORAL MAJORITY INC. STANDS ON TODAY'S VITAL ISSUES:

1. We believe in the separation of church and state.

Moral Majority Inc. is a political organization providing a platform for religious and non-religious Americans, who share moral values, to address their concerns in these areas. Members of Moral Majority Inc. have no common theological premise. We are Americans who are proud to be conservative in our approach to moral, social, and political concerns.

2. We are prolife.

We believe that life begins at fertilization. We strongly oppose the massive "biological holocaust" which is resulting in the abortion of 1½ million babies each year in America. Some of us believe this from a theological perspective. Other Moral Majority Inc. members believe this from a medical perspective. Regardless, we agree that unborn babies have the right to life as much as babies that have been born. We are providing a voice and a defense for the human and civil rights of millions of unborn babies.

3. We are pro-traditional family.

We believe that the only acceptable family form begins with the legal marriage of a man to a woman. We feel that homosexual marriages and common-law marriages should not be accepted as traditional families. We oppose legislation that favors these kinds of "diverse family forms," thereby penalizing the traditional family unit. We oppose legislation that might promote homosexuals as a

9. We believe the E.R.A. is the wrong vehicle with which to obtain equal rights for women.

We feel that the ambiguous and simplistic language of the Amendment could lead to court interpretations which might put women in combat, sanction homosexual marriages, and financially

5. We are not a censorship organization. We believe in freedom of speech, freedom of the press, and freedom of religion. Therefore, while we do not agree that the Equal Rights Amendment would ultimately benefit the cause of women in America, we do agree with their right to boycott those states that have not ratified the Amendment.

2. By mobilizing millions of previously "inactive" Americans.

We have registered millions of voters and reactivated more millions of frustrated citizens into a special interest group who are effectively making themselves heard in the halls of Congress, in the White House, and in every state legislature.

3. By lobbying intensively in Congress to defeat any legislation that would further erode our constitutionally guaranteed freedoms and by introducing and/or supporting legislation that promotes traditional family and moral values.

The passage of a Human Life Amendment is a top priority on the Moral Majority agenda. Moral Majority Inc. supports the return of voluntary prayer to public schools. We oppose mandated or written prayers.

4. By informing all Americans about the voting records of their representatives so that every American, with full information available, can vote intelligently.

We are non-partisan. We are not committed to politicians or political parties; we are committed to principles and issues that we feel are essential to America's survival at this crucial hour.

5. By organizing and training millions of Americans who can become moral activists.

This heretofore silent majority in America can then help develop a responsive government which is truly "of the people, by the people, and for the people" instead of "in spite of the people," which we have had for too many years.

6. By encouraging and promoting non- public schools in their attempt to excel in academics while simultaneously teaching "bonafide minority" like women, blacks, Hispanics, etc. We do not oppose civil rights for homosexuals. We do oppose "special rights" for homosexuals who have chosen a perverted lifestyle rather than a traditional lifestyle.

4. We oppose the illegal drug traffic in America.

The youth in America are presently in the midst of a drug epidemic. Through education, legislation, and other means, we want to do our part to save our young people from death on the installment plan.

5. We oppose pornography.

While we do not advocate censorship, we do believe that education and legislation can help stem the tide of pornography and obscenity that is poisoning the American spirit today. Economic boycotts are a proper way in America's free-enterprise system to help persuade the media to move back to a sensible and reasonable moral stance. We most certainly believe in and are willing to fight for First Amendment rights for everyone. We are not willing to sit back while many television programs create cesspools of obscenity and vulgarity in America's living rooms.

6. We support the state of Israel and Jewish people everywhere.

It is impossible to separate the state of Israel from the Jewish family internationally. Moral Majority members, because of their theological convictions, are committed to the Jewish people. Others stand upon the human and civil rights of all persons as a premise for support of the state of Israel. Others support Israel because of historical and legal arguments. Regardless, one cannot belong to Moral Majority Inc. without making the commitment to support the state of Israel in its battle for survival and to support the human and civil rights of Jewish people everywhere. No anti-semitic influence is allowed in Moral Majority Inc. Further, Moral Majority Inc. is committed to the human and civil rights of all persons everywhere.

7. We believe that a strong national defense is the best deterrent to war.

We believe that liberty is the basic moral issue of all moral issues. No one in Afghanistan is discussing abortion today. The only way America can remain free is to remain strong. We therefore support the efforts of President Reagan, Secretary Haig, and many others to regain our position of military preparedness — with a sincere hope that we will never need to use any of our weapons against any people anywhere.

8. We support equal rights for women.

We agree with President Reagan's commitment to help every governor and state legislator to move quickly to insure that during the 1980's every American woman will earn as much money and enjoy the same opportunities for advancement as her male counterpart of the same vocation.

penalize widows and deserted wives.

10. We encourage our Moral Majority state organizations to be autonomous and indigenous.

Moral Majority state organizations may, from time to time, hold positions not held by Moral Majority Inc.

WHAT MORAL MAJORITY INC. IS NOT:

1. We are not a political party.

We are committed to work within the two-party system in this nation.

2. We do not endorse political candidates.

Moral Majority Inc. informs American citizens regarding the vital moral issues facing our nation. We have no "hit lists." Some members of the media attempt to group Moral Majority Inc. with all so-called "new right" organizations. While we fully support the constitutional rights of any special interest group to target candidates with whom they disagree, Moral Majority Inc. has chosen not to take this course. We are committed to principles and issues, not candidates and parties.

Many organizations, called the "new right" by the media, are doing a noble work addressing political, domestic, and economic issues not addressed by Moral Majority Inc. We congratulate them on this contribution to America's renaissance. However, Moral Majority Inc. restricts its involvement to the moral issues defined above. For example, Moral Majority Inc. has no official position on the Panama Canal Treaty, Taiwan, or South Africa — as we are often falsely charged by our critics.

3. We are not attempting to elect "born again" candidates.

We are committed to pluralism. The membership of Moral Majority Inc. is so totally pluralistic that the acceptability of any candidate could never be based upon one's religious affiliation. Our support of candidates is based upon two criteria:

(a) The commitment of the candidate to the principles which we espouse, and

(b) The competency of that candidate to fill that office.

4. Moral Majority Inc. is not a religious organization attempting to control the government.

Moral Majority Inc. is a special interest group of millions of Americans who share the same moral values. We simply desire to influence government — not control government. This, of course, is the right of every American, and Moral Majority Inc. would vigorously oppose any Ayatollah-type person rising to power in this country.

Likewise, we feel that all Americans have the right to refuse to purchase dollars from manufacturers whose advertising dollars support publications and television programming which violate their own morality code.

6. Moral Majority Inc. is not an organization committed to depriving homosexuals of their civil rights as Americans.

While we believe that homosexuality is moral perversion, we are committed to guaranteeing the civil rights of homosexuals. We do oppose the efforts of homosexuals to obtain special privileges as a "bonafide minority" and/or attempt to force their lifestyle upon our children. We view heterosexual promiscuity with the same distaste which we express toward homosexuality.

7. We do not believe that individuals or organizations which disagree with Moral Majority Inc. belong to an immoral minority.

However, we do feel that our position represents a consensus of the majority of Americans. This belief in no way reflects on the morality of those who disagree with us.

HERE IS HOW MORAL MAJORITY INC. IS CONTRIBUTING TO BRINGING AMERICA BACK TO MORAL SANITY:

1. By educating millions of Americans concerning the vital moral issues of our day.

This is accomplished through such avenues as our newspaper called the Moral Majority Report, a radio commentary by the same name, seminars, and other training programs conducted daily across the nation.

traditional family and moral values.

There are thousands of non-public schools in America which accept no tax monies. Some of these schools are Catholic, Fundamentalist, Jewish, Adventist, etc. Some are not religious. But Moral Majority Inc. supports the right of these schools to teach young people hot only "how to make a living," but "how to live."

Moral Majority Inc. does not advocate the abolition of public schools. Public schools will always be needed in our pluralistic society. We are committed to helping public schools regain excellence. That is why we support the return of voluntary prayer to public schools and strongly oppose the teaching of the religion of secular humanism in the public school classroom.

THE TIME FOR ACTION IS NOW:

Now is the time for all Americans to stand up for what is right in our nation and attempt to change that which is harmful and injurious.

Millions of Americans have already joined Moral Majority Inc. and have pledged their time, talent, and treasure to the rebuilding of this Republic.

The pornographers are angry. The amoral secular humanists are livid. The abortionists are furious. Full-page ads, employing McCarthy-like fear tactics, are appearing in major newspapers. The supporters of these ads, of course, are attempting by these means to raise funds for themselves.

The opposition has every right to legally promote their goals and attack ours. But, certainly, we have that same right.

Therefore, we invite you to join our ranks. Moral Majority Inc. is a non-profit organization and does not give tax-deductible receipts for contributions. It is supported by Americans who are willing to invest in their country. We are spending millions of dollars at this time to return this nation to the values and principles on which it was built.

If you would like to receive a free copy of the *Moral Majority Report* newspaper, simply complete and mail the coupon below.

☐ **YES!** Please send me a free copy of the Moral Majority Report.

Name _____

Address _____

City _____ State _____ Zip _____

Mail to: **Moral Majority Inc.**
National Capitol Office
P. O. Box 190
Forest, VA 24551

WSJ

This ad is made possible by gifts from generous friends of the Moral Majority. If you wish to help, please send your check to the above address.

Figure 8

A DIVERSITY OF OPINIONS REGARDING ABORTION EXISTS AMONG COMMITTED CATHOLICS.

A CATHOLIC STATEMENT ON PLURALISM AND ABORTION.

Continued confusion and polarization within the Catholic community on the subject of abortion prompt us to issue this statement.

Statements of recent Popes and of the Catholic hierarchy have condemned the direct termination of pre-natal life as morally wrong in all instances. There is the mistaken belief in American society that this is the only legitimate Catholic position. In fact, a diversity of opinions regarding abortion exists among committed Catholics:

- A large number of Catholic theologians hold that even direct abortion, though tragic, can sometimes be a moral choice.
- According to data compiled by the National Opinion Research Center, only 11% of Catholics surveyed disapprove of abortion in all circumstances.

These opinions have been formed by:

- Familiarity with the actual experiences that lead women to make a decision for abortion;

sity of opinion within the Church, and that Catholic youth and families be educated on the complexity of the issues of responsible sexuality and human reproduction.

Further, Catholics — especially priests, religious, theologians, and legislators — who publicly dissent from hierarchical statements and explore areas of moral and legal freedom on the abortion question should not be penalized by their religious superiors, church employers, or bishops.

Finally, while recognizing and supporting the legitimate role of the hierarchy in providing Catholics with moral guidance on political and social issues and in seeking legislative remedies to social injustices, we believe that Catholics should not seek the kind of legislation that curtails the legitimate exercise of the freedom of religion and conscience or discriminates against poor women.

In the belief that responsible moral decisions can only be made in an atmosphere of freedom from fear or coercion, we, the undersigned* call upon all Catholics to affirm this statement.

- A recognition that there is no common and constant teaching on ensoulment in Church doctrine, nor has abortion always been treated as murder in canonical history;
- An adherence to principles of moral theology, such as probabilism, religious liberty, and the centrality of informed conscience; and
- An awareness of the acceptance of abortion as a moral choice by official statements and respected theologians of other faith groups.

Therefore, it is necessary that the Catholic community encourage candid and respectful discussion on this diver-

To assist in our work please check one or more boxes below and send this coupon to:

The Catholic Committee c/o
Catholics For A Free Choice, Inc.
2008 17th Street N.W.
Washington, DC 20009

☐ I want to help you reach more people with this message. Here is my tax deductible contribution of $ _____

☐ Please send me additional literature.

☐ Please add my name to your Catholic Statement on Pluralism and Abortion.

NAME _____

ADDRESS _____

CITY/STATE/ZIP _____

PHONE _____

This ad is a project of the Catholic Committee. It has been paid for by Catholics For A Free Choice, Inc. Make your check payable to Catholics For A Free Choice, Inc.

CATHOLIC COMMITTEE ON PLURALISM AND ABORTION

Anthony Battaglia, Ph.D., Associate Professor, California State University • Roddy O'Neil Cleary, D. Min., Campus Ministries, University of Vermont • Joseph Fahey, Ph.D., Professor, Manhattan College • Elizabeth Schüssler Fiorenza, Ph.D., Professor, University of Notre Dame • Mary Gordon, M.A., author of Final Payments and Company of Women • Patricia Hennessy, J.D., New York City • Mary Hunt, Ph.D., Women's Alliance for Theology, Ethics and Ritual • Frances Kissling, Executive Director, Catholics for a Free Choice • Justus George Lawler, Executive Editor, Academic Bookline, Winston-Seabury Press • Daniel C. Maguire, S.T.D., Professor, Marquette University • Marjorie Reiley Maguire, Ph.D., Fellow in Ethics and Theology, Catholics for a Free Choice • J. Giles Milhaven, Ph.D., Professor, Brown University • Rosemary Radford Ruether, Ph.D., Professor, Garrett Evangelical Theological Seminary, IL • Thomas Shannon, Ph.D., Professor, Worcester Polytechnic Institute, MA • James F. Smurl, Ph.D., Professor, Indiana University

OTHER SIGNERS

Agnes P. Albany, M.A., Chestnut Hill College, PA • Everett Bellmann, Minot State College, ND • Michael H. Barnes, Ph.D., University of Dayton, OH • Barbara Bernache-Baker, Ph.D., Loomis Institute, CT • Kathryn Bissell, Wider Opportunities for Women, MD • Mary C.I. Buckley, S.T.D., St. John's University, NY • Ronald Burke, Ph.D., University of Nebraska at Omaha, NB • Mary J. Byles, Ph.D., Maryville College, MO • Ann Carr, Ph.D., University of Chicago Divinity School, IL • Rev. Joseph M. Connolly, S.T.L., pastor, Archdiocese of Maryland, MD • Margaret Cotroneo, Ph.D., University of Pennsylvania, PA • Patty Crowley, Chicago Catholic Women, IL • Barbara A. Cullom, Ph.D., Quixote Center, VA • Maryann Cunningham, S.L., Colorado • Mary Louise Denny, S.L., MO • Daniel DiDomizio, Marian

College, WI • Maurice C. Duchaine, S.T.D., San Francisco, CA • Emmaus Community of Christian Hope, NJ • Margaret A. Farley, Yale Divinity School, CT • Darrell J. Fasching, Ph.D., University of South Florida, FL • Barbara Ferraro, Sisters of Notre Dame, WV • Maureen Fiedler, Ph.D., S.L., Catholics for the Common Good, MD • Silvio E. Fittipaldi, Ph.D., Pastoral Institute of Lehigh Valley, PA • George H. Frein, Ph.D., University of North Dakota, ND • Lorine M. Getz, Ph.D., Somerville, MA • Kevin Gordon, Director, Consultation on Homosexuality, Social Justice and Roman Catholic Theology, CA • Jeannine Gramick, School Sisters of Notre Dame, NY • Christine E. Gudorf, Ph.D., Xavier University, OH • Terry Hamilton, Woodstock/St. Paul Roman Catholic Community, NY • Jack Hanford, Th.D., Ferris State College, MI • Kathleen Hebbeler, Dominican Sister of the Sick Poor, OH • Patricia Hussey, Sisters of Notre Dame, WV • Caridad Inda, Council of Women Religious, MD • Dorothy Irvin, S.T.D., Dunbar, NC • Fr. Jerry Kaelin, O.F.M. • Nelson Keating, Yale University, CT • Pat Kenoyer, S.L., Loretto Women's Network, MO • Joseph E. Kerns, S.T.D., Center for Christian Living, VA • Paul F. Knitter, Th.D., Xavier University, OH • Joseph A. LaBarge, Ph.D., Bucknell University, PA • Eleanor V. Lewis, Ph.D., Baltimore, MD • Wayne Lobue, Ph.D., Gilmour Academy, OH • Agnes Mary Mansour, Ph.D., Lansing, MI • Roseann Mazzeo, S.C., NJ • Bro. Ray McManaman, F.S.C., Lewis University, IL • Kathleen E. McVey, Ph.D., Princeton Theological Seminary, NJ • John A. Melloh, S.T.L., Milwaukee, WI • Joe Mellon, M.A., University of Notre Dame, IN • Diane Neu, M.Div., S.T.M., Co-director Women's Alliance for Theology, Ethics and Ritual, Washington, DC • Jeanne Noble, National Assembly of Religious Women, MD • Margaret Nulty, Sisters of Charity of New Jersey • Kathleen O'Connor, Ph.D., Maryknoll School of Theology, NY • Margaret A. O'Neill,

Ed.D., Sisters of Charity of New Jersey, NJ • Ronald D. Pasquariello, Ph.D., Marist Brothers, Washington, DC • Richard Penaskovic, Ph.D., Auburn University, AL • Gerald A. Pire, M.A., Seton Hall University, NJ • Stanley M. Polan, S.T.L., Franklin Pierce College, NH • Dolly Pomerleau, Catholics for the Common Good, MD • John E. Price, S.T.L., Evanston, IL • Donna Quinn, National Coalition of American Nuns, IL • Jill Raitt, Ph.D., University of Missouri, MO • Maureen Reiff, Chicago Catholic Women, IL • John G. Rusnak, Ph.D., Phoenix, AZ • Mary Savage, Ph.D., Albertus Magnus College, CT • Jane Schaberg, Ph.D., University of Detroit, MI • Mary Jane Schutzius, Federation of Christian Ministries, Association of the Rights of Catholics in the Church, MO • Ellen Shanahan, Ph.D., Rosary College, IL • Emily Ann Staples, University of Minnesota, MN • Marilyn Thie, Sisters of Charity of New Jersey, Colgate University, NY • Sr. Rose Dominic Trapasso, Lima, Peru • Sr. Margaret Ellen Traxler, National Coalition of American Nuns, IL • Marjorie Tuite, Church Women United, NY • Alan F. Turner, Association for the Rights of Catholics in the Church, Valley Forge, PA • Judith Vaughan, National Assembly of Religious Women, CA • E. Jane Via, Ph.D., J.D., University of San Diego and Superior Court of San Diego, CA • Gerald S. Vigna, Ph.D., Pennsauken, NJ • Ann Patrick Ware, M.A., National Coalition of American Nuns, NY • Sallie Ann Watkins, National Coalition of American Nuns, CO • Mary Jo Weaver, Ph.D., Indiana University, IN • Virginia Williams, S.L., MO • Arthur E. Zannoni, Ph.D., University of Notre Dame Extension Program, IN

*Organizational affiliations are listed for purposes of identification only. Partial listing. This statement has been signed by many other Catholics. In addition, 75 priests, religious and theologians have written that they agree with the Statement but cannot sign because they fear losing their jobs.

Figure 9

THE NEW YORK TIMES, SUNDAY, FEBRUARY 6, 1983

A DECLARATION OF WAR

The time has come to draw the line. Political Action Committees (PACs) have put Congress on the take. And *you're* being taken for a ride. Consider your health: PAC money from doctors helped convince Congress *not* to pass a bill that would help keep your hospital costs from skyrocketing. Consider your protection from fraud: PAC money from auto dealers helped convince Congress *not* to pass a bill that would require used car dealers to tell you what's wrong with the second-hand car you're buying. Consider your savings: PAC money from the dairy industry has helped to convince Congress, year after year, *not* to make needed cuts in dairy subsidies, which artificially inflate the price of the milk, butter and cheese you buy. Consider yourself *mute.* Your voice is being *drowned out* by the ringing of PAC cash registers in Congress.

Senator Robert Dole, Chairman of the Senate tax writing committee, says, "When these PACs give money, they expect something in return other than good government." These are contributions with a purpose—a legislative purpose. And **the PAC system works according to the golden rule, says former Congressman Henry Reuss: "Those who have the gold make the rules."**

We're not talking about illegal campaign contributions of the sort that ten years ago created a national scandal called Watergate. We're talking about $80 million in campaign contributions that are *perfectly legal,* creating a new national scandal corrupting our democracy. And *that* is a crime.

Unless we change our system for financing Congressional campaigns and change it soon, our representative system of government will be gone. We will be left with a government of, by and for the PACs.

We can't let that happen. We *won't* let that happen. Common Cause has declared war — a war on PACs. Ours has always been a government of, by and for the *people.* We must keep it that way. Common Cause.

But We Need Your Help!

Because even though there are Members of Congress who have spoken out against the PAC system, a majority have been unwilling to change it. It suits a special interest *they* have: getting re-elected. As Congressman Jim Leach says: "Clearly the collective judgment of Congress is that it's pro-incumbent to keep the current system, or they would have changed it by now."

Well, the only way they are going to change it is if enough citizens demand a change ... fight for a change. And that's what we're doing. Because what's at stake is our democracy.

Join us. It's *People* against *PACs.* Plain and simple.

Please make your check payable to Common Cause and send to Common Cause, 2030 M Street, N.W., Washington, D.C. 20036. Thank you.

NAME

ADDRESS

CITY STATE ZIP

☐ I know that when citizens speak out together — like we did during Watergate — we *can* turn things around. Please sign me up on the "People" side of your war against PACs.

☐ To help this critical effort I am enclosing a special contribution of:
☐ $20 (Annual Dues) ☐ $10 ☐ $35 ☐ $50 ☐ $100 ☐ $250 ☐ Other

☐ I am a member of Common Cause. QNY283

Residents of New York may obtain a copy of our last financial report from New York State Dept. of State, Office of Charities Registration, Albany, NY 12231

Figure 10

Table 1
Types of Advocacy Advertising

Recognition of Sponsor Interest	*Themes of Advertising Copy*	*Nature of Adversary*
1. *Disinterested sponsor:* Sponsor's interest is carefully disguised.	General issues of public interest or with an ideological or philosophical content: support of free enterprise system, association of profits with growth, reduction in budget deficits, rational federal government regulation of business.	Government agencies and legislative bodies, news media, opinion leaders, academic institutions, public apathy, and ignorance.
2. *Benevolent sponsor:* Sponsor's interests are presented as indirectly related.	Issues of interest to sponsor presented within the framework of overall social problems and suggestions for their solution. Public is exhorted to make sacrifices voluntarily.	Government agencies and legislative bodies, news media, opinion leaders, academic institutions, public apathy, and ignorance.
3. *Acknowledged vested-interest sponsor:* Sponsor's identity and interests are directly associated with the advocated programs.	Open defense of self-interest, downgrading of opponents and their arguments.	Government agencies and legislative bodies, environmental and other public interest groups, other companies and industries opposed to the sponsor's interests, news media, and in the case of voluntary nonprofit groups, the business community and the power establishment.
4. *Participation sponsor:* Sponsor's interest is carefully disguised.	Issues presented as problems common to industry and in the public interest; for example, regulation of our industry.	Governmental agencies and legislative bodies, public interest groups, competing industries, or firms that stand to gain from such regulation.
5. *Elusive sponsor:* Sponsor's identity and interest are carefully disguised to convey an image of conscious disinterest. Group names are selected to indicate a broader public constituency.	Issues are tailored to identify them with public benefit and general social concern, without any mention of sponsor's interests.	Sponsors of legislative programs or advocates of changes in current policies and political programs, be they governmental agencies or private groups, or business and industry groups.

Source: S. Prakash Sethi, *Advocacy Advertising: Concepts, Strategies and Applications* (Cambridge, Mass.: Ballinger, 1987), p. 73.

by a single company or a group of companies that are illustrative of this approach include Drexel Burnham on tax reform and W.R. Grace on federal deficits (figure 11).

Benevolent Sponsor. The sponsor's name is identified in the advertisement, but is presented only as indirectly related. The issue is presented as of broader public concern. Where solutions are suggested, the sponsor's role is minimized in a causal relationship with the problem, but emphasized in the solution. The advocacy appeal

WHICH TAXES THE COUNTRY MORE, THE BILL OR THE WAITING?

Everyone's talking about tax reform. And that's the problem.

Because nobody's doing anything about it.

So while the controversy over the proposals rages, key sectors of the investment economy are coming to a screeching halt.

And no wonder.

Why make capital improvements if the very incentives for them are eliminated? Or even in doubt.

Why invest if the incentives for succeeding are reduced? Or even in doubt.

What are we saying about the fight against inflation, if indexing becomes a cornerstone of tax policy? No doubt there.

It may be years before real tax reform is legislated in this country.

But it's only a matter of time before the effect of that delay is felt.

Hopefully, the Administration will act responsibly and with speed.

Because the longer we wait for a tax bill, the less we may have to pay taxes on.

Drexel Burnham
Drexel Burnham Lambert Incorporated

Figure 11

is of a general nature; the audience is exhorted to perform some voluntary action of self-help or self-sacrifice. A large number of industry-sponsored campaigns fall into this category. Examples can be found in the advocacy ads sponsored by the Chemical Manufacturers Association, the Canadian Petroleum Association, the Savings and Loan Foundation, the Edison Electric Institute, the United Steel Workers, and the New York Medical Liability Reform Coalition on the high costs of medical malpractice insurance (figure 12).

Acknowledged Self-Interest Sponsor. The sponsor is directly identified and openly associates its interest with those of the programs advocated in the message such as ads by utility companies about air pollution standards promulgated by the Environmental Protection Agency. The reader is asked to take action that would be of immediate help to the sponsor, but would ultimately benefit the reader. Advocacy advertisements sponsored by Todd Shipyards, the League of Voluntary Hospitals and Homes of New York, and the Grumman Corporation are illustrative of this approach. This approach also has been used by Lone Star Industries and Mobil Oil Corporation, among others. Variation of this strategy can be found in advertisements where incumbent corporate management beseech their stockholders to vote for their plans in situations involving unfriendly or hostile takeover attempts (figure 13).

Participative Sponsor. The sponsor's identity is apparent, but its interests are carefully disguised. Issues are presented as problems common to industry and also in the public interest. Advocacy campaigns by voluntary organizations and public interest groups fall in this category, along with many industry and trade group campaigns. Ingersoll-Rand Corporation's advertisement on acid rain and its alleged causes is an illustration of this approach (figure 14).

Elusive Sponsor. The sponsor's interests and even identity are carefully disguised to convey an aura of conscious disinterest. Issues are tailored to reflect public benefit without any mention of the sponsor's interest. Many single-interest groups, social activists, ideologically-oriented organizations, and industry groups suffering from low public credibility or fighting adverse public opinion on an issue are likely to resort to this approach.

Intensity of Advocacy

This dimension measures the intensity with which an appeal is being made and ranges from emotional to reasoned persuasion and information. Emotional appeals are often identified with ads that fall into the categories of acknowledged vested interest and elusive sponsors. Emotional appeals often involve intangible or esthetic concerns and contain few specifics about what might be done or who should do it. Their emphasis is on building the reader's sympathy for the sponsor's action or position on an issue.

Thank You, New York Times.

The New York Times FRIDAY, APRIL 26, 1985

What's the Cure for Bad Medicine?

In the opinion of New York actuaries, the medical malpractice insurance business is hurtling toward a disaster that could impair the medical-care system. Governor Cuomo is sympathetic, but offers a bill that would provide only symbolic relief. He and the Legislature need to think harder about the problem.

The costs of malpractice suits are rising nationally as medicine grows more sophisticated. Nowhere is the problem more severe than in New York City and its suburbs. In the 70's, the cost of malpractice claims increased 20 percent annually. In the 80's, the rate is curving alarmingly toward 30 percent. What especially worries the actuaries is the time it takes to settle a suit: now more than eight years. Claims being paid for past malpractice average about $150,000 today. Inflation will push the figure to $450,000 for malpractice occurring now.

•

Such figures spell deep trouble for the Medical

avoids the tougher measure probably needed to contain the explosion in costs: a ceiling on damages for pain and suffering.

Such a ceiling would present difficult moral and practical issues. Would a limit wrongly squeeze the most severely injured victims the most? Should doctors be singled out for special protection? Nevertheless, a ceiling is not unprecedented. Courts in Indiana and California have upheld caps on liability, and the principle is recognized in worker's compensation and insurance of nuclear power plants.

The state trial lawyers' association, already campaigning passionately against even Mr. Cuomo's modest bill, insists no such stringent action is necessary. Why are doctors so upset, the lawyers ask, when most still pay only small percentages of their incomes for insurance? And how can the medical insurer be in trouble when it is making all of its payments with investment income?

The questions are disingenuous. Low malpractice premiums apply mainly upstate. Except for

Liability Mutual Insurance Company, the doctor-owned concern that insures 16,000 of New York's 22,500 private physicians. Its reserves total $1.15 billion but its potential liabilities may be $750 million more. The state insurance department recently authorized a premium increase of 55 percent, pushing the average cost to more than $20,000 a year in the metropolitan area and as much as $60,000 for some specialists on Long Island. Yet even such enormous increases may not be enough to keep the malpractice insurer afloat.

The prospect that doctors may thus not be able to find insurance at any price prompts state officials to consider "tort reform" — legislated limits on attorneys' fees and awards. The Governor's bill includes some curbs on fees and awards, but it

some successful specialists they are a genuine problem in New York City. They discourage doctors from some specialties. They drive up costs for middle-income patients. And they make it even harder to provide medical care in poor neighborhoods. As for paying claims out of investment income, the malpractice insurer is only 10 years old and hasn't yet had to pay out much; most of its cases are nowhere near settlement or verdict. Further, the high interest rates it has been earning are headed down, while inflation of payments heads ever higher.

The courts can't provide much justice for malpractice victims unless the malpractice insurance system works. That system is teetering. The crisis is real, and putting a ceiling on awards may be a sound remedy.

We Could Not Have Said It Better.

New York Medical Liability Reform Coalition
96 South Swan Street, Albany, New York 12210

Alliance of American Insurers
American Association
of Neurological Surgeons
American College of Obstetricians
and Gynecologists, District II
Business Council of New York State
Hospital Association of New York
State

Hospital Underwriters Mutual
Insurance Company
Medical Liability Mutual
Insurance Company
Medical Society of
the State of New York
Nationwide Insurance Company

New York Chamber
of Commerce and Industry
New York Conference
of Blue Cross/Blue Shield Plans
New York State Society
of Anesthesiologists, Inc.
New York State Society
of Surgeons

Figure 12

Most advocacy campaigns have one or more ads with primarily emotional appeals, or individual ads containing emotional appeals along with reasoned persuasion. Ad campaigns with environment and ecology as their primary theme are generally loaded with emotional appeals. Reasoned persuasion has been used in campaigns where sponsors attempt to identify their interests with those of their readers. The theme is "We are all in this together" or "We're doing our share, but we can't accomplish much unless everybody else does his share." Some information or data to appeal to one's reason is always provided so that a decision can be rationalized, although the actual reasons for making a given decision may be less than totally objective from the reader's perspective. Advocacy advertisements by public interest groups invariably contain a high level of emotional intensity, with an attempt to engage the reader's sense of morality and indignation against the adversaries identified in the ads.

Specificity in Identifying the Adversary

The adversary can be classified into one or more of four categories: the general public, governmental agencies, competitors, and public interest or social activist groups. When the sponsor is a public interest group, the reverse would be the case. In many instances, the ultimate adversary may be someone or something other than that identified in the ad. The objective of the advertisement is to change attitudes in groups of people who may be in a position, either directly or indirectly, to influence the actions of the sponsor's adversaries in directions preferred by the sponsor.

Implementation Strategies for Advocacy Advertising

An effective advocacy campaign must have a clear focus in terms of its long-term objective and the intended target audience. The strength of advocacy advertising for its sponsor lies in two elements: (1) the content of the message is defined in a manner most favorable for the sponsor; and (2) the environment of the message is carefully controlled, so that the message is disseminated in a more hospitable environment. Even the most potent ideas may go awry if they are not communicated properly. An analysis of various advocacy campaigns, both in the United States and abroad, suggests that successful implementation involves several steps discussed next.

Setting Campaign Objectives

A careful delineation of the sponsor's objectives is critical to the development of an effective campaign strategy. Two important issues must be borne in mind in establishing campaign objectives. An advocacy campaign, more than most other types of advertising campaigns, not only influences existing public opinion, but

Six compelling reasons why the Arleigh Burke destroyer must be built on the West Coast.

The United States Navy will soon begin rebuilding its aging destroyer fleet with up to 61 ARLEIGH BURKE (DDG 51) class guided missile destroyers. These ships, equipped with the highly successful AEGIS combat system, will incorporate the most advanced technology available in antiair, antisubmarine, antisurface, amphibious and strike warfare capabilities. In conjunction with 28 AEGIS-equipped CG 47 class guided missile cruisers, 13 of which are already under contract at two Eastern yards, they will provide an impenetrable shield against surface, missile and aircraft attack as elements of the aircraft carrier battle groups so vital to our national defense.

There are six compelling reasons why the DDG 51 class lead ship must be built on the West Coast:

1 **Maintain a geographically-dispersed AEGIS shipbuilding base.** The two classes of AEGIS ships are too important to the Navy's forward defense strategy, and that strategy is too important to our national security, to concentrate all building resources in one geographic area. Selection of a West Coast shipyard for construction of the DDG 51 to supplement current CG 47 class cruiser construction facilities on the East and Gulf Coasts will avoid the financial and strategic risks of AEGIS program disruption or delay and ensure mobilization "surge" capacity.

2 **Reduce "choke point" risk.** All newly constructed aircraft carriers, submarines and AEGIS cruisers assigned to Pacific Fleet duty must be deployed by way of the Panama Canal since all of these ships are currently built only in Eastern yards. In addition to the long distance deployment bottleneck and logistics problems this situation can create, what is the alternative if access to the canal is threatened or denied in the future? Establishment of a West Coast source for AEGIS ship construction now will reduce rather than expand reliance on this potentially dangerous "choke point."

3 **Establish AEGIS know-how on the West Coast to support the Pacific Fleet.** Many AEGIS-equipped destroyers and cruisers will be stationed in the Pacific and will need convenient, capable facilities to provide service and repairs in minimum out-of-

service time. Because the shipyards that build these sophisticated ships will be the best qualified–in fact, the only ones able–to service them effectively, this capability must be developed as quickly as possible on the West Coast to be available when the first AEGIS combatants go into Pacific Fleet service in 1985.

4 **Keep defense programs competitive.** The Navy's policy of maintaining competition among private shipyards on combatant ship construction programs has resulted in lower cost, improved quality and faster delivery, as exemplified by the FFG 7 class guided missile frigate program in which two West Coast yards and one East Coast yard shared in the construction program. Millions of dollars have been saved on this program and fleet readiness has been significantly improved through a procurement policy that mandated two-coast competition and building yard capability to directly support this class on both coasts.

5 **Minimize total program cost.** Support services (overhaul, repair, modernization, maintenance, etc.) over a ship's 30-year expected life cycle far exceed initial construction costs. Over the full term, cost-effective maintenance of Pacific-based DDG 51 class destroyers by the West Coast building yard will more than offset possibly higher acquisition cost caused by differences in regional wage scales, in addition to minimizing out-of-service downtime.

6 **Capitalize on an available, qualified private sector resource.** Todd's modern Los Angeles Division, which has an outstanding schedule and cost performance record on the FFG 7 class guided missile frigate program now winding down, backed by 25 years of experience in surface combatant construction, is fully qualified for the lead ship DDG 51 contract. Since 1976, Todd Shipyards Corporation has spent $120,000,000 of its own funds to create this technologically-advanced facility and its highly productive work force, an investment that will fully benefit the DDG 51 program.

The Navy needs AEGIS-equipped surface combatants, the Pacific Fleet needs experienced AEGIS support capabilities and our national defense urgently requires maintenance of a strong, knowledgeable West Coast AEGIS shipbuilding mobilization base.

The solution is obvious.

Todd Shipyards Corporation
One State Street Plaza, New York, NY 10004

DELIVERING THE SHIPS THE U.S. NEEDS–WHEN IT NEEDS THEM.

This advertisement appeared in THE WALL STREET JOURNAL, THE WASHINGTON POST and THE WASHINGTON TIMES.

Figure 13

Coal can keep the lights on.

America must start preparing now for the growing energy demands of the next 20 years or the outlook could be rather dark, indeed. The Department of Energy has pointed out: Even though conservation of gasoline consumption is taking place, with a corresponding decline in dependence on foreign oil, the increasing growth in demand for electricity (approaching an annual rate of 3%) is creating a gloomy forecast. If this significant growth rate continues or increases, by the mid-to-late 1990's *it will be too late to fulfill it*. To meet even our nation's minimum additional requirements, the necessary power plants ought to be on drawing boards *today*.

The Department of Energy further estimates that by the year 2000 we will have to replace 25 to 30 percent of our total generating capacity—the equivalent of 150 new nuclear plants or 250 to 300 coal-fired plants.

What's our energy picture today?

The goal of our country's National Energy Policy Plan is to provide *an adequate supply of energy at a reasonable cost;* enough to meet our present and future needs. Our resources include energy reserves stockpiled or in the ground, such as oil, natural gas or coal; or proved sources, including nuclear and hydro-electric power; along with developing technologies that make use of solar power, wind, geo-thermal sources and biofuels.

This variety of resources represents the second objective of our energy policy; "to promote a balanced and mixed energy system."

Which energy source can we rely on?

The Secretary of Energy of the United States cautions, "The single most critical energy issue confronting this nation is our continued dependence on foreign oil. If I were a businessman making decisions regarding my future energy supply, I would not be willing to gamble on low-cost oil."

For generating baseload electricity, coal and nuclear energy are more economical over the long term than either oil or natural gas. However, the immediate future of nuclear power seems uncertain. What's more, reserves of oil and natural gas are decreasing while the costs of finding new reserves continue to rise.

Solar energy, wind energy, hydro-power and geothermal systems essentially are technologies of the future and can, collectively, provide only about 11 percent of all the electricity generated by the year 2000.

Coal—a vital resource in the "balanced energy mix".

The U.S. possesses the world's largest recoverable reserves of coal, enough to provide the energy we need for centuries, at current and projected rates of demand.

According to the National Energy Policy Plan, coal production should increase more than any other fuel between now and the year 2000. But coal consumption has not grown in the last 5 years, and the future is unclear. In fact today, despite low oil prices, almost half (about $60 billion) of our trade imbalance of $130 billion per year is paid to import 5.4 million barrels per day of foreign oil. Think of the serious impact on our energy availability and our

Ingersoll-Rand speaks out for the Coal Industry.

The advertisement on these pages is one of a series prepared by Ingersoll-Rand's Mining Machinery Group that deals with vital energy issues confronting our country today— and the steps that must be taken to insure an ample supply of energy for centuries to come.

Appearing over the next few months in The Wall Street Journal, these ads address a number of key issues in order to show how coal can contribute significantly to our country's balanced energy mix. Ingersoll-Rand's Mining Machinery Group is pleased to stand up for the coal industry by bringing these critical issues to the attention of America's financial and industrial thought leaders. Add your voice to this cause; send today for the brochure and information packet offered in the advertisement.

economy when there is another oil shortage or prices again rise.

Coal's share of electric generating capacity is expected to grow from about 50% at present to 59% by the year 2000. But if we don't start plans now, we'll still have to depend on imported oil to meet our energy needs even then. It is also estimated that before 2000, oil and gas will be priced out of most utility markets. Thus, our nation *must* turn to coal for a continuing supply of energy.

If we expect to be prepared to respond to energy emergencies of the future—and the future starts today—we must recognize how essential coal is to the balanced energy mix. In order to help you understand the role of coal in our energy mix, we've prepared a booklet entitled, *Coal. America's Best-Kept Secret.* After receiving it, you may want to join your voice with others in taking a more firm stance on coal. Just return the attached coupon for your copy.

Ingersoll-Rand has pledged its resources to help propel American concern about our energy future into concrete action. Among other products, we manufacture machinery used to mine coal. But, that's not the only reason we're involved: mining companies will require equipment even if our energy

policies go unchanged. We're involved for the same reason you should get involved: because America must address its energy future, and act now.

Ingersoll-Rand
Mining Machinery Group
4201 Lee Highway
Bristol, VA 24201
Please send a copy of *Coal. America's Best-Kept Secret* and related materials to:

Name

Company

Address

City   State   Zip

INGERSOLL-RAND®
MINING MACHINERY

Figure 14

also affects public expectations of the type of information about the sponsoring organization and its level of performance, both of which may turn out to be different than the sponsor is willing to provide. Moreover, once aroused, people may become cognizant of nonadvertised facets of a sponsor's activities and may evaluate them within the framework of pleadings made by the sponsor in an advocacy campaign. Another facet of this issue has to do with the changes in public policy being advocated in an advocacy campaign. Robert L. Dilenschneider of Hill & Knowlton observes:

> How high does one raise the public's level of expectation through advocacy advertising, and then, what programs are in place to fulfill that level? If a change in a law or regulation is being advocated, is that really possible, and what is the effect on overall public good? If a modification is being suggested in a company or in society, is that feasible, and how will that be effective over the long range? If expectations are raised to a level that cannot be realized, then the advocacy advertising itself is doomed to failure.[4]

The second important issue in establishing campaign objectives has to do with the proper role for advocacy advertising in a total communications effort. This effort also includes other forms of communication, notably unpaid communications, incorporating news media relations that generate favorable publicity for the sponsor's policies and programs. A number of respectable public relations practitioners, and even corporate executives, have expressed misgivings about overreliance on advocacy campaigns to carry a sponsor's message on controversial issues of public policy.[5]

The objective of a campaign must be defined in two dimensions:

What public policy issues are to be communicated, and how well are they understood by the public or the target audience groups?

What does the sponsor expect to achieve from the advocacy campaign?

For example, a sponsor who merely wishes to create public awareness of a public policy issue will opt for a long-term educational campaign; choose opinion leaders as the target audience; and develop messages using single or multiple authenticating sources as spokespersons. This approach has been successfully used by companies such as Dresser Industries, LTV, and Smith-Kline Beckman. However, a company might wish to promote a variety of ideas, thereby identifying the sponsor as a public-sprited organization, for example, United Technologies and the LTV Corporation.

Another campaign objective may be to change public opinion on a specific issue within a short time. This campaign strategy will be quite different, depending on whether the sponsor stands to benefit from the advocated position or is acting primarily as a concerned public citizen. The advocacy campaigns by W.R. Grace, the Savings and Loan Foundation, and British Rail exemplify this approach.

Sponsor's Public Credibility

An important element in the success of an advocacy campaign is the public perception of the credibility of the sponsor. Although a sponsor may effectively control the content of a message and carefully define the communication environment, the adversary nature of advocacy advertising makes it imperative that sponsors strive to make their messages credible to an otherwise skeptical and even hostile audience.

A stance of pure opposition-opposition as an end in itself, rather than some larger, positive social commitment, is self-defeating, and likely to be short-lived. Herbert Schmertz, vice-president for public affairs of Mobil Oil and the architect of that company's advocacy campaign, appreciates this concern when he says that his company has made a fundamental decision to make a significant intellectual commitment to the subject matter in its ad campaign, rather than giving it a superficial treatment: "We probably lose readers. But in the long haul, unless you are prepared to put yourself on the line both intellectually and philosophically, you will never gain long-term leadership and recognition of substance."[6]

We receive our communication cues from a variety of sources, most of which are not, and cannot be, controlled by the sponsor. Similarly, we interpret a particular message based on our prior attitude toward the sponsor and opinion on the subject being discussed. It is therefore not surprising that the oil industry's defense of its activities during the oil shortages of 1972 to 1973 had little effect in changing the public's opinion of the oil companies or the believability of their public statements.

A new campaign by R.J. Reynolds follows somewhat similar logic. Designed to counter the public's growing hostility toward smoking and smokers, the ads use a reasoned approach to provide scientific information to correct the public's attitudes about the "second-hand smoker." It will be interesting to see whether such a campaign has any influence in changing public opinion about smoking hazards and public attitudes toward tobacco and cigarette smokers. Another advertisement sponsored by Philip Morris Incorporated protests the raw deal smokers are getting because many anti-smoking campaigns create discrimination against smokers by denying them use of public places in which to enjoy smoking, and by fostering a general bias against and hostility toward smokers.

In the long run, the sponsoring institution must develop a political position, a position that is not merely self-serving, but that clearly embodies the public interest. The campaign by AIMS of Industry in the United Kingdom exemplifies the approach. Advocacy campaigns also must reflect the long-term nature of the educational and attitudinal change in a sponsor's communication program. Campaigns developed on an ad hoc basis, under crisis conditions, invariably suffer from low public credibility because they project a self-serving image in a hostile external environment. However, if a sponsor continues to speak objectively on issues of social importance in which it has a vital stake, it builds a reservoir of credibility that can stand in good stead when it attacks inaccuracy or bias in the public statements of its critics.

Developing a Campaign Strategy

Advocacy advertising should be an integral part of a sponsor's total communication program, which in turn must bear a close relationship to the activities of the sponsor, the role it projects for itself in society, and the expectations of society for its performance. Too often, advocacy advertising is confined to what the sponsor wants the world to hear, rather than what the world wants the corporation to talk about. It should be a continuous program built around the long-range objectives of the sponsor.

Many institutional advocacy campaigns place a heavy burden on the mass media component of the campaign. All other elements of the communication mix are designed to promote the advocacy tactics, rather than the total objective of the campaign. This is unfortunate, because such an approach tends to skew the reach of the message toward one segment of the targeted audience and may also distort the perception of the message. Instead, an advocacy campaign should be viewed as an integrated project in which different elements of the communications mix— press relations, direct mail, lecture circuit, and mass media are carefully evaluated for their relative contributions to the overall campaign. The campaigns by W.R. Grace and the Edison Electric Institute demonstrate the success of such an integrated approach.

Selection of Target Audiences

Many advocacy campaigns, especially those oriented toward raising the threshold of public awareness and understanding of public policy issues, aim generally at the educated populace without any attempt at the careful targeting common to product and service advertising. There are, however, two exceptions:

A sponsor may target its messages to those segments of the potential audience considered undecided and therefore "persuadables" on a particular issue. Bethlehem Steel, for example, developed an interesting approach to segmenting its audience in this manner. This approach also influenced that company's choice of media.

A sponsor may want to reach influentials, such as political leaders, indirectly through their constituents or the general public, who will be encouraged to write to their elected representatives. This approach is generally used by sponsors who seek immediate action on a legislative issue and use the mass media to put pressure on decision-makers.

Development of Message Content

Advocacy campaigns dealing with specific ideas, whether of a short- or long-run nature, are unique, one-of-a-kind phenomena. They are more like editorial messages or pleadings that must reflect the magnitude and scope of the public issue under discussion; the tone of the time, the nature of the place; and the character of the sponsor, the intensity of its commitment, and the opposition to the sponsor's viewpoint and position.

Creativity, therefore, is very important in such campaigns. Moreover, since greater emphasis has to be placed on message substance than manner of delivery, development of message or ad copy requires significantly large resources for researching the issue. This is in sharp contrast to product advertising, especially consumer product advertising, where research emphasis is focused on the audience end, and messages are designed based on that research. There is also relatively more weight given to graphics and visuals—the manner of delivery rather than the message itself.

A serious question therefore arises as to whether an advocacy campaign should be developed in-house or by an outside full-service advertising agency. This is not just a philosophical issue, but could be critical to the success of a campaign. Advocacy campaigns in which advertising agencies have played a larger creative role have been generally long on graphics and color, have low-key messages, and have greater visceral than cerebral appeal. They also tend to use electronic media much more than campaigns developed in-house. Thus, it is quite easy to distinguish advocacy campaigns where ad agencies have played a major creative role. Campaigns by the Chemical Manufacturers Association, the Canadian Petroleum Association, Lone Star Industries, and the Association of American Railroads are illustrative of this genre of advertising. It should also not be surprising to see that most industry trade association campaigns fall in this category.

One reason for the failure of many advocacy campaigns may lie in the confusion that exists between the process of education, the procedures of advertising, and the purposes of propaganda. The purposes of education are to foster growth in comprehension of abstract ideas and concepts; to raise questions about prevailing beliefs; and to encourage intellectual inquiry. The purpose of propaganda is to inculcate a belief through differing information—and even false information—if necessary. Advertising, however, is intended to provide answers that are definite and specific; to persuade people to do things; and in general, to minimize inquiry and uncertainty in a society whose expectations have changed.[7]

Measuring the Effectiveness of Advocacy Campaigns

One of the most difficult problems with advocacy campaigns is determining their effectiveness. Many advertising executives, both within and outside corporations, have argued against advocacy advertising on a number of grounds, but especially that it is not cost-justified. Those using advocacy profess to be satisfied with the outcomes of their campaigns. Naturally, most of the criticism comes from those who have not engaged in advocacy advertising. Critics suggest that advocacy advertising, like other types of institutional advertising, is a "good time" phenomenon.

Businesses do this to claim that they are responsible corporate citizens when profits are rising and companies are prospering, only to discontinue it when they face hard times. There is some truth to this allegation, as can be seen from the cases of Bethlehem Steel and SmithKline Beckman, both of which have reverted to conventional corporate-image advertising after having been in the forefront of developing novel approaches to the use of advocacy advertising.

Evaluating the effectiveness of advocating advertising entails some of the same problems confronted by all advertising; its effect is invariably combined with all other communication activities undertaken by a sponsor and therefore cannot be easily isolated. Furthermore, unlike product advertising, advocacy campaigns are designed for very different purposes that make conventional effectiveness measures of limited relevance.

Long-Term Editorial or Omnibus Campaigns

Advocacy campaigns that are primarily of an educational nature and designed to increase public understanding of a particular issue have to take a long-term perspective. Their success cannot be measured in traditional bottom-line terms. For example, how do we know the impact of an informed public on the Federal government's expenditures for defense and national security or regulation of business? A cynic might ask why one individual corporation, or a nonbusiness group for that matter, should concern itself with such issues, and even if it does, will it really make any difference?

The proper question, however, should be whether private institutions in a democratic society, corporations included, can afford to be passive about fundamental values that underlie the foundations of society. To put it differently, should we be concerned whether individuals vote or understand the values of a free society? Ray D'Argenio of United Technologies makes this point quite cogently:

> Every company has the responsibility to engage in an intellectual dialogue with the public. And it must be done consistently and over a long period of time. You have an obligation to yourself and to the nation to do that. There are times when business is under attack for keeping its mouth closed, and by not expressing its point of view.

Changing public opinion and attitude is a slow process and may have no direct or discernible relationship with traditional measures of awareness or recall of an ad immediately following its appearance. And yet, by more enlightened criteria, many of these campaigns have been successful not only in terms of improving public understanding of the issues involved, but also in gaining public good will for the sponsoring corporation.

The LTV campaign, which presented opposing viewpoints on specific issues in its ads (including findings of public opinion surveys) was very successful. It generated more than 35,000 requests for additional materials on issues discussed in the ads. The advertisements in the *Wall Street Journal* alone generated more than 6,000 unsolicited letters in a single year.

The Edward Teller ad on nuclear power sponsored by Dresser Industries generated more than 5,000 requests for copies. Various groups and corporations reprinted the ad in local newspapers and other in-house publications at their own expense. Dresser Industries estimates it reached over 9 million readers.

Similarly, United Technologies' now classic "That Girl" ad was a phenomenal success. It generated great response from women's organizations all around the country and has been the subject of numerous newspaper and television stories, in addition to thousands of copies being distributed all over the world. SmithKline Beckman's two-year advocacy campaign generated more than 82,000 requests for additional information. Most companies engaging in educational or informational advocacy campaigns put a high value on letters from their readers, especially when these letters express individual viewpoints and seek additional information about the issue.

Specific Issue-Related Campaigns

Advocacy campaigns in this category include, among others, those of Kaiser Aluminum, Rodale Press, Bethlehem Steel, AFSCME, and Edison Electric Institute. When companies are launching campaigns that focus on specific issues linked with a company's activities, benchmark studies are sometimes carried out to determine the target audience's knowledge and understanding of those issues and their opinions of the company. The success of a campaign is then measured in terms of shifts in people's opinions on certain dimensions from the benchmark. Some of the major advocacy campaigns have used this approach: Bethlehem Steel, Commercial Union, Canadian Petroleum Association, Chemical Manufacturers Association, American Association of Railroads, SmithKline Beckman, British Railways Board, LTV Corporation, and Kaiser Aluminum. They offer excellent approaches to the use of benchmark studies prior to a campaign launch. Canadian Petroleum Association, for example, went so far as to establish specific targets for shifting people's opinions on various issues following different phases of its advertising campaign. Each phase of the campaign was tied into the previous phase accomplishing its objective. While benchmark and other follow-up studies are important, placing too much emphasis on them in determining campaign strategy may have serious drawbacks.

> The measurement is viewed only in terms of positive movement from the benchmark data. However, in a hostile external environment, the mere arrest of a decline in people's opinion on a given issue may be an important and worthwhile result.

> Public opinion studies measure current opinion and how it might have been influenced by an ad campaign. However, this measure is unstable, especially

when no other measure exists that would link a change in opinion to a specific action. Attitude changes on public policy issues evolve slowly and one cannot predict at what point a person's attitude will have been influenced by the message of an ad. A person may claim not to have been influenced by an ad at one time, but may evaluate the same information differently at a future time in view of other information that later came to his/her attention. Campaign decisions made on the basis of pre- and post-studies may actually suggest incorrect conclusions.

Short-Run Single-Issue Campaigns

These campaigns involve persuading the target audience to take certain actions, such as to write to their elected representative to vote for or against a particular bill or proposed law. The success of these campaigns is easily measured in terms of whether a particular law was enacted. The examples of the Savings and Loan Foundation in the case of the "All Savers Certificate" and the W.R. Grace campaign to lower capital gains taxes are illustrative of the great success that can be achieved through this strategy. There are, however, certain caveats:

> Both campaigns used a multiplicity of communication channels, print advertising in the mass media being only one of them.

> There was strong public support, although there was official antipathy to the issue. Thus, it was a question of mobilizing public opinion to bear on a reluctant political leadership.

> Even the best campaigns will not succeed where there is strong public hostility toward the sponsor or against the policy position advocated by the sponsor. All efforts of the oil companies were unsuccessful in preventing the passage of the windfall profits tax during the Carter administration.

> Studies show that while both the tobacco and bottling industries have had occasional successes in referendum fights against legal restrictions against smoking in public places and for bottle-return deposit laws, it has been largely a losing battle as more and more communities have been enacting some form of legislation affecting these industries.

Conclusions

Since the mid-1970s, there has been a significant increase in the quality and sophistication of the advocacy campaigns undertaken by corporations. This is especially true of the print media, where advocacy ads seem mostly to have discarded emotional messages. Instead, they concentrate on discussing issues in terms of expert opinion, corporate viewpoint, or even both-sides viewpoints from responsible and highly credible spokespersons. Most of this effort is sincere, honest, and open, and its growth has enriched the public debate.

At the same time, there has been a great increase in the number and diversity of nonbusiness groups using advocacy advertising. And some of the business and nonbusiness groups have been resorting to advocacy advertising not to raise the level of public debate, but to demean it; not to improve the quality of public decision making, but to deteriorate it by manipulating public opinion through the use of disinformation and emotional rhetoric.

Increased access to the marketplace of ideas carries with it an obligation to use such access in a responsible manner. The business community has the most to lose from public misinformation and so should take every step to improve the quality of public information and debate. Large budgets and air time are unlikely to buy happiness and credibility for corporations unless this opportunity is used intelligently and in a manner that will earn the business community public respect and trust.

When properly employed, advocacy advertising contributes to greater understanding by the public of the sponsor's position in meeting society's expectations. None of this, however, will come to pass if restraint is not exercised in the use of advocacy advertising. If we are content primarily to pursue partisan propaganda in our communications, the consequences could affect every aspect of our society. It will not reduce the scope and conflict, but enlarge it. It will not contribute to the quality and diversity of public information, but worsen it. In the final analysis, greater freedom to talk would be a pyrrhic victory indeed if in the process public trust in the sponsor's credibility is lost. There would be greater noise, but not necessarily more intelligent discussion. Critics of the business community, who also engage in advocacy campaigns, deserve no more respect if they continue to label all business claims as self-serving and contrary to public interest while they refuse to recognize any other viewpoint as representative of the larger public interest except their own, or to be interested in hearing viewpoints that are not variations of their own. We would thus create an environment where mutual distrust is fostered and the public interest is poorly served.

As Mr. Robert L. Dilenschneider comments:

> If this nation continues to receive an ever increasing glut of advocacy advertising, we are putting the readers of such ads in a position where, (1) they tune them out; or (2) they are interested and then have to choose sides. In choosing sides we set up a controversy that, if propelled to the extreme, could be quite unhealthy. Specifically, right now America appears to be at peace with itself. The populace, based on all of the polls, appears to be saying, "we are happy with our country, we are happy with the direction in which it is headed, we are happy with our leadership." I certainly don't want to comment on our leadership on a pro or con nature. But advocacy advertising that continues to suggest "things are wrong" will upset the mood of the nation after a prolonged period of time. I don't think the United States can afford right now to slip back into a period like the 1960s.[8]

Notes

This article is adapted from the author's forthcoming book, *Handbook of Advocacy Advertising: Concepts, Strategies and Applications,* to be published by Ballinger Publishing Company (in press).

1. S. Prakash Sethi, *Advocacy Advertising and Large Corporations* (Lexington, Mass.: D.C. Heath, 1977).
2. Testimony of S. Prakash Sethi before the Commerce, Consumer, and Monetary Affairs Subcommittee of the House Government Operations Committee, July 18, 1978, pp. 14–18; Testimony of Victor L. Lowe before the Subcommittee on Commerce, Consumer, and Monetary Affairs, House Government Operations Committee on Tax Deductions for Grassroots Lobbying, May 23, 1970; Auditing of political advertising by Electric Utilities and Gas and Oil Companies, July 16, 1976.
3. For an analysis of the bases on which these estimates were arrived, see S. Prakash Sethi, *Handbook of Advocacy Advertising* (Cambridge, Mass.: Ballinger, in press).
4. Robert L. Dilenschneider, president and chief operating officer, national operations, Hill & Knowlton, Inc. Letter to the author dated December 31, 1984.
5. Observers like David Finn of Ruder, Finn and Rotman; William P. Mullane, Jr. of AT&T; Kalman Druck, public relations counselor; and Robert Dilenschneider of Hill & Knowlton acknowledge the importance of advocacy advertising as a part of an integrated public communications campaign. However, they maintain that its impact and value are overblown, and that a sole or even primary reliance on it, may even be counterproductive in the long run.
6. Sethi, *Advocacy Advertising.*
7. Irving Kristol, "On Economic Education," *Wall Street Journal,* February 18, 1976, p. 20.
8. Dilenschneider, note 4.

Business and the News Media: The Paradox of Informed Misunderstanding
S. Prakash Sethi

It seems now almost an article of faith with businesspeople that bias in the news media and among journalists prevents fair and objective exposure of the business viewpoint. They contend that their access to the various media is grossly inadequate when compared with the importance, to business and society, of the issues being covered and the space and air time devoted to discussing opposing viewpoints. With disapproval of its activities increasing, business's need to defend itself has become more tense and its criticism of the media more acrimonious. One outlet for frustration that many firms have employed is advocacy advertising, the purchase of advertising space to express a viewpoint on controversial issues of social importance.

Media spokespeople by and large deny the charge of bias. They maintain that amount of coverage is a question of editorial judgment and that the complaints of businesspeople are no different from those of any group under social attack.

The objective of this article is to examine the nature and sources of this conflict between business and the news media, to analyze the positions of both sides, and to evaluate some of the approaches taken by various corporations and the news media to improve the quality of business news coverage. Finally, certain measures are considered that might ensure better public exposure and understanding of business's viewpoint on issues affecting business and social policy. (Unless otherwise specifically noted, all direct quotations are from personal interviews or written communications with the author during the period of January to April 1976.)

Business Complaints

Business charges against the news media can be grouped into three categories: the "economic illiteracy" of most journalists, inadequate coverage, and antibusiness bias among newspeople. Donald S. MacNaughton, chairman of the Prudential Insurance Company of America, feels that American journalism has been lacking in the professional tradition of self-correction:

> With freedom comes responsibility, and in the opinion of many, that sense of responsibility has been lacking. Most of us are fed up with glib, shallow, inaccurate reporting and editing—tired of journalistic tastes which prefer sensationalism above the fundamentals—which allow a thespian to pose as a newsman.[1]

Raleigh Warner, Jr., chairman of Mobil Oil, says that the purpose of the Mobil advocacy advertising campaign is to defend the company against slander. "We've been willing to react because we feel we've been treated unfairly."[2] Herbert Schmertz, a Mobil vice-president and the architect of its advocacy campaign, believes there is too much accusatory journalism. Frederick W. West, Jr., president of Bethlehem Steel Corporation, in a speech before the American Newspaper Publishers Association, echoed a similar complaint by saying that many reporters are out to get business and that some of them are over their heads when reporting business news. However, he believes that the reporting "that gets our blood up is probably more muddled than it is malicious."[3]

> Anyone who reads the daily press or listens to the news should know better. Corporations are constantly under attack from every quarter. Charges by consumer groups, Congressional Committee and Subcommittee Chairmen, individual Congressmen and the various organs of federal, state and local government get front-page headlines. . . . Silence by a company in the face of attacks upon its policies

and practices is interpreted as an admission of guilt. Corporate advertising provides one avenue of self-defense.[4]

In a recent speech, Louis Banks of MIT, a former editor of *Fortune,* suggested that although there had been significant improvement in the comprehension of economic matters on the part of good news editors, in the case of everyday news coverage:

> We are fed a daily diet of authoritative ignorance, most of which conveys a cheap-shot hostility to business and businessmen. Here is where the nation sees a persistently distorted image of its most productive and pervasive activity, business. . . . The reporters and editors in the general media are woefully ignorant of the complexities and ambiguities of corporate operations, and being so, are easy targets for politicians or pressure group partisans with special axes to grind at the expense of business.[5]

Other industry spokespeople and corporate executives have been equally vocal about the inability or unwillingness of the news media to give a fair presentation and exposition of their viewpoint on important public issues.

Business complaints against the broadcast media are similar to those made against the print media, but sharper. Herbert Schmertz contends that the structure of television news programs prevents adequate coverage of a complex issue. The demand for a large audience makes any news coverage, in part, a type of entertainment: "Put the two of them together and you've inadequate coverage and inadequate information." Moreover, he contends that there is nothing sacred about the way television covers the news: "There is no law that says it has to be that way. This is their approach to the problem. There is nothing to prevent their giving in-depth coverage to a particular topic." Some representatives of the print media concur with the charge of poor and inadequate coverage of news on television. On the end of the spectrum is Robert Bleiberg of *Barron's,* who says:

> There is no doubt in my mind that there is antibusiness bias in a good deal of reporting. Television, notably the network news programs and documentaries, goes out of its way to exaggerate the flaws of business and minimize the achievements. Television bias has been amply documented by such groups as Accuracy in Media and the National News Council.

The Media Response

Predictably, most of the news editors and broadcast media executives I interviewed dismiss the charges by businesspeople as unfounded. Some go so far as to accuse business of blaming the media for its own faults, of trying to muzzle bad news instead of correcting the causes, and of making broad generalizations about the deficiencies of the media with no supporting facts.

It will facilitate our understanding of the media response if the print and broadcast media are treated separately. The two operate in different legal environments and have different technical capabilities that make them susceptible to different kinds of charges about their news coverage.

The Print Media

On the question of bias, Osborn Elliot, former editor-in-chief of *Newsweek,* says that his answer is "an absolutely flat categorical no" to the contention that "there is antibusiness bias, conscious or unconscious, in *Newsweek.* But there certainly is an anti-crooked business bias." John B. Oakes of the *New York Times* also denies the existence of any systematic bias in reporting of business news. Similar opinions have been echoed by Marshall Loeb, senior editor of *Time,* and Garth Hite of the *Atlantic Monthly.*

Bias in the News

A distinction should be made here between news reporting, editorials, and coverage in general-purpose newspapers and magazines such as the *New York Times* and *Newsweek,* on the one hand, and special-purpose business magazines such as *Fortune* and *Business Week,* on the other. We should also distinguish among small-town newspapers, newspapers of conservative orientation, and a few large newspapers considered liberal, such as the *New York Times,* the *Los Angeles Times,* the *Washington Post,* the *Milwaukee Journal,* and the *St. Louis Post Dispatch.*

When it comes to the news, opinions differ between the editors of general-purpose newspapers and magazines and the special-purpose, business-oriented magazines. What businesspeople generally allude to as bias is discussed as lack of objectivity and superficiality in reporting. Objectivity is a relative term, however. The very decisions about what news to cover, what prominence to give it, and what kind of follow-up to accord it require a process of deliberate selectivity based on the subjective assessment of an editor as to what is relevant and important for the audience of the medium. This argument is even more germane in the case of special-interest news media, where there is a greater identity of outlook between a medium and its audience. Thus, a magazine catering to business will not only provide more coverage (compared to other news media) of news that is of interest to its audience but more important, it is likely to look at the news from the business point of view. Although the magazine might consider its news coverage to be objective reporting, such a contention might be questioned by opposing groups. It is not uncommon to see a given situation reported differently in different news media. Facts themselves are seldom in dispute, but they assume a coloration from the environment in which they are presented. The role of a medium in presenting and even creating this environment is a crucial factor in influencing audience reaction.

What businesspeople call "bias" media people often describe as oversensitivity to adverse news. John B. Oakes of the *New York Times* states:

> Newspapers *will* publish news that is sometimes unfavorable to the interests of a particular corporation or industry—but that's part of the function of the newspapers. The reporter in writing a news story aims at giving balanced information for the objective reader. We would not be performing our duty as newspapermen if we did not present a story in all its relevant aspects. It is understandable that the affected businesses may not like what they read about themselves in the newspapers. They use the argument of news media bias in objecting to these stories. This alleged bias then becomes an excuse for publishing the kind of advocacy ads that we're beginning to see. The problem has developed more markedly since the oil crisis, when the oil and energy companies have become more aggressive in buying advertising space to respond to public criticism of their business.

Marshall Loeb of *Time* also thinks the business complaints have more to do with the type of news being covered than the manner in which it is covered:

> I have little sympathy for the lament of corporate executives that the media are biased. We are in an era when all institutions are under fire—the church, government, the press, medicine, etc. Business is attacked more than many other institutions because it is highly visible. Moreover, there have been some outrageous scandals involving business, and these have fanned the criticism.

A number of media spokespeople have ascribed the inadequate and indifferent coverage to the low priority assigned to coverage of business news and the poor quality of reporters rather than a deliberate bias on the part of the media. Lewis H. Young, editor-in-chief of *Business Week,* feels that business coverage in most newspapers is so bad that it's not even worth talking about:

> The problem is basically in the publications who like to think they are very liberal. And they think that one of the marks of being liberal is to show antibusiness bias. It starts with a feeling that business is probably not good. It's an educational kind of bias: The belief that business is prepared to do anything to make a profit. This is reemphasized by a lack of understanding of how business works by newspaper reporters, since most have never worked in a business.

David Finn of Ruder & Finn, one of the largest public relations firms in the United States, observes that a number of problems exist in this country because of the way the news media cover the news. "Even a most conscientious reporter can't spend days covering a story except in special situations. There's rarely enough time to get into it in great depth. The subject of a newspaper article is likely to feel that the whole story hasn't been told. On occasions a story may be so sparse and superficial that it gives a distorted view." Furthermore, he feels that bad news is good news for newspapers: "negative aspects of a story are more interesting to reporters than the positive aspects."

Bias in Editorials

The editors and executives of newspapers, magazines, and television (both network and independent stations) unanimously reject the bias charge as irrelevant. Editorials are by definition the position of the editors of a particular print medium or television news program. John B. Oakes of the *New York Times* has best expressed the general position of the various editors interviewed:

> Editorially, the *New York Times* has been very critical of many business practices, not only this year, but also in earlier years. Over the years, we have been editorially critical of every special interest group that exists. Newspapers wouldn't be doing their duty if they did not express their opinion. We reserve the right to express our views in our columns. If oil companies or any other group wish to call this bias, that is their privilege.

Marshall Loeb of *Time* says that corporations tend to interpret editorials that are critical of business to be antibusiness. "For each editorial cricitizing business [in the *Times*], the reader could find a pro-business editorial. The *New York Times* is a strong defender of the capitalist system, or private enterprise. In short, business gets a pretty good shake in the national media."

Inadequate Access

On the question of inadequate access, the media response falls into one or more of the following categories.

> Before a news story is reported in the press, its contents are checked for accuracy with all the interested parties, including businesspeople, and their views evaluated and reported.

> Where businesspeople disagree with a news story or are critical of an editorial, the "letters to the editor" columns are open to them.

> Many newspapers have special editorial space, such as the Op-Ed page in the *New York Times,* which is made available to outside spokespeople, including top corporate executives.

> A large part of the inadequate coverage results from the general unwillingness on the part of top corporate executives to talk with reporters.

John B. Oakes of the *New York Times* maintains that the inadequate access complaint is poorly founded. When reporting business operations in a story, the *Times* asks the particular firm about it. The company may not consider this to be sufficient because the headline may not be to their liking or the space allocated to their position may be deemed insufficient:

The *Times* established the Op-Ed page about five years ago, where not only businessmen but spokesmen for an infinite variety of other groups, or just plain individuals, have an opportunity to have their say in a broad philosophical sense, and to respond to whatever criticism they have received on our editorial columns or news columns—or anywhere else. . . . We have also published the pros and cons from many groups, business and otherwise, including heads of such corporations as General Motors, IBM and Ford Motor Company.

The letters to the editor column is the more traditional means for access to the media. Without exception, the media people interviewed indicated that they took special pains to publish letters critical of the positions taken by their publications.

Garth Hite of the *Atlantic Monthly* reflects the views of most print media—general and special purpose—when he states:

If we do a piece that is critical of an industry (a good example is the current issue of *Atlantic* on supermarkets), we give it an opportunity to answer. If it wants to write us letters we'll publish a whole section of letters, pro and con, about the article. . . . We have a right to control what goes into our product, but responsible publications always give the other side a chance to answer.

Yet newspapers and news magazines must limit the number of letters they publish because of space problems. The *New York Times*, for example, receives more than 60,000 letters a year and publishes between 4 and 5 percent, with strict limitation on length. However, Kalman Seigel of the *Times* points out that the space allocated every day to the letters is exactly the same as that devoted to the editorials. Some newspapers and magazines publish a somewhat higher proportion of letters because the volume of letters received is not as high. Other newspapers have less restrictive policies; some, like *Barron's*, have no limit on the length of the individual letters accepted for publication. But although *Barron's* has run letters longer than the original offending material, the newspaper does not have a specified space devoted to letters each day.

Most of the businesspeople interviewed are not happy with the access they receive through the letters to the editor column. They contend that often too much time elapses between the publication of the news item and the letter; the item may have been front-page headlines, while the letter is tucked away in the inside pages. The length requirements of the newspaper or magazine may impose an unreasonable burden on the letter writer. Some companies' leaders have felt frustrated enough to resort to buying ad space to publish their letters. A vivid example of this type of frustration was a letter that Mobil wanted to publish in the *New York Times* in response to a *Times* editorial of March 25, 1975, on the question of oil import quotas. The original letter was 700 words long. The *Times* indicated a willingness to publish the letter provided Mobil reduced it to 400 words. Mobil got it down to 500 words but would not cut any further and instead published the letter as an advertisement.[6]

The Broadcast Media

Representatives of the broadcast media disagree with most, if not all, of the business complaints. William Sheehan, president of ABC news, says that given the time constraints within which they have to work and the selection of stories they have to make, they handle things with fairness and balance. Therefore, any group that has a special interest probably will feel that its particular subject is not handled very well:

> We make a very concerted effort in talking to people on all sides. Most of the time it is not just two sides in a controversy—it is very hard to find an issue where there is a yes or no but three or four or five different positions, which makes it difficult. We try to give expression to all points of view.

William Small, senior vice president and director of news at CBS, concurs with Sheehan's viewpoint, saying, "We hear this from people who are unhappy with the flow of news when it doesn't go the way they want it to go." Although he does admit that past coverage of business and economic news has been inadequate at CBS, the situation has been remedied in the past two years. But Small says this is not what business is talking about. The kind of coverage business would like is friendly coverage: "The great flaw in their complaint and what is galling to us is that they always want it on their own terms." He adds that the record would show that business has had sufficient access to the networks; CBS, in fact, has had a great many businesspeople and economists on the air in the recent past.

ABC and NBC dismiss the complaints of inadequate coverage and lack of expertise on the part of their reporters and commentators. Business is not a monolithic entity, they argue. The oil business is not like the broadcasting business or the garment business. One can no more be an expert in business than he or she can be an expert on such diverse industries as automobile, steel, electronics, banking and insurance, retail trading, and transportation. By the same logic a news medium should have experts on such topics as monetary policies, international trade, foreign exchange, and economic development. A news reporter should know or find out who the experts are and then ask intelligent questions to dig out facts and stories that are newsworthy. And good reporters do just that.

Furthermore, broadcast media people have been almost unanimous in their complaint that top business executives have been generally unavailable to reporters to give their viewpoints. "Sometimes people on the business side of the fence don't want to be interviewed," says Benjamin D. Raub, vice president and assistant general attorney for NBC. It is not unlike the days of the civil rights issue, when networks were charged with having a pro-civil rights bias.

In those days it was hard to get anyone on TV who favored states' rights. Another spokesperson argues that when a corporation is in trouble and reporters want to interview the president of the company, they are given some junior public relations person instead. If that happens, business cannot claim lack of access or bias. William Small of CBS says that businesspeople want their views to be filtered through very high paid, very clever public relations people:

> Take the case of Red Dye No. 2. We went to the company for an interview. They wouldn't give an interview but would give a ninety-second statement if we promised not to edit one word of it. The whole function of journalism relates to proper editing of raw material. You don't just turn over a glob of time to an advocate and say that's yours.

Herbert Schmertz of Mobil Oil concedes that there may be some truth to the statement that a lot of companies just will not make their top people available for interviewing by news reporters. But he also feels that reporters have always been able to find ways to get at the news if they are persistent. For its part, Mobil has been making "diligent efforts to make our top people available to the press." The company organizes a weekly luncheon at which top management people meet with two or three reporters for on-the-record discussion. "I don't see a great interest on the part of top TV reporters to come to us over here," Schmertz comments, "I have written Dan Rather three or four letters. He has never even answered." Small of CBS retorts that reporters must pick their own stories and interview people of their choice: "We don't compel our people to sit down with a corporation president. I have difficulty with it ideologically. They want to brainwash people. If Schmertz considers that it is such a successful technique then every corporation in America would be inviting our people to lunch. We would be getting very fat and not getting much news."

The Question of Paid Access to the Broadcast Media

In the print media, businesses have been able to compensate for the inadequate coverage through the purchase of paid advertising space to present their positions and advocate a certain course of action without any restraint from the magazine or newspaper carrying that advertisement. The broadcast media, however, do not allow any advocacy on the air. This is because of the regulated nature of the media and also because of limited air time.

Since the amendment of the Communications Act in 1949, radio and television broadcasters have been required to present fair and balanced coverage of controversial topics under the "fairness doctrine." The current status of the fairness doctrine is given in the 1974 policy statement, in which the FCC presented a major change in the policy.[7] Commercials were classified as two distinct types: those that are editorial in nature and those for commercial products and services. Commercials that consist of "direct and substantial commentary on important public issues . . . should be recognized for what they are—editorials paid for by the sponsor." The fairness doctrine should be applied "only to those 'commercials' which are devoted in an obvious and meaningful way to the discussion of public issues."[8] The responsibility of the licensee was limited to making a reasonable common-sense judgment of whether or not the advertisement advocated a point of view on a controversial issue of public importance.

Aside from the issue of fairness is the question of access to the broadcast media. The right of access by commercial advertisers was severely limited by the FCC and later by the Supreme Court when it was decided that neither the Communications Act of 1934 nor the First Amendment requires broadcasters to accept paid editorial advertisements. In its decision in *Columbia Broadcasting System, Inc.* v. *Democratic National Committee and Business Executives Move for Vietnam Peace* v. *FCC*[9] the Court, in Chief Justice Burger's majority opinion, concluded that the intent of Congress in the 1934 Communications Act was "to permit private broadcasting to develop with the widest journalistic freedom consistent with its public obligations."[10]

In addition, the Court did not find any reason to require broadcasters to accept paid editorial ads and cited a number of "undesirable effects" of doing so, among them that the right of access would favor the wealthy or those with access to wealth; that the application of the fairness doctrine to editorial advertising would place a financial hardship on broadcasters; and that the granting of a right to access could dissipate journalistic responsibility among many advertisers rather than leaving it with the licensee.

The broadcast media, with the concurrence and support of both the Supreme Court and the FCC, have instituted a ban on accepting commercials of a controversial nature. This has not, however, ended the controversy. Environmental groups feel that some of the supposedly noncontroversial corporate image advertising on the air is indeed editorial advertising. Corporations feel that this policy has blocked them from correcting biased and erroneous programming on business-related issues, especially by network television. In this connection, Mobil's efforts to get access to the media offer a good illustration of how the television networks and the corporations view each other's activities in providing information to the public concerning business and economic issues. In the winter of 1972 to 1973, Mobil's chairman, Raleigh Warner, spent three hours with Walter Cronkite. The edited version of the discussion that later appeared on the air led Warner to complain that to those who edited the raw material, "fairness did not seem an overriding preoccupation." In another instance, Mobil responded with a twenty-two-page complaint with the National News Council charging ABC's closeup documentary series of March 20, 1974, which examined the energy crisis, with factual errors and unwarranted and unfair interpretations.

The latest incident in this running confrontation is a full-page Mobil ad entitled "Whatever Happened to Fair Play?" which appeared in the *Wall Street Journal*, the *New York Times*, and the *New York Daily News* in early March 1976. This ad was a response to a five-part series on oil prices that appeared on NBC's New York television station between February 23 and 27, 1976. The ad copy made seventeen points, decorated with seventeen hatchets to indicate that facts were emasculated by the program's reporter, Liz Trotta. Although there were indeed certain inaccuracies in Trotta's reporting, some of Mobil's complaints pertained not to the facts but to Trotta's interpretations of the crisis and to the solutions suggested by some of the oil industry critics.

Mobil has repeatedly tried to buy time on TV to express its views and also to respond to its critics. In opposing this, William Sheehan, president of ABC News, says:

> I don't think that advocacy commercials should be for sale. An advocacy ad deal-ing with an issue like energy conservation contributes a lot of imagery and heat, but not very much light, or intelligent discussion. I wouldn't like to see these things decided in just thirty-second or sixty-second commercials on TV or radio. It would be a bad kind of debate where the one with the most money would get the most time on the air. Either that, or the one with the most time on the air. Either that, or the one with the slickest presentation would have the compelling argument in the minds of the public. I think it's better to handle these things in the way that we are currently handling them.

Raub of NBC concurs with this notion, and adds that broadcasters should determine agenda: "Sale of time for that purpose would permit those with money to determine agenda." If the issue is important enough to be covered from the public's point of view, it should and would be covered through regular news pro-grams. Mobil's Schmertz responds that neither he nor his company is interested in setting agenda but instead would limit the discussion to answering criticisms made in previous NBC programs. Moreover, in case there is a problem with the fairness doctrine, Mobil would pay twice as much in order that its opponents could answer, provided the networks would take the ads without censorship. The net-works could select the critics. Schmertz also commented on network concern about protecting those without money: "Are they protecting the corner grocery store against A&P?"

William Small of CBS is not persuaded by these arguments:

> Networks have to be the judge of what they want to put on the air. If Mr. Schmertz wants a network he can form one. A network is not a licensed entity. Anyone can form one. Mobil has a lot of money and Mr. Schmertz can go out and get a hun-dred or two hundred stations and he will have a network.

He feels that by allowing commercial time for advocacy advertising, networks would be allowing people with money to buy air time and exposure: "The large corpora-tions would be buying the networks—I don't think that actually would happen, but that is the basic danger."

Analysis

Despite the all-inclusive nature of the criticisms leveled at the media by corporate executives, it seems their complaints are primarily directed at the three or four major newspapers, notably the *New York Times*, and the news programs and documentaries on network television. The efforts of the news media notwithstanding, there are indeed some limits of how much access can be accorded to business or other groups that wish to express their opinion of a particular news story or editorial. There is also some element of truth in business complaints. The need for dramatic visual impact in television news has made it a prey to "contrived events": news is created to attract television cameras, whose very presence becomes an integral part of the event or the news being covered.

But the picture is far from bleak. Business news media will generally provide fair coverage for the business viewpoint. No one would argue that the *Wall Street Journal* or *Business Week* is biased. Nor should there be too much concern for the vast majority of newspapers with primarily local orientation. Constrained by expenses from hiring a sufficient number of reporters and heavily dependent on advertising, they are only too happy to accept press releases from the public relations departments of various companies and print them as news stories. Similarly, a distinction should be made between the network news in television broadcasting and the news programs of local independent stations. The stations' programs generally concentrate on local news and seldom venture into national controversies on economic issues. Furthermore, these stations have been known to yield to pressure by business. It was reported that TV stations in some localities had either fired their consumer affairs reporters or changed their assignments when advertisers threatened to withdraw their advertising from those stations.[11] Recent reports indicate that when New York's nonprofit public television station WNET (Channel 13) sought industry support for its programming, it was forced to drop its investigative and muckraking programs as the price of funding for other programs.[12]

Nevertheless, business is in a dilemma. In its attempt to reach opinion leaders, it must use the media of its choice. But the environment in these media is hostile because of the many revelations of activities that business would like to describe as necessary evils but that other groups consider illegal, unprofessional, and unethical.

The issue of alleged news media bias and inadequate access has three important dimensions that need attention.

1. The general unwillingness of corporate executives to talk to journalists is a major problem. Executives find it disconcerting to be asked questions that appear to them to be hostile, insensitive, or lacking in proper understanding of the complexity of the issues involved. Moreover, they fear their views will be distorted or presented out of context. Thus, devoid of strong support from the corporation, journalists are forced to seek information from whatever sources they can find—and

602 • *Business and Society*

some of the most accessible may have an antibusiness bias. Businesspeople also lose their credibility by insisting that the press blandly swallow some of their pronouncements as gospel.[13] A "statement of truth" written primarily by the person involved in events inevitably reflects his or her view of the world. Thus, insisting that reporters accept only the businessperson's view to be more "objective" and his or her values to be more "relevant" has probably made reporters more determined to be independent—and in this context, more critical. Self-isolation by businesspeople in the belief that it is better to have less of a bad press than more of a good press runs the risk of having more of the former and none of the latter—and in the long run is counterproductive.

2. The suggestion that television and radio stations should accept opinion ads without restriction, denying the station right to edit, is likely to raise more problems than it would solve. As previously stated, the Supreme Court declared that the right to exercise editorial judgement belonged to the broadcasters and that any other alternative would dissipate journalistic responsibility for news reporting and analysis from the broadcaster to many self-serving advertisers, a not wholly desirable alternative.

At face value, Herbert Schmertz's suggestion would be tantamount to reducing the broadcast media to the status of a common carrier; air time would be sold on a nondiscriminatory basis subject to the constraint of ability to pay. And his contention notwithstanding, there would be no logical basis for limiting such sale of air time to those wishing to respond to the "inadequacies" of news programs previously aired by the media. It would still be the company that would decide what parts of a news program need responding to, regardless of their relative importance in the overall makeup of the original program.

This corporate contention also assumes that every other segment of society, especially those opposing business, is treated differently by the media. Mr. Small of CBS asks why business should have the right to have its view presented on the air unedited; why should not business "undergo the same process that others [government, consumer groups] have gone through, which is a critical examination by the journalists?"

3. Part of the conflict and misunderstanding between business and the news media arises because business does not fully realize the necessity for the news media to cater to a diverse and heterogeneous audience. Therefore, a large part of what business might consider unfair presentation might simply be a fair presentation of news seen from another person's viewpoint.

From Negative Defensiveness to Positive Activism—An Action Program

It is the role of the press to investigate, to interpret, and to report. There will always be differences in how one group sees reality and how it is reported by the press. There is, however, a great deal that the news media can do to improve the quality of business news coverage. At the same time, business institutions can facilitate the availability of business-related news to the media. The objective is to increase and maintain access to the public communication space for differing viewpoints so that an open and vigorous debate can take place in the marketplace of ideas. Issues of public policy can then be decided by an intelligently informed public. Many companies and news organizations have taken steps in this direction. They are summarized here. In addition, some new approaches are suggested that provide a basis for further action by corporations, the news media, and other interested social groups.

Actions for Business

There is a clear and urgent need for corporations to be more open and forthcoming in their communications with the public and the news media. A corporation expressing its views needs to maintain a high standard of integrity in the treatment of the subject matter or it will end up escalating the level of partisan squabbling.

Schmertz of Mobil Oil appreciates this concern when he says that his company decided to make the subject matter in its ad campaign intellectually significant rather than superficial. "We probably lose readers. But in the long haul unless you are prepared to put yourself on the line both intellectually and philosophically, you will never gain long-term leadership and recognition of substance."

Corporations could also decentralize their communications with the public. There need be no "party line" to which employees must adhere. Managements can trust their employees as intelligent, alert people, who can and do make sound judgments. Such a decentralized approach to public communication carries with it a risk that conflicting opinions might emerge on a given issue. But it would also show the corporation in more realistic terms and make it easier to concede errors of judgment when they occur. The company would not then be forced to defend every action, no matter how trivial, in terms of corporate survival, management prerogatives, or a defense of the free enterprise system. William Small of CBS maintains that if businesspeople

> want to have a favorable image and report on their activities they must get in the public arena. You can't hire stalking horses to do it for you. If I were a head of a corporation . . . I would much rather have the opportunity to talk with the "reporters" and persuade them of our position than to ignore them and let them go away with hostility. American business as a whole would gain a lot more from constant attempts to tell their story than from hiding in a shell expecting public relations men to handle it all for them.

Reaching media may be a matter of corporations' having to learn how to get coverage. Robert Dilenschneider, a senior vice president in the public relations firm of Hill & Knowlton, feels that news media would give corporations more coverage if the companies talked in terms of what is in the public's interest, that of consumers, senior citizens, minority groups, unemployed, or people in general. Companies should not talk about problems but about solutions. News media look for solutions, and if there are none they are likely to come up with a negative story.

Improvements for the News Media

The news media can contribute to improved reporting of various viewpoints by setting up additional internal standards for checking into the type of news coverage provided. As John B. Oakes of the *New York Times* states:

> Newspapermen have a special obligation to retain public confidence through conscious and deliberate effort to open ourselves to the public to pay particular attention to complaints of unfairness, inaccuracy, bias, vindictiveness—that is, to make ourselves *voluntarily* accountable. Some newspapers have already gone a considerable distance in doing just this but not many and certainly not enough.[14]

One approach to attaining this objective is the installation of an in-house critic who would question the relevance and direction of various news stories covered in that particular newspaper or magazine, or on the programs of that radio or television station. To date, only one major newspaper (the *Washington Post*) has installed such a critic. More recently, CBS rejected a proposal that it hire an in-house critic with the "responsibility of receiving and investigating complaints from the public about unfair and inaccurate programs." The proposal was made by Accuracy in Media, Inc., a Washington-based organization. In rejecting the proposal CBS Chairman William S. Paley alluded to the high degree of independence and integrity achieved by the journalists employed by CBS News and indicated that it would be "way off base" to give one person "such control and high degree of authority over a worldwide news organization."[15] I do not believe that the in-house critic should have authority to investigate reports of inaccuracy or bias in specific news stories. These should be handled through normal channels. Moreover, I have faith in the diversity of viewpoints and integrity of individual newspeople. My perception of the in-house critic's job is to question any systemwide tendencies in covering certain types of news and the manner in which they are covered. The emphasis is on the long-term trends rather than specific items; such a person is not an ombudsman for readers investigating individual complaints.

A National Council for Public Information

Business has the most to lose from public misinformation. Improving the quality of public information and debate should therefore be in its interest. One way to do this would be to establish a National Council for Public Information (NCPI). This council would receive its major financial support from business corporations and trade groups. In addition, it would receive contributions of ad space and commercial air time from the news media. The news media contributions would come from what the various media allocate to public service advertising and commercial announcements. Corporations might allocate funds equal to, say, between 25 to 50 percent of the amount spent by them on advocacy advertising to be used for purchasing advertising space for public expression of those viewpoints which, though important, would not receive exposure because of lack of funds.

A policy of supporting the public expression of alternative viewpoints is *not* contrary to the corporation's self-interest. Instead, it should help in the development of a company's planning process, and also contribute to its public credibility. David Finn of Ruder & Finn provides one rationale for corporate support by saying:

> It would be very wise to show that a corporation is listening to what the other fellow is saying. If the company pays for time to let the other fellow make his best presentation, the president of the company will certainly read what appears in his space. And he will listen. He will overcome a lot of half-information that comes in newspaper articles or from his advisors who may be telling him what they think he wants to hear. Serious critics are also frustrated because their viewpoints do not come through. If a corporation really means what it says and wants to do what is best for the society—I believe that's what most corporate executives really do mean—this would be one way to accomplish this.

The media participation could be around 25 percent of the ad space allocated by them to public advertising. The implications for participation, by the media in such a program can be briefly summarized as follows.

It would broaden the scope of viewpoints represented in public service advertising.

It would indicate a willingness on the part of the news media, especially the electronic media, to experiment with new formats. The electronic media have been criticized by both business and nonbusiness groups for their unwillingness to explore different alternatives in their public affairs programming and discussion of socially important issues.

There is no danger that participation in this program would in any way adversely affect the responsibility of the media in determining their news and editorial agenda. The media would have the sole discretion of accepting or rejecting an advertisement. It was noted earlier that the broadcasters feared that by controlling the type of message in their advocacy ads, a corporation would be able to control the type of response, and thereby determine the direction of public debate. The approach outlined here overcomes this objection. The news media in general, and the electronic media in particular, need accept only those ad messages that would add to the medium's own coverage of an issue.

In terms of the electronic media, this would apply not only to allocation of free time, but also to the sale of air time for discussion of those issues covered in regular public affairs programming. The objective is to *complement* and not replace a radio or a television station's, or a network's, efforts in the discussion of a public issue. A station or the network does not have to air a commercial on a given issue, if it feels that the station's own coverage has been adequate.

The problems of the fairness doctrine are minimized because the emphasis in the selection of ad messages will not be so much on opposing a specific course of action but on the discussion of alternative approaches to complex social issues. The NCPI's selection process for ad campaigns can be designed to achieve this end.[16]

Notes

1. Donald S. MacMaughton, "The Businessman Versus the Journalist," *New York Times* (7 March 1976), section 3, p. 14.
2. Michael J. Connor, "Arguing Back: Mobil's Advocacy Ads Lead a Growing Trend, Draw Praise, Criticism," *Wall Street Journal* (14 May 1975), p. 1.
3. Deirdre Carmody, "Reporters Chided on Business News," *New York Times* (5 May 1976), p. 38.
4. Letter to Senator Philip A. Hart (D., Michigan), dated 16 July 1974.
5. Louis Banks, "Media Responsibility for Economic Literacy," speech given at the Annual John Hancock Awards for Excellence in Business and Financial Journalism. "A Bicentennial Examination of the Free Market System," John Hancock Mutual Life Insurance Company, Boston, 28 October 1975.
6. The advertisement appeared in the *New York Times* (11 May 1975).
7. Federal Communications Commission, *Fairness Doctrine and Public Interest Standards, Fairness Report Regarding Handling of Public Issues,* 39 Fed. Reg. 26372 (18 July 1974).
8. Ibid., p. 70.
9. 412 U.S. 94 (1973); 450 F. 2d 642 (D.C. Cir. 1971) rev'd sun nom. *Columbia Broadcasting System, Inc.* v. *Democratic National Committee* 412 U.S. 94 (1973). For a discussion and criticism of the FCC and Supreme Court decisions, see Nicholas Johnson and Tracy A. Westen, "A Twentieth-Century Soapbox: The Right to Purchase Radio and Television Time," *Virginia Law Review* **57**(1971): 547; and Gary William Maeder, "A Right to Access to the Broadcast Media for Paid Editorial Advertising—A Plea to Congress," *UCLA Law Review* **22**(1974):258.
10. *CBS* v. *DNC*, 412 U.S. 94 (1973) at 110.
11. Liz Roman Gallese, "Boston's Sharon King Becomes Local TV Star by Knocking Products," *Wall Street Journal* (20 October 1975), p. 1.
12. "Riding Out the Storm at Channel 13 with Jay Iselin," *New York Times* (9 November 1975), Section 2, pp. 1, 29.
13. Thomas Griffith, "Must Business Fight the Press?" *Fortune* (June 1974), p. 214. See also Enno Hobbing, "Business Must Explain Itself," *Business and Society Review* (Fall

1972); Adler Norman, "The Sounds of Executive Silence," *Harvard Business Review* (July–August 1971), p. 100; R.W. Armstrong, "Why Management Won't Talk," *Public Relations Journal* (November 1970), p. 6; and Max Ways, "Business Needs to do a Better Job of Explaining Itself," *Fortune* (September 1972).

14. John B. Oakes, "Confidence in the Press," *New York Times* (5 May 1976), p. 37.

15. "CBS Lists Record Profits, Rejects an In-House Critic," *New York Times* (22 April 1976), p. 49.

16. For a discussion of the organization structure and modus operandi of NCPI see, S. Prakash Sethi, *Advocacy Advertising and Large Corporations* (Lexington, Mass.: D.C. Heath, 1977).

11

Corporations in a Global Economy

Changing Rules of International Corporate Behavior

S. Prakash Sethi

The role of multinational corporations (MNCs), especially as regards to their operations in the Third World, has been a subject of long-standing public policy debate and critical analysis. Like a tidal wave, this criticism has gone through many phases and has focused on different aspects of MNC operations covering such issues as corporate control, cultural adaptability, profit repatriations, technology transfer, and interference in host country's internal affairs. This article is not intended as an all-inclusive treatise on the historical critique of MNC behavior. Instead, we would look at the changes that have more recently been taking place in the global economic and political environment. Our objective is to evaluate the impact of the changes on MNC operations, and the economies and polities of the countries where they operate.

I believe we have entered a new era of conflict surrounding MNC operations, especially as they pertain to the Third World countries. This era has been accompanied by a rather significant change in the sociopolitical global environment that would make the direction of future conflict qualitatively different—where historical stereotypes are likely to be irrelevant and may actually lead to erroneous strategies with unfortunate consequences for all concerned. Therefore, we focus our attention primarily to the changing rules of international corporate behavior, and the events that have led to these changes. Finally, some new issues that should concern us are discussed because they arise out of these new rules of the game, and have hitherto not been subjected to careful inquiry.

No vision of the future is ever totally perfect, and only the passage of time and events will determine the impact of what has been wrought. We are captives of our imagination, which is constrained to a large extent by our living environment. Instant history has its uses, since neither now nor in the future can we ignore the recent past. It provides us with a point of departure from which we can measure progress or deflection therefrom. We are encumbered by it in our perceptual biases about the behavior and motives of the people and institutions we must deal with. And most importantly, the recent past influences the goals we wish to achieve and the means we would like to employ. History repeats itself precisely because we have short memories.

Globalization of Business-Society Conflict

Most observers of the international economic scene involving MNCs, international organizations, and the Third World countries, are familiar with the controversy in the 1980s pertaining to the marketing of infant formula in the Third World countries that led to a worldwide boycott of Nestle products and the passage of an international marketing code under the aegis of the World Health Organization. What is not generally appreciated is the extent to which the controversy provides us with a mirror to see that our institutional stereotypes are no longer valid—both as institutions perceive themselves and as their opponents portray them.

   The infant formula controversy, more so than any other event, has crystallized the growing internationalization of conflicts between corporations and host country governments, with the intervention of both international organizations and public interest groups representing different constituencies and viewpoints. For example, until recently social activism was a major force primarily in the United States, and an important influence in some western European countries, at essentially a local level. It has now emerged as a significant element at the international level where social activists are building effective networks across national borders, and coordinating their activities to confront multinational corporations in the international arena. In the process, they have escalated the level of conflict to its diversity and magnitude—they have built alliances with different governments—and they have politicized many international organizations such as the World Health Organization (WHO), UNCTAD, UNICEF, UNESCO, and FAO, which had been primarily technical or program-oriented agencies. A somewhat simplified version of the new external environment of multinational corporations (MNCs) is presented in figures 1 and 2.

   Figure 1 shows that up until the 1960s, the primary elements of the MNC external environment, with a measure of direct control over MNC behavior, were the host country and home country governments. International organizations—United Nations–based and others—drew their resources and authority to act directly from their member states. The United Nations even then had become highly politicized and was losing its capacity for action. Notwithstanding, most of the technical and program agencies were still devoting their energies to carrying out their program mandates in the areas of scientific research and information dissemination, and carrying out field programs of assistance in various countries needing help.

   Of the four components of the external environment, that is, nonmarket intervenors, MNC has had a large measure of familiarity and experience in dealing with home country and host country governments. Hence, within the constraints

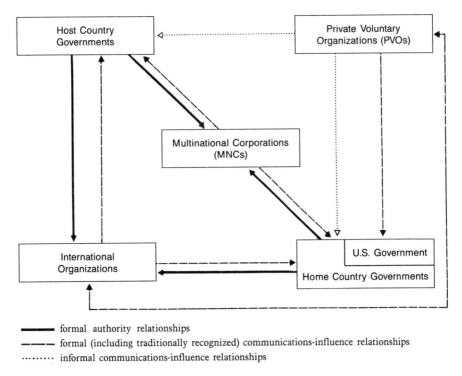

- ━━━━━ formal authority relationships
- ━ ━ ━ formal (including traditionally recognized) communications-influence relationships
- ⋯⋯⋯⋯ informal communications-influence relationships

**Figure 1. International Sociopolitical Environment of Multinational
Corporations, Pre-1970s**

of national sovereignty, MNCs have developed sophisticated coping mechanisms. They rely on the control of technological, financial, and marketing resources available to the MNC; the host country's needs for these resources; and the options available to MNCs for investing its resources among countries seeking such investments.

While there is a perception among the less developed countries (LDCs), that the balance of negotiating power, aided and abetted by MNCs' home country governments, has historically rested with the multinationals, this is not always the case. Multinational corporations are not a homogeneous group, and have different corporate goals and investment and marketing strategies, that are based on their asset dispersion, market penetration, and propensity to take risk. Thus, in many cases, a lack of bargaining power on the part of a host country may be the outcome of insufficient interest for MNCs to invest in a particular nation because of poor investment opportunities commensurate with perceived risk. Where host countries offer desirable investment opportunities, even the poorest among the LDCs have been known to negotiate mutually satisfactory agreements.

LDCs have available to them the resources of many international agencies, for example, the World Bank, and even private consulting firms of international repute, to provide legal and technical assistance in dealing with multinational

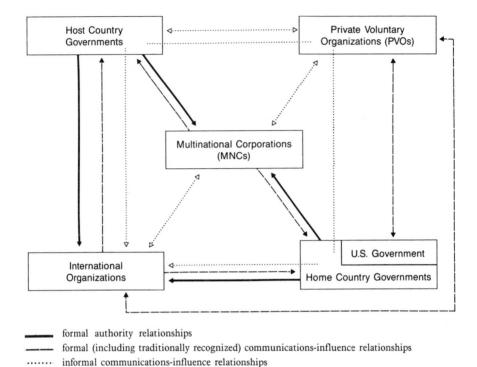

formal authority relationships
formal (including traditionally recognized) communications-influence relationships
informal communications-influence relationships

Figure 2. International Sociopolitical Environment of Multinational Corporations, Post-1970s

corporations. Certainly the OPEC nations have not lacked technical or marketing skills in dealing with the multinational corporations and Western governments on their own terms. A growing number of multinational corporations, based in developing countries such as South Korea, Taiwan, Philippines, India, and Pakistan, and many of the OPEC-related Middle-Eastern nations, have been successfully competing in international markets with their Western counterparts. All this is not being stated to suggest that LDCs do not need help. However, we should also disabuse ourselves of the notion that these countries lie in a state of total helplessness, and are easy prey to the greed and cunning of multinational corporations.

Nonmarket Intervenors—International Organizations

A type of nonmarket intervenors is various international organizations, notably United Nations' (U.N.) organizations and affiliated agencies. Until the beginning of the 1970s, there was very little formal direct contact between international organizations and MNCs. Nevertheless, industry was represented in many technical groups created for such purposes as standard setting and information sharing, and working as part of, or in association with, international organizations. Since then there has been a significant change in the situation (figure 2). The increasing number of newly independent nations has altered the character of many of these organizations. Politically conscious, yet economically backward and sorely in need of technological and financial resources of the industrially advanced countries, the LDCs have used their numerical power in the UN organizations and agencies to redress the economic imbalance that they perceive to be existing in the marketplace where capitalistic countries and private enterprises are said to hold inherently advantageous positions. Working as political power blocs, less developed and newly developing countries have proclaimed the need for a New Industrial Economic Order (NIEO). It blames all problems of the LDCs on the exploitative policies—both past and present—of the Imperialist West. Even the repressive character of many of the LDCs dictatorial governments and their poor management of their own economies is blamed on the Western governments and MNCs. The NIEO declares that LDCs have a right to a share of all the world's resources, and demand that Western nations and MNCs must provide LDCs with technology as a matter of moral and historical right. At the same time, any excesses on the part of LDCs are justified as their effort to catch up with the Western World. In this they find Soviet bloc countries willing allies. The issue is not solely of the LDCs' legitimate and rightful expectations of economic assistance and cooperation from the Western World, but that of reciprocal obligations and internal and external accountability, to ensure efficient utilization of resources that are available to them.

The politicization of many international organizations has been one manifestation of this approach. Thus, these organizations are being increasingly driven by a political agenda, comprised as they are of member nations, and, therefore, must reflect the emerging power alignments—even when their mandates are primarily humanitarian and scientific-technical. Until recently, this process of politicization has progressed largely unabated because of the unwillingness or inability of the industrialized nations to confront the new reality in terms of its larger implications for democratic societies. In a world where many of the LDCs operate under dictatorial rule, and with little respect for basic human rights of their own people, their accusations of oppression against Western nations and foreign multinationals have begun to lose their biting edge. We are also beginning to see the development of a new and less acquiescing response pattern on the part of governments of many industrialized nations.

The WHO Code of infant formula marketing practices is one example of a more active and interventionist approach on the part of international organizations. Other examples can be found in the current efforts to develop a code of ethics for multinational corporations, and international codes for marketing pesticides and pharmaceuticals. The changing role of international organizations raises two important issues, that is, of process and outcomes. The scientific character of these agencies called for a strong role to be vested in the organizations' bureaucracies because it was assumed that technical decisions were best made by scientists and professional experts who were shielded from undue political pressures. However, the political nature of intervention—both in terms of regulation formulation and implementation—calls for a closer scrutiny of the process itself, and the role of the organization's staff. The evolution and modus operandi of these organizations, as they affect the global operations of MNCs, have not fully developed, and their future shape and success remain largely undetermined. It is not clear how their relationship with the industrialized nations of the free world will evolve in the long run.

Nonmarket Intervenors—Private Voluntary Organizations (PVOs)

Private voluntary organizations (PVOs) or nongovernmental organizations (NGOs) in the parlance of United Nations represents one of the most significant changes in the MNCs external environment. At one end of the spectrum, PVOs include scientific and professional organizations with a legitimate stake in the deliberation of issues involving their respective professions or scientific expertise. Somewhere in the middle are institutions representing organized religion; consumer groups with long standing concern for the poor and under-represented; and other affiliated groups advocating causes and positions on humanitarian and ethical grounds. At the other end of the spectrum are special interest groups and social activists, whose sociopolitical and ideological orientations cover the entire spectrum of values and beliefs. These groups often do not represent constituencies of people in the conventional sense of the word, but instead represent constituencies of ideas or a vision of a different and, what they perceive to be, a better world. They seek legitimacy and operate through other more established groups, and above all, are identified through a common adversary, for example, the MNC. This is not necessarily the outcome of an ideological animosity against the capitalistic system or private enterprise, but it is the obvious reason that most of the issues of concern to these groups are rooted in the behavior and activities of the multinational corporations. MNCs also offer the most fertile cachet of resources that are claimed and desired by their constituencies. Therefore, MNCs have become the focus of attention on the part of a large number of these activist groups.

The influence of these groups on domestic political decisions and national agenda in the United States has become amply manifest over the last two decades. U.S. corporations have come to accept this influence as a fact of life. Consequently, an analysis of the role of PVOs is increasingly becoming an integral part of strategy development by the U.S. corporations because a failure to deal with PVOs can have a devastating effect on corporate survival, profitability, and growth. Figure 2 shows the changing role of these groups in impacting international political and public agenda. There has been a shift in the relative influence of different types of PVOs and NGOs. The scientific and professional groups are losing their former preeminent position, while nonscientific activist groups are gaining in ascendancy.

The role of PVOs at the international level is more recent and not well understood. And yet their impact on MNC operations can be even more far reaching and traumatic. The most recent examples of these efforts can be seen in the successful enactment of the International Marketing Code for Breastmilk Substitutes

(WHO's Infant Formula Code). In one single swoop the PVOs accomplished on a worldwide basis what they had been unable to gain at the individual country level. In the process they also handed MNCs a devastating defeat as to the latter's objectives and strategies for managing a corporation's external environment. Other ongoing efforts involving international organizations, Third World countries and PVOs, include those of the Law of the Sea, technology transfer, international code of conduct for multinational corporations, and efforts to enact an international code for the regulation of the pharmaceutical industry.

Therefore, it is of paramount importance that we understand the changing nature of our sociopolitical environment; its impact on the relative power and authority of various institutions in commanding a society's physical and human resources; and the constraints it imposes on institutions in the exercise of that power. At the micro level, a failure to perceive accurately the changing nature of these power relationships can cause us to react and respond incorrectly to external challenges with often disastrous results for all concerned. Even more fundamentally, at the macro level, changing institutional power relationships will not only affect business-society conflicts, they will influence and shape the very character of international and national geopolitical arrangements, and the nature of political order in democratic societies.

The Changing Role of Multinational Corporations

We must, therefore, begin to appreciate anew the changing role of private economic institutions, including multinational corporations, the uses of their economic resources, and their contribution to human welfare. We also look at the adverse consequences that accrue both as a direct result of corporate activities and also as second-order effects of corporate actions that may expose people and communities to unnecessary harm, notwithstanding the fact that these harms were unintended and their impact unforeseen. Such an assessment is important. For regardless of our ability to control the activities of MNCs and redirect their resources, there would follow an inevitable loss in aggregate growth in the Third World, efficient production, and even more equitable distribution, if we ignore the market constraints within which MNCs must operate, and without which they would cease to exist as viable economic entities.

This assessment has two dimensions. The first one deals with the conventional aspects of multinational operations in the Third World and their effect on the welfare of people in these countries both as MNCs project it and these nations perceive it and experience it. It is this gap in the relative perception that perhaps accounts for greater antagonism between MNCs and LDCs than the purported harm caused by MNCs to the Third World people through their sins of omission and commission. Our ultimate objective is to define a proper role for the MNC and how one might maximize the Third World welfare without at the same time creating prohibitive and, therefore, self-defeating barriers to their overseas operations.

The second aspect of the new MNC reality has to do with the radical changes in manufacturing technology brought about by electronics, computers, and information processing. These changes have dramatically altered the ground rules of international competition by: (1) shifting emphasis in cost structure where traditional economies of scale have become less relevant; (2) bringing about a change in the competitor mix where multinational companies from Japan and newly industrializing countries of Asia are entering the international competitive arena; and (3) making the traditional sources of comparative advantage and cheap labor on the part of Third World countries less important.

The influence of these factors is twofold:

1. The new MNCs have a different set of core values, ideologies, and operating philosophies that do not lend themselves to criticisms similar to those inflicted Western-based MNCs.

2. By changing the notions of competition, these factors have lessened the potential dependence of MNCs on LDCs either for the former's physical resources or inexpensive labor, thereby lessening the potential bargaining power of the Third World countries to influence MNC behavior.

The Traditional Role of MNCs in Less-Developed Countries

One aspect of the role of multinational corporations has to do with their functioning in less developed countries and the impact of their activities on local people and societies. At the aggregate level, the assumption that MNCs serve public interest in host countries through their activities in the private sector is largely supportable and easily defended. We have the example of such industrializing nations as South Korea, Taiwan, and Singapore. There is also strong evidence to suggest that in the Third World, the countries that seem to have made the least progress in improving their people's economic and social welfare are also the countries that have restricted the growth of private enterprise—domestic and foreign—and have relied primarily on state-owned enterprise and government-to-government assistance.[1] Moreover, even China has more recently recognized the strength of private enterprise and foreign investments in improving its economy and its population's standard of living and welfare.

The munificence of the multinational corporation is not an unmixed blessing, however. At the aggregate level problems arise simply because the objectives of privately-owned multinational corporations in investing abroad may not always agree with those of the host countries, especially the poor and less-developed ones. Nor do these countries always have the choice in terms of significant alternative sources of foreign capital and technology. The host country may have built an unrealistic expectation of what it can expect, or extract, from the multinational corporation within its borders. There is a whole body of scholarly literature and polemical-political publications listing the MNCs' sins of omission and commission.[2] The movement for a New International Economic Order (NIEO) is in fact one response by the Third World nations to seek a larger, and what they consider to be a more equitable, share of this world's resources from the industrialized world.[3]

There are some other problems that arise at the level of a single company or industry in the Third World as a consequence of MNC operations. These may have to do with the inappropriate or ill-conceived transfer of technology or plant operations in less developed countries. The most recent, and by far the most tragic example of this kind occurred in December 1984 in Bhopal, India. The accident caused the death of over 2,000 people while injuring another 200,000. The specific causes of the gas leak, the exact nature and extent of Union Carbide's culpability, and the size of damage awards remain to be determined and may never be completely known. The important thing, however, is to realize that the Bhopal accident was not a natural disaster that could be foreseen and, therefore, prevented. It was not the price of progress that must be paid. From all accounts, it would appear, however, that the accident was not caused by the unforeseen failure of some highly sophisticated and complex piece of machinery. It was instead a combination of small errors, postponed maintenance, and poorly trained personnel whose cumulative effect resulted in the ensuing catastrophe. One should expect that the expected can be prevented. No responsible corporation would deliberately create systems that were prone to major failures. However, it is the unexpected, the small, the insignificant and therefore routine, that should have been anticipated and taken into account in any prudent operational system.

None of the factors leading to the accident should have been a surprise to Union Carbide or for that matter any other MNC with operating experience in less developed countries. The lack of an industrial culture, poor emphasis on preventive maintenance and training, and a general disregard for safety procedures are a fact of everyday life in these countries. Therefore, their presence cannot be used as an excuse for the accident but should be considered proper grounds for demanding an explanation from the management for their lack of prior action.[4]

Therefore, while a multinational corporation may not have deliberately violated any laws, its normal business activities can and do have unintended, but nevertheless undesirable, social consequences. Each individual action pursued in enlightened self-interest does not always lead to collective good. In other words, rational micro actions may and do cause irrational macro outcomes. A single individual leaving an empty can on a vast beach may not consider his action particularly consequential, but when thousands of individuals do the same thing, we have dirty beaches with no one responsible for clean-up. Thus, rational individual actions lead to irrational collective outcomes, which had we known before the fact, we would not have wanted to cause.[5] We become victims of the tragedy of the commons where collective responsibility becomes total irresponsibility.[6]

All marketing activities of individual firms have second-order effects that extend far beyond the boundaries of the parties to their immediate exchange. Quite often, these effects are far more pervasive in their collectivity than visualized by individual firms when making simple transactions. The infant formula controversy is one such example. Other cases and industries involved in similar issues where their marketing practices are perceived to cause unnecessary harm include, among others, the pharmaceutical, processed foods, and agribusiness industries.[7] Thus, while the users of the product or those indirectly affected by it are unable to seek adequate remedy and relief in the marketplace, the cumulative effect of their dissatisfactions results in transferring the issue from the private to public domain. The solutions thus arrived at are essentially political in nature; are externally imposed; may be quite inflexible to accommodate specific peculiarities of the individual MNC operations; and, in the long run, may not be the optimal solutions for the MNCs or the LDCs involved.

Once again, the infant formula controversy and the WHO Code provide us with a vivid illustration of the fallacy of the MNC stereotypes as economic behemoths whose enormous economic power make them impervious to the needs of people in countries where they operate and whose governments—notably those among the LDCs—are afraid and unable to control them.[8] Having power alone is not enough, for its exercise rests largely on its political legitimacy. In a free society, this legitimacy accrues from the consent of people and social institutions that represent other spectrums of political will. Corporations are no exception. The degree to which they can exercise their economic power rests largely on society's judgment that its use is prudent and is directly related to its intended purpose, that is, welfare of the owners of the corporation.

The power of the multinationals—to the extent that it can be associated with their command of economic resources—has to be exercised rationally, that is, in response to market opportunities determined largely by people exercising free choice. It is unreasonable to blame the multinationals for all the economic and social ills of LDCs. To expect them to exercise their economic power in a manner that is radically different than the wish of political authority is impossible. The argument is based on inconsistent logic. To exercise such a power, MNCs must have political support, and yet it is against the prevailing political will that we expect MNCs to assert its power. Economic power can be abused only when it is exercised irrationally, illegally, or under the aegis of political dictatorships and command economies, where people's freedom to assert their economic will is subjugated to the dictates of centralized authority.

Therefore, the extent to which a corporation can and must deviate from this narrow mandate depends on society's changing expectations of the functions and performance of economic institutions. Democratic societies impose tremendous constraints on the use of economic and political power on the part of its holders. Therefore, it is not surprising that we impose strong procedural and review constraints on those we authorize to use power. Power also imposes its own discipline. It must be wielded in a restrained manner or the holder loses its legitimacy.

The New International Competitive Environment

In terms of market competition, the world has become truly a global village. The new entrants from the Asian countries, notably Japan, into the international competitive arena have radically altered the competitive equation. The new reality of a different competitive environment can be accounted for by two broad sets of factors: changes in production and manufacturing technologies, and the changes in the composition of competitors.

Technological Changes

The intensification of global competition[9] has been brought about by a revolution in manufacturing processes that have radically changed the economics of manufacturing. Economies of scale, based on large production runs of standardized products, together with the use of low-skilled labor, no longer deliver lower product costs measured in terms of consumer-driven product attributes. Although the present system creates production economies through lower unit manufacturing costs, it also leads to greater specialization, longer production runs, and a certain rigidity in the types of products manufactured.

The emerging computer-integrated manufacturing technology, however, creates greater flexibility. It makes possible shorter production runs and facilitates the creation of more customized products. It offers faster responses to changes in market demand. It provides for greater control and accuracy of processes and reduced manufacturing in-process time. It requires greater emphasis on manufacturing engineering rather than operations management.[10] The new technology radically alters the terms of trade-off between change-over and inventory costs in favor of the former, with profound implications for corporate strategy. By providing greater flexibility in creating product differentiation and shorter response times, it creates tremendous new marketing opportunities for the corporation.

The new international competition centers around manufacturing efficiency. There is tremendous emphasis on quality. In comparison with U.S. companies, the foreign competitors have been able to deliver a higher quality/price ratio. The new technology also offers greater innovation and product variety. For example, one of the major strengths of the Japanese companies has been their emphasis on integrated manufacturing processes. They have exploited this advantage by building greater option—added value—into their production, thereby increasing product variety. When combined with better quality controls, the Japanese have been able to compete both at the lower and the higher ends of consumer products markets and in many of the smokestack basic industries. The new competition of the 1980s is not in mass produced and highly standardized products, but in more specialized goods available at reasonable prices to highly segmented markets. The result has been a secular decline in the United States' comparative advantage in standarized products manufactured in highly capital intensive plants, using relatively unskilled labor.

The miniaturization of products and automation of manufacturing has resulted in successively reduced use of commodities and minerals, on the one hand, and number of workers required to produce a given amount of output, on the other hand. Thus, the old notion of macro-level comparative advantage located in the Third World countries, and based on availability of raw materials and cheap labor, is becoming less important. Instead, increasingly the greatest source of value-added is coming from knowledge and knowledge-based skills that are traditionally in short supply in the Third World countries.

The New Competitors

Corporations from different countries bring with them their own institutional baggage in terms of philosophies of competition and cooperation, factor endowments, propensity for risk taking, desire for market entry, and corporate objectives as to pay-back periods and acceptable rate of financial rewards. At the same time, different tax systems and governmental supports for exports and overseas investments make them into competitors that are qualitatively different from competitors in one's own country. Consequently, they call for different strategic responses in the marketplace.

The Emerging International Environment

Not all the changing trends in the international economic and sociopolitical environment have stabilized to the extent that their mutual interaction and impact on MNC operations can be predicted with a high degree of certainty. Nevertheless, it is quite reasonable to expect that during the next ten years MNCs will be confronted with a large measure of turbulence in their sociopolitical environment that will call for the development of new rules of behavior on the part of various players in the international arena.

International Organizations

International organizations, both U.N.-affiliated and regional blocs, for example, the Common Market, would continue to emphasize a greater monitoring role for themselves in the regulation and guidance of MNC activities. At last count, there were at least thirty codes of conduct at different stages of development and enforcement.[11] These codes generally fall into two categories. The first category of international codes deals with MNC operations that are primarily in the Third World, or where the Third World economic interests are pitted against those of the industrialized nations, for example, WHO Code of infant formula marketing practices, the U.N. Code of Conduct for Transnational Corporations, and the

Law of the Sea. The motivation behind these codes is not only economic, but also ideological and political. Therefore, their enactment, even by overwhelming majorities, may largely reflect political grandstanding and not necessarily be an indication of the prospect of their being implemented either by the host countries, or MNCs and their home countries. Alternately, they languish interminably in the corridors of international bureacracies as hostages to one power bloc or another.[12]

Notwithstanding, the very process of the formulation of international codes raises public awareness of the underlying issues. These codes afford opportunities to various political groups to form coalitions and thereby develop joint strategies against MNCs and Western industrialized nations. Moreover, their propaganda value can not be underestimated. Although, the solutions advocated in these codes may not be totally inappropriate to the problem, they do indeed become a rallying point because the MNCs in the past had chosen to ignore many of the legitimate complaints of the Third World that became the basis of early reform movement. While they may not seriously adversely impact the interests of the MNCs in the short run, their long-term potential for damage to the freedom of MNCs can not be ignored. Therefore, MNCs must become sensitive to the problems of their overseas operations as they emerge rather than wait for them to become acute. Otherwise, they run the danger of antagonizing public and political opinion not only in the Third World but also in their home countries, and thereby invite further regulation of their activities.

The other type of international regulation involves primarily industrially advanced countries, and relates to regulating behavior that impacts international investments and trade, for example, Common Market's regulations prohibiting anti-competitive behavior.[13] These codes are generally promulgated after long periods of negotiations and discussions, and have had a higher degree of success in compliance. Moreover, these codes do not call for changes that are contrary to the precepts of free markets, international competitive behavior, or good business practices. In many cases they strengthen international commerce by harmonizing trade and investment practices in different countries of MNC operations.

Private Voluntary Organizations

It appears that the Reagan administration has not seriously diminished the influence of private voluntary organizations (PVOs) in the United States. In fact PVOs have been quite successful in thwarting many of the Reagan administration's initiatives in the areas of environment and conservation, such as off-shore leasing. PVOs also have been quite active in the worldwide anti-apartheid movement against South Africa. In the United States they have consistently kept the issue in the limelight. Furthermore, in cooperation with a variety of state, city, and labor pension funds, they have put pressure on the U.S. multinational corporations and banking institutions to abide by the Sullivan Principles in their South African operations. The more aggressive of these groups have called for total withdrawal of U.S. companies from South Africa if that country's government does not completely dismantle its apartheid structure and grant full citizenship rights to its black majority in the foreseeable future.[14]

PVOs are becoming more active and influential in countries such as the United Kingdom, Sweden, Denmark, Norway, and West Germany. Their influence is especially noticeable in areas of pharmaceuticals, chemicals, nuclear power, and other industries that adversely affect the earth's physical environment. In the international arena, activist groups have continued to form power coalitions with various Third World political blocs on issues of common interest. The groups find sympathy among the professionals of U.N. agencies who must depend on the growing voting power of the Third World countries and their allies for political support.[15]

The success of PVOs, especially those affiliated with the organized church, has created its own backlash in the form of criticism from more conservative groups who have charged these groups with leftist orientation, selective moral outrage against social injustices, and undermining the values of capitalism and even democracy. To date, the influence of these groups in restraining the activities of PVOs has been, in my opinion, rather negligible, although it has raised public consciousness about the types of criticism that can be leveled against church-affiliated PVOs.[16]

The Less-Developed Countries

The less-developed countries (LDCs) are being buffeted by a variety of conflicting forces. At the ideological front there is increasing emphasis on self-sufficiency and an aversion to dependence on foreign capital's unfettered operations. The ideological and political counterpart of New Industrial Economic Order is the liberation theology and dependency theory. The LDCs argue that a dependence by the poor countries of the Third World on the capitalist countries and their agents, the MNCs, is both morally and politically unacceptable because it destroys the cultural underpinnings of those societies through the import of inappropriate, and culturally incompatible technologies.[17] The liberation theology first found expression in Latin American countries where an activist Roman Catholic church sided with the poor and the oppressed against the atrocities and inequities of an authoritarian political order.

It is unfortunate that the rise of the liberation theology is found in those countries where poverty is at its worst and political dictatorships are rife with corruption and prone to excesses in human rights violations. Since these regimes also controlled large economic enterprises and used them as vehicles of corruption and self-enrichment, capitalism came to be viewed in these countries as a source of exploitation. This experience is historically at odds with that of the United States and Western Europe where democracy and individual freedoms are inextricably tied to private enterprise and capitalism. The authoritarian regimes also provide a stable—albeit a repressive and coercive—political environment that appears less risky to many MNCs who chose to invest in these countries without adequate regard to future implications of such an association when there is a change in the political power in these countries. It is often argued that MNCs provide jobs and other benefits through their investments even under these repressive conditions. However, since these benefits are the secondary and not the primary motive for investment, these investments are viewed by MNC critics as merely after-the-fact rationalizations and, therefore, not highly credible. Thus, the poor masses and radicalized clergy see private enterprise, in general, and foreign private enterprise, in particular, as the instruments of evil that must be banished if they are to achieve liberty from the tyranny of the military and their foreign allies.

Multinational Corporations

The MNCs face an uncertain future in a changing sociopolitical international environment. However, this is not entirely without its positive aspects. There is growing awareness among many less developed countries of the important role that private capitalism and MNCs can play in the development process. Evidence of this tendency can be seen in shifting trends in China, India, and Ceylon. At the same time, changing technology and manufacturing processes have made MNCs less dependent on cheap labor and mineral resources of the Third World. The mix of MNCs has been changing with more MNCs coming from Third World and Asian countries. These MNCs not only bring a different time perspective and risk orientation to their overseas investments, but they carry a different institutional baggage about the treatment of their overseas workers and the management of their enterprises.

At the same time, the LDCs are becoming more sophisticated about their economic and social needs and the variety of sources available to them to meet these needs. The challenge for the MNCs would be to find a role for themselves that would take into account these new realities. These would involve an awareness of the increased information and negotiating ability of the LDCs, the growing power of these countries in the international arena to raise issues and exchange information, making it all but impossible for the unscrupulous among the MNCs to hide behind legal or technological considerations or raise the flag of defense of free enterprise.

MNCs will have to become more sensitive to the entire spectrum of technology transfer that will take into account the profit maximization aspects of the MNC enterprise, and even more important, will contribute to the stability of the society and its cultural values, as well as to growth that is accompanied with more equitable distribution of income. It is only when the interests of the MNCs and the countries involved are in harmony, and can stand the test of public scrutiny, that the MNC will be able to survive and grow in the new international environment. Investments will have to be justified simultaneously for their economic efficiency, political legitimacy, and moral sufficiency. It is hoped that MNCs will indeed be able to rise to this challenge and develop new modus vivendi that will contribute to a better world for all concerned.

Notes

1. P.T. Bauer, *Equality, the Third World, and Economic Delusion* (Cambridge, Mass.: Harvard University Press, 1981).

2. See for example, Richard J. Barnett and Ronald E. Muller, *Global Reach: The Power of the Multinational Corporations* (New York: Simon & Schuster, 1974); C. Tungendhat,

624 • Business and Society

The Multinationals (London: Penguin, 1973); Raymond Vernon, *Storm Over the Multinationals: The Real Issues* (Cambridge, Mass.: Harvard University Press, 1977); Kari Levitt, *Silent Surrender: The Multinational Corporation in Canada* (Toronto: Macmillan of Canada, 1970); F.G. Lavipour and Karl Sauvant (eds.), *Controlling Multinational Enterprises: Problems, Strategies, Counterstrategies* (Boulder, Colo.: Westview Press, 1976); Lee A. Tavis (ed.), *Multinational Managers and Poverty in the Third World* (Notre Dame, Ind.: Notre Dame University Press, 1982).

3. Willy Brandt, *North-South: A Program for Survival* (Cambridge, Mass.: The MIT Press, 1980); Karl V. Sauvant and Hajo Hasenpflug, *The New International Economic Order* (Boulder, Colo.: Westview Press, 1977).

4. S. Prakash Sethi, "The Inhuman Error—Lessons from the Union Carbide Plant Accident in Bhopal, India," *The New Management* (Summer 1985), pp. 41–45; Larry Everest, *Behind the Poison Cloud: Union Carbide's Bhopal Massacre* (Chicago, Ill.: Banner Press, 1985); Paul Shrivastava, *Bhopal: Anatomy of a Crisis* (Cambridge, Mass.: Ballinger, in press); Alfred de Grazia, *A Cloud Over Bhopal* (New Delhi, India: Kalos Foundation, 1985); Ward Morehouse and M. Arun Subramaniam *The Bhopal Tragedy* (New York: Council on International and Public Affairs, 1986).

5. Thomas C. Schelling, "On the Ecology of Micromotives," *The Public Interest* 25:59–98 (Fall 1971).

6. Garrett Hardin, "The Tragedy of the Commons," *Science* 162:1103–1107 (December 13, 1968).

7. Mike Muller, *The Baby Killer*, supra note 1. See also, Andy Chetley, *The Baby Killer Scandal* (London: War-on-Want, 1979); Andrew Chetley, *Taming the Transnationals: The Experience of the Baby Milks Campaigns* (in press); Andrew Chetley, *Cleared for Export: An Examination of the European Community's Pharmaceutical and Chemical Trade* (London, England: Coalition Against Dangerous Exports, 1985); J. Braithwaite, *Corporate Crime in the Pharmaceutical Industry* (London: Routledge, Kegal Paul, 1984); Garry Gereffi, *The Pharmaceutical Industry and Dependency in the Third World* (Princeton, N.J.: Princeton University Press, 1983); Charles Medawar/Social Audit, *The Wrong Kind of Medicine?* (London: Consumers Association and Hodder & Stroughton, 1984); Diana Melrose, *Bitter Pills* (Oxford, England: OXFAM, 1982); Mike Muller, *The Health of Nations* (Boston: Faber & Faber, 1982).

8. Bauer, *Equality, The Third World, and Economic Delusion*; Vernon, *Storm Over the Multinationals*.

9. The discussion in this section is largely based on the ideas developed in S. Prakash Sethi, Nobuaki Namiki, and Carl L. Swanson, *The False Promise of the Japanese Miracle* (Marshfield, Mass.: Pitman Publishing Co., 1984), pp. 281–297.

10. J.D. Goldhar and Mariann Jelinek, "Plan for Economies for Scope," *Harvard Business Review* 61:141–148 (Nov.–Dec. 1983); See also Donald F. Barnett and Louis Schorsch, *Steel: Upheaval in a Basic Industry*, (Cambridge, Mass.: Ballinger, 1983).

11. Mary A. Fejfar, *Regulation of Business by International Agencies*, Center for the Study of American Business (St. Louis, Mo.: Washington University, 1983); "Current Status Report: Selected International Organization Activities Relating to Transnational Enterprises, 1984," Office of Investment Affairs, Department of State, Washington, D.C., 1984; Seymor J. Rubin, "Transnational Corporations and International Codes of Conduct: A Study of the Relationship Between International Legal Cooperation and Economic Development," *The American University Law Review* 30:903–922 (Summer, 1981); Servass van Thiel, "U.N. Draft Code of Conduct on Transnational Corporations," *Bulletin of International Fiscal Documentation* 39:29–33 (January, 1985).

12. S. Prakash Sethi, *The Righteous and the Powerful: Corporations, Religious Institutions and International Social Activism—The Case of the Infant Formula Controversy and the*

Nestle Boycott (Cambridge, Mass.: Ballinger, in press); Timothy W. Stanley, "International Codes of Conduct for MNCs: A Skeptical View of the Process," *The American University Law Review* **30**:973–1008 (Summer 1981).

13. Rubin, "Transnational Corporations"; Stanley, "International Codes of Conduct for MNCs."

14. There is a growing body of literature about the South Africa debate that is too voluminous to cite here. The reader's attention is directed to a special issue of *Business and Society Review* (Spring 1986), which is entirely devoted to a discussion of the South African apartheid policies and the role international economic and political institutions can play in bringing about a change in those policies.

15. Sethi, *The Righteous and the Powerful*; Burton Y. Pines (ed.), *A World Without U.N.* (Washington, D.C.: The Heritage Foundation, 1984); Tobi T. Gati (ed.), *The US, the UN, and the Management of Social Change*, (New York: New York University Press, 1983); Chetley, *Cleared for Exports*, supra note 2; Charles Medawar and Barbara Freese, *Drug Diplomacy* (London: Social Audit, 1982); Dianna Melrose, *Bitter Pills: Medicines and the Third World*, (Oxford, England: Oxfam, 1982).

16. Thomas C. Oden, *Conscience and Dividends: Churches and the Multinationals*, (Washington, D.C.: Ethics and Public Policy Center, 1985); Enrest Lefever, *Amsterdam to Nairobi: The World Council of Churches and the Third World*, (Washington, D.C.: Ethics and Public Policy Center, 1979).

17. For a better understanding of the ideas and concepts underlying liberation theology and dependency theory, the reader is directed to: Cornel West, "Religion and the West," *Monthly Review* **36**:9–17 (July–August 1984); Phillip Berryman, "Basic Christian Communities and the Future of Latin America," *Monthly Review* **36**:27–40 (July–August 1984); Allan Boesak, "Black Theology and the Struggle for Liberation in South Africa," *Monthly Review* **36**:127–137 (July–August 1984); Joel Kovel, "The Vatican Strikes Back," *Monthly Review* **36**:14–27 (April 1985); Sol W. Sanders, "The Vatican Gets Tougher on Nicaragua's Liberation Theology," *Business Week* (August 27, 1984), p. 47; A.J. Conyers, "Liberation Theology: Whom Does it Liberate?" *Modern Age* (Summer/Fall 1983), pp. 303–308; George Hunsinger, "Karl Barth and Liberation Theology," *The Journal of Religion* **63**:247–263 (July 1983); Enrique Dussel, *Ethics and the Theology of Liberation* (Maryknoll, N.Y.: Orbis Books, 1978); Gustavo Gutierrez, *A Theology of Liberation*, trans. Bernard F. McWilliams (Maryknoll, N.Y.: Orbis Books, 1973); King Paul and Dave Woodyard, *The Journey Toward Freedom: Economic Structures and Theological Perspectives*, (Rutherford, N.J.: Fairliegh Dickinson University Press, 1982).

Peter Evans, *Dependent Development* (Princeton, N.J.: Princeton University Press, 1979); Andre Frank, *Critique and Anti-Critique; Essays on Dependence and Reformism* (New York: Praeger, 1984); Doran et. al., *North/South Relations: Studies of Dependency Reversal*, (New York: Praeger, 1983); Chilcote Johnson, *Theories of Development* (Beverly Hills, Calif.: Sage Publications, 1983); Gary Gereffi, "Power and Dependency in an Interdependent World: A Guide to Understanding the Contemporary Global Crisis," *International Journal of Comparative Sociology* **25**:91–108 (1984); Adrienne Armstrong, "The Political Consequences of Economic Dependence," *Journal of Conflict Resolution* **25**:401–428 (September 1981); Michael Timberlake and Kirk R. Williams, "Dependence, Political Exclusion, and Government Repression: Some Cross-National Evidence," *American Sociological Review* **49**:141–146 (February 1984); Volker Bornschier, Christopher Chase-Dunne, and Richard Robinson, "Cross-National Evidence of the Effects of Foreign Investment and Aid on Economic Growth and Inequality and Survey of Findings and a Reanalysis," *American Journal of Sociology* **84**:651–683.

American Business in South Africa: The Hard Choices

Sal G. Marzullo
Chairman, Industry Support Unit Inc.
to the Sullivan Signatory Companies

The growing escalation of violence and the increasing racial division taking place in South Africa forces us to address this issue in a most urgent and compelling manner. People of good will understand that there are many legitimate strategies for dealing with this issue, but I think one may honestly question the basic thrust of the debate on South Africa as it presently exists in the United States. The fact that this is a highly emotional and complex issue demands more from each of us than the passion that racial oppression and injustice rightly evoke. One cannot argue with passion. Apartheid is an evil and oppressive system that must disappear from South Africa; that ultimately will disappear from that country. All our energies should be directed toward meeting that objective. The debate and strategy all Americans should be focusing on now is how best to create those coalitions that will bring structural change and economic equality about quickly, peacefully, and democratically. Violent revolution will only make the chances for the emergence of a nonracial, democratic, just society less likely, and economic sanctions could prove to be not only counterproductive but highly dangerous as well in searching for ways to diffuse black rage and white fear and move toward racial accommodation and reconciliation.

The Moral Underpinnings of Pragmatic Choices

The corporate philosophy for remaining in South Africa is both a moral and pragmatic one. Corporate presence is better than corporate absence. Such presence allows companies to shape and be participants in those dynamic forces present in the South African environment that can lead to the erosion and final elimination of apartheid. It is very much in order at this point to stress what companies can and cannot do since they are accused by some of being cosmetic and by others of trying to undermine the sovereignty of the South African state.

U.S. companies have never claimed to be able to do more than they could deliver. The Sullivan Principles by themselves were not meant to be a guaranteed and sure method of providing quick and simple solutions to the grave and fundamental injustices that exist in South African society. Companies have been and can continue to be an effective catalyst for change by working with and supporting local institutions in that society that are having an impact on initiating and accelerating the process of change. These groups have, in their own way, begun to perceptibly change attitudes among many white South Africans who understand that fundamental structural reform and absolute equality for South Africans of all races is essential to the long-term survival of that country. What, then, has been done? From 1977 through June 1985, U.S. Sullivan companies have spent more than $158 million in the areas of health, education, community development, training, housing and black entrepreneurship. Companies cannot bring about genuine change alone, however, so they also support institutions like American Friends of Community Development—PACE; The Cape of Good Hope Foundation; Friends of SOS Children's Village, Inc.; Get Ahead; Institute of International Education; Institute of Natural Resources; Lawyer's Committee for Civil Rights Under Law; Medical Education for South African Blacks (MESAB); St. Barnabas; South African Legal Services and Legal Education Project, Inc.; U.S. Committee for the Friends of Baragwanath; United States South African Leadership Exchange Program; United States Zululand Education Foundation, Inc.; University of Cape Town Fund, Inc.; The Urban Foundation, Inc. and many others that can work more efficiently than they can in particular areas in securing justice for all of South Africa's racial groups. This support will continue.

Beyond the traditional support areas companies have now moved to new challenges. American companies, both in the United States and in South Africa, have unequivocally urged the South African Government to take action in the following areas. These movements forward are an expansion of the Sullivan Company Fourth Amplification originally announced by the Rev. Dr. Leon H. Sullivan in Washington, D.C., on November 8, 1984. Companies are calling for:

1. The elimination of Influx Control and the Group Areas Act of South Africa.
2. The establishment of an equal national education system.
3. The end of apartheid in the work place, including the elimination of the pass laws, and the last job reservation remaining in the mining industry. It should be noted that on April 8, 1986, President P.W. Botha announced that the pass laws controlling where blacks can live and work would no longer be enforced. He also ordered the release of all blacks jailed on charges of violating these much hated laws. All South Africans he has said will now carry the same identity documents and influx control will be scrapped.
4. The establishment of freehold rights for all South Africans regardless of race.
5. The establishment of a unified health delivery system available to all races.
6. The elimination of residential segregation and forced removals, and the promotion of black land ownership in all areas of South Africa.
7. The maintenance of the existing independence and integrity of the South African judicial system.
8. The development of the leadership abilities of all black South Africans so they can work for the elimination of apartheid and be prepared to assume their rightful role in the running of that society.

The transition from company involvement with the local workplace and community to regional and national issues lasted from 1982 to 1984, when the presence of U.S. companies in South Africa became an increasingly emotional and partisan U.S. political issue. Three separate developments, in the United States and South Africa, helped to publicize and polarize this complex issue. First, was the awarding of the Nobel Peace Prize to archbishop-elect of Cape Town, Desmond Tutu, a powerful religious and moral voice of South Africa's oppressed people, who warned of the dangers of mass violence if blacks were not given the rights of free men in the country of their birth.

Second, anger was growing among South Africa's black population at being excluded from the 1984 constitutional dispensation that opened political participation to the country's "colored" and Asian populations. The exclusion of black South Africans from any political process whatever led to a growing demand for sanctions against South Africa. The third development leading to increased domestic pressure on the South African issues was the 1984 U.S. presidential campaign. The involvement of U.S. politicians in South African issues was raised to its highest level by the Rev. Jesse Jackson's campaign for the presidential nomination. The creation of a Free South Africa Movement (FSAM) helped provide a way for U.S. politicians to exert political clout on an issue (the removal of apartheid) about which most Americans agree. South Africa and change in South Africa became a full-blown domestic political issue.

U.S. companies in 1985 and 1986, responding to those pressures, became far more public and vocal in their advocacy of change. For example, American companies in South Africa in September 1985, in newspaper ads that were printed in both South Africa (figure 1) and the United States, unequivocally called for:

1. The abolition of statutory race discrimination wherever it exists.
2. Negotiation with acknowledged black leaders about power sharing.
3. The granting of full South African citizenship to all South Africa's people.
4. The restoring and entrenching of the rule of law for all of South Africa's people.

The companies also have declared that they continue to reject violence as a means of achieving change and support only the politics of negotiation and reconciliation.

This call for political change and the extension of human rights for all of South Africa's people was renewed by the U.S. Corporate Council for Change in South Africa (formed in September, 1985) (figure 2) in October 1985 in newspaper ads run in major newspapers all over the United States. Examples of these ads are shown here. Later in November 1985, a meeting in London of selected Council members and South African business leaders occurred and a frank exchange of views took place. South African business leaders conveyed the views of U.S. business calling for the rapid elimination of apartheid directly to State President Botha. In January of 1986, Mr. W. Michael Blumenthal of Burroughs Corporation, and Mr. Roger Smith of General Motors, cochairmen of the council, met with Bishop Desmond Tutu for a full discussion of South African issues, including that of the role of U.S. business in South Africa. In March, selected council members met in England with Dr. Leon Sullivan and business representatives from five other countries to discuss South African problems and possible solutions to those problems.

Business Actions in the International Arena

The International Chamber of Commerce (ICC), representing over 7,000 companies all over the world, in its hearings before the United Nations on September 16, 1985, proclaimed its total opposition to apartheid and its support for the passage of laws leading to its elimination. The declaration states:

> The ICC condemns racially discriminatory policies and practices anywhere in the world. Consequently, it opposes the South African system of apartheid and believes it should be abolished as quickly as possible. This system is morally indefensible. It is also economically counterproductive and fundamentally irreconcilable with the principles of free enterprise.
>
> The international community as a whole has a responsibility to engage in such positive action as may help to eliminate apartheid in South Africa. The international standards of business behavior set by TNCs in South Africa are a force towards this end. Efforts of individual companies operating in South Africa, through compliance with the Sullivan Principles, or the EEC Code of Conduct, or other instruments of that nature, or through their own guidelines, have contributed to: promoting racial equality in employment practices; training and developing black managers and skilled and educated black manpower at all levels; developing a free trade union movement open to all races; generating the fundamental attitudinal changes necessary to bring about racial reconciliation and greater social equality; improving the quality of life of people in the region through social actions at the community level, particularly through assistance to education and housing.

Actions of the South African Business Community

The South African business community has itself actively begun to challenge rather than to accept government policies. I would call the attention of the nonbusiness world to an *Action Program of South African Business* issued by the Federated Chamber of Industries in South Africa in January of this year. This Charter of Social, Economic and Political Rights for all South Africans is truly a unique document for South Africa and for many other countries of the world as well. It should be read carefully by all those seeking to learn how both South African and American business are pressing for political change in South Africa. It should be noted that U.S. business firms in South Africa are members of these national business groups calling for change in that country. A section of this South African Business Charter of Social, Economic and Political Rights states:

Sunday Times, September 29, 1985, Johannesburg, South Africa

p.8

"There is a better way"

As responsible businessmen committed to South Africa and the welfare of all its people, we are deeply concerned about the current situation.

We believe that the reform process should be accelerated by:

● **Abolishing statutory race discrimination wherever it exists;**

● **Negotiating with acknowledged black leaders about power sharing;**

● **Granting full South African citizenship to all our peoples;**

● **Restoring and entrenching the rule of law.**

We reject violence as a means of achieving change and we support the politics of negotiation.

We believe that there is a better way for South Africa and we support equal opportunity, respect for the individual, freedom of enterprise and freedom of movement.

We believe in the development of the South African economy for the benefit of all of its people and we are, therefore, committed to pursue a role of corporate social responsibility and to play our part in transforming the structures and systems of the country toward fair participation for all.

Name	Title	Company
L.C. ABRAHAMSE	Chairman	SYFRETS TRUST LIMITED
E.J. ABRAHAMSEN	Chief Executive	NEDBANK GROUP LIMITED
R.D. ACKERMAN	Chairman	PICK 'n PAY STORES LIMITED
C.S. ADCOCK	Managing Director	TOYOTA S.A. LIMITED
PROF. G. ANDREWS	Director	GRADUATE SCHOOL OF BUSINESS WITS UNIVERSITY
P.J. BADENHORST	Chief Executive	UNITED BUILDING SOCIETY
C.J. BALL	Managing Director	BARCLAYS NATIONAL BANK LIMITED
B.P. BARNETT	Chairman/Managing Director	STERNS DIAMOND ORGANISATON LIMITED
J. BEARE	Chairman	BEARES LIMITED
A. BERMAN	Joint Managing Director	NATAL CONSOLIDATED INDUSTRIAL INVESTMENTS LIMITED (THE FRAME GROUP)
A.H. BLOOM	Chairman	PREMIER GROUP HOLDINGS LIMITED
W.G. BOUSTRED	Chairman	ANGLO AMERICAN INDUSTRIAL CORPORATION LIMITED
L. BOYD	Chairman	S.A. MOTOR CORPORATION LIMITED
I.D. BRITTAN	Chairman	BOUMAT LIMITED
D.G.S. CAMPBELL	Chairman	FRASERS CONSOLIDATED LIMITED
P.L. CAMPBELL	Managing Director	METAL BOX S.A. LIMITED
A. CARLEO	Managing Director	PUTCO LIMITED
T.N. CHAPMAN	Chief Executive	THE SOUTHERN LIFE ASSOCIATION LIMITED
J. CLARKE	Managing Director	IBM S.A. (PTY) LIMITED
R.K. COHEN	Chairman	AMALGAMATED RETAIL LIMITED
T.G. COULSON	Chairman/Managing Director	BLUE CIRCLE LIMITED
Z.J. DE BEER	Chairman	ANGLO AMERICAN PROPERTIES LIMITED
C.S. DOS SANTOS	Managing Director	SCORE FOOD HOLDINGS LIMITED
J.C. DOUGLAS	Chairman/Managing Director	S.A. GENERAL ELECTRIC COMPANY (PTY) LIMITED
C. DUKE	General Manager	ABBOTT LABORATORIES (S.A) (PTY) LIMITED
D.J. ENGLISH	Managing Director	RANK XEROX (PTY) LIMITED
A.J.F. FERGUSSON	Chairman	THE PRUDENTIAL ASSURANCE COMPANY OF S.A. LIMITED
R. FERES	Managing Director	KODAK S.A. (PTY) LIMITED
D.T. FLETCHER	Chairman/Managing Director	CALTEX OIL (S.A) (PTY) LIMITED
J.A. FRANKEL	Joint Managing Director	TIGER OATS LIMITED
M.R. FURST	Managing Director	HEWLETT-PACKARD S.A. (PTY) LIMITED
S.M. GOLDSTEIN	Chairman	S.M. GOLDSTEIN LIMITED
E.H. HART	Chairman	WHITEHALL PRODUCTS (S.A.) (PTY) LIMITED
DR. W. HASSELKUS	Managing Director	BMW S.A. (PTY) LIMITED
M.S. HERMAN	Joint Managing Director	PICK 'n PAY STORES LIMITED
M. MILKOWITZ	Managing Director	LIBERTY LIFE ASSOCIATION OF AFRICA LIMITED
J.B. HODGSON	Chairman	DARLING & HODGSON LIMITED
G.W. HOOD	Managing Director	OK BAZAARS (1929) LIMITED
J.R. HOUSTON	Managing Director	NCR CORPORATION OF S.A. (PTY) LIMITED
L.J. JACOBSON	Chairman/Chief Executive	TRADE & INDUSTRY ACCEPTANCE CORPORATION LIMITED
P.H. JACOBSON	Chairman	BRADLOWS STORES LIMITED
E.J. JAFF	Chairman	DELSWA LIMITED
A. JAFFE	Chairman	CURRIE FINANCE CORPORATION LIMITED
J.K. JOHNSON	Managing Director	KELLOGG'S LIMITED
R.I. JOWELL	Chairman	TRENCOR LIMITED
C.R. KAPLAN	Chairman	MICOR HOLDINGS LIMITED
J. KING	Managing Director	S.A. ASSOCIATED NEWSPAPERS LIMITED
M. KING	Managing Director	KIRSH TRADING GROUP LIMITED
D.C. KROCH	Executive Deputy Chairman	LEGAL & GENERAL VOLKSKAS ASSURANCE LIMITED
S. LEWIS	Chairman	FOSCHINI LIMITED
P. LLOYD	Managing Director	BEER DIVISION, S.A. BREWERIES LIMITED
S. LURIE	Joint Managing Director	NATAL CONSOLIDATED INDUSTRIAL INVESTMENTS LIMITED (THE FRAME GROUP)
I. MACKENZIE	Chairman	AFRICAN FINANCE CORPORATION LIMITED
J.A. MACKNESS	Managing Director	CNA GALLO LIMITED
D.M. MAHONEY	Managing Director	CONTROL DATA (PTY) LIMITED
D.R. McCARTAN	Chairman	NAMPAK LIMITED
P.W. McLEAN	Managing Director	THE ARGUS GROUP
P.J. MEYER	Senior Vice President	THE COCA-COLA EXPORT CORPORATION
H.W. MILLER	Executive Chairman	THE ARGUS GROUP
P.R. MORITZ	Managing Director	S.PECTANAMID (PTY) LIMITED
T. MOOLMAN	Joint Managing Director	CAXTON LIMITED
M.N. NEWMAN	Executive Chairman	S.A. BIAS HOLDINGS LIMITED
G.W. NOCKER	Chief Executive Officer	COLGATE-PALMOLIVE LIMITED
J. OGILVIE THOMPSON	Chairman	DE BEERS CONSOLIDATED MINES LIMITED
H.F. OPPENHEIMER	Executive Chairman	OVENSTONE INVESTMENTS LIMITED
A.D. OVENSTONE	Joint Managing Director	NATAL CONSOLIDATED INDUSTRIAL INVESTMENTS LIMITED (THE FRAME GROUP)
S.R. PRIMER	Chairman	THE PROPERTY GROUP OF S.A. LIMITED
B.P. RABINOWITZ	Chairman/Managing Director	MOBIL OIL S.A. (PTY) LIMITED
G.P. RACINE	Chairman	ANGLO AMERICAN CORPORATION OF S.A. LIMITED
G.W. REILLY	Chairman	GRAND BAZAARS LIMITED
M. SACHAR	Chairman	THE TONGAAT GROUP LIMITED
C.J. SAUNDERS	Chairman	NAMPAK TISSUE DIVISION
R.J. SCHMITT	Managing Director	VOLKSWAGEN OF S.A. (PTY) LIMITED
P. SEARLE	Managing Director	SEARDEL INVESTMENT CORPORATION LIMITED
A. SEARLL	Chairman	W & A INVESTMENT CORPORATION LIMITED
M. SIMCHOWITZ	Managing Director	AECI LIMITED
B.J. SMALE	Managing Director	JOHNSON & JOHNSON (PTY) LIMITED
C.A. SPALDING	Managing Director	AFRICAN OXYGEN LIMITED
A.M. SPITZ	Executive Chairman	N S S SPITZ FOOTWEAR HOLDINGS LIMITED
J.R. SUTHERLAND	Chairman	AFRICAN OXYGEN LIMITED
P.R.S. THOMAS	Managing Director	THE UNISEC GROUP LIMITED
L. VAN DER WATT	Chairman	ASSOCIATED FURNITURE COMPANIES LIMITED
G.H. WADDELL	Chairman	JOHANNESBURG CONSOLIDATED INVESTMENT COMPANY LIMITED
C.N. WEIL	Managing Director	CHECKERS STORES LIMITED
DR. A. WESSELS	Chairman	TOYOTA S.A. LIMITED
P.D. WHARTON-HOOD	Managing Director	THE PRUDENTIAL ASSURANCE COMPANY OF S.A. LIMITED
R.A. WHITE	Managing Director	GENERAL MOTORS OF S.A. (PTY) LIMITED
PROF. N. WIEHAHN	Director	GRADUATE SCHOOL OF BUSINESS UNISA
C.T. WOOD	Managing Director	CITIBANK LIMITED
P.G. WRIGHTON	Deputy Chairman	PREMIER GROUP HOLDINGS LIMITED
W.S. YEOWART	Immediate Past President	ASSOCOM.

Figure 1

On September 29, 1985, ninety-one leaders of the South African business community spoke with one voice:

JOHANNESBURG SUNDAY TIMES   September 29, 1985

"There is a better way"

As responsible businessmen committed to South Africa and the welfare of all its people, we are deeply concerned about the current situation.

We believe that the reform process should be accelerated by:

- Abolishing statutory race discrimination wherever it exists;
- Negotiating with acknowledged black leaders about power sharing;
- Granting full South African citizenship to all our peoples;
- Restoring and entrenching the rule of law.

We reject violence as a means of achieving change and we support the politics of negotiation.

We believe that there is a better way for South Africa and we support equal opportunity, respect for the individual, freedom of enterprise and freedom of movement.

Today, we add our voice to theirs.

We believe in the development of the South African economy for the benefit of all of its people and we are, therefore, committed to pursue a role of corporate social responsibility and to play our part in transforming the structures and systems of the country toward fair participation for all.

[A list of South African signatory names and corporations appears here, largely illegible.]

The U.S. Corporate Council on South Africa strongly supports the ideas and initiatives of this group of responsible businessmen. We pledge to play an active role in peacefully achieving their goals.

W.H. [signature]   [signature]
ROGER B. SMITH
Chairman & CEO, General Motors Corporation
Co-chairman USCCSA

W. MICHAEL BLUMENTHAL
Chairman & CEO, Burroughs Corporation
Co-chairman USCCSA

STEERING COMMITTEE

John F. Akers
President & CEO
IBM Corporation

Robert A. Hanson
Chairman & CEO
Deere & Company

John S. Reed
Chairman & CEO
Citicorp

Rawleigh Warner, Jr.
Chairman & CEO
Mobil Corporation

James E. Burke
Chairman & CEO
Johnson & Johnson

Reuben Mark
President & CEO
Colgate-Palmolive Co.

David S. Tappan, Jr.
Chairman & CEO
Fluor Corporation

Howard V. Vergin, Jr.
Chairman & CEO
Caltex Petroleum Corp.

COUNCIL MEMBERS

Warren M. Anderson, Chairman & CEO, Union Carbide Corporation
James E. Burke, Chairman & CEO
Willard C. Butcher, Chairman & CEO, The Chase Manhattan Corporation
Colby H. Chandler, Chairman & CEO, Eastman Kodak Company
John W. Culligan, Chairman & CEO, American Home Products Corporation
E. Mandell de Windt, Chairman & CEO, Eaton Corporation
Joseph L. Dionne, President & CEO, McGraw-Hill, Inc.
Charles E. Exley, Jr., Chairman & CEO, NCR Corporation

C.C. Garvin, Jr., Chairman & CEO, Exxon Corporation
Philip H. Geier, Jr., Chairman & CEO, The Interpublic Group of Companies, Inc.
Richard L. Gelb, Chairman & CEO, Bristol-Myers Company
Roberto C. Goizueta, Chairman & CEO, The Coca-Cola Company
John M. Henske, Chairman & CEO, Olin Corporation
Thomas A. Holmes, Chairman & CEO, Ingersoll-Rand Company
John L. Horan, Chairman, Merck & Co., Inc.
Edward G. Jefferson, Chairman, E.I. du Pont de Nemours & Co., Inc.
David T. Kearns, Chairman & CEO, Xerox Corporation

Robert D. Kilpatrick, Chairman & CEO, CIGNA Corporation
William E. LaMothe, Chairman & CEO, Kellogg Company
William C. Norris, Chairman & CEO, Control Data Corporation
Roy T. Parfet, Jr., Chairman & CEO, The Upjohn Company
Donald E. Petersen, President & CEO, Ford Motor Company
Robert P. Luciano, President & CEO, Schering-Plough Corporation
Thomas A. Holmes, Chairman & CEO, Ingersoll-Rand Company
Donald R. Melville, Chairman & President, Norton Company
Philip Dodge, Chairman & CEO, Federal-Mogul Corporation

George A. Schaefer, Chairman & CEO, Caterpillar Tractor Co.
Edson W. Spencer, Chairman & CEO, Honeywell Inc.
Eugene J. Sullivan, Chairman & CEO, Borden, Inc.
Donald Taylor, Vice Chairman & CEO, Rexnord
Henry Wendt, President & CEO, SmithKline Beckman Corporation
Alton W. Whitehouse, Chairman & CEO, The Standard Oil Company
Joseph D. Williams, Chairman & CEO, Warner-Lambert Company
John A. Young, President & CEO, Hewlett-Packard Company

Listed above are those who have joined the Council as of October 15, 1985. Council membership is expected to grow as more Sullivan signatory companies respond to our invitation to join.

U.S. CORPORATE COUNCIL ON SOUTH AFRICA

Figure 2

Every human being has the right to recognition as a person before the law.

Everyone is equal before the law, and is entitled to equal protection of the law without any discrimination on the basis of race, color, language, sex, religion, ethnic or social origin, age, property, birth, political or other opinion, or economic or other status.

Everyone has the right to freedom of association and freedom of peaceful assembly.

Everyone born in South Africa or the independent or national states, or naturalized in accordance with law has the right to South African citizenship.

I truly believe that the efforts of the U.S. business community and the business community in South Africa have been successful in changing white attitudes and in encouraging the passing of legislation by the South African Government to remedy some of the inequities and injustices that unfortunately still exist—much remains to be done and at a faster pace. I believe that this assessment is based on more than hope or wishful thinking. Some Sullivan company task group chairmen and I recently returned from a three-week trip to South Africa. In meeting after meeting, we all listened to much that was critical but these same critics also told us privately that they do not seek disinvestment, that what they want is a continuation of corporate efforts leading to jobs, mobility, equality, training, housing, and community development. They urged us to be more outspoken, to deal more directly with challenges to the laws that still keep black South Africans out of the mainstream of both political and economic life.

Of course, some blacks support disinvestment; many however also advocate continued and even expanded foreign investment. We in business have a role to play and we accept pressure to do more in South Africa. But we cannot agree with the forced withdrawal of the American business presence or with the imposition of economic sanctions. This is why we oppose legislative proposals seeking to impose these measures. Yes, we share the objective of the proponents of such legislation—peaceful change as quickly as possible—but we seriously doubt that this objective will be the result of American withdrawal or South African isolation.

This is a time of great frustration with the existing conditions in South Africa, but it is also a time of challenge and hope. Growing numbers of people within South Africa begin to demonstrate a commitment to change. Let us pursue honest and sincere policies of support for the unification of these groups—businesses, labor unions, educators, students, church people, and others—in the peaceful pursuit of change, rather than pursue strategies that will have a strong potential for further polarization.

1986—The Critical Year

The year ahead in South Africa could be one unfortunately of protracted struggle, violence, and risk. But it can also be one during which steps can be taken to bring about genuine power sharing and negotiations leading to full citizenship for all of South Africa's people. Alan Paton, one of South Africa's great writers, is a man of uncompromising principles. He reflects the torment of his torn land. He writes: "If the nations of the West condemn us, they will only hinder the process of our emancipation from the bondage of our history. But if they stay with us, rebuke us, judge us and encourage us, the chances are that we shall do better."

One must listen to the many black voices speaking for freedom and power sharing in South Africa including that of Mangosuthu G. Buthelezi, chief minister of KwaZulu, president of Inkatha and the South African Black Alliance. On July 5, 1985, he greeted a group of American black leaders. Among his comments to them were the following:

> I am not heard in the United States when I say that apartheid is far more vulnerable to democratic opposition now than it has ever been before, and that apartheid is certainly far more vulnerable to democratic opposition than it has ever been to the politics of violence. I am not heard when I say that the scales are tipping in favor of the politics of negotiation, and that America more than at any other time in history should be strengthening the democratic process. They should be strengthening the circumstances which favor the continued growth of democratic opposition to apartheid, and they should be strengthening those who have made it their task to hold political violence at bay, and to employ the forces of democracy to bring about real change.
>
> The escalation of violence both on the part of the State and by those who oppose the State, can only lead to ever diminishing prospects of salvaging this country from destruction. I am not heard in the United States when I say that we must increase white dependency on blacks; that we must tip the scales even further in favor of the politics of negotiation; that we must increase black bargaining power and that these things must be done by increasing the rate of industrialisation in South Africa.

In summary, any effective leverage to induce peaceful change in South Africa requires a business presence. Business withdrawal would neither bring down the South African government nor affect the policies of that government, except perhaps to make it more rigid and truculent as it feels itself more isolated. To the extent that sanctions or isolation or withdrawal seek to govern the actions of South African affiliates of American companies, they place these companies in an impossible situation between two governmental authorities at a time when engagement of a more active character remains one of the last hopes for a peaceful resolution to South Africa's problems.

Americans must not be passive actors in this South African drama, but we must be careful that we do not exaggerate our ability to influence the course of events in South Africa by ourselves. Only South Africans themselves can be the key actors—black and white alike. We must work to bring the races together so they can negotiate their future peacefully. Withdrawal would be a disaster for all of South Africa's people and exacerbate the tensions that sadly already exist. Pretoria must quickly and unequivocally make the ultimate commitment to ending apartheid and to begin a process of negotiation with all of its people for a transition to true democracy in that country. We must certainly help in that process, not by isolating South Africa, but by pushing and prodding her and showing that change can come peacefully.

This may be South Africa's one last chance for a peaceful resolution to an environment increasingly turning to violence. Nobody, for whatever reason, should seek to diminish or create obstacles to any honest effort leading to peaceful change. Nobody in South Africa, black or white, will benefit from the mass destruction sure to result if there is mass confrontation between the racial groups of that country. In the midst of the pain and violence that exist in the anguished country, all of us who seek peaceful change may yet see the emergence of a politics of negotiation in South Africa. It must happen. It can happen. It is that process we should press for and encourage, not sanctions, not mindless confrontation, which will bring about only mass violence and increased racial division. This is what we must avoid at all costs if the struggle for equality is to succeed.

Note

Index

List of Contributors

James M. Carman, University of California, Berkeley

Archie B. Carroll, University of Georgia

Gerald F. Cavanagh, University of Detroit

Anthony J. Celebrezze, Jr., Attorney General of Ohio

Thomas Howard Chase, American Telephone and Telegraph

W. Howard Chase, Howard Chase Enterprises, Inc.

Robert Chatov, State University of New York, Buffalo

Niels Christiansen, American Council of Life Insurance

Philip L. Cochran, Pennsylvania State University

Eddie Correia, United States Senate

Thomas Dunfee, University of Pennsylvania

William C. Frederick, University of Pittsburgh

R. Edward Freeman, University of Minnesota

Daniel R. Gilbert, Jr., University of Minnesota

George S. Goldberger, Citizens Against Government Waste

John Hall, University of Georgia

Robert G. Harris, University of California, Berkeley

John M. Holcomb, University of Maryland

Frank Hoy, University of Georgia

Ian Maitland, University of Minnesota

Steven Markowitz, Multistate Associates, Inc.

Sal G. Marzullo, Industry Support Unit Inc. to the Sullivan Signatory Companies

Sharon Meluso, The Futures Group

Michael Novak, American Enterprise Institute

James O'Toole, University of Southern California, Los Angeles

Rafael D. Pagan, Jr., Pagan International

Mark Pastin, Arizona State University

James E. Post, Boston University

Lee E. Preston, University of Maryland

E.S. Savas, Baruch College

Paul Steidlmeier, State University of New York at Binghamton

Steven J. Twist, Chief Assistant Attorney General of Arizona

Kenneth D. Walters, California Polytechnic State University

Steven L. Wartick, Pennsylvania State University

Murray L. Weidenbaum, Washington University

Oliver F. Williams, University of Notre Dame

Donna J. Wood, University of Pittsburgh

About the Editors

S. Prakash Sethi, internationally known for his work on corporate social responsibility and business and public policy, is professor of management at Baruch College, CUNY. Prior to joining Baruch College he taught at the University of California–Berkeley and the University of Texas at Dallas. He has authored, coauthored, or edited 18 books and published over 100 articles in scholarly and professional journals. Among his books are *Up Against the Corporate Wall*, *The Corporate Dilemma*, *The False Promise of the Japanese Miracle*, *Handbook of Advocacy Advertising*, and *The South African Quagmire: Search for a Peaceful Solution to Democratic Pluralism*. His writings have also appeared in national and international news media, including the *New York Times*, the *Wall Street Journal*, *Business Week*, the *Evening Standard* (London), and the *Cape Times* (South Africa). He received his Ph.D. in business from Columbia University.

Cecilia M. Falbe is assistant professor of management at the State University of New York at Albany. She has also taught at Baruch College, CUNY. She has published several articles in leading management journals. She has a Ph.D. in sociology, with a specialization in organization theory, from Columbia University.